PRAISE FOR

Becoming Richard Pryor

An Amazon "Best Book of the Month"

"Absorbing, incisive. . . . With skill and insight, Saul shows how both the best and the worst of Pryor could merge into a great body of work unmatched by anyone who was ever paid to make people laugh."

—Gene Seymour, *USA Today* (four out of four stars)

"Masterful." —*Newsweek*

"A book that breaks new ground. . . . Saul details the amazing way that Richard found his way out of the life for which he seemed destined and into the world of the performing arts."

—Janet Maslin, *New York Times*

"Sharply observed. . . . Lays out the case that Pryor was not only a comic genius but 'a bellwether of the great changes of postwar American life, some of which he helped incite.' . . . Riveting."

—Lev Grossman, *Time*

"A gripping read. . . . The only book you need on its subject."

—*Sunday Times* (London)

"A pop-culture masterpiece of exhaustive reporting, psychological insight, and elegant writing." —*Cleveland Plain Dealer*

"An always fascinating, sometimes horrifying look at the catastrophes and cunning that formed one of our most wicked, smartest comic minds." —Patton Oswalt, comedian and author of *Silver Screen Fiend*

"Revelatory." —Jeet Heer, *The New Republic*

"The most detailed and rigorously researched work on the comic's life and performances. . . . Pryor was both the quintessential hipster and the vulnerable, damaged witness of his age. . . . *Becoming Richard Pryor* captures these dimensions of the persona and the man behind it very well."
—Gerald Early, *Washington Post*

"A fascinating, exhilarating read. Saul dives deeper and comes up with more treasure than previous biographers; he deftly traces the stamp that Pryor left on American culture at one of its more impressionable moments. . . . I didn't want to put the book down and couldn't wait to get back to it."
—Michael Chabon, bestselling and Pulitzer Prize–winning author of *The Amazing Adventures of Kavalier and Clay*

"*Becoming Richard Pryor* is a compulsively readable book that sets a new gold standard for American biography. Scott Saul's research is extraordinary; his writing is taut, elegant, and insightful; and he captures both the hilarity and pain that made Richard Pryor such a towering figure."
—Debby Applegate, winner of the Pulitzer Prize for biography and author of the forthcoming *Madam: The Notorius Life and Times of Polly Adler*

"Insightful and expansive, Scott Saul's remarkable biography of the now legendary comic chronicles how a sensitive brilliant man with a hardscrabble past mined his personal life for American entertainment, revolutionizing stand-up along the way."
—*Playboy*, "This Winter's Best Books"

"Piquant. . . . Richard Pryor's journey from the 'instabilities of his childhood' to his supreme but shaky fame is of commanding interest."
—Liesl Schillinger, *New York Times*

"*Becoming Richard Pryor* captures Pryor at his most vital, in and out of drug addiction and all too brief marriages, while testing the limits of comedy with brutal honesty and candor. . . . Terrific."
—*The Daily Beast*

"Magisterial. . . . Brilliantly reveals the glorious highs and lows of Pryor's life. . . . *Becoming Richard Pryor* reveals itself to be not simply a biography, but the compassionate map of a terra incognita."
—Bonnie Greer, *The Independent* (London)

"[Saul] is an excellent critic, always willing to analyze and generalize and just plain do historical work. . . . Whatever Pryor is involved with—brothels in postwar Peoria, high-school dropout rates for black teenagers in that time and place, an African-American G.I.'s chance of getting a date in Germany in the late fifties, the coffee-house scene in Berkeley in the sixties, the Black Power movement in Oakland in the seventies (and that's just the beginning—forget all the later and much more complicated business of working in nightclubs and TV and movies)—Saul has studied it all." —Joan Acocella, *The New Yorker*

"With umpteen prior biographies, what could a new book possibly add to what we know about the iconoclastic stand-up comic? A great deal. Drawing on new interviews and previously unseen material, Scott Saul approaches Pryor as one might a biography of a president. His meticulous research, startling insight, and empathetic prose take us so close to his subject, it's as if he is offering a brilliantly edited volume of Pryor's diaries." —*Empire* (London), five out of five stars

"Scott Saul's *Becoming Richard Pryor* is like manna from heaven: a painstakingly researched and crisply written biography with an eye on clarification and demystification. . . . [Saul] strikes a balance between biography, commentary, and history—and in the case of this unique performer, that's harder than it looks." —*Flavorwire*

"[Saul is] an eloquent synthesizer and a first-rate analyst (he's especially good at breaking down everything about a classic bit: how it was built, why it landed, and where it came from in Pryor's tormented history). In the wake of the downfall of moralist-in-chief Bill Cosby, it pays to follow Saul into the brain of the painfully honest hot mess who truly expanded comedy's borders." —*Vulture*

"Fascinating. . . . A clear and gripping narrative that at times reads like a novel, especially in its depictions of Pryor's many battles with network and casino censors, managers, and an ever-revolving cast of wives and mistresses as his career gained in momentum and chaos. . . . One of the book's great triumphs is how skillfully Saul is able to interweave the personal, the professional, and the historical dimensions of his tale. . . . Much is debunked in the biography, and much is revealed." —*Paste*

"The Richard Pryor biography we've been waiting for." —*Deadspin*

"With *Becoming Richard Pryor,* Scott Saul gives us the fullest picture yet of a great and puzzling American figure. What starts as a procedural on the making of an artist becomes a story of a man desperate to be free."
—R. J. Smith, author of *The One: The Life and Music of James Brown*

"Pryor has had the good fortune to fall into the hands of a writer with the smarts to understand both his greatness and his madness. *Becoming Richard Pryor* is a first-rate biography."
—Peter Biskind, author of *Easy Riders, Raging Bulls*

"*Becoming Richard Pryor* takes you on a wild, tumultuous ride. Scott Saul's superb storytelling is a perfect match for his subject—he keeps you mesmerized, laughing, crying, stunned, hungry, and, above all, surprised."
—Robin D. G. Kelley, author of *Thelonious Monk: The Life and Times of an American Original*

"A well-executed study that gives Pryor due credit as pioneer, intellectual, and artist. Better written and more thoughtful than David and Joe Henry's *Furious Cool.* The latter remains worth reading, but this book is the place to start." —*Kirkus Reviews*

"Saul delivers an intimate look at how Pryor's crackling personality, biting sense of humor and complicated life fueled his daring and enduring comedy."
—Donna Seaman, *Booklist,* Top 10 Multicultural Nonfiction of 2014

"Drawing on interviews with family and friends, unpublished journals, and court records, Saul jauntily chronicles the year-by-year, and almost day-by-day, evolution of Richard Pryor. Glaringly honest, Saul shines a light on a revolutionary stand-up comic who perfected the art of dramatizing his own imperfections, and the world's."
—*Publishers Weekly*

BECOMING RICHARD PRYOR

BECOM
RI
PRY

SCOTT SAUL

ALSO BY SCOTT SAUL

Freedom Is, Freedom Ain't: Jazz and the Making of the Sixties

ING
CHARD
YOR

HARPER PERENNIAL

NEW YORK • LONDON • TORONTO • SYDNEY • NEW DELHI • AUCKLAND

HARPER PERENNIAL

A hardcover edition of this book was published in 2014 by HarperCollins Publishers.

FIRST HARPER PERENNIAL EDITION PUBLISHED 2015.

Designed by William Ruoto

Frontispiece: Michael Ochs Archives/Getty Images

The Library of Congress has catalogued the hardcover edition as follows:

Saul, Scott.
Becoming Richard Pryor / Scott Saul.—First edition.
pages cm
Includes bibliographical references and index.
ISBN 978-0-06-212330-5
1. Pryor, Richard, 1940–2005. 2. Comedians—United States—Biography.
3. Actors—United States—Biography. I. Title.
PN2287.P77S38 2015
792.7602'8092—dc23 [B] 2014034682

ISBN 978-0-06-212332-9 (pbk.)

15 16 17 18 19 OV/RRD 10 9 8 7 6 5 4 3 2 1

TO MAX

CONTENTS

PART THREE IN THE HOUSE OF PAIN

PART FOUR KING OF THE SCENE STEALERS

PART FIVE THE FUNNIEST MAN ON THE PLANET

A trickster does not live near the hearth; he does not live in the halls of justice, the soldier's tent, the shaman's hut, the monastery. He passes through each of these when there is a moment of silence, and he enlivens each with mischief, but he is not their guiding spirit. He is the spirit of the doorway leading out, and of the crossroad at the edge of town (the one where a little market springs up).

—Lewis Hyde, **TRICKSTER MAKES THIS WORLD**

The world around us is crumbling to make way for new life.

—Richard Pryor, in a 1977 interview

AUTHOR'S NOTE

On Monday, March 19, 2007, at 11:00 a.m., I drove up a hill to the parking lot of the Phillip and Sala Burton Academic High School, where I took in a startling view of San Francisco from its southeastern corner. The public radio station KALW was housed within one wing of the school; I had an appointment to meet Alan Farley, a KALW DJ who, thirty-six years earlier, had been Richard Pryor's housemate in Berkeley.

Farley welcomed me to the station. His face was framed by a full head of white hair that he parted down the middle; he spoke with the silky grace of an experienced DJ and the quavering tones of a man in his seventies. Farley was one of those intercessors whom biographers dream of finding. He had stuck close to Pryor in 1971, recording for posterity everything he could and carefully labeling and dating each reel-to-reel tape. At KALW, he spread out before me eight hours of unreleased Richard Pryor recordings. I couldn't take them home, but was allowed to listen to them in Farley's presence and make notes. As I recall, Farley spent much of his downtime that afternoon lying on the radio station floor—he was suffering just then from a debilitating attack of gout—while I tapped out page after page of notes on my laptop.

My listening session with Farley was the culmination of a

two-month quest to figure out what had happened during Pryor's enigmatic, if crucial, sojourn in the Bay Area. Pryor himself declared that he'd reinvented himself in Berkeley, experimenting with his act as never before, but he was fuzzy with the details. His previous biographers couldn't even agree on when he landed in the Bay Area. They placed his arrival somewhere between 1969 and 1971—somewhere between, that is, his beginnings as a winsome comedian in the mold of Bill Cosby and his breakthrough as the most fearless stand-up comic of the 1970s.

Since I was based in Berkeley, I'd begun my Pryor research by delving into this mystery. I interviewed those who had known him and scoured various archives for the traces he left. (It turned out that he spent seven months, February to September 1971, in the area.) I discovered that Pryor had DJ'ed a bit for KPFA, Berkeley's Pacifica affiliate, and it was that station's archives that led me to Farley; over the course of a ninety-minute interview, he revealed, among other things, that he still had his cache of Pryor-related tapes. So we arranged the rendezvous at KALW.

The tapes offered a fascinating jumble of material. They encompassed Pryor's programs on KPFA, his concerts at local clubs, his ideas for unproduced screenplays, his attempts at spontaneous poetry, and even an avant-garde sound collage. Listening to them over the course of a long afternoon, I could hear how Pryor, having come to Berkeley without a clear sense of his future, had absorbed the countercultural energies of his new home and tried out different versions of himself: serious actor, guerrilla filmmaker, poet, political satirist. His struggle was that of an artist searching for his true medium, not of a comedian polishing his material. He sparred with his audience; he riffed to himself; he spun out wild scenarios for films that seemed unfilmable. His Bay Area interlude, formerly hazy, now popped into focus. I felt I'd been raptured to Biographer Heaven.

The "Farley tapes" launched me on a quest to understand Richard Pryor anew—a quest that has pulled in biographers before me and no doubt will pull in others in the future. A man burns himself up as he ascends to the sky: this is the myth of Icarus, the story of Richard Pryor, and a tale whose meaning begs to be unraveled. Pryor revolutionized American comedy with his improvisational approach, his frank talk about sex and race, and the psychological depth that he brought to the stand-up stage. Consigned to bit roles and cameos in Hollywood, he improvised his way, literally, to become a top box office draw and the most powerful black movie star of his time. Meanwhile, he led his life with the same incisive imagination that he poured into his comedy, and with the same gamut of troubling emotions. He was intensely memorable: those who spent time with him tend to spill over with stories about this or that incident, quip, or cutting remark. And since Pryor's comedy was frequently autobiographical (in fact, he might be said to have *initiated* the autobiographical turn in stand-up comedy), there's a justifiable sense that the secret to his genius must be located within the story of his life. We long to know how he turned the confusions of his life into the complexities of his act—and how the brilliance of the act was not enough to save him.

At the same time, Pryor has proved to be an elusive quarry for the biographer. For all his openness about his life onstage, he was guarded about the facts of it offstage. He hated the standard format of Q&A interviews. Often he refused to play it straight with reporters: asked about his comedic influences, he might offer up J. Edgar Hoover. During his heyday, he wanted to reserve for himself the prerogative to tell his own story on his own terms. Even late in his life, he had the same proprietary sensibility: when film critic Elvis Mitchell tried pitching a major Pryor biography to publishers in 2004, an ailing Pryor announced he would scoop him by pitching a second memoir of his own.

Pryor's earlier biographers ran into another sort of wall when they tried to fill out his story by approaching his family with questions about his background. Pryor's elder relations were tight-lipped with outsiders to the family—a habit of circumspection they'd acquired from years of operating in Peoria's underground economy, where much business was kept off the books. When, in 1983, the

Pryor biographer John A. Williams hired a private detective in Peoria to get his bearings on the world of the Pryors, the detective warned him off the enterprise and confessed that he'd found little. "It's hard to get information from these people," he said. "It's hard even to find them."

Given the caginess of the family and of Pryor himself, earlier accounts of his life left unexplored the space between how Pryor understood his life as it unfolded and how we readers might understand it in the fullness of history; the legends of his life tended to be burnished rather than scrutinized and investigated. John A. Williams was the one early biographer who challenged Pryor's own account of his life, refusing to take it on faith. He wouldn't believe, for instance, that Pryor grew up in brothels unless he could independently confirm the fact. He tried to contact the Pryor family; they rebuffed him. He tried to find a record of the Pryor "family business" in the *Peoria Journal Star* and city directories, and came up short. So he came to question this most basic fact of Pryor's childhood. It was a bold stand—and a wrong one, as my own research has established. But it's easy to understand why, given the smokescreen he passed through, Williams might have suspected that there was, in fact, nothing to see beneath it—that the smoke was all there was.

This book is different from other Pryor biographies. It's different partly because it was written in a different, freer moment than the earlier ones that were published in Pryor's prime. By the time I began my research in 2007, the elder Pryors had passed away, as had Richard Pryor himself, and any statute of limitations had run out on the illegalities of the 1940s, '50s, and '60s. Younger relatives of Pryor, such as his two half-sisters, were willing to share their memories. And there were many more people, friends and lovers and collaborators of Pryor, who wanted to talk, too—to fill in the gaps in Pryor's own account of his life, or add a missing dimension, or dispute some piece of it. This book is built, in no small part, on the memories of the eighty-some people I have interviewed, many of whom were generous enough to speak for hours, and often over several days, about Pryor. From the person who literally shared a crib with Pryor to the musicians who played behind him at his first club dates; from those who acted alongside him in Hollywood to those who tried to build a life with him—these were my sources, and their contribution to this book has been essential.

The book is different, too, because it approaches Pryor as a historical figure and uses a historian's tools to reconstruct his life and unpack its meaning. Pryor and his family were powerfully dramatic people, and the drama of their lives left an extensive paper trail—though often the documents were not so easy to locate. I needed to constellate my own "Pryor archive," since Richard Pryor, for all his gifts, was not exactly the most punctilious record keeper; he left no set of papers on deposit. To fill out the story of Pryor's early years, I combed through old issues of newspapers like the *Decatur Herald*, the *Peoria Journal Star*, and the *Chicago Defender*; I asked the Peoria county clerk to dig up the divorce records of Pryor's parents and any records of criminal proceedings that involved his family; I procured, with the help of his widow Jennifer and the respective registrars, Pryor's school and army records.

Though a few intervals in Pryor's life remain less documented (for instance, his time on the road in 1962), these were the great exceptions. From the time he began performing as a comic in New York City in 1963, Pryor generated copy—whether in the press, the diaries of those who knew him, the archives of the film productions he worked on, or the files of the Los Angeles district attorney and the FBI.

With these materials in hand, I could follow Pryor's life from month to month and sometimes even day to day. The chronology of his life, formerly nebulous, could be clarified immensely; inflection points—for example, the moment he began speaking publicly of growing up in a brothel—could be isolated. Just as important, I could now place him within the larger tides of history: the boom of the home front during World War II, the struggle to desegregate the Midwest in the 1950s, the burgeoning of underground culture in mid-1960s Greenwich Village, the rise of the Black Power movement, the opening of "New Hollywood" in the 1970s, and so on. Filled out by these larger histories, Pryor's story took on a new resonance. He could be seen both as the exceptional comic genius he was and as a bellwether of the great changes that defined postwar American life, some of which he helped incite.

Finally, this book is different because it aims to trace, meticulously, Pryor's evolution as an artist. A recent documentary film on Pryor took the subtitle *Omit the Logic*, as if his life were disjointed to the point of absurdity. I beg to differ: though Pryor's life was certainly tumultuous—full of extreme swings of mood and violent reversals of fortune—it can, and does, make sense. Pryor developed as an artist in step with the times he lived through and the circles he inhabited. Many critics and audience members, at their first experience of Pryor, might have wondered, "Where did this man come from?," but the essential truth is that he didn't come out of nowhere. He was, first, a product of Peoria, Illinois, and of a family that was shrewd, loving, and bruising—a family of survivors. As he grew from a child into an artist, he kept himself open to everything (an important source of his genius as a performer). He learned from whoever could provide him inspiration, whether it was a garrulous wino on the street or a drama teacher at a community center, whether Jerry Lewis or Bill Cosby, Huey Newton or Mel Brooks.

In this book, I trace Pryor's artistic education up to that point, in the late 1970s, when the roles were definitively reversed—and he became the teacher from whom everyone else learned. Another sort of biography would cover the last, sobering years of Pryor's life more dutifully. I've chosen to focus on those hungry decades when Pryor was wondering who he might become and when no one, least of all Pryor himself, could anticipate what would happen next.

PROLOGUE

My grandmother is the lady who used to discipline me," says a slender man in his late thirties, wearing a collarless red satin shirt, black slacks, and gold shoes. "You know, beat my ass," he finishes with a chuckle. His face flickers between the confident look of a storyteller in control of his audience and the haunted look of a child who recalls *how* he was beaten more than *why*. Before him, at Long Beach's Terrace Theater, sits a crowd of three thousand. They're watching what will become, after the film is released, the most celebrated stand-up comedy performance of all time: *Richard Pryor: Live in Concert.*

"Anyone here remember those switches?" the comedian asks his audience. "You used to have to go get the tree yourself and take them leaves like that?" A roar of "yeah!" comes back at him. He demonstrates by reaching upward and groping to strip off a branch, suddenly a little boy agonizing over the task before him. For the rest of the sketch he'll flip effortlessly, with a jazzy rhythm, between boy and man.

"I see them trees today," he says, "I will kill one of them motherfuckers. I will stop the car—say, 'Wait, hold it.'" He strides over to the microphone stand and starts throttling it with a rage that's absurd—arbicidal. "'*You ain't never gonna grow up. You won't be beating nobody's ass.*'"

Then he pauses, returning to the perversity of his past and finding some belated pleasure in it: "That's some hell of psychology—to make you go get a switch to beat your own ass with, right? My grandmother said, 'Boy, go get me somethin' to beat your ass with.' And that would be the longest walk in the world."

He pivots so the crowd can see him in profile, a boy inching forward with a frozen look of fear on his face. "You be thinking all kind of shit 'cause you know you done fucked up, Jack," he says. The boy turns his eyes upward as if in prayer, and whimpers, "'Maybe it'll snow before I get there. Maybe she'll have a heart attack and won't be able to whup me. I don't want to get no whuppin' 'cause it's going to tear it up.'"

"You get them switches and they start cutting the wind on the way home. Make you start crying before you get in the house," the comic says.

Shwoo-shwoo.

"Ma-ma!" The boy's whimper has opened into a full-on wail.

Shwoo-shwoo.

"'Ma-ma! I don't want. . . . Mama, please! Mama, please!'" The boy starts darting from one place to another, cowering while dodging blows that seem to rain over his entire body. "Mamapleasemama-pleasemamaplease!" he howls, his voice the same pitch as a baby's scream.

At this point the routine takes the less expected tack. It would be easy for the comic, looking back at the beatings that framed his childhood, to paint his grandmother as the villain of this tale. He does not. When he plays her, his voice assumes a honeyed drawl, a more confident register, as if he were relishing her strength.

"*'Get your ass out—'*" his grandmother hollers when the boy tries to escape her wrath by putting himself to bed early. "*'Put your hand down! Don't you run from me! Don't you run from me!'*" Then, giving one downward clout to her grandson's body with every syllable: "*'Long . . . as . . . you . . . black, don't . . . you . . . run . . . from . . . me!'*" The crowd roars at this last line—at the wallop of it, the double truth about the boy's life it relays. Try as he might, there's no outrunning the twin forces of his fate, the squeeze of his race and the squeeze of his grandmother's discipline.

The next morning, the boy faces the woman who struck him, and is given a lesson in the peculiarity of love. "'Morning, Mama,'" he says softly, his mouth fixed in a grimace from the welt that has taken over his face. "'Come here, baby,'" she says, then looks at his bruises tenderly, fixing them up. "'You see, you shouldn't do that, goddamn it. I told you not to—just sit still now.'" She's still administering to the bruises when Richard Pryor delivers the last line of the sketch in her voice: "'And next time you do it, I'm going to tear your ass up again.'"

The comedian laughs, waits for the applause to die down, moves on. The instabilities of his childhood—the confusions of love and violence—have shaped him into the kind of person who is never at home with peace. A tangle of competing impulses, he cycles not just through moods but through whole personalities, of which the ingenuous child and the avenging adult figure among the most prominent. Offstage, these personalities flow through him with a volatility that makes him hard to handle, if not bewildering. One of his many wives, a few months into her short-lived marriage to him, says that getting to know him is like getting to know "25 or 30 different people." Onstage, he is mesmerizing. You feel, in the audience, that you're plugged into the socket of life—that you're seeing not a single man onstage but rather an entire world in roiling motion, animated through a taut experiment in creative chaos and artistic control.

For the comedian, though, the stakes are more personal. The stage is the place where he can set his contradictions in motion and play the full array of his many selves. If he's having a good night—if the "comedy gods" smile upon him, if he finds his form—Richard Pryor can own all these personalities as much as they own him.

PART ONE

UP FROM PEORIA

CHAPTER 1

Dangerous Elements

Decatur, 1899–1931

The matriarch on the town: Marie Carter Bryant, Richard Pryor's grandmother, in a Peoria tavern with her son Dickie, circa 1945. (Courtesy of Barbara McGee)

On the morning of October 19, 1929, a twenty-nine-year-old black woman named Marie Carter Bryant walked into a confectionary in Decatur, Illinois, with trouble on her mind. She'd just heard that a young black boy, probably one of her sons, had been slapped in the confectionary, only a few blocks from her home, and she brought with her a sort of cudgel for the purpose of evening the score. When she found Helen Pappas, one half of the Greek American couple who ran the store, behind the counter, Marie unloaded her fury: a battery of blows to Pappas's head that opened up a flesh wound. Pappas ran out of the store in a panic. Marie held her ground.

It was unusual, to say the least, for a black woman to assault a white shopkeeper in 1920s Decatur. The city's black citizens were expected to stay "in their place"—in a small area south of downtown, and on the lower rungs of the local economy—and they were expected to be quiet about it. When Marie unsettled those expectations with her cudgel, the Decatur police responded as if a bank had been robbed. Five policemen were summoned to rush the confectionary and subdue her. They found her inside, biding her time before their arrival, and arrested her on a charge of assault.

Marie Bryant was Richard Pryor's grandmother, the woman who raised him and took up residence in his psyche ever afterward, imprinting upon him her pride, cunning, and raw, bottom-dog outlook on the world. Born to a poor family that lived outside respectability, abused by her husband as a teenager, Marie had transformed herself by 1929 into a force of nature: a woman who protected herself with her own big hands and took no guff from anyone, whether they were lovers, husbands, shop owners, or policemen. A bootlegger in Decatur, she became a still more daunting presence when she moved eighty miles to Peoria, Illinois, where, as a madam in that city's thriving red-light district, she kept order in her establishments by threatening to pull out a straight razor she reportedly stashed in her bra.

The riddle of Richard Pryor's personality begins with the story of Marie and her hard-won transformation into a woman to be respected—if not out of esteem, then out of fear. The true story of her upbringing rivals any story that her grandson told from the stage.

Richard's "Mama" was born Rithie Marie Carter on October 31, 1899. Of the nine children her mother had birthed by 1900, only three survived—a punishing ratio even for a black woman at the turn of the century.

Marie's grandfather Abner Piper had been a Union volunteer in the Civil War and, paralyzed later in life, lived at home with Marie when she was a young child. He was one of many black veterans who bore witness to the limits of what the Union victory had achieved for blacks in northern cities like Decatur, the self-styled "Pride of the Prairie." Decatur had been carved out of the fertile farmland of Central Illinois, where the prairie grasses grew so tall and thick that early settlers felt as if they were alone in an ocean of the stuff, and it prospered by attracting cereal mills and breweries, furniture makers and textile plants. It was a city that celebrated its local manufacturing, a town that took pride in having invented the flyswatter and the refrigerated soda fountain. But black Decaturites were shunted to a shabby part of town and kept on the margins of its economy. Black women usually worked as domestic servants or laundresses. Black men were all-purpose laborers who, like Marie's relations, worked intermittently as hod carriers, teamsters, cooks, janitors, and the like.

Even more troublingly, blacks were subject to the vigilante justice of lynch law—made to feel that their lives were cheap and that a single case of mistaken identification could put them in the fatal clutch of a noose. The lynching of Samuel Bush in 1893 had left a deep stamp in the memory of local blacks. Police arrested Bush, an itinerant laborer from Mississippi, after a two-week search for a man who had attacked a couple of white women. Bush protested his innocence, yet many of the county's leading white citizens rushed the jail to kidnap him, backed by a mob of a thousand. The mob stripped Bush naked, strung him to a telephone pole, and hanged him. Sheriff's deputies stood nearby, intervening only after the hanging itself, when members of the mob tried to riddle Bush's dead body with bullets. That was where white lawmen in Decatur drew the line—at the desecration of a body they had let twist in the wind.

The lynching was meant to cow the city's black population into submission, but black Decaturites took a more productive lesson from it. A year later, after a black porter was arrested for attempting to rape a nineteen-year-old white domestic worker, a hundred blacks with rifles and army muskets patrolled the central business district, on the lookout for the first sign that a lynch mob was forming. For three days and nights, defying hostile coverage in the press, they guarded the streets surrounding the courthouse where the prisoner was being kept. The feared lynch mob never materialized; even the father of the victim urged local whites to let justice take its course. This astonishing act of armed self-defense was part of a broader history of local blacks mobilizing to advance their interests and protect their rights. Black political organizations, such as the Afro-American Protective League, the Negro Liberty League, and the NAACP, abounded in Decatur from the 1890s through the 1920s.

Richard Pryor's Decatur ancestors had an oblique relationship to these organizations, benefitting from their accomplishments but not investing in them personally. His kin played little role in the formal political life of the town—though they certainly absorbed the lesson that it was best to be armed if you wished to defend yourself. When the secretary of the local NAACP wrote a ten-chapter history of the city's black population on the occasion of Decatur's centennial in 1929, she enumerated seemingly every black family that had migrated to the city from its founding through the turn of the century, trumpeting their accomplishments as the stuff of Decatur's progress. Yet Richard's paternal ancestors—two large families that had arrived from Missouri and Southern Illinois and filled out the ranks of Decatur's working poor—appear nowhere in her annals. It is as if they never existed. Their dubious achievements were too often in full view for anyone reading the police blotter, and had no place in a story about the colored race's dogged pursuit of a better day.

Marie's father, Richard, had a well-earned reputation for lawlessness: he worked as a bouncer in the city's brothels and was arrested, variously, for beating his wife, whipping his wife, assaulting someone with brass knuckles, yelling obscenities in public, and pointing a firearm at his brother. But no Pryor ancestor cut a broader swath through Decatur than Marie's uncle "Tip," who, like her father, made his money in Decatur's underground economy. A tall, wiry amputee who brandished his crutch as a weapon, Tip Carter had his finger in perhaps every illegal business in town. He bootlegged liquor industriously. He turned his own home into a gaming room and ran a pool and billiards room that doubled as a gambling den. In 1909, when

Congress passed the Opium Exclusion Act—the nation's first shot in its war on drugs—Tip was among the first generation busted. Police nailed him for running an "opium joint" after finding a pipe, oil, and opium ashes among the cases of beer and whiskey in his illegal drinking hideaway.

Named in 1910 as a "disturbing element in Decatur for twenty years," Tip lived, alongside Marie's father, in a demimonde where white women and black men partnered up, sometimes in pleasure and sometimes in crime. In 1899 he was arrested simply for taking a room with a white woman. Four years later he was involved, with a white female accomplice, in a robbery that was striking for its twist of personal brutality. One night, a drunken visitor from a nearby town clambered into a carriage driven by Tip. Soon two white women were invited into the carriage, too, presumably to sweeten the party. When the visitor woke up from his revelry at 2:00 a.m., he was lying on the street in a pool of blood, wearing nothing but his underclothes. His face was mauled and his mouth throbbing with unbelievable pain. According to police and a grand jury, Tip had stripped him of his clothes and all his gold—twenty-five dollars in gold money, his gold watch, and twenty-five dollars' worth of gold in bridgework on his teeth.

Even before being imprisoned for this act of amateur dentistry, Tip Carter had been arrested a stunning 150 times. Yet Decatur was a loose enough town, and Tip Carter a capable enough person, that he seemed rather to prosper while drifting in and out of jail. He kept himself busy and salvaged a decent reputation for getting the job done: when he threw a "cakewalk" party during the dance's vogue, the *Decatur Herald* felt obliged to note that he "is himself not a cake walker, but is recognized as a good manager."

Decatur's city fathers seemed to look more kindly on an illegal operation if it was well run and its violence didn't spill over to civilians in the community. As even the local newspapers had to admit, there was a double standard of justice in Decatur: a stiffer one for blacks, a more lenient one for whites. "It is a noticeable fact that the uneducated, good-for-nothing colored man who rattles the bones for a few pennies gets himself in jail," observed the *Herald Dispatch* on the occasion of one of Tip's many gambling arrests. "The well dressed gambler who rattles bones not only for dollars but for hundreds of dollars never is locked up. He 'gets out before he gets in' and pursues his avocation on the same night he is arrested." Given how the hammer could fall on you if you were black, it was important—even while running a bordello or bootlegging operation—to be conscientious, deliberate. You had to be a man, or woman, of your word. Such was the moral instruction Marie Carter received from her uncle Tip.

On the evening of August 15, 1914, Marie Carter became Marie Pryor, the families of the bride and groom coming together at the home of the pastor of the Church of the Living God. Roy Pryor was a laborer and chauffeur. He was twenty-six; Marie, fifteen. The Pryor clan had some respectable elements—Roy's brother William was a great supporter of the Pentecostal-based church—but Roy had a dark, willful streak that may have attracted him to the notorious Carter family, and vice versa. He was the sort to be arrested for "using bad language" in public—the second of Richard Pryor's ancestors to be sent to jail on an obscenity charge. Four years before he married Marie, Roy had gotten into an altercation with a police officer. He had been arguing with another man in front of Decatur's Nickelodeon when the officer ordered him to "shut up and move on." Roy preferred not to, and instead transferred his argument to the police officer. The paddy wagon was called, and Roy sent to jail.

Marie and Roy's marriage soon produced a child, LeRoy Jr., or "Bucky," born in June of the following year. But from the start Marie found herself on the wrong end of her husband's temper. Sixteen months after their wedding, Marie attended a "grand ball" without the company of Roy. Mad with jealousy, he assaulted her and threatened to kill her. (Charges were filed; Roy pled guilty and paid a fine of $5.30.) Two years later, Marie had Roy arrested on another assault charge. In yet another incident, perhaps related to domestic violence, her brother Jim swore out a warrant for Roy's arrest, charging him with carrying a revolver.

Marie possessed a fighting spirit: she refused to be passively enmeshed in an abusive relationship. In this way, she took after her mother, aunt, and sister-in-law, who had all fought their husbands' abuse with a number of instruments at their disposal, bringing in the law when they weren't simply reaching for the closest household weapon. When Marie was four, her uncle Tip attacked his wife and paid a high price: his wife struck him on the head with a common hammer, bloodying him so much that Tip claimed to the police, believably, that he had been kicked by a horse. When Marie was six, her mother, Julia, came home to discover her father "on a ripsnorter," having consumed more than a pint of whiskey. When he refused to let his wife into the house, she called the police to put him in jail.

After she married Roy, Marie could refer to the example of her sister-in-law Blanche Carter, stuck in a volatile marriage with Marie's brother Jim. A madam herself, Blanche held her own in a marriage to a man well known in Decatur for his nitroglycerine temperament. After her husband struck her with a club and opened up two deep gashes in her head, she pressed assault charges. In another drag-out fight, in 1916, she went even further: after her husband broke a chair over her head and threw a lamp at her, she snatched up a bread knife and plunged it into his back. It was, the *Decatur Review* reported several years later, "the only time that he ever got the worst of it in a fight." Jim's wounds healed, but the marriage continued to unravel. Two years later, Jim shot an elderly man who refused to let the married Jim court his seventeen-year-old daughter at a dance—an incident that led the *Decatur Review* to argue for the incarceration of all the human powder kegs in town. ("Why wait until they kill?" the *Review* pleaded.) Blanche Carter had had enough: she filed for divorce not long thereafter. Perhaps it was one thing to be abused, and quite another to have your husband making a criminal fool of himself in pursuit of a younger woman.

Marie looked around at the women she knew, then, and saw the battle before her with her husband Roy: how to hold on to her life and her children in the presence of a man who could explode at any time? Yet she managed the impressive feat of outmaneuvering her formidable husband on at least one significant occasion. It was November 18, 1916—half a year after her sister-in-law stabbed her brother Jim in a fight. Her own husband was no longer living with her, having moved out shortly after she gave birth to Bucky, Richard Pryor's father. On a Saturday night, she took their year-old baby to a "gathering of the colored brethren" at a local meeting hall, and her husband showed up. Roy played with the baby and then (his crucial mistake) started to carry Bucky home with him. Not so fast: Marie brought the law into the picture. She pressed assault charges against her husband, which meant that he would be put in jail and the baby released back to the guardian who was not incarcerated—in this case, his mother, Marie.

It's a curious thing to consider: Marie was willing to use the police against her husband, repeatedly, but not willing to divorce him just yet. Marie and Roy had three more children together—Maxine in 1918, Richard (or Dickie) in 1920, and William in 1921. Here she was following the lead of her mother, Julia, who stuck out her marriage to Marie's father well past his abandonment of the family, his liaisons with other women, his return to the family, and his continued abuse. But then Julia died, on May 4, 1921; she'd been married for thirty-three years, since the age of nineteen. Perhaps the death of Marie's mother triggered some second thoughts about what it meant to remain with a dangerous man for one's whole adult life. Roy had continued to get in hot water with the law—he'd been arrested in a sting on their home for running a gaming house there—and there was realistically no end to the struggle.

In April 1922, Marie filed for divorce from Roy, charging him with cruelty and asking for full custody of their four children. The children ended up with Marie. A few years later, while working as a cook at a restaurant, Roy got into an argument with his boss and assaulted him with a heavy cooking utensil; the restaurant owner responded with a fusillade of knives, forks, and plates, and when they didn't connect, he threatened Roy's life with a gun while Roy hid behind the stove. (An inquiry by the state's attorney determined that Roy was at fault.) In 1928, in another matter, Roy pled guilty to grand larceny and was given probation. By that point, the vicissitudes of his life may have been of little interest to Marie. She had a new man and a family to protect. Her children kept Roy's last name, but she went back to her maiden name of Carter. She was done.

The new man was Thomas Bryant, a light-skinned black man who wore wire-rimmed spectacles, a pencil-thin mustache, and a soft, sometimes inscrutable expression on his face. Six years older than Marie, he was, like her, a veteran of a collapsed marriage. He had married his first wife, Blanche, in 1920, when he was twenty-seven and she was fourteen; they divorced seven years later, and he lost custody of his two children after being accused of drunkenness in the proceedings. The charge may have been a screen for another set of difficulties. Just before the divorce filing, Thomas Bryant was convicted of selling liquor and spent three months on the Vandalia prison farm in Southern Illinois, where he milked cows and grew corn with his fellow inmates.

The newly single Bryant would have met a considerably different woman from the teenager whom Roy Pryor married. Somewhere between her wedding and her divorce, Marie Carter had become a redoubtable woman: bigger, tougher, and more independent-minded. Her marriage to Roy had salted her with fire, giving her a sense of what she could abide and what she could not. She had absorbed some of the aggressive energy of her husband and the rest of her family: in 1919, she was arrested for fighting with another black woman on Main Street in Decatur. And for a while she stepped out of Roy's shadow by managing a little down-home musical duo, the Jazz Bone Minstrel Company, in which one man made music with a comb while the other blew a jug—a sign that the abuse from her husband had hardly robbed her of her sense of fun.

In September 1925, at the age of twenty-five, she had lost the second of her two parents. Her father, Richard, had been working in the Wabash rail yards when he was crushed between two train cars as they switched tracks. Marie's father had mellowed in his last few years: his obituary noted that he had served as a steward of the African Methodist Episcopal Church and was a member of the Knights of Tabor, a black fraternity. But according to Pryor family legend, his devil-may-care side reasserted itself one last time after he was struck by the railcars. Rather than request medical attention after the collision, the old man staggered to a nearby speakeasy and ordered himself a drink. A few hours later, he was pronounced dead.

Free of her former husband, deprived of her parents, and partnered up with a man with bootlegging experience, Marie turned entrepreneurial: she became a bootlegger herself. Decatur had been an on-again, off-again dry town in the first two decades after 1900, a swing city in the fight by temperance forces to abolish alcohol in Illinois. The passage of national Prohibition, in 1919, turned Decatur over to the "drys" and transformed thousands of saloon-going Decaturites into would-be criminals craving a banned substance. Many Decaturites started drinking "canned heat," a legal cooking fuel made from denatured and jellied alcohol, even though it could cause them to go blind or die. The city's police chief challenged anyone who doubted the extent of the problem to inspect the Sterno trash mounds distributed across the city, thousands of empty cans piling up as evidence of a collective desperation. Some bootlegging establishments in Decatur mixed their drinks with the stuff, straining the resulting liquid through a loaf of bread to reduce its traces of poison. Dangerously adulterated whiskey was, for many, better than no whiskey at all.

It didn't take much—a bottle, two chairs, and a dash of chutzpah—to open a speakeasy. Marie followed the standard practice, developed in black neighborhoods like Harlem, of converting her private apartment into a small-scale drinking establishment. Twelve-forty East Sangamon Street became what was known elsewhere as a "buffet flat." Unfortunately, little is known about Marie's Decatur speakeasy except that she was busted, once, in a raid on her home on a Sunday night in mid-October 1929. Marie was arrested for possession of intoxicating liquor, the charge affixed to a bootlegger when the police were not able to buy a bottle and leave the establishment. She pled guilty and, rather than face jail time, chose to pay a fine of $28.15.

It was just a week after her bootlegging bust that Marie ran into more trouble with the law when, out of some mixture of maternal instinct and racial pride, she stormed into a neighborhood confectionary and exercised her wrath upon the woman behind its counter. When the shopkeeper, Helen Pappas, pressed assault charges, Marie did not back down: she pleaded not guilty and struck back with a countercharge a week later. The shopowners, Michael and Helen Pappas, she claimed, were the ones guilty of assault. It's unclear what exactly Marie told the police to get the Pappas couple arrested: perhaps she was standing up for the boy who had been slapped, pressing charges on his behalf; or perhaps she was clearing the way for her own defense by asserting that she hadn't been the one who started the fight; or perhaps she was fabricating an incident to rile the Pappas couple. In any case, Marie was not one to let her adversaries land the last blow; as with the police at the confectionary, she held her ground. "Tit for Tat," read the headline in the *Decatur Herald*.

Yet there were limits to how much a strong-minded black woman could bend the city of Decatur to her will; Marie eventually lost in court. After her opening plea of not guilty, she switched to one of guilty three weeks after her arrest and was fined fifty dollars, which she paid. All told, between the bootlegging fine and the assault fine, Marie lost the equivalent of around a thousand 2014 dollars. Michael and Helen Pappas entered a plea of not guilty to the assault charge Marie had filed, and seem to have escaped being fined a cent.

At the same time that Marie's assault charge was working its way through the Decatur courts, Wall Street was beginning to totter. On October 28, 1929, or "Black Monday," the Dow lost 13 percent of its value. The next day, Black Tuesday, it lost another 12 percent.

By July 8, 1930, stocks had declined 89 percent from their peak. It's highly unlikely that Marie and her new husband, Thomas, belonged to the 16 percent of American households that invested in the stock market, but they would have noticed the shattering effect of the crash nonetheless. Decatur's industrial base shriveled, with factory payrolls plunging 37 percent between the mid-1920s and 1932. Class war broke out in the streets: when around two hundred miners picketed the Macon County Coal Company in 1932, the police dispersed them with shotguns, tear gas, and axe handles. As was true across the country, Decatur's black community was especially hard hit. The few blacks who held on to work were usually the hired help of affluent whites: domestics and chauffeurs.

Meanwhile, eighty miles away in Peoria, a river city with a vice district that bustled even in hard times, a business opportunity was opening up for Marie. In the small hours of September 29, 1930, a man named Joe Markley kicked in the door of a well-appointed brothel operated by "Diamond Lil," a stout black madam known for the twelve stones, each at least a carat, embedded in the top row of her teeth. Markley demanded to see Lil. Rebuffed, he rushed to the stairs that led to her bedroom. Before he could get there, Lil herself appeared at the top of the stairs pointing a six-shooter down at him, the gun belt and holster wrapped around her nightgown. Markley moved for Lil's gun; in the ensuing scuffle, he got shot twice in the chest. Lil was convicted of murder and given a fourteen-year sentence in the state penitentiary in Joliet. Her club the Oasis, a brothel known as the "largest and liveliest black and tan resort" in Central Illinois, closed soon afterward.

Lil's Oasis was located at 200 Eaton Street, in the heart of Peoria's main red-light district. Marie moved to 130 Eaton Street, just a few doors down from where Lil's establishment had been, and set up her own brothel there. Her recent trouble with the law in Decatur probably motivated her decision to relocate and her choice of destination. *The Christian Century* called Peoria "the sinkhole of midwestern vice, the place to which prostitutes can flee when driven out anywhere else." This "sinkhole" was Marie's safe haven, a hospitable base of operations. She could take refuge in a town where gambling was big business, black madams commanded a public stage, and the longtime mayor and his cronies ran city politics out of an old houseboat dubbed the Bumboat.

She brought her whole family—her new husband, Thomas, and her four teenage children—to Peoria with her. Soon her son Buck and a young woman fresh from Springfield would make her a grandmother for the first time. Her grandson would be given the name of her father: Richard.

CHAPTER 2

The Backside of Life

Peoria, 1932–1946

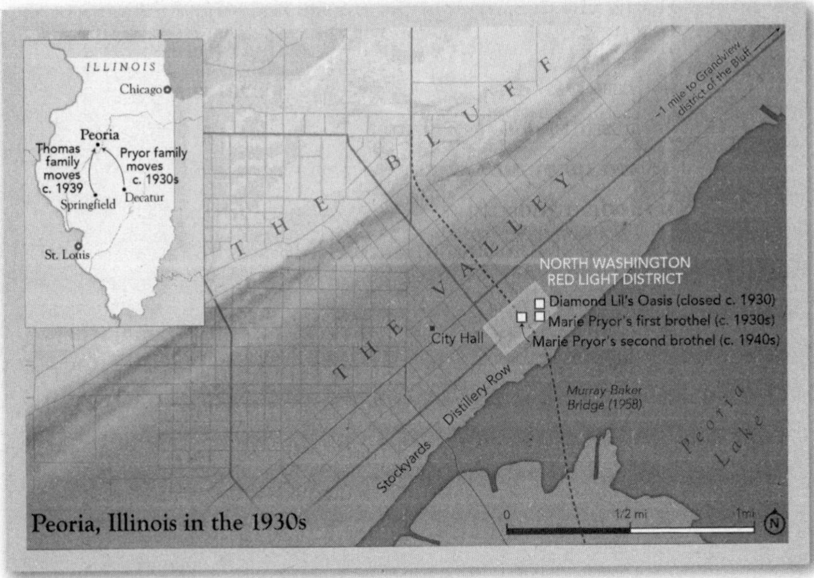

Peoria, Illinois in the 1930s

There's something about the sound of "Peoria" that makes people think that they know the city when they simply know the cadence of its name. "Sweet as far-off bugle note / Fall the syllables and float— / Peoria!" gushed a New Hampshire poet in 1890. On the vaudeville circuit in the early twentieth century, "Peoria" became the setup to a joke about a heartland city that was the most boring place on the planet. "Do you know Peoria?" "Oh, yes—I spent four years there one night." Or: "Why did you two get married?" "We were in Peoria and it rained all week."

By the 1930s, when Richard Pryor's grandmother arrived in Peoria, the jokes about the land of "the rube and the boob" bore only the thinnest relationship to the actual city. Far from a blandly typical midwestern town, Peoria was perhaps America's most unchecked sin city, a bold experiment in squeezing maximum profit from the pleasures of the flesh. Peorians were different, looser: they "talk[ed] about corruption the way people elsewhere talk about baseball," one reporter noted, and divorced at a rate double that of Illinois and the rest of America.

A hundred seventy miles southwest of Chicago, Peoria rose up from the western bank of the Illinois River, which connected it to the Mississippi and points beyond. In the early nineteenth century, it was settled by homesteaders from Virginia, Kentucky, and Maryland; in the 1840s, a wave of German immigrants brought with them their native fondness for beer and their recipes for how to brew it. Beer and whiskey became the economic cornerstones of this "city of good spirits." Though only a midsize city, Peoria began boasting of its unmatched achievements. Starting in the 1880s, it hosted the largest distillery in the world; its breweries and distilleries required so much corn from the nearby Corn Belt that Peoria became the largest corn-consuming market in the world. In the era before the federal income tax, Peoria, through the whiskey tax, was responsible for fully half the federal government's internal revenue, by one estimate. (Chicago was second in whiskey tax revenue, Cincinnati third.) Later, the arrival of Caterpillar's headquarters and the LeTourneau factory made the city the earth-moving capital of the world, too.

Yet Peoria was a city of violent contrasts, disparities so extreme that they begged to become grist for satire. The city was divided geographically and culturally between its industrial valley, which skirted the river, and the bluffs that looked down from a height of three hundred feet on the valley below. On the bluffs at night, a pair of lovers might bask in silvery moonlight; below, their valley equivalents might inhale a yellow fog that carried distillery fumes and the aroma of hog intestines. Above: magnificent estates inhabited by the city's managerial class. (Theodore Roosevelt was so moved by the area's palatial homes, gentle curves, and expansive vistas that he called its main street "the world's most beautiful drive.") Below: streets thick with the modest homes and outhouses of machinists, carpenters, salesmen, and waitresses.

The politics of the bluffs were the politics of "reform": its inhabitants hoped to scrub city politics clean as a whistle. One of its noted residents, the industrialist Robert LeTourneau, took as his slogan "God Runs My Business." The politics of the working-class valley were "liberal," which in the parlance of the day meant open gambling, open drinking, and open prostitution, all held together by a network of underworld businessmen who followed a principle of mutual self-interest. In Peoria, "live and let live" meant, according to the local paper, "Don't bother my racket and I won't bother yours."

The bluffs controlled the manufacturing economy of Peoria, but for the first half of the twentieth century the valley controlled its politics, and for a simple reason: it had the votes. From 1902 until 1945, the face of "Roarin' Peoria" was the thin, flushed, cigar-chomping mug of Ed Woodruff, who served as the city's mayor, off and on, for twenty-four years. Woodruff operated an ice company and lived in an unfashionable part of town. His philosophy, which he made into his city's, was "Peoria likes to live and doesn't want to be told what to do and what not to do all the time." A self-fashioned man of the people, he held court on the steps of city hall, which, under his tenure, became a place avoided by the decent folk of the bluffs. Feminist pioneer Betty Friedan, a native Peorian and self-styled decent person, recalled with disdain that "bums cluttered its steps and threw their empty bottles into the courthouse yard."

Peoria of the 1930s was "wide open as the gateway to hell," wrote the *Peoria Journal* twenty years later—"a city where every sordid passion had its willing handmaidens." This was not just vivid hyperbole. The sex trade was a mainstream affair. Hustling women cruised the downtown bars, offering patrons a quick visit to a hotel room or the backseat of a parked car. One downtown restaurant even supplied, for its customers, a group of vacant parked cars in a lot in the back; once bidden, a young woman could enter a car and earn half a dollar for her services. A professional criminal familiar with the Capone organization landed in Peoria and was shocked. "When I had left Chicago," he said, "well, things had been pretty wide open, but they weren't as wide open as they were in Peoria. Which was something for me to look at—wide-open gambling, wide-open prostitution, everything running wide open. With no interference from the law."

In fact, the city worked out a set of formal protocols with its underground entrepreneurs. Madams like Diamond Lil were required to register their girls with the city and get them regularly checked by a doctor for venereal disease. Slot machine operators paid city hall a rate of twenty dollars a month per machine and were free to place the machines in newsstands and neighborhood drugstores, even near local schools (the latter being penny machines—in Peoria, it was never too early to learn how to gamble). Walk across the street from the police department and you'd be in the city's most elaborate casino. Walk across the street from city hall and you'd be in a high-stakes, protected dice game. Every Monday, a messenger from local operators carried to city hall a sealed envelope stuffed with cash, which was recorded in the municipal budget under the title "Special Miscellaneous: Madison Novelty Co." "Madison" referred to the street where city hall was located; "novelty" seemed to wink at the peculiarity of Peoria's arrangements.

Unfortunately, the "liberal" ethos of Peoria did not extend to the realm of civil rights for its black residents, who were 3 percent of the city's population in 1940, the year of Richard Pryor's birth. Like many northern cities before World War II, Peoria was legally integrated but, on a practical level, segregated from top to bottom. In housing, black Peorians were concentrated in districts known before 1900 as "Watermelon Wards." Soup Alley, Tin Can Alley, Pig Ear Alley—these were the nicknames attached to the black parts of town, and the preponderance of "alleys" was no coincidence, since black Peorians were made to live in narrow straits. None of Peoria's hotels admitted blacks; many of its laundries would not take clothes worn by blacks; only two restaurants downtown served blacks; and most movie theaters seated blacks only in the mezzanines, while two movie theaters banned them entirely.

For blacks, liberal Peoria was a city of grudging compromises. There might be black policemen, but they did not patrol white areas and could not arrest white people. There might be blacks admitted into the city-run swimming pools, but only one day a week. Blacks might be able to attend integrated schools, but no matter how well educated, they were pushed into menial jobs or shut out of the workforce entirely. In 1940, 40 percent of black Peorians were out of work—a sobering statistic made comprehensible by the number of employers who essentially refused to hire blacks. Caterpillar Tractor, the largest employer in Central Illinois, had no blacks on its payroll before World War II; the local power utility had one. And while policemen may have looked the other way at organized crime in Peoria, they were ever vigilant at the first sign of "trouble" from blacks in town. A full two-thirds of black Peorians reported, in 1940, the persistence of police brutality.

Yet while there may have been many better places in America to be black, arguably there was no better place to be a black madam. The same white men who refused to hire blacks in their businesses were happy to gamble away their money or hire a prostitute in a black madam's brothel. Since the 1870s, there had been a line of black madams who swaggered and threw their weight around town: Adaline Cole, the "queen of Peoria's half world" in the decades before the rise of Diamond Lil, cut quite the figure riding with her girls through the streets of Peoria, her elegant black carriage pulled by a team of sleek black horses. An enterprising, poorly educated black woman in Peoria could look at her main options, prostitution or domestic service, and reasonably conclude that prostitution offered a more likely path to a higher station in the world.

When the Pryor clan first arrived in Peoria, the rest of Marie's family found jobs outside the world of brothels. Marie's husband,

Thomas, worked as a butcher; Buck, Richard's father, as a chauffeur; his aunt Maxine, as an entertainer; his uncle Dickie, as an elevator operator. But by the early 1940s, when Marie opened a second brothel on North Washington Street, the red-light district's main thoroughfare, everyone appears to have been integrated into the "family business" and fallen into their respective roles. They lived and worked in what Richard Pryor later called "the backside of life."

Settling into a role that fit her well, Marie was the family's madam in chief. She was a boulder of a woman—six feet tall, over two hundred pounds of immovable flesh—and she was in charge of establishing the law of the house. Thomas, or "Pops," tended to work on the sidelines: when the Pryors had a legitimate business on the side, like a tavern or a pool hall, Pops would be found there. Buck was the muscle of the operation, having won a Golden Gloves boxing tournament in Chicago when he was eighteen. Dickie and Maxine were more sociable types and could be counted on to do the work of recruiting the girls and the johns. All Marie's children were large people—Maxine was close to six feet tall; Buck, six foot two; Dickie, six foot four—and cumulatively, they had the sort of heft that could make any trouble go away.

As a madam, Marie had a motto, "Don't mess with my money," by which she meant that you shouldn't mess with the money in her hand, the prostitutes whose bodies she owned, and the johns whose cash she was seeking. The color of money was more important than black or white: while black customers predominated on Marie's block of North Washington, whites were not to be harassed. To enforce the law of the house, Marie had her straight razor. Prostitutes would meet the razor if they tried to cheat her of her customary 50 percent share of the take; johns would be sliced on the face if they tried to leave without paying. (One childhood friend of Richard Pryor's recalled "a lot of men" walking around Peoria "with nasty scars around their face.") In later years, Marie upgraded to a pistol, which she carried strapped to her leg. Most of the time, she didn't need to draw her weapon or even use her fists. She simply said, referring to her size-twelve shoes, "I'll put my twelves up in your ass," and the trouble went away.

"I was raised to hate cops," Richard Pryor once told a journalist. "We ran a whorehouse, and I was raised to not trust police." But through the 1940s, Marie, like other madams in Peoria, appears to have reached an accommodation with the authorities, who gave her free rein to run her business as she saw fit. Richard remembered that, during election season, "all the political people would come to the whorehouse to try to win votes, to tell all the whores that there wouldn't be no busts and shit like that." Woe betide the rookie cop who decided to take down Marie. According to family legend, Marie's brothel was once raided by a group of young policemen who were unaware that the house was off-limits. "As fast as they would come in," remembered family friend Cecil Grubbs, "she would throw them out the door. She said, 'You tell your chief, you don't go bothering me.' And before they could get back to the station, she'd been there, talking to the chief, and her place wasn't bothered anymore."

Marie's toughness and working relationship with the cops might have been savored, from a distance, as the stuff of family lore, but the scene was considerably uglier up close. One of Richard's neighbors recalled being devastated, as a young girl, by what she saw on the sidewalk of North Washington Street, right in front of Marie's brothel. Marie was whaling with her fists on the body of a black woman, most likely one of her prostitutes. Buck the boxer was standing on the sidelines. The woman would struggle to get up; Marie would knock her back down, hard enough to draw blood. As this one-sided melee unfolded, a police car rolled down the street and continued on its way; Marie kept whaling. Looking on, the young girl cried uncontrollably.

Even in Peoria, where the red-light district was integrated into the political and social life of the city, it was no place for the tender emotions of a child.

The historical record sheds only a bit of light on the background of Richard Pryor's mother, Gertrude Thomas. Unlike the paternal side of Pryor's family, the maternal side kept clear of the law and left few traces. Born in 1919, Gertrude spent her first years on a farm in the small eastern Illinois township of Pilot, where her father, Robert, worked land that he did not own. As the Great Depression deepened, Gertrude's family was part of the migration off of farms and toward cities, leaving Pilot for Springfield, Illinois. Her father started working, like her future husband, as a chauffeur. Though her family was part of the working poor, Gertrude was likely exposed in Springfield to a more glamorous lifestyle. Her father's employer lived in the tony neighborhood of Leland Grove and was the business manager and personnel director of Illinois's State Division of Highways, administering one of the larger money pots in Illinois government. A more attainable sort of glamour was on display at Rosalie's, a two-story brothel with a black madam and black prostitutes, a few blocks away from Gertrude's home. En route to her high school, Gertrude would have passed Rosalie's and noted the spectacle: the deep red paint of the house, the neon sign with a red rose, the girls dressed in the latest fashions.

Around 1939, the Thomas family relocated to Peoria: Gertrude's father found work there as a driver. The twenty-year-old Gertrude struck out on her own and took a room in a fateful location downtown: across the street from the apartment building where two of Marie's children, Maxine and Dickie, were staying. She was launching herself in the world, and it's likely that they introduced her to Marie as a girl who could work in her brothel. Gertrude was light-skinned, small if solid, and moon-faced, with sad, expressive eyes. An added bonus, from Marie's point of view, may have been that she was fresh from Springfield: Peoria madams preferred to take their girls from out of town. In Marie's brothel, Gertrude reportedly took on the professional name of Hildegarde, a nod to the elegant supper club singer of the period.

And what did Gertrude see in front of her when she met her future husband, Buck? The twenty-four-year-old son of the madam who was bringing her into the business; a tall man with the muscled body of a former boxer, now settling a bit; heavy-lidded eyes that rested all their weight on whatever they focused on; a well-trimmed mustache over a mouth that, at least in photos, gave out a thin smile. The various features added up to a man, good with his hands, who enjoyed his vices, did not deny them for himself, and radiated a hustler's tough confidence. His softer side was expressed through his love of music: he adored the Ink Spots' 1939 ballad "If I Didn't Care," and loved to sing it. Perhaps Buck wooed Gertrude as he wooed another woman who would carry his child, a year after Richard was born, by singing onstage at a local tavern.

The two began sleeping together, and when Gertrude became pregnant and wanted to keep the baby, Buck let her. He did not have much choice: Marie took Gertrude's side in the matter.

Richard Franklin Lennox Thomas Pryor was born December 1, 1940, in Peoria's St. Francis Hospital. There was no birth announcement in the local newspapers because Pryor's parents were unmarried and the papers did not trumpet births that could not be attached to a "Mr." and "Mrs."

The circumstances surrounding Richard's arrival in the world remained a mystery to him later in life. "I wish I would've asked my mother more about how I came to be, but didn't," he admitted in his memoir. "Why didn't you, Richard?" It's easy to understand the older Richard's frustration: he had only a fleeting relationship with his mother, Gertrude, and it was concentrated in the first five years of his life, when his memories were few and hazy. Raised by a grandmother who "made it her job to scare the shit out of people," he could not help but wonder what it might have been like to grow up around someone whose oversize shoes were not always threatening to kick your ass.

"At least Gertrude didn't flush me down the toilet as some did," Pryor reflected in a hard-bitten aside. "When I was a kid, I found a baby in a shoe box—dead. An accident to some, I was luckier than others, and that was the way it was." As he was growing up, his father never let him forget that he was fortunate simply to have been taken in by the family. "I chose you, so be cool," Buck repeatedly advised the young Richard. "You could be in an orphanage." Buck's other children—four more, by four different women—may not have been sent to orphanages, but neither were they raised within the family.

A year after the baby arrived, the onset of World War II gave a great jolt to the family business. Caterpillar jumped into high gear, manufacturing tank transmissions, howitzer carriages, and bomb fuses; its tractors leveled the landscape of South Pacific islands for airstrips and cleared the rubble from London during the Blitz. Cash was everywhere on the table in Peoria. Factory hands had steady work again, and soldiers streamed in on weekend passes, looking to spend their wages on a good time. After the opening of nearby Camp Ellis in April 1943, that stream into Peoria became a deluge. There were so many soldiers sleeping off their hangovers on the courthouse lawn in the center of downtown that Peoria County opened up its jails and let the soldiers crash on beds brought from the camp.

Politically, the war sharpened Peoria's divides, emboldening the city's "reform" elements while handing windfall profits to the operators of its red-light districts. Regional military officials noticed that soldiers were picking up venereal diseases on their lost Peoria weekends, and in early 1942, they threatened that the city would be denied defense contracts and declared "out of bounds" for soldiers and defense workers if its brothels were not padlocked. Peoria's Junior Chamber of Commerce organized a mass meeting on the theme of "Why Peoria's Vice District Must Go!" Venereal disease, chaplains declaimed, was a form of wartime sabotage on a par with Nazis wrecking machinery in defense plants. In response, the foxlike Mayor Woodruff practiced a strategy of public acquiescence and private obstruction. When the reform-minded city council passed ordinances closing brothels, Woodruff assented but kept the city's health department and police from pursuing the work with any vigor. And even when judges clamped down on prostitution, levying a two-hundred-dollar instead of a five-dollar fine on brothel keepers, the local madams found a way to keep the profits rolling in. They jacked up their prices three- or fourfold, and the unlucky soldiers, who sometimes had not been to a city in two or three months, paid the new tariff. According to Richard Pryor, his grandmother had her own strategy for skimming a little extra from servicemen in her brothel: she'd ply them with liquor and turn up the heat in the winter months, then have a young boy like Richard search their combat boots for money while they were sound asleep.

The war years were boom times for Marie and her family. A good number of Camp Ellis men were black, and so found their way to the block on North Washington Street where Marie ran her brothel. Soon she expanded her operation to include another brothel two doors down and a tavern on Adams Street just an alley away: men who came to the tavern looking for action could easily be funneled to one of her houses. She copped the tavern's resonant name, the Famous Door, from a pair of well-known clubs in New Orleans and New York. The place might have been simple—a handful of tables, drinks but no food, a small bandstand—but it had aspirations. The family was joining together and going "legit," carried there by the money sluicing around wartime Peoria. A photograph of the Famous Door, taken around 1945, is a family portrait—and perhaps the only surviving picture that places Richard's mother, Gertrude, with his grandmother, father, uncle, and aunt. Framed in the center of the ensemble, Marie has the happiest face in the picture, one lit up with a den mother's pride.

Then Buck received his draft notice, and the war was more than just an economic godsend. Buck married Gertrude on December 24, 1943, in Peoria, seven days before he was inducted into the U.S. Army in Chicago; the Pryor family now claimed the three-year-old Richard officially. Buck and Gertrude were probably motivated, like so many wartime couples, by practical concerns as much as any desire to cement a romance. As a war bride, Gertrude would receive a fifty-dollar monthly allotment for herself and a twenty-dollar monthly allotment for their son; and if Buck were killed in the war, she would be the beneficiary of the army's ten-thousand-dollar life insurance

The Pryor family at the Famous Door. Bottom row from left: Gertrude Thomas Pryor, Dee Pryor. Top row from left: unidentified woman, unidentified man, Marie Carter Bryant, Dickie Pryor, LeRoy "Buck" Pryor. (Courtesy of Barbara McGee)

policy. Death in battle was a palpable threat: on their wedding day, the Peoria newspapers announced that Gen. Dwight Eisenhower had been selected to head up a second Western Front, a huge human mobilization that would be launched six months later, with the D-Day invasion of Normandy.

Buck did not last long as an enlisted man. Well before his time in the army, he had bristled against shows of discipline: as early as 1931, he was arrested in Decatur for disorderly conduct. The army was a poor match for a man of his temperament and ego. After seven months, in July 1944, it gave him a Section 8 discharge ("mentally unfit for service") at the height of the military's large-scale deployments in Europe and the Pacific. It was as if he had been declared unsuitable even as cannon fodder. One intriguing detail from the traces he left in Army records: Buck's pay was docked for ten days of lost time. By whatever means—going AWOL, drinking too much, taking too many drugs—he had absented himself from his military obligations for that interval. Buck returned to Illinois with $68.72 in back pay, cut off from veteran's benefits: no unemployment benefits, no education benefits, no home loans, no disability checks, no military burial—none of the entitlements that helped lift so many working-class veterans of World War II into the American middle class.

Judging from his subsequent actions in Peoria, Buck didn't come back from his tour of duty with much respect for military men. On the afternoon of February 12, 1945, a black sergeant from Camp Ellis was strolling down North Washington Street, a block from Marie's brothels, with a billfold carrying $106 in cash. Buck and another man jumped him, dragged him into a sunken space off the sidewalk, pummeled him, and took his money, wristwatch, Ronson lighter, and pocketknife. Buck was indicted by a grand jury for assault and robbery. The sergeant had been staying at the exact address where Buck's brother and sister let rooms, so it's possible that Buck was tipped off to look out for the black soldier with a wallet stuffed with money.

For the most part, Buck's post-service violence was directed at a closer and easier target: his wife. They worked together at the Famous Door—Gertrude as a waitress, in a close-fitting white uniform; Buck as a bartender—but at home they fought constantly. Typically, in the heat of argument, he would knock her down, then leave the room with her still splayed on the floor. In the space of one month in late 1945, according to Gertrude's divorce papers, Buck once struck her and kicked her in the face; once beat her so badly that she was "compelled to seek refuge with friends"; and once threw a chair at her before beating her face and body, again forcing her to take refuge. Gertrude's flights went unexplained to the young Richard. Even later in life, he half-blamed his mother for abandoning him: "Gertrude drank a lot. She'd be home for six months or so, then one day she'd leave the house as if she was going to the store, say goodbye and be gone for six months. How'd that make you feel, Rich?"

Though her divorce filing painted her as the victim of domestic abuse, Gertrude was sometimes capable of throwing a few punches herself. On at least one occasion, according to Richard, she managed to get the better of her husband through a supremely well-aimed swipe. Buck, wearing undershorts and a T-shirt, had been beating her in their bedroom, and finally Gertrude drew the line: "Okay, motherfucker, don't hit me no more." Buck hit her again. Gertrude shot back, "Don't stand in front of me with fucking undershorts on and hit me, motherfucker"—and then, lightning-quick, she clawed his crotch. Buck ran to his mother's brothel two doors down, and the four- or five-year-old Richard saw him bust in, his undershorts wet with blood, crying, "Mama! Mama!" The boy struggled to reconcile his father's panic and his mother's air of satisfaction. When, soon after, she hugged Richard and rubbed his head, she "confused my ass just by being so nice to me."

All told, Richard's sentimental education was none too sentimental. Just as a young Marie and a young Buck had watched their respective parents go at it, so Richard now watched *his* parents do the same; he absorbed the message that love was tangled up in violence. He believed to the end that his father truly loved his mother: "He felt that deep kind of love that doesn't ever do a person good, that ends up kicking you in the ass, leaving you crying and tormented." This was love in the spirit of the blues—crazy love, love as damnation, love as possession by devils, with little tenderness to act as a countervailing force. Buck eventually admitted to Richard that "he was glad Gertrude had gone. He loved her so much, he said he probably would've killed her."

On December 31, 1945, Gertrude decided she'd had enough. She fled North Washington Street with her son, telling no one in the Pryor family where she was going. She wanted a clean break for both of them: no more Buck or Marie, or the family business. The Pryors scrambled to find her and Richard, to no avail: Gertrude was no longer in Peoria. Many days later, she disclosed her whereabouts—in Springfield, seventy miles away—when she filed a legal petition for divorce.

The divorce was ugly, with the custody of the five-year-old Richard at the center of it and the two sides jousting for the judge's sympathies. The stakes for Richard's future were stark: would he end up with Gertrude and her parents on the rural outskirts of Springfield, sharing space with livestock, or would he remain with Buck and Marie, surrounded by the sex trade? The court battle was a curious shadow-puppet show where no one could mention the fact that they had all been involved in illegal activities—and, more specifically, that Buck's family ran a brothel where Gertrude had worked. Both parties presented themselves to the judge as upstanding citizens and fine parents. In her suit, Gertrude claimed that she had "always conducted herself in a manner becoming an affectionate and virtuous wife," while Buck had acted with "extreme and repeated cruelty." She asked for custody and some financial relief.

In his counterclaim, Buck denied everything—that Gertrude had ever been compelled to leave for fear of her safety, that he had ever struck her on any of the days enumerated—and went on the offensive. Most likely he benefitted from the strategic counsel of Marie, who had learned in Decatur how to bend the law to her own use. Exploiting Gertrude's professional life to undercut her suit, Buck argued that she had "committed adultery with divers other persons to your counter-plaintiff unknown." (Notably, Buck alleged that she had committed adultery on the exact same day when, she claimed, he had struck her; he let the judge draw his own conclusions.) He labeled her an unfit mother, accusing her of child abandonment under cover of "taking refuge." By leaving Peoria with Richard in tow, Buck argued further, she had essentially kidnapped the child. Last, he added that as an army veteran, he was a fit person to take custody of Richard.

This final claim was simply too much for Gertrude. How could someone who'd been kicked out of the army draw upon the great reservoir of gratitude felt toward those who had served honorably? Her one formal response to Buck's counterclaim was an "affidavit of non-military service" clarifying that Buck was no longer with the army. But Gertrude did not contest, on paper, the substance of Buck's suit. She did not bring up, for instance, how he had fathered a child by another woman. Nor did she make what seems the most obvious claim for custody of her child: with her, Richard would not be raised inside a brothel.

On March 26, 1946, Justice John T. Culbertson (a future Illinois Supreme Court judge) heard the case in Peoria County Circuit Court. Richard sets the scene vividly in his memoir: Buck and Marie dressed him up in his Sunday best and coached him to tell the judge that he wanted to stay with Marie, not Gertrude. In court, he remembered saying exactly that—"I'd like to be with my grandma, please"—and remembered feeling shattered by the experience. "I broke my mother's heart," he wrote. "But, Ma, I thought that they were going to kill me if I said that I wanted to live with you."

If Richard Pryor had ever consulted the records of his parents' divorce, he would have discovered that this recollection—of betraying his mother and asking the judge to give custody to his father—was a trick of his memory. He thought he was ten at the time when, in fact, he was only five, and the testimony of a five-year-old child would hardly have been the decisive factor in awarding custody, then or now. (The judge's three-page ruling does not mention Richard having any preference for his guardian.) In an even greater discrepancy, the judge's decision stated that Richard was living in Springfield "at the present time." If true, then it seems improbable that he was coached in any testimony by his father and grandmother, as he was not living with them before the court date.

In his ruling, Judge Culbertson came down hard on Gertrude. Though there was generally a presumption, in custody battles, that the mother would be better fit to care for young children, Culbertson did not give Gertrude an inch of sympathy. Buck was a "true, loving, affectionate and dutiful husband"; Gertrude, an adulterer and a mother who had repeatedly deserted her child. Culbertson decried how, at the time of the hearing, Richard had been "abandoned" in Springfield, though most likely he was simply staying at the home of Gertrude's parents. He awarded the full "custody, control and education" of Richard to Buck, and explicitly prohibited Gertrude from "any interference" in Richard's upbringing; she had no visitation rights. After his ruling, Gertrude would be involved in her son's life only at Buck's discretion.

It seems a curiously extreme ruling in retrospect. The testimony of the gentler parent was deemed a fraud; the testimony of the more abusive parent was taken on faith. Sole custody was given to a father who never found a way to talk to his son—a man whom Richard later summed up this way: "He had a child but he didn't need a child." But Culbertson was responding to the panic stirred up, at the tail end of World War II, by a perceived spike in adultery among war brides: in one notorious case, a sailor came home from the Pacific to discover another man wearing his old clothes and living with his wife and son. Such stories offered a quick explanation for a divorce rate without precedent in American history. In 1940, one in six marriages had ended in divorce; in 1946, with so many wartime marriages unraveling upon the husband's return, the ratio stood at one in four. It was tempting to believe, as Culbertson simplified matters in his ruling, that the adultery of a wife like Gertrude was the root cause of a marriage falling apart, and that a man cuckolded was a man who deserved the indulgence of the court. To find the source of trouble, *cherchez la femme.*

Why would Richard have fabricated a memory of having betrayed his mother in court? Possibly, at some point, his father or grandmother had suggested that he was living with them, not Gertrude, because he had *chosen* them, and that suggestion swelled into a story in the young child's imagination. Or possibly, like many children of divorce, Richard felt that he was somehow at fault for the unhappiness of the parents, and so he invented a scene where he was responsible for his mother's distress, grasping for a strange kind of power in a situation that made him feel powerless.

It's easy to understand, though, why Richard's mind would have circled back to the courtroom and the judge's decision to send him to his father and grandmother. It was the pivot point of his early childhood. It deprived him, for good, of his right to be a child, but gave him in return his material as an artist. "I got my bizarre sense of humor from the fact that I was scared," he observed. Unlike his soft-edged mother, Buck and Marie were extraordinarily gifted at instilling fear; their livelihoods depended upon it.

Instead of remaining on a farm next to a garbage dump, in a city that revolved around state government, Richard was headed back to Peoria, brothel bound.

CHAPTER 3

The Law of the Lash

Peoria, 1946–1952

From an early age, Richard gravitated toward the movies, spending as much time as he could in the cool, dark sanctuary of Peoria's downtown cinemas. The curtains would open at movie palaces like the Madison, Majestic, and the Rialto, and Richard would drift into his dream of being a leading man. In his mind, he assumed the lean of John Wayne, the musculature of Tarzan, the fiery look of Kirk Douglas, the uncanny force of Boris Karloff. He was promiscuous with his fantasies, quickly projecting himself into another place, another time, another persona. For an hour or two, it no longer mattered that his home life was chaos or that he was expected to sit in the back of the house just because he was black. His affection extended even toward a theater he called the Funky London, where cockroaches and rats vied for a nibble of his popcorn. "I used to live in the movie houses," he remembered. "No movie opened that I didn't sneak in to see."

In his pantheon of cinematic heroes, one star loomed largest: Lash LaRue. "I wanted to be just like him, I wanted to *be* him," he said. Lash LaRue may have been the most unlikely leading man in 1940s Hollywood, and was certainly the odd man out when it came to Westerns of the time. Unlike John Wayne or Roy Rogers, LaRue dressed head to toe in black—black Stetson hat, black cape, black neckerchief, black shirt, black pants, black boots—and rode a black horse. He looked and sounded like Humphrey Bogart, bringing a city kid, gangster inflection to his roles on-screen. He had a gangster's sense of style as well, cocking his Stetson at a jaunty angle and strutting in high-heeled boots. His eighteen-foot bullwhip, ever coiled above his six-shooter, was his weapon of choice. One flick of the wrist and—*snap!*—the whip would snatch a gun from the hand of a villain. Another flick and—*snap!*—the whip would loop around the legs of another villain and bring him to the dust. In "quality" Westerns, it was the villain who sported a whip, perhaps because a whip is less efficient than a gun and more of a plaything. LaRue was strictly B-grade, his heroics verging on camp. He was the sort of fellow who'd woo a lady by grabbing a bouquet of flowers for her—with his bullwhip.

The young Richard found in Lash LaRue the perfect alter ego. Here was an actor whose everyday looks didn't keep him from being a star; a man who could wear black from head to toe and punish his enemies brutally yet remain broadly sympathetic; a hero with so much panache that he punctured the seriousness of the films he starred in, turning them into parodies of themselves. (Fans of *Blazing Saddles*, take note.) Most of all, here was someone who, in claiming the whip hand himself, was never humiliated, never burned, by the sting of the lash.

In the films Richard loved, violence had a purpose. In his home life, violence was often both senseless and inexplicable. One of his strongest memories of growing up in his grandmother's brothel was of being woken in the middle of the night by screams, without knowing where they came from. Were his mother and father at each other's throats again, or was one of his "aunties" getting roughed up by another strange man? It was so confusing, so bewildering, this world where screams could come from anywhere and mean anything or nothing, and where the people you loved were always disappearing behind closed doors.

Marie specialized in score settling and ass whupping: when she wanted to, she was good at getting screams to stop. But she was not gifted at explaining her world to her grandson. His childhood was "hell," Richard said, "because I had nobody to talk to." When asked, by an interviewer in 1979, who cared for him, Richard answered, "Richard Franklin Lennox Thomas Pryor the Third." Which is to say, no one but himself. "It was somehow assumed that I knew everything, maybe because I saw so much," he wrote to himself in a late 1970s diary entry. "Things were told to me in a way that left me with the impression that I was not to ask again." When his otherwise indomitable grandmother seemed to shrink at his questions, Richard reckoned with a child's magical thinking that they must be extremely dangerous, capable of "bring[ing] down every whorehouse in this world." He learned to keep his questions to himself.

An irony for the annals of child rearing: the comic who later seemed most able to unzip his brain, without fearing what would spill out, grew up completely zipped. "It's so much easier for me to talk about my life in front of two thousand people than it is one-on-one," he reflected. "I'm a real defensive person because if you were sensitive in my neighborhood you were something to eat." Something to eat, or something to be taken away by child services: Richard also lived in fear that, if anyone discovered he was growing up in a brothel, he would lose the only family he had. Though Marie had worked out an "understanding" with Peoria authorities, the young Richard still felt himself at risk. "You had to be an adult," he recalled. "[Y]ou had to be very careful about what you said because the police might take you away at any moment."

Since he was not going to talk, Richard learned to observe, and observe closely. His grandmother's brothel at 317 Washington had a "strange, dark, big feel" and "stood amid whole blocks of such places." Formerly a dance hall, it sported a large central room where the girls lingered at its bay windows, exhibiting their wares. His grandmother's girls would "peck on the windows with quarters—tap, tap, tap—for customers." Cajolery would ensue: "Hello, it's me, baby." The customer would file in, partner up with the girl of his choice, then follow her upstairs to the bedrooms where Marie's girls lived and worked.

Starting around age four, Richard shared one of these bedrooms with "Pops," Marie's husband Thomas, so was well placed to peep and eavesdrop on the brothel's more intimate goings-on. He knew there was secret knowledge there, and he sought it out by peeking through keyholes and peering over transoms, "watching things when I didn't exactly know what they were." Once, probably when he was around eight or nine, he scooched into a vent and watched a prostitute and her john "attack[ing] each other, humping and pumping with a furiousness I'd never imagined"—and grew so excited that he popped out the vent and stuck his head into the room. But if the brothel's keyholes and vents initiated him into the mystery of sex, its larger operations also stripped it of its mystery, turning the sex act into a matter of coldhearted calculation. In a 1977 interview with the *New York Times*, when asked how his wealth suited him, he jabbed back, "I saw my mother turn tricks for some drunk white man when I was a kid. I saw my father take the money, and I saw what it did to them." In the brothel, "feelings" were nonsense, and money was all.

Growing up in a brothel had an ambivalent effect, then, on the young Richard. It made him a cynic for life, with a piercing appreciation of the games people play on others (and sometimes on themselves); and it made him an undefended romantic, his heart hungry for a purer connection. His childhood "messed me up sexually for a minute because I'm afraid sexually," he confessed. Thirty years after the experiences of his childhood, he yearned to tell a lover, "Hey, this scares me. What we're doing together, it scares me." He knew "the act" that was sex, had learned "how to be fake," but the tenderness of love—"the real thing, the real deal, when you're laying with someone and you touch someone, you stroke them or something, touch them, make magic"—was left unrevealed. From an early age, Richard felt both that sex was a motor force in the world and that there had to be a softer form of intimacy, of which he knew next to nothing.

If Marie's brothel defined Richard's sense of home, the other establishments on North Washington Street, a mix of taverns and brothels, defined his sense of neighborhood. His family's friends were fellow brothel owners and hustlers, all finding their niche in Peoria's underground economy. They were also larger-than-life characters who, while they gave young Richard few answers, furnished him with countless stories.

Next door to Marie lived Harold and Margaret "China Bee" Parker, the power couple of Peoria's black underworld. Harold was a heavyset, light-skinned Creole whose elegant suits seemed personally tailored, but his suavity was matched by a gangster-like approach to business. Once, after a waitress at his club made a one-dollar mistake with a customer, he slapped her down with a blackjack; when another waitress came to her defense, a bouncer threatened the second waitress with a gun and clocked her in the mouth with *his* blackjack. Harold's wife, China Bee, also a Creole, was Peoria's best-known black madam in her day and ran a tight outfit, sending her girls regularly to a doctor to be inspected. China Bee had her own sense of style: her brothel was decorated with plush wine-red furnishings and Chinese lanterns that cast a soft glow on the operations of the house; her fifteen girls dressed exquisitely and shopped at Peoria's finer department stores. They were reputed to provide "anything you needed, sexually."

Down the block, at 405 North Washington, Cabristo "Bris" Collins ran a tavern that was notoriously freewheeling. Bris was a tough, bullnecked businessman who wore thick spectacles and was the type to employ an unsmiling three-hundred-pound bouncer-chauffeur named "Bulldog" Shorty. Over the span of his career, Bris was variously a boxing manager, a drug runner, a purveyor of fried chicken and barbecued ribs, a club owner, a procurer, a counterfeiter, and an alleged kingpin of a hundred-thousand-dollar numbers racket in Chicago. (His name surfaced during the Kefauver investigations into organized crime in the early 1950s, and he spent time in military and federal penitentiaries on the drug and counterfeiting charges.) Bris was not a sharp dresser like Harold Parker, but he threw around his money with flair. If he were stuck in a losing streak at a craps table at the Elks Club, he would put hundreds of dollars in the hands of a young lad and make him shoot the dice. According to musicians who worked for him, Bris was straight up in his business dealings if you fell on the right side of them and nasty if you didn't: he liked to shake down deadbeats and then brag about it afterward. When police raided Bris's Washington Street tavern in 1953, they confiscated a large cache of gambling paraphernalia and a decent arsenal of guns: four .38-caliber snub-nose revolvers, one .45-caliber revolver, one .25-caliber automatic, and one Spanish-made automatic. Two bartenders had been packing heat; the rest of the guns were stashed behind the bar for backup.

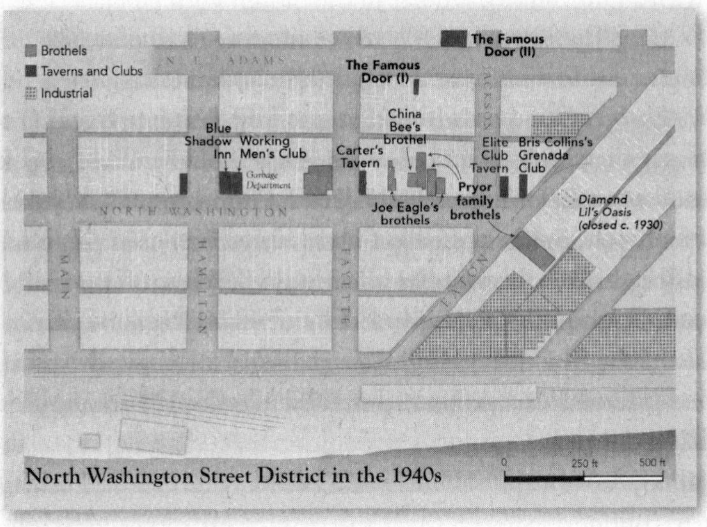

North Washington Street District in the 1940s

The Famous Door, the Pryors' tavern, was another lively neighborhood hub, and another place where the underage Richard was exposed to a very adult carnival. "As a comedian," he recalled, "I couldn't have asked for better material. My eyes and ears absorbed everything. People came in to exchange news, blow steam, or have their say. Everybody had an opinion about something. Even if they didn't know shit about sports, politics, women, the war. In fact, the less people knew, the louder they got."

Richard's memories of the Famous Door have the half-lurid, half-comic tone of the best blaxploitation movies. A drunk man comes in, cursing out Richard's grandmother; Buck defends her honor by shooting him full of holes with a pistol—and the man not only survives but crawls across the floor to slash Buck in the leg. A few months later, the man is back at the Famous Door nursing a drink. Or an angry marine starts raising hell, only to be jumped by Richard's father and uncle Dickie; the three spend a half hour duking it out—and when they've exhausted themselves, they laugh and share drinks together. Or a guy gets knifed in the stomach during a barroom brawl, and rather than wait for an ambulance, he screams for someone to escort him to the liquor store down the street. Richard: "Come on, man. The ambulance is coming. Why don't you lay there?" Man with guts spilling out: "Shit, I'm going to get me a half pint." Richard's takeaway thoughts: "I wondered where he going to put that half pint. If he drank it, I thought he'd die instantly. Of course, that's what I thought. But I found out different. Assholes don't die. They multiply."

Family photographs of the Famous Door do not capture its wilder aspects, but they underline how special the tavern was. Located on the more respectable address of North Adams Street, just a block away from Marie's brothels, it was surrounded by an eclectic mix of businesses—a barber shop, a laundry, a chicken hatchery, a butcher shop, and the local Salvation Army—that would never have been found in the red-light district proper. And after it expanded to a larger location, at 319–21 North Adams, the Famous Door had all the accoutrements of a smart business: elegant colored lettering on its front picture window, a bar gleaming with rows of glasses, bartenders and waitresses dressed all in white, and a bandstand that featured small jazz-blues combos.

And then there was the Famous Door's clientele, which departed sharply from the Peoria norm. Especially after 1:00 a.m., when other bars closed, white Peorians would drift to this black-owned establishment and fraternize on equal terms with black Peorians. A family photograph of the club's interior preserves a spectacle exceptional in late 1940s America: a table with two couples who appear to be interracial, black men with white women, encircled by a seemingly interracial crowd. Everyone is togged out for a night on the town, the men in suits, the women with corsages on their dresses and flowers in their hair. A white woman on the left looks pleasantly at the camera; a black man eyes it more warily, as if unsure where this photograph will end up. A Creole man holds his arm leisurely around the back of his white date, so confident that he doesn't need to be possessive. It's Harold Parker, Richard Pryor's neighbor and one of the smoothest operators in Peoria.

A night out at the Famous Door: a candid photo of two couples at the Pryor family's tavern. (Courtesy of Barbara McGee)

Among the underground entrepreneurs of black Peoria—the Pryors, the Parkers, Bris Collins—there was a sense of camaraderie throughout the 1940s. The money was good, abundant enough to go around, and together they were opening up Peoria in a way that even the most progressive civil rights leaders of the time hardly dreamed of: by creating a world where blacks and whites might pair up as lovers without consequences. (As late as 1947, interracial marriages were illegal in thirty states; in the eighteen other states, they were frowned upon.) Of course, many of the assignations at the Famous Door or the brothels of North Washington Street were the very opposite of love, the product of stone-cold business, and need not be romanticized.

While the red-light district, from one vantage point, showed how taboos existed to be flouted, Marie made sure that her grandson Richard never lived in a moral vacuum. She may have been a madam, but she was also a mother who took care of her family, and a churchgoing woman. After the scorching revels of Saturday night, there was always Morning Star Baptist Church on Sunday morning, where Marie and her grandson felt the congregation rock with the righteousness of the Lord, singing and praying and testifying in waves of enthusiasm. And when Marie's professional duties relaxed during the week, she would run the family kitchen like a master, whipping up a soul kitchen feast of barbecued coon or chicken, candied yams, potato salad, and coleslaw. She aimed to provide for her kin and seems to have kept the whole family in reasonably solid financial shape. The young Richard always dressed nicely and in childhood photos, he was kitted out in the type of clothes bought for special occasions: a sailor outfit, a suit complete with a brightly patterned bow tie. Sometimes he even felt embarrassed by how nice his clothes were: when he got a pair of new shoes, he would step in mud to dirty them up and keep his friends from noticing their shine.

Marie also impressed her grandson with a profound sense of personal dignity, one that would resonate in his comedy. She constantly told him, "Son, one thing a white man can't take away from you is the knowledge"—the knowledge of who you are, which you keep separate from how other people might treat you. Richard applied this maxim not just to himself but to everyone he saw who lived in the shadow of other people's preconceptions: "You take some 63-year-old cat on the street—ugly, spit coming out his mouth—he's still got something you can't have. You can't say he didn't see that gutter or he didn't drink this wine. That's the knowledge."

For Richard, though, "the knowledge" came at a price. Marie's approach to parenting was old-school, strict. A boy had to respect his elders, never talking back and always calling them ma'am or sir. (Even as an adult, Richard followed this latter protocol with older men and women.) He had to perform his chores well or else be sent back to perform them again. And he had to do manly things or else risk being turned into a "sissy"—as when Marie took him out fishing to test his sexual orientation. "If you couldn't put the worm on the hook, you was a faggot," Richard recalled. "I always identified with the little worm because it seemed like he was talking—*no, don't put me on the hook!*" Marie insisted, "Boy, put that worm on that hook!" Richard complied. Marie crowed, "See? I told you he wasn't no sissy," and Richard learned to keep his misgivings to himself. "The worm," he couldn't help but notice, "didn't like it."

In Marie's household there was no space for a child's ambivalence, no wiggle room. Richard knew that if he disobeyed his grandmother, she would try to beat his disobedience out of him, using anything from a birch switch to an old hot water bottle that doubled as a douche bag and smelled of vinegar. He grew accustomed to living in a state of fear, telling a reporter later in his adult life, "Anything you want to know about fear, you got the right person." Thirty years later, in his film *Live in Concert*, Richard evoked his grandmother's beatings as if they were still fresh—and still the moral touchstone of his early childhood.

On the plus side, Marie's beatings were predictable and, relatively speaking, limited in scope. Richard walked on eggshells with his father, never knowing when Buck would detonate in his presence or nonchalantly slay him with a cruel remark. When Richard struggled to pick up the saxophone through music lessons, Buck told him, "You don't have to take 'em no more. The guy says you have no soul," a comment that left Richard feeling "destroyed. I took the horn and tried to flush it down the toilet." Matt Clark, one of Richard's childhood friends, remembered that Richard was "scared to death" of Buck, "afraid to make a sound" in his presence. Buck could strike fear into his son with the smallest of gestures. From his easy chair in the living room, he might simply rustle and straighten out his newspaper—*fffsshtt!*—and Richard would drop whatever he was doing.

In his early comedy, Richard managed to find humor in his father's bouts of humorlessness. Most parents, he noted, warned their children "If you don't go to sleep, the bogeyman will get you." In his family, the dialogue was considerably different.

> **BUCK** [*deadpan*]: "Richard, you want me to kill you?"
> **RICHARD**: "No, sir."
> **BUCK**: "Then go to sleep."

When other kids in the neighborhood said they never got spankings, Richard would chime in and say he never got a spanking, either. And he didn't: he got *beatings*. His father would brag, "My son never cries when I whup him," but there was a simple explanation for that: one punch from Buck, and Richard was out. Richard joked that there was no limit to how far Buck would go, but he may not have been simply joking. A Peoria police officer speculated that Richard could "never have gotten into *real* trouble. At the first sign of it, I'd just march him up to his father and he'd kill him."

Even when Buck was not disciplining Richard, he dispensed a brand of hard-edged wisdom that was difficult for a kid to swallow, especially one drawn to toying with his world. Once, Richard trapped a few rats by luring them with some cheese into his grandmother's blue-speckled oven roaster and then clamping the lid down on them. He then threw the rats into a kitchen sink, full of water, to watch them swim around. ("I was weird," he admitted when recounting this story to TV host Mike Douglas.) Buck walked in and cut his son to the quick: "Kill them. Take the broom and kill them." Richard gulped: "I can't kill them. Not like that." "Then let them go. Don't play with them." And that, as so often happened when Buck got involved, was the end of the story.

There may have been a deeper reason, beyond sheer perversity, for

Richard wanting to see rats skittering in the sink, clutching for their lives; why he was so curious about the look of fear when a powerless creature faced its powerlessness. Around the age of six, he had been playing by himself in the alley behind North Washington Street, casting stones at trash cans to push rats out of their hiding places, when an older teenager named Hoss stepped into the alley. "Right away, I knew he was trouble," Pryor recalled forty years later. "I saw it in his bloodshot eyes . . . I should've run. But I didn't. Because he was right about me in that sense—I was a little chickenshit." Hoss slammed Richard into a darkened corner where no one could see the two of them. He unzipped his pants and told Richard, "Suck it." Richard did as he was told; Hoss walked off a happy man. He left Richard feeling dirty, humiliated, and ashamed.

As with his parents' divorce, Richard felt complicit in his misfortune. Whom would he tell? His grandmother, with her birch switches and vinegary douche bag? His father, with his KO fists? His mother, seventy miles and a universe away in Springfield? A few nights later, in the middle of dinner, his father started serenading the table with his personal version of "I'm Forever Blowing Bubbles": "I'm forever blowing bubbles, pretty bubbles in the air . . ." Richard "felt a shiver of embarrassment and mortification run up and down my spine like rats in a wall. What the fuck? Did he know, too?" Richard never asked his father why he chose the song or if he was aware of who had blown whom in the alley; he had never confided in his father, and wasn't about to start with the story of Hoss and the darkened alley. Like other victims of abuse, Richard became warier, more suspicious of the motives of others, and kept his secret for five decades, until the writing of his memoir *Pryor Convictions* unlocked it.

At least his family let him repair to the movies, where he could fall into a dream life. His heroes tended to be orphans, like Tarzan, or rootless loners, like Lash LaRue or John Wayne, or comic fools lost in a world of their own, like Red Skelton. He initiated a lifelong fascination with cartoons, where violence was anarchic and acceptable and magically exaggerated into slapstick comedy; his favorite comedians, too, had more than a touch of the cartoonish to them. At some Saturday matinees, he would sit through as many as twenty-five cartoons in a row, reveling in the antics of Bugs Bunny, Porky Pig, Mickey Mouse, and the Road Runner. He studied their poses and facial expressions with the eye of an artist and would delight himself by drawing goofy cartoon characters on sketch pads. Each tilt of an eyebrow, each curve of a lip, made such a difference—a lesson the future comic internalized in his own facial muscles. Once, he went around for days imitating the Road Runner.

Though Richard generally identified with leading men, there was one glorious exception: the character of Little Beaver, the Navajo orphan who served as Red Ryder's loyal, spunky sidekick in a series of Republic westerns through the 1940s. Little Beaver had a compelling backstory, one that offered easy entrée for a black boy feeling cornered by his own family. Beaver was the grandson of an Indian chief, an outsider by birth, but gave up his claim to chiefdom so that he might stay at the side of his surrogate father, a solitary Anglo cowboy so charmed by Beaver's pint-size moxie that he adopted him as his ward. With his trousers always falling down, Little Beaver was a child stuck in a man's world, but he was also an indispensable presence in it, rescuing Red Ryder time and again with his sly intelligence. (In one film, he procures a skunk to foil a villain.) The granite-faced Ryder cared for Beaver and needed Beaver, in ways that may have felt delicious to a child beaten or ignored by his own taciturn father.

Yet Richard's infatuation with Little Beaver also set him up for a pointed lesson in the foolishness of openly confusing fact and fantasy. After losing himself in the Red Ryder serials, he grew convinced that Little Beaver had to be behind the screen, waiting to meet him. Once, when the picture ended, he went to the back of the theater and discovered no trace of Little Beaver, or even the actor Bobby (later Robert) Blake, the white boy who played him. Instead, he came upon an angry crew, who chased Richard from the premises. It was, Richard said, "one of my first big traumatic experiences": the discovery that characters were not real just because he ached to believe in them.

Around this time, Richard fell into his first performance as a comic. In his memory, his first stage was the brothel's backyard in the mid-1940s; his first prop, a pile of dog poop. He was wearing a spiffy cowboy outfit his grandfather had given him and was sitting on the edge of a brick railing, looking for all the world like a miniature version of his heroes John Wayne or Lash LaRue. Then he threw himself on purpose off the railing, and his family broke out in laughter. A few more falls, and the laughter didn't stop. The comedian-in-the-making conceded that his routine was over and ran to his grandmother, but along the way, he slipped on the pile of dog poop. Again, roars of laughter. Eager to please, he did what any attention-craving child would have done: he repeated his pratfall, dog poop and all. "That was my first comedy routine," he said. "And I've just been slipping in shit ever since." If comedy was partly the art of self-humiliation, early on Pryor realized he had a knack for it.

His elementary school became his first public stage, though he grew to have qualms about his audience there. At home he was in the violently controlled dominion of Marie; at Irving School, he was in a white-oriented world where the realities of his life were unmentionable, if not unimaginable, for his teachers and fellow students. Richard was one of a minority of blacks at Irving: the school drew predominantly from the white working-class population of Peoria's valley, families that lived paycheck to paycheck and looked anxiously at the influx of blacks to Peoria during its wartime boom. If his white classmates knew anything about black life, it was most likely refracted through the cartoon versions of it in circulation, the minstrelsy behind popular radio programs like *Amos 'n' Andy*. (In fact, the white actor playing Andy had been born and raised in Peoria, and discovered blackface comedy in the city's theaters in the 1910s.) Richard felt his way through school by turning his own sense of himself as a misfit into the stuff of comedy. If his white classmates expected an act from the skinny, excitable black kid, he would give it to them—and then some.

Richard did not begin as a class clown, though. He started simply as a boy out of sorts, having trouble adapting to the strictures of school. At the end of first grade—by which point he had witnessed his parents' divorce and been sexually abused—his teacher made a special note in his record: "Apparently unstable emotionally." He received an F in "conduct" and similarly low grades in every subject except English, where he earned a C. Irving decided to hold him back a year.

During the middle of his second try at first grade, for reasons that remain unclear, Richard left Peoria and lived for half the school year with his mother and her family on the outskirts of Springfield. "The farm," he recalled in his memoir, "was paradise, a playground where my imagination could go wild. At night, I listened to crickets instead of creaking beds and moans, and in the morning, I woke to the sound of roosters crowing and the smell of hot biscuits and fresh-brewed coffee." The setting, in a neighborhood on the eastern edge of town, might have appeared to others as a rural slum, with its shotgun houses and unimproved land. But to Richard, it was a slice of heaven. Even the garbage dump next to the farm, where his grandfather hauled the trash he picked up during the day, enchanted Richard. He would wander down to the dump and pretend he was a cowboy or soldier, firing rounds from a .22-caliber gun at any rats that made the mistake of crossing his path. "Yes, sir, I fucked up some rats," he said. He called this interlude the happiest time of his life.

And then it ended: by September 1948, he was back in Peoria schools, now promoted to second grade. By third grade, in 1949, Richard suffered constant bullying from boys who hailed from the valley's white Protestant blue-collar families. They ganged up on him in the vacant lot across from the school, sometimes giving him flimsy grounds for their attack, often not. Slight in stature, Richard fought back most impressively with his mouth. Bottled up tight at home, elsewhere he was loose, and mimicking the kind of salty talk he heard at Marie's brothel and the Famous Door. And he had the good fortune to befriend two other kids who were similarly outsiders and similarly targeted: the pint-sized Michael Grussemeyer, whose family was middle class (not blue collar), and the wavy-haired Roxy Eagle, whose family was Italian American and Catholic (not Protestant). Roxy also happened to be the son of Joe Eagle, who ran the sole brothel with white prostitutes on Richard's block of North Washington Street.

Repeatedly the three fended off the bullies in the vacant lot and developed a strong sense of togetherness, so much so that Richard started calling Michael and Roxy "nigger" as a term of endearment. Richard seemed to recognize, early on, that there were some white people who could be smuggled into the circle of black identity—the exact white people who could be called nigger and hear it as a compliment. They were "three oddball brothers," in the words of Michael Grussemeyer, and proud of it.

Third grade marked the beginning of the end for Richard's academic career. Despite relatively decent grades (three Bs and four Cs) the year before, he took a nosedive, now ending up with two Cs, four Ds, and one F, again in "conduct." And that was about as good as it would get. For the rest of his time in school, his grades would never rise above Cs, with an increasing concentration of Ds and Fs. Given an intelligence test, he scored a 100—perfectly average. Conventional testing could little recognize unconventional talent.

Richard's poor grades in "conduct" were tied to his increasing propensity for mischief. Often he was simply disruptive, a prankster on the loose. He threw spitballs and went through a Tarzan phase where, from out of nowhere, he would erupt into his imitation of Johnny Weissmuller doing his yodeling call or would gibber like the chimpanzee Cheeta. But he also fell into a reverberating discovery: that he could use his failures to transfix his audience. When he was caught without his homework or when he lost his books, Richard would not make a quick, shamefaced confession and be done with it. Instead, he seized the opportunity for a disquisition about how, exactly, he'd arrived at this sorry outcome. The teacher might not like ceding control of her classroom, but the other kids delighted in Richard's freewheeling spiels—even the ones who, outside class, attacked him on the vacant lot.

Richard started testing boundaries, treating rules as playthings, monkeying with expectations. He tried out for, and made it onto, Irving School's basketball team. His inspiration? The Harlem Globetrotters, who visited Peoria every year to play an exhibition game at a local high school and who, despite their name, actually hailed from Chicago. The Globetrotters were the toast of the black community at the time. They had just defeated the Minneapolis Lakers, the dominant team in the all-white world of pro basketball leagues, in two exhibition matches—victories that were as sweet as black heavyweight Joe Louis's knockout of Max Schmeling a decade before. In his mind, Richard was channeling the spirit of Goose Tatum, "Clown Prince" of the Globetrotters and ball handler extraordinaire. At practice, he tried to dazzle and entertain his teammates rather than demonstrate basic skills. The reaction was swift. The coach felt he'd lost control of his team and would have none of it; style was not at a premium in his version of the game. Within a week, Richard was kicked off the team.

In fourth grade, Richard found trouble in a whole new way, though this time he had no idea he was crossing a line—he didn't even know there was a line. He had noticed that, while the white boys in class kept their distance, the white girls were more welcoming; they seemed to enjoy seeing him whip out his drawing pads and sketch his cartoon characters. He fell for one girl in particular and gave her a scratch board—the kind covered with a plastic sheet that, once lifted, would erase the drawing—as a token of affection. She was thrilled. It was, she swore, her new favorite toy.

The next day, her father appeared in their classroom, scowling as he held the scratch board and demanding to know which "little nigger" had given it to his daughter. The teacher fingered Richard.

"Nigger," the girl's father shouted, "don't you ever give my daughter anything." Richard recoiled in shock. "Why was he calling me a nigger? Why did he hate me?" he wondered to himself. In his memoir he wrote, "If I was four and a half feet tall then, the girl's daddy cut six inches off. Zap. Six inches of self-esteem gone. That was my indoctrination to the black experience in America." The meaning of Richard's blackness was coalescing: being a "nigger" meant keeping his affections to himself when they involved a white girl or else face certain humiliation. The liaisons he'd observed around North Washington Street were taboo elsewhere; what happened at the Famous Door stayed at the Famous Door.

There was, however, an unexpected upside to the whole thing. For once Richard saw his father unleash his anger in his defense rather than against him. Buck came to his son's classroom the very next day and confronted the teacher.

"How could you do that?" he asked her. "How could you not say anything to that man?"

The teacher looked down and shook her head, as if to telegraph that she was ashamed of her own behavior, and Buck softened, patting her on the back in an unusual show of tenderness. Then he turned to the little girl whom Richard adored. "Did you get his present?" Buck asked.

"Yes," she whimpered, "but he wouldn't let me keep it."

At which point Richard, trying to ease her pain, interjected, "That's okay." Of course, it wasn't.

This unpleasant interlude was just one of many during fourth grade, Richard's most troubled year at Irving School. He skipped school more often and was suspended for misbehavior on a near-weekly basis. A ritual developed: Richard would act up and get sent home; a family member would drag him by the ear to the principal's office and ask for him to be reinstated; the principal would comply; Richard would act up again and the cycle would repeat. "You could almost set your watch by it," recalled his friend Michael Grussemeyer. By the end of that school year, Irving's administration seems to have given up on him: a note was placed in Richard's file reading, "S[tudent] can't return."

Richard's frustrations at school pushed him deeper into the realm of private fantasy at home. He listened to his grandmother's Doris Day records and confected a Doris Day scenario in his mind, placing himself alongside a cast of beautiful people. He played with Popsicle sticks and imagined they were living characters acting out a Hollywood drama in front of his eyes. "I'd write a lot," he remembered. "I'd lock myself up in my room for two or three days at a time without eating or sleeping, just writing about life." He gathered photos of theater marquees from *Life* magazine and Peoria newspapers, then wrote "RICHIE PRYOR" on a strip of paper and pasted it onto the marquees. Flopped on his bed on the top floor of his grandmother's brothel, he threw himself into the wildest of fantasies—that he was destined for stardom—even though he had little practical sense of how he might be plucked, like his beloved Little Beaver, out of one life and into another.

On the bright side, Richard had someone new in his corner at home: a stepmother named Viola Anna Hurst, whom everyone called Ann. Born in New Orleans in 1921, Ann had arrived in Peoria after the war and slipped into work as a prostitute at China Bee's, the classiest black brothel in town. She was a freckled Creole, so light-skinned she might have passed for white if she had wanted to, and dressed smartly, forties style, in wide-brimmed hats and elegant dresses cinched with belts. Sociable and lively, she charmed her North Washington Street neighbor Buck, who married her on August 16, 1950. For a while Ann assumed some responsibility for taking care of Richard: more often than not, she was the one who pleaded with the principal to let Richard return from suspension during fourth grade. Richard, already familiar with mothers who made their living on the horizontal, took quickly to calling her "Mom." He liked the look of her and was heartened by the fact that, compared with Marie or Buck, she was no disciplinarian.

But Ann had her principles, and tried to instill them in Richard. A practicing Catholic, she took Richard to catechism on weekends and helped enroll him in a private Catholic school for fifth grade, since Irving was no longer an option. The school offered the promise of a fresh start, and Richard seemed to welcome that. He made new friends, took school seriously, and impressed his teachers with his intelligence. Halfway into the school year, though, a whispering campaign put an end to his fresh start. Someone complained about

Sociable: Richard's stepmother Ann (second from left) at a Peoria nightclub, circa 1950, with saxophonist Vy Burnside, trumpeter Tiny Davis, and an unidentified friend. (Courtesy of Barbara McGee)

how Richard's family made its living, and the school told Richard he was no longer welcome there.

"Why'd they kick me out of school? What did I do?" he asked Marie, devastated. "Nothing, baby," Marie replied. "Some people just don't know right from wrong, even though they think they wrote the book."

As Richard struggled in school, his elders were facing a stiff headwind of their own. Just as the politics of wartime Peoria had favored the expansion of the brothel business, so the politics of postwar Peoria favored its contraction. To survive, the family would have to improvise: the 300 block of North Washington Street, which the Pryors called home, would soon be demolished, and the heart of the red-light district would go with it.

The reversal of fortune began in February 1945, when Peoria's longtime mayor was defeated by a reform candidate in an election where the middle-class bluffs outvoted the working-class valley by 15 percent. Shortly thereafter, the new mayor cleared out the city's slot machines and started putting the squeeze on casino gambling. Then, in July 1948, the reformers picked up more steam when the head of a local syndicate was murdered outside his favorite tavern by a sharpshooter hiding in some nearby underbrush. The gangster's widow avenged his death by releasing a bombshell to the press: a recording of an emissary from the county attorney's office in the process of extorting a twenty-five-thousand-dollar bribe from her late husband. Suddenly, the "bad morals" of Peoria were everywhere, impossible to ignore. After the county attorney was indicted by a grand jury, Illinois's attorney general launched a sweeping investigation into gambling and prostitution in Peoria, aiming to eliminate organized vice root and branch. Although a rump of gamblers resisted—the home of the new county attorney was bombed a year after his predecessor's indictment—the casino world, which had been the most profitable sector of Peoria's underground economy, soon became a ghost of its former self.

With gambling out of the way, the reformers targeted prostitution as the next social evil to be scrubbed from the valley. Their cause was joined by a large number of ex-GIs returning to Peoria with hopes of raising families there. Seasoned by their military experience, these men became, collectively, a powerful force for reform: they felt it was their patriotic duty to serve their city by cleaning it up. They won seats on the city council and the county board of supervisors, breaking the hammerlock that an older generation had long held on local politics. They longed to put madams like China Bee and Marie Pryor on notice: when the reformers finally captured city hall in full in 1953, within its first few months in office the new administration made a point of launching thirty-five raids on established brothels.

Before that moment of complete electoral triumph, the reformers hit upon a less explicit strategy for destroying the red-light district: they could help the government build an interstate highway through it. Since the early 1940s, Peorians had been clamoring for the construction of a second bridge connecting Peoria to East Peoria. In 1951, the State Highway Division recommended that the project begin at North Washington Street on the Peoria side. The Pryors and their fellow residents of the 300 block, the black-oriented portion of the red-light district, found themselves at the very center of construction. Fourteen buildings, all within the vicinity of the district, were demolished in the initial phase, and no one seems to have paused with the bulldozer. Richard's block was "blight." Three-quarters of its dwellings lacked a private bathroom or were deemed dilapidated by the 1950 U.S. Census; one in six had no running water.

For the underground entrepreneurs of 300 North Washington Street, the construction of the bridge meant the end of their neighborhood. In late 1951, Marie and her family left behind her brothels at 313 and 317 North Washington Street, a few steps ahead of the wrecking ball. The Famous Door had closed two years before, along with a beauty shop Marie had run next to it for two years. With the disintegration of the friendly relationship between Peoria's police and its madams, the family needed to regroup. Marie chose to move her family to the 2400 block of South Adams—four and a half miles away from the old red-light district, in an undeveloped part of town that had few black residents but offered cheaper rents and less ramshackle housing stock. The family loosened up, subdividing into its various specialties. Richard's grandfather devoted himself to his new pool hall; Richard's uncle Dickie turned to drug running and counterfeiting; Buck and Ann remained connected to prostitution; and Marie went back to bootlegging, hanging up her spurs as a madam at age fifty-two.

An era, Marie's era, was drawing to a close. Richard enrolled in the nearly all-white Blaine-Sumner elementary school, smarting from his most recent expulsion, and reached for another chance at a fresh start.

CHAPTER 4

Glow, Glow Worm, Glow

Peoria, 1952–1956

Mrs. Margaret Yingst, sixth-grade teacher at Blaine-Sumner elementary school and a woman who looked and dressed like an older version of Snow White, had a problem on her hands. When she took attendance after the ringing of the morning bell, there was usually a hitch at the *P*s. "Richard Pryor? Richard?" No answer. Half an hour later, Richard ambled into class and sat down at a desk in the first row. He looked ragged, as if he'd been up half the night.

"Richard," Mrs. Yingst asked finally, "you leave home early enough to get to school on time. Just why does this tardiness continue day after day?"

Richard played with his fatigue, converting it into a bit of shtick. "Well, you see, Mrs. Yingst, it's like this. (*yawn*) I get on the bus. The ride makes me oh (*yawn*) so sleepy that (*yawn*) I just shut my eyes and ride on. And on. When the busman comes back to my corner a second time, he tells me to get off and get to school." He stretched his jaws into one last yawn to close off his act.

Margaret Yingst felt sorry for the misfit in front of her. He was one of the only black kids at the school and seemed isolated on the playground, connecting with other kids only by performing his wacky pantomimes for them. So Mrs. Yingst struck a deal with him: if he arrived at school on time, he'd be rewarded with his own Friday-afternoon comedy set—ten minutes to entertain the classmates who, by and large, shunned him. He was rarely late for school again.

In the company of Lincoln: Richard dressed up for a sixth-grade field trip to Springfield, Illinois. (Courtesy of Margaret Ruth Kelch)

For his Friday-afternoon material, Richard borrowed liberally from the rubber-faced comedians of the day. He loved Red Skelton and Sid Caesar, whom he watched avidly on his family's new TV, and was especially inspired by Jerry Lewis, with his child-man persona and his mix of the kinetic and the clumsy. In his sixth-grade pantomimes, Richard might pretend to be holding a steaming hot bowl of soup, and then would yowl and slurp his way through the meal. His comedy was solo slapstick, Lewis

Mrs. Margaret Yingst, the first teacher who gave young Richard a stage. (Courtesy of Margaret Ruth Kelch)

sans Martin. "Oh my, he could roll those eyes back," remembered Yingst.

His Friday-afternoon slot soon grew into a prime-time show, with a new venue and a bigger audience. In the spring of 1953, lunchtime at Blaine-Sumner offered a veritable revue. Margaret Ruth, one of Richard's only friends, had banded together with three other girls to form a singing group called the Glow Girls, and they helped pull in an audience for Richard. (Their name came from their signature

Richard's best friend Margaret Ruth (left) and their friend Gladys. (Courtesy of Margaret Ruth Kelch)

song, "The Glow Worm": "When you gotta glow, you gotta glow / Glow little glow worm, glow.") The entrance to the gym served as an amphitheater, its steps as risers for an audience of twenty-five or more kids. An alcove around the corner formed the wings of the stage, where the acts could make their dramatic entrances. The Pryor–Glow Girls double bill had a theatrical run of around fifteen impromptu performances, and won the admiration and encouragement of Mrs. Yingst.

Richard felt himself coming into his own. "When I heard their laughter," he said, "I felt good about myself, which was a pretty rare feeling." He became so comfortable with Mrs. Yingst that he teased her about his prospects with her daughter, who was around his age. "Maybe we'll get married," he joked. "Then you and I will be family." The episode with the scratch board might have sharpened Richard's awareness of the color line that separated black boys and white girls, but it also had left him wishing to play with it.

"Oh, Richard," Mrs. Yingst said sweetly, taking his audacity in stride. In the end, she gave him roughly the same report card as other teachers (Cs in reading, writing, and English; Ds and Fs in everything else), but in Richard's memory, Mrs. Yingst remained a hallowed figure from his childhood, the one schoolteacher who pushed him, ever so gently, in the right direction.

Then Richard graduated from Blaine-Sumner and moved for seventh grade to the recently opened Trewyn School, and the bottom fell out again. While at Blaine-Sumner there had been a sprinkling of black students, at Trewyn Richard was the only black in a school with hundreds of students, the vast majority of whom were middle class. All the Glow Girls except Margaret Ruth had moved on to different schools, so he lost his opening act, the quartet of perky white girls who had given him cover as a performer. Mrs. Yingst was succeeded by Miss Dempsey, a gawky, bespectacled woman with dull brown hair, little sense of humor, and even less sense of understanding. And the other boys at Trewyn weren't any more welcoming either, teasing and attacking Richard on the playground for being different.

And different, he was; the world of his family bore little resemblance to, say, the world of Margaret Ruth's. In April 1953, his uncle Dickie was the target of a federal narcotics sting—"the first major crack-down on narcotics traffic in Peoria in many years," according to the *Peoria Journal.* Arrested for selling heroin on North Washington Street, Dickie was slapped with heavier charges; the federal agents argued that he was the "king pin" of a multicity narcotics ring that had been under investigation for two months. They raided a house that was reported to be his headquarters, arrested the seven alleged drug addicts they found there, and upon searching the premises, came away triumphantly with twenty-nine heroin capsules, a bunch of hypodermic needles, and a large quantity of marijuana. Dickie was sentenced to several years in a federal prison in Michigan, but considered himself lucky nonetheless: when he was apprehended on North Washington Street, he had also been carrying a box of counterfeit money and, just before being cuffed, had nonchalantly placed the box on top of a garbage can, where it remained undiscovered. The funny bills were likely connected to his old North Washington Street confrère Bris Collins, who ran a counterfeiting operation in Peoria and who, in 1954, followed Dickie to the federal penitentiary, busted in a sting of his own.

Like the men in his life, Richard felt marked, too. One afternoon he came to Miss Dempsey with his clothes torn, his lower lip smudged with blood, and his cheeks wet with tears. "What happened?" she asked.

"Those kids out there called me a nigger," Richard said.

Miss Dempsey answered loud enough so others could hear her, in a tone that was perfectly matter-of-fact: "Well, Richard, that's what you are. Why are you so upset?" Lunchtime was drawing to a close; she couldn't be bothered. She pointed him to sit at his desk with the other students.

The experience was no doubt chastening for Richard, but perhaps less unnerving than this: the same Miss Dempsey who acted as if it were normal for Richard to be a "nigger," also acted as if it were normal for him to be an entertainer. And so she followed the precedent, established by Mrs. Yingst, of ceding her classroom floor to Richard for his weekly monologues. His performances at Trewyn were double-edged, moments of triumph that he purchased at the price of heightened ambivalence. Part of him needed an audience that another part of him begrudged.

The neediness was evident to his one ally in Miss Dempsey's class, ex–Glow Girl Margaret Ruth. "He wanted to be included, he wanted to be part of the group, he wanted to be in everything," she recalled. He came, alone, to all of Trewyn's basketball games and sock hops. In eighth grade, he ran to become his homeroom's elected representative for Student Council—and won. But except when he lit up for his comedy routines, he looked defeated, as if the social isolation was taking its toll. When the school day ended, he would walk home with Margaret and choke up. "Why did I have to be born black?" he asked, leaning on her for comfort.

Though well meaning, Margaret herself played a role in deepening his pain. When her mother, who was southern born and bred, spied Richard and Margaret walking home together, she had a conniption over their association, and so Margaret pulled away from Richard. Their walks continued, but the two of them would separate before she neared her family's house; boundaries had to be maintained. And when Richard discovered that Margaret had feelings for another student, a white boy, he took it not only as a personal rejection but also as a fresh racial insult. Sitting next to her on a three-hour-long bus ride for a school field trip, he kept circling back to a single theme: if only he were white, he said, then she might have fallen for him. If only.

Richard hated Trewyn so much that he was willing to risk the wrath of his grandmother to escape the dreaded place. One day, Marie received a phone call from Richard's school, advising her that Richard had not been in Miss Dempsey's class for twenty-odd days. That was strange, Marie thought; she hadn't noticed a change in Richard's school-day routine. In the morning, she would give him money for lunch and he would leave with books under his arms; in the afternoon, he would return home and act as if he'd had another fine day at Trewyn. So Marie put a black policewoman on Richard's tail. The policewoman tracked him down to a vacant lot covered with horseweed, whose tall shoots offered good camouflage for a thirteen-year-old on the lam. Richard was bedded down in the weeds, whiling away his hours with the assistance of a superhero comic book and some soda and cigarettes he'd bought with his lunch money. Marie was none too pleased.

Richard escaped Trewyn permanently in late 1954, when, for unclear reasons, he moved out of his grandmother's home on the edge of Peoria's valley and into his father's home downtown. He was placed in Roosevelt Junior High, his sixth school in seven years. Suddenly Richard was in a much blacker element: Roosevelt was closely split between white and black students. Still, in another sense, he never left Blaine-Sumner or Trewyn behind. His later crossover comedy returned to the psychic scenes of his sixth- and seventh-grade classrooms, where there were no other black faces in the room and he had to play to an audience that could not intuit where he was coming from. When he saw whites in his audience, he might wonder if he was performing for the likes of Mrs. Yingst or the likes of Miss Dempsey, and then devise tests—little barbed teases, like his gambit with Mrs. Yingst over her daughter—to sort the two groups apart. For the right kind of person, the barb was an invitation to a friendship that had the flavor of a conspiracy. For the wrong kind of person, it was simply a barb, and was meant to stick under the skin.

In the spring of 1955, Richard walked into the George Washington Carver Community Center, a squat, unassuming brick building that had formerly housed the phone company's maintenance division. He was looking for Carver's Youth Theater Guild; he found, in Miss Juliette Whittaker, the person who showed him his future.

Carver was, in the words of teacher Kathryn Timmes, "the Mecca of the black community." Situated at the heart of the neighborhood where three-quarters of black Peorians lived, the center opened in 1944 as a "teenage hangout" and, by Richard's arrival, had become much more. Black kids at Peoria public schools tended to be, like Richard, excluded from the mainstream of social life, so they converged at Carver after school and on weekends to find a world of their own. Carver had its own proms, its own carnivals, its own athletic teams. Young children played checkers or marbles or basketball, sang in its "Cherub Choir," learned to tap dance, or worked on crafts. Teenagers shot pool, played chess and Ping-Pong, joined jazz bands such as the Rhythm Rockets or the Blue Dukes, and learned the basics of everything from modern dance and set design to cooking and sewing.

Nondescript on the outside: the George Washington Carver Community Center in 1954. (Courtesy of the author)

It's telling that it took Richard fourteen years to reach this Mecca, and that even then, he did so at the behest of a friend rather than his family. The red-light district of North Washington Street was only a mile away from Carver, but in spirit, the two places were light-years apart. Carver had emerged out of the prewar efforts of Peoria's Colored Women's Aid Society, which aimed to put young black Peorians on the path of moral improvement—which is to say, a path that led away from brothels such as Marie's. Carver's teachers and administrators channeled the ethos of the black women's club movement by running a tight ship. Obscenities were abhorred. Chaperones were on hand so that the social dancing didn't get too heavy. In the minds of Carver's staff, black boys and girls were there to learn how to work and play with dignity and, eventually, how to join the world of the middle class.

Juliette Whittaker, who ran Carver's theater program, was the rare adult there who had a more flexible sense of what "moral improvement" might be. Slim and petite, she had a dancer's posture—the straightest of backbones—but an easy gap-toothed smile that, as

A sketch artist: Juliette Whittaker, Pryor's first professional mentor, demonstrating the art of theatrical makeup. (Courtesy of the Peoria Journal Star*)*

Richard recalled, "made you forget about things." Juliette was the center's bohemian, the never-married teacher who wore radiant, flowing dashikis well before they were fashionable, knew her way around bongo drums, and piped from her office a steady stream of music ranging from Tchaikovsky to Miles Davis. She kept a bohemian's hours, too, arriving at Carver in the late morning and often keeping her theater workshop open until the wee hours. "When you're putting a play together," she explained, "you don't stop simply because twelve o'clock comes. You're working on scenery, you're doing costumes . . . We'd go home, sometimes dawn was coming up." Juliette paired her matchless work ethic—she'd graduated from high school at age fourteen, from college at eighteen—with a deep-seated sense of racial pride. Her parents had both held their heads high in the world—her mother as a teacher; her father, a Harvard Law alum, as the attorney who ran the principal black law office in Houston.

When Richard first arrived at Juliette's Youth Theater Guild, the young actors were rehearsing a new version of *Rumpelstiltskin* that Juliette had concocted. Richard watched, spellbound, then walked up to the edge of the stage and said, "I can do that!" Juliette apologized: the play had already been cast. "I don't care. I'll do anything, I'll do anything," he begged. She gave him a bit part as a servant—someone who walks onstage and sneezes—and Richard accepted. It would be his entrée to stardom. When the actor playing the king was a no-show at rehearsal, Richard pleaded with Juliette to take over the part. He was never a good reader so couldn't study scripts like other actors, but he had an inspired grasp of character and could memorize dialogue by ear.

Starting with this, his very first role onstage, he refused to play things straight. His new king, modeled after his uncle Dickie, was a mack daddy who made the kind of sweet promises to the miller's daughter that a pimp might make to his best earner: "Hey baby, you keep on spinning that straw into gold for me and I'll get you a car. Something fine. Something for your mama. I'll make you my woman . . ." The kids and Juliette split their sides with laughter.

When the other boy returned to rehearsals, Juliette convinced him to watch Richard's performance and decide for himself who should get the part. "Yeah, it's true, he does do it better," the boy conceded. Richard was the new king. Or as Juliette often encapsulated the story, "That's the way Richard got on the throne of comedy, and he hasn't been down since."

Starting with *Rumpelstiltskin*, Richard took a crash course in theater production from a woman who did everything: writing, directing, choreography, set design and construction, costume design and creation. Juliette never believed in excuses; a poverty of resources never justified a failure of imagination. For *Rumpelstiltskin*, her workshop built the scenery from discarded window shades, and the multilevel stage from tossed-out lumber and orange crates. And she refused to think of children's theater as a hokey, feel-good exercise for the kids: it was art. Her *Rumpelstiltskin* had "an eerie quality not often found in amateur performances," wrote a columnist for the *Peoria Star.* "I got the feeling of seeing an old folk tale, combined with the freshness and delight of a park in Paris with the audience watching a Grand Guignol of 'Punch and Judy.' "

Carver's other teachers couldn't imagine a future for Richard, the kid who had no stomach for self-discipline, kept flunking out of schools, and seemed half-crazy. "His elevator doesn't go to the top floor," they joked. Some wanted to "slap him away, like an annoying mosquito": he was not on the Carver program of moral uplift, much less on his way to being the next president of Caterpillar, Inc. But Juliette saw him as potential incarnate. For a precious year or so, Carver became the nurturing home Richard had never had, and Juliette became his surrogate mother. With one proviso attached: his real home was not to be discussed. Juliette never knew Richard had a father, because "I never even heard him mentioned in all the time I knew Richard"—this despite the fact that Richard was living with Buck at the time.

The two spent countless hours in Juliette's small corner office on the second floor, planning the shows that Juliette had written and would direct herself. Juliette was Richard's first cowriter, and the two settled into a dynamic that he would later repeat with actor-writers such as Mel Brooks and Lily Tomlin: Richard would spin a yarn and keep riffing, and Juliette would try to give the riffs a structure and setting. When they had polished the story to a nice sheen, Juliette would holler, "We've got a new one!" to Kathryn Timmes, the teacher who handled Carver's "girl's department" downstairs, and Timmes would hustle upstairs and be treated to a twenty-minute monologue, Richard's extemporized version of the tale. "He could make up a lie quicker than you could blink your eye," said Timmes. "Honest to Pete. And it just had me on the floor, because I had never heard things like that before."

Juliette aimed to enlarge Richard's sense of the world along with his sense of imagination. She sat in her office's big chair and spoke with him about race in America, or city politics. She wanted him to explore beyond his neighborhood, so she took him on field trips to local plays and Peoria's Lakeview Museum. At times, too, she had to drag him forcibly out of his old world when inertia got the best of him. More than once, Richard did not show up for rehearsal. Another sort of teacher might have thrown up her hands at the backsliding child, but Juliette went on a reconnaissance mission to "Pop's Pool Hall," where Richard could be found racking balls and sweeping the floor for his grandfather. "When I would come into that pool hall," she recalled, "it was like a church—you could hear a pin drop. And this man would be standing against the cash register—and he's huge—and he'd back up. I'd say, 'I've come for Richard, it's time for his rehearsal,' and he'd say, 'Take him, take him!' He wanted me out of there so the game could continue. Because nobody was doing anything when I was there."

Juliette tried to slip in some moral instruction, too, in a crafty, indirect manner that contrasted with the brute-force methods of Richard's father and grandmother. In Richard's next play for her, *The Vanishing Pearl*, he played a thief who schemes to steal a pearl. But when the thief finally lays his hands on the jewel, it disappears—the moral of the tale being, according to Juliette, that "in order to be worthy of something, you have to work for it." In another instance, Juliette monkeyed with Richard and a group of his friends when they stalked another kid who, they suspected, had stolen something from Juliette's desk. Thinking that they were defending Juliette's interests, they jumped him in the park and beat him up. "Confess!" they demanded—but he wouldn't. So they brought him to Juliette. The supposed thief continued to insist, "I didn't do it, Miss Whittaker." Juliette stared at Richard and his friends, then announced, "Well, if he didn't do it, one of *you* did it," raking her finger across the group. In fact, Juliette had no clue who was the thief. But she meant to teach them a lesson about the importance of presuming innocence—by having them experience the presumption of guilt.

Richard took in Juliette's method of teasing moral instruction and made it his own, upping its trickster quotient. Once, he, Juliette, and Kathryn Timmes were sitting together in Juliette's office, chatting about how black children needed to leave their comfort zone and see the world. Timmes, who taught third-graders at the nearby Douglass School, rued that her students' lives were so bounded by the rim of the housing projects where they lived. A college graduate herself, she wanted to take her students on a field trip to a black-owned grocery store so they could aspire to more in life. Richard offered to accompany her and her class, and said he knew a special route. "They'll see people they've never seen before," he offered. "They should know everything"—wasn't that the idea?

On the day of the field trip, a fourteen-year-old Richard Pryor escorted the class of third-graders down a peculiar side street. The ladies of its houses, who tended to linger at their front windows, were surprised at the parade of children in their neighborhood and came out on their porches. Richard, who knew the women, introduced them with a smile to Mrs. Timmes and her class. To the teacher's eyes, they were the nicest of black women—humble, yes, but ever so friendly, offering lemonade to her charges and waving hello with such enthusiasm. The children waved back, beaming. The field trip was a great success, she thought, thanks in no small part to Richard's contribution. When she came home, she was still puffed up from the experience and described it to her husband, a policeman familiar with the vice beat. He stopped her short: "You're the biggest fool I've ever laid eyes on." Richard had led her by the nose down a street lined with brothels.

Shortly thereafter, she confronted Richard. He fell out laughing. "I knew you didn't know where you were going!" he said.

"I'm going to get you for that, if it's the last thing I do," Timmes said.

Richard kept up the teasing. "I'm gonna tell people where you were!"

"If you do, I'll whip you!"

"Mrs. Timmes, you're not going to whip me!"

"I'm going to whip your ass!"

At that last word, Richard laughed triumphantly. He not only had pulled the high-minded Kathryn Timmes into the red-light district, but had broken the façade of her propriety, too.

Timmes jumped on Juliette next: how could she have let Richard fool her? The master smiled at the work of her pupil. "It's good sometimes," she said, "for people to become familiar with who they are after they think they know everything."

Though he adored Carver and Juliette's Youth Theater Guild, Richard's apprenticeship as a stage actor was surprisingly brief. Juliette had begun writing a play especially for him, *The Magic Violin*, in which an Italian boy charms his listeners with his music, turning them into better versions of themselves. But this love letter to a boy's artistry was never completed. Richard began spending more and more of his time at a local gym, training as a boxer, to the delight of his father, who proudly remembered his own time in the ring.

Juliette kept up a brave face, but the loss of Richard was a mean disappointment, one that she chalked up to the gender norms of the day. The trappings of Juliette's theater—the fanciful costumes, the cosmopolitan themes, the general indulgence of the imagination—had no place in the meat-and-potatoes outlook of most Peorian men, much less the cynicism of men like Buck. Juliette, though, was nothing if not a fighter herself, and she had the will to lure Richard back from the boxing ring. "I would have gone to hell itself to get that boy," she said.

Ultimately, she just had to promise him the spotlight—the role of emcee at the regular talent shows she organized. These shows were a main event for Peoria's young blacks. Carver's auditorium would be packed with hundreds of kids, all straining to see who would win the prize for best singing or music group. Local gangs would even settle their rivalries at the shows: a singing group from the old projects would battle against a singing group from the new projects, and the outcome would determine which gang could hold its head high the next day. Richard loved the crowd—it was his first time performing his comedy for a large black audience—and the crowd loved him back. In little time, he'd built up a following. At his first show as emcee, he simply had five minutes, enough time for a riff or two. Then Juliette decided to design the shows around Richard, who was in a class of his own, the only comedian at the center. "The kids would come to rehearsal like you would expect them to come to a performance. The auditorium would be packed," Juliette recalled.

At the later talent shows, perhaps because he had more time to extend himself and perhaps because he drew on his recent work with the Youth Theater Guild, Richard started taking on characters more fully. He did "impressions" of well-known figures from the community, and the audience howled in recognition of how Richard captured their quirks and body language. His favorite character, though, was an invention of his own: a black superhero too poor to buy his own suit, who went to rummage sales and put one together out of used pantyhose, a cape (which he stole), and a pair of shoes that were clownishly large: "The Rummage Sale Ranger." Like Juliette Whittaker, who built her stage out of tossed-out orange crates, the Rummage Sale Ranger made an art out of making do. He was the comic book hero of Richard's imagination and a mirror for everything he adored about the improvisational spirit of Juliette.

"Miss Whittaker was just a magic lady," Richard said in a 1974 interview, a note of wonder creeping into his voice. "She just makes you feel like there's something in life." He loved her tutelage, but his own capacity for troublemaking soon pushed him out of it.

CHAPTER 5

The Boot

Peoria and the Army, 1956–1960

In September 1955, Richard transferred to Central High for ninth grade and found himself back in a nearly all-white environment, one of 9 blacks in a class of 340 students, most of whom hailed from Peoria's affluent bluff. All Central's teachers, administrators, and even its custodians and cafeteria staff were white. Still, there were fewer brawls at Central than at Roosevelt or Trewyn, and Richard at first adapted to its controlled environment, buoyed by his experiences two miles away in Carver's afterschool programs. "Richard had something he could really get into," said Juliette Whittaker, "a positive approach to himself. He was being appreciated [at Carver], and that minimized the problems he was having in class." In the fall of 1955, he earned by far his best marks since second grade: a passel of Cs and the first A ever to appear on his transcript, in Physical Education—a subject, perhaps more than any other, in which it was possible to get an A for effort.

At the same time, Richard hit a hard, unyielding wall at Central in the person of his science teacher, Mr. Fink. A former air force colonel who still experimented with model airplanes, Walter Fink brought a military sensibility to the domain of the classroom. Standing perfectly rigid and tall, Fink looked like a sharp-nosed Gregory Peck. He was the straightest of straight arrows, a man who "didn't put up with foolishness," in the words of Richard's friend Loren Cornish. Richard, meanwhile, was foolishness incarnate, the clown in permanent residence in the classroom's back row, always cracking wise, desperate to keep his classmates in stitches.

One day in mid-March 1956, Mr. Fink reached his limit: he interrupted a Pryor performance by seizing Richard by the scruff of his neck and removing him bodily from the classroom. Richard, in response, took a swing at him. That punch was grounds for Richard's expulsion from Central High. Richard lasted 129 days in ninth grade—82 more than Frank Sinatra, who endured only two restive months in high school, and roughly the same interval as Roseanne Barr, a comic whom Richard later inspired to take the stage. At age fifteen, he was done with his formal education.

Though Richard couldn't help but take the expulsion personally, as a verdict on his fitness for school, in another sense the expulsion wasn't personal at all. It was business as usual—Peoria's educational machine separating the wheat from the chaff or, more precisely, the white from the black. None of the eight other blacks who entered Central with Richard were still there by the end of eleventh grade. Whether because they left school voluntarily to join the working world or, like Richard, ran afoul of school authorities, black teens in Peoria were extremely unlikely to finish high school. A black population of over ten thousand produced a paltry crop of thirty high school graduates per year, reflecting a dropout rate higher than ghetto-bound Chicago's, even.

Buck absorbed the news of his son's expulsion without registering the faintest surprise. "It's okay," he said. "But I'll tell you this. If you don't put nothing in the pot, you don't get nothing out." Richard had a grace period of exactly one family dinner. The next day, he needed to find work; he would no longer be free to develop his muse at the Carver Center in the afternoons. He had skipped ahead to his statistical fate as a black male, born in Peoria in the 1940s: backbreaking work, and not enough of it to earn a good living. A mid-1950s survey of employment in Peoria discovered that blacks were overrepresented in only two occupations, as laundresses and janitors, where they cleaned up the messes left by others. There was exactly one black doctor and one black engineer in Peoria, and no black accountants, lawyers, or writers. Having completed only eighth grade, Richard looked extremely unlikely to finesse his way out of the world of manual labor.

He started by working as a janitor at a strip club, but soon lost the job when the club's manager noticed the women rising from the stage with dirt and grit stippling their bodies. "I can do the sweeping, but I can't do no mopping," Richard admitted. "My arms too skinny."

He lasted longer at the shoeshine station of the Hotel Pere Marquette, a downtown showpiece designed by the same architect who had conceived New York's Ritz-Carlton and Harvard's Widener Memorial Library. The architecture of the Pere Marquette, with its high-domed grand lobby, marble staircase, and crystal chandeliers, captured the ambitious, free-for-all spirit of Peoria in the 1920s. At the hotel, Richard bent over the shoes of conventioneers and, in his recollection, "made the shine cloth crack like a bullwhip." He entertained his customers with jokes and banter, and even enjoyed himself a bit. But he knew he had only a bootblack's upturned view of the glamour around him. He told friends that he always dreamed of having enough money to take a meal at the hotel's restaurant, whose tables looked onto Main Street through large picture windows. He yearned to be the man whose shoes were being polished, the man who sat above the crowd.

Richard loved getting paid and feeling "the jingle-jangle of possibilities in my pocket"; he sensed himself growing into independence. But to his grandmother and father, he was a mere teenage boy, still living at home and still to be handled as a child. Over and again, Richard declared that his grandmother and father needed to treat him with respect—and over and again, they whittled him down to size. Once, his grandmother told him to clean a skillet, as had been the custom. Richard refused, and added preemptively, "Hey Mama, don't hit me no more. I'm a *man*!" Marie asked, "Yeah, nigger?" then answered her own question by grabbing the skillet and cracking Richard on the head with it.

On another occasion, Buck found Richard in the housing projects, so drunk that he defied his father when Buck ordered him into his car. Two decades after the incident, Marie relished its denouement on *The Mike Douglas Show*:

> So I'm sitting on the front porch. The car drove up, I see two people in there. Bucky said, "Come on, get out of here!" And [Richard] come out, reeling and rocking, he was so drunk . . .
>
> I looked at him and said, "What are you doing drunk?"
>
> He said, "I wanted to drink some wine, and I drank some wine."
>
> I said, "You did, did you?" So I dragged him, I said, "I'm going to take care of you, I'm going to tear you to pieces."
>
> I grabbed him and throwed him on the dining room table, and got me an ironing cord. And I wore him out.

Tellingly, when Marie spun out this story on the talk show, Richard exploded in laughter next to her, wiping tears from his eyes. It was as if he recognized the paradox of his childhood: that when Marie punished her grandson for pretending to be the man he wasn't, she made him into the man he became.

Buck remained a more baleful antagonist, the epitome of brute force to the teenage Richard. In *Live in Concert* (1979), Richard re-created a faceoff with Buck over the state of his manhood. Threatened with a beating, he announced to Buck, with a breaking voice, "I'm not takin' any more ass-whupping. This is it!" Buck replied, "What? You a man now, motherfucker?"—and like Marie, he didn't wait for an answer to the question.

> He hit me in the chest—hard.
>
> He hit me so hard my chest caved in and wrapped around his fist, and I held on to it with my chest [*look of excruciating pain*].
>
> I would not let go so he could hit my ass again. And everywhere he moved his arm, I was hanging on.

Understandably, Richard added a dose of magical realism to the tale, bouncing around the stage with his arms stiff at his side, as if his chest had the power to swallow Buck's fist. The unreality took the edge off the pain.

Still, it may have been a different side of Buck, the sexual cynic, that wounded the teenage Richard the most. Around the summer of 1956, Richard met a girl his age, "an attractive little package," and managed to turn his parents' garage into a bare-bones lovers' hideaway. A few months later, she told Richard she was pregnant, and he crumpled emotionally: he was eager to fall in love, but not ready to be a father. He ran into his house in a panic and broke the news to Buck. His stepmother Ann rushed into the dining room, saw the tears on Richard's face, and asked, "What's wrong with the boy, Bucky?" Buck answered, "Ain't nothin' wrong with him. Got some girl pregnant." Richard started heaving with sobs.

At that point Buck and Ann took Richard into the living room and convened a family meeting, where Buck, who himself had fathered four children out of wedlock, questioned whether the child was Richard's. Richard decided to follow the path that his father had himself followed. A baby girl was born in April 1957, but Richard kept his distance.

By the time of the baby's birth, Richard appears to have left behind his job as a shoeshine at the Pere Marquette and turned to more demanding physical work. For a while, he helped his father and uncle with their recently launched trucking business. On one memorable job, his uncle drove a truck loaded with coal and dumped it onto the street; Richard's task was to shovel the coal into a cellar. "I never knew there was so much coal in the world. From then on, I stuck to oil heat," he quipped a decade later. After his trucking job, he found steady work at a local slaughterhouse, shaking and folding hides and loading them onto Chicago-bound trains. "It was nasty work," Richard observed. "All the shit that got on me during the day, the rock salt, water and whatnot, froze in the cold. By quitting time, my pants were as stiff as a board."

Belittled at home and ground down at work, Richard spent as much time as possible with his posse of black friends, woofing away the hours on the streets of Peoria. Richard was the kid with the frail body and the smart mouth: he radiated fear even when he wasn't in the orbit of his family, and he radiated sass even though he lacked the physique to back it up. If you gave him a ride on your scooter, he would start crying when the scooter accelerated too fast for his comfort. He needed a shield like his friend Matt Clark, a solidly built kid who, a decade before, had bonded with Richard over their shared love of cowboys. Clark knew how to handle himself in a crowd, having grown up in a family of seventeen kids, and he could intercede when Richard's mouth rubbed other kids the wrong way. The two had, in Clark's estimation, "the perfect friendship. I protected him from danger, and he made me laugh."

Richard practiced his stand-up routines wherever he could. Though he looked to many like a garden-variety cutup, he dreamed big: he made his barber cut his hair so that he looked more like Harry Belafonte, one of America's first black matinee idols. He stationed himself in front of his uncle Herman's pool hall and told jokes with enough flair that passersby would sometimes linger for half an hour or more. Often he hung out with his friends at State Park, in the center of downtown Peoria, performing for an audience that appreciated his material but never gave him a free pass. They shared bottles of Silver Satin, a cheap and sweet white wine, and watched movies that the city projected on the wall of the neighboring Lincoln School. State Park was their preferred locale for a simple reason: it had clear sight lines that allowed Richard and his friends to spot any police cars before the cops could reach them and bust them for violating the eleven o'clock curfew.

The curfew was, for black teenagers, an ever-present threat—a nightly reminder that, just by trying to have a good time, they risked being hauled into custody by the police. Because they tended to gather indoors and outside the curfew's enforcement area downtown, white teens were not much affected by it; the law plainly targeted young black teens like Richard, who hung out on the downtown streets. Thirty minutes before the curfew, horns in the housing projects would blare a reminder. At eleven o'clock, police cars would sweep through downtown, and black teens would scatter and run.

They lived in fear that they'd be picked up and hauled "down to the river"—the Illinois River, which curved around the edge of downtown—and take a beating there. They were right to be afraid: the policemen, who were themselves black and Arab-American (and thus not allowed to patrol the white parts of town), wanted to scare the kids straight. They would bring a curfew violator to the river, ask him to "drink it," then dunk his head in the water.

Richard, according to his act a decade later, would wait "until three minutes before eleven" to head home, "so that the guys would think [he] was brave." A block from home, a police car would come screeching to the curb.

> "Get your hands up, black boy!"
>
> "I didn't do nothin'!"
>
> "Shut up, punk, and put your hands against the wall!"
>
> "There ain't no wall!"
>
> "Find one!"
>
> "Put the handcuffs on him, Fred."
>
> And they'd put the handcuffs on me. And I was really skinny and they'd slip off. And the guy would get mad.
>
> "Put them on his ankles, his chest, or something!"
>
> And they'd handcuff my thighs—and hop me to the car.
>
> Then they'd call my father up . . .
>
> "Mr. Pryor, we have your son here in jail. What would you say we do with him?"
>
> "Let him escape and shoot him in the back."

The sketch was an absurdist scenario, not a transcription of Peoria reality, but it captured something crucial about how Richard experienced his years after his expulsion from Central. He felt himself a harmless soul mistaken for a criminal, a victim of impossible demands, a son who could expect absolutely no sympathy from his father. The entrapment was so total that, from the proper angle, it made a darn good joke.

On April 13, 1959, Richard Pryor went to Chicago and reported for his induction into the U.S. Army. For black teenagers in Peoria, the army promised a steady paycheck and, better still, passage to the wide world beyond their families and their hometown. For Richard, the army offered him a chance to be a man, finally, and to escape the dead-end routines of a city he knew all too well. Peoria felt like a closed circuit: a third of its restaurants still refused to serve black customers, and around this time Richard himself was turned away from the Pantry, a downtown fixture, when he tried to get a hamburger with friends after a late-night movie. He regularly spent half his take-home pay at a tavern next to his grandmother's home, enjoying a steady diet of pickled pig's feet, ice-cold beer, and barroom palaver. In a best-case scenario, he speculated, he might move up to a job at Caterpillar and achieve a semblance of financial stability. The formula for the good life in Peoria: "Work, pension, die."

Meanwhile, Richard had met returning black GIs who crowed about the freedom of life overseas. "Yes, I was in Deutschland and it was a gas." "Man, when I was in Germany, I had three white chicks!" The army was easy to romanticize from afar. His friend Matt Clark had lied about his age so that he could suit up for the army at age sixteen. Richard was only four months past his eighteenth birthday when he volunteered. He had little clue where that decision would take him.

At his induction, Richard took a battery of aptitude tests and swore that he wasn't a member of any subversive organizations. He claimed he was in good physical and mental health, suffering from nothing more than occasional cramps in his legs. The army physician noted that Richard had flat feet and, at five foot ten, was terribly skinny, at 126 pounds, but judged him ready for service. The army signed him up for a two-year tour of duty and shuttled him off to the Ozarks—boot camp at Fort Leonard Wood, Missouri, which specialized in training the army's construction-oriented Corps of Engineers, and was known among black GIs to be "one of the most racist bases in the country." Richard was being tracked, as he had been in Peoria, into the role of general laborer.

In the summer of 1959, Richard enrolled in "basic combat training," or what he called "kill class." "It really blew my mind," he said later, "because I thought the Army was things like hunting, camping, a little fishing"—summer camp with guns. The naïf was soon schooled: "I learned to kill from a guy who killed in World War II, and then they couldn't stop him. So they gave him a job. *'Can't let him on the streets, so we'll let him train these guys for World War III.'* "

In a late-1960s routine, Pryor would re-create his kill class, turning his instructor into a cartoon of the wounded warrior. "When I was in World War II, I killed some and I was killed some," the corporal barks. "That's right, I was wounded thirty-two times." The corporal urges Private Pryor to demonstrate a "leg-thrust kick to the groin," and the reluctant but eager-to-please Richard obliges by administering a killer kick to the corporal's own groin. "Class dismissed," the corporal squeaks.

There was a good deal of wishful thinking behind this routine, and some psychic payback, too. During basic training, Richard was not kicking the army in the balls; he was cracking under its discipline. In mid-August, he submitted to another physical, and this time he reported that he suffered from motion sickness, vision problems, depression, nerves, difficulties with teachers, and those persistent leg cramps. He was hardly in shipshape condition on the eve of being shipped out. Perhaps because he was deemed less than A-grade material for the front, the army formally assigned him to a specific support duty, one that would keep him out of high-risk situations. His job? Plumber. Some military men might have exulted that they were not going to be thrown into combat, but Richard took his new assignment in a spirit of ripe irony: "Once again I was covered in shit."

On September 3, 1959, Richard embarked from an army terminal in Brooklyn and, ten days later, arrived in the port of Bremerhaven, West Germany. Like many of the thirty thousand black GIs deployed annually in Germany in the 1950s, he came there with an appetite for adventure and with the hope that he was putting an ocean's distance between himself and Jim Crow. Some black GIs, like those Pryor had met in Peoria, found Germany a charmed place. Colin Powell, America's best-known black soldier, came to Germany a year before Pryor and remembered that "For black GIs, especially those out of the South, Germany was a breath of freedom—they could go where they wanted, eat where they wanted, and date whom they wanted, just like other people. The dollar was strong, the beer good, and the German people friendly, since we were all that stood between them and the Red hordes. War, at least the Cold War in West Germany, was not hell."

Powell, though, had served in Gelnhausen, a picturesque town not far from Frankfurt. Richard was dispatched to southwest garrison towns in the former Nazi stronghold of the Rhineland-Palatinate, desolate places that now welcomed the American military presence as before they had welcomed the Nazis. According to Richard, three days before his job was to start, he phoned the sergeant who was to be his commanding officer and advised him that he was going to report for work on Monday. "It's about time you got here, boy," the sergeant replied in a southern accent. "I've been working with one of those niggers and he's stolen everything that isn't nailed down." "Oh, God," Richard thought to himself—and kept thinking to himself all weekend long. When he reported for work, the sergeant couldn't believe his eyes. "You Private Pryor? The guy I talked to on the telephone? I hope you don't get upset about anything I say. You can ask all the people around here, especially the colored folks. They know I'm a nice guy."

Kaiserslautern's commanding officers hailed largely from the South, and while the army had been officially desegregated in 1954, the Kaiserslautern base felt to its black soldiers as if it were ruled by a Mississippi-ish double standard. A white soldier who showed up late for duty might get a free pass, but a black soldier who did the same would get disciplined and perhaps demoted—part of a system that managed to keep blacks in the lower ranks. Many black GIs felt intensely isolated: they were struggling against the same discrimination they faced at home, but without their family or larger community to offer distraction or support. It was not an easy place to be a black comedian, either. When, in 1958, the black entertainer Timmie Rogers arrived late for a show in Kaiserslautern, one major became so incensed that he slugged Rogers and kicked him while he was on the floor, breaking a rib. The major claimed that he'd been provoked, that Rogers had insulted him by asking, "What's the matter, man?"—not "What's the matter, officer?" These were the sorts of men to whom Richard reported.

The surrounding towns of the Rhineland-Palatinate offered no easy social escape. Upon their arrival in the area, white GIs had threatened German bar owners with an economic boycott if they served a drop to blacks, and the bar owners acceded to the pressure. The same Germans who had earlier embraced the Nazi Party, which made "miscegenation" punishable by death, and who now made the Rhineland-Palatinate the only German state to have a proud neo-Nazi in its legislature, found segregation quite palatable. As a result, these garrison towns had two sets of bars—one for white GIs, another for their black counterparts. In Kaiserslautern the black bars were confined to a single street, known as "Little Harlem." And while, by the late-1950s, white GIs might freely carouse with German women, black GI bars were often raided by American military police and German authorities. Any German woman who frequented a black GI bar was assumed to be a prostitute and so could be hauled off to jail. (Kaiserslautern's Little Harlem was also known as "Bimbo City.") In one town, three-quarters of women prosecuted for prostitution were in the company of black GIs—an astonishing figure, given that blacks were only 15 percent of the army population. Even steady girlfriends of black GIs had a hard time escaping punishment.

Private Pryor stumbled into this German version of Jim Crow when he visited a local club early in his tour of duty. Before he could order his first beer, two white soldiers started scuffling. Then he heard someone yell "Nigger!" and looked around, only to discover that he was the only black person in the bar. The scuffle had shifted its focus to him. He ran upstairs to escape the fight and, landing in a room where the club's strippers changed their clothes, begged for help from the first girl he met. Her face twisted into a sour expression. She told him, "Get out of here. I call police." Soon after, the MPs arrived. Richard sneaked outside and scrambled back to his barracks, one step ahead of the law.

It was an all-too-typical incident in these southwestern garrison towns. Many barroom brawls were the result of a new black recruit wandering into a place where he was not welcome—not by white GIs and not by German civilians. When military police arrived at the scene of an interracial fight, they responded by tracking down the black GI and beating him into submission; Richard was lucky to escape a rendezvous with their nightsticks. At least once, not long before his arrival in the area, the violence between black and white soldiers had exploded into a full-fledged race riot. On New Year's Eve in 1955, in the neighboring town of Baumholder (where Richard would soon be transferred), hundreds of white and black GIs clashed in the town's center until "blood was running in the gutter," according to the local police chief. Scores were wounded, and an unknown number of soldiers died in the melee—unknown because the military command refused to release information about the incident.

A month after his arrival in Germany, Richard went to the dispensary at his base. He feared that he was losing his mind: he was being woken up in the middle of the night by horrible dreams. The dispensary recommended that he be transferred to the army hospital nearby and given an emergency psychiatric consult. The army psychiatrist reassured him that he was normal: it was normal for a soldier to worry and lose sleep. He suggested that Richard return for a follow-up exam, but he never did.

On December 9 he was transferred out of Kaiserslautern and sent thirty-five miles away, to Baumholder, known variously as the Siberia of Germany (in recognition of its remoteness and cold winters) or, more simply, as the nation's armpit. It was a cow town whose peasants still hauled goods on horse-drawn wagons. Soldiers stationed in Baumholder fell into a numbing routine: rise and shine, reveille, long jogs, classroom drills, three meals, and occasional visits into the town at night. Richard seems to have coped with the stress by smoking and eating. By the time he left the service, eight months later, he was up to one and half packs a day and had gained twenty-six pounds from his first physical.

In Baumholder, Richard's military career unraveled. He was assigned to a job so dull that it was grueling to endure: maintaining a Nike missile up a hill on the fringe of the camp, far from any mess halls or amenities. Soldiers in missile battalions were there to push the red buttons if an emergency arose, but mostly they just sat around and dithered in the "ready room," a barracks with bunks and a lounge area. For Richard, the missile battalion's plumber, the only emergency he could anticipate was a stopped-up toilet. His enthusiasm for the service waned. On January 4, 1960—the first Monday after New Year's Eve weekend—he missed morning reveille and was slapped with the punishment of seven days' restriction to the missile area and a distant mess hall. On January 12, just after serving the last day of his restriction order, he missed formation and was given two weeks of extra duty, an extra shift at the end of each endless day.

Richard never cottoned to boredom: he had an antic personality that created high drama out of thin air. In the late afternoon of January 24, one hour before he was to begin his overtime shift, he started insulting the corporal of the guard in the ready room.

"Gringo monkey!" he yelled. "*Chingada madre!*"

Why Richard called his superior officer a "gringo" and a "motherfucker" in Spanish will always retain an element of mystery. Maybe Richard had been posing as a Puerto Rican recruit to dodge the worst of army racism—he suggested as much in a later routine—and perhaps the Spanish obscenity was part of the masquerade. The insult may have baffled the man who was its target, too: the army record does not report any response from him.

"Are you tired of living?" Richard sneered as a follow-up. The man asked what he meant by that. "Maybe you'll die tonight," Richard answered.

For his less than deferential behavior, Richard was disciplined officially and demoted a grade. In the paperwork, the captain in charge of Richard's unit laid the groundwork for an eventual discharge from the army. Private Pryor, he wrote, "lacks the ability to perform his duties as expected of a good soldier." And then, piling on: "Further, this individual lacks effectiveness in performing his assigned duty as a plumber." In the eyes of the army, Richard was good for nothing, a nuisance.

Richard hung on for a while nonetheless. Like many black GIs, he picked up some basic German on his jaunts into town, where he found comfort in the arms of fräuleins who were not local to Baumholder but who'd traveled there because they sensed an opportunity. The local priests and burghers might have labeled all such women prostitutes, but their motives were decidedly mixed. Some took cash for specified sexual services. Others formed liaisons with black GIs that lasted as long as their partner's tour of duty. A few landed a spouse and a ticket to America. For Richard, who was familiar with what it meant to live in such a ripely compromised world, the red-light districts adjacent to his army base probably felt more like home than the base itself.

With one German fräulein, Richard had a sexual experience he would never forget. It was an experiment in rebellion, a refusal of his uncle Dickie's solemn advice: "Boy, don't you ever kiss no pussy. I mean that. Whatever you do in life, don't kiss no pussy." Richard asked the woman if he could go down on her, and she said yes. The experience was "a revelation, something that changed my life, because until then, my family only fucked in one position—up and down." Having strayed from the Pryor family nest, he was straying from its mores, too.

Seven months after the "*Chingada madre*" incident, Richard was booted from the army for good. Yet his own account of the trouble is so out of kilter with the testimony lodged in the official record that one is tempted to say that, on the night of July 9, 1960, when Richard drew a switchblade on a specialist fourth class, he did so enveloped in the fog of war.

According to Richard, his unit had been watching the film *Imitation of Life*—a lush melodrama of the time, starring army pinup Lana Turner—when a white soldier "laughed at the wrong spots." *Imitation of Life* is a film that, unusually for its time, smuggles a profound story about racial ambivalence and self-loathing into what appears, at first, to be a simple morality tale about a negligent white mother. In its last half, most of its energy flows into the saga of Sarah Jane, a light-skinned young black woman who, leaving home, passes for white so that she can chase dreams of white glamour: being a showgirl in a glossy production, having a well-off white boyfriend. Her quest ends tragically, with her black mother dying from the heartbreak of their separation.

Laughing at *Imitation of Life* was equivalent to laughing at the sorrows of black life—or of Richard's. Didn't he, like the character of Sarah Jane, long to shake off the fate of a hardscrabble life? Didn't he dream, like her, of achieving escape velocity as a star? And didn't he understand, from his failed courtship of Margaret Ruth to his most recent trysts in Germany, the pull of romance across the color line? Small wonder that he would have been willing to risk his army career, in effect, to defend the film's honor.

According to Richard's memoir, a friend of his started slugging the white GI who had laughed at the film. A crowd gathered outside the enlisted men's club to watch the fight. But when it became clear that the white GI would win, Richard reached into his pocket, drew out a switchblade, and stabbed the white GI six or seven times in the back—to no effect. The white GI appeared indestructible. Petrified, Richard ran away and flung his knife into the bushes. Soon after, an MP arrived at Richard's barracks, accused him of having stabbed a fellow soldier, and tossed him in the stockade.

The army's version of the tale is considerably less colorful, lacking as it does any testimony from Richard. According to the military, Private Pryor had, for no reason, stabbed a Specialist Fourth Class in the chest outside the enlisted men's club. The stabbed specialist had pursued and caught Pryor, but Pryor had jerked away and fled, only to return a few minutes later to issue a threat: "Man, you hit me. I have a long knife, and when you come out, I'm going to cut you!"

The absence of Richard's testimony from the official record is no happenstance. Like other soldiers brought up on discipline charges, Richard chose to sacrifice any legal representation and leave the service "under honorable conditions" rather than face a court-martial and possible prison time. Black soldiers were particularly liable to land in this predicament: a decade later, the NAACP charged that military stockades in Germany resembled prisons in America, with blacks making up more than half of inmates.

For the army, Richard's "elimination" was an open-and-shut case. He "has a history of violence," wrote the major who commanded his unit. "His retention in the service would be detrimental to unit moral[e] and the personal saf[e]ty of the men forced into contact with him." Richard had performed poorly in all three units where he served, the major added, and had "been counseled and corrected without avail." He was an inveterate troublemaker, and an unpopular one at that: "He does not get along with other men and he continually feels he is being 'picked on.'" Race often went unmentioned in reports like these, as commanding officers were likely to be blamed for racial friction between their troops but were simply doing their job when they eliminated unsuitable men from their unit. Richard's file was no exception. By the evidence it contained, Richard had a persecution complex.

Confined to a cell with a concrete floor, a single lightbulb, and little else, Richard had plenty of time to ponder what he would do after his service ended. He was held in Baumholder for a full month after the stabbing incident, during which time he was given another physical. He ticked off a host of ailments: eye trouble, shortness of breath, pain in his chest, heart palpitations, leg cramps, motion sickness, stuttering, insomnia, anxiety, and depression. The army had taken a rail-thin teenager, put meat on his bones, and turned him into a mess of a man.

But in one regard, the army had cleared Richard's head and straightened his vision. At his exit physical, he was asked to list his occupation. On two previous occasions, he had responded to that prompt by referring to his work with his father and uncle, and had called himself a truck driver. This time, he looked to his future more than his past. He took up the pen and wrote, in the wobbly script that reflected his interrupted schooling, "actor."

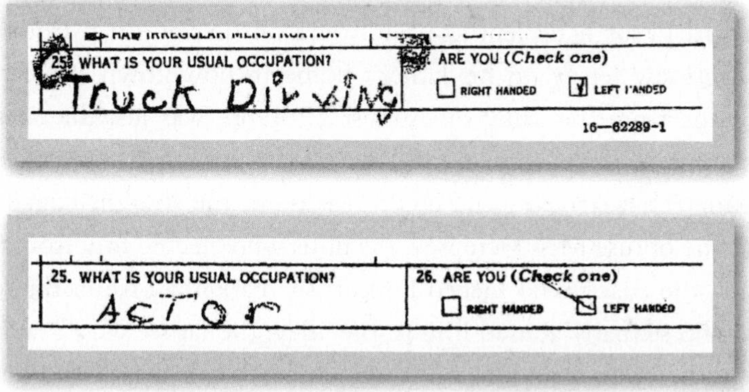

25. WHAT IS YOUR USUAL OCCUPATION? Truck Dirving
ARE YOU (*Check one*) ☐ RIGHT HANDED ☒ LEFT HANDED
16—62289-1

25. WHAT IS YOUR USUAL OCCUPATION? Actor
26. ARE YOU (*Check one*) ☐ RIGHT HANDED ☒ LEFT HANDED

Changing jobs: Pryor's "occupation" upon entering the US Army in 1959, and upon exiting it in 1960. (Courtesy of Jennifer Pryor)

CHAPTER 6

The Measure of a Man

Peoria, 1960–1962

Richard Pryor had plenty to mull over on the long trip from Fort Dix, New Jersey, to his father's home in downtown Peoria. His discharge from the army on August 27, 1960, was just the latest in a chain of humiliations and rejections that stretched as far back as his nineteen-year-old mind could reach—to the straight-edged Mr. Fink, the obtuse Miss Dempsey, the nuns who ejected him from their school, the coach who kicked him off the basketball team, the teenager who sexually abused him in the alley, the father who beat him, the mother who abandoned him. He arrived in Peoria with twenty-five days of back pay in his pocket and used the money to play the part of the conquering hero. He took his half-sister Barbara to a movie, then called a cab to whisk her home, even though she lived just three blocks away. He broke out a few snatches of German to impress local girls. If everyone assumed that he had prospered from his time in the service, he was not going to disabuse them of the illusion.

The money went only so far. Soon enough, Richard was back under Buck's roof, living in an expanded household that included his uncle Dickie and half-sister Barbara in addition to his father and stepmother. Ann had been diagnosed with cancer of the mouth, and the family struggled to make ends meet. When Buck and Dickie couldn't find much work as truckers, it was Ann herself who took up the slack, going out into the cold and returning with a white man in tow, whom she led into a bedroom so they could close the deal. While she turned tricks, Buck sat quietly in the front room—counting the money in his head, perhaps. A little while later, Ann would emerge with "just enough [money] to fix us some food for that day," Barbara recalled. "She'd put out a big pot of chicken—I don't know what it was, but it was good—and we'd live on that for two or three days." With money so tight, Buck looked down on his underemployed son, and his son looked away. They barely talked to each other directly.

Since he didn't have the resources to get his own apartment, Richard simply made himself scarce. On weekends, he often slept on the couch of his friend William Bradley, curled up in a black trench coat. There he became acquainted with his five-year-old half-sister Sharon, who was Bradley's stepdaughter and one of Buck's four "outside children." (Buck had no relationship with Sharon at the time.) "I came up to him and he gave me a hug," Sharon said, remembering her initial encounter with Richard. "That was the first time I had ever known what thirty-five cents was. It was a quarter and a dime, and that was all he had in his pocket."

With so little money to his name, Richard warmed to the kindness of this alternate family. He ate spaghetti at their house and performed amateur magic tricks for Sharon and her brothers and sisters. An aficionado, even in his young adulthood, of cartoons such as *Woody Woodpecker* and *Baby Huey*, he would loll in the Bradley family's living room on Saturday mornings in front of their TV set, or escort Sharon and her siblings to the Rialto Theater, where a local weatherman hosted an auction called "Bids for the Kids": kids would collect milk cartons to earn points, then pool their points to bid for a bicycle or toy. Sharon and her siblings were always disappointed, never able to win the prizes they coveted, but for Richard the auction was merely the run-up to the main event, a morning of nonstop cartoons. "We had to sit there through all them cartoons while Richard was laughing, laughing at everything," Sharon grumbled in retrospect.

One of the gifts of Richard's childhood, which translated into one of the strengths of his comedy, was that he had no snobbery; he moved easily between vastly different worlds. If, on some mornings, he spent time with his friend's children, during the afternoons and evenings he frequented the Blue Shadow, a tavern famous for serving a hangover-cure chili so spicy that its mere aroma sent customers into a sweat. There he held down a stool with his friend Wilbur Harp, the rare black man in Peoria who was openly gay and openly effeminate in his manner.

In the wee hours of the night, Richard might wander over to the Villa, a large club outside the Peoria city limits, run by his buddy Hank Hansen. With its mixed-race house band, the Villa drew a lively and mixed crowd, but for Richard the real action was in the casita that served as a gambling house out back. The scene was a comedy sketch waiting to happen. Among the *dramatis personae* were "Big Irma" Anderson, a huge lady who used "Kiss my ass, nigger!" as the equivalent of "Hello"; Sylvester "Weasel" Williams, for whom insults were a prelude to a hustle ("You funny in that hat . . . That hat went out with Dick Tracy. You can go look funny if you want to, but I got a hat out in the car that's a bitch"); and an older, unnamed black man who stood on the fringe of the gambling but made more noise than anyone else ("Now what you gonna do, nigger?! You done fucked up the game!"). Richard observed later that Hank's Place was "a beautiful place with beautiful people. Everybody was an individual."

When he couldn't afford a stool at a tavern or a stake at a table, Richard simply took up residence on the streets of Peoria. He remained loyal to the sweet white wine of his teenage years, the citrus-flavored Silver Satin. And he discovered that the street, like the back room at the Villa, was full of characters, none more compelling than a grizzled drifter known as "Preacher" Brown. Brown spent much of his day walking and talking around Peoria, often ending up in the heart of its soul district—near Pop's Pool Hall and Wade's Inn, a country kitchen that served up a fine plate of beans and neck bones. Brown was social but did not socialize, exactly: he wasn't the sort to drink with a close-knit group of friends on the street corner. Instead he preached with a bottle in his hand, stopping traffic, schooling youngsters in their no-good ways, and telling stories about his illustrious past.

A decade later, Preacher Brown would manifest onstage as one of Richard's breakthrough characters, "the wino":

Man, I know Jesus. Shit, he lived over there in the projects. Nigger ain't shit. I knew the boy's mama personally. That's right—Mary. The girl with big titties. Pretty black girl, man. Had personality all over her face. Well, that's right. I knew her. I'm the one responsible for that girl. She wasn't no virgin either, 'cause I know a couple of niggers eased up there and got some. . . .

I remember when her son Jesus was born 'cause her husband Joe damn near killed her. 'Cause she told him God made the baby. He beat her with a pool stick. Said, "Bitch, you gonna tell me who the daddy of this baby is." Damn near broke that bitch's neck. She fessed up—found out it was Jimmy Walker. . . .

Shit, I been around. I ain't no fool, I study peoples. I know where peoples comin' from. Shit, I'm a people-ologist.

In Preacher Brown, Richard found a riveting companion, and one who put absolutely no demands on him other than to listen and observe—to conduct his own form of "people-ology." Which is what Richard did, without condescension or even that much distance. Richard was on the skids himself, and it didn't take too much imagination to think that, thirty years down the line, he might wind up in Preacher Brown's shoes, holding forth to anyone who would indulge him. That was an obvious trajectory for a black kid with a spotty job history, a taste for sweet wine, and an unquenchable love for the stage, any stage.

Happily for Richard, his family had well-placed friends in Peoria's nightclub world, friends earned through two decades of shared dealings in the city's underground. He dropped in on his old neighbor Harold Parker, who now ran a club on one of the few blocks of North Washington Street to have survived urban renewal. Richard told him he was looking for work.

"What do you do?" Parker asked.

"I sing and play piano," Richard said.

"How much you expecting to make?" Parker followed up.

"Not much," Richard said.

"That's good," Parker said. "'Cuz you won't."

There were a two small problems with Richard passing himself off as a Nat King Cole disciple: he had none of Cole's savoir-faire onstage and knew his way around only four chords on the piano. At his nightclub debut, Richard sat down at the piano and fingered those four chords, then sang some nonsense words to fill the space. Sweat poured from him. The people in his audience—not for the last time—wondered if Richard was messing with them or was simply a mess himself. To his everlasting credit, Parker appreciated the courage behind the bluff. "You've got more nerve than anybody I've ever seen," he said, and offered Richard two jobs—one as a bartender and another filling the fifteen-minute intermissions between sets. Richard had stumbled into his first paying job as a professional comedian. For much of the night at Harold's Club, he worked behind the bar in a red vest and bow tie. Then, when the musicians left the bandstand, he removed his bar costume and assumed the stage. Sometimes he sang, to mediocre effect, but more often he used his short sets to make people laugh. When his fifteen minutes were up, he returned behind the bar and retied his bow tie, put his vest back on.

Arguably, Richard could not have found, in all of Peoria, a better venue than Harold's Club or a more influential sponsor than Harold Parker. Parker had seen his own star rise over the previous decade: in 1959, the *Chicago Defender* christened him the "Boy Wonder of Peoria" and dubbed his nightclub "the hottest thing this side of Khrushchev." After years entangled in prostitution, Parker was making a bid for respectability. He'd divorced his wife, China Bee, Peoria's best-known black madam, and married a Chicago-bred chorus girl. In early 1961 he even ran, albeit unsuccessfully, as a Republican candidate for alderman, campaigning as the underworld's enemy and promising to "give ward residents an honest and impartial representation in our city administration."

Harold's Club was the centerpiece of Parker's new class act: the swankiest black-and-tan nightclub in Peoria, modeled after Chicago

A club like no other in the Midwest: Harold's Club, with its proud proprietor at the center. (Courtesy of Harold Parker Jr.)

showplaces like the Regal Theater. An evening at Harold's promised a "package entertainment." Chorus girls strutted through choreographed routines and a series of costume changes over the course of the evening (with fishnet stockings being one constant). Musicians suited up in matching tuxedos to perform. From the diamond-patterned parquet floor to the sprays of flowers that sat atop the piano, the design of the club was elegance itself. Not only was the ladies' room set up as a powder room, but even the men's room was designated a "men's lounge," in the upscale idiom of the time. For its clientele, an evening at Harold's Club was a night of stepping out on the town. With its cover charge and dress code, it attracted a mixed-race crowd (about one-third white and two-thirds black) who had money to spend.

Presiding over this festival of swank was Harold Parker himself, a pencil-mustachioed dandy who left a scent of cologne trailing after him. He had such beautiful skin that he seemed to wear cosmetics, and reminded at least one musician of the zoot-suited Cab Calloway. Parker's framed portrait hung above the bar—the Boy Wonder paying

The "Boy Wonder of Peoria" on an off night: Harold Parker Jr., in a 1961 mug shot. (Courtesy of the Peoria Journal Star*)*

tribute to his own wonderfulness. Yet Parker was also a stone-cold businessman who, according to pianist David Sprattling, bribed the musicians' union so that he would not have to pay union scale to musicians—if he paid them at all. "Sometimes when he didn't pay the musicians anything, they'd go in there and loud-talk him," Sprattling said, "and he'd have his bodyguards whup you up a little bit."

Richard Pryor, who had reason to be grateful to Parker, called him one of the "meanest cats" he had ever known. In the early years of Harold's Club, Parker's own mother played the part of enforcer, adding an odd tinge of menace to the club's smart ambience. Night after night, from the moment the music began at 9:00 p.m. until the club closed at 4:00 a.m., the sexagenarian sat like a statue at the bar, dressed in black and carrying a large black handbag. In that large black handbag, everyone knew, was a large black gun. No one was going to double-cross her son or otherwise endanger his livelihood.

The incongruities of Harold Parker—his ruthlessness matched by his grace—played out in his club, which smuggled an "anything goes" attitude into an atmosphere of controlled elegance. "It had that very clean, very organized feel, but with people who were out of control," recalled Fred Tieken, who fronted a mixed-race rock 'n' roll group there. "The crowd was one of the most mixed [crowds I've ever seen], and I'm not just talking racially mixed. There were gays, straights, cross-dressers, business guys in suits, young people, old people . . . every form of life you could possibly imagine." According to Tieken, the composition of the audience shifted around 1:00 a.m., halfway into the night's entertainment. "People who had responsibilities—a day job—were heading home, and a whole new crowd of nightlife people would be there, jumping up on stage." Once, after Tieken hopped on the piano to play a saxophone solo, a black woman started grabbing his ass in excitement. "The women were very suggestive, in terms of the way they dressed and in terms of their makeup. And some of them were actually guys."

The freewheeling atmosphere of Harold's Club suited Richard's comic style, which, partly because of his lack of experience and partly because of his inclination, was fluid and exploratory. He assumed different characters over the course of the evening, some of whom were drawn from the streets of Peoria, others merely lifted out of his imagination. He might pretend to be Santa Claus, squeezing himself down different chimneys. Or the jackleg preacher who partied on Saturday night only to clean himself up on Sunday morning. Or the car salesman who put over a lemon on an unsuspecting customer.

Thanks to the hours he spent among the likes of Preacher Brown, Richard had a wino character in his repertoire, and he invented shambolic conversations between him and his friends on the street corner. In one bit, he pantomimed how the wino acted the fool until the police arrived on the scene, at which point he stood up straight as a soldier and sober as a priest. When the police left, the wino returned to his old self, cutting the monkey with his friends again. Already Richard's stand-up leaned toward multicharacter theater, with Richard the comedian a recessive presence in the overall drama. And already, too, it was the down-and-outers, the marginalized, who assumed center stage in his imagination.

As he groped toward his own style, Richard did not aspire to be a comedian in the mold of Bob Hope, who chose his lines from an overstuffed catalog of gags (most of them written by jokesmiths in his employ). In sensibility, he leaned toward his idol Sid Caesar and his fellow midwesterner Jonathan Winters, two comics who submerged their real selves beneath the outlandish characters they created. Both Caesar and Winters were averse to jokes; they were performers, not commentators. They were interested in the absurdity of so-called normal life. Caesar specialized in nutty professors and squabbling husbands; Winters, in squares and hayseeds. Richard had his own body of material—the people he'd observed in Peoria's pulpits, used-car lots, and working-class bars—and his comedy inclined to the off-kilter and the zany.

In tone, he was closer to these mid-1950s comics than to the fiery, experimental comedian he would later become: he was trying hard to make the patrons of Harold's Club laugh, and so excised any details that might make them squirm. His wino was not yet a foul-mouthed blasphemer, just a man in his cups. When he acted crazy onstage, it was "crazy" in quotes, kooky rather than unglued. He didn't yet have the confidence to mine the memories of his Peoria upbringing for their brutal pathos, or the artistic intuition to start digging. No one in the audience—not even the house musicians who performed with him night after night—knew much about the real life of the kid who turned himself inside out to become other people, and he wasn't telling.

Offstage, Richard was in bloom, and in trouble. In the spring of 1961, he fell for Patricia Watts, a seventeen-year-old, auburn-haired transplant from the small river town of Louisiana, Missouri. The two made for an unlikely couple. Richard was lanky as an exclamation point; Pat, sturdy and curvy. Richard had been raised among pimps and prostitutes in a brothel; Pat, among livestock on a farm. Richard dreamed of becoming a comedian; Pat, of becoming a mortician. ("Dead people never hurt you," she said often. "The ones you need to be afraid of are the ones who are alive.") Yet they shared enough—a zest for life, a fondness for alcohol, a sense of mutual attraction—and the two became an item.

Shortly thereafter, Pat discovered that she was pregnant. Richard hankered to have a happy family, one devoted to one another "for better, for worse, and forever"—a vision of family he'd gathered from *Father Knows Best*, a TV show he watched avidly. Pat, meanwhile, wanted to be sitcom star Donna Reed: happily ironing, doing the dishes, and taking care of her man and her kids. When Richard asked Pat to marry him, she accepted. His grandmother Marie supplied the ring, a Pryor family heirloom with a series of flat-cut diamonds set over its gold band.

As the ceremony neared, Richard wavered. The "forever" part of the wedding vows started seeming less abstract and more forbidding. His father pulled him aside and dispensed the same advice he'd given his son before his military service, when Richard supposed that he'd gotten his first lover pregnant: "Son, you don't have to do it." Buck didn't question the paternity of the child, as he had before, but he underlined how ill equipped his son was to support a family. Earlier, Richard had bowed to his father's counsel; this time he defied it. "If Buck hadn't said that, I might have chickened out," he reflected later, "but to spite him I said, 'Shit, I'm going through with it.' "

On June 11, 1961, Richard and Pat were married in a short, informal ceremony in the living room of Marie's home on South Adams Street. Fewer than ten people attended. Buck picked up Richard's sister Barbara on the way to the wedding, and by the time they arrived, the ceremony had already ended. The eighteen-year-old Barbara was surprised to discover that, in her purple dress, she was dressed more formally than the bride.

With Richard earning only fifty dollars a week, the newlyweds saved money by moving into Marie's home, four miles from downtown. No longer a madam, Marie made a living by selling liquor out of her home during the week and by converting a room, over the weekends, into a modest restaurant that served fried chicken and fish to a few customers at a time. Meanwhile Richard and Pat struggled for bare essentials. When Richard wanted to write down an idea for a comedy routine, he would strip the paper from clothes hangers. Pat pushed him to hold down a regular job, but he resisted. After she sent him off to a hospital so that he could fill out a job application—her parents both worked as housekeepers in local hospitals—he came back empty-handed. The hospital had been closed somehow, he explained weakly.

The daily grind took its toll on their marriage. Pat cooked up potatoes day after day—boiled potatoes, fried potatoes, mashed potatoes—and one day, Richard reached his limit. "I'm sick of potatoes," he cried, and started beating Pat in frustration. Marie, who, like Pat, had been married in her teens, took the younger woman under her wing. "The next time he hits you," Marie told her, "you pick up something and hit him back, and he won't bother you any more." Pat did as instructed: when Richard exploded next, she grabbed a pan and walloped him so hard that he tottered and fell onto Marie, seated nearby. Marie, in turn, scooted her feet back so that Richard tumbled to the floor. Her baby had to learn his lesson, even if it meant landing hard on his backside.

The lesson didn't take, despite the fact that Richard was under new pressure to play the role of supportive husband. Pat suffered a miscarriage just after their wedding, then quickly became pregnant again. The two newlyweds were heading, with deliberate speed, for the responsibilities of parenthood. But Richard was easily distracted. At one point, Pat stopped into Harold's Club to watch her husband perform onstage. He broke into a song and looked in her direction, and Pat brightened at her husband's serenade. How romantic! Then she realized that his gaze was fixed not on her but on a white woman sitting at a neighboring table. That was Pat's breaking point, her own "I'm sick of potatoes" moment. She dragged the other woman into a knockdown fight, toppling over chairs and sending glasses crashing to the nightclub floor. At the end of the week, Richard had even less money than usual to bring home: Harold Parker had garnished most of his pay to cover the damage.

Richard and Pat's marriage ended, effectively, soon after. Around September 1, 1961—eighty days after their wedding—Pat moved back into her parents' home on Fourth Street. Richard left his grandmother's house and returned to his parents' home. If he was going to be broke, he figured, it was better to be broke downtown, close to the action. He sank deeper into the nightlife offered by Harold's Club, the Blue Shadow, Hank's Villa, the Elks Club, Blackie's Archway, and other Peoria hotspots, sometimes staying out well past sunup. Sonny Stenson, a drummer who worked at Harold's Club and a slender, smooth operator, introduced him to marijuana and amphetamines. "It's part of show business," Sonny said. Richard didn't need much of a sell: he took instantly to the buzz, the relaxation, offered by pot and the rush offered by uppers. The drugs "eased my pain and insecurity, erased the fear, turned me into a whole new man," he remembered. "Sometimes I stayed up two or three days straight, feeling so cool and jive." He loved the uppers so much that he sometimes doubled the dose, which felt great until, on the second or third day of wakefulness, it felt horrible. "There's an Indian playing a drum inside me. Tell him to stop," Richard told Sonny. "That's your heart," Sonny replied, laughing.

At first, the drugs were merely one ingredient in the jangling carnival of Richard's days and nights. Unanchored, he drifted from scene to scene—and nearly lost his life one Sunday morning, at the tail end of an extended Saturday night.

On April 1, 1962, Richard and a musician from Harold's Club were about to exit the Elks Club through its front door when the club's bouncer, James King, insisted they step back. There was danger waiting outside that door: a sixty-eight-year-old man named Albert

"Goodkid" Charles, who felt he'd been cheated of his money at the club and had now returned with a .12-gauge shotgun in hand. The bouncer—himself a father of five and the leader of the choir and Sunday school of his Baptist church—came onto the front steps of the club and appealed to Charles to put down his gun. Charles replied by shooting him point-blank in the groin. "Goodkid, why did you shoot me?" were King's last words. The man who had saved Richard's life was lying in a pool of blood on the steps.

On April 10, a week after the shooting, Richard and Pat's child, a son, was born. In the hospital, Richard stared at the baby, taking in his features. He told his father that his son "looked like a little ape."

Buck wasn't one to gild the lily, either. "So did you," he said. "Like a little gorilla. That's what Mama said about you."

"Yeah?" Richard said under his breath. "Then I guess he's mine."

The boy was named after his father: Richard Jr. For a few months, Richard stopped by the home of his in-laws, checking in with Pat and playing games with the baby. But his mind and heart were elsewhere.

On May 17, 1962, Harold Parker lost his liquor license, which was tantamount to losing the lease on his nightclub, and Richard was forced to find a new job. Parker had been dogged by the law for several years, but he was effectively nailed when he allegedly bribed a police officer who had written him up for a liquor code violation. (Parker claimed he'd been entrapped.) Peoria mayor Robert Day prosecuted Parker with a vengeance: after the Illinois Liquor Control Commission ruled in favor of Parker in 1961, Day filed a lawsuit against the commission and against Parker. When Day's lawsuit succeeded, the wild and styled world of Harold's Club was no more. In a matter of years, the entire vice district of North Washington Street, the seedbed of Richard's childhood, would be wiped off the map in its entirety. In a striking cultural about-face—the military-industrial complex edging out the underground economy—the Caterpillar Corporation would build its sprawling international headquarters on the block where Harold's Club had stood. Harold

Parker left Peoria for Chicago, where he died a few years later of a heart attack.

When Harold's Club shuttered in May 1962, there was still one survivor from the old days: the resourceful Bris Collins, who had operated a tavern at 405 North Washington Street since 1939. Collins and the Pryor family had been tight for decades. When Collins was sent to prison for a year on counterfeiting charges in 1954, Richard's grandfather Pops took over the operation of the tavern in his absence. Eight years later, Collins repaid the favor by giving Richard a steady job, for seventy-two dollars a week, at Collins Corner, the nightclub he had recently opened on the spot of his old tavern.

Collins may have been, like Harold Parker, a hard-nosed hustler who always made sure to get his cut, but in his own way he was also a pillar of the community, supporting the Carver Center financially and refusing to carry any liquor from Hiram Walker as long as the distillery did not employ blacks outside of menial jobs. Collins Corner was, unlike Harold's Club, a nightclub oriented primarily to black Peorians. With the exception of the white strippers who straggled into Collins Corner after their own clubs closed for the night, no more than a handful of whites ever wandered in—and when they did, they had to endure an evil eye or two. The house band played jazz in the bebop mode of Charlie Parker and Miles Davis, but people found a way to dance to it anyway. And despite the intimidating presence of Collins's three-hundred-pound bouncer, people found a way to tear up the place in barroom brawls, too. Pianist Jimmy Binkley observed that the fights were cinematic in scope, MGM-grade. "Bris Collins would say, 'Play louder, Jimmy, play louder!'" Binkley recalled. "In the back of the room, they sometimes had two or three fights going on at one time."

For Richard, Collins Corner was a return to the all-black audience he had last experienced at the Carver Center, loosened up by a liberal dose of alcohol and an even stronger one of working-class irreverence. He continued to refine his characterizations of his wino, his hustler, and his preacher, three stock figures that would have been familiar to his audience. His comedy was often uproariously physical—as when, after heavyweight champion Floyd Patterson suffered an infamously quick first-round defeat to Sonny Liston in September 1962, he imitated Patterson by tumbling off the foot-high bandstand and rolling into the back of the audience, scattering chairs along the way.

The physical comedy was not simply wacky, though. The best of it expressed his vulnerability, his tenacity, and the depth charge of his resentment, and gave a stronger hint of the comedian to come. It was at Collins Corner that Richard developed his impersonation of "a baby being born," an extended pantomime in which a spirited baby attempts, and mostly fails, to escape the womb. The baby begins in the fetal position; he touches his face and, in the act of exploring its contours, catches some sticky goo on his fingers. He tries to widen the opening of the womb, and the breach slams shut like a pair of subway doors. He tries again, with trembling hands, and succeeds in catching a glimpse of the outside world—which is a horrible thing; his face assumes an expression of raw terror. Undeterred, he gathers himself and attacks the breach again, and this time it tightens around his neck like a noose. In a rage, he slips out of the noose and assaults the breach again—only to be stuck there, halfway born, his legs in a vise. He starts hearing things: a doctor saying, "Ooh, that's one ugly baby"; a mother chiming back in agreement. Everything—biology, society—seems to conspire against this poor baby. But rather than admit defeat, he musters his courage and finally clears the breach. His reward for entering the world: he begins his life on the outside with a full-on cry.

At this point in his career, Richard steered clear of talking about his personal life onstage, but this routine offered his psyche in miniature: innocence mixed with cynicism, wonder spiked with fear, anger heated by the sense that he was fundamentally alone. And if we were to substitute "Peoria" for "the womb," we might see that the birthing sketch was a nakedly autobiographical retelling of the first twenty-two years of his life. Richard had tried hard, in mind and body, to leave the world he'd been born into, and had slammed against barrier after barrier—until it was tempting for him to believe that there was no escape, just new ways of being mortified and entrapped. The world was a horror show, a noose, a vise, an insult.

In the fall of 1962, despite the fact that Richard was pulling down steady money from his gig at Collins Corner, Buck decided that his son should take on the family business. Like a master guildsman instructing an apprentice, he set up Richard with a prostitute, expecting him to profit from the experience. One day, after earning a little money, the prostitute gave some cash to Richard and asked him to beat her. "Hit me, hit me," she screamed. Richard didn't understand that she wanted him to rough her up and show his control, but not hurt her seriously. "She hit me and I started fighting—for my life," he told an interviewer. "I had no idea what she was talking about. I went berserk. I didn't know there was any romantic connotation to physical violence."

The bruised prostitute ran to Buck, who approached Richard, steaming. "What the fuck are you doing?" he asked. "You don't know how to beat a whore." The apprentice had learned so little from living with his master's example.

"But she said to hit her," Richard said in his defense.

For Buck, this remark was the last straw. His son the comic didn't understand women, didn't grasp the basics of pimping, and didn't deserve the indulgence of anyone.

"Get your ass outta here!" Buck said.

Richard scrambled to gather a few things—some clothes, some money, an alto saxophone, a typewriter he'd borrowed from his sister Barbara, under the pretense that he wanted to script a Western with a black cowboy at its center. The screenwriting was put on hold: the typewriter, along with the saxophone, was pawned for some quick cash.

His head swimming, he headed over to Collins Corner and bunked for a while at the club. But where would he go from there? In conversation with his mentor Juliette Whittaker, Richard had confessed that his dream was to be on *The Ed Sullivan Show*, and Whittaker urged him to head east: the stepping-stone to *Ed Sullivan*, she said, was Grossinger's in the Catskills, not any club in Peoria. Then one night, all the performers at Collins Corner arrived at the club to discover a nasty surprise. The club had been closed without any notice, an apparent casualty of fiscal mismanagement. The performers looked at one another, stunned, and talked about what to do next. A choreographer of a burlesque revue offered, "Let's all go to St. Louis. I think I can get a job for all of us." The musicians in the house band stayed back; they had prospects still in Chicago. Richard told Pat he needed to follow his dream and pointedly did not invite her along for the ride.

When Richard had earlier told his friends, "One day you'll pay to see me," they had laughed at his bravado. Now that he was in fact leaving, they expected him to return, humbled, after a few weeks. In their defense, it was hard to foresee a dazzling future for a young man who was leaving home to emcee what turned out to be a *South Pacific*–style burlesque show of female impersonators at a Chitlin Circuit club in East St. Louis.

At Richard's departure, there was no love lost between him and Buck. Four years later, Buck would brag that kicking Richard out of his house was "probably the best thing we ever did for him—make him go out on his own." And in a twisted way, he was right: Richard may never have found the courage of his convictions if he had not been cut off from the abusive relationship that defined his childhood. His eviction from his father's home not only made him desperate; it also gave him his freedom.

For Richard, Peoria would always be the scene of his childhood's ghosts, of unutterable feelings and unbearable pressures. Peoria had made him and unmade him both. When a Peoria journalist asked him, in 1993, if he had a message for the folks back home, he took on the voice of the demon in the film *The Amityville Horror* and rasped, "*Get out!*" He got out, in late 1962, and for the next decade rarely returned for more than a few days at a time—usually when there were loved ones to bury. He needed to leave Peoria, and needed to keep leaving Peoria, so that he could metabolize what he had experienced there. So he began his journey: as a wayfarer on the road known as the Chitlin Circuit, with no final destination in sight.

PART TWO

MAN OF A THOUSAND RUBBER FACES

CHAPTER 7

In Search of Openness

New York City and the Road, 1962–1964

When he first hit the road in the fall of 1962, Richard Pryor had reason to think he might spend the rest of his working life on it, touring the sort of showplaces, nestled in black communities, where "good Negro folks would never venture and stepping on a brother's Florsheims has meant hospitalization." An earlier generation of black comics—Redd Foxx, Moms Mabley, LaWanda Page, Pigmeat Markham—had ridden the Chitlin Circuit for the whole of their careers. With white-oriented clubs and TV networks closed to their style of gutbucket humor, Foxx, Mabley, and the rest had traveled from one "Bronzeville" to another, entertaining boisterous crowds between floor shows and R&B combos, and making a meager living at it. "We was so poor even poor folks didn't speak to us," said Page. "We traveled by bus or train, couldn't afford hotels most of the time. Stayed in boardinghouses in the Negro neighborhoods. Every once in a while you'd get lucky and stay in somebody's house. But most folks wouldn't let you, because most of those show people would steal."

Richard lived hand to mouth on the road for months at a time, working any venue that would have him. He bused, trained, and hitchhiked from Chicago to Cleveland to Pittsburgh, and picked up a few tricks along the way. "Every day was different, a surprise, an adventure through uncharted territory, and it forced me to sharpen my skills and learn my craft," he remembered. It was a time for experimenting with material and delivery, for shaping what was admittedly a rough-hewn stage persona. In Youngstown, Ohio, he dressed down a hostile audience: "Hey, y'all can boo me now. But in a couple of years I'm gonna be a star, and you dumb niggers will still be sittin' here!" An emcee in East St. Louis advised him, "You've got to talk to the people. You always look like you want to kill them."

By his own account, Richard's time on the road was full of miscues and misadventures. He learned the hard way to be suspicious of his fellow show people when, after a three-week gig in East St. Louis, he woke up to discover that his "friends" had given him the slip and taken his clothes with them. In Youngstown, after suspecting that the owners of the Casablanca club were going to stiff him, he burst into their office and tried to claim his earnings. According to an embellished version of the incident that he performed onstage, he brandished a blank pistol to intimidate the owners of this "mafia club," but found that he'd succeeded only in making himself a laughingstock. "Hey, do it again, Rich!" they said. "Put the gun away and do it again. Say 'stick 'em up.' Ha-ha-ha-ha! You fucking kid."

In December 1962, Richard was in Pittsburgh when he discovered that his idol Sammy Davis Jr. had just headlined its Civic Arena. Desperate for work and hungry for advice, he tracked Davis down to his hotel room and knocked on the door. Davis's handler wouldn't let him in. Playing for time, Richard drew up a chair and camped outside the door. The handler called the police. When a couple of officers arrived, Richard put on his best adult voice and faked them out: "Officer, about that young fellow—he has lit out, so take it easy. But if he comes back, I'll give you a call." The police moved on. Richard sat back in his chair, awaiting his idol with an empty stomach.

Hours later, Davis came out for a breath of fresh air and, finding Richard parked in the hall, invited him into his room. Richard asked for a job. Davis let him bum a cigarette, then gave him a quick bit of perspective. Even for a major star like him, Davis admitted, the business was "a hard grind at best." Still, what was to be done? "Daddy, swing—take it easy," he counseled the young man.

Richard heard the advice and took solace in it, but hardly took it easy. While in Pittsburgh, he started dating a singer and, in an ill-considered moment, bragged that he was collecting cash from her, as pimps do from their girls. Six hundred miles from Peoria, he was still shadowboxing with his father. When the singer caught wind of Richard's boast and confronted him backstage, he panicked and gave her a beating so as to avoid, he thought, getting a beating himself. On January 1, 1963, police rousted Richard in the rooming house where he lived, charged him with aggravated assault and battery, and dragged him to jail. In court, he was given a suspended sentence, but appears not to have been able to pay the costs levied by the verdict—which meant his first extended stay in a jail cell, thirty-five days of incarceration.

The misadventures persisted when, sprung from jail, Richard tried his luck at clubs that weren't on the Chitlin Circuit. On one hapless jaunt in the middle of 1963, he crossed the border to Canada and faced white audiences who, he remembered, were less receptive to his act. In Windsor, Ontario, he played a "hillbilly bar" where the audience, eager to see the voluptuous singer next on the bill, booed him off the stage in the middle of his James Cagney impression. At a Toronto nightclub, he was upstaged as well as thumped by his competition: a bear that guzzled beer before wrestling with customers. The bear "got a little bit carried away with the wrestling," Richard recalled. "He went after me. You know—a bear's a bear. You can't out-wrestle a bear, especially a bear that's had a few. And then the bear would get gentle, and stroke you and sit on you." Meanwhile, at his hotel, he observed a group of huge, gay wrestlers acting much the same as that bear, swinging between violence and tenderness. "I couldn't believe it," he said. "I mean, you'd see them brutally murdering each other in Saturday-night wrestling matches. And then you'd see them back at the hotel, kissing and holding hands. It was bizarre."

Frustrated in Toronto, Richard caught yet another surprise. He flipped open *Newsweek* and was startled to read about a "smart new 24-year-old Negro comic." The young comic, *Newsweek* observed, had begun his career onstage with some racial humor—by imagining, for instance, what would happen if a black man were elected president. ("Everything is OK," says the black president. "Just a lot of 'For Sale' signs on the street.") But then this comic—an athletic, handsome type by the name of Bill Cosby—made a name for himself by scrubbing all race-related jokes from his repertoire. His signature routine revisited the first conversation between God and Noah, turning it into theater of the absurd:

> **GOD**: I want you to build an ark.
> **NOAH**: Riiight . . . What's an ark?
> **GOD**: Get wood. Build it 80 cubits by 40 cubits.
> **NOAH**: Riiight . . . What's a cubit?
> **GOD**: Let's see . . . A cubit, a cubit. . . .
> **NOAH**: What's going on?
> **GOD**: I'm going to destroy all the people from the face of the earth.
> **NOAH**: Riiight. . . . Am I on *Candid Camera*?

Cosby was sly and wry, threading observational humor into shaggy-dog stories with little explicit political content. His act was a clear departure from the "sick" humor of comedians like Lenny Bruce and Mort Sahl, who had laced early 1960s stand-up with strong doses of vinegar, gall, and topicality. "I'm trying to reach all the people. I want to play Joe Q. Public," Cosby told *Newsweek*.

Richard was devastated. "Goddamn it," he said, "this nigger's doing what I'm fixing to do. I want to be the only nigger. Ain't no room for two niggers." Cosby represented literally the road not taken: rather than build his audience by working the Chitlin Circuit, where Richard had concentrated his energies, Cosby had focused on hip cafés in Philly and New York City. His big break had been a 1962 summer residency at the Greenwich Village café the Gaslight, where, according to the *New York Times*, his audience was "composed mainly of Bohemian youths in beards, college girls who discuss medical care for the aged, and tourists who are alternately bewitched and bewildered by what they believe is the 'dolce vita' of New York." That audience had been Cosby's pathway to the talent bookers and, from there, to national exposure via *The Tonight Show*. Cosby had been a pioneer in his approach not only to comedy, but to his career as a whole.

Though Richard would later be seen as the anti-Cosby—funky, experimental, and provocative where Cosby was clean, predictable, and safe—he had reason in 1963 to identify with Cosby's quest for a crossover style and a crossover audience. Having grown up in a city where blacks were about 10 percent of the population, a microcosm of America as a whole, he was accustomed to maneuvering through largely white institutions and communities. At least since third grade, he had brought white friends and teachers into his world by teasing them with half-barbed invitations; later, at Harold's Club, he had grown comfortable working a mixed audience. And even after his months on the Chitlin Circuit, Richard's comedy still hewed closer to the models of his childhood idols (physical comedians like Red Skelton, Sid Caesar, and Jerry Lewis) than to profane comics like Redd Foxx, who played to largely black audiences. Given his childhood, Richard might never have described himself as "Joe Q. Public," but now that Cosby had taken on the role, it probably sounded like an appealing title, or at least a good alias.

Posthaste, Richard bought a train ticket to New York City. He arrived there with ten dollars in his pocket and patent leather shoes on his feet, hoping to glide through the door that Cosby had opened. But first he had to find it. He had only the faintest idea where to start looking.

At the train station, Richard took a shower, threw on his well-worn suit, knotted his skinny tie, and splashed on some Canoe cologne. He walked out into the open air and felt dizzy beneath the crush of Manhattan—the skyscrapers, the press of Checker cabs on the avenues, the people racing down the sidewalks as if they all had an urgent appointment with destiny. "It was a lot to take in for someone with no place to go," he remembered. "I heard alarms go off in my head and wondered what the hell I'd done."

His first priority, above even finding a place to stay, was to get a gig. He was familiar with only one venue in Manhattan, the Apollo Theater, so he grabbed an uptown bus, which dropped him off at

Uncertain charms: one of Pryor's first head shots, not long after his arrival in New York City. (Courtesy of Getty Images)

125th Street in Harlem. Ah, Harlem, the home he was looking for: "In two blocks, I saw more black people than I'd ever seen in my life. Just two blocks, and it was beautiful and it was exciting. And I looked and I felt it and I loved it, and I wanted to be part of it. Everyone talks about 'Don't walk in Harlem.' I felt safer than I ever felt in my life."

He'd landed in the cradle of blackness—or had he? At the Apollo, he met the theater's booking agent, who looked put-upon when Richard asked for work. "Yeah, right. Why don't you try down at the Village?" the agent said. Richard looked at him uncomprehending; he'd never heard of any village in New York. "Downtown," the booker explained, and pointed him out the door and out of Harlem.

So much for the soft cushion of the cradle. But Richard had the good fortune, after catching a downtown bus, to arrive in Greenwich Village at a choice moment in its scrappy history. "It was a time," actor-writer Buck Henry remembered, "when every doorway late at night had someone standing in it who would later be famous." With America sitting on the edge of the cultural changes that came to be known as "the sixties," bohemia was becoming, more than ever before, the incubator of the new comics, the new singers, the new talent.

In 1963, when Richard arrived, the *New York Times* described the Village as having a "Coney Island, carnival atmosphere," complete with barkers who promoted their establishments to passersby. Coffeehouses offered a smorgasbord of artistic experiment, their freewheeling spirit typified by the twisted proverbs on the menu of the Bitter End: "One good mistress deserves another," "Grasp the eye by the monocle," "Cold meat lights no fire," and so on. Bookshops stayed open until midnight, coffeehouses until dawn, and revelers kept the streets alive until the wee hours of the morning. The local avant-garde effervesced: it was the season of Andy Warhol and Pop Art's explosion, of happenings galore, of art world productions like Carolee Schneemann's *Eye Body*, in which the artist covered herself with grease, plastic, and chalk and had herself photographed nude with two garden snakes writhing up her torso. Buses filled with tourists crawled bumper to bumper through its narrow streets in a steady parade, their passengers looking down on the action. Performers in the Village in 1963 could justifiably feel that they were both on the edge of society and within its very nerve center.

Richard fell into a small bohemian pocket of the Village. With his friends he tried every drug the Village had to offer: he smoked reefer, got a codeine fix by buying terpin hydrate over the counter at a MacDougal Street drugstore, raided whipped cream cans at Village cafés for their nitrous oxide, and eventually found his way to cocaine. Meanwhile, he and his friends honed their chops in the Village's hootenanny scene. The "hoots" were loosely structured amateur nights, where folk musicians and comedians performed in the hope of catching the eye of someone who would offer them a regular booking. Richard played the circuit, starting with the Café Wha? on Monday nights and the Bitter End on Tuesdays, where he sat nervously on a bench with the other comics awaiting their turn—among them, Joan Rivers, who remembered him wearing a coat "with jacket sleeves lengthened so many times, he looked like an admiral." He appeared to be still, at age twenty-two, in the midst of an awkward growth spurt. Though he became a regular at its cafés, he felt ill at ease in the Village whirl. He made the decision to rent a small, dark apartment on the other side of the East River, in Brooklyn, rather than locate himself in the Village proper. "I didn't make the Village scene," he said. "[P]eople were very snobbish to me in the Village—I don't know why."

Part of that awkwardness came from his inability to tap into his past. On the one hand, he had a fund of experience, from his first twenty years in Peoria, that made the most "far-out" adventures of the avant-garde seem thin by comparison, mere playacting. On the other hand, the prevailing zeitgeist, in the form of Bill Cosby, was blowing him in the exact opposite direction—away from his underworld past and toward a squeaky-clean future. Before arriving in Greenwich Village, Richard had been transfixed by Cosby's example; after catching him in action, in between his own sets at the Cafe Wha?, he was stunned by his talent. "The man was amazing. Truly amazing," Richard recalled. "Do you hear me? I was amazed."

For a few months he tried to remake himself as "Richard Cosby," studying Cos's records to divine the secret of their success. Much of Richard's act had been made up of impressions—"screaming take-offs," wrote the *Philadelphia Tribune*—of Alfred Hitchcock, character actor Walter Brennan, and Sammy Davis Jr. Now he would slip mid-act into the kind of storytelling that Cosby was known for, in an unattributed impression of his new idol. Here's how, in one routine, he described the arrival of a burglar in his home:

I grabbed the crook. That was the wrong move.
He threw me down—I got up.
He knocked me down—I got up.
He kicked me down. He said, "Get up!" I said, "heh, heh."

> Then my wife threw him across the furniture, and the police came. She beat them up, they took her away. Now me and the crook are living happily ever after.

The rhythms, the make-believe scenario, the wacky, absurdist ending—these were pure Cos. When his fellow comics confronted Richard on his raiding of Cosby's act, he had a simple reply: "I'm going for the bucks."

The critics picked up on the bald act of emulation, too. In what may have been the first media coverage of Richard's career, on March 19, 1964, the *New York Herald Tribune* declared that "Comedian Richard Pryor has got guts. He uses Bill Cosby's style, mannerisms, inflections, and much of Cosby's material without batting an eyelash. Be yourself, Richard, so we can pan (or applaud) you on your own." Manny Roth, the owner of the Café Wha? and Richard's first manager, gave him a more profound version of the same advice. Roth told him, "You can't be Cos, you just can't be Cos. It's going to be hard enough just being Ritchie, Richard Pryor . . . You'll never be Cosby in a million years. But you know what? You're going to be bigger and better than Cos."

Bigger and better than Cos? Bigger than the *Tonight Show* performer whose first album had soared up the charts? In 1964, such soothsaying was hard to fathom, much less credit. Yet the insight behind the advice was unimpeachable. Temperamentally, Richard could never hope to become Cos, whose strength onstage came from his preternatural composure. Cosby's relaxed intensity made his audience trust that they could lean back in their seats and enjoy the ride. Richard's strength, on the other hand, was his supersensitivity, his ability to tune into the lower frequencies of human interaction. Unlike Cos, Richard never took on an air of unqualified success; he was forever an underdog, and had all the anxiety and embattlement that followed that fate. If Richard wanted to live up to his promise, he needed to channel his anxiety rather than run away from it.

Richard found camaraderie, and a partial solution to his dilemma as a comic, among "a bunch of hobos looking for work"—the comedian friends he made in the Village. Together, they scraped for their ten minutes onstage and passed around a hat afterward for loose change. Though some hailed from more comfortable backgrounds, all of them were hungry—for experience, for action, for a break. They made a ragged army of individualists: Henry Jaglom, a loquacious actor-comedian who came to the Village by way of his parents' luxury apartment building on Central Park West; J. J. Barry, an earthy, hefty performer once described as an "upright hippo of a man"; Bob Altman, a shaggy-browed stock analyst who would soon give up his day job and become the frenetic comic known as Uncle Dirty; Martin Harvey Friedberg, a sweet-tempered man who brought pathos to scenes of utter hilarity; and Burt Heyman, who worked for the United Jewish Appeal before committing to comedy full time. Richard was the one black performer in the bunch, but in observance of an unwritten rule of bohemia, the comics focused on their common present rather than on their multiple pasts. All of them were in transition from one life to another, where it was hoped the old rules wouldn't apply.

The group found a second home at the Improvisation, a coffeehouse that had opened in the spring of 1963 at Forty-Fourth Street and Ninth Avenue, two miles north of the Village. (In an early *Village Voice* advertisement, The Improvisation called itself the home of "everyone you haven't seen since they left the Village.") Later known simply as the Improv, the café started as an after-hours hangout for the Midtown theater set. The *Herald Tribune* found it a "happy espresso oasis" where "local 'gypsies' (show business people)" went to "unwind after the curtain"; the likes of Judy Garland were known to give impromptu performances, singing and swinging until 7:00 a.m. Soon comedians like Richard and his gang started taking over the club, whose loose-jointed feel served their purposes, too. In the early hours of the morning, when the Improv's audience dwindled to what Henry Jaglom called "the dregs"—a nightlife crew of "the hookers and the cab drivers and the drunks"—Richard would tell his friends, "Come on up, let's get up and fool around," and then two or three or four of them would take the stage, performing for nothing other than the joy of performance. Thus was born an important, if rarely noticed, experiment with the form of group improv.

In part, Richard and his fellow improvisers took their cues from the innovative exercises, or games, developed by the Chicago theater group the Compass. These games were designed, in the words of one critic, "to almost fool spontaneity into being": they asked actors to surrender to the flow of interaction, to collaborate with the audience as well as their fellow performers, and to rely on their bodies to put over their character's story.

For Richard, who had felt the limitations of his written material, group improv unlocked his genius as a performer. "He would just investigate. The commitment was very full," said Jaglom. In one sketch at the Improv, Richard had played a fortune-telling vending machine that answered someone's questions about their future in installments, one dime's worth at a time. With other comics, the sketch had lasted three minutes; with Richard as the vending machine, seducing and goosing the paying customer, it lasted forty. During another bit, Richard started removing his shirt in an apparent non sequitur. A beat later, his shoes came off. Then his pants. And then, to everyone's astonishment, he pulled off his underwear. "That was against the law at that point," Jaglom reflected. "I was screaming, and other people were screaming, with laughter. Other people were really mad: 'Put your pants on! What are you, crazy? They're going to close us down.' I remember clearly saying in my journal, 'This guy has no limits. He's free.'"

Though Richard's improv often came out of these theater games, it frequently had less of a pretext or conceptual frame. Much of it was high-concept larking—the result of someone's brain flash. Richard and his buddies might pretend to be an officer and his platoon of soldiers, a Mafioso and his mark, or a fellowship of samurai warriors (anticipating Richard's famed samurai hotel sketch with John Belushi

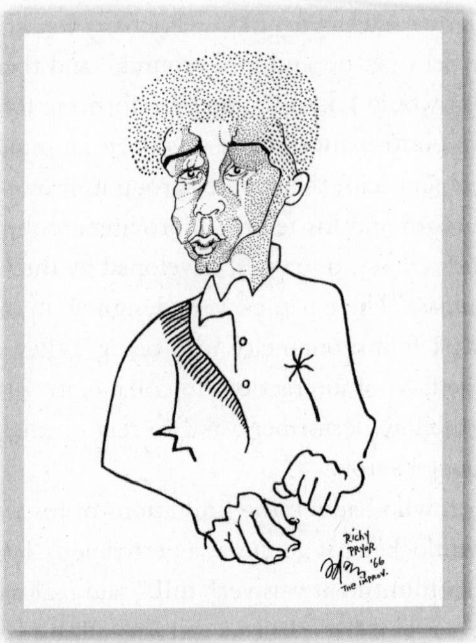

Present at the creation: sketch by Henry Jaglom, "Richy Pryor '66 The Improv." (Courtesy of Henry Jaglom)

on *Saturday Night Live*). Or they might go outside the club and transform the Improv's picture window into a make-believe aquarium, the sudden setting for a four-man water ballet. In their improvs, all lines were to be crossed, including the one that separated "onstage" from "offstage." Once, Richard and his comic friends sat eating an entire meal, of rice pilaf and chicken, under the lights onstage, with the audience watching. After a while, Richard started eating with his hands, touching off an avalanche of anarchy: soon all the comics were acting like cavemen, licking their dishes and throwing them on the floor. Budd Friedman, the Improv's owner, charged the stage; the comics expected him to scold them. "So that's the way you feel about it, hunh?" Friedman said—then yanked away the tablecloth so that absolutely everything crashed to the ground.

Richard and his friends probably wouldn't have considered themselves avant-garde, but their improv was taking them close to the edgier performance scenes of the Village, where it was more important to create a spectacle than to advance a well-made plot. At the same time that they had their caveman banquet, flouting social decorum onstage, the Village avant-garde had the "flesh jubilation" of *Meat Joy* (1964), a ritual play where men and women, stripped to their underwear, writhed together and rubbed raw chicken and sausage on their bodies. With their affection for improvisation and their frank sensuousness, Richard and the avant-garde were on parallel paths to points unknown.

The Improv was generally a hospitable home for Richard's explorations, with Budd Friedman and his then-wife, Silver, happy to stoke the merriment and the madness. At the Improv's first birthday party, an after-hours party for regulars in the spring of 1964, Richard disappeared into the men's room near the tail end of a set by a self-serious chanteuse and emerged having ditched his button-down shirt, sports coat, pants, and underwear. Clad only in his felt hat, shoes, and socks, he pranced sweetly across the stage, exposing his nether parts to his audience and toying with their expectations about how black men were supposed to measure up. "Well, there goes another myth," quipped Silver, in the spirit of Richard's escapade.

Yet not every audience at the Improv could match the freewheeling spirit of the guests at the Improv's birthday party. One night on the early side of a weekend evening, Richard sat next to Silver and eyed the Improv crowd for several minutes. "I think I'll go downtown," he said finally.

"Not enough action for you?" she asked.

"Maybe later."

"What are you looking for?"

"Openness." Then he lit off in search of it.

Richard found a type of openness in his unexpected friendship with Henry Jaglom. Later known as a director of more than fifteen independent films, Jaglom came from a spectacularly wealthy Jewish family: his father, formerly the finance minister of the Free City of Danzig, had been so important to the German economy that Hitler wished to make him an "honorary Aryan" so he might keep brokering trade between the two territories. Henry himself was a student at the University of Pennsylvania and the Actors Studio in Manhattan, and had been affiliated with an offshoot of the Compass theater group in Boston; by temperament he was an intellectual and an idealist, involved with the Congress of Racial Equality's effort to desegregate Madison Avenue. Just two years before, Richard had been living under his father's roof with a stepmother who tricked to put food on the table. Now he was Henry's regular guest at the Jagloms' luxury apartment on Central Park West, where Louis XV furniture decorated the rooms, Renoir and Degas paintings hung on the walls, and family dinners were elaborate affairs with servants setting out finger bowls. Richard played it cool, as if he were to the manner born. He never admitted any disorientation to his well-off friend.

Precisely because of the unacknowledged distance between the two of them, Richard and Henry made a perfect bohemian pair: the black outsider bonding with the artistic son of a Jewish import-export financier. Richard had been born into the sex trade and had flunked out of it; Henry had been born into money and had felt himself an imposter. They met up, providentially, on the stage of the Improv, where creativity required no credential.

Their friendship revolved around the pursuit of comedy. They took long walks around the city until sunrise, debating a seemingly trivial question ("What's more funny, a chicken or a duck?") as if it got at the finer points of their art. They lingered at the Improv after everyone else had left for the night, and competed to see who could make the other one crack up. On one occasion, Richard started spilling condiments on his face to get a rise out of Jaglom. Ketchup spattered his ears—no laugh from Jaglom. Mustard splattered his eyes—no laugh. Finally, Richard took the entire tray of condiments and dumped them over his head, so that he was dripping with a chaos of color. Still no laugh. Then Richard delicately picked up a small napkin and, in the middle of this mess, dabbed a corner of his mouth with the utmost elegance. "I fell on the ground in what I still remember as the hardest, longest laugh of my life," Jaglom said. "His instincts were always brilliant and they always topped everyone else's."

At Jaglom's home or at a friend's apartment in Hell's Kitchen, the two smoked dope together and brainstormed their future. They put special effort into developing a comic TV show, inspired by their peripatetic travels around New York City, that would star the two of them as a pair of detectives. If it had been picked up, it would have been the first of the interracial buddy comedies that Richard would develop. Unfortunately the show went nowhere, and eventually Richard and Jaglom were scooped by the ubiquitous Cosby, whose shadow seemed to envelop Richard even when he was not chasing it. In November 1964, it was announced that Cosby and Robert Culp would star as a black-and-white pair of world-traveling CIA agents in a show titled *I Spy*.

Richard and Jaglom's friendship had a dynamic equilibrium, one occasionally troubled by the great social gap that separated the two of them. With his connections to the Compass theater ensemble, the Actors Studio, and (ironically) the black-led Congress of Racial Equality (CORE), Jaglom was plugged into larger institutions—and Richard was a lone integer, struggling to find his own voice as an artist and a man. Once, Jaglom complained to Richard about performing before a cold audience with the Compass; the troupe was skewering JFK from the left, Jaglom said, and the audience refused to go there. Richard immediately put the focus on the race of the performers: "I bet there's nobody black in the show." Jaglom drew back. For all his civil rights involvement, he hadn't thought twice about the all-white cast to which he belonged.

Politics gradually turned into a sore spot in their friendship. Starting in the summer of 1963, New York's CORE launched a series of direct-action protests, most notably against the city's all-white building trades. CORE leaders anticipated that white construction workers and the New York Police Department might harass their rank and file, so they set up training workshops in the practice of nonviolent protest. Jaglom tried to convince Richard to go up to Harlem with him so they could train and be activists together. He admitted that he had his own doubts about whether he had the right temperament for nonviolence. If people spat on him, Jaglom thought he might "get killed because I couldn't control my temper."

Richard responded, "You're all fucking crazy. You just pull out a gun and shoot 'em." He was the grandson of Marie Pryor, who believed in the power of razors, guns, and big hands.

Jaglom replied that the brave ones were those, like Martin Luther King Jr., who controlled themselves for the sake of the movement. Himself, he didn't think he could handle the abuse.

"Of course you can't," Richard clinched the conversation. "Who the fuck wants to be able to do it?"

Richard had taken so much abuse already—much more than Jaglom knew or, for all his worldliness and right-thinking politics, could imagine—and he wasn't about to sign up for another dose. He was ripe for something other than the civil rights movement of 1963. His progressive Jewish-American friend might find resonance with Martin Luther King Jr. and his insistent idealism, but Richard was waiting for a movement that would call upon America's fear of payback, not just its conscience; a movement that would not be shy about wielding a gun.

For Richard in the mid-1960s, improv became more than an art form to be practiced onstage. It was a way of life, a survival tactic, a means of turning his frustration and rage into the stuff of a joke. When he and his comic buddies gathered at each other's apartments, they would play improv games until daybreak. Richard would raid a steamer trunk full of props for inspiration. If he took out a hammer, one of his comic friends might grab it and riff, "What kind of toothpick is this? I'm not going to be able to get the meat out of my teeth with this thing," then pass it on to the next comedian.

On one occasion, Richard removed a toy gun from the steamer

trunk and told J. J. Barry that he was going to shoot him unless Barry convinced him otherwise. For a full hour, it seemed, Barry begged, pleaded, and sweated for his life, until everyone assumed that Richard would put the gun away. Instead, he shot him—and Barry bounced against the walls, writhed, and groaned for another half hour, his life leaking out of him drop by drop. Finally he seemed dead, truly dead.

Then his body twitched—at which point Richard shot him again, quickly, perhaps to put him out of his misery or perhaps just to make sure the deed was done. The rest of the comics sat mesmerized. Richard had stayed in character through all of Barry's theatrics—even as no one knew what his character was, exactly. He was singular and mysterious, and nothing like the funny young fellow "Joe Q. Public" that his idol Cosby played onstage and that he had himself tried to incarnate for a while. There was power in being honestly unpredictable, he was discovering, though he was not yet an expert at tapping it. The honesty part was the sticking point.

CHAPTER 8

Mr. Congeniality

New York City, 1964–1965

Manny Roth met Richard Pryor when the "scared little black kid" washed up at the Cafe Wha? asking for him by name and looking for a spot on his stage. Despite the twenty-two-year age difference that separated the two of them, they felt a special affinity with each other. Roth, one of the Village's many Jewish entrepreneurs, had been raised in Newcastle, Indiana, part of an Orthodox Jewish family in a tiny blue-collar town thick with churches, not far from the northern hub of the Ku Klux Klan. His parents, like Richard's family, operated a makeshift midwestern tavern, serving beer, pickled pig's feet, and pickled ham on the bone to workers from the local Chrysler plant. (Roth's mother, who tended the bar, grimaced every time she had to handle the nonkosher ingredients.) The young Manny grew up sensing that Jews and blacks shared something, if only by way of other people's enmity. When, in the mid-1950s, he moved to Greenwich Village and set up his first café-theater, he made a point of welcoming black theater artists such as Sidney Poitier and Lorraine Hansberry to his establishment.

Roth's Cafe Wha? didn't look like much. Bob Dylan remembered it as "a subterranean cavern, liquorless, ill lit, low ceiling, like a wide dining hall with chairs." But what it lacked in ambience, it made up for in variety. Dylan, who like Richard played his first gig in New York City there, remembered catching, in its afternoon shows, "a comedian, a ventriloquist, a steel drum group, a poet, a female impersonator, a duo who sang Broadway stuff, a rabbit-in-the-hat magician, a guy wearing a turban who hypnotized people in the audience, [and] somebody whose entire act was facial acrobatics." In other words, "anybody who wanted to break into show business."

Richard began as just another young performer taking advantage of the Wha?'s open mike, but soon Roth promoted him to a slot in the evening shows at fifteen dollars a set, or seventy-five dollars a week. Not long after, Roth offered to serve as Richard's manager—the first (and last) time he took on that sort of job. He saw in Richard's search for himself, in his desperate hunger for success, a mirror of his own inner struggle. "I was the craziest of the crazies when I hit the Village, the neediest of the needy," Roth said. "I was just as lost as he was." Perhaps, in helping Richard find his path, he might chart his own. His friends Roy Silver and Fred Weintraub had groomed Bill Cosby into a crossover phenomenon (in part by pruning the racial humor from his act), and Roth hoped for a piece of their action. Higher motives mixed with the frank pursuit of a payday.

Manny worked hard to prime Richard in mind and body, to prepare him for the break that could change both their lives. "What Pryor needed most was a father figure, and I became that father figure by default—certainly not by choice," Roth observed. A health nut himself, he took the comic to the YMCA, where they swam and lifted weights. Together they pored over the daily newspapers, looking for headlines to weave into Richard's act. They rehearsed Richard's routines over and over, refining jokes and sharpening his delivery. Manny warned Richard not to amble like Cos, not to dawdle. "Faster, faster! Pick up the pace!" he advised Richard at the first sign of a *longueur.* "You need to crank it up." He hoped Richard could match Cos's success, but suspected that he would arrive there only by way of a hyperkinetic style all his own.

When, in March 1964, Richard landed a gig at the Living Room, a Midtown club frequented by showbiz types, it seemed their efforts were going to reap some rewards. Manny classed up Richard's act by buying him a couple of suits and shirts, ties, socks, shoes, cufflinks—a whole new professional wardrobe, "everything for the big time." They even traveled up to Harlem together to get Richard's hair set in a fresh conk.

On the Living Room's stage, Richard opened his act with an effusive tribute to his wonderful manager, Manny. Then he crashed onstage, stumbling through "a half-assed show" that, as Manny recalled, was so embarrassing that both of them "walked out with our tails between our legs." Doubling the misfortune, the gig attracted Richard's first notice in the trade press. *Variety* praised his "avant garde viewpoint," "healthy instinct for irreverence," and "feel for expression," but counseled him to proceed with caution in his career: "there is still much for him to learn before he can go into commercial rooms. He is still in the coffeehouse stages as far as this audience was concerned on his opening night. He has the approach of an intellectual entertainer, and [his] writing seems to be for clever effect rather than laughs."

And so the big time was put on hold. Richard returned to the clubs operated by Manny's friends in the Village—the Village Gate, the Bitter End, and the rest. He had no choice but to follow *Variety*'s counsel and hone his chops among the bohemians. Meanwhile, Manny discovered that, as Richard's manager, damage control was a considerable part of his job. When he was once ruffled onstage at the Cafe Wha?, Richard attacked someone in the audience with a fork. (Fortunately the Wha? carried only plastic cutlery.) Then there was Richard's relationship to money, which seemed to jump out of his pockets and land in the hands of others. He could be shockingly mercenary: in the middle of a pro bono gig for NYU students, he stopped mid-show, wondered out loud why he was performing for free, then walked offstage. He often asked Manny for small amounts of cash, and if he didn't get the money, he would threaten to skip his gigs. Perennially broke, he would sign contracts without reading them so that he could get a ten- or twenty-dollar advance. Once he dropped into the Wha? and asked Manny for some cash to pay a cab fare. Manny gave him five dollars for the fare, which was a dollar and fifty cents. Richard handed the driver the full five and said, "Keep the change."

Five months after the Living Room gig, Richard was given a second chance to impress a mainstream audience when he appeared in a late-August taping of *On Broadway Tonight*, a televised variety show hosted by crooner Rudy Vallee. The program was designed as a showcase for young performers: its studio audience was sprinkled with "America's leading starmakers," there to judge the talent in the room and work their starmaking magic on anyone they favored. (Producer David Susskind, who had boosted the careers of black actors Sidney Poitier, James Earl Jones, and Cicely Tyson, was on hand for Richard's TV debut.) Vallee introduced Richard with a set of fibs that most likely had come from Richard himself: the young comic was a former army paratrooper; his comedy had been broadcast by the U.S. government; and he was proudly indebted for his talent to his father, Leroy, "a song and dance man back in those wonderful days of vaudeville." Richard's past had been rewritten so that he came off as a plucky, patriotic, and natural-born entertainer, the sort of Yankee Doodle Negro whom Rudy Vallee and his show's middle-aged studio audience might clasp to their bosoms as one of their own.

Once introduced, Richard Pryor strutted onstage, wiped his nose, fidgeted with his tie, cleared his throat—and kept the lies coming:

> I'm going to tell you a few things about myself because a lot of you probably don't know me. I'm not a New Yorker. My home's in Peoria, Illinois. I'm from an average-type family—eleven kids. No mother and father, just kids . . .
>
> I had a wild neighborhood because my mother's Puerto Rican, and my father's Negro, and we live in a really big Jewish tenement building in an Italian neighborhood. Every time I go outside, the kids say, "Get him! He's all of them!"

There were some serious misrepresentations here: Richard was raised an only child, not one of eleven kids; his mother was a light-skinned black, not Puerto Rican; and his family lived in brothels and houses, not tenements. The jokes were confected out of a New York state of mind, the Puerto Ricans belonging to Spanish Harlem and

"I'm from an average-type family": keying into the expectations of his audience. (Courtesy of the author)

the multiethnic tenements to the Lower East Side. It was as if Richard could talk onstage about his childhood only by relocating it to New York City, the new home he'd chosen for himself.

The rest of Richard's seven-minute routine skittered from one joke to another at a rapid-fire clip. The setups were quick, the punch lines coming every ten seconds—just like he and Manny had planned—and often punctuated by a goofy look on Richard's face:

> I like [Village coffeehouses] because they don't serve booze. Just coffee, ice cream, weird pills [*cross-eyed, hands jerking back and forth*].
>
> I hate to take the subway because the first thing you see when you

Man of a thousand rubber faces, a different one for each punch line. (Courtesy of the author)

walk down into the subway is some guy saying, "Gimme a nickel" [*eyes bug out, body bends down and weaves*].

> Nothing works in the subway, right? Candy machine doesn't work, Coke machine doesn't work. It's not the subway's fault, but it don't work. You ever drop a dime in the Coke machine and your Coke comes pouring out—no cup? [*Looks down at the ground, dejected, as if following the spilling drink.*]

When the audience broke into applause, Richard seemed uncomfortable with the delay it posed to his routine, cutting through it with "Wait, I got some more to tell you" or bending down in a mock curtsy, as if the applause had turned him into an abashed debutante.

His main persona was the bungler or schlemiel. He was the bachelor who sliced himself when he tried to cut open a can of coffee, and who stabbed himself when he tried to pry open a can of evaporated milk. He was the straphanger who, when he tried to foil a pickpocket, ended up socking the dentures out of an eighty-year-old lady instead. He was someone—only incidentally a black man—who was trying to navigate the big city, yet always falling into its traps. He was Bill Cosby's younger, skinnier brother, the one who blew his cool as much as Cosby kept his.

In only one joke did the race-conscious Pryor make a cameo appearance, and the joke's racial subtext was probably lost on the studio audience:

> You can't get a cab in New York City. Especially when it rains, all the cabs are owned by one company: "Off Duty."
>
> If you're lucky enough to get a cab, you get in and say, "I want to go to 78th Street." The driver says, "I'm not going that way."
>
> "What do you mean? I wanna go to 78th Street."
>
> "Are you going to give me a tip?"
>
> "I'm going to tip your cab over if you don't take me to 78th Street!"

This time the punch line wasn't accompanied by a goofy look. Richard's eyebrows lifted and his eyes widened in anger, as if to suggest that the threat was not an empty one. And then, before anyone could absorb the shift in tone, his face recomposed itself into a mask of congeniality, and he was on to the next joke.

After Richard's turn on *On Broadway Tonight*, the starmakers did not call. Even Richard's folks back home in Peoria had little to say: they had tuned their TV to the wrong channel, they told him, and by the time they discovered their mistake, his performance was over. If his Improv friends had seen his TV debut, they might have been startled by the conventionality of his act: he stuck to his script, delivered his punch lines, and remained clearly within the bounds of decency. He did such a fabulous job of blending into the woodwork that, in the end, no one noticed him at all.

The Bitter End hired Richard for the entire month in October when he and Manny returned to the Village. The Café au Go-Go—a large brick-walled cellar where Lenny Bruce was notoriously arrested by the NYPD for obscenity—picked Richard up for a few shows, and installed him in the spring of 1965 as its house comic. But despite his success in the Village, Richard had begun to question the terms of his crossover act.

He wasn't alone. In the mid-1960s, many black artists and intellectuals started wondering if they'd lost course by catering too much to white expectations of what was "proper" for black folks. Nationally, the alliance between blacks and white liberals—an alliance that had undergirded the civil rights movement and been embodied in Richard's friendships with Henry Jaglom and Manny Roth—was cracking under the pressure of events such as the September 1963 bombing of a church in Birmingham, Alabama, that killed four black girls and convinced many black Americans that nonviolent protest was not enough to protect their community.

In New York City, black activists were disillusioned to discover that local whites, no matter how sympathetic to Martin Luther King Jr.'s actions down south, balked when the civil rights movement showed up at their doorstep. After a black-led boycott in early 1964 pulled hundreds of thousands of children out of their schools (the largest civil rights boycott of the era), the *New York Times* advocated a "self-imposed curb on speechmaking" and opined sourly that "A racial balancing of all the city's schools remains as impossible after the boycott as before." Black activists looked at the difficulty of the tasks ahead—turning broken schools into engines of opportunity, slums into livable neighborhoods—and felt a combustive sense of urgency. White liberals, and some black liberals, too, were chastened by that same difficulty. They looked to study the problems, grasp their complexities, and find a workable, targeted approach to them. Meanwhile, the middle ground between these two positions seemed to be disappearing. In July 1964, the month before Richard's debut on TV, the shooting of a black ninth-grader by a white policeman touched off several days of battles between black Harlemites and the NYPD, with black rioters hurling Molotov cocktails and bricks at armed officers, who shot back.

Richard's political feelings in this period are hard to trace with exactitude, perhaps because they weren't well defined. He was more a tongue-tied witness to events than the trenchant commentator he would become. But in his acquaintance with poet-playwright LeRoi Jones, a fellow black bohemian, he felt the pull of a certain articulacy, a slashing anger that put the white world on notice. At the time, Jones was known primarily for his play *Dutchman*, an Off-Broadway sensation in which a white woman propositions a black man on the subway, inflames him into a rage, then stabs him in the chest and enlists the other passengers to throw his body off the train. Though married to a Jewish woman himself, Jones had an astringent view of the undercurrents of jealousy and desire that ran between blacks and whites in America. And he had an uncompromising vision of how honest an artist had to be: "[The artist] is a man who would say not only that the king has no clothes," he wrote, "but proceed from there to note how badly the sovereign is hung. Such a man is, of course, crazy. . . . We're all ravers, in one fashion or another." By mid-1964, Jones had become a prominent voice of black radical disenchantment.

It was Henry Jaglom, ironically, who introduced Richard to Jones, by taking him to an intimate staging of a Jones play at the Actors Studio. In the post-play discussion, Jaglom attacked what he saw as the play's slanted treatment of race, and Jones responded with a stark challenge and an ad hominem attack: he was not prepared to listen to anything Jaglom said about his play or race in America; Jaglom was part of a system of oppression and had no right to comment on his work unless he was prepared to kill his own parents. Jaglom was shocked. He was coming at the race issue from a progressive angle, he felt. And his parents, as Jews escaping the Nazis, had only recently come to America—how could they be held responsible for slavery and its legacies? Jones was unperturbed. He repeated that if Jaglom wanted to be taken seriously, he needed to be willing to kill his parents. At this point, Jaglom looked to his good friend Richard—his collaborator onstage, his partner in dreaming, his political sounding board—for some moral support. To Jaglom's chagrin, Richard kept his silence. It was a turning point in their relationship, a sign that they were not just *compañeros* in comedy, but separate particles: white and black, legit and illegit, rich and not rich at all. That night the two migrated from the Actors Studio to the Improv, where they assumed the stage as if nothing had happened. But "something had been broken," Jaglom reflected.

Near the time of the face-off at the Actors Studio, Richard met Jones, this time without Jaglom, at the well-heeled apartment of the publisher of *Kulchur*, an avant-garde magazine for which Jones served as music editor. The apartment was a hipper version of the Jagloms' luxury residence: original paintings by Picasso and Modigliani, rather than Degas and Renoir, hung on the walls. Richard, Jones, and the son of *Kulchur*'s publisher were talking politics, and the publisher's son wanted to know how he might become more involved in the cause, whatever that entailed for a young white radical. "What can I do to help?" he asked Jones.

"Cut your father's throat," Jones said. It was a well-practiced, all-purpose answer to white would-be allies in 1964.

Richard started to interject something, but Jones cut him short with a look and one word: *"Richard."*

The son hemmed and hawed; Richard watched. He was entranced by the power of Jones's sharp cruelty, by the paralyzing effect it had on the white kid in the room. The kid who seemed to have everything in the world, who seemed born into knowingness, was suddenly and indelibly at a loss.

"Reality is best dealt with," Jones told Richard privately at another moment. It was professional advice in the form of a Zen koan, and Richard tried to straighten his head so that he might follow it.

On February 21, 1965, Malcolm X was assassinated in Harlem's Audubon Ballroom, killed by a shotgun blast that ripped a seven-inch hole around his heart. For LeRoi Jones, as for many black radicals, the death of Malcolm was a shattering event: the most charismatic spokesman for black liberation had been cut down at the very moment when his message felt most vital. Within a few weeks, Jones left behind his Jewish wife, their two children, and their world of friends in Greenwich Village and moved to Harlem, a neighborhood he had never known from the inside. There he founded the Black Arts Theatre Repertory/School, an all-black cultural organization that aspired to be the handmaiden of the black revolution. His dalliance with bohemia behind him, he was now fully committed: "[b]ack in the homeland to help raise the race."

Richard Pryor wasn't there yet. He had an affinity with Jones, but it was hard enough to be a struggling comedian without taking on the revolutionary struggle, too. And while Jones had been a resident of bohemia for a full decade, Richard was just starting to sample its freedoms—not least among them, the freedom to date white women.

In early 1965, Richard fell for one in particular, an Audrey Hepburn lookalike by the name of Maxine Silverman. Maxine was a savvy bohemian with a hard-earned sense of independence. Her parents—working-class Jews from Boston, a cabdriver and a department store clerk—had expected their daughter, first, to be well behaved. When she wasn't, they tried to pound the mischief out of her with an ironing cord, or locked her in a closet to teach her a lesson. (Throughout her

A vivacious beauty: Maxine Silverman at the beach in 1961, posed with Phillip Wylie's Opus 21, *a novel of sexual and political discovery. (Courtesy of Elizabeth Pryor)*

life, she went to sleep with the TV on, as she couldn't stand to be in the dark.) By sixteen she had had an abortion. By age twenty-one she had split for New York City with a girlfriend and become a devoted follower of jazz, Lenny Bruce, and haute couture. Holly Golightly had Tiffany to spark her dreams; Maxine had Henri Bendel, where she could eye, but not buy, the latest dresses and accessories.

Maxine was a prickly, vivacious beauty. When she first caught Richard onstage, she saw him as a Lenny Bruce wannabe: he'd dropped the word *shit* into his routine, and she thought it was a cheap way to get a laugh (and told him so). But she warmed to his aura of innocence—he seemed to her like the sweetest, most darling person she'd ever seen—and not long after they met, she was willing to ditch her then-boyfriend and take a chance on love. Richard thought Maxine was "the cutest white girl I'd ever seen," who "grooved right along with me in treating life like a party" and "knew things, sophisticated things that I'd never learned, like which forks to use at a nice restaurant." After he caught some commercial breaks, they moved in together, in a classy doorman building at Fifty-Seventh Street and Ninth Avenue.

Their relationship was high drama. It began as a comedy of misrecognition—Maxine taking Richard's sweetness as the whole of his personality, Richard taking her vivacity as the whole of hers—and evolved into something considerably darker. Both of them had grown up in homes where abuse and affection were mixed up like feathers in a whirlwind, and they practiced on each other what had been practiced on them, probably without knowing why. Petty quarrels flared into knock-down, drag-out fights, fanned by Richard's discovery of a different kind of "white lady": cocaine.

In his memoir, Richard recalls one of the few occasions when Maxine got the last jab. An actor friend broke into their apartment late at night and shook Richard awake. Richard's signature, it seems, had been illegible on a two-hundred-dollar check he had written so that his friend could fly out to LA for an audition—a check that would have cleaned out his bank account, and that Maxine had asked him not to write. The bank had sent the actor back to get another signature.

Richard did not wake easily. "I'm sleeping. Ask Maxine," he said.

The friend woke Maxine, who became incensed—that Richard hadn't listened to her, that the argument was coming around again, that he was fobbing this actor off on her—and ended up on their apartment's balcony, screaming. Soon there was a roundelay of rage: Richard "angry at Maxine for getting angry while this actor was angry at both of us for fucking up his big chance."

In the heat of the moment, Maxine grabbed a knife and fumed, "I'm gonna cut you, motherfucker."

Richard egged her on. "Go ahead, bitch."

She sprang at Richard, swiping across his left arm with a slash of the knife, cutting half an inch into the flesh.

Blood spurted out. Richard, in a fugue state, staggered to his friend Bruce Scott's apartment upstairs. "Holy shit, she nailed you good!"

Scott exclaimed. He brought Richard inside, where, in silence, he cleaned the wound and wrapped it in gauze. Finally, Richard asked, "You want to come along? I'm going to rent a car and drive around." Scott feared that Richard might, with his hundred-yard stare, drive himself off some forlorn cliff in suburban New Jersey, and so, around seven in the morning, the two found themselves in a rental car tooling aimlessly around the Garden State. Richard sat quietly with his gauze-packed arm on the wheel, mulling over something and revealing nothing on the long ride. He wanted a companion who would put no demands on him—who would just be there.

Usually the violence between Richard and Maxine went the other way. Richard could be brutal, and she never knew how far he might go. Two years later, when they lived together in Beverly Hills, she wrote a secret message on the back of a picture in their home: "If anything happens to me, Richard Pryor did it." He might put her in the grave somehow, she thought bleakly, but he wouldn't get away with it.

Still they considered themselves, for a while, husband and wife. Maxine called herself "Mrs. Maxine Pryor" early in their relationship and never dropped the title; Richard called her his wife, though he hadn't yet divorced his first wife, Patricia. In the manner of bohemians, they preferred informal vows to any official ceremony in a church, temple, or city hall. Cigar bands, not wedding bands, were exchanged between them. Richard cried out to be taken care of, and Maxine tried to take care of him, in her fashion. When Richard debuted on *The Ed Sullivan Show* in May 1965—the biggest break of his early career—he turned to Maxine to pick out his tie.

The routine that opened the doors in Richard's professional life was a five-minute farce, a version of his theatrical debut in a children's production of *Rumpelstiltskin*. "Rumpelstiltskin" was his calling card as a comic, a work of mini-theater that he used successfully to audition for Ed Sullivan's and Merv Griffin's shows. And like much of his early act, it was an elaborate scrambling of the facts of his life.

At age fourteen, Richard had made his stage debut at the Carver Center in a production of *Rumpelstiltskin* that had lived up to Juliette Whittaker's exacting standards of professionalism and artistry. In his routine, Richard backdated the routine to his kindergarten year at Irving School, substituted a nasally white "Mr. Conrad" for the elegantly black Miss Whittaker, and converted his fellow performers from aspiring thespians to "little kiddies" who can't seem to get their lines or characters straight:

> **RUMPELSTILTSKIN** [*squirrely kid's voice*]: My name is Rumpelstiltskin and I'm a meanie! My name is Rumpelstiltskin—uh-oh! I hear the sound of horsey hoops. I will hide behind a rock or tree.
>
> **NARRATOR**: Bookety-bookety-bookety-bookety-bookety . . .
>
> **PRINCE** [*overacting*]: Whoah, horsey. Whoah, horsey. Ho, ho, ho, man! I saw something hidin' in the woods behind a rock or tree. Go look, captain of the garbs.
>
> **CAPTAIN OF THE GUARDS** [*haltingly*]: Prince . . . you did not see anything. It must have been a menage.

And so it goes, in this burlesque of a fairy tale. The boy playing the fairy godmother introduces himself as the fairy "godfather," then confusedly corrects himself. Rumpelstiltskin brags about the wicked power of his magic dust, then blows it by mistake into his own face and gasps.

For Rumpelstiltskin, Richard drew upon that part of himself that had stayed forever in kindergarten, the part that was not wised up and that wanted to believe in fairy-tale happy endings. (His kindergarten year at Irving School marked the moment, in his life, of his parents' divorce and his separation from his mother.) The sketch was a hilarious portrait of the guilelessness of children, rendered by a comedian who hankered after innocence even as he knew how absurd it was to walk innocently among the wolves of the world. With his narrow shoulders and pipe-cleaner legs still suggesting the gawkiness of adolescence,

Richard *looked* young, too—young enough that the years seemed to melt away when he played kindergarteners. And unlike Bill Cosby, whose sketches often revolved around children, too, he didn't seek to correct their behavior or interject himself as an authority figure when they misbehaved and struggled to stay "on script." There was joy in their comedy of errors, delight in how they slipped out of the roles they were given. The only grown-up in the sketch, the self-important teacher Mr. Conrad, was the character who came off most poorly.

Artistically, "Rumpelstiltskin" was a watershed for Richard. With it, he found a way to collapse the techniques of group improvisation he'd learned at the Improv into his solo act as a stand-up comedian. Instead of joining a handful of actors onstage to play a theater game, he became all the actors himself and made the rules of the game into the premise of the routine. "Rumpelstiltskin" set the template for later virtuosic sketches such as "T.V. Panel," "Prison Play," and "Hank's Place," in which he effortlessly seemed to incarnate character after character and spun the anarchy of their interaction into comedic gold. Though these sketches were carefully crafted and sometimes repeated word for word from performance to performance, they had a bracing sense of spontaneity built into them. They *felt* improvised even if they weren't, perhaps because the people within them, like all children and all good improvisers onstage, tended to be searching for the truth of their character rather than in possession of it.

Practically, "Rumpelstiltskin" marked a new stage in Richard's career, and for a very simple reason: both Ed and Merv loved it, and loved him. Right after his debut with Merv Griffin, he became a regular, notching more than twenty appearances on the show in less than a year. After he performed "Rumpelstiltskin" on *Ed Sullivan*, he was signed to a multi-show contract that kept him on the program every two months. The television exposure changed his life: he left behind Manny Roth, who, after all, had the Café Wha? to attend to, and teamed up with General Artists Corporation, a powerhouse talent agency that represented everyone from the Beatles and the Supremes to Nancy Sinatra and fellow up-and-comer George Carlin.

Soon Richard would be recognized as a "lean, literate, quick-witted kook," the man with "the most elastic face in show business." He had graduated from the coffeehouses of the Village and was becoming a national, not just a local, act. *Jet* reported, breathlessly, that this "newest and youngest of the Negro comics" was "being stormed by teen-agers every time he does a TV show." As the appearances piled up, he found himself in an unprecedented situation: making more money than he could spend.

Back in Peoria, Richard's family was dealing with legal trouble more serious than the cat-and-mouse games of his early childhood. The police were cracking down on the Aiken Avenue area where Peoria's brothels had migrated after the bulldozing of North Washington Street, and for the first time in twenty years, his father and stepmother faced the threat of prison time.

The trouble began on May 28, 1965, when Sheriff Ray Trunk was fiddling with a padlock at 405 Aiken Avenue, a house shuttered by court order. He heard a tapping sound from the house next door, at 409 Aiken; a woman was knocking on the window and signaling him to come over. He approached, and the front door cracked open; the woman invited him to sneak around to the back. Instead, Trunk pushed open the door and arrested the two women he found in the front room as suspected prostitutes. He explored the house and, coming upon Richard's stepmother Ann in another room, asked if she ran the place. When, according to Trunk, she said yes, she was hauled off to jail on prostitution charges.

Three months later, the Pryors suffered another impromptu raid at 409 Aiken. On September 18, an undercover Illinois state trooper wangled his way into the house; a twenty-one-year-old working girl propositioned him, and, after money changed hands, he revealed himself as an officer of the law. The trooper was ill prepared for what came next. Several people—among them Buck Pryor, fifty years old and built like a refrigerator—grabbed the girl and ran into the streets. It was a lucky if impulsive move. Buck eluded capture for a day, and though he was charged with being the brothel's proprietor, in the end there was not enough evidence to substantiate the charge. He got off with just a twenty-dollar fine, for resisting arrest.

Richard's stepmother was not so fortunate. On October 6, 1965, a Peoria judge declared Ann guilty of operating a brothel, and the assistant state's attorney recommended a three-month jail term. Ann's lawyer pleaded in court for a fine, not jail time, and put his client on the stand to make a case for extenuating circumstances. She was dying of oral and nose cancer, Ann said; she had recently been operated upon in a hospital in Chicago, and her condition required regular follow-ups there. She also testified that she was out of the game, a madam no more, and pointed to the fact that she was attending night school at Midstate College of Commerce, studying typing and office work.

Ramrod-straight Peoria had no sympathy for Ann. The president of Midstate College of Commerce, indignant to have been used for an alibi, dismissed her from its rolls after the story of her announced reform hit the newsstands. "If we had known her identity, we would never have accepted her," he said, and refunded her tuition forthwith. In late October the judge quadrupled the sentence recommended by the state's attorney, imposing the maximum of a one-year prison term for her offense. If his sentence stuck, Ann was likely to die in the Illinois State Reformatory for Women, ninety miles from her home.

The Pryor family rallied to her cause, quickly raising two thousand dollars for her bail. Their lawyer shot off an appeal to a higher court, and Ann was free pending its resolution. She was playing out her string, though it was far from clear how much string she had left.

For Buck and Ann, their son Richard—once a nuisance and irritant in the household—was now a source of consolation. In the days after the judge pronounced his sentence, Richard was headlining the Blue Angel in Chicago, and the two drove the three hours to watch him perform. "Sure enough, high above in big lights was the name Richard Pryor," Buck recalled to a reporter in 1966, playing the proud father. "We knew then that he had found what he'd always wanted." And Buck got a piece of what he wanted out of Richard's success, too: twenty thousand dollars in cash, handed freely from Richard so that Buck could buy a new home in Peoria, separate from the Aiken Avenue house that had just been raided twice.

For Richard, the generosity of that gift was inversely proportional to the amount of time he wished to spend in Peoria. He was trying to become the name on a bigger marquee, the star twinkling above his family and their troubles. Except in the controlled world of his imagination, he had not returned to his home in the three years since he left, and that was how he liked it.

CHAPTER 9

An Irregular Regular

Los Angeles, New York City, Peoria, 1965–1966

L*ate October 1965, an apartment in a West Hollywood high-rise*: Henry Jaglom, still an underemployed actor, is writing furiously in his journal with different-colored pens, having just dropped acid for the first time. He had been given the stuff—little known outside certain bohemian circles in Hollywood and San Francisco, and still perfectly legal in California—from a friend at Jane Fonda's July Fourth bash in Malibu, and had held on to it for months, hesitant to experiment with his own psyche. Now he feels his world buzzing. The celestial harmonies of Bach are manifesting to him in a wash of color; flowers are growing out of the walls and the colored pens he's holding. He looks at himself in a mirror and observes that he has undergone the most stunning metamorphosis. His hair is blond and flowing, his neck elongated, his back sprouting wings until he seems like a cross between a swan and an angel.

An interruption: the phone rings. It's his friend Richie Pryor, in town for a set of gigs down the hill at the Troubadour, a hotbed of the new comedy and folk-rock.

"I've got something that is so incredible," Jaglom says. "It will make you feel so great." Richard hardly needs that strong a sales pitch.

Later that night, Jaglom is lying naked on the bathroom floor when he hears a scream from the living room. He emerges from the bathroom to find Richard howling at the window, getting ready to hurl himself six floors down. The living room carpet now seems to Jaglom like high grass, taller than his body, but he runs across it, feeling like a knight on a horse, charging to save the princess—only

Richard is the princess he needs to rescue. Arriving at the windowsill, he grabs Richard's ankle so tightly that his fingernails break through the skin, and he holds Richard there for what seems, in LSD time, like an eternity.

Why has Richard tried to climb out the high window? It's not so much that he's aiming to kill himself—nothing so coherent as that—but rather a sign of how intensely the acid has unhinged him. He's crying, raving: about the ugliness he feels, about the pain he's seen since he was a child, about the meanness of his life. When he looked in the mirror, at Henry's well-intentioned suggestion, he had glimpsed the opposite of what Henry had seen. There had been a devil looking back, the devil inside. The window had been his escape route.

How differently these two friends traveled through the high times they shared! Henry was cushioned by his privilege and his optimism; Richard, always at risk of falling—or throwing himself—into the abyss. And so the same LSD that had heightened Henry's love affair with himself, enveloping him in a nimbus of glory, had trapped Richard at the top of a dark tower, swarmed by memories from his past and anxieties from his present. Dropping acid together, the white actor and the black comic had never been farther apart.

Back home in New York City in late 1965, Richard put on his game face. He was writing new material constantly, and for good reason: with near-weekly appearances on *Merv Griffin*, he needed to keep his act fresh. He prepped for the shows with his agent, Sandy Gallin, an energetic player who would later manage Dolly Parton, Lily Tomlin, and Michael Jackson, and who took on many of the duties of a manager with Richard. "What are you going to do with him?" Gallin had been asked when he first signed Richard to General Artists Corporation. "He can't put three sentences together without saying 'fuck' or 'nigger.'" Gallin was charged with trimming the swear words from Richard's act.

By the time Richard appeared on *Merv*, the rougher edges of his humor had been sanded down. His spots on the talk show were often fish-out-of-water routines, revolving around the misadventures of a small-town youth adrift in the big city. Sometimes he hinted at the peculiarities of being black in Manhattan, but only to dramatize his perplexity, not to lodge a protest:

> I cannot call a waitress. I go to a restaurant like Sardi's, and I know that the only time I'd get into a restaurant like Sardi's, if I wasn't in show business, would be if I was cleaning it up. So I go in there and you can't call a waiter. So I always go . . . [*flutters his fingers, mouths some silent words to attract the waiter's attention*]
>
> And they always come over: "Do you want a shot?"

On *Merv* and other TV shows, Richard presented himself as a classic klutz. He was the sort to get anxious at other people's homes and knock over gravy boats or ashtrays—or ashtrays full of gravy. And he was at his clumsiest when he tried to pick up women by mimicking the suave motions he'd observed in cosmopolitan types. His "Cary Grant thing" involved arching his eyebrows like a clown doing warm-up exercises and gesticulating wildly until the drink he held flew out of his hand. Trying to light a woman's cigarette, he burned his thumb instead.

Perhaps because of the pressure to keep his act clean, Richard started working a vein of silent, absurdist pantomime in these early TV appearances. He honed an extended series of cockeyed "impressions," in which the setup was as far out as the punch line. At the time, Richard was watching Jerry Lewis movies in marathon sessions at the all-night theaters of Forty-Second Street, and these "impressions" took Lewis's zany physicality into the realm of surreal fantasy. Richard impersonated "the first man on the sun" by yowling and jumping with every step he took, as if the floor of the stage were now the photosphere. He became an amateur scuba diver in some imaginary "shark-fighting championship," doffing his fins and goggles and swimming in slow motion toward the shark, then harpooning his own belly by mistake. He became "a Japanese robot who's a karate expert," his arms slicing through the air with beeps and whirrs—

The comic and his talk-show foil: Richard Pryor and Merv Griffin in 1965. (Courtesy of Getty Images)

until, in a glitch of computer programming, he karate-chops his own body to the ground. Or he puffed up into the world's strongest man, "Novocain Martinovich," and went through the motions of hefting seven hundred fifty pounds: the show-offy flexing of his muscles; the guttural groan to rally his strength; the stricken look when the imaginary barbell refuses to budge; the hyperventilating surge that hoists the barbell up above his head; and, finally, the wide-eyed panic when the barbell falls behind his back and takes his body down with it.

Merv acted as a straight man for Richard, his steady-as-she-goes foil. His aw-shucks demeanor put Richard at ease when they "unraveled" together (as Merv termed his creative conversations with his guests). "I just want to thank you, Merv," Richard confessed in an early appearance. "You've been really nice to me. You were the first one to have me on." And Griffin deserved the compliment. For all his midwestern ingenuousness, he was a canny programmer who did not shy away from controversy: in 1965, just as he was welcoming Richard on his program, he invited British philosopher Bertrand Russell to discuss, and attack, the United States' involvement in Vietnam. (The in-studio audience booed.) And unlike Johnny Carson, Merv regularly took a chance on unknown comics, establishing a direct pipeline between the Improv and his show.

Still, Richard was starting to chafe at the limits of his TV work. At countercultural clubs like the Café au Go-Go and the Troubadour, his "impressions" were considerably more freewheeling than on *Merv*—as in his "impression of my sweater talking to my ass." The matter of sex, nowhere to be found in his TV routines, was popping up increasingly in his work onstage. He might talk about a "nudie" movie theater he patronized on Forty-Second Street: "five hundred guys would be in there, with coats on their laps," transfixed by a movie about a runaway brassiere. Or he might tell a dirty joke, especially one with a tinge of absurdity to it:

> Did you hear the one about the guy who was in the hospital, dying?
>
> So the doctor runs outside and says, "Nurse Jones, come here. There's a man in the room, dying, and he wants to see the Vice President and the President before he dies. And I hear that you have a tattoo of the Vice President on your left leg, and a tattoo of the President on your right leg. How about going into the room, letting the man see them, and in his delusion, he might really think that's who it is?"
>
> So the nurse goes into the room, pulls up her dress, walks up to the bed. And the man sees the Vice President and the President, and he kisses the Vice President, and he kisses the President. And he looks up to the nurse and says, "Now can I bid Castro goodbye?"

Maybe the greatest difference between his TV comedy and his live act was that, in a club, Richard could fool with his audience in real time. He was free to improvise and, like the jazz musicians he loved, free to succeed or fail in the moment. When his fellow comic Bob

Altman asked him how he was able to create so many "hunks" of new material, often with no thought of using them again, he said, "You ever take a long ride in a car, and your mind just goes out there . . . you're driving but your mind is somewhere else? I can let my mind out and I don't care where it takes me. I ain't ashamed of where it takes me."

At this time, Richard often opened his act by speaking in a stage whisper, as if confessing to a secret desire: "I would like to make you laugh. I would like to make you cry. I would like to *make you.*" Sometimes he skipped the two opening phrases and just left the last one hanging in the air, which made the confession all the more stark. "I would like to make you . . .": it was a slippery, half-slangy expression, which probably explains why the audience laughed. Partly Richard was flirting with his audience, admitting he wanted to lay them en masse, and partly he was hinting at another desire—that he wanted to *re*make his audience, as a novelist might rewrite a character. They were part of his medium of expression, part of his search for himself. He made the confession disarmingly, but it was audacious, nonetheless: he may have been, in mid-1960s America, the only black man who admitted openly that he hungered for a soul kiss with his audience.

He was developing a kind of authority, couched in vulnerability but sometimes revealing its prickliness. In February 1966, at his first engagement at the hungry i nightclub in San Francisco, he introduced his audience to a game:

> This is a game that I'm going to play with you because I would like to play with you. The name of the game is 'Improvisation' . . . [Y]ou name what you would like, and I do it. Sometimes it's great, sometimes it's not bad, but it's never boring.

Boredom was the great enemy: better to create a memorable failure than grab a predictable laugh. When someone in the audience suggested that he tell a joke or two, he shot back, "Why don't you go to

Vegas? They got millions of comics doing that." He laughed dismissively, and moved on.

There was a final problem with Richard's prefab work on TV: the wrong people—white folks—seemed to enjoy it most. In August 1965, he was excited to be featured on a bill launching a new theater season at Harlem's Apollo Theater—so thrilled, in fact, that he convinced Bill Cosby to take a cab uptown so they could see Richard's name on the marquee. During the cab ride, Cosby counseled him to act properly at the Apollo: he wasn't to cuss or play the fool.

"But I'm being paid to be a fool," Richard said.

"You know what I mean," Cosby said.

When the cab pulled up to the curb of the Apollo, Richard and Cosby got out and gazed at the marquee:

• •

BILLY ECKSTINE
AND
OPENING ACTS

• •

"Where's your name, Rich?" Cosby asked. "I see Billy Eckstine's. But not yours."

"Right there. Underneath."

"I don't see it."

"What do you mean? Right there. 'Opening Acts.' "

The Apollo crowd could be brutal to black comedians whose humor was oriented to white audiences: Godfrey Cambridge, at his 1962 debut, was heckled so mercilessly that he scurried off the stage with tears running down his cheeks and felt compelled to cancel, midweek, the rest of his engagement there. Richard fared better than Cambridge: he survived his week under Eckstine, his zaniness an easier sell than Cambridge's witty patter, but he hardly connected as he'd hoped. According to singer Jerry Butler of the R&B group the Impressions, Richard was "making faces and all kinds of funny sounds"—the pantomimes of his TV act—and "running back and forth across the stage." The Apollo's management didn't ask him back.

Half a year later, in March 1966, Richard returned to Harlem in the company of Redd Foxx. The two had just taped a *Merv Griffin* show together downtown, and then they hit uptown, the older comic guiding the younger on a tour. Time and again Richard heard people hollering Redd's nickname: "Hey, Zorro!" Richard didn't hear his name, which surprised him. Near the *Merv Griffin* studio, he had been the celebrity and Foxx the unknown. "Wait a minute," he thought to himself. "I'm in the wrong place, I'm in the wrong town. I want to be here. I want people to talk to me like they talk to Redd."

His people, by not speaking his name, were calling.

It was one thing, however, to hear the call, and quite another to answer it. Ever since Richard had landed in Greenwich Village three years earlier, he had been chasing after crossover success, and the stakes had been rising with his every breakthrough. He had begun by constellating around himself a crew of comedian friends, savoring with them the camaraderie of being young, keen, and on the move. Then he had proven himself with tastemakers such as Merv Griffin and Ed Sullivan, the cultural gatekeepers of middle America. Now his agent, Sandy Gallin, was dangling another business opportunity in front of him: Bob Banner Productions wanted Richard to appear as a recurring special guest on the *Kraft Summer Music Hall*, a prime-time variety show taped in Los Angeles. The show threatened to be as cornball as could be—its host was John Davidson, a squeaky clean, dimpled performer who played the banjo and whose mother and father both were Baptist ministers—but it was also billed as a "showcase of rising young stars." The "spontaneous and multi-talented" Richard was to be the special guest kicking off its premiere.

He accepted the gig without hesitation, eager not just to work on a prime-time show but also to move out to Los Angeles, where he could more easily audition for film and TV roles. Instead of subletting his Fifty-Seventh Street apartment or letting it sit vacant for the three-month gig, he chose to give it up. He was leaving New York City behind; it would be the scene of his apprentice years, not his future.

He journeyed out to LA in the spring of 1966, with Maxine at his side and their possessions stuffed into a car. By one piece of evidence, their relationship seemed to be deepening: on March 4, Richard had officially filed in Peoria County Court for a divorce from his first wife, Patricia, presumably to free himself up to marry Maxine. But on their cross-country drive out to LA, they bickered, the accusations and counteraccusations flying until, at a Chicago hotel, one of them punished the other in a spectacular fashion: by dumping a suitcase of clothes into the hotel swimming pool.

Not long after arriving in LA, they settled into a home on Ferrari Drive, in the uplands of Beverly Hills, where their neighbors were guaranteed to be white and well-heeled. (As late as 1980, Beverly Hills had a black population of 1 percent.) If Richard felt a twinge of regret about leaving Harlem behind, the feeling wasn't strong enough to make him choose a racially integrated neighborhood like Baldwin Hills, the affluent mid-city enclave favored by black entertainers like Earl Bostic and Ray Charles.

A photograph taken by *Ebony* the following year catches the mad force of his desire for mainstream success. Richard is airborne, leaping high underneath the street signs marking the intersection of Hollywood and Vine, dreamland's epicenter. His whole body is tense with the effort—his eyes wide, his mouth open, his arms shooting out from his sports coat to reveal his cuffs, his legs splayed out. He looks like someone crazed, and a little terrified, with his own eagerness.

For all his antic energy, Richard smoothly infiltrated the Hollywood in-crowd. After rehearsing the *Kraft Summer Music Hall* during the day, he wandered at night to the Daisy, a private Beverly Hills club run by fashion maven Jack Hanson, who had, with his Jax slacks, created a line of tight pants that clung "like oil to water" to the slim hips of stars such as Audrey Hepburn and Candice Bergen. Pryor, himself a fan of the lean, pipe-cleaner fit, befriended Hanson and his wife, Sally, and was soon part of the club, part of a world that updated Old Hollywood glamour for

A flying leap: Pryor at the iconic intersection of Hollywood and Vine, 1967. (Courtesy of Johnson Publishing Company, LLC)

the mid-1960s moment. On a typical night at the Daisy, *Doctor Zhivago*'s Omar Sharif might be found shooting pool, Tony Curtis sipping an Irish coffee at the bar, Natalie Wood relaxing after a vigorous Frug on the dance floor. The club limited its membership to around four hundred; paparazzi and autograph chasers were banned. "The Daisy, on any given night, is a noisy, frenzied circus of the most gorgeous women imaginable," wrote one reporter granted entrée, agog. "It is a place where this great montage of thigh-high miniskirts and glued-on Jax pants are doing the skate, the dog, the stroll, the swim, the jerk, the bomp, the monkey, the fish, the duck, the hiker, the Watusi, the gun, the slop, the slip, the sway, the sally and the joint. Like all good Beverly Hills children, Daisy dancers never even sweat. . . . Compared to The Daisy, all other discotheques are slums." For Richard Pryor, who had known actual slums, the Daisy was alluring and probably a little unreal. It became his favorite haunt, and the incubator of his new Los Angeles life.

On Sunday afternoons, Richard joined a select group of Daisy regulars who gathered at Barrington Park, in nearby Brentwood, to play a game of sandlot baseball. The weekend games breathed in an air of casual Hollywood luxury. Jack Hanson (manager-shortstop) and actor Peter Falk (centerfield) rolled up in their Rolls-Royces; actor Kevin McCarthy (team photographer), in his Porsche convertible. No one sported a uniform: some wore polo shirts, some pajama tops, some no shirts at all; one player went sockless and shoeless in the outfield. The Daisy team faced off against a team organized by a lumber broker, also filled out with Hollywood types—actors and producers and executives. Singer Bobby Darin and actor Ryan O'Neal were Richard's teammates. When he wasn't on the diamond, Richard presided over the PA system as a play-by-play announcer, announcing every "sensational catch" or "tremendous triple" or "dazzling throw" as if the World Series hung in the balance. Nancy Sinatra, Suzanne Pleshette, and any number of young women cheered from the bleachers. The games ended, typically, with scores too high for anyone to have kept track, and everyone was treated with coffee and ice cream courtesy of La Scala, a restaurant favored by the film colony. Over the next six years, no fewer than three of Richard's fellow ballplayers—Aaron Spelling, James B. Harris, and David Wolper—would cast him in films they produced.

Richard's day job on the *Kraft Summer Music Hall*, meanwhile, was a letdown. He joked with Sandy Gallin about the utter squareness of the show, which always ended with host John Davidson serenading older audience members with the Tin Pan Alley songs of their youth. Given how retro the program was, and how geared toward a white audience, Richard may justifiably have felt like he was back at Peoria's Blaine-Sumner Elementary School, the fly in the buttermilk. He kept his distance from the other cast members and sometimes skipped rehearsals, which fueled speculation that drugs were keeping him away. Richie Pryor seemed "really in his own world," Davidson remembered.

Matching outfits: on Kraft Summer Music Hall *with host John Davidson. (Courtesy of the author)*

Viewers of the TV program, though, would have had a hard time detecting any disaffection on Richard's part. He wore the same crew-neck sweater, white slacks, and white buck shoes as every other male performer on the show, and carried himself in general like the happiest goofball in the world. "Smile a happy face and sing your cares away": so the cast sang in chorus at the show's opening, and when Richard was introduced as a guest performer, he went cross-eyed, stuck out his tongue, and waved like a child, with both hands, at the camera. In the show's segments, he played well with others. For a medley of "river songs"—"Shenandoah" and so on—he added his voice to the three-part harmony and tap-danced with abandon when the spotlight fell on him. In another bit, where the cast performed some hokey children's circle games, he slapped his thigh to the beat and recited a rhyme that would never have played in Peoria's red-light district: "My girl, she went a-golfing, and boy did she have fun / She wore her new silk stockings and got a hole in one." His guest stand-up segments were variations on his TV-friendly work for *Merv Griffin*: "Rumpelstiltskin," the pantomimes, his failure as a pickup artist. Though familiar to Richard, they were deft enough that his fellow cast members were struck by how much he moved the straitlaced audience. As he'd learned to do at Blaine-Sumner, he had gauged his surroundings and donned the mask of class clown.

In the August 1 program, Richard had the courage to let that mask slip for a few minutes. Davidson announced that, though Richard "had been a guest many times" and "had always been a clown," he had learned that Richard's "secret desire" was "to be a singer," so he yielded the stage to Richard Pryor, crooner. The last time Richard had bared this side of himself, he was auditioning for Harold Parker at Harold's Club in 1961, and his vocals had been a mess. Not this time. Accompanied at first only by a stand-up bass, he launched into a slinky rendition of the blues standard "Nobody Knows You When You're Down and Out," a song about a man who splurges on his friends when his money is rolling in, only to find himself deserted when he goes broke. As the horns arrived to punctuate the chorus, Richard raised his voice by a full octave and belted the song's cynical moral with showstopping energy and utter conviction. "Nobody wants you, nobody needs you when you're down and out": a strange thought, perhaps, for someone who had just moved into a new house in Beverly Hills and been awarded membership in the most exclusive of social clubs. But Richard seemed to feel the fragility of his success. Even as he was flying high, he reminded himself what it would be like to plummet to the ground.

Richard's fantasy of being a torch singer was probably stoked by his budding friendship with one of his sandlot baseball teammates, the singer Bobby Darin, who took Richard under his wing not long after they shared their first Daisy baseball game. Darin was the most connected, and the hippest, entertainer to sponsor Richard's career yet. Through "Splish Splash" and a raft of Hollywood films, Darin

A "wing-dang-doodle" of a time: Maxine Silverman Pryor, Bobby Darin, and Richard Pryor at the party Darin hosted in his honor. (Courtesy of Harry Langdon)

had established himself as a teen idol; through "Mack the Knife" and his incandescent cabaret act, he had become a sensation among older audiences. He was also a self-styled industry iconoclast—a performer who followed up his smash hit "Mack the Knife" with a heartfelt R&B tribute album to Ray Charles, then albums of country-and-western and folk music. By August 1966, like Richard, he felt himself veering off from the core of his audience, the folks who filled New York City's Copacabana or Las Vegas's Flamingo Hotel to hear him perform Tin Pan Alley standards. He had just recorded the folk-rock "If I Were a Carpenter," a song that wondered aloud: would you still love me if I wasn't who I appear to be?

Darin promoted Richard with characteristic élan. He signed him up as the opening act for his August 1966 return to the Flamingo hotel—a gig that promised $2,400 a week, more than Richard had ever made—and in anticipation of the gig, staged a party at his elegant Bel

Air home to fête his new protégé. The invitation declared that, according to astronomers, a new star was to descend upon Darin's home, a star that hailed from "the constellation Talent" and was named Richard Pryor. Darin promised everyone a "wing-dang-doodle" of a time, and the party itself was a head-turning celebrity summit. Old-school comedians Milton Berle and Groucho Marx were there, with cigars poking from their pockets or cradled in their fingers. Singers Connie Stevens and Diana Ross tripped the light fantastic with Darin, who seemed liberated by the recent announcement that his wife, Sandra Dee, had filed for divorce. He was looking as sharp as ever, with a matching polka-dot ascot and pocket handkerchief. Meanwhile, Richard, the guest of honor, seemed uncomfortable with all the attention. He arrived wearing a cable-knit sweater over a T-shirt, dressed not for his "coming out" party but for a casual night at home, spent parked in front of the TV.

Early in the evening, Richard discovered he was right to be nervous. Sitting across from him was Groucho, who had seen Pryor's recent appearance on *The Merv Griffin Show*, where Richard had met his idol Jerry Lewis for the first time. After an earnest moment in which Richard had praised Lewis as "the god of comedy," the two had regaled Merv's audience by spitting water on each other.

"Young man, you're a comic?" Groucho asked Richard.

"Yes," Richard replied, walking into the trap. "Yes, I am."

"So how do you want to end up? Have you thought about that? Do you want a career you're proud of? Or do you want to end up a spitting wad like Jerry Lewis?"

"Huh?" Richard stammered. His idol a spitting wad?

"Do you ever see plays?" Groucho asked.

"No."

"Do you ever read books?"

"No."

The questions, and Richard's humbling answers, hung in the air. After the party, he turned over Groucho's slap-down in his mind. Here he'd been, breathing the same oxygen as the entertainers who had defined American comedy for twenty years, and what did he have to show for himself? *The Kraft Music Hall*? He'd left one kind of brothel for another. "Wake up, Richard," he told himself. "Yes, you are an ignorant jerk, pimping your talent like a cheap whore. But you don't have to stay that way. You have a brain. Use it."

It was hard for Richard to use his brain when his ego was being so insistently, and distractingly, stroked. A few days after Darin's party, he arrived in Vegas and marveled with Maxine at seeing his name in lights on the Flamingo marquee. It was, he said, "as big a thrill" as he'd had "up to that time." He delighted, too, in the Strip's "around-the-clock hustle": by the mid-1960s, Vegas had evolved, as a sin city, into the best world that money could buy, a startlingly upscale version of the Peoria of Richard's childhood. The just-opened Caesars Palace had reclaimed the banner of imperial Rome for the age of Populuxe. From the outside it looked like a fourteen-story Coliseum, while from the inside it looked like the largest bachelor pad in existence, with waitress "goddesses," in tunics and sandals, instructed to introduce themselves with "I am your slave." The Flamingo itself was the first luxury hotel on the Strip, and had already become iconic. The Rat Pack had robbed its casino in *Ocean's Eleven*; Elvis and Ann-Margret had frolicked around its pool in *Viva Las Vegas*.

Being an opening act for Bobby Darin at the Flamingo meant basking in an air of complete adoration. During the first week of their engagement, Darin demolished the all-time attendance record for the Flamingo's showroom. The sellout crowds welcomed Richard's act, which, despite Groucho's advice, remained a smooth amalgamation of the sketches he performed on *Merv Griffin*: spoofs of New York, "Rumpelstiltskin," and the rest.

Yet if Vegas offered itself as a blank canvas for Richard's fantasies, he grew indifferent about painting it. Sure, *Variety* praised his "wonderfully kookie style," but he was still being lumped into "the Bill Cosby school of reminiscing and identifiable storytelling." Don Rickles, ostensibly coming backstage to praise his act, merely slipped in the knife. "It's uncanny," he said. "You sound just like Bill Cosby."

It was the same connection Manny Roth had made two years ago and a world away, during Richard's first hungry months in Greenwich Village, when he still had the excuse of being the freshest arrival in town.

Back in LA, Richard was both making it and not making it—getting his first roles as an actor in TV and film, and then struggling with what to do with them. He took a supporting part in *The Busy Body*, a Sid Caesar vehicle that offered him the chance to work with one of his childhood heroes. He leapt at the opportunity, playing a circumspect, fumbling police detective to Caesar's blabby, fumbling mobster. It was a part that Cosby would have invested with his reserves of calm and competence. Richard tried to give the role an inflection he'd crowd-tested in his work on *Merv*—the "cool guy" who always seems on the verge of a crack-up.

Unfortunately, he suffered a crisis of confidence on set. He felt himself "tiptoe[ing] around the cameras [and] lights," and wondered, "What the fuck am I doing here?" Acting in a film didn't come as naturally as he'd expected. "I did every actor that I'd ever seen in the movies in this one role. I walked in the door like Steve McQueen. I took my hat off like John Wayne, even did some Charlton Heston." The end result was a muddle: he voiced the role in an artificially deep register, as if he were a kid playing a grown-up. His performance was mannered, jokey—like pretty much every other performance in the film. A mashup of *It's a Mad, Mad, Mad, Mad World* and Hitchcock's *The Trouble with Harry, The Busy Body* lacked the star power of the former and the control of the latter, and it found little favor with audiences or critics. *Time* dismissed it as a "tasteless Runyonesque rehash." The *Chicago Tribune* complained, "Producer-director William Castle . . . used to make supposedly horror movies that in actuality were funny. In 'The Busy Body,' he has made a supposedly funny movie that in actuality is a horror." The film did nothing to elevate Richard among the ranks of working actors.

His first role in a TV series—a background part on the fall 1966 premiere of *The Wild Wild West*—suggests that he was not exactly being choosy in his auditions. Richard played a dim-witted ventriloquist, outfitted in red turban and magenta dashiki, part of a group of carnival show assassins. It was no one's proudest moment: at one point, the show's hero exercises his wit by asking Pryor's character, "Who's the ventriloquist and who's the dummy?" To *Variety*, the episode was patently ludicrous. "For real-life stuff," the critic jibed, "viewers will have to turn the dial to 'Green Hornet' or 'Tarzan.' "

Fresh from these experiences as an actor, Richard traveled back to Peoria for the first time since he'd left in 1962, and was received with a warmth so novel that it felt disorienting. His old friends, who had doubted his prospects, hailed the conquering hero. The cops who had treated him like a juvenile delinquent now vowed that they had believed in his talent all the while. His father, an unsentimental character for as long as he could remember, told a *Peoria Journal Star* reporter that when he and Ann first caught Richard on TV, "the thrill of our son making it good tugged at our hearts and brought a tear or two." Richard tried to reconnect with Peoria and embrace his new stature: he played cards, went fishing, got drunk. He pulled three or four friends over to the Pere Marquette Hotel, where he had worked as a shoeshine, and finally achieved a dream he'd held inside himself since he was a boy. He sat at the picture window of its restaurant, where he could enjoy a lordly view of Main Street, and ate a lordly lunch.

Still, bitterness leaked out of him. He lashed at a *Journal Star* reporter when she suggested that blacks were getting more exposure on TV. "It's a sham," he said, "a trick that deludes. You see more Negroes on TV because what they are selling, sells to the Negro. Now, they are getting worse parts, but more of them." It's not hard to divine the sources of Richard's frustration, given his recent work on the *Kraft Summer Music Hall* and *The Wild Wild West*.

He was in a more positive frame of mind when discussing how he developed his comic material. "I can walk two blocks down the street and see funny things, comical happenings all around me. Now, I can put these local, human, real things into a skit, and they come out funny," he said, noting that this method had taken him two years to hone. "I have a lot of people to thank for these funny bits," he continued. "My grandma, the boss of the whole family, has lots of material there. I've got a 13-year-old cousin, Denise, who they say is just like me. She's a source with her little jokes. My uncle, Richard, and my grandpa Tommy Bryant—what they do gives me material. I called my grandpa to tell him I was going to be on TV. All I said was 'grandpa' and without letting me finish, he said, 'I ain't got a quarter,' then hung up."

It was the first time Richard had publicly articulated the change he felt brewing in his comedy, the turn to the close observation of his family and neighborhood. There was a good bit of premature optimism in his self-assessment: when he discussed his family or his social life onstage over the last two years, he'd still tended to present a fantasy version of his life—for instance, in the oft-repeated joke about belonging to a family with eleven kids (repeated on the *Kraft Summer Music Hall* in June), or in his self-presentation as the most harmless of souls. And he had exercised his imaginative license for good reason: the *Kraft Summer Music Hall* was not about to lend its stage to a comic who pulled back the veil on Peoria's brothels, replicated his obscenity-laced bull sessions with his friends, delved into his violent relationships with women, or described the psychedelic horror show of an acid trip.

But if Richard misstated, to the *Peoria Journal Star*, what he'd already achieved in his comedy, his remarks pointed with clarity to the journey that lay ahead of him. He was poised to discover whether the larger following he'd built—a crowd that ranged from the dope-smoking hipsters of the Troubadour to the elderly gents and ladies in the *Kraft Summer Music Hall* audience—would follow him or abandon him as his comedy turned to the nitty-gritty of his life. Would Ed Sullivan, or even Bobby Darin and Henry Jaglom, remain simpatico if his comedy itself were no longer so congenial in spirit? His hurtling journey toward success was turning into a hurtling journey to find himself, and the velocity was becoming severe.

CHAPTER 10

The Person in Question

Los Angeles and Las Vegas, 1967

The summer of 1967 may have been known, to flower children in San Francisco, as the Summer of Love, but for black Americans it was a long hot summer of reckoning. Ghetto residents looked around and wondered whether, for all the promises of the civil rights movement and Lyndon Johnson's Great Society, their lives had really changed. Jobs were still scarce, their schools still substandard, and their streets still patrolled by police forces with the air of an occupying army. The political temperature was rising steadily. "If America don't come around," black militant H. Rap Brown threatened at a rally in Cambridge, Maryland, in July, "we should burn it down, brother." He pointed to a nearby school as a sign of America's moral dereliction. Later that night, flames enveloped the school and the nearby business district.

More than a hundred cities across America burned, in fact. In Newark and Detroit, blacks tangled with police, National Guardsmen, and paratroopers in battles that left twenty-six and forty-three dead, respectively. By the fall of 1967, the mood of black America had turned urgent and desperate. "Violence is as American as cherry pie," "These rebellions are but a dress rehearsal for real revolution": so declaimed Brown, and his cynicism and zeal proved infectious. "On certain corners in American cities," *Ebony* reported, "black brothers can be heard kidding one another about being tuned out of the revolution if they haven't yet purchased a Butane gas lighter." The revolution called for action, even as it was unclear—aside from setting one's neighborhood on fire—what form that action might take.

Richard Pryor was living in Beverly Hills and West Hollywood, not Watts, but the summer of 1967 was his season of reckoning, too, scissoring his life in half. On the one side was the accommodating, fresh young fellow who was Bobby Darin's protégé; on the other, a man who felt the pulse of black America in his own racing heartbeat and saw no way to express the truth of his experience without resorting to a healthy dose of obscenities. Richard's comic act was in transition to something unforeseen, something rooted in the sense of emergency all around him.

While opening, in January 1967, for the upbeat cabaret act of Steve Lawrence and Eydie Gormé at the Sands hotel in Las Vegas, Richard made his first bold move of 1967: he criticized the Vietnam War from the stage. The Sands was no countercultural hole-in-the-wall like the Café Wha?. The clientele of its Copa Room supped on prime sirloin, French peas forestière, and Boula Boula Amontillado, and expected their entertainment to be similarly rich, buttery, and smooth. The crowd booed and hissed Richard; a woman whose son was posted in Vietnam stood up and ripped him to shreds. Richard was shaken by the vehemence of the response—and though Bobby Darin was on hand to console him afterward, he couldn't hold himself together. His agent, Sandy Gallin, remembered fielding a call from Jack Entratter, the bearish, Mob-connected president of the Sands, who screamed into the phone that Richard was "fucking crazy. He's right now swinging from chandeliers in the lobby."

Gallin somehow got Richard on the phone and tried to reason with him. He was playing "the top place in the United States"—did he really want to burn his bridges? On this occasion, Richard took the path of conciliation. He patched himself up and, this time, left Vegas with his reputation intact.

A month later, Richard was whipped by headwinds coming from the exact opposite direction. He stepped into a role on the hour-long TV special *A Time for Laughter: A Look at Negro Humor in America*—and was given a trenchant lesson in the politics of culture, courtesy of singer Harry Belafonte, the show's producer, and William Attaway, Belafonte's creative partner and the show's main writer. Both Belafonte and Attaway had strong radical credentials, the former as Martin Luther King Jr.'s confidant and the benefactor behind 1961's Freedom Rides, 1964's Freedom Summer, and much else; the latter, as a writer with roots in the proletarian literature movement of the 1930s. Their shared frame of mind was defiant. "A whole people has been disenfranchised, subhumanized and put through culturally crippling experiences," Belafonte argued in an *Ebony* interview. "How did we as a people survive? We have survived through our dignity and integrity and a rich sense of humor." Attaway laid out the aims for the show in related terms: "Negro humor has often been loud and bitter. In the show we tried to give the reasons behind the bitterness and what has grown out of the bitterness."

For *A Time for Laughter*, Belafonte and Attaway brought together a comic wrecking crew without precedent on American television. Their cast stretched from Chitlin Circuit veterans like George Kirby, Redd Foxx, Pigmeat Markham, and Moms Mabley to relative newcomers like Dick Gregory and Godfrey Cambridge. Foxx and Mabley, who had seventy-five years of stage experience between them, were making their prime-time TV debuts—proof of the cultural segregation the program sought to challenge. According to Richard, he snuck into the project through the back door. "They wanted Bill Cosby," he explained sheepishly. "He was contractually committed so they took me. There was a time in my career when it wouldn't have mattered. For about a year I was Bill Cosby."

A Time for Laughter schooled Richard in his own history, his own dilemmas. Narrated by Sidney Poitier, the show suggested that, when it came to blacks, comedy in America had developed along two tracks. One track was the tradition of blackface minstrelsy, here presented as a story of theft and caricature. The program began with the legendary meeting, around 1830, of black stable hand Jim Crow and the white minstrel "Daddy" Rice: it showed Rice emulating Crow's dance steps, then scoped outward to a gang of white minstrels blacking up with burnt cork, creating a grotesque counterfeit of what they had seen. When Jim Crow protested, "That ain't fair," the blackface minstrels responded unnervingly, "Now that ain't fair, yuk, yuk, yuk." The echo telegraphed a larger, weighty history of unequal interchanges, in which questions of fairness were laughed away. At the close of the segment, a chorus of blackface performers belted out, "And dat's how darkies was born"—a shockingly harsh illustration of how white audiences had wrested black images away from actual black people.

The second track of black comedy, infinitely preferable by the lights of *A Time for Laughter,* encompassed the performances that blacks had reserved solely for themselves. "Negro humor has stayed home," Poitier explained. "And through generations of fermentation it has become a heady wine rarely tasted by the outside world." *A Time for Laughter* announced that now, in 1967, the time had come for everyone in America to put away the cheap imitations and sample the real stuff. It entered a pool hall, where Redd Foxx was irreverently dressing down the civil rights movement: "Somebody hit you upside the head with an axe handle, and all you're supposed to do is lay there and hum, 'We shall overcome'?" It sat in the courtroom of Judge Pigmeat Markham, who delivered his verdict by whacking the plaintiff with a bladder balloon. It dallied in a barbershop, where a manicurist and a Black Muslim bantered freely. If blackface minstrelsy tended to flatten black life into a cartoon of itself, *A Time for Laughter* revealed the variety of the black community and the streetwise wit of those within it.

Richard might genuinely have wondered where he fit into this two-track model of black comedy. Alone among the comics assembled for the special, he was a crossover performer first and foremost, with a taste for physical comedy and surrealism that was easier to link to the hash-brownie spirit of the counterculture than to the "heady wine" of the black tradition. He wasn't shucking and jiving, exactly, but neither was he in the company of older comics like Foxx, Markham, or Moms Mabley. Nor did he fit in with the more recent "humor of the revolution." There was nothing in Richard's act that compared with the defiance of Dick Gregory, recounting from a jail cell his tussle with a southern cop: "He said, 'You'll make this march over my dead body.' I said, 'Baby, that wouldn't be a bad route.'"

On the special, Richard played a version of his frequent *Merv Griffin* persona, the novice out of his depth. Here he was a young funeral director fumbling through the eulogy of a man he never knew, casually taking up a seat on the coffin and crossing his legs to make himself comfortable. Mostly he was a victim of his own improvisatory spirit, his inability to stick with the safety of cliché. "The Lord giveth and he taketh away," he started. "You might say he's a sort of an Indian giver. Life is not a bowl of cherries. No, life is just a big bowl and it's up to us to fill it up with anything we want to fill it with. Now John—he chose to fill his bowl with old beer cans. That's his bowl!" Richard's performance was a solid piece of character-based humor, but in its goofy tone, it was also an outlier in the special. As the *Chicago Defender* judged, it "would be equally at home in any color scheme."

A Time for Laughter cut Richard to the quick. Observing his fellow comics do their thing, he felt that his career had been missing a dimension. "Working in a show like the Belafonte special has convinced me I've got a long way to go to really make it," he told TV critic Harvey Pack just after the show wrapped.

A few months later, in an *Ebony* interview, Richard chose to speak the truth about his past for the first time with a reporter. Whether he'd experienced some sort of political awakening or had simply grown frustrated by the game he'd been playing, he let go of the usual euphemisms and canned answers. When asked the standard question about where he came from, he answered that he had lived in a brothel until he was fifteen. The interviewer, a black woman, was "shocked by his lie." Richard laughed hysterically. The reporter implored him to be serious, and he parried by reading the situation perfectly. "Your serious and my serious are two different seriouses," he told her. It wasn't just white America that couldn't absorb, or stomach, the truth of his life.

The interviewer might be forgiven for thinking that Richard was pranking her. In the hours they'd spent together, he had, variously, run into the middle of the intersection of Hollywood and Vine and started directing traffic (for which a motorcycle cop awarded him a ticket); hopped into an empty bathtub fully clothed to demonstrate his creative process; and "proven" that he was making a documentary on dogs by training the lens of his sixteen-millimeter camera on a coil of excrement on his lawn. Still, a more contemplative Richard was poking out of the hijinks. When asked to reflect on his career, he said, "I never thought about not making it," then paused. "But the *it* has nothing to do with show business. The *it* I'm trying to make is me. Who am I?"

After *A Time for Laughter*, Richard's life took two dramatic turns. Onstage he delved into the more color-coded parts of his past, developing what *Billboard* called "vignettes of a boyhood in a not-too-genteel neighborhood": his first sketches on his Peoria circle of friends and their struggles with the curfew date from this period. Personally, he spun into a crisis without compare, in length and severity, with his life's earlier rough patches. Drifting away from his earlier act as a comedian, he also drifted away from his commitments in toto, consequences be damned.

His relationship with Maxine, nine months pregnant and about to give birth, was the first to go. While she focused on the child-to-be and the future life of their family, he acted as if he had no obligations to her, haunting nightclubs and gambling with friends until the early morning. In his defense, Richard claimed that he "could barely commit to being me. How could I give her more? But the more I said no, the more adamant she became. The only reason we stayed together was because neither of us had any other place to go." The relationship hit its breaking point when, just a matter of days from having their child, Maxine went on a reconnaissance mission to the Daisy and caught Richard with another woman in his arms. At that, even the adamant Maxine finally threw up her hands.

On April 24, 1967, Maxine was at a friend's home and, feeling the pangs of labor, was rushed to the hospital; she gave birth soon after. Richard, meanwhile, was in a world of his own—wandering outside that evening, his eyes trained on a gently looming harvest moon that looked like a "big orange balloon" or a "big orange titty" and was teasing him: "Hey, Rich, what's going on? Why don't you come and get me?" He jumped in his car and chased the full moon south toward Mexico. He drove as if "holding on to a rope," and that rope pulled him back to the red-light districts of his past. By the time the moon disappeared in the light of day, Richard was in Tijuana, drinking and partying with a few "pretty little whores." He was looking to blot out Maxine—her demands, the pressures of building a family—and the partying did the job. For four or five days, he devoted himself to oblivion.

U.S. Customs officers killed his high, and quickly, when at the border they searched his car and person for drugs and found an ounce of pot—part of a crackdown on the Tijuana–San Ysidro border that seized more than sixteen thousand pounds of marijuana in 1967. Richard disputed the charge in his memoir: "I was black and I'm convinced that was the reason I got stopped. . . . There wasn't even enough to roll a joint." Whatever the material evidence, he soon found himself in jail, charged with possession of marijuana. Richard stewed in jail for six days before he was reminded, by a deputy, that he had been booked with thousands of dollars on his person, more than enough to post bail. He bought his way out of jail time.

When he arrived back in Los Angeles, it was as the father of a baby girl named Elizabeth—and it was without a place to live. By splitting the first two weeks of their child's life between a Tijuana brothel and a San Diego jail, Richard had done an unparalleled job of demonstrating his unfitness for parenthood, and Maxine made him leave their Beverly Hills home. He decamped to the Sunset Towers West, a complex that claimed to provide "the most luxurious apartment[s]" on "the famed Sunset Strip," with "country-resort living" and hotel-quality service for its residents. Richard remembered it, by contrast, as a "home for a hodgepodge of Hollywood dreamers, schemers, and hustlers," and he seems to have been dead-on about the desperation in the air. In the year after he lived there, one resident—a producer of *noir* and horror films—shot himself in the head. Another resident, also a Hollywood producer, would later hijack a Chicago-bound plane and demand half a million dollars in small bills and safe harbor in the Bahamas. (He got neither.)

Richard was himself a sharp-elbowed wreck during his stay at the Sunset Towers West. He hooked up with a drug dealer he called Dirty Dick, and it was not unusual for him to snort as much as two hundred dollars' worth of cocaine a day, or roughly the full amount he commanded for a night's work. Around 11:30 on the night of July 26, 1967, Richard walked into the lobby of the Towers fresh from a session at Dirty Dick's and "fairly well fucked up." He asked for his messages and his mail. Fabian Tholkes, the hotel's auditor and night clerk, gave him his messages but couldn't give him his mail right away: the mailbox required his key, which the Towers management had taken from Richard for nonpayment of his rent. Richard was discovering, for the first time, that he had been locked out of his room. Tholkes offered to talk to the manager about the missing key and began to patch through the call, but before he could follow through, an older white woman asked Tholkes for *her* mail. Tholkes made the fateful decision to give Rose Pritcherson her mail before settling the matter of Richard's key.

In an average tone of voice, Richard muttered a single word: *discrimination.* It was his last restrained action of the night. He reached across the hotel desk, grabbed Tholkes by the necktie until he gagged, and punched the bespectacled clerk in the left eye. The lens shattered, and pieces of glass sliced into Tholkes's eye. By this point, Sunset Towers manager Wayne Trosper had picked up the phone call from Tholkes. Instead of hearing Tholkes's voice inquiring about Richard's mail key, he caught the sound of commotion. Trosper, a former Las Vegas policeman, rushed into the lobby and, seeing Richard only, asked what the trouble was.

"Who are you?" Richard asked back.

"The manager," Trosper answered. He caught sight of his hotel clerk, slinking in the background with a bloody towel held over his face.

Richard asked Trosper, "How would you like some of the same thing?"

Trosper got off the best line of the evening: "Not in my lobby. I just redid it today." He laid his suit jacket on a safe—as cautious about his suit as about his renovated hotel—and told Richard not to leave.

Richard went outside and stood on the hotel entrance's top step. Trosper circled him and stood on the bottom step, blocking his way. The two traded insults.

Without warning, Richard lunged at Trosper and smashed Trosper's face with his fist. Then he ran to the street and paused at a newspaper vending box. Juiced by the cocaine, Richard picked up the vending box and tried to heave it at Trosper; it was chained to the ground, and clattered at his own feet. The Battle of the Sunset Towers West had progressed from intemperate explosion to blustery farce, with Richard reprising the role of failed weight lifter from his pantomimes. Sirens could be heard approaching from the west.

Richard pulled a knife from his pocket and told Trosper, "I am going to kill you." He slashed Trosper across his cheek, then pulled out a fork to complete his utensil set. Trosper grabbed Richard's arms, twisted them backward at the wrists, and removed the fork from one hand and the knife from the other. Weaponless, Richard ran down Sunset Boulevard—and into the arms of the Sheriff's Department. He was saved, for the night, from his own capacity for making trouble.

It was a night of random wastage that was, in other ways, not random at all. In the army, Richard had rehearsed the threat "I am going to kill you." At the Café Wha?, he had rehearsed attacking someone with a fork. Throughout his life, he was cursed by the combination of his sensitivity to racial prejudice and his combustible temper. For Richard, "discrimination" could explain so much—how quick Trosper was to lock him out of his room, or how slow Tholkes was to settle the matter of his mail box key, or how matter-of-factly Trosper handled Richard in the lobby and outside. In cross-examination at a preliminary hearing about the incident, Richard's lawyer suggested that Trosper had been terminated by the Las Vegas Police Department for police brutality. (The judge never let Trosper answer the allegation.) And in his memoir, Richard claimed that Tholkes taunted him into a fight with "Come on, nigger. Come on and try it."

The court record, however, does not mention that statement. And it's also true that, under the influence of cocaine, Richard was not exactly the most reliable narrator. Tholkes ended up with a lacerated cornea and permanent loss of vision in his left eye—an injury disproportionate to the slight Richard suffered, whatever it was. Booked on suspicion of assault with a deadly weapon, Richard was silent as Tholkes, Trosper, and Tholkes's ophthalmologist gave testimony in his preliminary trial. Whether because he was advised against it by his attorney or because he couldn't, in his current state, give a good account of himself, he was not deposed to offer his side of the story.

Three days after his mute performance at the preliminary hearing, Richard ran out of words in a still more perilous location—onstage at the Aladdin hotel in Las Vegas. It was the primal scene of his comic development, full of shock and shame and feelings of indecent exposure. He would return to the ill-fated act again and again in interviews, as if his failure there held the secret to his future success. In the words of journalist Mark Jacobson, the incident is "the pith of Pryor legend." But Richard was loose with the details, which has lent an air of mystery to the legend. He dated his crack-up anywhere from 1967 to 1970. Sometimes, as in his memoir, he turned the episode into a story about his own haplessness—how he walked onstage, stared at his audience, wondered whom they were looking at, and walked off to find the answer. Other times, he turned it into a story of half-crazed defiance—how he stripped naked, ran into the casino, jumped onto the 21 table, and announced himself with a single word, "Blackjack."

Richard's incident at the Aladdin, it turns out, was really two different incidents: an onstage nervous breakdown and a bold, if kamikaze-like, career move, separated by ten days of normal routine. All told, his two-part Aladdin fiasco was more complicated and audacious than he let on, or than the received myth suggests.

The Aladdin was upmarket but loose-limbed, and hardly as strait-laced or middle American as Richard's stories would later imply. It had opened only the year before and had made a name for itself as one of Vegas's most extravagant hotels. It boasted a cavernous interior decorated in Ali Baba reds and blues, an eighteen-hole golf course, and (its signature) a fifteen-story sign, in the shape of Aladdin's lamp, that required forty thousand lightbulbs to operate. Yet, in its programming, the Aladdin was on the adventurous side. Redd Foxx was a Bagdad Room mainstay. Other comics who preceded Richard to the five-hundred-seat Bagdad Room included Godfrey Cambridge, the tart and sophisticated black stand-up, and Rusty Warren, the "risqué redhead" who drew an audience of brassy older women with her tales of men who couldn't perform and women who couldn't get enough. Foxx and Warren even recorded two adults-only albums in 1967 in the same theater that was the scene of Richard's mental disintegration—an indication that playing the Aladdin was not the same as playing the *Kraft Summer Music Hall*.

The full bill during Richard's run at the Aladdin was a typical mix of comedy, novelty, and sexual sizzle. He was scheduled to share the stage with Pat Collins, a curvy hypnotist known as the "blonde beguiler," and the hotel's in-house topless revue. He would earn three thousand dollars a week, or double his usual rate for nightclub work, for three weeks of work at the regular Vegas grind. Two performances a night, seven days a week. The full shows were to run like clockwork from 9:00 p.m. until 5:00 a.m.

In mid-September 1967, Richard was not equipped to be a gear in someone else's clockwork. A little after 1 a.m. on opening night, after the first seven minutes of his second set, he lost himself. According to Dick Kanellis, the Aladdin's entertainment director, Richard left the stage and drove back to Los Angeles without the courtesy of an explanation. His own account corroborates Kanellis's, but offers some measure of his rationale. "I was doing material that was not funny to me," he told the *Los Angeles Times* in retrospect. "I saw how I was going to end up. I was false. I was turning into plastic." Or, as he told *Rolling Stone*, more picturesquely: "The life I was leading, it wasn't me. I was a robot. 'Beep. Good evening, ladies and gentlemen, welcome to the Sands Hotel. Maids here are funny. Beep' . . . I didn't feel good. I didn't feel I could tell anybody to kiss my ass, 'cause I didn't have no ass, you dig. My ass was on my face."

According to his memoir, Richard had spied Dean Martin at one of the front tables, staring at him and waiting expectantly for the first laugh of the evening. "Who was Dean looking at?" Richard wondered, then staggered for the answer. His eyes traveled across the sea of faces, all staring back at him. "I didn't know who Richard Pryor was. And in that flash of introspection when I was unable to find an answer, I crashed," he recalled. Rather than have compassion for himself, he considered his tuxedoed self with a cold eye: "I imagined what I looked like and got disgusted."

After a pause, he asked the crowd, "What the fuck am I doing here?" No answer was forthcoming, so he turned and headed off the stage. But even his exit was a botch: he had wandered to the side of the stage that had no true opening, just a narrow ledge beside the curtain.

Someone yelled, "You can't get through there!"

"I can get through there, believe me!" he screamed back. Richard wasn't about to cross the stage again. He crept along the thin lip of wood, hugging the curtain as if it were a sheer rock face, toward an Exit sign that beckoned weakly.

He emerged on the other side some interminable seconds later, his nose scraped and bleeding. "Fuck, fuck, fuck" was all he could say. He picked up his clothes backstage, climbed into his '65 Mustang, and pointed it straight for Los Angeles.

Richard soon heard from Jim Murray, his agency's man in Las Vegas. Murray was twenty years older than Richard and his regular agent, Sandy Gallin, and had a show business sensibility shaped by the likes of Frank Sinatra and Don Rickles. He had shrugged off Richard's bad behavior at the Sands, but this was too much. "You'll never work in this town again," Murray threatened, then thought aloud about the blowback from Richard's behavior. "What about us? What about our reputation?"

Richard was unyielding. "Everybody was worried about themselves. I said, 'Fuck all you motherfuckers, I'm worried about *me*.'" And in response to the demand that he needed to go back to the job, he scoffed. "I just knew I couldn't work, not then, not that way," he said. He needed to look after himself, and if that meant giving up the "big time," he was ready to let it go. In Richard's burnished version of the story, he faced the consequences of his actions: no more gigs in Vegas, no more work in the big time. Banishment to what *Rolling Stone* called "the minors—the low-paying, no-cover hoot-niteries you find in some major cities and college towns." In Richard's telling, his flame-out at the Aladdin became a parable of the suffering artist: he was the artist at war with his audience, his handlers, and the person he had been, and fated to be wounded grievously in each of those battles. "I was blackballed by most of the industry for two or three years after that," he said.

There are two major problems with Richard's account here. First, Richard was hardly blackballed by the entertainment industry. Post-Aladdin, he kept Sandy Gallin as his agent and, with Gallin's help, continued to land steady work in the most mainstream of venues. In 1968 he appeared on *The Tonight Show* four times, *The Ed Sullivan Show* twice, *The Pat Boone Show* five times, and the über-square *Kraft Summer Music Hall* once. He entertained soldiers at three army bases as a regular on the TV show *Operation Entertainment*. Even Vegas forgave him quickly: he returned in August 1968 to play Caesars Palace with Bobbie Gentry and José Feliciano—and he played it well. All told, his career jumped up several notches the year after the supposed fiasco. He gained a powerful manager in Bobby Roberts, who also worked with the Mamas and the Papas, and recorded his self-titled first al-

Not blackballed: Pryor onstage at Caesar's Palace in August 1968. (Courtesy of the author)

bum, for which he received a hefty advance. Though Richard wished to think of himself as the victim of a narrow-minded industry, he had a gift for ingratiation, and enough undeniable talent, that booking agents were willing to indulge him as the price of doing business.

There's a second, even more startling discrepancy between Richard's account of the Aladdin debacle and the tale told by its paper trail: he came back to Vegas. After a brief sojourn in LA, he returned to the Bagdad Room to fulfill the terms of his contract, making himself presentable for a while. The *Hollywood Reporter* enthused on September 21—six days after he walked offstage on opening night—that Richard and Pat Collins were making "just the right pairing for the Aladdin."

But after a week of performing according to script, that delicate something in Richard snapped again. According to the Aladdin's

Dick Kanellis, Richard started becoming "abusive to his audience," "crowd[ing] his dialogue with four-letter words." He insulted Vegas and the Aladdin with the sorts of obscenities that were unacceptable even in the room where Redd Foxx and Rusty Warren recorded their "adults-only" albums. As the person responsible for the hotel's entertainment, Kanellis warned Richard "at least four times" that he had to rein himself in, but to little effect.

On Sunday, October 2, Kanellis decided to roll tape on Richard's show. He wanted incontrovertible evidence of Richard's obscenities—evidence that could be presented to the American Guild of Variety Artists, in case Richard challenged the decision to terminate his contract. Kanellis got what he was looking for: Richard delivered, in the words of the *Hollywood Reporter,* enough four-letter words to "blister the ears off a longshoreman." Three days before he was set to complete his engagement, Richard was fired, with cause.

Now that the laws around obscenity have loosened dramatically, it's easy to judge Kanellis a timid soul who placed himself on the wrong side of history. But he wouldn't have been wrong to be afraid for himself and the Aladdin, and to worry about Las Vegas police shutting down the show. Richard's profanity-laced act was a great leap beyond even the blue humor of Foxx and Warren. In his 1967 Aladdin show, Foxx played with the line separating normal speech and profanity—with a shaggy-dog story about the "mother-frockers" and "cork-soakers" of New York City, and with a bluff that his name was spelled "F-U . . ."—but he never crossed that line. Any performer who, in 1967, spoke four-letter words onstage flirted with prison time or worse, and any impresario who presented such a performer could be on the hook, too.

The case of comedian Lenny Bruce stood as a fresh cautionary tale. Starting in the early 1960s, Bruce courted censure with his goring of a whole parade of sacred cows. He talked saucily about Eleanor Roosevelt ("the nicest tits of anyone alive"); stripped the recently widowed Jackie Kennedy of her halo (after her husband got shot in Dallas, she "was hauling ass to save her ass"); and suggested, through his Uncle Willie character, that the American family was a breeding ground for child molesters ("Let your Uncle Willie, tickle ickle ickle you . . . Don't tell Mommie or you'll break the magic charm"). In San Francisco, Los Angeles, Chicago, and New York City, the police responded by monitoring Bruce's act and locking him up for breaking the law. The comic lost his Chicago and New York City cases, and after New York City's district attorney succeeded in convicting and fining the club owner who sponsored Bruce, the comic was unemployable in Greenwich Village, his cultural base. His gigs became scarce, his performances overtaken by the minutiae of his legal troubles. On August 3, 1966, Bruce fell off the toilet seat in the bathroom of his Hollywood Hills home and collapsed onto the floor, a hypodermic needle in his arm. Police let reporters and camera crews mill around and "feed on the corpse," in the words of Bruce's biographers. The resulting photos were indelible: Bruce sprawled on the diamond-tiled floor, naked except for the blue jeans pooled around his ankles, silenced at last. His friend Phil Spector quipped darkly that the cause of death was "an overdose of police."

Strangely, Richard rarely talked about how, Lenny Bruce–like, he had unleashed himself at the Aladdin. His earlier breakdown onstage, for everyone to see, was seared into his memory with a vividness that made it easy to recall, and with a comic aspect—Richard's bumbling stage exit—that may have made it easier to retail, too. Yet while his first Aladdin breakdown pointed backward in his career, towards his struggles with the "Mickey Mouse material that [he] couldn't stomach any more," the second incident at the Aladdin was prophetic. It pointed forward, toward the comic Richard became in the early 1970s—the comic for whom profanity was the grease that lubricated his monologues and helped them move. This impulse within Richard put him on a parallel but separate path from Lenny Bruce, who used obscenities to spike his social commentary, and especially to bring the mighty down to earth. For Richard, obscenities were not usually leveraged for an explicit point; they were just an indispensable part of how he expressed himself, like meat cleavers to a butcher or roses to a florist.

It was telling that Richard turned to profanity onstage at the same time that he was committing, in his mind, to comedy that was character-driven and rooted in the black community. His trip to Peoria in October 1966 had cemented his sense that his family and old circle of friends deserved to be at the center of his comic material. His work on *A Time for Laughter* had deepened his awareness of the political character of black comedy, and had made him hesitate at what he saw as the inauthentic, pandering elements in his own act. He had desperately wanted to be on TV, but now that he was a regular player on variety and talk shows, he bridled at their restraining orders. Shortly before his engagement at the Aladdin, he complained to *Ebony*: "Be clean. They always say 'be clean.' They want you to be something that really doesn't exist at all." For Richard, life itself was unclean, profane. He couldn't be clean and be true to the characters he wished to portray. And the very first character he needed to portray, the first character he needed to approach with utter candor, was himself. *That* was who came onstage at the Aladdin on the night of October 2, ready to reveal himself, and it wasn't meant to be pretty.

In only one interview, with Cynthia Dagnal Myron of the *Chicago Sun-Times*, in 1978, did Richard tell a version of the Aladdin story that covered, from his perspective, the second part of the actual episode. According to Myron, her interview with Richard had an intense, focused quality from the start: it was as if Richard were speaking directly to her—a black female reporter almost exactly the age he was in 1967—rather than to the readership of the *Sun-Times*. Richard intuited that Myron was, as he had been, dazzled by the glittering prizes of a nearly all-white world, and he wanted her to understand how dangerous her path was, how fraught with suicide traps.

He told her that he had felt, in Vegas, like he was choking to death each time he walked through the kitchen "like a good little boy" to get to the stage. One day he decided he'd had enough. He told the Aladdin management that this would be his final performance, and beat back their protestations. Then he went onstage and delivered a performance so angry and profane that it was sure to offend, and it did: he was pulled offstage mid-act, and the Aladdin's staff rushed up to him. Richard braced himself and, lifting his chin, told them that he couldn't be a man and work for them anymore. They looked into his eyes, and whatever they saw disarmed them. They backed off.

Richard felt the hand of God in his life, raising him up and protecting him. After he went back through the kitchen and stepped outside, the world seemed transformed. For a precious moment, a calm settled over him. His eyes scanned the desert horizon. The trees, perhaps stirred by the wind, were bowing to him.

The magic moment didn't last long. In November, a scheduled appearance on *The Ed Sullivan Show* sent Richard into a nervous "flittamajitter," and he didn't show up—the showbiz equivalent of standing up the Queen of England. Sullivan treated Richard like a *monstre sacré* whose bad behavior was to be expected: an extra clause was simply stitched into his next contract, specifying that Sandy Gallin was required to be in New York City for every engagement and that Gallin was personally responsible for his client's appearance at rehearsal and taping. Richard remained in the show's good graces.

Whatever sympathy and forgiveness Richard experienced in his professional life, elsewhere it was harder to come by. In mid-November he was ordered by the court to pay Maxine's legal fees and a regular child support payment of three hundred dollars a month. A month later, on the first day of his trial on the Sunset Towers assault charge, he treated the court as he had treated Ed Sullivan, with a no-show, and the judge issued a bench warrant for his immediate arrest.

In Peoria, Richard's family was itself facing a sea of troubles. On the same day that Richard was ordered to pay child support, police raided his father's brothel at 409 West Aiken and charged him with being a keeper of a house of prostitution. Tough to the core, Buck took the harder legal route: rather than pay a fine, he demanded a trial by jury. Meanwhile, Richard's stepmother Ann was now so ill that, even though the Illinois Supreme Court had rejected her appeal of the previous year, the court order was apparently never carried out. She took her rest at home.

On the very last day of 1967, Ann received last rites, then expired. For twenty years she had been a prostitute and a madam, but she was also a member, in good standing, of Peoria's Catholic community, and the local priests reserved St. Patrick's Church for her service. Peoria's most prominent black mortician readied the body.

When Buck called Richard with the news, his son expressed his condolences but balked at attending the funeral. "Dad, I ain't going," he said. He wasn't in a frame of mind to handle the weight of the family he'd tried so hard to escape.

"That's all right, son. You don't have to come," Buck said, baiting him. "But the next time you be on *Ed Sullivan*, it'll be a duo."

"What do you mean?"

"It'll be you telling jokes and me kicking your ass."

Richard quickly booked two plane tickets to Peoria. One was for himself, the other for the woman who accompanied him out of the destructive chaos that was 1967 and into the productive chaos that was 1968.

PART THREE

IN THE HOUSE OF PAIN

CHAPTER 11

The King Is Dead

Peoria and Los Angeles, 1968

When Richard arrived for Ann's funeral with a young white woman named Shelley Bonis at his side, he brought convincing evidence of how far he'd traveled in the six years since he'd left Peoria—and how far American culture had traveled with him.

The two had met a few months before in a bar, both togged in the costumes of the times. Shelley had pulled off a stunning go-go look: honey hair spilling to her shoulders, miniskirt levitating above her tall white-leather boots. Richard looked like some combination of hippie, pimp, and journalist. He carried a notepad and pen, and wore bell bottoms with a wide belt, from which dangled a "huge, Mad Hatter–style watch," as Shelley recalled. His pickup line was to ask for the time.

Shelley walked away, moseyed to the dance floor, and started doing what she had done, professionally, for the cameras of *Hollywood a Go-Go*: danced by herself. Richard followed the tease by approaching her with the notepad and pen.

"So what're you writing on that little notepad of yours?" Shelley asked. "You're not trying to steal my dance moves, are you?"

"Dance moves! I'm working on my act, girl."

"What kind of act?"

"My comedy act. I'm a comedian."

Something squared in Shelley's head—she was under contract with Columbia Pictures and plugged into the industry—and she said, "You're the guy who walked off the stage in Vegas. I dig that."

Richard was intrigued, and riled, by whites playing black. "You 'dig' that? Now where you comin' from, girl, talking the talk. You don't look like no nigger I know. You're not some kind of freaky bitch, are you?"

Shelley punched back that she was simply "hip to change": "The Man ain't the Man no more—dig?"

"Don't get all political on me, bitch," Richard said. "I know who the fuck I am. I'm a nigger. And I know who the fuck you're not: a nigger."

"You don't know a thing about me, funny man. Not a thing."

Richard didn't know, for instance, that Shelley was the daughter of Danny Kaye's manager, a child of liberal Hollywood. Or that she was the sort of Brooklyn-born Jewish girl who loved black culture more than her own—that she felt herself a "sister" in her very soul. Or that she had already fallen for him with his first ridiculous question about the time, and was ready to take a deeper plunge.

Just days after they met, Shelley moved into the small cottage, at the tail end of Wonderland Avenue in Laurel Canyon, where Richard had settled after the Sunset Towers fiasco. The cottage was only a three-mile ride up from the Sunset Strip, but it was a world away from that neon carnival. The Canyon was rusticated—home to screech owls, coyotes, and a pack of folk-rock troubadours hoping, in the famous words of one of their own, to "get ourselves back to the garden."

It was steadily becoming home, too, to the "heads and "freaks" of LA's counterculture (*head* and *freak* being terms much preferred, within the community, to the epithet *hippie*). Music engineer Robert Marchese, who later produced Richard's first album, lived nearby in what he called a "classic psychedelic pad." Each room was painted scrupulously, or fanatically, with a different color scheme: Marchese's bedroom was split between orange and magenta down to the mismatched screws—one orange, one magenta—on the light switch. A few months after Shelley joined Richard, musician Frank Zappa came to the Canyon and settled into a dim, cavernous house known as the "Log Cabin," which quickly became, according to the Canyon's chief chronicler, a "rock-and-roll salon and Dionysian playground," drawing a steady stream of freaks from the San Fernando Valley to Hollywood. Its goings-on became part of a richly embroidered legend of rock 'n' roll decadence: "Talents as imposing as Mick Jagger and as whimsical as Alice Cooper were stabled, jam-sessioned, fed, and fellated while the undisputed master of the house . . . reigned as the 'freak daddy' of the whole show."

Richard was neither freak nor freak daddy, but he and Shelley inhaled the Canyon's heady romantic spirit. Shelley lit incense, wore love beads, pattered around barefoot, and, in Richard's words, "made me feel free." They made a sport of the rocks lying around the cottage—giving them as presents to one another, kissing them, imagining them in conversation—and then laughed at the deliriousness of it all.

Then the world outside their cottage came calling—threatening, in the person of Buck, an ass-kicking for good measure—and the lovers packed themselves off for Ann's funeral in the dead-of-winter Midwest.

On the day of the funeral, the temperature fell to fourteen below. Two hundred friends and relatives filled St. Patrick's Church; a soloist's voice rose above the hum of the organ. Ann was laid out in a fur-lined coat, her usually straightened hair braided in cornrows.

Buck was neither a religious man nor one to stand on ceremony. Inside the limousine as it traveled to St. Joseph's Cemetery, Richard held his father and tried to give him strength: "Pop, don't cry, please." Buck cut the tender moment short: "Okay, son. But if it get any colder, they're going to have to bury the bitch by themselves."

At the cemetery, the pallbearers hoisted Ann's casket to the grave site. They wore gray gloves, and after lowering the casket into the grave, they removed their gloves and dropped them into it. The preacher began delivering a eulogy over the casket, only to be interrupted by a shivering Buck. "The dirt. The dirt. Throw the dirt," he muttered through clenched teeth. "It's cold, preacher. The dirt." Even at his wife's funeral, Buck would be Buck—"brutally honest," as his son later observed.

After the service, the whole family repaired for a reception at the large house that Richard had bought for his father a few years earlier, at 1319 Millman. A photograph from the reception suggests how Ann's death rippled differently across the family. Buck and June, Ann's daughter from earlier in her life, sit in front, their faces drawn and tight-lipped in grief. Behind them, Shelley and Richard's aunt Maxine beam at each other as if sharing a private joke. Richard's teenage cousin Denise smiles with a look of nervous excitement. Richard wears a powder-blue turtleneck and white windbreaker, and connects to the camera with confident eyes and an easy grin, ready even in hard times for his close-up.

A family reshuffling itself after Ann's death. Front row: LeRoy "Buck" Pryor and Ann's daughter June. Back row: Barbara McGee, Denise Pryor, Maxine Pryor, Shelley Bonis, Richard Pryor. (Courtesy of Barbara McGee)

With Ann buried, there were some new introductions to be made. Buck had fathered three children with three different women while married to Ann, and as long as she was alive, he had been able only to watch those children from afar—by standing across from a schoolyard while one of them played, or from the inside of his station wagon. Now they could be brought into the fold.

Buck's daughter Sharon came timidly to the door at 1319 Millman. She knew that Buck was her father, but aside from an overpowering hug at Ann's viewing—"he squeezed me like he was going to squash me to death"—she had never had any physical contact with him in her thirteen years. A small white poodle yapped at her ankles. She saw Buck sitting with the family at a table near the entrance to the house.

"Let my baby in," he said. "Look at my baby!" Buck, who needed comforting, comforted her. "Come on over here—that dog ain't going to bother you." She skittered over, and he led her around the house, introducing her with great pleasure to the extended family. Marie was ministering to a kettle of neckbones in the kitchen; Richard and Shelley were nesting together like lovebirds in the living room. Then Buck sat down again and put Sharon on his lap, where she stayed.

When Sharon was leaving, Buck insisted to her mother, "Please don't let this be the last time I see her." Sharon was in sixth grade and, in the eyes of her school and her mother, who had ten other children to handle, she was a problem child, always tilting against figures of authority. The freshly bereaved Buck soon took her under his wing. "Baby, everything's going to be all right," he reassured her when they spent time together in the next few months. "Ain't nobody gonna mess with my little girl again."

On January 13, Richard and Shelley were married in a quick impromptu ceremony at a small chapel in Las Vegas. They consecrated, in the city of Richard's recent embarrassment, a relationship that sometimes played out as a political allegory of late-1960s America. Shelley was the white romantic, Richard the black cynic. It was Shelley who had avidly read Malcolm X, Angela Davis, and the Black Panthers, and who believed that a new day was dawning and that the love she felt for Richard was proof of it. Richard, meanwhile, had been hardened by his family and his struggles with school, the army, and show business—every institution he'd come into contact with. He tended to shield himself from disappointment by expecting the worst—of people and of his country.

Still, a piece of Richard longed to believe, as Shelley believed, in what was pure between them and how it might spill beyond their cottage in Laurel Canyon—and here, again, the two lovers were emblematic of larger hopes and tensions. Around the country, the Black Power movement and the largely white counterculture were engaged in a delicate, circling dance, as each group wondered what they might give to, or gain from, the other. In Los Angeles in 1967, white hippies had sought to bring together "the city's two hip communities" by organizing two "love-ins" at parks in Watts, with tellingly mixed results. The first love-in drew a crowd of seven thousand whites and blacks, who danced together to a mix of blues and rock groups; the alternative paper *Open City* raved that the hippies "short-circuited the ghetto's mental hate syndrome with smiles, freaky renaissance clothes . . . and an open attitude which became contagious." The second love-in, more poorly attended, was disrupted by a stone thrown at a white photographer and a "get whitey" speech from the stage—and the hippies, discouraged, left Watts for good.

For their part, black militants looked at the counterculture and saw two things at once: some of the least racist and most engaged people in America, and some of the most privileged and committedly naïve people in America. A case in point: the *Los Angeles Free Press* and *Open City* ran some of the most detailed and sympathetic coverage of the Watts riots and the Black Power movement, but they also published articles like "Hippie: The New Nigger" or "Diggery Is Niggery," which appeared to turn black suffering into someone else's plaything. H. Rap Brown expressed a typical ambivalence when, in a 1967 interview, he called the hippies "politically irrelevant," but added that he wished "all white Americans were like the hippies, because they ARE peaceful, and that's more than can be said for most honkies."

Richard's stand-up was one of the great beneficiaries of this dance between Black Power and the counterculture. In 1968, performing for Troubadour audiences that, for him, were half white and half black, he invented a style that was as far-out as Frank Zappa and as defiant as H. Rap Brown, and was catalyzed by the fusion of the two movements. On the one hand, the freewheeling ethic of the counterculture shaded Richard's act with irony, making his more political moves seem provisional and subject to revision. On the other, the militancy of the Black Power movement sharpened his zaniness, giving it a point: his improvisations could cut you open with their poignancy or shock you with their bitterness. For years, Richard's comedy had set itself apart from the conflicts of the times; now it drew on the energy of those tensions and played them out in spectacular fashion.

He needed his art because, offstage, the chaos was sometimes too much. When news of Martin Luther King Jr.'s assassination reached Richard on April 4, 1968, he was between sets at Mister Kelly's nightclub in Chicago. The second set was immediately canceled, and everyone was warned to take caution and head home. Richard did the opposite. He smoked a joint with Jeff Wald, the booker at Mister Kelly's. Then the two hopped in a car and "drove around Chicago like lunatics," Wald remembered. They felt aimless, high on grass and miserable about the state of the world, and were curious to see where their careening would take them. Richard was sobbing uncontrollably; he couldn't believe how crazy America had become. The two heard shots fired around them but raced through the streets anyway. It was the beginning of a riot that would wreathe the streets in smoke and tear gas, and leave at least nine black Chicagoans dead.

The death of King reverberated in Richard. He canceled a scheduled appearance on *The Ed Sullivan Show* and returned to Los Angeles, where two weeks later he performed in front of an audience of ten thousand at a Martin Luther King Jr. memorial benefit at the Hollywood Bowl. The tone of the King event was set by actor Rod Steiger, who proclaimed that "we are here today because of a man with a purpose and a dream. We are gathered for one reason and one reason alone—to raise money to help fulfill that dream and that purpose. We mean to guarantee that a future shall exist without ignorance and without prejudice." These were high-minded thoughts, and Steiger was joined in his solemn tribute by entertainers ranging from Jimmy Durante and Edward G. Robinson to Bill Cosby and Barbra Streisand.

Richard punctured the mood. He looked out at the largest live audience of his career, one assembled to mourn one of the most grievous losses in American history, and spoke with the brazenness of his father at his stepmother's grave. "All these people here are giving money," he observed, "but if your son gets killed by a cop, money don't mean shit." There was a collective gasp at both the four-letter word and the bitter sentiment it carried. The show, after all, was meant to embody King's vision and raise money for King's Southern Christian Leadership Conference and the Urban League, two organizations that represented the civil rights establishment. Richard, meanwhile, was refusing to turn the other cheek. He was pointing his audience's attention to those, less sainted than King, who had been killed by police bullets in the riots following King's assassination, and he was refusing to forgive.

For Richard, it was almost like a public "coming out": no one with a decent pair of ears could mistake him for Bill Cosby any longer. Forty-five KLAC listeners withdrew their pledges in protest at his remarks.

The death of Martin Luther King Jr. marked the beginning of an extraordinarily productive four months for Richard as an artist. His manager, Bobby Roberts, had negotiated a fifty-thousand-dollar, two-album contract with Mo Ostin's Reprise Records, and Richard generated a flurry of new routines for his vinyl debut. For the first time since his breakdown at the Aladdin, he was able to pour his volatile emotions into the channel of comedy, where they remained so intense that his act took on fresh vitality, audacity, and outrage. The salty characters of his teenage years in Peoria glided and swaggered on the stage of the Troubadour, where they were joined by a wild assortment of Uncle Toms and black militants, faith healers and mainline ministers, prison guards and stage directors. And at the center of this new world was the newly unbuttoned character of Richard himself. "Strange, unconked and outspokenly glib, Pryor exudes the essence of every street-corner gang comedian who ever did his schtick while keeping one eye out for a prowl car"—so wrote Nat Freedland in the *Los Angeles Free Press* in April 1968, catching in print for the first time the stage persona that made Richard famous.

At his most freeform, the new Richard might work an angle like a jazz soloist working a motif. In one riff during his mid-April engagement at the Troub, he tried to describe how he felt:

> [*Funky scat-singing*] Bam-da-boom, bippidy-bop bop-da-boom!
> I got the feeling! Hunh-da-doo!
> I got the feeling, yeah! Hey!
> I feel like a . . .
>
> [*Deep-voiced, imitating Paul Robeson*] "Sometimes I feel like a . . ."
>
> [*Halting*] I feel—I don't know how I feel, man. I don't know. All I know is I feel.
>
> [*Church woman's voice*] "I feel!"
>
> [*Warming up*] I don't know how I feel, but I just—unnhh!—I feel. I feel. I really feel. Bing-bing-bing! I really feel, man.
> Them energies are coming.
>
> [*Loud sound of waves traveling down a tube, being sucked into a vacuum, then escaping into the air with the fading vibration of a tuning fork.*]
>
> And it's cool. It's cool. Hey, wow! God, man.

That's what I feel—I feel like, I feel like—God. That's a groovy feeling.

The comic had cycled, in exactly a minute, through several forms of black identity (funky dude, Paul Robeson, church lady); aligned himself with the freaks in the audience by experiencing a trip before their eyes; then lightly sent up the spiritual pretensions of that set by mocking his own sense of godhood. And while the pinballing of his mind made him seem one of the freaks himself, Richard denied that he was high, then ended by underlining his own love-hate relationship to drugs: "Dope just cut out, and leave you hanging there. Dope say 'later!' and you say, 'But dope, I wanna go *with* you." Despite the seeming randomness of the improvisation, it was all of a piece: Richard had a mind that established quick affinities, then just as quickly located the comic downside of every one—until the identity he'd just assumed had turned into an embarrassment, or a trap. No one was spared the thrust and parry, least of all him.

While "I Feel," as this bit was called, was a loose and playful mind bend, other riffs had more bite. Instead of whitewashing his past, Richard hung it out to dry. He recalled, as a child, how he didn't hesitate to use the term *nigger baby* for a small black licorice candy. For Richard, that candy, which he loved to eat, opened onto a parable of his childhood: "I used to play a game, 'Last one to the store is a nigger baby' . . . I used to run like hell myself. I didn't want to be it. I didn't know that I'd lost before the race started." He had a sharp eye for the hustle, and for what it meant to be the dupe.

The most elaborate of Richard's new sketches were around ten minutes in length, built on the multi-character template of "Rumpelstiltskin" but considerably more adult in theme. In "Prison Play," a kind of play within a play that Richard performed for an imagined audience of the incarcerated, a black blacksmith has his bicep squeezed by a swooning southern belle in an upside-down version of *Gone With the Wind*. The blacksmith gently asks her if she'd like to feel his ass, and then the belle nearly faints, joined now in her swooning by her mother. The play within a play races to an unexpectedly happy ending: the blacksmith proposes to the belle, and the belle's brother, a cavalier of the old sort, approves the union in the name of "true freedom and true love." That's the breaking point for the redneck prison guard, though, who stops the performance, having been advised beforehand that "the nigger dies." "Nobody leave," he shouts. "I want a dead nigger out here!" Richard pauses, then reveals through the character of this prison guard the madcap logic of scapegoating: "If I don't get me a dead nigger here, we gonna hang one of them homosex-u-als!"

Richard's creative explosion now had to be brought to market—recorded, edited, packaged, sold—and here the complications began. His manager, Bobby Roberts, hired Robert Marchese, a recording engineer who had apprenticed with Phil Spector, as the producer of Richard's album, and the two felt a quick bond: Marchese had grown up in a tough, racially mixed inner-city neighborhood in Pittsburgh, and he was game for Richard's wildest and most provocative flights. At their first meeting, Marchese promised Richard a "motherfucking dynamite album" and pledged that "you'll hear everything you say, and it'll be live." Marchese then recorded four nights of Richard's shows at the Troub in late July 1968.

Afterward, Marchese had a surplus of material to work with. At the Troub, Richard had performed, in addition to "Prison Play," a number of other newly conceived playlets. "T.V. Panel Show" was a calmer, if equally iconoclastic, sketch in which Richard impersonates a potpourri of guests—a bloviating anthropologist, a sheepish minister, a fiery black nationalist, a still-jumpy woman who has given up narcotics for God—on a late-night interview show. Their solemn conversation about the origins of man and the relationship between man and God is a thinly disguised bull session. Everyone is on this side of outlandish, and a target for satire: the former addict for her brittle devotion to God; the anthropologist for his self-serious nonsense ("Man was begat by raindrops, grew out of the grounds, uprooted himself and just walked away"); the black militant for blowing his top at the slightest provocation ("Why didn't you introduce me first, sissy?"); and the minister for his too-intimate rapport with the deity ("Often God touches me—at night. I lay in bed and I feel God touching me. It's quite marvelous").

"T.V. Panel Show" bore Richard's stamp as a satirist, which was to smuggle some sharp insights into the mouths of his all-too-human characters. God "has been cleaning up every Sunday for the last thousands of years with that religion crap. And we all know it's patootee-patootee, don't we?" remarks the anthropologist, who turns out to be a skeptic first, a blowhard second. The black militant responds with a blast of counterintuitive wisdom, one that transforms God from a huckster into something much more vulnerable: "God was a junkie, baby! He had to be a junkie to put up with all of this, you know what I mean?" Here the militant is surprisingly seconded by the minister: "God probably did take some sort of outside medication. As it states in chapter six, verse thirty-two, 'I will take unto myself what is needed.'" Strange alliances were being made in Richard's countercultural theater of the absurd. No doubt the Troub's audience relished the suggestion that God, like them, had suffered through the chaos of this world and, like them again, had found his way to dope.

Richard also performed, for Marchese's recording equipment at the Troub, the comic masterpiece of this period in his career. In the eleven-minute "Hank's Place," he took his audience into the inner sanctum of this after-hours joint in Peoria and evoked the atmosphere of his misspent youth: a world of hustlers, prostitutes, gamblers and every other form of trickster black Peoria had to offer. Character after character presents him- or herself to a young and timid Richard, who drinks in their words and their style. There is, for instance, Mr. Perkins, a carpenter who hopes Hank, as the joint's proprietor, will hire him to reupholster his craps table. His cajoling sales pitch is a soliloquy:

> See how you got them cushions up there? Now see, those cushions ain't but *that* thick . . . You got to have four to five inches of cushion up there,

> Hank. You get that cushion up there, and those dice got to come off there and tell the *truth*. They got to come off *straight* . . .
>
> Most of those guys—they get that velvet down and crease it. I'm gonna take some satin and I'm gonna whup over the top of it. I'm going to pull it tight over the table. I'm gonna put in them big four-inch tacks in there—big ones, thick enough to hold that wood together. And [those dice] can't do nothin' but tell the truth every time they come off there.

Mr. Perkins, like many of the characters of "Hank's Place," is a bullshit artist, but an artist nonetheless. He hammers on the word *truth* while speaking a language full of invention.

"Hank's Place" also marked the first time Richard brought to life a pimp onstage—and the first time he took up in his act what it meant to grow up shadowed by the world's oldest profession. "Coldblood" struts into Hank's Place and, like Richard's own father Buck, makes the young Richard feel small, pointedly calling him "Little Dick" and trapping him in a corner of the room, where the young Richard has no choice but to listen to his spiel. Yet Coldblood is, beneath the surface, a bundle of need. In a silky but wheedling voice, he appeals to the young Richard:

> You smart. You don't say nothin'. I been diggin' you. See, a lot of these niggers talk, they don't walk. But you can handle yourself.
>
> Got any money? I don't know, I thought maybe you'd get a little blow or something, might snort up something. Find out where we at or something. Might tell me something. I need to *know* something.

In "Hank's Place," Coldblood gets his comeuppance when he ventures beyond the safe audience of the powerless, voiceless Little Dick. After a shambly cop named Torsey wanders into Hank's Place, Coldblood baits him, demanding that Torsey take off his badge if he wants to prove himself in a fight. Torsey obliges in a stuttering panic of machismo ("I can take this badge off qui-qui-quicker than a bitch")—and decks Coldblood in a matter of seconds. The smooth-talking pimp is revealed to be all talk; the stammering cop, a worthy antagonist.

In Richard's version of after-hours Peoria, no one was quite the man he appeared to be.

Despite the comic riches of "Hank's Place" and the other extended sketches, Marchese didn't have an easy time assembling the "motherfucking dynamite" album he'd promised Richard. During the editing of the tracks, Richard's manager, Bobby Roberts, kept asking, worriedly, "Why didn't he do 'Rumpelstiltskin?'" Roberts wanted the *Merv Griffin* version of Richard Pryor, a comedian no more topical than the Bill Cosby of *Why Is There Air?* He agreed with the slant that *Variety*, with its distance from the counterculture, had taken on Richard's Troubadour shows: that his new material flirted with making his audience "uncomfortable or perhaps even hostile" and that "[F]or Pryor to climb into the upper brackets, he faces the difficult task of polishing his gab enough for the jabs to still penetrate, but to tickle more than they do."

So Marchese and Roberts struggled for a month to define the shape of Richard's first album. Every obscenity was cause for battle, with Roberts inevitably prevailing. The routines in which Richard ventriloquized Peoria's black community—routines in which *shit* and *motherfucker* made an occasional appearance—were deferred to the second album of Richard's contract. The first would be called, simply, *Richard Pryor*, and though it would be fashioned around the centerpieces of "Prison Play" and "T.V. Panel Show," it would be filled out with some earlier routines, like Richard's take on his time in the army. Marchese and Roberts skirmished, finally, over how the album would end. Marchese wanted to drop the curtain with a back-and-forth between Richard and a black audience member who had demanded that Richard impersonate a black militant, and who then had complained about Richard's accent. "There you go again," Richard had riposted, "telling us how to be." Roberts wanted to close on a less political yet zanier note: Richard's impression of Frankenstein's monster on LSD, in which the monster evolves from groaning lout to burbling child to Lyndon Johnson ("mah fellow Americuns"). Roberts won again: "Frankenstein" was the closer.

For all the losses in the editing suite, the album did capture the multidimensionality of Richard's comedy, his ability to throw himself into characters both ridiculous and sympathetic, and to operate outside the framework of established routines. And while "T.V. Panel" and "Prison Play" may have been less innovative and revelatory than "Hank's Place," they also expressed a demographic truth about the world Richard had inhabited for the past two years in LA. Like Black Ben the blacksmith or the black militant on the TV panel show, Richard had been a lone black man in a white-dominated world, fighting to flip the scripts he'd been given and turn his cameo into a leading role.

The "new Richard" of 1968 was perhaps showcased most vividly not on the tracks of the album but on its cover, a collaboration between Richard and the design team of photographer Henry Diltz and art director Gary Burden. An executive at Reprise Records had cautioned Burden to "be careful": Richard was "out there" and might go "off the deep end," and the company needed a "real record cover to sell the record." Fortunately, Diltz and Burden didn't take the warning too seriously. At a first photo shoot, in Burden's garage on June 1, Richard wore a Native American bead necklace and a white tunic top that was cousin to the Nehru jacket. After a few shots with the tunic, he took it off, then vamped in front of a giant American flag left over from a folksinger's photo shoot—extending his arms as if crucified, putting up his dukes, smiling while a gun was pointed at his head, and picking his nose as if that was all the respect the Stars and Stripes deserved. A watermelon was nearby, so Richard played with it, too, cradling it while giving a "Heil, Hitler" salute to the flag, and hoisting it like a quarterback aiming for an end zone thirty yards away.

These photos were satiric but also hammy and obvious, and Diltz and Burden, once they developed the film, were left wanting something more. They arrived at Richard's house in the late morning on June 29, only to find Richard asleep and in no mood for a photo shoot.

Hamming it up: Pryor in a crucifixion pose for his first album's cover shoot. (Courtesy of Henry Diltz)

"Let's do it right here in bed. This will be the album cover," Richard said lazily. Diltz and Burden balked. Richard sat up and suggested that if he were to do it, the premise would have to be something "rootsy." Burden offered to visit a friend's antique shop, which carried an assortment of aboriginal weapons and jewelry—"real authentic stuff"—and Richard brightened. For his part, he knew of a little cave in a park above Beverly Hills where they could stage the shoot.

An hour or two later, near the mouth of the cave, Burden gave Richard a loincloth, and Richard stripped and put it on; Burden gave him a bow and arrow, and Richard took the weapon; he gave Richard, more hesitantly, a brass nose ring, and Richard enthusiastically clipped it in his nose. Richard did the rest. His costume complete, he submerged himself fully into the character of the native alone on the dry plain. He squatted next to a few burnt sticks, the markers of his ostensible hearth and home, and scanned the horizon for predators. He grunted vaguely; he lifted his bow, strung it with an arrow, pointed it. Diltz snapped away with his camera. Richard didn't acknowledge the camera's presence except in the overall paranoia of his demeanor. It was as if he were trapped inside an improvisation to which he was committed with deadly seriousness.

The figure at the center of the resulting photographs—the one who was taking seriously a ludicrous premise, detonating a stereotype by embracing it with total commitment—seemed a world away from the prankster with the flag and the watermelon. Even Richard's face had changed. In the earlier photos, as in every photograph up to that point, he had been clean-shaven and fresh-faced. Four weeks later, he had raised the first scrub of a moustache and a beard. He no longer looked considerably younger than his twenty-seven years.

On the night of September 27, Richard's father, Buck, planned a private celebration for himself, his daughter, Sharon, and a tall, dark-skinned nineteen-year-old woman named Ginger who was one of four prostitutes working out of Buck's Aiken Avenue brothel a half mile away. It was a Friday night, and as was his custom on Friday nights, he indulged himself with some Kentucky Fried Chicken—a

In character: the native on the plain, embattled. (Courtesy of Henry Diltz)

meal that ran against his doctor's orders, as he'd recently been hospitalized for gastritis and advised not to eat greasy foods. Friday night was for letting go.

While his teenage niece Denise sat downstairs in the living room of 1319 Millman, Buck set the mood in his bedroom. He put on some soft jazz—he was a fan of Etta James and Nancy Wilson—and mixed his favorite drink, a highball of Seagram's Seven whiskey and 7-Up. He offered some to Ginger, his prime moneymaker after the death of Ann, and she downed a few. Then he plied his thirteen-year-old daughter with the cocktail, and though Sharon had never touched alcohol in her life, she drank it down, too.

For Sharon, the evening was the crossing of a final threshold. In the nine months after Ann's death, she had surrendered to Buck—surrendered not unlike the women who had given Buck his livelihood for twenty-five years. "I clinged to him," she remembered, "because he wasn't the one who was going to whup me or holler or scream at me, whereas my mom took action." About a month after their first meeting, Buck initiated a sexual relationship with his daughter, a sixth-grader who had not yet menstruated. After sex, he would tell her, "This is our secret, and you know Daddy loves you."

He asked her to move into his home, where she could always be but a few footsteps away, and she did. Sharon felt her mind going blank with confusion: "Why did I love him and hate him, all at the same time? Why?" Life at 1319 Millman was a string of associations: Buck sitting in his La-Z-Boy, lord of the manor; the guns decorating the walls of the house; the pretty women, with names like Ginger and Delicious, who took refuge at the house after the Aiken Avenue brothel was raided. And everywhere, the press of odors: the brackish smell of the boat Buck kept in the backyard and of the river fish that he caught, then cleaned on the porch; the musky, "whorish smell" of Buck himself, the scent of sex.

Before September 27, Sharon's relationship with her father had always been, as Buck insisted, their secret. That night he decided to pull Ginger into the conspiracy. The older girl had resisted the move—

"She's just a child," she said of Sharon—but ultimately relented. The lights were turned off, and the three were left in pitch-black darkness.

In the middle of sex, a naked Buck let out three loud belches, then collapsed as if stricken. He lay facedown on the bed. Ginger and Sharon ran downstairs in a panic and brought Denise back to the bedroom. The fingers of Buck's left hand were gripping the sheets in agony. Denise straddled her uncle from the back—Buck was so heavy that all three of them wouldn't have been able to turn his body over—and pressed below his shoulder blades with the weight of her body, hoping to release some gas from his chest and save him. But Buck never came back from his agony. By the time the ambulance arrived with his body at St. Francis Hospital at 11:25 p.m., he had died of cardiac arrest.

Or maybe, as Sharon suggested from the distance of forty-three years, he had died at the hands of the Lord: "God said, 'This is it. I'm going to take you where they take anyone in their badness.' And He took him."

The death of Buck spun the Pryor family into a welter of grief and confusion. He had, with his blunt strength, organized the force field of the family for so long that it was hard to imagine life without him. The next day, Marie was disconsolate, searching for answers. "What happened to Bucky?" she asked everyone at 1319 Millman. "Somebody tell me what happened to Bucky!"

Sharon kept her silence. She thought that if she were to tell her grandmother the truth, Marie would kill her. Her body was still in shock. Shortly, a doctor would recommend for her a course of sedatives, which she took to get through the next few days.

After Marie discovered that Buck had been in bed with Ginger, her grief ratcheted into white-hot anger. She fixed on the idea that the nineteen-year-old girl had stolen money from him—money that was now due her, since she was the Pryor family backstop. It had been sixteen years since she ran a brothel herself, but the old reflexes kicked in. She took out the gun she often kept strapped to her stocking.

"I know you got more money than this, bitch," Marie told Ginger. "You gonna give me that money." Then she was on top of Ginger—beating her, pistol-whipping her face in the same bedroom where her son had died the night before. A bruised Ginger packed her bags and left.

By the time Richard fielded a phone call from his grandmother, the death of Buck had somehow been processed into the family mythology as an example of devil-may-care swagger, with the inconvenient detail of Sharon's presence nowhere to be found. Buck had died while having sex with five women, Richard learned. (Or, as he later quipped about his father, "He came and went at the same time.") Upon hearing the news, Richard collapsed into Shelley's arms, and tears streamed from his eyes. After a while a phrase lodged in his head: "The king is dead," he mumbled. "Long live the king." There was a power vacuum and a crown being passed, it seemed, if he wanted to wear it.

When he traveled with Shelley to Peoria—their second funeral there in less than a year—the extended family was gathered in mourning at 1319 Millman. Richard's aunt Maxine, known for her warmth, approached Richard and caustically summed up her brother Buck: "Your father fucked everything. Just be glad he didn't fuck you."

"Tender thought," Richard wrote in his memoir, dripping sarcasm. But Maxine's barb might have been the most direct acknowledgment Richard ever received of how dangerous his father was, and how the abuse he took from Buck was a mere fraction of the violence Buck meted out to others over his lifetime. Richard never appears to have discovered that his father molested his sister. But it seems Maxine knew, at the least, what her brother was capable of.

In Peoria it fell to Richard, the prodigal son returned, to make the funeral preparations and pay for them. He went to the funeral home and picked out an average-looking casket, then was accused by his family of being cheap—What kind of casket is that? Did you try to save money? Didn't they have anything fancier?—when his choice was made public. "It was as if they were beating me up because they didn't know what else to do," Richard speculated. So it had been with his family when Buck was alive; so it was now that he was dead. Richard was the whipping boy who, when he tried to make good, just set himself up for another thrashing.

Buck's funeral rites were curious, if fitting for a man of his character. Since Buck had never been a churchgoing man, much less a Catholic, he could not be given a church service at St. Patrick's Church like his wife, Ann. And since he had received a Section 8 discharge from the army, he could not be honored with a veteran's burial. Phone calls were made, and a compromise was found: the funeral would be held in the gymnasium attached to St. Patrick's parochial school.

Six days after Buck's death, his open casket was placed at center court at 10:00 a.m. The bleachers were pulled in to accommodate the hundred people who came to pay their respects, no small number of whom were prostitutes. Richard later claimed on *The Tonight Show* that there was a basketball team practicing layups on the side of the gym during the service—a blatant exaggeration. But as in much of his comedy, the exaggeration magnified the truth as much as it distorted it. Buck was a man who held nothing sacred, and even his funeral was profane to the core.

Richard himself felt that his father wasn't quite dead, couldn't be dead. When he visited the casket for the last time, he expected his father to wink at him. Instead, he saw Buck laid out in his finest suit, motionless. He bent down and stashed a little money in Buck's pocket, "just in case there [was] any action up there." Money was what people everywhere seemed to appreciate, and what Richard had. After the priest who had arranged the gymnasium service concluded the burial, Richard slipped him a single five-hundred-dollar bill, the most stunning honorarium of the priest's forty-five-year career.

The burial put the body of Buck in the ground, but it couldn't remove Buck from Richard's head, where he was more alive than ever, more approachable and engaging than ever. When Richard was a child, Buck had been a source of terror. When he shared a roof with Buck as a young adult, there had been little back-and-forth, just exchanges punctuated by "yes, sir" and "no, sir." But now that Buck was dead, Richard found that "the conversation flowed" and that he "couldn't stop talking to him." Buck had transitioned fully into the spirit realm of Richard's imagination, where, like all Richard's characters, he spoke freely, without a muzzle, and traveled freely, without a leash. He wouldn't go away.

CHAPTER 12

Black Sun Rising

Los Angeles, 1968–1969

In "Super Nigger," one of his favorite routines from 1968, Richard gave a hint of the double life that he started leading after his father's death:

> Look—up in the sky! It's a crow! It's a bat! No, it's *Super Nigger!* . . .
>
> Announcer's Voice: We find Super Nigger, with his X-ray vision that enables him to see through everything except Whitey . . . disguised as Clark Washington, mild-mannered custodian for the *Daily Planet*, shuffling into Perry White's office.
>
> "Hey, man, I'm quitting, baby."
>
> "Great Caesar's Ghost! I can't talk to you now."
>
> "Talk to me, Jack. 'Cuz I'm ready to quit, man. You dig? I'm tired of doing them halls. Every time I finish, Lois Lane and them come slipping and sliding down through there and I got to do them over again. You dig it, baby? I'm through. Fire me?!"
>
> "I can't talk to you now. The warehouse is on fire!"
>
> "What warehouse?"
>
> "Warehouse 86."
>
> "Damn. That's where I got my stash. This looks like a job for Super Nigger!"

On its surface, the routine was another one of Richard's media spoofs, like his snoozer of a talk show or his war movie where Marines attack a beachhead screaming, "Apple pie!" and "Mother!" In this satire of the whiteness of superhero comics, the reporter Clark Kent was demoted to the janitor Clark Washington, shuffling in the time-honored manner of a blackface minstrel; Superman was demoted to Super Nigger, a superhero at first mistaken for the "crow" in "Jim Crow." In the routine's major twist, Richard's superhero was both less and more than the Man of Steel—less community-minded and more interesting. He fought not to advance "truth justice, and the American way" but to protect the interests of number one; the fire might destroy half of Metropolis and wouldn't bother him a bit if it didn't threaten his private cache of drugs. Super Nigger was a trickster in the tradition of Brer Rabbit, a creature of wit and appetite, comically and guiltlessly amoral.

Below the surface, Richard's routine was a parable about the trap he felt himself falling into—and the freedom he craved. The character of Clark Washington stood for the outer life that Richard, like so many working-class black men, had assumed as his fate. (Richard had even mopped the floors of a strip club as a teenager.) For all Richard's success, he felt that he was still wearing a mask of mild-mannered subservience, still cleaning up someone else's mess. What better evidence than the film and TV roles that were coming his way? The bit player supporting someone else's star production, that was Richard—the one black comedian in a variety show's stable of performers (*Kraft Summer Music Hall*), the one black musician in a rock star's entourage (*Wild in the Streets*), the one black henchman in an arch villain's crew (*The Wild, Wild West*). It didn't help that these productions were too cornpone or blinkered to connect with his artistic imagination. No wonder Clark Washington wanted to quit his day job.

Super Nigger, meanwhile, represented Richard's hidden self, the all-powerful black trickster, as marvelous as Captain Marvel and as disreputable as the *N*-word itself. "Super Nigger" was what Richard called himself when he snorted cocaine and became the life of the party. It was also what he imagined himself becoming at his best moments as an artist: the comedian who sucker-punched America in the gut when it expected to be tickled in the ribs. He yearned not just to be a star but to be like no star ever before; not just to win over Hollywood but to overturn its conventions.

There were a number of signs, heading into 1969, that Richard was growing weary of the Clark Washington role. In April 1968 there was his blunt and bitter admonition, to those assembled at the Hollywood Bowl for the Martin Luther King Jr. benefit, that "money don't mean shit." The subsequent assassination of Robert F. Kennedy, the escalating Vietnam War, the police riot in Chicago during the Democratic National Convention in the summer—all these fed, for Richard as for many others, a deepening pessimism about the American experiment. In November 1968, on a Canadian talk show as part of his first album's promo tour, he refused to engage in niceties when the conversation turned to American politics. Asked if he dreaded the possibility of segregationist George Wallace becoming president, Richard shrugged and said, "Wallace is president. Wallace has always been president."

When the talk focused on racial problems in Mississippi, Richard raised his finger and offered to draw his own personal outline of the shape of Mississippi. It was the shape of the continental United States. "The United States won't be the United States much longer," he prophesied. Democracy had been hollowed out. Even whites were becoming "slaves, just like the black man. Chicago proved that. Chicago proved the people don't matter." But wasn't he, the interviewer probed, an example of the opportunities open to blacks in America? "Sure, I made it big as a comic," Richard replied, "but I couldn't as a brain surgeon. You can make it if you think white, but not if you think black."

Faced with the stark choice, in his mind, between "thinking white" and "thinking black," Richard explored both options over the course of 1969 and 1970. He pursued two careers at once, a decision that split his personality in two. On the one hand, he kept taking on acting roles in middle-of-the-road entertainment—ABC Movies of the Week, *The Partridge Family*—even though he was uneasy with the compromises entailed. On the other hand, he committed himself to the cultural underground. He lent his talent to causes such as the Sky River Rock Festival, an outdoor music event that was held on an organic raspberry farm outside Seattle and served as the blueprint for all the let's-get-naked-and-dance festivals to come. He canceled contracts with clubs that asked him to avoid obscenities and performed at smaller clubs to largely black audiences. And he made a movie himself, called *Uncle Tom's Fairy Tales,* in which the black revolution and the sexual revolution were supposed to meet and strike up sparks. Hoping to become Super Nigger and superstar, he worked as the film's screenwriter, producer, director, and lead actor, and spent more than a year on this visionary if shambolic project.

A few weeks in late 1968 were typical of Richard's mixed itinerary. Just after Thanksgiving, he chatted with Johnny Carson on *The Tonight Show,* sharing the guest slots with comedienne Lucille Ball and then-California governor Ronald Reagan and his wife, Nancy. Two weeks later, the counterculture had its turn: Richard headlined a benefit in Long Beach for the Los Angeles chapter of the Diggers Creative Society, an anarchist group that aimed to usher in a world beyond capitalism and the profit motive, and that was known for staging happenings that blended free theater, free food, and free love.

A week later, it was Squaresville again. He traveled to Fort Leonard Wood, Missouri, for *Operation: Entertainment,* a patriotic variety show taped in front of a live army audience. Perhaps it was the dissonance of performing for troops about to be shipped out for a war he didn't support, or maybe it was the strangeness of returning to the army base where, a decade earlier, he had gone through basic training, but almost as soon as he arrived, Richard snapped. He demanded to see the commanding officer. His room was not satisfactory. Richard's agent, Sandy Gallin, received a panicked call from the show: Richard was threatening to quit. But later, when the cameras were rolling, Richard assumed the stage, dusted off his zany "Kill Class" routine, with its wooden-eared corporal barking orders and taking a kick to his groin—and performed it with total conviction. He acted as if the new Richard, the Richard who thought American democracy a fraud, were a figment of someone else's imagination.

In the drama of his double life, it was the trickster who offered the greater fantasy of power and deeper experience of intoxication, and 1969 and 1970 were the years in which Richard lost himself in that alter ego, whose amorality allowed for nastiness as well as artistic derring-do. The nasty side came out, behind the scenes, in Richard's dealings with his manager, Bobby Roberts. Richard begrudged Roberts for diluting the force of his comedy: he said he wished people could play his first album's *cover* rather than the album itself. He grew frustrated with the poor sales of the album, which didn't even crack the Top 100, and he blamed Roberts, who was co-owner of the album's imprint on Reprise, for this, too. Meanwhile, Richard's lifestyle, with his cocaine habit siphoning off his money, made him hungry to get paid.

In a conversation with the album's producer, Robert Marchese, in Laurel Canyon, Richard wondered aloud: why, if he had signed a two-album, fifty-thousand-dollar contract, had he gotten so little money up front? Marchese explained that the amount did not include the expenses that Reprise deducted for the production of the first album, and that Reprise was still holding on to a good deal of the total amount, waiting to see how much the second album cost.

"What am I going to do about this?" Richard asked.

Marchese answered that Howlin' Wolf, "the greatest blues singer ever," made sure to bring his gun into his negotiations with the Chess brothers, who ran his record label. And he usually got his money.

Richard apparently proceeded to follow the lead of Howlin' Wolf, as he understood it. At a meeting with Bobby Roberts over the first album's royalties in Sandy Gallin's office, Richard pulled out a gun and, without too much of an explanation, pistol-whipped his manager. It's unknown if Richard walked away with money as a result, but other results were more clear cut. Reprise Records would not record a second album, and Richard and Bobby Roberts were no longer a team. For a while afterward, the industry deemed Richard literally unmanageable. Sandy Gallin tried to pick up the slack as best he could, but Richard's nightclub work took a noticeable dive in frequency.

Richard's falling-out with Roberts was an index of a broader change in his life. He was leaving Hollywood and hunkering down in a much blacker world, a world in which his new friend Paul Mooney, a fellow comic, was both his ballast and shadow partner. The two had met, about a year before, at a crowded party at Mooney's bungalow on Sunset Boulevard. Without so much as an introduction, Richard looked at the woman who was with Mooney, considered the woman on his own arm, and then proposed, "Let's all get in bed and have a freak thing!" (The "free love" ethos of Laurel Canyon seemed to have rubbed off on him.) The orgy never materialized: Mooney's "woman" was in fact his half-sister. But the misfire set the terms for the friendship that followed. From the get-go, Mooney saw Richard as uninhibited and "without guile"—"selfish with the innocence of a four-year-old," he recalled, always living in "Richard Pryor's Eternal Present."

Perhaps it was their rhyming family backgrounds that led Mooney to appreciate Richard's wicked wit and accept his adolescent selfishness. Like Richard, Mooney was raised by a grandmother who dispensed hard discipline and earthy wisdom. The moral center of the family, Mooney's "Mama" had a phrase for every occasion. When a child started getting out of line, she announced, "I'm passing out lollipops and whoopin's, and I'm fresh out of lollipops." If she spotted a con artist in her midst, she warned, "A cow always knows where the weak fence is." If she thought someone too deferential, she advised, "A dog that will bring a bone will take a bone." And like Marie Pryor, Mooney's grandmother was tough-minded about sex and money. If the women of the family were too loose with their favors, she might say, "A hard dick knows no names" or (Mooney's favorite) "A wet pussy and a dry purse don't match."

Starting around the fall of 1967, Pryor and Mooney grew closer, bonding through a mixture of friendship and creative collaboration. For the next two decades, Mooney was at the center of Richard's inside circle. He was the audience member whose hearty laugh rang out from the crowd and emboldened Richard onstage; the sounding board who, after a show, rapped with Richard for hours about which lines killed and which lines died; the quick-witted conversationalist who supplied Richard's comic act with some of its most unforgettable lines (for which he was compensated generously). He was also the drug-free confrère who could be counted on to handle the logistics—Where's the party? Where's the car?—that Richard had no head for. And Mooney did so without judgment; he didn't press his relatively clean lifestyle on Richard or anyone else. Quite the contrary. When Mooney inevitably declined an offer of coke, Richard had a customary response to the purveyor. "I get Mooney's share," he would say merrily, and snort it up in full.

With Mooney at his side, Richard began haunting black-oriented clubs like Maverick's Flat and the Redd Foxx Club, and feeding on the energy in their rooms. John Daniels, the owner of Maverick's Flat, had aspired to open, in the words of the *Los Angeles Times*, "a black Playboy Mansion, with comfortable pillows and good-looking boys and girls dancing to the beat." He ended up with something even more interesting: a club, on black LA's Crenshaw Strip, that was wholesome and decadent, psychedelic and soulful, fun-loving and experimental. On the wholesome side, Maverick's Flat served ice-cold Coca-Cola, not alcohol, and was open to teens. It hosted beauty pageants, casting calls, and a conference on the redevelopment of the ghetto. It was unpretentious enough that visitors like Diana Ross, when told there were no seats available, would sit on floor pillows; loose enough that Muhammad Ali would take over as a DJ, dropping his rhymes on the audience. But Maverick's also had a very adult vision of sophistication. It stayed open until 4:00 a.m. and drew everyone from Stokely Carmichael and Sidney Poitier to Robert Mitchum and Marlon Brando (who was almost kicked out for not wearing shoes). One of Maverick's exquisitely decorated walls featured an image of a nude black couple nesting with intertwined legs in a celestial love seat, four long-stemmed wineglasses at their side, a red planet blazing in the distance amid twinkling stars. The Temptations' "Psychedelic Shack" was inspired by the club's décor.

Meanwhile, the Redd Foxx Club, on La Cienega Boulevard in the Mid-City neighborhood, returned Richard to the days of his first performances at Collins Corner. Foxx wielded a switchblade and a small black Derringer to keep his employees in line (and to protect himself from overeager creditors). Richard judged that Redd "ran the club like a gangster, treating friends like relatives and enemies with scorn. People were beat up regularly." In other words, it felt like home. The room was so intimate that Bill Cosby described it as "an aisle." As at Collins Corner, the nearly all-black audience at Redd's place was rambunctious and free with its backtalk: according to one performer, "a comic with his wits about him could stand there and do fifteen or twenty minutes just trying to slow them down long enough for him to tell one planned story or do one planned piece of material." Some comedians might have clenched under the pressure; Richard surrendered to it. "I loved getting on that stage and just tripping—ad-libbing new routines and so on," he recalled. And the club was free in another way, too: Richard remembered snorting so much cocaine with Redd in the small hours at the club that he felt they were competing in "the coke Olympics."

Onstage at Maverick's or the Redd Foxx Club, Richard could say anything he wanted. It was an extraordinary feeling, this sensation of creative freedom. For him, the worm was turning: those parts of himself that had been buried, by shame or censorship, were now his creative fuel. According to Mooney his two favorite words at Maverick's, in order of frequency, were *motherfucker* and *nigger.* Richard's use of the *N*-word, in particular, was a stark sign of where his newfound freedom was taking him. *Nigger* has been called "the nuclear bomb of racial epithets," and comics before Richard, such as Lenny Bruce and Dick Gregory, detonated the word sporadically in their act. Richard leaned on it often, and found more flexible uses for it. He might use the word, while in character, to sharpen an insult ("Say, nigger, what the fuck wrong with you? You gonna slam the door in my face, as much money as I spent in this raggedy motherfucker?"). Or he might use it, in his own voice, as a blanket term ("Niggers nowadays be serious. The same niggers who was winos is in the Panthers now, doing something for the community"). Though it served occasionally as a punch line, especially if Richard pronounced it as a white person might ("Look up in the sky . . . it's Super Nigger!"), usually it was a basic form of oral punctuation, something between a comma and an exclamation point—there to supply a pause and underscore his latest poke at the audience.

Richard's use of the *N*-word kissed his entire audience with lightning. Instantly, it established a rapport with those blacks who had never heard a comedian address them in the language of their closest friends and family, and who, in the age of Black Power, were eager to leave *Negro* behind in pursuit of blackness. Less obviously, it connected Richard to those white audience members who wanted to eavesdrop on the black community's inside language, letting them join his black fans in a grand gesture of refusal. Whenever the *N*-word came out of Richard's mouth, it expressed a basic stance to the world of the kibitzers and star makers, the world of Bobby Roberts and the Aladdin hotel. It was the same stance taken by Clark Washington to his boss: You can't fire me, I quit. I'll make it on my terms, or on no terms at all.

A jazz critic for the *Oakland Tribune* judged that Richard "had an act the like of which has never, to my knowledge, been done before in a conventional nightclub." Bill Cosby remembered that "Richard would walk in [the Redd Foxx Club], and he'd blow Foxx away. He'd blow me away, with no problem. That was mainly because Richard was bringing in a new kind of language at the time—not really bringing it in, but using it and using it well." "Using it well": Cosby appreciated that Richard was not simply dropping *N*-bombs and *F*-bombs willy-nilly. He'd found a way to control their power.

In a dope-fueled brainstorming session with Paul Mooney, Richard announced that he was going to make a movie. TV was too confining—his last speculative foray in that medium had been his untimely idea, with Henry Jaglom, of an interracial buddy comedy—

but filmmaking was opening up to anyone with a sixteen-millimeter camera.

"We'll get our friends together and do it," Richard told Mooney.

"Where we gettin' the money?" Mooney asked.

"Me," Richard said. "I'll put it up. I'll produce."

"Who's gonna direct?"

"Me."

"Who's gonna be in it?"

"Everybody we know."

From the start the film was powered by an insane level of ambition on Richard's part; he supposed that he would be the film's writer, director, producer, and star. He founded a production company and gave it the resonant name of Black Sun.

Richard had toyed for a while with the idea of making his own film. During his Greenwich Village days, he had bought a sixteen-millimeter camera: Manny Roth remembered him wandering around New York City for a full day and night, his camera trained on whatever sights and sounds snagged his interest. And just in the two years since he'd moved to Los Angeles, the barriers to independent filmmaking had been lowered dramatically. Several new types of low-budget movies competed with the glamour films churned out by the major studios. Director John Cassavetes pioneered a mode of personal filmmaking that was untidy, urgent, and actor-driven. Skin flick auteur Russ Meyer produced grindhouse classics such as the S/M melodrama *Faster, Pussycat! Kill! Kill!* (1966) or *Mondo Topless* (1966), in which a group of "busty buxotic beauties" (San Francisco strippers) perform and discuss the realities of sex work. On the exploitation end, American Independent Pictures (AIP) dominated the field, latching onto the counterculture with a boomlet of motorcycle gang and hippie films.

In Richard's case, it was his involvement with the AIP film *Wild in the Streets* that both inspired and goaded him to sit in the director's chair. His fascination with the process of moviemaking deepened on its set. "I can spend hours watching people on the set do their 'thing,'" he said. "Everybody here has their certain 'thing' and it's amazing to watch their concentration. Take the makeup man. You'd think that his work was the only thing seen on the screen. The same with all the people here. I guess that's why American pictures have the reputation of being so technically perfect."

It seems likely, too, that the tabloid quality of the film itself helped spur Richard to believe in his own tilted vision. *Wild in the Streets* was a mad parable about a groupuscule of young rock musicians (including Richard's Stanley X) who convince an opportunistic politician to lower the voting age in America so that teens can vote. The franchise thus expanded, psychedelic chaos ensues: LSD contaminates the nation's water supply; the leader of the band gets elected president on the motto "Down with experience!"; everyone over thirty is packed off to concentration camps, where they pass their lives in a stupor, dazed by the daily dose of acid they're forced to drop. The movie feels as zonked out as its characters, delighting in rapid plot reversals, kaleidoscopic cinematography, and a tone that oscillates between comedy and horror before landing squarely on the latter.

Yet *Wild in the Streets* also gave Richard a taste of the limits of independent filmmaking. *The New Yorker*'s Pauline Kael called the film a "cheap commodity," which "in its blatant and sometimes funny way of delivering action serves to remind us that one of the great appeals of movies is that we don't have to take them too seriously." Richard certainly valued irreverence, but the on-screen evidence suggests he did not enjoy how much *his* character wasn't to be taken seriously. As Stanley X, drummer and "author of *The Aborigine Cookbook*," Richard was a trivial, token presence in the white rock star's entourage—the black militant there to balance out the gay guitarist, the vegetarian acidhead, and the teenage Japanese masseuse. He was part of the scenery, and he intoned his few lines with an aloofness that suggested he wasn't going to fight to become something else. After one particularly limp moment of repartee ("You've got a big mouth"; "You've got a square head"), the camera focuses on Richard, who puts his hands together on his lap, rolls his eyes up to the ceiling with a look of scorn, and lays a heavy topspin on his single word of dialogue: "Wow."

Worse was the unthinking racism that, according to Paul Mooney, came at Richard from the same below-the-line technicians whose professionalism he admired. Hanging out on the set with Mooney, Richard observed some set decorators spraying the streets with a shiny substance that made them glisten with the look of fresh rain. "What's that stuff?" Richard asked.

"It's called 'nigger-size,'" a set decorator answered. His tongue didn't pause over the word; his eyes didn't meet Richard's to gauge his reaction.

"Nigger-size?" Mooney asked.

"Yeah, it's what we nigger-size the streets with." This was established Hollywood lingo, it seems. The two black men on set looked at each other and shook their heads.

When asked later about the film that went variously by the name of *Uncle Tom's Fairy Tales*, *Bon Appetit*, and *The Trial*, Richard told the *Peoria Journal Star* that "an angel is helping finance it." It was a coy remark that papered over the serious political ironies that underlay the production of his film and shaped his marriage to Shelley.

By the fall of 1968, their marriage was fraying at the ends. If their relationship had originally been conceived as a countercultural experiment in interracial loving, it was colored now by the brooding vision of Black Power, in which battles between black and white were taken as the baseline of American politics. Mooney called Richard and Shelley's home the "House of Pain"; arguments began with insults and ended with Richard administering blows. Lady Cocaine, along with various other women, had supplanted Shelley in Richard's favor. He spent long nights at the home of his drug dealer, racking up debts and becoming deeply hooked. On one occasion, when Shelley flushed Richard's cocaine down the toilet, he jabbed her, with a boxer's efficiency and strength, in her head and pregnant belly, knocking her to the floor just as Buck had knocked down Gertrude. Shelley was at a loss—unsettled by his cocaine binges, demoralized by his faithlessness, shaken by his physical abuse.

What to do? She hit upon an inspired idea: she could invest her parents' wedding present—thirty thousand dollars, waiting in a bank account—in the Black Power screenplay that had become Richard's pet obsession. By working together on the film, she hoped, the two of them could breathe new vitality into their marriage. When she proposed the idea, Richard quickened: he was happy to take the money and lose himself in a movie of his own creation.

And so his vision of the black revolution would come to cinematic life through a cash infusion from Herb and Bunny Bonis. Super Nigger depended, in material terms, on the white wife he cheated on and, behind her, on the white in-laws who regarded him with suspicion. If that irony weren't rich enough: Herb had earned the money as the personal manager of Danny Kaye, the effervescent Jewish comedian who came up from the Borscht Belt, and who had made his stage debut Jolson-style, in blackface, in his Brooklyn kindergarten's production of *The Watermelon Fantasy*. It was an intergenerational, interracial transfer of funds, from the center of the political spectrum to its leftward edge.

The production gradually took shape over the course of 1968 and early 1969. In its first outline, *Uncle Tom's Fairy Tales* was propaganda pure and simple. When art director Gary Burden visited Richard's home in June 1968 for the cover shoot of Richard's first album, he observed that Richard was brainstorming "a documentary . . . of black people taking over the world, and he had all these storyboards on the wall of black warriors mowing down the white pigs." But the project took a surprising turn in the wake of the trial of Black Panther Huey Newton, cofounder of the Black Panther Party. That trial was the major Black Power media event of 1968, a political shocker in a summer of shockers, and Richard's creative imagination was jolted by its electricity.

The trial was touched off by an arrest gone wrong. Nine months earlier, Newton had been stopped on the streets of Oakland by police officer John Frey, who contacted headquarters to notify them he was stopping a "known Black Panther vehicle." In Newton's account, he took out a criminal law textbook and questioned whether Frey had reasonable cause for the arrest; Frey snarled, "You can take that book and shove it up your ass, nigger," then punched Newton in the face with a force that sent him tumbling to the ground. A struggle ensued, and when it ended, Newton had taken a shot in the abdomen; a supporting officer had been shot in the arm, knee, and chest; and Officer Frey had died from bullets to his leg, chest, and stomach.

In another time, another place, the death of a white police officer in a firefight with a black radical would have been an open-and-shut case, and Newton would have picked up a one-way ticket to death row. But the Black Power movement had cleared open a space in the American legal system, broadening the relevant "facts of the case" until they encompassed the larger social forces that had sent a young black radical and a young white police officer on a collision course. In a striking reversal, Newton's trial put the American status quo, more than Huey Newton himself, up for cross-examination: in the words of legal historian Mark Weiner, defending Newton meant "questioning the assumptions that made his acts criminal in the eyes of the law." Newton's lawyer Charles Garry did not even touch on the shooting incident until a few days before he called Newton to the witness stand, convinced that "the only way Newton could be defended was to take him in the context of his world and see the facts from that viewpoint."

The Newton trial was high rhetorical drama, with Newton's life hanging in the balance. Garry audaciously compared Newton to Jesus Christ, likening the Panther message of self-defense to the instructions found in the Gospel of Matthew: "Think not that I come to send peace on earth: I came not to send peace, but a sword." In his closing argument, Garry called for not just the exoneration of his client but the abolition of the ghetto:

> White American, listen, white American, listen! The answer is not to put Huey Newton in the gas chamber, it is not the answer to put Huey Newton and his organization into jail. The answer is not that. The answer is not more police. The answer is to wipe out the ghetto, the conditions

> of the ghetto, so that black brothers and sisters . . . can walk down the streets in dignity.

Garry's argument worked, in part. In its verdict on September 8, 1968, the jury held that, while Newton had shot Officer Frey, he had been provoked by the lawman. It lowered the charge from murder to manslaughter; instead of facing execution, Newton faced a potential sentence of two to fifteen years.

In the aftermath of the Newton trial, Richard began contributing significantly to the Black Power movement. In January 1969, during his run at Mister Kelly's nightclub in Chicago, the Black Panther Party chapter of that city courted his support, and he responded warmly, donating a thousand dollars in cash to the cause. He agreed to make a special trip to Peoria to perform a benefit for the city's fledgling Afro-American Black Peoples' Federation. And he headlined a Congress of Racial Equality fund-raiser at the Apollo Theater at a moment when the organization championed black nationalism and community control.

Yet in his art, Richard rarely traveled a straightforward route. He ripped the premise of *Uncle Tom's Fairy Tales* from the headlines of the Newton trial, but he also turned history upside down in his imagination. Scribbling his screenplay in a spiral notebook with tattered pages, he created an odd mixture of pornography, black comedy, and Black Power agitprop. The trial of a black man in a white man's courtroom became the trial of a white man in a black man's courtroom. No longer a grandiose vision of black people taking over the world, the film shrank to the scale of a chamber drama and become less programmatic, more offbeat. Richard recalled:

> The film opened with a black maid having her pussy eaten at the breakfast table by the wealthy white man who owned the house where she worked. Then, a gang of Black Panther types burst into the house and took him prisoner. As he was led away, the maid fixed her dress and called, "*Bon appétit*, baby!"

After that memorable kiss-off, the white man was put on trial "for all the racial crimes in U.S. history." He pled his case in a basement courtroom, in front of a black judge and a jury stocked with pimps, prostitutes, winos, and drug addicts. The judge had a plate of cocaine and a bottle of liquor in front of him; the jury was similarly well furnished.

Uncle Tom's Fairy Tales was half lurid, half loopy, and fully avant-garde. In one scene, the white man was stripped to his underwear and made to lie on the floor in the courtroom. A gang of black men arrived with sponges and buckets of water. They soaped him up and rinsed him off—an event billed as a "car wash." When the time came for the jury to reach its verdict, it didn't deliberate over the man's fate but yelled out his sentence like members of a lynch mob: "Kill the motherfucker!," "Hang him!," "Shoot him!" In his cocaine-whirred imagination, Richard had conceived a vision of revolution as a travesty of justice, a kangaroo court. Blacks were granted a fantastic power, only to abuse it.

Tellingly, Richard set himself up to perform two opposing, color-coded roles in the film: he was both the lawyer for the defense, kitted out in white hat and long white leather coat; and the lawyer for the prosecution, resplendent in darker duds. He played out his own internal drama, becoming the white man's closest ally and his most committed antagonist. For Richard, there was no golden mean, no middle ground. Between his assumed identities as defense lawyer and prosecutor—as between Clark Washington and Super Nigger—there was only an unbridgeable gap.

Now, as the director of a film moving into production, he faced the challenge of finding a form that could contain the energies splitting him, and his country, in two.

CHAPTER 13

Irreconcilable Differences

Los Angeles and Peoria, 1969–1971

Around the turn of 1969, Richard Pryor strutted onto the UCLA campus in a broad-brimmed hat and ankle-length brown leather coat. He was hailed by two young people, film student Penelope Spheeris and her then-boyfriend, who recognized Richard from TV and asked him why he was on campus.

"I'm looking for film students to do a movie," Richard answered.

"You just found them," Penelope replied. She worked at the tech office of the film school—the first woman employed there—and could arrange to borrow some equipment for a while. It was the first of many acts of creative generosity that Richard received from a woman who later became known as the sharp-eyed director of off-beat music documentaries like *The Decline of Western Civilization* and mainstream comedies like *Wayne's World* and *The Beverly Hillbillies*. Spheeris signed up to work the camera; her boyfriend, the sound recording. Soon after, Richard recruited the cast from the UCLA student body and his circle of friends, many of whom didn't require makeup or costuming, according to Spheeris, "to look like pimps and whores."

Shooting began in February 1969 at a soundstage in Gayley Studios in Westwood and at a private home in Beverly Hills, where Richard staged the abduction of the white man by several Black Panthers. But not long after the film fell together, it started falling apart. Richard had his screenplay in that spiral notebook, but he preferred to improvise. What worked at 3:00 a.m. in a New York comedy club, though, didn't translate so well in film production: Richard had little concern for such crucial technical matters as continuity and coverage, to say nothing of the cost of film. And then there was the influence of cocaine, which made him believe his every brain flash was pure inspiration, regardless of the film's prevailing arc. "[Richard] would go out and shoot a couple more days and come back," recalled Spheeris. "When you're doing a bunch of coke like that, you can't really make a cohesive story. . . . You think of so many things and you try them all, and nothing is cohesive enough to make sense."

It was one thing to have a trickster as a character on-screen, where his amorality could be a source of delight, and quite another to have him installed in the director's chair, where that same amorality had considerable drawbacks. Production funds were diverted into the bottles of Courvoisier and mounds of cocaine that Richard kept on hand. One actor on the film recalled that Richard promised him two dollars per hour on set and, after seventeen hours of work, wrote him a check for thirty-four dollars. Somehow Herb and Bunny Bonis's thirty-thousand-dollar wedding gift had dwindled or been misplaced; the check bounced.

In the film's early months of production, though, Richard was upbeat about what the film signified for his career. In March 1969, when he traveled to Peoria to headline a benefit for its Afro-American Black Peoples' Federation, he told the *Peoria Journal Star* that he was shifting away from nightclub work and into film; his production company, Black Sun, was gearing up for more; his career had achieved escape velocity. He boasted for the benefit of the hometown audience, "I can make whatever I want—$300,000, $400,000 a year." The *Peoria Journal Star* commented, with a touch of hyperbole, that Richard had experienced "the most meteoric rise in show business of any single entertainer in many a year."

The trip to Peoria was a rush job, a whirlwind visit that lasted only a matter of hours. It was Richard's first return since the death of his father, and he didn't choose to linger among the ghosts of his past, even as he was brushed with intimations of another loss to come.

He arrived at the Peoria airport just before noon and was whisked to Methodist Hospital to visit his mother, Gertrude. After Buck's death six months earlier, Gertrude had reentered the Pryor family circle, living at 1319 Millman with her former mother-in-law, Marie, and three other members of the Pryor family. In the twenty-three years since her divorce from Buck, she had remarried a man by the last name of Emanuel, though she was no longer with him; had filled out in weight and lost several of her front teeth; and had contracted a cancer that was sapping her strength. No more than fifty, she had been ravaged by time but strove to keep up her appearance. Before Richard's visit to her hospital room, she had put herself together as if it were Sunday.

Richard hadn't dealt much with Gertrude for decades. Still, he felt the impulse to shield her and care for her. When, a few years earlier, she had arranged to attend a performance of her son on *The Merv Griffin Show,* he had taken her shopping at Bonwit Teller and Saks beforehand to buy a new pocketbook. He wanted her to look nice, to feel nice, he said. But during the taping, when the camera found her and lingered, Richard went rigid, wanting to protect her from the scrutiny. "You've got it on her too long. Turn it off," he snapped.

Now Richard tried to make the best of his precious few minutes with his mother in the hospital. "Hiya, mom," he said softly. He gave her a hand mirror he had brought as a present, then enveloped her with a hug and kiss. She lay back down in her bed. Two photographs hint at the mixed emotions that seem to have washed over him in the hospital room. In one, he looks at Gertrude warmly and appears to have just cracked a joke; her eyes are crinkling at the edges, her mouth wide with laughter. In another, he clasps Gertrude's hand but is turned away from her, his eyes blank and distant, his face a mask of resignation. The two photos suggest a son torn between his desire to boost his mother's failing spirits and his confusion over what he was truly capable of doing. He told the *Peoria Journal Star* that he aimed to fly Gertrude out to Los Angeles so she could live with him. It was an impractical idea: Richard could hardly attend to his pregnant wife, much less care for his dying mother, and the "House of Pain" was unlikely to serve as a good hospice. But after the deaths of Ann and Buck in the space of a year, Gertrude was his last living parent, and he must have felt a stab of dutifulness.

Yet Richard had less than two hours before he was supposed to be onstage at the Carver Center. He rushed from the hospital to visit other family—his granduncle Herman, his grandmother and grandfather at their pool hall. (His five-year-old son, Richard Jr., was not on his itinerary.) Then he was off to the auditorium that had fed his early dreams.

Richard's benefit performance at Carver, his first in Peoria since his father kicked him out of his house in 1962, recalled performances past. His old Carver mentor Juliette Whittaker beamed from the front row. As in the old talent shows, he was the sole comedian, sharing the bill with local singing groups and bands. But how much had changed since his debut in "Rumpelstiltskin" thirteen years before! The name of the group sponsoring the benefit—the Afro-American Black Peoples Federation—hinted at how Peoria had been swept and shaken up by its local civil rights revolution. The Nation of Islam had put down roots, opening its first local temple on Peoria's South Side a month before Richard's visit. Twelve black men with guns, organized under the auspices of the "Afro-American Service Patrol," now watched over Peoria's black community on a nightly basis—and did so with the blessing of city hall and the *Peoria Journal Star*, who appreciated its tough-on-crime stance. Black high school students, under the auspices of the local NAACP, were pressing for school reform, boycotting classes and advocating for more black teachers and black-oriented history books. And just two days before Richard arrived in town, Bradley University bowed to student pressure and established a black culture theme house. Even the bands that now shared the bill with Richard at Carver had names redolent of black pride: the Struts, the Ace of Spades, Peggy and the Soul Setters.

"I'm so happy, so excited," Richard told the 175 people in the audience. "Nobody ever asked me to come here before." He thanked the Afro-American Black Peoples Federation and offered that he was proud to be black himself, and proud to do what he could for the black community. He did some quick, hilarious impressions—of LBJ, of Nixon, of being born—and performed a few routines that touched on his childhood, name-checking friends in the audience and local institutions such as the Irving School, the Carver Center, and State Park.

After twenty minutes onstage, he left to catch a plane for Chicago, where he was performing that night at the Hilton. As was customary in his life, there was little time for reflection; he doesn't appear to have stopped back at the hospital for a last good-bye to his mother. One of his relatives remembered that, shortly after Richard's visit, Gertrude left for New York City—to die there. The plan to resettle her in LA was scuttled for reasons unknown, and Gertrude vanished from Richard's life just as she had vanished after his parents' divorce. She left little trace: while Richard revisited the deaths of his stepmother and father onstage and in print, evoking their impact on him and his family, he would never mention Gertrude's passing. It's hard to tell if the irrevocable loss of his mother was too sore a subject or, given the turbulence of his life at the time, no subject at all.

While Richard burrowed into the making of his underground movie, his former amateur baseball teammate, producer Aaron Spelling, came calling with a different sort of opportunity. ABC had signed Spelling to create ten "Movies of the Week," and Spelling thought of them as "*Playhouse 90* on film," a revival of the 1950s anthology program but with the resources of a small film production. A maestro of the mainstream, Spelling sensed he could carve out a niche for these prime-time movies by using them to put a human face on the political troubles of the late 1960s. He came to cast Richard in two Movies of the Week whose plots revolved around racism: *The Young Lawyers* (1969), a generation-gap drama about two jazz musicians railroaded by a bigot for a crime they didn't commit; and *Carter's Army* (1970), a *Dirty Dozen*–style film in which a ragtag all-black World War II platoon is sent on a suicide mission behind German lines.

Spelling's TV movies telegraphed a broader change afoot in prime-time programming, as network executives made a bid for the younger viewers they feared lost to rock music and films like *Bonnie and Clyde* and *Easy Rider*—hipper forms of entertainment. The late 1960s had brought a trickle of youth-themed programs: *The Smothers Brothers Comedy Hour* smuggled an antiwar and countercultural sensibility into the genre of the variety show, for instance, while the Aaron Spelling–produced *Mod Squad* featured three young "hippie cops" on the drug beat in LA. In 1970 the trickle became a cataract. Network executives premiered a host of TV shows, following the template of *The Mod Squad*, in which young and idealistic characters grappled with issues like inner-city poverty, antiwar resistance, and drug addiction, usually with the help of some crusty authority figure. *Storefront Lawyers*, *The Young Lawyers*, *The Young Rebels*, *The Interns*, *Dial Hotline*—these gave the 1970/71 season the nickname the "Season of Social Relevance."

Richard's career got a notable boost from the trend. He played a drug-running trumpeter with Miles Davis mannerisms in *The Mod Squad*, a Detroit nightclub owner in trouble with the Mob in *The Partridge Family*, a jazz musician who steps into the wrong cab in *The Young Lawyers*, and a black GI who flirts with desertion in *Carter's Army*.

Most of these shows were as formulaic as *Uncle Tom's Fairy Tales* was freewheeling, turning the murk of late 1960s politics into brightly lit morality tales. The sniper who tries to pick off Richard's trumpeter is brought to justice by the Mod Squad; the gangster named "Heavy," happy to crush the ghetto's spirit of community, is sunk when feisty red-haired Danny Partridge joins forces with the Afro-American Cultural Society; the bigoted father attempting to cover up his affair with his son's wife is exposed by a salt-and-pepper team of young lawyers. After the initial surprise of these shows' topicality, there was little surprise in their execution, the dastardly villain always foiled by a team of heartwarmingly interracial heroes.

Carter's Army was an exception, the best of the lot by far—"one of those curious flicks," in the words of the *Philadelphia Tribune*, "which made you hate yourself for liking it." A black World War II service battalion, used to serving food and digging latrines for white GIs who see combat, is called upon to secure a strategically vital bridge. The white officer put in charge of the mission, Captain Carter (Stephen Boyd), is a drawling southerner who low-rates his men's potential and is given to such lines as "Boy, don't let me catch you 'round no white women."

Sure enough, the black GIs pull out a squeaker of a victory and the white officer comes to respect them as men, but the movie squeezes some compelling drama out of its familiar premise. Its script is tight, its ensemble cast of six black actors delivering a nuanced portrait of a company of men. Richard's character, the weak-willed private Jonathan Crunk, finds gusto in his friendship with the mountainous Big Jim (Rosey Grier); the tightly coiled lieutenant (Robert Hooks) bonds with an older physics professor (Moses Gunn); the hotheaded Harlemite (Billie Dee Williams) toys with knife-throwing, while the dreamy kid (Glynn Turman) writes in his diary about scenes of combat he's never experienced. It may have been part of the formula for the six to dwindle to five, then four, then three, but the strength of the acting meant that each death evoked a shudder of loss.

Carter's Army took risks, too, with its surprisingly astringent ending, which might have earned the Black Panther seal of approval. After the black brigade captures the bridge in a death-defying maneuver, a caravan of Allied troops comes streaming by. The first truck bears a Confederate flag on its hood. A white soldier yells, "What you boys standing around for?"; another adds, "Hey, boys, you better get some latrines dug!" and tosses a shovel at their feet. Richard's Private Crunk, coughing a bitter laugh, throws down his rifle. What was he risking his life for, exactly? In the film's final moments, the white captain (a now-former bigot) breaks the shovel in two and hands the rifle back to Crunk. He'll be needing that rifle, it seems, for whatever war comes his way.

For Richard, *Carter's Army* was an initiation into the guild of black actors, just as *A Time for Laughter* had initiated him into the guild of black comedians two years before. Hooks and Gunn were experienced stage players who had recently helped launch the Negro Ensemble Company, a New York theater group that sought to offer black writers and actors the chance to explore black life with a free hand. "We got to calling ourselves 'the soiled six.' There was a great feeling of togetherness," Richard said. "At one point in the picture, one of the men in the unit is killed en route to the dam. When the actor who played him didn't come into work the day after that scene was filmed, I think we all thought that he had really died. It was one of the most unusual experiences I've ever been through."

The intensity on the set registered in Richard's performance, his meatiest dramatic role to date. "I play a coward and that was the hardest thing I've ever done," he said. "My natural instinct is to be funny and I really had to fight with myself not to make the character a lampoon." He won that struggle: in a raw four-minute scene that anticipates Richard's later indelible portrayals of fear in *The Mack*, *Blue Collar*, and elsewhere, his Private Crunk is so terrified that he sees Germans in the waving branches of a darkening wood and fires wildly at the phantoms. When no Germans fall at his feet, he crawls into a ditch and huddles in the fetal position, crying out, "Shoot 'em!"

Richard's fear had little in common with the eye-popping, teeth-chattering, 'feets-don't-fail-me-now' cowardice of earlier black and blackface comedians. It was immense but not cartoonish, and hinted at something tragic and new from a black male actor in the age of Black Power: a near-total vulnerability. Richard was physically lean but never seemed to flex his muscles with total confidence, and was convincingly fragile on-screen. After his various crackups and breakdowns of the past few years, he had the capacity to bring a trembling energy to his roles as an actor—if only a director knew how to use it.

On July 16, 1969, Shelley gave birth to a daughter, and the parents named her Rain, after the weather of that summer day. For the first time in his life, Richard made it to the hospital, flowers in hand, for the birth of one of his children. But his dedication as a father was short-lived. Five days later, Shelley waited in vain to be picked up from the hospital. After a cab dropped her off at their home, she walked in to discover Richard in bed with their housekeeper. She locked herself in the bathroom and sobbed; Richard remained outside, unapologetic. Later, he would bring other women to their home, flaunting his infidelity to the point of inviting Shelley into a threesome. His attention remained fixed on his needs rather than on his baby and her around-the-clock demands.

Meanwhile, Richard and Shelley had a visitor who lived, during daylight hours, in the den of their two-story Hancock Park home. For twelve hours a day, five days a week, Penelope Spheeris sat parked in front of a Moviola editing machine, trying to give shape to the shapeless *Uncle Tom's Fairy Tales*. According to Spheeris, the atmosphere in the house was claustrophobic, crackling with tension. Richard had a collection of samurai swords above the fireplace, and he passed the hours standing above Penelope at the Moviola, tossing out ideas in his bathrobe, his Courvoisier and cocaine near at hand.

At times the line between art and life would collapse, the plot dynamics of the film bleeding into the dynamics of Richard and Shelley's marriage. Working at the Moviola, Penelope might be wrestling with a snippet of dialogue like "Get out of here, you pig-faced motherfucker!" while in the kitchen Shelley labored to cook soul food for Richard and his circle of black friends. "Come on, get our food together! Can you make some chitlins, Miss Shelley?" they razzed her as they trooped en masse through the kitchen, playing the race card with the same abandon as the film's characters. Paul Mooney liked to call Shelley "the White Lady" to her face, and when he did, Shelley grimaced and Richard cackled. She had reason to feel, like the white protagonist in the film, that she was being put on trial for all the racial crimes in American history.

By December 1969, Penelope had about forty minutes of film that was, at best, experimental, and Richard and Shelley had a marriage that had gone sour. One day, when Shelley came downstairs and saw a too-familiar tableau—Penelope in front of the Moviola, Richard sitting nearby with his Courvoisier and coke—something in her broke.

"I'm sick of this movie and sick of your shit," she said. "You have a wife and daughter. It would be nice if you would acknowledge us from time to time."

Richard was apparently sick of the movie, too: he rose to his feet and attacked the Moviola, yanking the film's one two-thousand-foot reel out of the bin. He ripped it to pieces in a whirlwind of effort, returning the film to the incoherence in which it had been born. Penelope sat motionless in the editing chair, too dazed to stop him. Months of her work lay in tatters; some scraps of celluloid were no more than four inches long.

Shelley repaired to the bathroom, where she undressed to take a shower. Richard, like his film, was at loose ends: he dashed out of the house and made for his car. According to Spheeris, Shelley noticed him leaving and, playing her own mad part in their *folie à deux*, ran naked to his car. He was pulling out of the driveway, so she threw herself on the car, her body plastered on the hood, her face looking at Richard's through the windshield and the car motoring away as though everything were normal.

Penelope grabbed an extra coat, jumped into her car, and took off in pursuit. Richard's car traveled a block and a half with a nude Shelley on top, until finally he reached a red light at Wilshire Boulevard. Shelley scrambled off the car and ran around to the window, banging on it and begging him to come back. Richard looked past her; the light changed to green, and he peeled away. By the time Penelope caught up with Shelley and offered her the coat, Richard was gone.

Astonishingly, this was not quite the end of Richard's film or his marriage; both limped on. Penelope spliced back together a working print, and Richard arranged a private showing of the film in a UCLA screening room for Bill Cosby, who Richard hoped would finance a final edit. Around the same time, Cosby had, without batting an eyelash, put up a fifty-thousand-dollar loan to help director

Melvin Van Peebles launch another off-center, X-rated exercise in black guerrilla filmmaking, *Sweet Sweetback's Baadasssss Song.* Despite his wholesome persona onstage, Cosby was sympathetic to black artists who strayed from the snug spot in the American mainstream that he had seen fit to occupy.

Cosby watched Richard's film at UCLA and managed just one sentence when the lights came back on: "Hey, this shit is weird."

It was to be the last verdict on the film. *Uncle Tom's Fairy Tales* was shelved for good; only a few minutes of soundless footage remain. Richard had attempted to bring his own vision of the black revolution to the screen and had been outdone in militancy by an Aaron Spelling TV movie in which he costarred. He felt scooped, too, by director Robert Downey Sr., a fellow low-budget absurdist who had trained his gimlet eye on the racism of corporate America in *Putney Swope.* "I liked it very much," Richard told an interviewer, "and I was mad that a white cat did it. See, nigger, you let a honky beat you at your own game. . . . He took a chance, see, and the gods favored him."

Black Sun Productions was defunct; Richard's marriage, heading for a similar fate. Not long after their dramatic argument over his film, he moved out of the home he shared with Shelley, distancing himself from his responsibilities as a husband and father. In June 1970, Shelley finally filed for divorce, citing "irreconcilable differences." Her action meant that a full trifecta of women had recently taken Richard to court: in 1969 his first wife, Patricia, and his companion Maxine had separately sued him for child support, the latter case producing a year-long bench warrant for his arrest when he defaulted on paying legal fees.

Richard let his phone be disconnected, went incommunicado with the world, courted the void. He couldn't be found when Shelley's attorney tried serving him with a copy of her legal complaint.

In 1970, Richard was in danger of becoming a second-string character actor, called up whenever there was a part for a streetwise black dude. He rarely worked the nightclub circuit anymore. He had rung in the New Year, in fact, by cutting off his relationship with Mister Kelly's, the Chicago nightspot that was the premier supper club between New York City and Las Vegas. When its owner asked Richard, in advance of a multi-week holiday engagement, to "keep it clean," Richard replied that he would do the same act he was performing elsewhere, or no act at all. When the owner called his bluff, Richard pulled out of the gig at the last minute, to the owner's fury. Other clubs, such as Lennie's on the Turnpike, decided to drop Richard, too. The gigs Richard did play had a new spring-loaded tension, his white audience sometimes squirming in their seats at the "niggers," "bitches" and "motherfuckers" whizzing in their direction. "Just listening to nigger bum talk can get them uptight," Richard told the *Washington Post*, reflecting on the new atmosphere at his shows. "The deeper you get, the more uptight they get. It scares them. They haven't heard this stuff. But it's the truth."

Still, it wasn't just the "uptight" club owners or audience members who started doubting Richard's ability to deliver as a performer. The black critic Charles Brown, who had earlier enthused about Richard's comedy, suggested in the *Los Angeles Times* that Richard "could use some self-discipline" and complained about his "confused and erratic" delivery: "He would start a story, drift to another, forget what he was talking about, and at last ask the audience to refresh his memory." In May 1970, Redd Foxx groused that Richard was too often a no-show at Redd's nightclub, a venue where the younger comic was free to use whatever language appealed to him. And from still another angle, a white critic from the countercultural *Los Angeles Free Press* accused Richard, in a review of a Bitter End West show that drew a nearly all-white audience, of "pandering"—of "keeping up the Stepin Fetchit image" for "all the $4.00 cover-plus-one-drink-minimum hip liberals." All those *N*-words, the *Free Press* said, were simply Pryor's way of "using our prejudices to work for him." The problem was not that white audiences became uptight (as Richard saw it), but that they loosened up, flattered themselves for their open-mindedness and tolerance, over the course of the show.

The rumbling chorus of complaint narrowed Richard's options considerably. By 1971 there were only four clubs "in the world," he felt, whose doors were still open to him: the Cellar Door in Washington, DC; Maverick's Flat in LA's Crenshaw corridor; Basin Street West in San Francisco; and Mandrake's in Berkeley.

With no manager to help him handle his business decisions and with his debts to his drug dealer mounting, Richard turned for help to Louis and David Drozen, the father-and-son team behind Laff Records, an independent label that specialized in bawdy comedy records from the likes of Skillet and Leroy, LaWanda Page, and Mantan Moreland. Laff reveled in raunch, and given the saltiness of Richard's new act, there was a decent fit between his comedy and a label that zestily pressed albums with titles like *Elsie's Sporting House*, *Mutha Is Half a Word*, *Two or Three Times a Day*, and *That Ain't My Finger*. But Richard wasn't exactly negotiating with the Drozens from a position of strength. "When we signed Richard Pryor," David Drozen remembered, "we gave him an advance of five thousand dollars. He had to have it or otherwise he was going to get killed. He said 'if I don't get this I'm going to die.' "

The four-album contract Richard signed with Laff on December 9, 1970, was a harsh comedown from the $50,000 two-album contract he'd signed with Reprise two years before. Laff agreed to pay him $1,000 immediately and another $4,000 upon the recording of his first album for the label, and then another $27,500 for the next three albums. In return, Richard gave them exclusive rights to his comedy for two years, along with the option for two more years, during which time Laff would release a minimum of three more records. Richard had generated one comedy record in his first thirty years; now he was looking at generating at least seven albums in the next four. One imagines that, feeling the heat of his unpaid debts, he didn't trouble himself with such niggling details.

The fruit of Richard's desperation was *'Craps' (After Hours)*, an album that later became a cult classic and a creative touchstone for generations of black comedians. It was his *Sun Sessions*, the small-label effort that revealed the shape of his creativity when he was performing for himself above all. Mostly recorded at the Redd Foxx Club, *'Craps'* was casual, scatological, and scalding in its originality. Unlike Richard's first album, which was sequenced as a series of short polished plays, *'Craps'* felt intimate and conversational, with Richard rapping about the facts of life and the facts of *his* life. His first album had seven tracks; *'Craps'* had thirty-two—and was only six minutes longer.

Instead of going high concept, Richard mostly went low. There was the eleven-second "Masturbating," for instance, with its quick riff on how women put up a sexual smokescreen ("That vibrator is for my *back*"), followed, twenty minutes later, by the pointed seventeen-second confession of "Jackin' Off" ("People don't talk about nothin' real . . . like jackin' off . . . I used to jack off so much I knew pussy couldn't be as good as my hand"). Although *Uncle Tom's Fairy Tales* had stalled out as a production, the comedy on *'Craps'* was conceived alongside it and did what that film had aspired to do: it brought together the sexual revolution and the black revolution in a madcap mésalliance. Unlike the film, *'Craps'* didn't have to be coherent. It just had to be funny—and it was.

The best routines found a dark vein of comedy in the same racial injustices that elsewhere were occasioning sit-ins, rallies, and boycotts. Richard had been performing some of them since 1966, but once collected together and pressed on vinyl, they seemed to chart a decade in the life of a young black man growing up in the pincers of the law. The subject matter was militant, but Richard's routines winked at life's absurdities. When he and his teenage friends were entrapped by Peoria's curfew, it was the black cop who was their nemesis, and for good reason: "The black cop had to do more shit to keep his job. He had to whup more niggers than the white cop. *'I ain't gonna lose my pension, nigger!'* " Richard spoofed police lineups, inventing one where the suspects acted like they were "in show business":

> *[Cop voice] Alan T. Johnson, suspected of grand theft auto. Step forward.*
>
> I'd like to say something about that. I thought that was my mother's car. I went downtown. My mother told me to pick the car up at 1:30,

and it was in front of the bank. . . . I dug this white lady sitting next to me screaming and shit. I didn't know *what* was happening. I thought it was a stick-up. In fact, I want to press charges against her 'cause she scratched my hand, and yelled in my ear and hurt my ear. And I have medical reports to prove that—

You want an ass-whuppin'?

Then there was the gloss on human anatomy that Richard felt compelled to deliver as a result of being strip-searched himself. "You talk about degrade a nigger," he said. "They degrade you immediately. I don't know what they be looking for. What you be looking for in my *ass*? Ain't nothing in my ass. If I had a pussy, I might dig it because you can hide something in your pussy. But in your ass—what am I going to hide in my ass? A pistol? We'll come out with a .45? *'Up against the wall, motherfucker'*?"

Balanced against Richard's account of his skirmishes with the law was an unvarnished portrait of the black community's chippies, hustlers, jackleg preachers, and winos. He took his audience to the inner sanctums of the black experience—the "members only" all-night clubs, storefront churches, barbershops—and captured the human variety he found there, channeling voice after voice with an ease that suggested there was no limit to their number. The exponents of Black Power claimed there was a fundamental difference between white life and black life in America; Richard brought that difference to vivid life, his every *N*-word a stabbing reminder of the American caste system. And he openly punctured the optimistic talk of interracial fellowship:

We used to think that we could all sit in the same club, white and black, and not understand each other.

NEWSCASTER VOICE: It's amazing. It could only happen in America.

Or, as he quipped in another performance at the time, "Blacks are the same as whites . . . except the whites have all the money and guns."

In the four decades since the release of *'Craps,'* many critics have noted how the album brought the language of the street to stand-up, but fewer have observed the equally fundamental change it registered: Richard was now using the ugly details of his intimate life as fodder for his comedy. Previous to *'Craps,'* his autobiographical skits tended to be ironically observational, in the manner that *Seinfeld* later made famous, or backward looking, with Richard reliving his childhood. On *'Craps'* he put his marriage to Shelley up for examination and poked its sore spots:

> Being married is hard, 'cause we fuck from memory now. We have some great fights, though. Do you ever have fights with your woman? Me and my woman have some serious fistfights. Not like on TV, where you be arguing. 'Cause she hurt my ego and I punch her out.
>
> Me and her fights our ass off upstairs 'cause I found that if you be with a woman, if you don't fuck in a week, you've got to fight. You either fuck or fight, one of the two.

The sexual candor, the capacity for violence that Richard owned up to, the mix of vulnerability and menace that radiated off him as a result—these were new ingredients not just in his stand-up but in American comedy as a whole. The battle between the sexes might have been at the core of stand-up since the heyday of Henny "Take my wife, please" Youngman, but Richard's confessional comedy drew blood—as when, in the struggle for a butcher knife, his wife scratches his neck and denies the damage, provoking Richard to retort, "Nail polish, my ass!"

Richard couldn't have spoken so frankly about sex if the counterculture hadn't challenged older ideas of discretion; *'Craps'* might have been banned if it had been released just a few years earlier. Still, Richard's vision of sex had more in common with the topsy-turviness of the blues than the free-love ethic of Woodstock. He acted for his audience as a voice of skeptical wisdom, a guide to the familiar troubles that persisted after the sex-and-drugs revolution had supposedly freed people from their hang-ups. Sexual competition: "I don't have no advice for married people except don't take them on an orgy, because they always say things like 'you never touched *me* like that.'" Jealousy: "I had to quit [smoking dope] too, since I'd wake up in the middle of the night and say to her, 'Are you fucking the paper boy?'" In an absurd reversal, the multiplication of sexual partners meant simply that there were more ways to be betrayed: "I got the guilties after [me and my wife's best friend] fucked. I had to tell my woman because I thought she knew. . . . 'I did it! I fucked Ethel!' 'You fucked Ethel?' She went and kicked Ethel's ass. She was fucking her too."

There was a strange dynamic here: in detailing his failed connections with his various lovers, Richard was reaching for an unpredictable intimacy with his audience. "I was the only dude in the neighborhood who would fuck this faggot," he said in a quick but shocking aside. He let down his guard and confessed to the unmentionable:

> A lot of dudes don't play that shit. In the daytime [they say] *"I don't fuck no faggot, man!"* At night you catch them [*sound of door knocking*].
>
> *But it's embarrassing because I met the dude ten years later.*
>
> [*Campy effeminate voice*] "Hi, Rich!"

A bundle of need, Richard presented himself as someone driven to have sex with a man, black macho be damned. But there was another level of need directing him onstage: the need to admit his embarrassment and, through his rapport with his audience, move beyond embarrassment, beyond shame.

With *'Craps'* in the can, Richard had produced an album unlike any other, but his life was still bottoming out, consumed by the chase for the next high. He was living in the Sunset Tower, a thirteen-floor Art Deco gem that rose grandly over the Strip and had once been a haven for the Hollywood film colony, with residents ranging from John Wayne and Marilyn Monroe to Preston Sturges and Frank Sinatra. Over the course of the 1960s it had lost much of its aura and was now known for having the best-kept prostitutes in Hollywood.

If Richard had chosen, on January 29, 1971, to flick on his TV and watch the episode of *The Partridge Family* in which he guest-starred, he would have caught a perfect parable of the limits of his career at the time. He played A. E. Simon, a Detroit entrepreneur who, along with his brother, Sam (Lou Gossett Jr.), has sunk his ambitions into a club that represents the ghetto's dreams of uplift and self-reliance. "We started this place out to be a community club, a place for our people to go," says Sam, sitting in an oversize cane chair that replicates the chair Huey Newton used as a would-be throne in an iconic photograph. "They don't have much, so we don't charge much." But the soul brothers' dream is foundering: their club is in hock to the Mob, and since the lily-white Partridge Family, instead of the Temptations, have been sent to perform at their club, there's little chance that they can raise the funds to save it.

Fortunately, the can-do spirit of the Partridge Family saves the day—saves the ghetto, in effect. The Partridges brainstorm the idea of hosting a benefit in the form of a block party; Keith Partridge (David Cassidy) writes a song—"sort of an Afro thing"—for the occasion; the Partridges and Sam fan out through the neighborhood, collecting donations; and the braggadocious Danny Partridge (Danny Bonaduce) enlists the help of the local Afro-American Cultural Society, whose paramilitary airs and black berets are cribbed from the Black Panther stylebook. As might be expected, the block party is an extraordinary success, the Mob rebuffed, the club saved.

Yet there's more, a final joke at someone's expense. As the Partridge Family bus is about to pull away, the leader of the Afro-American Cultural Society sprints over, breathless, to meet up one last time with Danny. He commands Danny to stand at attention, then unrolls a scroll and proclaims, "For your dedication and service in helping our community, I'm hereby making you an honorary member of the Afro-American Cultural Society." He hands the scroll and a black beret to Danny, who enthuses to his mother, Shirley, "Look, Mom, I'm official. Maybe I can start my own chapter at home." The ever-indulgent mother replies, to a burst of canned laughter, "We'll talk about that in the bus, Danny."

One didn't need the supersensitivity of Richard Pryor to wonder: Why were the Panther stand-ins so free and easy with their berets and their blackness? Why, when Black Power made it onto prime-time TV, did the Partridge Family have to swoop in to save the ghetto? And less abstractly: Why, even when Richard was a "special guest star," did he have to play second fiddle to the likes of David Cassidy and Danny Bonaduce? Richard's frustration could be seen edging into his performance. When Danny swaggers with puffed chest alongside members of the Afro-American Cultural Society—so happy to be black!—Richard shoots Lou Gossett Jr. an incredulous look that says, in the words of an autobiographical screenplay Richard composed shortly afterward, "This can't be happening to me." And yet it was.

Around forty-two seconds after 6:00 a.m. on February 9, 1971, Richard was lying naked in his bed in the Sunset Tower when he was awakened, along with the rest of Los Angeles, by a wrenching of the earth. His windows started rattling and popping out of their frames. He reached for his trusted companions—a samurai sword and a fifth of whiskey—and dragged himself outside. Los Angeles had become "the valley of the damned," he recalled. Everyone was on the streets, alone, and shooting curious smiles at him—the black man left standing after the apocalypse—as if he "knew God or something."

The Sylmar Earthquake, as it became known, was the most powerful American temblor in two decades, the most destructive since 1933. It was so terrifying that eight of the fifty-five people whose lives it claimed died from heart attacks. Two hospital buildings crumbled; twelve overpasses collapsed into freeway lanes; broken gas lines set off hundreds of fires; and the aftershocks kept coming—at least sixteen big ones by the end of the day. Oddly and ominously, the tremor was centered in an area where no fault had previously been detected.

For Richard the earthquake sealed his intuition that he was doomed in Los Angeles. "It was as if I was stuck to a funnel cloud that was tearing a path of destruction everywhere I went," he remembered. "I sensed catastrophe around the corner and knew I had to get out."

At a show soon after, he was approached by Alan Farley, a gentle, shaggy-browed young man and one of his most erudite fans. Farley had a math degree from Cal Tech and, though white, had been chairman of the math department at the historically black Morehouse College; now he was living in Berkeley, working as a production assistant for the Pacifica flagship KPFA. When Alan casually offered Richard a ride up to the Bay Area and said he could crash at his Berkeley apartment for a spell, Richard took him up on both proposals. The Bay Area was the scene of Huey Newton's trial and other countercultural spectacles; most important, it was not Los Angeles. Richard quickly scrambled his plans to make the move possible: a gig at the Gaslight in Greenwich Village was canceled, a week-long gig at San Francisco's Basin Street West arranged in its place.

After dreaming so big for half a decade in LA, Richard was ready to dream small, or just to sleep. He lay down in the backseat of Alan's car as they drove up to the Bay Area and conked out. He brought with him not much more than the clothes on his back—traveling as light as when he had left Peoria, a no-name bound for the Chitlin Circuit, eight years before. Untethered, again.

CHAPTER 14

I'm a Serious Mother

Berkeley, 1971

When Richard arrived in Berkeley in February 1971, he pursued his own version of the simple life. The trappings of his showbiz ascent—the Sunday baseball games with Aaron Spelling and Bobby Darin; the nights at the Daisy with the likes of Natalie Wood and Tony Curtis; the coke Olympics at the Redd Foxx Club, in which he competed with Jesse Owens–like intensity—he left behind in LA. In Berkeley, the mecca of the counterculture, he would try to whittle his life down and "learn to live on the least possible." He would subsist, he said, on fruit—"an apple a day. And wear Levi suits and drive in a '49 Packard and still be comfortable with it and not be uptight because of (my) surroundings." He wanted to find his "lost soul" and thought the best way to start was "to cast off everything but the bare essentials . . . to renounce the past in order to discover the future." As he wrote in his memoir: "House, car, clothes, women, friends—I tossed them all away."

Berkeley was a peculiar if perfect place for Richard to strip his life to the core—peculiar in that the city was a clamorous carnival of delights and distractions; perfect in that Richard was, like so many who migrated to Berkeley in the late 1960s and early 1970s, a seeker in search of himself. Starting in the fall of 1967, Berkeley's Telegraph Avenue had replaced San Francisco's Haight Street as the main stem of hippie life in the Bay Area. It was the sort of street where drivers might find themselves taunted by someone in a bullfighting cape; where a police officer stood a fair chance of being tripped while in pursuit of a suspect on foot; where a long-haired man of college age couldn't walk a few blocks without being propositioned by people dealing grass, speed, acid; where a group of street people sold tea from samovars and called themselves the Persian Fuckers. Novelist Ishmael Reed, who befriended Richard in Berkeley, remembered that the city was "crackling with information and ideas," "sizzling" with the apocalyptic sense that "something great, something dramatic, was going to happen."

By 1971, the left in Berkeley was numerous, various, and pulsing with energies it could scarcely contain. The black revolution, the third-world revolution, the sexual revolution, the drug revolution, women's liberation and gay liberation, the student movement, the prisoners' rights movement, the environmental movement—all had put down roots in the city. The week that Richard arrived in town, the underground *Berkeley Barb* reported that three hundred demonstrators had protested FBI raids on two Berkeley communes by rushing the local FBI bureau, pounding on office doors, and baiting FBI agents with shouts such as "Come on out, motherfuckers!" and "You ripped off our dope. We want our dope back. What are you doing in there, getting high with our dope?"

Even more telling, in its fervor and confusions, was a large-scale antiwar event held five days after the FBI protest. A crowd of more than three thousand took to the streets of downtown Berkeley to demonstrate against Nixon's expansion of the Vietnam War into Laos. A phalanx of the Women's Brigade led the march, raising Pathet Lao and National Liberation Front flags and chanting, "Smash the State!" When a policeman grabbed a protester who had knifed the tire of a police car, half a dozen people clobbered the policeman until he had released his prisoner. When another police officer seized one of the clobberers, he was surrounded by a knot of protesters who ripped off his helmet, struck him to the ground, and kicked him in the head until he was lying in a pool of his own blood. Marchers felt an explosion, saw a soaring plume of black smoke: someone in their ranks, it seems, had stuck a fuse into the gas tank of an Atomic Energy Commission car and lit it.

Yet for all the protest's combative power, even the countercultural *Barb* judged it a failure. The crowd, it reported, acted like "a schizophrenic with multiple personalities, all at war with each other, crippling the whole body." Rally organizers used their microphone time to attack one another, exposing the brewing feud between those who embraced violence and those who abhorred it. The two parties couldn't agree on strategy—where to lead the people?—and so the rally dribbled to a close, the crowd dispersed with tear gas and wooden bullets. Ultimately it was just another day in Berkeley. A young woman composed a poem on a patch of lawn. The street musicians sang, without skipping a beat, "Hey, hey, the sun is shining bright, and I'm so very happy that I can't keep myself from loving you." Eight thousand miles away, the war in Laos pounded on, unchanged.

In Berkeley, Richard found a mirror of his hopes and his disenchantment, and curiously enough, it may have been the feeling of shared alienation that was more galvanizing on a creative level. In Greenwich Village and the countercultural precincts of Los Angeles, he had already felt his audience's appetite for the offbeat and had discovered his capacity to feed that hunger in ever-inventive ways. In the Bay Area, audiences were more than "far out." They shivered with recognition at Richard's bitterness about the American political scene, and thrilled when he sharpened his attack on their favorite targets—the war machine, institutionalized religion, the shallowness of the American dream—and twisted the knife.

For the next seven months, Richard delved into his own agonies, exploring them from the inside out, revisiting the traumas of his life with an unblinking stare. He had been hurtling forward for eight years, trying desperately to hurtle upward; now he pressed the Pause button. He crawled into himself and ruminated. He experimented—in routines onstage, in bids at spontaneous poetry, in screenplays and in an avant-garde sound collage—with being *un*funny. Death haunted his imagination. He fell into darker circles, let go of his obsession with the main chance, and reached for a new complexity in his performances, a new strength.

Richard's home base, at first, was the one-bedroom apartment of his fan Alan Farley, located in the downtown flatlands west of the University of California campus, not far from where the police fired tear gas a week before. Serendipitously, Richard had planted himself in the very epicenter of the Berkeley cultural earthquake. Known for its low rents, Richard's new neighborhood attracted a fertile mix of Cal graduates looking to stay in the area on the cheap, hippies fleeing the high cost of living in San Francisco, and black locals with little stake in "the system." In a survey of the electoral preferences of Berkeley's black population in 1971, two political scientists found that the most radical blacks (those who supported, for instance, a separate police department for black Berkeley, with strong community control) lived in those mixed areas, like Richard's, with a sizable infusion of young whites. Overwhelmingly black districts voted in a liberal, rather than radical, direction. The politics of Richard's new neighborhood spoke, then, to a distinctive form of countercultural chemistry—the chain reaction where black groups like the Black Panther Party catalyzed the dreams of white radicals and, more surprisingly perhaps, the experiments of white radicals accelerated black political awakenings. Each group felt buoyed, or vindicated, by the convictions of the other.

Richard and Alan's relationship played out this chemistry on an intimate scale. A refugee from academia, Alan was remaking himself as a fledgling social critic, writing a "Media Monitor" column that stood up for the principle of free speech and attacked the timidity of network TV programming; Richard was free speech incarnate and someone who himself could benefit from Alan's connections to KPFA, a hub of the Bay Area left, and other local institutions. During the workday, Alan managed the operations of KPFA; in his off-hours, he managed the operations of Richard. He gave Richard his bedroom, cooked meals for him, ferried him to friends' homes at night, and made the odd business arrangement with a club owner, the press, or the radio station. Fortunately for posterity, he also followed Richard with taping equipment, recording his gigs, interviews, and radio shows, and lending the equipment to Richard when the aspiring auteur wanted to work out his ideas in real time.

Richard kicked off his Bay Area sojourn on a triumphant and revealing note, with a successful weeklong engagement at the San Francisco nitery Basin Street West. Five years earlier, the *Examiner*'s Phil Elwood had complained that Richard was "unfunny and not original," and was "insecure and ill at ease, despite his projected hipness." Now Elwood, a high-profile critic of Bay Area nightlife, was knocked out by Richard's performance, writing arguably the best review Richard had yet received—the sort of review that a performer clutches to his chest while falling asleep. Elwood pronounced Richard "a major figure among contemporary hip theatrical figures of American society," an artist whose "stance, eyes, head, arms, cigarette-prop and even his pratfalls are handled with grace and perfect timing."

Elwood did more than praise Richard's artistry, too. He underlined the political stakes of Richard's new persona: "In the vernacular, he is one of the 'baddest niggers' around. That is, he's one of the favorite acknowledged and respected spokesmen for the younger black community." Elwood was probably exaggerating Richard's "bad nigger" renown—*'Craps'* had yet to be released, and Basin Street West was one of the few nightclubs still open to Richard's act—but his review had the assured air of righteous truth. Elwood noted Richard's liberal use of "rough, raw and colorful words" and offered a ringing defense: "He will be offensive in vocabulary and theme only to those who are upset by words in themselves, or by reality."

Elwood was no outlier in praising Richard extravagantly. The San *Francisco Chronicle*'s Ralph Gleason crowned him "the very best satirist on the night club circuit." Alan Farley took to the pages of the *KPFA Folio* to praise Richard's "endless creativity" onstage, his "uncanny ability to perceive, evaluate and portray people and their attitudes accurately," and his courage in facing the truth even though "it hurts him and it hurts us." (The fact that Alan and Richard were housemates went unmentioned.) And Grover Sales, *San Francisco* magazine's theater and film critic, hailed Richard regularly and vividly in his monthly column, calling him the "master of a hundred voices" and a "nervous, light-brown ferret" who "exposed the sickness of our time" by wielding "the salty, spermy motherwit of a black ghetto poolhall." Bay Area critics all took Richard seriously as an artist and social commentator—and were among the local forces pushing him to take himself seriously, too.

Richard soon demonstrated just how serious he could be. While staying at Farley's apartment, he was approached by a producer at PBS to contribute some material to *The Great American Dream Machine*, an eclectic anthology program that mixed reportage with off-center comedy from the likes of Albert Brooks, Chevy Chase, and Marshall Efron. Targeted at younger viewers, the show cultivated a tilted sense of irony: a segment about the elderly utopia of Sun City might be set against, say, ten minutes of barroom palaver hosted by Studs Terkel or a pseudodocumentary about the "Famous School for Comedians," where bow-tied lecturers demonstrated how to target someone with a cream pie ("Make sure that you hit one of three desirable areas"). Writing on spec for the show, Richard delivered "Uncle Sam Wants You Dead, Nigger," a screenplay in tune with the antiwar rally that greeted his arrival in Berkeley. It was a scathing parable about a wasted life, and a veiled meditation on Richard's own family life and his stint in the army.

Richard's screenplay tracked the life of Johnny, a young black man who's set upon by voices: his father dismissing him as "just a heartache to me and your momma"; his mother lamenting that he dropped out of school; and a militant, named Dashiki, bidding him to fight his own fight and "join our army." Johnny decides to enlist in the U.S. Army, partly to appease his father (to whom he'll send his allotment money) and partly to live out his own dreams of grandeur. "I'm gonna get me some of them gooks, too, Jack," he tells himself, "so when I go home, I'll be a hero." The screenplay then shifts to a field in the Vietnamese countryside, where a group of a farmers wave to the U.S. Army truck of Johnny's regiment. Johnny thinks they're simply waving, but his commanding officer thinks they're signaling to bring on mortar fire and orders Johnny to kill them, which he does. Next, Johnny is ordered to harvest their ears for a body count, which he agrees to do, too, though with great reluctance.

At the climax of the screenplay, Johnny looks at the bodies of his victims and sees the bodies of his own family, lying there dead. Before he can mutilate the bodies as ordered, a Vietnamese sniper in a distant bush fires at him; Johnny begins falling in slow motion. In the short film's coda, we hear three voices marking his death as his body continues to fall to the ground: a black preacher eulogizing him with empty clichés ("he lived a good life, um hm"); a white guard at a graveyard, refusing to admit the body ("We don't bury no niggers"); and Dashiki, with the last word, putting a harsh twist on the traditional military recruiting poster ("Uncle Sam wants you . . . dead, nigger").

It was Richard's most straightforward political statement yet. It underlined that the Vietnam War was an atrocity, a travesty that claimed the Vietnamese and young black Americans alike as its victims. It traced the violence not just to the officers ordering the killing but also, less obviously, to the black church, the black family, and a culture that preferred simple lies to complicated truths. And judging from a recording Richard left of the screenplay in which he acted out the film himself, it seems he intended the film as a showcase of his virtuosity, wherein he might play multiple roles in the manner of Alec Guinness in *Kind Hearts and Coronets* or Peter Sellers in *Doctor Strangelove.* The silver-tongued preacher, the hard-ass father, the fire-breathing radical—these were familiar characters from his stage routines. Johnny was a version of his Private Crunk from *Carter's Army*, lifted out of the context of the Good War and dumped into the horror of Vietnam. While Richard had played two roles in the ill-fated *Uncle Tom's Fairy Tales*, here he proposed doubling the challenge to four.

Yet, like so many of Richard's funky experiments from this period, "Uncle Sam Wants You Dead, Nigger" was not to be. *The Great American Dream Machine* rejected the script, perhaps because it was bleak rather than quirky. Its producers may have expected the Richard of the mid-1960s, the creator of light-fingered takes on the army and the media. In any case, they turned it down flat. Instead of seeing his film produced, Richard would have to settle for seeing his screenplay in print. At Alan Farley's suggestion, he sent his treatment to *The Realist*, a San Francisco–based underground magazine that had just published the notorious "Disneyland Memorial Orgy," a baroquely detailed image in which, among other things, Goofy penetrates Minnie Mouse, Doc sodomizes Dopey, and the remaining five dwarfs work on Snow White. Paul Krassner, *The Realist*'s irreverent editor, was more than happy to print Richard's piece in the April/May issue.

If the rejection of "Uncle Sam Wants You Dead, Nigger" by *The Great American Dream Machine* was one sign that Richard's Bay Area sensibility had trouble traveling outside the Bay Area, another was his late-April gig at the Improv, his old New York City stomping ground, in front of a largely white audience. Richard was approached by Improv regular Michael Blum, a young would-be director, who asked Richard if he might film a show for a sample reel, something that Blum could shop around to get more work for himself. Richard agreed.

In Blum's film, released fourteen years later under the title *Live and Smokin'*, Richard is jittery, his face beaded with flop sweat, as he rolls out material that slayed mixed audiences at Basin Street West. According to Blum, "the room was filled with a lot of people who looked up to Richard" but remembered him as "a sweetie with these all-white gloves"; they were blindsided by the Richard of *'Craps.'* When Richard describes how the white johns of his childhood were conned by the faked enthusiasm of the black prostitutes he knew, the crowd reacts with befuddled silence. When he riffs on sexual taboos—how a fringe benefit of "being a Negro" was "fucking white girls," how he tried to keep his sex with gay queens on the down low—he is met with murmurs, side talk. "This ain't as funny as we thought it would be," he observes.

Richard was usually a master at curing a sour atmosphere in a room. At other shows, when audiences sat stone-faced to provocations like "Remember the old days, when giving head wasn't cool?", he might snap back with "Oops! Guess those days ain't old!," throw out his body in an ironic buck-and-wing, and save the moment. He could be cruelly ingenious, too, at silencing hecklers. When one woman kept complaining about a jibe of his, he performed an elaborate pantomime in which he grabbed, stomped, shredded, and pulverized her; sprinkled her into make-believe rolling papers and smoked her; then finished her off by announcing, "This ain't shit!" to the hoots of the crowd.

At the Improv show captured in *Live and Smokin'*, though, Richard seemed at a loss. After some audience members made a move to leave, he cracked, "I hate to see folks leave when I be talking. I hope y'all get raped by black folks with clap, and ain't nothin' worse than the black clap." The cruelty was there, but the ingenuity was not. Richard needed an audience who knew how to play off him, who would follow his cues even if it meant that everyone was staggering and tripping, fumbling for a foothold together. At the Improv, he staggered alone.

On the night of May 21, 1971, Richard was caught in another jam: stuck on a delayed flight from New York City, unable to reach a gig at Mandrake's, the music club just a half mile from Alan Farley's apartment in the Berkeley Flats. Unbeknownst to Richard, he was also running late for a rendezvous with his Berkeley destiny, the clock ticking down to an encounter that would both ground him and help set him free as a black artist.

Mandrake's itself was another case study in the interracial give-and-take of the counterculture. Its owner was Mary Moore, a white woman married to a black jazz saxophonist. Named after a root fabled for its magical properties, the club paid tribute to the black roots of American music, its programming a mix of the best jazz and blues artists (Thelonious Monk, Ornette Coleman, Muddy Waters, John Lee Hooker) and groove-oriented bands (Commander Cody and his Lost Planet Airmen, Country Joe and the Fish) that drew a younger, whiter audience. Whatever the music, the club's atmosphere was loose, feel-good, participatory: the audience prided itself on being adventurous. A week before, jazzman Roland Kirk walked out the door while still blowing on his saxophone, and the audience followed him into the street and around the block, happy to have discovered their very own Pied Piper.

It was a good crowd for Richard, in other words. But where was he? Mary Moore called to the stage Country Joe McDonald, who found a guitar and tore into "Louie, Louie," trading the song's famously unintelligible lyrics with a delighted audience.

In the middle of "Louie, Louie," Country Joe was cut off; Richard had manifested himself. "A slim shadow slipped on to the stage," recalled novelist Cecil Brown. "He then crossed the stage into the little spotlight and came out of the shadow. . . . We fell under the spell of Richard's voices." For Brown, who was teaching English classes at UC Berkeley at the time and had never seen Richard perform, the show was a revelation: here was a brilliant satirist in the line of Juvenal, Jonathan Swift, and Mark Twain. And yet he was also a living, breathing link to the black oral tradition, a descendant of Langston Hughes and Zora Neale Hurston, an avatar who took folklore and made it dynamic and new. Brown felt a special connection: "I was one of the only blacks in the audience and Pryor glanced over at me through the entire routine as if I were a witness to what he was telling this white audience."

After the show, Brown followed Richard to the parking lot, looking the picture of hipness himself, with his black leather jacket, black knitted cap, and "Free Huey" button. They clasped hands in the Black Power handshake.

"How long are you going to be performing in Berkeley?" Brown asked.

"I live here now," Richard replied, upbeat. "You can come by and hang out with me."

The friendship would be a consequential one, cutting a window onto a new reality for Richard. Brown was, like Alan Farley, extremely well educated (with an MA in English from the University of Chicago), but unlike Farley, he shared with Richard a raucous and fearless sense of humor: the two were fellow provocateurs, with a common affection for the con man, the player, the teller of tall tales. Brown had recently published *The Life and Loves of Mr. Jiveass Nigger,* an incendiary novel that the *New York Times* described as "a nightmare dreamed on a bed of nails." The novel's protagonist, George Washington, was cousin to Richard's Super Nigger, a mischief maker in the age of Black Power, living by the motto "All is jive." He jives his way from Harlem to Copenhagen, mastering his world through lies, put-ons, and superior cocksmanship, until he realizes he has been screwing himself all the while, surrendering to other people's fictions of him. Trying to let go of his final illusions, he dreams of publishing a book seven hundred pages long, with each page blank except for the phrase "KISS MY BLACK ASS" and a footnote on the bottom reading "MY BLACK BALLS TOO." *Jiveass* was extremely piquant—"flimflamboyantly erotic," in the words of the *Times*—and it struck an exposed cultural nerve. For a brief period in 1970, Brown was the writer of the moment, fielding raves for his best-selling novel, appearing on *The Tonight Show* with Bill Cosby and Jane Fonda, and selling the book's screen rights. His house in the Berkeley hills hosted the sort of parties that brought together novelists and actors, professors in tweeds and hipsters in beads.

Brown and Richard became running buddies, and through Brown, Richard was drawn into a circle of black intellectuals who breathed in the Bay Area's bohemian spirit: Ishmael Reed, Claude Brown (no relation to Cecil), Al Young, and others. "He had never been around highly educated, professional black writers and artists of that stature," reflected his Berkeley friend Joan Thornell. "I think he was fascinated by that." Richard noted later that his new friends were "uncompromisingly black," but it was perhaps more important that they were uncompromisingly artists, dexterously exploring the tangle of sex and race in American life, and lobbing rhetorical bombs at the pieties of the left and the right.

Chief among the bomb throwers was Reed, a free-ranging satirist who spoofed black literature classics like *Invisible Man* in his first novel (*The Free-Lance Pallbearers*), parodied the Western genre in his second (*Yellow Back Radio Broke-Down*), and was in the middle of writing a third (*Mumbo Jumbo*) that turned the detective novel inside out. Richard and Reed traded notes, giving themselves an education that, in Reed's words, "was not on the curriculums when we were going to school." As part of that education, Reed gave Richard a biography of Bert Williams, the black vaudevillian who wore blackface but imbued his act with pathos and complex hilarity. Richard felt a special connection, too, with Claude Brown, author of the best-selling *Manchild in the Promised Land*, the autobiographical story of a Harlem boy who is pulled out of his childhood and into a life of drug dealing and petty crime. Richard and Brown's friendship began with a 3:00 a.m. phone call placed from Cecil Brown's home, in which Richard came on the line with the impertinent question "Hey, motherfucker—is all that shit (in *Manchild*) true?"

All these new friends were artists who, like Richard, had found a way to turn the language of the streets into the language of art, but more than Richard, they could step back and give an intellectual account of their style. Claude Brown in *Esquire* in 1968: "Perhaps the most soulful word in the world is 'nigger.' . . .'Nigger' has virtually as many shades of meaning in Colored English as the demonstrative pronoun 'that,' prior to application to a noun." Ishmael Reed, in the introduction to a 1970 anthology *19 Necromancers from Now*: "[T]he great restive underground language rising from the American slums and fringe communities is the real American poetry and prose."

The old justifications Richard had given for his act—getting paid, making people laugh—seemed tired and worn out by comparison. He grappled with his limitations. "I don't think I have a style yet, that's what I'm working on," he told *Good Times*. "Something special. A tone. I blow good but I haven't got the tone yet." In the meantime, he introduced himself by way of a disclaimer: "People think I'm funny. But that shit ain't true. I ain't funny. I'm a serious mother."

Not long after meeting Cecil Brown, Richard stopped crashing at Alan Farley's apartment and moved a few blocks away, to a $110-a-month rental in a dingy clapboard rooming house where the doors were secured by padlocks. He had a bed, some clothes, a TV, a portable record player, and a single copy of Marvin Gaye's "What's Going On," which he spun over and over until he considered it "the soundtrack for my life." He hibernated and retreated into himself, trying to unriddle his life's inner mystery. He read and reread the collected speeches of Malcolm X, whose story of ascetic self-transformation reverberated in him. Malcolm stood as an emblem of the courage that Richard hoped to gather. A week after his Mandrake's gig, he recorded an arresting riff on Farley's tape recorder:

> Dracula, Frankenstein, the Wolfman, the Invisible Man and Hercules don't scare me. The FBI, the Anti-American Committee, J. Edgar Hoover, President Nixon, President Johnson . . . the Bank of Manhattan, Chase Manhattan, Rockefeller—none of these people scares me. What scares me is that one day my son will ask me, "What did you do, daddy, when the shit was going down?"

And what was Richard, holed up in his bare apartment, to do about the shit going down all around him? He had largely given up on TV work, his main vehicle for reaching a larger audience, explaining to a Bay Area interviewer that being on TV was "like drinking out of two cups." (The reference was to Paul's stern warning in 1 Corinthians 10:21, "Ye cannot drink the cup of the Lord and the cup of the devils.") He took a more relaxed attitude to booking gigs, trying to escape the Hollywood mentality: "I'm using the money, the money ain't using me." And perhaps because he was now surrounded by writers, he made an unprecedented commitment to writing, experimenting with genres he had never before tackled, in an effort to express new thoughts, new visions, new tones. It was, he later reflected, "the freest time of my life."

Sometimes he'd sit down by himself, "very high"—in his words—

"on cocaine and whiskey and insecurity and guilt," and try to improvise poetry into being. A snatch of one stream-of-consciousness poem, recorded in the fall of 1971, captures the blend of disillusionment and yearning, exhaustion and ambition, that filled Richard during this interval. His voice on the recording is scratchy and eerie, like a phone call from beyond the grave:

Back up on myself and dim the lights
Poetic justice stems from my lips . . .
A fading car goes by, it whispers in my voice
A creakiness untold that I haven't heard before
A challenge to me to stay here who I am
To be, to live, to realize
Not to justify, not to inherit,
I lay claim to all and nothing
I survived from my will,
My will to survive in life's endless bloody dream.

If life was an "endless bloody dream," Richard was pursuing a certain wakefulness within it. The boy who had grown up in a brothel was looking to be reborn in a state of purity—to find that, in his heart, he had "no crimes, no sins, no guilts." He withdrew all claim on the "things that have been willed to me": for the would-be ascetic, less was more; the man without possessions was free to be full of life. Yet Richard's performance of the poem, his graveyard voice, pulled against the triumphant message. It was as if he recognized that there might be wisdom in renouncing the world, but not so much in the way of pleasure.

In fact, "pleasure" was far from the center of the creative work Richard produced in Berkeley, starting with a number of film scenarios he devised in the wake of seeing director Melvin Van Peebles's *Sweet Sweetback's Baadasssss Song.* With his wild fable of black payback, Peebles succeeded where Richard failed with *Uncle Tom's Fairy Tales.* The film—about a professional sex stud who kills two policemen in defense of a Black Panther, screws his way out of handcuffs, then screws his way out of the clutches of a female biker gang—was the surprise hit of 1971, taking in over five million dollars and launching the blaxploitation boom. The movie divided black critics fiercely: Huey Newton celebrated it as "the first truly revolutionary Black film made . . . by a Black man," while *Ebony*'s Lerone Bennett Jr. wrote, in a crisp takedown of its politics, that "F★★★ing will not set you free. If f★★★ing freed, black people would have celebrated the millennium 400 years ago."

Richard watched *Sweetback* over and over. "I was sad I wasn't in it. I envied the people that had parts in it," he said at the time. Then he praised the "phenomenal" movie with a resonant analogy: "That was as exciting to me as it must have been to Walter Cronkite when the cat landed on the moon." Van Peebles was a black Neil Armstrong, planting a flag in *terra incognita*, a spot formerly thought unreachable; Richard was exulting in the transmission from a world away.

Sweetback revived Richard's dreams of being a filmmaker. He brainstormed one day, on Alan Farley's tape recorder, a short film titled *The Assassin*, set five years into an apocalyptic race war. The film would follow a day in the life of a black guerrilla, stalking through a forest and armed with a rifle, bayonet, and hand grenades. The guerrilla is implacable, indifferent. He sees two white children picking flowers in a meadow and garrotes them with a wire before killing their mother and father, too. He steals into an army stockade where he sees seventeen bodies, people accused of anti-American activities, swinging in the breeze, then kills the army officers responsible. At sundown he sees a white female hippie taking a bath naked in a stream; she dreamily invites him to smoke some grass and lay her. He kisses her, then stabs her in the stomach with the bayonet. Finally, he walks to the top of a mountain, surveys his world, and says to himself, "There be mornings," before falling asleep and beginning the cycle anew.

The Assassin was not much—a creative burp that came out of Richard's political dyspepsia, reflecting his hunger to be righteous and his sense of being utterly alone. He invested more energy into *This Can't Be Happening to Me*, his first attempt to translate his Peoria upbringing into film. The screenplay survives only in fragments, but those pieces suggest how, as Richard delved into the enigma of his identity, he was brooding over the scenes of his childhood, tinting them with a tripped-out imagination that made his projected film cousin to a midnight movie like *El Topo*. If the Richard Pryor of the mid-1960s underplayed the difficulties of his childhood, and if the Richard Pryor of the late 1960s turned them to comedic account, the Richard Pryor of the early 1970s, in Berkeley, remade them into a show of horrors. His feelings of humiliation and loss ran like a bright red thread through whatever he wrote.

The screenplay begins with the teenage Richard stabbed in a chaotic fight in his grandmother Marie's brothel. Shocked at seeing her grandson wounded, Marie fires her gun "in fear and excitement," but the bullet goes wild; she literally shoots Richard in the back, killing him. Before he passes into oblivion, though, the scenes of Richard's life flash painfully before his eyes: his mother servicing a john while his father spies on the scene from a keyhole; visiting a priest after being kicked out of parochial school for having a mother who works as a prostitute. "Why is this happening to me?" he asks during the latter. Doves perch all over the priest's head and body, covering him with their excrement; the priest answers Richard's appeal gravely and hesitantly, spitting out bird droppings every few words. When the camera pulls away from the shit-spattered priest, we see that, as he has been dispensing sober advice, he has also been masturbating into a vat of holy water.

In its last act—Richard's funeral and wake—*This Can't Be Happening to Me* strikes a different, calmer note. If the earlier scenes are brutalizing, seeking to traumatize the viewer as Richard has been traumatized, these are suffused with resignation. We see a diamond-ringed preacher eulogizing Richard, then pull back to discover the church empty except for the preacher and a naked Richard. The scene takes up the eternal gnawing question "Will they be sorry when I'm gone?," and answers it in the negative. There is nothing left for Richard but to cremate himself. He walks into a furnace and comes out as ash.

In the screenplay's final scene, Richard at last gets a proper send-off when the preacher gathers together Richard's friends—"pimps, whores, dudes"—and mixes his ashes into ten pounds of cocaine. Everyone snorts and reminisces. Richard, reconstituted and now wearing what's described as a "Super Nigger" outfit, looks on with satisfaction. But the "Super Nigger" costume, we discover, is merely another version of a clown suit. Richard announces, "Everyone knows Super Niggers can't fly," and shambles off toward the darkness. When he turns his back to the camera, he reveals that his suit has a large hole at his rear end. He departs bare-assed from his life, and his film.

This Can't Be Happening to Me never happened; it ended up in some producer's slush pile, if it ended anywhere at all. But the screenplay stands as a revealing X-ray into the mind of Richard during his Berkeley sojourn. He might still wear a "Super Nigger" suit, but he no longer believed in the bravado of the act. He was reconnecting with the fragility he'd felt as a child and lingering with it, searching for answers and finding only more questions.

As the final scene of *This Can't Be Happening to Me* suggests, Richard never quite gave up *all* the things willed to him in the world. In Berkeley he kept his cocaine close, while being extremely generous with it. Claude Brown remembered a drug dealer visiting Richard with a fresh shipment and asking, "How much you want?"—to which Richard replied, "How much you got? Just leave it there. I'll see you tomorrow." The cocaine was so pure that the two of them needed to steady themselves with shots of overproof rum when they snorted it or else they'd lose their grip. "We'd be up at dawn and going for two or three days," Brown said. "I used to have to keep away from him to get some sleep." On his benders, Richard took to wearing an old kimono, wooden sandals, and the conical hat of a rice farmer, looking, in his words, "like a deranged wizard." At one point on Telegraph

Avenue, he popped a quarter into a newspaper kiosk, removed all the newspapers, and then tried handing them off to pedestrians nearby. When they wouldn't take the papers, he started throwing them—at people, at cars. Someone familiar with the neighborhood's denizens might have mistaken him for one of the Persian Fuckers.

Yet in his stage act at the time, Richard was honing one of his greatest routines, a sharp and unsentimental portrait of drug addiction. Berkeley may not have released him from his drug habit, but it gave him enough critical distance on it to distill the life of an addict into a riveting version of his "Wino and Junkie" routine. The ironic stance of his intellectual friends, who claimed the authority of street knowledge but refused to be reduced to their blackness, resonated in his stage act. Asked by an interviewer how he found his material, Richard lit on a curious comparison: "You know how Dracula has to suck blood? I go out and get vibes, find out what it's about. Revitalize, re-energize myself, get back with the people. I get high. I suck up the vibes." Like some benign vampire, Richard was a boundary crosser—of the streets and beyond the streets at once.

Richard's "Wino and Junkie" was his showstopper for years to come, and it is both as experimental and as finely calibrated as anything he ever performed in his stage act. The routine always began with the familiar character of the wino, whose low social position is no bar to his braggadocio. For two or five or ten minutes, Richard would play this self-proclaimed "people-ologist" of the ghetto, spinning off unbelievable riffs on how he had worked for the FBI, or how he knew, from personal experience of the man, that Jesus could never have risen from the grave ("Shit—he wouldn't get up in the morning").

Then the routine would hang and take on a more unpredictable rhythm, as if it were losing itself in the confusions of the street:

> **JUNKIE** [*Body weaving; grimacing and struggling to form sentences; unclear if he's addressing himself or the wino*]: What's happen . . . what's happening, mother . . . What's happening? Hah . . .

[*Picks something off his pants*]

Caked all up and smells . . .
What's happening? Shit!
I see you, you old motherfucker, "I'm the man, motherfuck these cars, I'm directing this shit."

[*Suddenly becomes animated and fluid as he mimics the wino's efforts to direct cars like a traffic cop.*]

[*Reverts back to his strung-out self*] Say, man, I feel bad enough to drink some milk. You got anything?

WINO: Yeah, boy, I got some—I got some advice for your ass. You better lay off that narcotic, nigger. It done made you null and void. You better try to go to work, get a job, be somebody respectable. Fuckin' around here in the streets like a fool. You could help the community, get it together.

JUNKIE: "Get it together. You better get it together, get a job."

[*Looking glassily into the distance*] What's happening, shit. Motherfucker. I used to work, motherfucker, I worked for five years in a row when I was in the joint, pressing license plates.

[*To an unseen antagonist*] Kiss my ass, truck!
Where the fuck a nigger going to get a job out here in the street, pressing license plates, man? You understand, motherfucker.

[*Sobs, puts his hand over his face*] Kiss my motherfuckin' ass, nigger. Kill me, motherfucker! Hah.

In his performance, Richard floated free of the rules of stand-up comedy and into some nether realm, the land of living hell. The punch lines—"I feel bad enough to drink some milk," "Kiss my ass, truck!"—have no conventional setup. The junkie, stuck as he is in life, is largely stuck in language, too, fixed on two basic phrases: "What's happening?" and "motherfucker."

Yet what complexity Richard wrings as a performer out of those two phrases! In his memoir, Richard said that at Mandrake's or Basin Street West he sometimes experimented self-consciously with tiny shifts in tone—"I repeated a single word like 'bitch' or 'motherfucker,' but gave it fifty-seven different inflections"—and this routine suggests why his audiences didn't just boo him off the stage. There was an emotionally acute method to the madness. Here "What's happening?" is the phrase the junkie uses when he wants to put on a brave face and engage his friend; the phrase he uses when he looks at his dirty clothes and wonders what's become of himself; the phrase he uses when he considers the forces that lock down the ghetto and keep people like him from finding a decent job; and more. Feelings of camaraderie, hopelessness, and rage churn through that casual scrap of language.

Richard's junkie is the sort of person who might sob through curses like "Kiss my motherfuckin' ass!" and "Kill me, motherfucker!," but he also has the capacity to step back from the brink of despair and laugh with one last "hah" at his own melodramatic imagination. He's unlike other junkies ginned up in the media in the late 1960s and early '70s—neither a tabloid villain nor an object of middle-class pity. He may be desperate, but he can't be reduced to his desperation.

Richard always ended the routine by converting it unexpectedly into a tenderhearted father-son drama. The two men were revealed to be ghetto yin and yang: one old, one young; one drawn to the past, one thinking of his future; one full of swagger, one drained of self-confidence. When they collide on the street, they complete each other. At the routine's close, the junkie confesses he "need[s] someone to talk with me and walk with me" so he "can handle this white world" until his next fix, and the wino softens up as Richard's own father never did, announcing "I'm going to walk with you, because I believe you got potential. You could be somebody if you had opportunity, like I had."

That last sentence struck a perfectly bittersweet chord, and Richard delivered it as the final punch line, performance after performance. He seemed to like the question it left hanging in the air: What opportunities were in the offing for people like his junkie, who represented the future of the ghetto as much as his wino represented its past?

On the morning of September 9, 1971, over two thousand miles away at the Attica Correctional Facility in upstate New York, an inmate pulled a lever on an open lockbox and freed another inmate, who had been confined to his cell for allegedly throwing a soup can at a guard. Prison authorities tried to crack down in response—and Attica exploded into riot. More than a thousand inmates seized control of the grounds, taking forty-two hostages from the prison staff and appealing to New York state officials to negotiate a series of demands, from better living conditions to the federal takeover of the prison and the removal of its warden. (In a prison that housed twice the number of inmates it was built for, inmates were allotted one shower every seven days and one roll of toilet paper every five weeks.) Four days later, Russell Oswald, the head of New York State's prison system, gave the order for state troopers to storm the facility. The result was the bloodiest prison confrontation in American history: ten hostages and twenty-nine inmates killed by troopers. In the aftermath—what a federal court later called an "orgy of brutality"—guards forced inmates to crawl naked over broken glass while clubbing them with nightsticks. One inmate, who was wounded in the legs and couldn't get up, was sodomized with a Phillips-head screwdriver.

When the news arrived from Attica, Richard was roosting in Sausalito, an artsy enclave just across the Golden Gate Bridge from San Francisco. Not long before, he had packed his few possessions into the tiny, bright yellow Porsche of his new flame, Patricia Heitman, a smart-looking blonde with a passing resemblance to *The Mod Squad's* Peggy Lipton, and moved into her apartment in a converted mansion built by the founder of Bank of America. After half a year of the simple life, Richard was ready to step up and out. (Not incidentally, Sausalito was also where he went to meet his drug connection.) Heitman lived in another world from that of Richard's black Berkeley friends. She was a longtime Pan Am stewardess who, by her own admission, had never really "talked to a black man, let alone kissed one, let alone . . . please!" At a party on a Sausalito houseboat on the night they met, Richard made an impression by snatching a pair of Janis Joplin's shoes from one of Joplin's lovers, who had been crying over them. "What the fuck are you doing?" Richard cracked at the grieving lover. "They're fucking shoes!" He threw them in the bay. On that unsentimental note, he captured the fascination of Patricia and maneuvered into what would become one of the most durable, if troubled, relationships of his life.

The story of Attica—a group of largely black prisoners fighting for their dignity, then being crushed by the state—was a hammer blow that threw Richard back to Berkeley and his experimental circles there. He had just been given his own biweekly show on KPFA and decided to devote his first two shows to the insanity of Attica, composing poetry, new stage routines, and even a sound collage in the heat of his indignation. It was the last burst of creativity of his Bay Area sojourn, and capped the most politically militant stretch of his career.

He led off his first program, broadcast two days after the suppression of the riot, with the admission that it was "really hard to be funny with what's [gone] down at Attica." Then he launched into a vitriolic poem he'd written:

Murder the dogs,
The mad, frothing-at-the-mouth dogs
With expensive capped teeth
And fat bellies full of babies starving.

No, don't wait until they die—
Kill them now

The anger was scalding, the politics of Attica boiled down to a life-or-death struggle against a pack of rabid dogs who, if allowed to "die a natural death," would eat your children "whole—flesh, bones, and soul." Onstage at Mandrake's a few days later, Richard confessed, "I can't think of nothing to do to motherfuckers that you hate, but kill them and forget about it," then backtracked as he re-thought the impulse: "You know, it's easy for me to say. I ain't never killed nobody—except emotionally. That's the way I get even with white folks."

Richard spent much of his KPFA airtime trying out ways to "get even with white folks." Mockery was his foremost tool, as he circled around the question of how the white public justified the carnage at Attica. He lambasted the take-it-slow rhetoric of those who defended current conditions, arguing that they had "been saying that since 1954, when they were supposed to let black children go to their white schools, to go work in their Ford company. Niggers should go to their own schools and learn their own things." Attica, he said, was a town of "2800 white citizens" whose "industry is other people's misery."

In his second and last KPFA program, Richard focused on the complicity of white liberals in the Attica debacle. He began his show with "The Button Down Mind of Russell Oswald," a fifteen-minute sound collage he had constructed with Alan Farley, introducing it as part of a new album made by the "famous Attica comedian." Richard and Alan had spliced applause and gut-busting laughter into a long, rambling speech by the prison commissioner, who announced his high-minded belief in rehabilitation even as he defended the lethal raid he'd authorized. By inserting their own punctuation into the speech, Richard and Alan managed to unravel it. Oswald's hand-wringing sense that he had made "the most agonizing decision of my life"; his defense of prison guards as a "pretty fine lot"; his accusation that Attica's "hard-core" inmates "preferred not to accept that I was going to change things"—all these were made to seem laughable on their face.

Likewise, Richard put his scorn for mealymouthed liberals at the center of a Mandrake's performance he taped for KPFA, a concert that became his onstage farewell to the Bay Area. "The liberal white folks that are on our side," he offered, "are the most dangerous motherfuckers in the world," because "after a while they start telling you how to think." Then he ventriloquized the squishy thinking of Attica apologists, the excuse-making that allowed them to let themselves off the hook:

> [*Nasally*] Well, I know what happened is terrible and all, but, gosh, you've got to realize that Oswald was in a hell of a position. You've got to realize the trouble that man went through. . . . It wasn't actually a mistake. Not exactly. It wasn't exactly a mistake as much as it might seem. It *seems* to be a mistake only because it's *obviously* a mistake that *seems* to be committed—but it's a confused mistake.

As Richard put it in a memorable aphorism onstage, "wrong is perfect, right fucks up all the time." The worst people, like Oswald, were protected in a bubble of privilege and doubletalk—perfectly sealed off—while everyone else was exposed and vulnerable, their misdeeds magnified, their human failings held against them.

The largely white crowd at Mandrake's cheered Richard's satire of liberal weakness and hypocrisy, and not just because it was well delivered. In 1969, thousands of radical Berkeleyites had taken over an unused university-owned parcel of land, greening it with sod and christening it "People's Park," only to watch in horror and anger as police bulldozed the land and National Guardsmen patrolled the area with bayonets drawn. Their liberal would-be allies, such as the chancellor of UC Berkeley, had acted like Russell Oswald, temporizing just enough to give his conscience a rest, then stepping out of the way once martial law was declared. After the lost battle over People's Park, Berkeley radicals broke with liberals, propelling a regime change in city politics: in April 1971, right after Richard arrived in Berkeley, radicals captured the city's mayoralty and ended more than fifty consecutive years of Republican rule.

Through Attica, then, Richard and his audience experienced a meeting of the minds: they were all enemies of the liberal establishment, and all enemies of the state. Richard's audience at Mandrake's may have been the only white audience in America that could listen to his drubbing of Oswald and his account of police harassment—the officer barking, "Let's see that little shuffle!," Richard rejoining, "Mr. Officer, can I help you search myself?"—and hear it clearly as a version of their story, too.

Richard and his Mandrake's audience, one might say, occupied a bubble of their own. They lived in a Berkeley bubble of goodwill, funkiness, and enthusiasm for the experimental life, in which suspicion was reserved for those who, out of ignorance or principle, operated outside its hash-scented atmosphere. For seven months, Richard had enjoyed the freedom of that bubble, stretching out as a writer and performer. Released from his own need to succeed in the grandest terms, he had taken the liberty to explore the touchiest parts of his past and his present, hone the political edge of his satire until it was razor-sharp, and renovate his stage act.

Then, not long after Richard's second show on KPFA, the bubble popped. He had plans to tour some college campuses and work on a small independent film, but they were dropped when Berry Gordy's Motown Pictures approached him about a bit part in the Billie Holiday biopic *Lady Sings the Blues*—a day player role, but one that placed him outside the universe of comedy. Richard felt lured back to Los Angeles: Berkeley was a sideshow, not the main event. He pushed Patricia Heitman to give up her stewardess job at Pan Am and move down with him to LA, and she did.

Now Richard faced a new challenge: how to take his Berkeley self out of Berkeley, where the outré was the norm and the avant-garde the ideal. He had no agent, no manager, no driver's license, no bank account—just a restless ambition. "I talked about being a star all the time," he remembered. "Not because I saw myself as a star. I just had all this juice inside me, this swirl of emotions that I felt could be brought on the big screen." He girded himself to breach Hollywood for a second time.

PART FOUR

KING OF THE SCENE STEALERS

CHAPTER 15

The More I Talk, the Less I Die

Los Angeles, New York City, Oakland, 1971–1972

One of Richard Pryor's first moves, upon returning to LA, was to phone his old agent, Sandy Gallin, with the hope that Gallin might be enlisted to serve as his manager. When his secretary announced the call, Gallin felt his whole body tense up: Richard had been out of touch for nearly a year, and Gallin's life had been an oasis of relative peace in the interim. When Richard asked Gallin to come on board, Gallin respectfully declined. As with him, so with others: a well-connected friend contacted the major talent agencies on Richard's behalf, and each of them gave Richard the brush-off. Among those who controlled the traditional levers in Hollywood, he had no traction. Isolated, he started questioning what his stand-up gave his audience, exactly. "I don't know what they're laughing at. I think it's the suit," he told Norman Steinberg, a writer he'd met on the set of *The Flip Wilson Show*. So he stopped wearing the suit: he took a leave of absence from stand-up comedy and tried to pick up gigs as a writer and film actor instead, using whatever channels he had open to him.

Fortunately for Richard, the machinery of Hollywood was getting overhauled: the traditional levers were no longer the only levers. Starting in 1969, the studios had entered the throes of an economic crisis so deep as to feel existential. Box office attendance had slumped from its record high of 78.2 million a week in 1946 to a low of 15.8 million a week in 1971. "The movie industry was more on its ass than any time in its history, literally almost wiped off the face of the earth," said Peter Bart, Paramount's vice president of production in the 1970s. The heads of the studios had tried to replicate the blockbuster success of mid-1960s family entertainment like *The Sound of Music* with musicals like *Doctor Dolittle, Sweet Charity*, and *Paint Your Wagon*, and had discovered that, after the cultural revolution of the sixties, they no longer knew how to bring together young and old at the movie theater. They laid one major egg after another. "These were aging gentlemen who did not remotely understand where their audience had gone," said Ned Tanen, who headed up Universal's just-created youth division. "They looked at a movie like *Easy Rider*, and they said, 'What in the hell is this?' It's against everything they thought was a value in the country; they were still worshipping the grand ol' flag. But suddenly they were looking at these movies where everybody was dropping acid, was fucking in the park. Even I, who was much younger, didn't know who was a star anymore."

In a desperate search for new ideas and new energies, the studios started seeding low-budget experiments. Screenwriter-director Paul Schrader recalled, "Because of the catastrophic crisis of '69, '70, and '71, when the industry imploded, the door was wide open and you could just waltz in and have these meetings and propose whatever. There was nothing that was too outrageous." Or, as Columbia's Peter Guber put it, "It was like the ground was in flames and tulips were coming up at the same time."

Richard became one of those tulips. Within a year of his return to LA, he would ad-lib his way from a bit part to a supporting role in *Lady Sings the Blues*, one of 1972's top-grossing movies; would put his stamp, as a screenwriter, on Mel Brooks's *Blazing Saddles*, a smash hit that would generate a new formula for Hollywood comedy; and would inject his share of inspired madness, as both actor and writer, to *The Mack*, the film that brought "the pimp" to mainstream America. He entered into three very different productions—a biopic, a genre parody, an urban drama—and skewed them so that they broke free from their original trajectories.

He could do so because Hollywood was cutting loose from its old moorings, in terms both of the stories it told and of the people it trusted to supervise the telling. In "New Hollywood," a production might be driven forward by a music executive like Motown's Berry Gordy (*Lady Sings the Blues*); it might be tied to a comedy auteur with a zinging spirit and a track record of spotty art house success, like Brooks (*Blazing Saddles*); it might be helmed by a red diaper baby who, after growing up around Harlem, had developed into a filmmaker with a love of cinema verité, like Michael Campus (*The Mack*). These were the mavericks who reached out to Richard, willing to risk, in Brooks's words, the "bananaland" where he would take them.

Richard's companion of the time, Patricia Heitman, attributed to him an almost supernatural disruptive power. "Believe it or not," she said, "if he would have a watch, the crystal would break within twenty-four hours. It was this energy field that Richard had on his body."

"Toothsome twosome": Richard Pryor and Patricia Heitman at the NAACP Image Awards dinner in 1974. (Courtesy of the Institute for Arts & Media, Cal State, Northridge)

Around the start of October, the couple had arrived in Los Angeles in style, the two of them zipping around town in Patricia's new car, a red Ferrari, and settling temporarily at the Mediterranean Village, a large West Hollywood apartment complex populated by a complement of actors and high-class prostitutes. But as the two waited for filming on *Lady Sings the Blues* to begin, their relationship became more asymmetrical, uncomfortably close in its bare outline to the relationship Richard had witnessed between his father and stepmother. Earlier, Richard had forced Patricia to quit her job; now he helped himself to what she had salted away from a decade of working for Pan Am, dipping into those savings to support his cocaine habit.

It was not the smart move to have an addict in charge of the household budget. Paying for coke took first priority; food was an afterthought. At one point, their cash depleted, Richard ordered Patricia to go down to their local supermarket and bring back some food. Dutifully she trooped over, in a lynx fur coat, and stashed a tomato and an onion in one coat pocket and a potato in the other: the noblewoman in furs reduced to a petty thief. Her Ferrari was shortly stripped from her, too—sold off to plug another financial hole.

While Richard's nights were spent in search of the perpetual party, his days were soon spent performing a sharply ironic role, as the confidant of a great artist destroying herself through drugs. When he was first cast in *Lady Sings the Blues*, the glossy biopic of jazz singer Billie Holiday, his part had exactly one scene and one line. He was the piano player who, after a young Billie fumbles an audition as a dancer, implores the exasperated nightclub owner to try her out as a singer: "Hey Jerry, give the girl a chance." It was a thin role, but Richard projected a personality onto it, modeling his character after Jimmy Binkley, the upbeat jazz pianist he'd known at Collins Corner a decade before, in Peoria. He cocked his fedora at a rakish angle and, when the cameras rolled, gave his line a wry topspin.

The gambit worked. *Lady* producer Jay Weston recalled that

Richard delivered his single line "in such a funny, drawling way that when we looked at the dailies that night, someone said, 'Let's keep him in the scene tomorrow, where she sings her number.'" Given more room in the scene, Richard improvised a stream of patter on camera—"You've never heard ['All of Me'] like this. *Church! Take you home!*"—with a spieling delivery that the *Village Voice*'s Andrew Sarris later called "mumbly-magical."

The movie's creative team set about revising the script as the film was being shot. The originally nondescript "piano man" became Billie's best friend "Piano Man," and his scenes gradually expanded to a third of the film. His death at the hands of two drug dealers—with Billie looking on, powerless—became, astonishingly, the movie's emotional climax, the event that sends her into a final tailspin. Richard ended up the third-billed star on the picture, just beneath Diana Ross and Billie Dee Williams, its two romantic leads.

Richard was glad to pick up the extra work. Signed originally for five hundred dollars, he started receiving multiples of that amount every day to improvise in tandem with Diana Ross and develop his character in real time. The two found a groove, both of them stretching outside their comfort zone—singing for Ross, stand-up for Richard—and seizing the chance to act. "We became real close," Ross remembered. "Every day, it wasn't a job. We just worked together really easily."

In his scenes Richard was, alone among the film's actors, given the freedom to ad-lib his entire performance, and the character who emerged from that improv was both the Jimmy Binkley facsimile he originally intended and much more. Quick with a quip, his Piano Man brought out the earthy humor of the jazz world. After Billie shuddered at the sight of nightclub singers using their private parts to pick up tips from customers, Piano Man jibed about one performer: "Don't worry about her—what she misses on the top, she picks up on the bottom. One day she picked up the tabletop." When put in the place of toasting Billie on the happy occasion of her anniversary at the club, he took the opportunity to roast the club owner:

> We got old cheapie to spring for something. . . . Everything's beautiful. He even paid the band since you been here. A beautiful year! Look at the girls, look at their uniforms. Even the hos are making money!

Without Richard's Piano Man, *Lady Sings the Blues* would have had no leavening agent; the down-home humor of Billie Holiday's world would have been sacrificed on the altar of the film's high production values.

Yet Richard may have left his greatest imprint by adding a layer of emotional and ethical complexity to a film that put forward, as its moral hero, Billie's husband Louis McKay (a choice much disputed by those familiar with the real-life Billie, who wrote, of the men in her life, "I was as strong, if not stronger, than any of them"). As played by Billie Dee Williams, McKay was magnetic and suave, a do-right man who aimed to steer Billie away from drugs and toward a conventional family life. The movie's villains, like the masked southern Klansmen who ram an American flag through the window of Billie's tour bus, were drawn with a similarly broad brush.

As long as Richard's Piano Man was alive and on-screen, he stood for a middle way between the hero-villain poles of this melodrama. His attitude—hip, sympathetic, vulnerable—suggested that it was possible to live with the struggles of Billie Holiday and not be ensnared or defeated by them. Usually Billie looked pathetic when high on drugs—slack-jawed and slumped in a bathroom, say, her hair a mess. With Piano Man, she found a disjointed camaraderie in her high. In the scene in which they take heroin together, the dialogue is loose:

> **BILLIE HOLIDAY**: Hey, you know what?
> **PIANO MAN**: Chicken butt!
>
> [*Billie sings "God Bless the Child" while Piano Man accompanies her on harmonica.*]

BILLIE: You got your own harmonica. [*Rubbing her nose*] I got my own harmonica.

PIANO MAN: I got my own high, too.

The scene doesn't glamorize drug use, but neither does it condemn it. It's a scene of release for Billie and Piano Man—from everyday pressures, from logic, from the burden of performing for watchful eyes. Eventually there will be hell to pay—the dealers come after Piano Man, who has stolen the heroin for Billie, and beat him senseless—but in the moment, the drug offers Billie and Piano Man exactly what they're looking for.

Here and in other scenes, Richard's improvisations played into the hidden strengths of director Sidney Furie, who, before impressing Hollywood with the hit spy thriller *The Ipcress File* (1965), helmed *The Leather Boys* (1964), a gritty treatment of England's gay biker subculture. Piano Man's last three scenes with Billie Holiday felt almost as if they belonged to a different film, something closer to *The Leather Boys* than a mainstream musical biopic like *Funny Girl*: the scenes were open to emotional confusions and seemed as if they might go in any number of directions as they played themselves out. They were intriguingly off-balance, like the character Richard improvised into existence.

Despite Richard's achievement as an actor in *Lady*, there was a hall-of-mirrors quality to his playing Piano Man at this moment in his life. On-screen he was the addict's boon companion, hip and sweet. He'd shaved off his moustache and beard for the part, and looked again like the Cosby wannabe of 1965. Offscreen he was the addict himself, and in danger of falling into the same self-sabotaging traps that *Lady* largely warned against. One day on set, as the crew waited for Richard to perform the scene where Piano Man is beaten to death for stealing drugs for Billie, Richard shut himself in his trailer and wouldn't come out; he was incapable of being the consummate professional. According to producer Jay Weston, Berry Gordy broke the impasse by relaying a curt message to Richard through a production assistant: "Tell him if he doesn't come out right now, I will take a baseball bat and break his knee." Fortunately, Richard came out of his trailer—and performed the scene flawlessly. A perfectly happy ending: Richard avoiding a beat-down in real life by taking a beat-down in front of the cameras.

But Richard's addiction threatened others beside him. The night before shooting his scenes, he typically partied—drinking heavily, doing drugs—until three or four in the morning, waving away the fact that the Motown Productions limousine was set to arrive just a few hours later at his home, a former gardener's cottage on the grounds of Yamashiro, a jewel of a Japanese restaurant set in the Hollywood Hills. Day after day, when the limo pulled up, he was dead asleep, unwakeable.

One morning after a late-night card game, Patricia tried to rouse him.

"Bitch, if you touch me one more motherfucking time," Richard said, "I'm going to beat the shit out of you."

"The car is here," Patricia pleaded. "Richard, please."

Richard punched her in the face, and Patricia ran off, leaving the limo driver to handle him.

A half day later, he returned home from the day's shoot. Patricia was wearing a bandage on her nose; one of her eyes was bruised a shade of black.

"Who fuckin' did this to you?" Richard shouted. "I'll kill the motherfucker!"

After his work on *Lady Sings the Blues*, Richard spent the next six months settling with Patricia in their modest cottage on the grounds of Yamashiro. For all the brashness of his personal style, Richard was attracted to the serenity of Japanese gardens. At night, in his more solitary moods, he would pace around the restaurant's expansive grounds in a Japanese jacket and wooden clogs, the lights of Los Angeles spread out before him as he weaved through the gardens' concentric paths. There was no way for guests to drive up to the cottage entrance, and

Richard appreciated the extra bit of isolation; it was quiet, private.

Then writer Norman Steinberg called with an intriguing proposal, and Richard was whisked out of his isolation and into the Judeo-comic maelstrom that surrounded a short man by the name of Mel Brooks. Brooks had a problem on his hands, for which, he thought, Richard was the solution. Brooks was putting together a send-up of the Western for Warner Bros., in which the arrival of a hip black sheriff in town would expose all the clichés and double-talk of Hollywood's "Old West." "I decided that this would be a surrealist epic," Brooks said of the project that became *Blazing Saddles*. "It was time to take two eyes, the way Picasso had done it, and put them on one side of the nose, because the official movie portrait of the West was simply a lie."

When he reached out to Richard via Steinberg, Brooks had already assembled three Jewish writers to collaborate on the screenplay, and sensed he needed a black writer to complete his team. "If you have three Jews in a room," explained Andrew Bergman, who had written the original scenario and was the first writer to join Brooks's team, "you're going to be very skittish about writing jokes about a black man—what's permissible, what isn't permissible. . . . Richie gave us license, which was an enormous gift." Brooks was more specific on why he needed Richard: "I said, 'I can't say the *N*-word. I need him—he has to bless it. I need a black guy to bless that word.' "

For his part, Richard was thrilled. As a child, he had been enamored of B-Western star Lash LaRue, with his stylish black cowboy suit and whip-snapping panache, and as a teenager, he had fallen in love with Sid Caesar through *Our Show of Shows*, whose stable of writers famously included Brooks, Carl Reiner, Neil Simon, and Woody Allen. Now these two early love affairs were reawakened: Richard had the chance to create a cockeyed Western with an actual black cowboy at its center, and to do so with one of the creative geniuses behind the TV show he'd loved. Even better, Brooks was seeking to recapture, in his writers' room, the formula he felt had worked so well on *Our Show of Shows*: "lock a bunch of weirdos up together and come up with a great script." Richard eagerly accepted the job, with two small conditions. He needed train fare to New York City and a bottle of brandy waiting for him in the writers' room.

His first day on the new job at the Warner Bros. building at 666 Fifth Avenue, Richard arrived late. He settled into his chair in the sixth-floor executive conference room. Brooks started to explain how the film was shifting from its original conception. While he listened, Richard pulled out a little locket, opened it, tipped out some coke, and snorted it without missing a beat.

He pushed the locket over to Brooks: "Brother Mel?"

"Never before lunch," Brooks joked.

The other writers held their tongues, stunned; at least one of Richard's cowriters had no idea what this curious white powder was. They were nice Jewish boys, even if they had wayward imaginations. That night, Brooks phoned Andrew Bergman and asked, "Did you see that?"

Richard may have been the only *Blazing Saddles* writer to snort coke and kill a bottle of Courvoisier over the course of a day's work, but in one crucial respect he fit in perfectly: he had the fearlessness that comes from having nothing to lose. Later, *Blazing Saddles* would be seen as one of those smash hits that change the culture. It ushered in a wave of genre spoofs (*Young Frankenstein*, *Airplane*, *Top Secret*) that lent Hollywood comedy a new knowingness; it established a highbrow-lowbrow formula that has kept *The Simpsons* going for twenty years and counting; and not least and not best, it opened up the Pandora's box of fart jokes. But at the point of its conception, *Blazing Saddles* was a small studio movie, with no stars attached or to come, and the four men who gathered around its writers' table were either untested or on the skids. Steinberg was a fledgling writer with no film credits; Bergman, a history PhD who had just failed to land an academic job. Brooks himself felt washed up after the box office disappointments of *The Producers* and *The Twelve Chairs*; one reason he wanted to re-create the writers' room of *Our Show of Shows* was to shuck off his recent failures. Then there was Richard, who had made a name for himself, then decided it wasn't the name he wanted. Their response, as writers, to their shared precariousness was to go berserk, to forget about pleasing anybody other than themselves—or, as Brooks put it, to write "for two weirdos in the balcony. For radicals, film nuts, guys who draw on the washroom wall—my kind of people."

The writing process was spectacularly fitful. Sometime in the late morning, the writers would assemble, and the dialogue would start to fly. Both Richard and Mel Brooks were performer-writers: they thrived on acting out their riffs instead of dictating them. (During his gig on *Our Show of Shows*, Brooks said to himself, "My God, I'm not a writer, I'm a *talker*"—a self-assessment that could have applied equally to Richard.) Meanwhile a secretary would take notes, scrambling "like a one-armed paper hanger trying to keep some kind of order," Bergman recalled. "After an hour of working, we'd start perusing these [takeout] menus. Then we'd order lunch for about forty minutes, trying to figure out what we're going to get." After lunch, the script riffing would resume, and then, "at three o'clock, Mel would say, 'My brains are exploding, I can't do this anymore,' which was about right, and that would be it."

The screenplay that emerged from this month of spasmodic creativity was darker and more pointedly political than the original treatment, spiked as it was by the contributions of Richard, whom Brooks called "very brave and very far-out and very catalytic." In Bergman's original treatment, the black sheriff was a Bunyonesque figure who romanced the daughter of a railroad owner; Bergman's inspiration was the swaggering Panther spokesman H. Rap Brown, and the part originally fell to the grandiloquent actor James Earl Jones. By the time Richard and his fellow writers had finished with him, "Black Bart" was a trickster who fit more closely Richard's self-conception, a hero so deviously outrageous that his deputy Jim calls him "one crazy nigger."

This Black Bart "sports some violet shades" and "moves like a moist dream across the prairie." One of his first moves as sheriff is to crumple up and throw away a Wanted poster with a black man on it, reasoning, "He's got enough trouble without a bunch of honkies chasing his ass all over Mexico." He whiles away the time in his office by taking a black jockey ashtray and painting it white. After he and Jim clobber some Klansmen off camera, Jim asks him, "Did you *have* to stick the cactus up his ass?"—to which Bart replies, dreamily, "I had to." And Bart has sexual as well as political bluster. When Jim asks him what happened during his night with Lily von Shtupp, he quips, "I don't know, but I think I invented pornography."

In this first-draft screenplay, Richard's most personal contribution was a piece of street poetry that Bart performs on a scaffold in order to delay his hanging. Winking at the camera, he says, "The more I talk the less I die." Then he launches into a seventy-three-line recitation that might be titled "The Pimp's Lament." It begins:

My family was poor
My mama was a whore
And society held my father in contempt
And before I had bloomed
I knew I was doomed
To live the life of a pimp

Then it segues into Bart's success with a particular "sidewalk jezebel":

The girl turned out nice
She was doubling up twice
On the meeting and greeting scene
Why this whore would take on
Frenchmen, Puerto Ricans, henchmen
To her, they was all the same
And no son of a gun
Did this whore shun
Who could pay for her time and her frame

When the girl gets ill, Bart schemes to work her into a threesome with another girl and a white hillbilly, and she, feeling jilted, turns him into the police. Thus his final message:

So the moral of the story is
Your whore's your bread and glory
And I say this with tears in my eyes
Even if she's sick
And can't turn a trick
Don't leave your whore till she dies

Cut to: a tear rolling down from under the hood of Boris the executioner.

Richard's "pimp's lament" came out fully formed in the writers' room and surprised everyone. He told Norman Steinberg that he'd learned it in prison, and the poem is a textbook example of the kind of profane "toasts" that circulated among black men in barber shops, taverns, and jails—toasts that were first collected between covers, two years later, in Bruce Jackson's classic anthology *Get Your Ass in the Water and Swim Like Me*. For Steinberg, the poem was like nothing he'd ever heard. For Richard, it was the poetry of North Washington Street, the soundtrack of his childhood. And given what he witnessed growing up—his father and uncle playing the role of the pimp; his ill stepmother Ann pulling tricks in his father's home—its playful styling had deeper associations.

This poem at the scaffold, like many of the most explicit gestures in the original script, didn't survive the months of editing that whittled the 120-page script down to a more manageable size. But the final film carried Richard's imprint, not least through the uses it found for the word that punctuated his nightclub act: *nigger*. In the film, it's a word that comes as easily to an elderly white woman ("Up yours, nigger") as to a slave-driving yahoo foreman (who asks for a "good old nigger work song" from a group of exhausted railroad workers). It's also a word to be leveraged, jujitsu-like, against one's opponents. When the townsfolk pull out their guns to shoot Bart, he becomes a performer onstage much like Richard himself, able to encase the roles of perpetrator and victim in the same body. He is, suddenly, both a white bigot who holds Bart at gunpoint and a "cringing, whining plantation darkie" (in the words of the script). When the white gunman threatens, "Next man makes a move, the nigger gets it," the townsfolk lower their guns, touched by Bart's one-man melodrama. "We would never have done [that bit]," said Andrew Bergman, reflecting on how the other writers benefited from Richard's nerve. "It might've occurred to us, but we would have said, 'Uhhh . . ."

As much as Richard contributed to *Blazing Saddles* a scalding treatment of race in American life, the film gave him something in return. It allowed him to move outside his usual preoccupations, to shed his skin. Mel Brooks remembered that, instead of throwing himself completely into the part of Black Bart, Richard "concentrated on Mongo. He wrote most of the Mongo stuff; he loved Mongo. He came up with crazy stuff like 'Mongo only pawn in game of life.'" Like the rest of the writers on the film, Richard was free to ransack the clichés of the Western and twist them until he had wrung out their inner absurdities. He could, through the pressure of his imagination, reveal Mongo to be not just a dumb brute, but a sweet child and inadvertent poet—even someone who flirts with being gay (given his "deep feelings" for Sheriff Bart and, in the original script, his preference for dancing with men).

Still another gift of *Blazing Saddles* was that it gave Richard a taste of a creatively fruitful interracial collaboration—something he arguably hadn't experienced since his mid-1960s New York days as a comic at the Improv. "We all adored [Richard]," said Bergman. Steinberg remembered Richard happily goofing off for an appreciative audience: at one point, Richard dressed up in a housekeeper's outfit and feather-dusted the room. Some of that mutual affection found its way into the friendship of Bart and Jim, the relationship that grounds the film and balances out its wild, centrifugal energy. For

Bergman, that on-screen friendship was essential to the film's success. "You really believed that these two guys love each other. You really felt, with all the insanity, that there was a real relationship between them, which was amazing when you consider the things that are going on on-screen."

Within the writers' room, of course, there were limits to the friendship between Richard and the others, invisible boundary lines that went uncrossed. Norman Steinberg remembered that a woman once popped into the room and asked Richard for some money; her hand was in a cast.

"What happened?" Steinberg asked.

"I punched her," Richard said.

"You punched her in her hand?"

"She put it in front of her face."

In Steinberg's recollection, "We all thought, 'Okay, moving on . . . We weren't going to touch that." Likewise with Richard's indulgence of cocaine and Courvoisier: the friendship between him and the other writers, while based in mutual admiration and acceptance, was also a delicate thing, and sometimes strategically left untested.

In the film's original script, the delicate balance of Bart and Jim's friendship comes through in the shape of its happy ending. Bart rides off from Rockridge, leaving behind the townfolk and saluting them with a fresh honorific: "Keep the faith, niggers." Then he bumps into Jim, and the two negotiate the terms of their future:

JIM [*casually*]: Where ya' headin'?

BART: Nowhere special.

JIM: Always wanted to go there.

BART: Promise y'll stay sober?

JIM: Nope.

BART [*smiling*]: Come on.

[*They ride off together.*]

As with Piano Man and Billie, the love survives the addiction, even possibly deepens with it. This was wishful thinking, Hollywood-style, where wishes do come true.

With his fellow writers on *Blazing Saddles*, Richard started getting antsy. He caught a train back west after about a month of writing. "That was about as much *sitzfleisch* as he had," Bergman said. "*Sitzfleisch* means literally 'sitting meat'—that's someone who's going to sit and write for three months. He wasn't wired that way. We'd done pretty much most of the first draft, and he wasn't going to come back for another draft—that we knew." So Richard left others to tighten the script. He anticipated that, since Brooks had enthused whenever he performed as Black Bart in the writers' room, he'd be coming back later on the project—as an actor in its starring role. He felt, with some justification, that the film carried his sensibility as much as anyone's. When the first draft was completed and typed up in his absence, the names of the screenwriters were not listed alphabetically. "Richard Pryor" was placed second, just under "Mel Brooks."

According to the legend, the original script for *The Mack* was written, by former pimp Robert Poole, on toilet paper from within his San Quentin jail cell. A typed version, called *Black and Beautiful*, eventually traveled into the hands of tough-guy independent producer Harvey Bernhard, who was intrigued by the idea—a pimp using mind control to bind women to him—and had the chutzpah to think he could finance the project on Diner's Club cards if necessary. Bernhard estimated his budget at the Hollywood pittance of $120,000. The success of early blaxploitation films like *Shaft* and *The Legend of Nigger Charley* suggested that he could make a quick return on his overextended credit.

Though Bernhard bought Poole's script for its seductive premise, the script itself was a piece of agitprop that begged to be rewritten. Drafted in 1969, it was a flat transmission of the revolutionary politics of Black Power's zenith, much of its action centering on the protagonist's Black Nationalist brother. "Snipers, baby! The war has begun!":

so exults the brother in the movie's final line, his revolutionary brigade having just riddled a pair of dirty cops with bullets.

Bernhard first pulled in a young director named Michael Campus to rewrite the script top to bottom. Campus was still smarting from the flop of his sci-fi *ZPG*, about the dangers of population explosion. ("To say I was cold after 'ZPG' is an understatement," Campus said. "I was like a slab of ice.") He had an abiding interest in black working-class life and an enabling overconfidence in his ability to negotiate perilous situations. Raised by a Communist mother and father on the border of Harlem, he had grown up in a family knitted together by the idea of social justice. The young Michael sang the Internationale at summer camp; he cried with his parents over news of lynchings in the South; he saw his father, formerly chief radiologist at Harlem Hospital, blacklisted in the anti-Communist purges of the 1950s. He picked up a hunger for unsettling truths: when Campus went behind the camera in the 1960s, he was happy to take assignments that put him in a riot on the streets of Calcutta or in the back of a police car in New York City. When Bernhard pitched *The Mack* his way, Campus agreed to the project under one condition: that he be allowed to move to Oakland and see the culture of "players" for himself. He wanted to ground his film in the reality of pimping, not some ersatz fantasy dreamed up by Hollywood.

Campus considered several actors (Ron O'Neal, John Amos, Paul Mooney) for the central role of Goldie, but fatefully chose Max Julien, an actor-writer who could rewrite the role around his own sensibility. Julien's mother, a part-time minister, had just been killed in a robbery in the streets of Washington, DC, and Julien felt both devastated and free to take on a role he would have declined while she was living. He brought to *The Mack* a brash and long-standing self-confidence. By the time he crossed paths with Campus, Julien had traveled a complicated itinerary, embracing a series of roles: premed student at Howard; middling stand-up comic in New York City (where he met Richard, who informed him, "I don't know what you do, but it ain't comedy"); expatriate actor-filmmaker in Italy; and writer-producer of *Cleopatra*

Jones, a hit black action film with a shapely karate-chopping narcotics agent at its center. At the end of that journey of self-discovery, he was a committed radical, a close friend of Huey Newton and an artist dedicated to upending the stereotypes that Hollywood preferred. "There could be [a black cinema]," he argued in a 1971 interview, "if films start to deal with the psychological problems of the black man instead of repeating the one dimensional militant or Uncle Tom." His rewrite of Poole's one-dimensional Goldie would put his ambition to the test. "I can't play Goldie as a fop," he told Campus. "He has to be a real person."

Julien insisted that his friend Richard Pryor play Goldie's partner, Slim, and Richard in turn demanded that he be able to write all the dialogue for his character. Soon Richard was hosting all-night rewrite sessions at his cottage on the grounds of Yamashiro. More than Julien and Campus (who had yet to go to Oakland), he knew the world of pimps from the inside. *The Mack* gave him a chance to become on intimate terms, again, with the demons of his past. It remained to be seen whether, in revisiting the hard-edged world of his father, he would exorcise those demons or become their servant.

The three writers came together as a team—"the three musketeers," in Campus's optimistic view, each lending his individual talents to the project. Campus brought a sense of storytelling structure and, after he spent several weeks immersed in the world of Frank Ward, one of Oakland's leading gangsters, a familiarity with the rough characters who prospered in that city's underground. Julien inflected Goldie with his verbal bravado and the sensitivity that peeked out from underneath it. Richard gave the film his ear and his feeling for black street life. In his handwritten notes from the time, Campus described how Richard's creativity erupted in the rewrite sessions:

> Richie says nothing. He just doesn't talk, then suddenly, he says everything. The words tumble out, a river. Overlapping, caustic, furious, tough, sloppy, myopic, visionary, crude and always, always real. His life is chaos. But in the core, constant discovery. Realization.

As with his work on *Blazing Saddles*, Richard considered his cocaine a necessary stimulant on the job. At their first meetup, he visited the bathroom to take a hit; in later sessions, he made multiple trips. Always, when he came back into the room, he avoided the eyes of Campus, whom he called "White Boy."

Gradually, over several weeks of intensive writing, the film took shape. The characters retained their names from Poole's script, but otherwise bore little resemblance to their original form. Richard's character Slim, formerly a tough-minded mentor to Goldie, became his wobbly sidekick, macho in theory if not in practice. Goldie was reborn as a player of some complexity: preening in a maxi-length white fur coat, but devoted to his mother; quick with an insult ("Let me tell you something, you vicious-ass piece of jelly"), but liable to drift into a church to gather his thoughts; openhearted when the cash was coming in, but coldhearted when it was not. Through Richard's suggestions, he also became a more stylish sadist, injecting battery acid into the veins of a drug kingpin, forcing a rival to stick himself with his own dagger-tipped cane, or locking a "rat" into the trunk of a car that was teeming with the real thing.

All told, the arc of the film became more melancholy, less triumphant, its radical politics tempered by the disenchantment of 1972. The dirty cops were still righteously dispatched, but Goldie was left with nothing. At the beginning of the film, he came empty-handed to Oakland on a bus, and now he departed the film seemingly on the same bus, again empty-handed. Still, for a film about disenchantment, its dialogue crackled with the vitality of people teetering on the edge of disaster. "You shade-tree nigger. You ain't no pimp, you're a rest haven for ho's. You're a car thief, a car thief!"—so cries Pretty Tony, a pimp getting squeezed by Goldie's operation. Here, with his pitch-perfect sense of street talk, Richard's contribution was essential.

Richard couldn't have asked for a writing gig with more personal relevance, but the experience of rewriting *The Mack* was hardly idyllic. He had committed to it in a moment of faith—like Julien and

Campus, he wanted to see the film come to fruition—but they had never formally discussed credit or compensation, and the default position was for all of them to get none at all. Of the "three musketeers," he was the one most ill served by this arrangement: since Campus and Julien were the film's director and star, their fortunes would obviously rise with the film's. And then there was the irony that wasn't lost on Richard: wasn't he writing a movie *about* getting paid? Who was the mack but an expert in squeezing the last nickel from anyone who owed him?

"You're gonna pay me for doin' all this shit," he told Campus during one writing session, then started repeating it like a refrain. Campus shrugged: "I'm the director, not the producer, not the money guy."

At their last session, Richard stared at the pages of the script, taking in what they'd accomplished. Then, as Campus and Julien said their good-byes, Richard stepped back from the pleasantries. He lifted a key line from the script—what Goldie the pimp says to Lulu, the first woman in his stable, when she runs to him breathless and penniless, raving that a trick has just tried to kill her—and he made it his own: "Get me my money." Having written *The Mack*, Richard was trying to operate as one. Campus agreed to plead Richard's case, to "get him his money," but in his mind he already could hear Harvey Bernhard's response: "Screw Pryor."

"Richie is the human submarine," Campus jotted down in his notes at the time. "Everything below the surface but the rage periscope." Now *The Mack* had to move into production up north in Oakland and Berkeley, on a tight shooting schedule and with a fuming Richard as its costar.

One of the reasons *The Mack* lives on as a cult classic—a movie that has inspired filmmakers such as Quentin Tarantino and the Hughes brothers, and hip-hop performers from Ice Cube and Dr. Dre to Outkast and Jay-Z—is its texture, the way it evokes the feel of desperate nights in Oakland in 1972: Snoop Dogg has called it "one of the coldest movies in American cinema." That sense of hard-bitten reality was achieved at considerable risk. Campus was committed to filming on location—in Oakland's bars, nightclubs, barbershops, churches, and funeral parlors—at a moment when the larger location was dicey in the extreme, and not just on account of the expected complications that might arise when a film crew enters the inner city (for which *The Mack*'s bodyguards carried firearms). One day, when Campus set up his camera and maneuvered his actors into place for an outside shoot, bottles started raining down from the nearby rooftops. The crew scattered, shocked at the organized ambush.

Bernhard and Campus had entered, blindly, into an ongoing territorial battle between the Ward Brothers, who controlled the underground economy of the area, and the Black Panthers, whose organization was at a tender transitional moment. Just two months before *The Mack* started filming, the Panthers had narrowed their ambitions, declaring Oakland their sole "base of operations" and asking all party members to close down other local chapters. The party aimed to concentrate on "liberating the territory of Oakland"—from the police and from kingpins like Frank Ward. In public, the Panthers started putting on a fresh face and mobilizing to elect Black Panther chairman Bobby Seale as mayor of Oakland; much less publicly, they tried to muscle in on the Ward Brothers and get a slice of their action. When Campus had toured Oakland's demimonde with Frank Ward and then secured the Ward Brothers' protection for the filming of *The Mack*, he unwittingly took sides in this war for possession of Oakland. The fusillade of bottles was the Panthers' way of announcing, as Seale told Harvey Bernhard, "You're in Panther territory now, boy."

Bernhard reluctantly agreed to meet "the Man," Huey Newton, at his penthouse apartment overlooking Lake Merritt, and the next day at noon, he, Max Julien, and Frank Ward were sitting on lacquered seats in front of a Chinese table, waiting for Newton. Bobby Seale walked out in white pants and a black watch navy cap, and recited his poetry for twenty minutes. His recitation complete, Seale announced "I'm not going to rip you off for much"—just five grand. Bernhard pulled out his checkbook and wrote a check for the full amount, unaware that his own financing agent hadn't yet put up the money. After the check bounced, the war between the Panthers and the filmmakers escalated. The Panthers set up pickets at the Showcase Lounge, where *The Mack*'s crew hoped to film the essential "Players Ball" sequence. "The Black Community Will Not Be Exploited Anymore!" charged eight-foot-high banners. Seale demanded that all extras on the film receive fifty dollars, not the ten dollars for which they'd been contracted, and called films like *The Mack* a "silver coated form of oppression." This time, Bernhard wrote a check that didn't bounce—and that was funneled into a fund for extras.

At the same time that the filmmakers were fending off the Panthers, they hit an equally persistent spot of trouble with Richard, who appeared to have pushed a Self-Destruct button en route to the East Bay. His character, Slim, was written as an insecure player with a taste for the finer things, and sometimes it seemed there was little daylight between Richard and the role he had scripted for himself. He partied with three or four women through the night, getting high on coke and champagne, then treated the set like his private playground during the day. Once, he came out of his trailer with three ladies of the evening at his side, and staggered up to Campus.

Campus asked, "What are you doing? Who are you?"

Richard deflected the brunt of the question. "This is family. It's okay—these are my cousins."

The substance abuse, combined with Richard's insomniac sleep schedule, took its inevitable toll on his body. When acting out a scene of drunken camaraderie between Slim and Goldie at a bar, Richard was so wasted on booze and coke that Michael Campus needed to prop him up during filming. If Campus lost his grip for a moment, Richard hit the floor.

Meanwhile, Richard continued to simmer over his unpaid work on the film's script, his anger spilling out on set and off. In the early hours of September 27, at the tail end of a punishing day of filming, he told Campus, "I want my fucking scene now."

Campus snapped at Richard: the reason for the delay, he said, was that his two stars were talking too much. He turned away.

Richard snagged Campus's attention by insulting his mother—a cruel touch, as Richard knew she had died early and tragically, when Campus was a child. Then, without another word, Richard charged at the director and clocked him so hard on the jaw that Campus reeled and fell to the ground, unconscious.

"How'd you like that blow?" Richard asked the limp body on the ground. Then, to everyone: "Did I get him? Did I really get him?"

The security crew trained their guns on Richard, and Max Julien rushed to grab and protect him. "You can't shoot him. No, you got to shoot me," Julien said, making himself a human shield. The security crew stood down, and Richard was escorted back to the Marriott.

Yet he was not done with the day's mayhem. At 3:00 a.m., he knocked on the door of Julien's room, carrying a homemade weapon—a sock with some metal in it, some coins or some iron balls—and appealed to Julien to join him on a late-night visit to Harvey Bernhard. Julien demurred, and the two embraced. Richard said, "You know, sometimes even if you love people, you've got to cut them loose," and he wandered off on his lonely journey down the hall toward Bernhard's room, sock in hand.

"Harvey, you know I really love you and am sorry," he began with Bernhard. "I wanted to come in here and apologize for beating up Michael." Then, as if disgusted by his act of ingratiation: "I came in here to kill you." He swung the sock.

Bernhard was sitting, groggily at first but increasingly awake, next to a coffee table on which he'd left an extremely sharp knife, one he used to peel almonds. "I was going to throw the coffee table on top and cut his throat," Bernhard recalled. But before he could execute the maneuver, his wife walked into the room and started talking about the good heart of her husband, Harvey. The temperature in the room shifted; Richard's bravado collapsed. "I can't take this shit," he said, and left.

The next day, he borrowed fifty dollars from Bernhard's sister and went back down to LA. The manager of the Marriott pulled Bernhard aside so that he could see the state of Richard's room at checkout. It looked as if a hurricane had torn through it: broken lamps, broken chairs; a total shambles. As for the film, Richard's character, Slim, would have to be written out of his remaining scenes.

Perhaps the whole production cut too close to the bone, too close to the pain of Richard's past. Just as he had played second fiddle to his father, Buck, for two decades in Peoria, so here he was playing the mack's sidekick, the wannabe who voices the vulnerability that his emotionally armored friend cannot. In some of the film's most famous scenes—some of Richard's best acting work, too—Slim steals the spotlight with his cracked-up pain. In one, he refuses to walk away from two dirty cops who ask him and Goldie to beat it. Slim is perceptive enough to know that as soon as he and Goldie turn their backs, they might be shot for "resisting arrest," and bold enough to defy a shotgun pointed at him by a cop. But Slim isn't as collected as he is perceptive. He sucks in his mouth; his eyes widen with fear. "I ain't runnin' no fucking place," he says. "I ain't no track star."

The scene then sputters unforgettably, as if some actor in it were going off script (which Richard in fact was doing, improvising around Slim's pain). The cops leave abruptly when a group of onlookers—potential witnesses—appears. Goldie walks away somberly, bearing the weight of the world on his shoulders in the form of a hip brown suede cape. Alone now on the street, his friend receding into the distance, Richard's Slim can't stop talking, even though he's talking only to himself. He spits out the words with a teary-eyed fury:

> We're gonna get the motherfucker, 'cause he's a punk! You ain't shit! I'm gonna get him! Goldie, we gonna get 'em 'cause they pulled down on us! They didn't use that shit, baby! The motherfucker pulled a gun on me, man! I ain't bullshittin', brother! We gonna get him, punk-ass motherfucker!

As Slim raves on alone, talking about a "we" that doesn't exist, the camera gradually pulls back to reveal a new detail of his outfit: along with a pink floral shirt and gray satin vest, he's wearing a pair of crimson knee pants that seem designed for a child. Neither the pimping game nor these brave words have made a man of Slim; neither has restored him to himself.

In all, Slim's monologue furnishes one of the strangest half minutes in 1970s film. To fantasize about revenge is, for Slim, to fall apart—to become too intimate with his pain. But his defiance is, in its weakness, also exquisitely human. It connects him to those who've felt that they were living, literally or figuratively, with someone who pointed a gun in their direction; links him to those who have wanted to stand up for themselves but doubted their power to do so. Max Julien observed, "I know ladies who've been abused, and they saw that scene and they realized they didn't want to be abused anymore. It said, 'Don't touch me again.'"

The Mack could never escape being a fly-by-night production—its acting was uneven, its plotting forced—but with Richard's help, it fingered something raw and profound. Upon its release in the spring of 1973, it rose to become the fourth-highest-grossing movie in the United States, despite the fact that it was largely limited to inner-city theaters.

Richard seemed to live *The Mack* in his mind, to be possessed by the spirit of its script. In Los Angeles around the time of the film's production, he relayed to his girlfriend, Patricia, a version of what he had told Michael Campus. "Bitch," he said, "you've got to go out and bring back some money."

Shell-shocked, the former Pan Am stewardess drove to the Beverly Wilshire hotel and sat at its bar. She waited for something to happen, and when nothing did, she repaired to her car, on a side street off Wilshire Boulevard, and started sobbing. A group of men heard her crying and asked what was wrong. When she told them, one of the men, an actor, offered her a hundred dollars. She felt she couldn't take it under the circumstances.

When she came home empty-handed to their cottage in the hills, Richard flew into a rage. He had an empty bottle of Courvoisier in one hand and a mostly empty bottle of Courvoisier in the other, and started beating Patricia's head with them.

Patricia threw up her hands to shield herself. Richard yelled, "Be a woman! Put your hands down!"

Patricia pivoted, ran into one of the cottage's small bedrooms, and locked the door. A little while later, she heard a terrifying chopping sound. Richard had taken the small hatchet that she used to chop wood for their wood-burning fireplace and was attacking the door that stood between them.

The hatchet made short work of the door. "Please, Richard, I love you, I love you," Patricia said, in a naked bid to calm him.

Richard stood over her, addled by the drugs and agitated by his anger, and began choking her. When Patricia looked into his eyes, he seemed off in some faraway place.

Then, all of a sudden, he felt sick and doubled over, vomiting. He had shrunk into a helpless child making a mess on himself. "Mama, mama, help, help," he said, before passing out.

Patricia looked at herself. She was on her hands and knees; her white dress was smeared with blood, her lip swollen. She decided that she was through with Richard.

She saw a light outside, and left the cottage for it. She met a woman, who offered her some clean clothes—the woman's mother, a heavyset woman, had just died and left a closet full of them—and then the two drove to a hospital. There Patricia was treated for a broken nose and three cracked ribs. She contacted a writing friend of Richard's, who lent her enough money to return to Sausalito.

About a year after arriving with Richard in Hollywood, Patricia came back to Sausalito in a dead woman's oversize clothes, and crashed with an old friend.

CHAPTER 16

Black Goes First

Los Angeles, Marseilles, Cannes, 1972–1973

"There's probably a cobra crawling around in there," Richard said, pointing to a bale of hay. He was on the outskirts of the Chino men's prison, talking to a Paramount publicist and waiting for his scene. Flies buzzed about; cows lowed in the distance, their smell traveling over the wind. Inmates were gathering on the edge of the shoot, curious. Their rural prison worksite was being used as a location for *Hit!*, director Sidney Furie's follow-up to *Lady Sings the Blues*, and the inmates had stopped pitching hay for a moment to catch a glimpse of Hollywood in action.

The publicist was asking Richard about the arc of his career, and Richard had turned unusually reflective, musing on the traps into which he'd fallen. "I want to do something to show that I have depth," he said. "It's time to branch out, time to stretch my talents as far as they will go." He dangled a piece of hay between his fingers. "The happy-go-lucky comic—that's an act. I like to do parts. But I don't want to be one-dimensional, to lock myself in."

A crew member called Richard for his scene. His character, Mike Willmer, was supposed to spot the man (now a convict) who had raped and killed his wife, then attack him in a sort of fugue state. It was a scene in which Richard was expected to move, in a matter of seconds, from a state of guarded congeniality to one of throttling, homicidal rage.

Richard brushed the hay off his pants. "Being a character, man, that makes me come alive," he said. He spread his hands as if taking in a larger piece of the world. "You've got to separate who you are and who the character is. There's such excitement in that real moment when you achieve that character—it's like being in your conscious and your subconscious at the same time."

He then took off to prepare for his scene. The publicist watched him pace the length of the parking lot and noted his intensity: "Shoulders stooped, eyebrows furled, his movements suggest a rock that is about to precipitate a landslide."

Nineteen seventy-three seemed as if it might be Richard's landslide year, but it was instead a half-and-half year—of artistic breakthroughs and professional struggles. It was the year when he started being courted as a film actor, did some of the best TV work of his career, and, through his contribution to the landmark documentary film *Wattstax*, established himself as black America's most nimble color commentator. Perhaps most important, it was the year his self-understanding shifted, the year when he recognized—partly as a result of his brief and enchanted collaboration with Lily Tomlin—how much he loved falling into character. Sometimes that character was a wino or a junkie, a preacher or a cop, a pimp or an average Joe like *Hit*'s Mike Willmer. Sometimes it was a more vivid version of his ordinary self, raised through the magic of the stand-up stage into some combination of Everyman and avatar: the man who, by turning his life story into an act, gave it shape and resonance.

For this artist in love with character, the one thing he abhorred was losing the flow of character, the flow of dialogue between his "conscious" and "subconscious." From this point forward especially, Richard responded poorly—with frustration, rage, sabotage—when asked to hew closely to a script or, worse, to censor himself. Presented with a bale of hay, he couldn't help but imagine the cobra crawling around inside it.

For many in Hollywood, of course, Richard's irreverence was his great selling point. On a Saturday night in October 1972, director Mel Stuart caught a rare Pryor performance—in "a half-empty room" of a "dull-ass club" in a part of LA that Stuart had never visited—

and was convinced within three minutes that he was in the presence of "the comic genius of our time." And not just a comic genius: the performer who could fix his film *Wattstax*—rescue it from its baggy rough cut and give it a through line.

When Stuart arrived at that club, he was wrestling with only the latest of the many challenges that had dogged his film. *Wattstax* had been conceived, in the manner of the concert film *Woodstock*, as a celebration of a community drawn together through music—in this case, the thousands of black Angelenos set to attend a concert organized by Stax Records, the powerhouse soul music label. Stuart, a documentarian whose résumé included mainstream fare like *The Making of the President: 1964* and *Willie Wonka and the Chocolate Factory*, agreed to make the film "on one condition: I am the only white person on the set." Watts was a foreign world to him; he knew he needed the palpable sense of camaraderie that only black camera operators could provide. The community had exploded into riot just seven years before, and he felt it was justifiably wary of outsiders. But how to get blacks behind the camera? Hollywood's technical unions had only a tiny number of blacks on their rolls. The film's producers held an open call, drew on union apprenticeship programs and university workshops—and managed to recruit forty-five black technicians to film the concert, an unprecedented number on a Hollywood shoot.

On August 20, 1972, the Los Angeles Coliseum rocked to Wattstax the concert. Some ninety-two thousand people paid a nominal one dollar per ticket to see and hear Isaac Hayes, the Staple Singers, Rufus Thomas, and others. But after Stuart's editors sorted through the one hundred thousand feet of film that his cameramen had shot, he was left nonplussed (not unlike later film reviewers, who noted the music's lack of oomph on-screen). "It's a newsreel," he told the film's creative team. "I don't do newsreels." The music was there, but the spirit behind the music was not. So Stuart sent his cameramen out to Watts's soul kitchens, barbershops, and stoops, where they filmed hang-loose conversations about topics such as the blues, the police, and the black church.

It was an inspired decision. Partly because so many of the cameramen themselves hailed from South Central, the interviews had the feel of a neighborhood bull session, full of hyperbole, backtalk, and salty turns of phrase. In keeping with Watts's demographics, most of those captured on camera were folks struggling to make do. "There are directors I could name—black directors too—who wouldn't have wanted so many street people in the film," said Stuart at the time. "They would want more lawyers and businessmen. But our producers took the decision to show the language and attitudes of the people who have to hassle with the essential business of living each day just to get by." In other words: the film was keyed to the same slice of the black community that Richard took up in his comedy.

But even with these on-the-street interviews stitched into the film, Stuart still felt his film was incomplete. "Gentlemen, we need Shakespeare," he told the film's producers. The room became deathly quiet. "We need the chorus in *Henry V*." Stuart elaborated: "*Henry V* was so big and the pageant so big that [Shakespeare] couldn't put it all in the picture, so he needed some guy to tell you what was going on in France and England and in the war and everything else. We need somebody to be the chorus of this picture, someone who really knows the black soul and yet is funny."

This is where Richard entered the picture. Seeing him perform at the Summit Club at the top of Baldwin Hills, Stuart felt he'd found his chorus figure, the commentator who could convey the full pageant of black America. The next day, he returned to the Summit Club and set up his cameras. Richard spoke mostly off the cuff. He was given a single phrase, like "black men and women" or "black politics," and allowed to rap as long as he wanted, to let himself go. Several hours later, Stuart had his narrator, and Richard had improvised himself into another starring role in a feature film.

With *Wattstax*, Richard found a remarkable vehicle for bringing his stage act to a larger audience. Speaking to the camera as if to a friend, he seems like the liveliest of barstool raconteurs—a sit-down comic. He didn't have to mind the censors, as he did with his TV work. He didn't have to lose the visual nuances of his nightclub work, the montage of gestures and expressions, as he did on records. And given the focus of *Wattstax*, he had the freedom to dwell on the absurdity of race. In a double-edged bit—one that placed him as the descendant of black royalty and the upshot of a cosmic joke—he offered a history of the *N*-word in the form of a parable:

> I think that niggers are the best of the people that were slaves. That's how they got to be niggers—[the traders] stole the cream of the crop from Africa and brought them over here. And God, as they say, works in mysterious ways, so they made everybody "nigger" because we were arguing over in Africa about the Watusi, and the Buwalladah, and the Busawoono, and Zawoonga . . . And so he brought us all over here, the best, the kings and the queens and the princes, and put us all in one tribe: *niggers*.

While the larger film documents the early 1970s efflorescence of black pride—black beauty pageants, a black Santa Claus, a stadium full of black people chanting, "I am somebody"—Richard's commentary troubled the waters and pointed to the excesses of black militancy: how identity politics could go horribly awry, especially when the identity in question was subject to reinvention. After one of *Wattstax*'s "native informants" testified to the deep racial bond established by the soul handshake, Richard said, "Niggers change their shit all the time," then dramatized the soul handshake as a problem, not a solution:

> You be meeting the guy: *Thunk-bam-spun-spun* [*clasping his hand in the middle, then lower*]. But then six months later, the shit done change: *Chee-pun-chee-up-hunh!* You all down here [*reaching down to the ground*]: *Hey-hup-ho-chup!*
>
> And if you don't do that, then you ain't no nigger.
>
> The dude be, "You ain't black, motherfucker. You didn't know how to do—" [*points to both ears as if plugging them, points down, then runs his finger across his throat as if slitting it*].

At the same time Richard did not downplay the tribulations of being black; his satire of black militancy was aimed at its trappings, not its root causes. He lashed at police brutality ("How do you *accidentally* shoot a nigger six times in the chest?") or, through his wino character, portrayed the struggle to find work. Asked at the unemployment office for his occupation, the wino, fresh from the penitentiary, gave the ridiculously true answer: "license-plate presser."

In *Wattstax*, Richard could be "side-splittingly funny and at the same time tremendously sobering," as one critic observed, because the film itself struck the same fine balance. It was urgent and ironic both. On the urgent side: it showed the black audience at the Coliseum sitting listlessly through "The Star-Spangled Banner," as if trapped watching an endless commercial, then purposefully standing up and pumping their fists for the chant of "It's Nation Time" (the nation in question being the black nation). It drew out the defiant energy of the musicians onstage, whether it was the Staple Singers pressing the crowd to "Respect Yourself" or the Bar-Kays offering themselves as the descendants of detective John Shaft, one "bad motherfucker."

Yet *Wattstax* also reveled in the rich theatricality of black life. It lavished attention on the dashikis and dark glasses of the concertgoers; on Isaac Hayes's glittering mesh of gold chains and the Spandex pink tights that showed off his manhood; on Rufus Thomas's pink cape, pink sports jacket, and pink Bermuda shorts; on the matching blue fur coats of South Central's players, stepping out of a silver Rolls-Royce with the license plate FLA-VOR.

Wattstax intimated that these two aspects of black life, its political struggles and its extravagant theater, were two sides of the same coin. Director Melvin Van Peebles explained as much from the stage, linking the 1965 Watts riot to the festive air of Wattstax: "We're here to commemorate a revolution that started the movement and was one of the milestones in black pride. Some folks may find it a little strange that we laugh, we sing and we joke, but we're doing our thing the black way to commemorate." It was the summer of 1972—close enough to the radical upsurge of the late 1960s for him to speak of revolution in the air, far enough away that the demands for political commitment were less clear cut than organizing a protest or picking up a gun.

It was a moment, in short, when a provocateur like Richard could seem like the natural-born tribune of the black community. He had only to stylize the nitty-gritty problems of black life, not to solve them. A *Los Angeles Times* columnist, anticipating that *Wattstax* would push Richard to a whole new level, named him the "Here and Now Black Man of the Moment."

The heart is a curious, convoluted organ. Not long after Richard tried to choke the life out of Patricia Heitman in their Hollywood Hills cottage, he took a trip out to Sausalito, hoping to track her down, talk with her, and win her back. He brought, as enticements, a Mercedes-Benz, a floor-length black sable coat, and the dog that Patricia had loved but had left behind in LA. He speculated that she might still be haunting the Sausalito bar where the two of them met, and when he walked into it, he found her there.

Patricia was petrified when she first spotted Richard. Then she saw her dog—a happier reminder of the life she'd left behind. Richard begged her to come back to him, vowing to change his ways, and offered her the Mercedes and the fur coat as gifts. She wanted to believe that they could make a new life together, so she swallowed her misgivings and decided to give Richard another chance, moving back into the cottage with the hatcheted bedroom door. Instead of giving them a new door, their landlord simply put a new piece of wood over the part Richard had destroyed.

For two years, Richard had been drifting professionally, picking up work through acquaintances like Norman Steinberg and Berry Gordy or friends like Paul Mooney and Max Julien. He caught a boost when Ron DeBlasio, who ran a boutique label under the Atlantic umbrella and had worked with Helen Reddy and Tiny Tim, offered to serve as his manager. Now he had someone willing to hustle on his behalf—someone who could look out for his interests, strategize about his future, and fix any problems that developed along the way. With Richard's help, DeBlasio made a list of all those who liked Richard or owed him a favor, and all those whom Richard owed or had pushed away.

DeBlasio could also act as a buffer for Richard, whose ego was unstable, easily inflated or deflated. When *Lady Sings the Blues* premiered at the Directors Guild, Richard stayed home out of anxiety; DeBlasio attended without him. After the screening, DeBlasio couldn't contain his enthusiasm, so he went to a pay phone at a gas station and called Richard.

"Richie, you were a sensation, you were fantastic."

"What do you mean?"

"You were funny. The audience loved it."

"That's what you think. That's you—you're thinking that . . . Gotta go." Richard hung up.

Around midnight, DeBlasio's phone rang at home.

"Did I interrupt you?" Richard asked. "You're not fucking, are you? Listen, I was with some people tonight and they said the film was great—that I'm great." He gushed with enthusiasm at what he'd achieved.

The next day, Richard popped by DeBlasio's house with a special gift: a Dunhill lighter, dark blue with gold trim, the sort favored in James Bond films. Richard wanted his manager to be prepared for the big time. "You're going to have to look the part," Richard explained. "You're going to be smoking cigars and are going to need something to light your cigars with."

The momentum seemed to be gathering. The *Los Angeles Times*, *Chicago Tribune*, the *Village Voice*, and *The New Yorker* celebrated Richard's performance as Piano Man with fulsome praise. In mid-November the Pied Piper, a club in South Central, was packed with black celebrities and other well-wishers for a "Richard Pryor Salute." Richard felt himself on the brink of a breakthrough.

Alas, the Dunhill lighter went unused. In fact, Richard was dealt a considerable setback when he discovered, near the end of 1972, that the role of Sheriff Bart in *Blazing Saddles*, the role he'd written for himself to play, had gone to Cleavon Little, an amiable, classically trained actor then starring as a loopy doctor in the hospital sitcom *Temperatures Rising*. Mel Brooks said that after he saw Richard "acting out so many things so beautifully" in the writers' room, he "asked [Warner Bros.] on bended knee to let Richie do it." He even flew out to New York to meet with the studio's moneymen and beg for Richard. The studio's response: "Absolutely not. We like Cleavon's looks . . . [I]f you want to do the picture, it's with Cleavon." For the studio executives, Richard wasn't even in the running. "Very simply," Brooks said just after the film's release, "they're afraid to go with an unknown, unknown as far as they are concerned, vis-à-vis dollars and the public."

Twenty years later, Brooks revealed the true source of the studio's hostility toward Richard: "he was a known sniffer." Richard's co-writer Andrew Bergman explained: "Warner Bros. wouldn't touch him with a ten-foot pole because his reputation was so dubious in terms of reliability." It seems likely that the news about Richard's coke-fueled crackup on location with *The Mack*, just a few months earlier, had traveled to the Warner Bros. executive suite.

Richard spoke bitterly about his experience with *Blazing Saddles*, calling it "a thorn in my heart." He was skeptical that Brooks or anyone else had gone to the mat for him—"They used me and that's not fair"—and viewed the collaboration over the script with a jaundiced eye, claiming credit later for the film's most famous scene, the explosion of farts around the campfire. The other writers, by contrast, treasured their work on the film and felt there was plenty of recognition to go around. When asked if the campfire scene was Richard's brainchild, Norman Steinberg said, "Nobody takes credit for anything. I wouldn't even begin that discussion." Apparently, Richard hadn't gotten the memo.

The spiking of Richard as Black Bart is one of the great what-ifs of his career, not to mention of film history. *Blazing Saddles* was

Cleavon Little's shining moment. Would it have been Richard's, too? The two had such different personas as actors, Cleavon with his indestructible affability, Richard with his hurt and anger always threatening to break through the surface of his boyish charm. After the grandmotherly woman in *Blazing Saddles* responds to Bart's "Good morning, ma'am" with "Up yours, nigger," Cleavon's Bart acts as if simply dumbfounded by the exchange, his grin sliding into a blank expression. Richard's reaction as Bart, one imagines, would have been anything but simple. In other roles he manipulated the mask of his face so that it captured the quick-flying emotions—anger, fear, shock—that flashed over him and warred with one another. "Richie had a dark side and Cleavon didn't," summed up Bergman. Cleavon was too sweet to inhabit fully the role as Richard had imagined it, which goes some length in explaining why some of the more personal contributions Richard made, like the "pimp's lament," were cut.

A *Blazing Saddles* with Richard Pryor in the lead role would have been more cutting and psychologically complex, touching an extra exposed nerve or two. It would also have launched Richard and Gene Wilder as a comedy team three years before their debut in *Silver Streak*, and have given them better material than anything in their shared future. But the movie might have lost some of its winking staginess (perfect for Cleavon's style), and its jokes might have been less inviting to a mass audience. "Cleavon is not a threatening figure," said Bergman. "It's probably another reason that the movie was as successful as it was."

Dinged for the lead role in *Blazing Saddles*, Richard was disappointed with the scripts that did come his way. "I don't want to become Jack Oakie the rest of my life," he told the *Los Angeles Times*, referring to the rubber-faced actor of the 1930s and '40s—the epitome of the second or third banana, punching up scenes with a wisecrack or double take. "Always getting those parts, over and over, just to fill in. I don't want to do that."

Director Sidney Furie, just coming off *Lady Sings the Blues*, made

Richard the first offer he felt he shouldn't refuse: a supporting role as a mechanic-turned-assassin in *Hit!* The film reunited much of the cast of the earlier film, including Richard and Billie Dee Williams, and below the line, its cinematographer and editor. Conceptually *Hit!* was a "Lincoln-doctor's-dog of a movie," borrowing as many bankable formulas as possible. *The French Connection*, *Mission: Impossible*, *The Dirty Dozen*, *Death Wish*—all were blended together in its story of a federal narcotics agent (Williams) who, after his daughter dies of a heroin overdose, assembles an improbable team to assassinate the nine kingpins of a Marseilles-based drug syndicate. As in *Lady Sings the Blues*, Richard was there to give a comic accent to a film that otherwise threatened to become grim, and was allowed to improvise his dialogue in that vein.

During *Hit!*'s production in late 1972, Richard grew closer to Billie Dee Williams. On December 27, when Billie Dee married his girlfriend, Teruko, at a civil ceremony in Beverly Hills, Richard served as his best man and Patricia as Teruko's maid of honor. When the justice of the peace asked the group "Which ones of you are getting married?" Richard joked, "Me and Billie."

Their relationship, like most intimacies in Richard's life, was vexed. Richard was jealous of Billie, of his leading man looks and laidback, honey-voiced charm. (In his memoir Richard wrote, sparingly, of his frequent costar: "I didn't know anyone more aware of their image.") Meanwhile, according to Patricia, Billie craved Richard's creative understanding of character. During the filming of *Hit!*, he turned often to Richard for advice about how to play a scene; afterward, he called Richard a "genius" to the press. And then there was this bombshell, just planted and waiting to go off: what with all the evenings that the two couples spent together, playing dominoes and poker at each other's homes, Patricia and Billie were drawn into an affair around the date of Billie's wedding.

In the meantime, Richard and Patricia traveled together to Marseilles for the shooting of *Hit!*, arriving on New Year's Eve at an elegant old-world hotel that faced the Mediterranean. An orchestra was playing in the ballroom; Patricia felt she'd been transported to some version of Versailles. Then, one day, upon returning to their hotel room, she found Richard in bed with a prostitute. Brazen as ever, he insisted Patricia join in the action. When she refused, he beat her for spoiling his party, stripped off her clothes, and threw her naked out of the room. She found a sheet, wrapped herself in it, and, with the help of the hotel staff, settled in a separate room. Then, in a moment of inspiration, she recalled a conversation she'd had, when she and Richard had first moved to LA, with a call girl who'd evened the score with an abusive lover.

After getting her clothes and putting herself together, she went to a hardware store and bought a can of powdered rat poison. She stole into Richard's hotel room and sprinkled the poison in his socks and underwear; she'd heard that it stung terribly on contact with human skin. She knew Richard would be filming a scene the next day in a wetsuit and relished the idea of him being trapped in tampered underwear, his groin on fire. Then she folded up his clothes with care, concealing her handiwork; gathered her passport and things; and left for the United States. She wasn't around for the filming of Richard's scene, but was sure that her plot worked—that Richard felt his nether regions burning up.

Watching Richard's scenes from *Hit!* now, with an awareness of their backstory, he seems foiled less by Patricia's sabotage than by the film's too-stiff sense of itself. A pulp vigilante film with a tabloid sensibility, *Hit!* delivers some familiar pleasures—*New York*'s Judith Crist, one of the film's few defenders, said that "The secret of the film's success is professionalism"—but it is also ponderous where it cannot afford to be. In a typical pan, *The Hollywood Reporter* offered that director Sidney Furie had "made the bizarre choice of giving this thin, incredible story the look of a superproduction, thereby exposing its emptiness." Richard's character is stranded in the movie's humorless landscape, a jive non sequitur.

Film critics did pay attention to Richard's performance, and noted its peculiar angle toward the rest of the film. "Pryor's humor pierces through his characterization to mock the whole movie with energy and finesse," wrote *Time.* The *Hollywood Reporter* praised Richard's improvising, then chimed: "His work may relieve the tension of watching something so bad, but certainly doesn't add to the reality." It was easy to enjoy Richard's dialogue but hard to admire the craft of the scenes in which his character, Mike Willmer, was placed. Take this exchange between Willmer, who has just speared one drug kingpin with his harpoon, and his teammate, a willowy and whey-faced call girl:

> **MIKE WILLMER**: Take it easy—ain't nothing to it—killing some pigs, that's all.
> **CALL GIRL** [*frail and red-nosed, whimpering*]: Aren't you scared?
> **MIKE WILLMER**: Scared? Fuck no, I'm supernigger.
> **CALL GIRL**: I'm scared.
> **MIKE WILLMER**: You think you got troubles, nigger? I lost a motherfucking spear. Cost me forty-seven boxtops. I saved for six months. . . . Had a gold tip on it and everything.

As a whole, Richard's performance in *Hit!* was oddly split. In its first half, he seemed determined, as he told the Paramount publicist, to break new ground for himself as an actor: on-screen he was serious and reticent, as if husbanding his resources. In the second half, he became a comedian again. He relied on old reflexes—and old routines—to generate some energy for the film and fell victim to a hoary trap, the Jack Oakie syndrome that he was trying to escape.

On February 4, 1973, Richard spent three hours getting his hair braided and wrapped in leather so that he might arrive, at the Los Angeles Music Center that evening, resplendent: the cock of the walk in impeccable cornrows. The occasion was the premiere of *Wattstax*, one of the most singular openings in Hollywood history. It was the first premiere held at the cultural acropolis of downtown LA. And in keeping with the ambitions of the film's producers, it brought together the glamorous and the gritty, the powerful and the out-of-luck. A range of politicians—including Richard Nixon's staff assistant and the deputy chairman of the Republican National Committee—consorted with musicians like Isaac Hayes and Rufus Thomas, professional celebrities like Zsa Zsa Gabor, and, more strikingly, a collection of gang members and welfare mothers bused in from Watts. Because the recommended dress on the premiere's gold-plated invitation was "bizarre," the spirit of the evening was ghetto fabulous in its early '70s heyday. Redd Foxx peacocked in an orange-printed polyester knit suit, Raymond St. Jacques in a full-length orange monkey-fur coat, Jim Brown in a floor-length white wool coat over a jumpsuit. *Wattstax*'s producers had turned the Music Center into what the *Los Angeles Times* called "a fashion free-for-all."

For Richard, *Wattstax* marked a turning point in how he was perceived as a performer. Before *Wattstax*, he'd been largely a player on the fringe: the one black comic in countercultural productions such as *Wild in the Streets* or *Dynamite Chicken*, the kooky cameo player, the offbeat comic. After *Wattstax*, he had a new platform and a new authority—as an expert on the black "street." For all Richard's showbiz ambitions, it wasn't a larger role he had actively sought. "I'm not equipped politically to be a spokesman for an organization or a group," he said while promoting *Wattstax*. "I don't like giving my mind up. I don't like anybody in the back of my funnel closing off the sunshine. No, I always felt I was a revolution just by doing and speaking the way I speak and saying what I think and living my life the way I live it." And yet here he was in *Wattstax*, his private revolution setting the barometer for everyone else in the film. When the next Watts Summer Festival rolled around, "that crazy nigger" was asked to serve as grand marshal of its parade. And when Councilman Tom Bradley, on a trajectory to become LA's first black mayor, held a fund-raiser for his campaign, Richard was chosen to headline it. He was less radioactive than he'd been for years.

For film critics nationwide, Richard's *Wattstax* monologues were something of a revelation: few had heard *'Craps' (After Hours)* or seen Richard perform after he'd dropped off the nightclub and talk-show circuit in 1970, and so his new act seemed to come out of nowhere. To

Up and coming: Pryor shaking hands with soon-to-be-elected LA mayor Tom Bradley at Wattstax*'s premiere. (Courtesy of the* Los Angeles Daily Journal*)*

them, Richard was "wickedly funny" (*Newsweek*), or "breathtakingly irreverent and ironic" (*Los Angeles Times*), or "the most talented black comedian to emerge since Bill Cosby" (*Tulsa World*). Even those less captivated by *Wattstax* singled Richard out for praise. The *Boston Herald-American* judged that "Without Pryor's wise rudder, *Wattstax* would probably be a ship lost at sea": the film needed his complex stance to the world, "composed of equal amounts of self-love, self-hate and bemused irony." The *Seattle Daily Times* went so far as to suggest that "Perhaps Pryor should have directed 'Wattstax.' It needs more of his irreverent involvement." According to many, he had carried the film.

A bit abashedly, Richard plugged *Wattstax* with interviews in the press and on TV programs such as *Soul Train* and *Black Omnibus*, but despite his efforts, the film underperformed at the box office. Its producers had hyped it as an artistic and civic landmark, hosting premieres not just across the country and in London, but also at the United Nations (for African dignitaries) and in Washington, DC (for Nixon's White House and members of Congress). They had plugged it, in ads, with the tag line "You Can't Judge a Movie by Its Color," and tried to entice white viewers with the explicit promise that it would "be enjoyed by *all* movie-goers." Still, the white audience for the film didn't show.

In the final promotional push, the producers looked to a *Wattstax* screening at the Cannes Film Festival to generate some buzz. So Richard journeyed, along with his manager and the film's producers and director, to the Côte d'Azur.

It was a magical French interlude, the opposite of his troubled time in Marseilles the previous winter. The sun gleamed off the Mediterranean; the roulette wheels spun; and *Wattstax* coproducer David Wolper opened his deep pockets so that the entourage could luxuriate in the romance of Cannes. They stayed at the sumptuous Hotel Carlton, and at a certain point Wolper asked Richard if he wouldn't mind hanging on a few extra days so as to meet with a group of African directors. "We'll move you to one of the bungalows," said Wolper matter-of-factly. Richard and Ron DeBlasio were led to their new bungalow suite and started laughing at their absurdly good fortune. The sea was at their eye level; they were in the best room of the best hotel, they felt, in all of France.

With DeBlasio and his *Wattstax* compatriots, Richard relaxed and took in the Cannes parade. Ladies of the night were out in full daylight; aspiring starlets strolled the Croisette promenade in see-through swimsuits. Richard was garrulous and open. When, at the hotel bar, a sad-faced girl asked him if he wanted to buy a stuffed toy, he didn't brush her off, but gave her double the price.

It was a time to be proudly and playfully black. Richard talked with African filmmakers about how racism was not limited to the

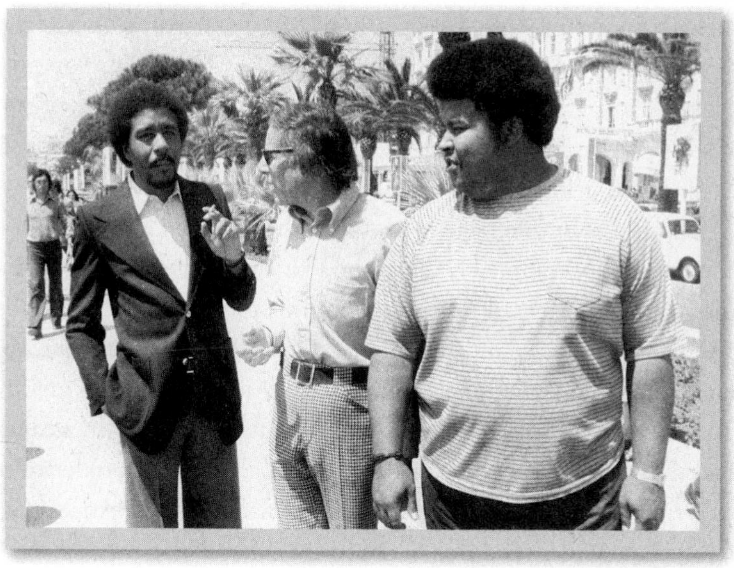

At Cannes: Pryor on the Croisette with director Mel Stuart and associate producer Forrest Hamilton. (Courtesy of Traverso Photos)

American South; he exulted at seeing writer James Baldwin. He gave a press conference that, according to the *Los Angeles Times*, was "one of the uproarious delights of the festival."

One day, at Richard's urging, he and director Mel Stuart sat down to play chess. Richard happened to sit in front of the black pieces and Stuart in front of the white ones.

When Stuart made the first move, Richard said, "No, black goes first."

"No, white goes first," said Stuart. "You can have white, I'll take black, but the white has to go first because the whole game, all the moves, the moves of the bishops and the pawns, they're all set in a certain pattern and everything's going to get mixed up and it's going to be hard to play."

"No, black goes first."

"No, white goes first."

"No, black goes first."

Stuart folded up the chess set and said, "No game today. We'll play tomorrow." The next day, he returned with a red and green set. Trickster had met trickster. Richard jumped into playing without a problem—and with, one imagines, a smile at how he'd managed to hold on to his principles.

Richard was in fine form, too, when the *Wattstax* entourage drove to Monaco to meet Grace Kelly at the Prince's Palace. Wolper was exquisitely well connected—he'd made films for both Lyndon Johnson and Richard Nixon—and had met Kelly on an earlier project, so he thought he could swing an audience with the princess. The group set off in a rented van large enough for forty but holding eight, and upon arrival they drove into the gates of the castle. There, an older official looked them up and down and informed them stiffly, "Princess Grace can't see you today. She's busy. But you can see the mosaics on the inner wall of the castle."

Entrance denied, Richard dropped into character. "Wait a second," he yelled up at the parapets in the thick voice of his wino. "I don't wanna see no goddamn mosaic! I wanna see Princess Grace! Now, Richard come all this way—shit, man, what am I supposed to do? *Grace! Richard's down here!*"

The palace guards came at Richard with their pikes. A hefty member of the *Wattstax* gang picked Richard off his feet and shoved him back into the van. "It was so true and so funny," remembered Mel Stuart. "We had come all this way, and we were going to look at the mosaics?"

They drove back to Cannes along the gentle curves of the Grande Corniche, a famously romantic road. The Alps were behind them, the Mediterranean spread in front of them, their bus sweeping along the ledge two thousand feet above the ocean. At the top of the route, they stopped at La Chaumière, an elegant restaurant with a fireplace crackling in the center of its dining room. During their meal, David Wolper—who paid for everything and had chosen the restaurant, one of his favorites—noticed tears running down Richard's face.

"What's wrong?" Wolper asked.

"Nothing," Richard said. "Spending this day in the South of France—I just never knew the world could be so beautiful."

A few days later, Richard was back at his low-slung cottage in the Hollywood Hills. Cannes was a waste of time, he told Patricia. There was good blow, and in steady supply, but the French didn't understand his sense of humor. No one knew how to translate *motherfucker.*

CHAPTER 17

Be Glad When It's Spring, Flower

Los Angeles, the road, 1973–1974

When invited to work with new collaborators in the early 1970s, Richard devised little experiments to see how his world would collide with theirs. With filmmakers like Mel Brooks, James B. Harris, and Mel Stuart, he would remove some cocaine from, say, a tinfoil package, as casually as one might unwrap a chocolate bar, snort a little for himself, then offer the astonished onlookers a toot for themselves. (One did not need to take the toot to pass his test, just refrain from judgment.) With actress Lily Tomlin, who hoped Richard might lend his talents as an actor to her first TV special, the tests were more elaborate. "I had to jump through hoops for him," Lily remembered. "I'm sure he was testing if this white girl was okay to work with."

He began with the neighborhood test. He took Lily to a black part of Los Angeles to observe how she behaved and was received. Lily had grown up in a working-class ghetto in Detroit, where success "meant, if you were a girl, not getting pregnant; if you were a boy, not going to jail." On the streets of black LA, she was at ease—and greeted with cheers of enthusiasm. People recognized her from *Laugh-In*, the comedy sketch show where she had developed unforgettable characters like Edith Ann, the most audacious of five-year-old girls, or Ernestine the telephone operator, pinch-faced and punchy, snorting to herself in self-amusement.

Satisfied with the results of the first test, Richard asked the loose-limbed actress to accompany him to a porn theater. He had probed her for any racial hang-ups; her sexual hang-ups were next. A committed feminist, Lily agreed to go but only if she could pay her own way. So

Soul mates: Lily Tomlin and Richard Pryor in a 1974 photograph by Annie Leibovitz. (Courtesy of Annie Leibovitz/Contact Images Press)

Richard escorted her, on this odd Dutch date, to the Pussycat Theater on Santa Monica Boulevard. Nearby, a sign winked "Nude Live Girls."

However Lily comported herself at the Pussycat, it worked. Soon after, Richard invited her to his Hollywood Hills cottage, where they brainstormed her TV special. "We had conversations that spiraled into the ozone," Richard recalled. "In minutes, we'd create enough characters to populate entire neighborhoods." Richard found in Lily a comedian who, like him, was wedded less to the pursuit of laughs than to the pursuit of character, and who was willing to lose herself in the act of imagination. "We are soul mates," Richard reflected in 1977. "I mean the characters we do literally take possession of us. You're O.K. as long as you keep an eye on what's happening, as long as you don't get scared or tighten up. Because then you lose control over yourself and the character takes over completely. I've never seen it happen to any other entertainers but Lily and me."

The collaboration between these two soul mates was brief, beginning in late 1972 and ending a year later, but it left a considerable imprint on Richard's psyche. Working with Lily enlarged his sense of himself: unguarded in her presence, he found new reserves of both fearlessness and tenderness. For the first time, he was working with a fellow performer who was equally committed to the battle for free expression—who was willing, even, to lead the charge to create something sharp and poetic on prime-time TV. "The networks feel [that] certain things don't belong in variety shows," Lily quipped at the time, "but what I've always hated about variety shows is that they have no variety." Together, the two of them produced some of the most remarkable television moments of the 1970s—scenes of interracial affection that didn't aim for Movie-of-the-Week "significance" and so, in their roundabout way, were able to achieve something more striking. They avoided the easy laughs and went for the hard ones instead. As the *Los Angeles Times* observed, Lily's TV work made "the 11 o'clock news afterward seem like a situation comedy."

From the start, Lily grasped Richard's potential as an actor. She urged her creative partner, Jane Wagner, to write a sketch that could tap into the full array of Richard's abilities, "something he'd be proud of." A white Tennessean by birth, Wagner was yet deft at capturing the flow and hardship of black life. She had earlier written *J.T.*, an unusually bracing TV movie about a black boy who, estranged from his mother and his school, devotes himself to nursing a wounded cat back to health. In a shocking departure from the usual formulas, Wagner had the cat get run over by a car. For Lily and Richard, Wagner delivered "Juke and Opal," about a woman who runs a hash house and the man who drifts into her establishment looking for some mixture of companionship and drug money. Three decades later, *New Yorker* theater critic Hilton Als hailed the ten-minute "Juke and Opal" as "the most profound meditation on race and class that I have ever seen on a major network." But when Lily submitted the draft of her special's script to CBS, the script came back with "Juke and Opal" excised by the producer the network had selected.

For this first special, titled *The Lily Tomlin Show*, Richard and Lily were left then with a more limited sketch, one that put Lily's Tasteful

Lady and Richard's wino together in an elevator for a short and unpredictable ride. The premise was simply to watch these two characters, a snob and a derelict with dignity, duel in an enclosed space. At rehearsal, the network was horrified at Richard's improvised sallies. "You ever kiss a black man?" his wino (here named Lightning Bug) teased. "You better get off of here before you get pregnant." To make matters worse, the staging of the sketch coincided with the premiere of *Wattstax*, for which Richard had styled his hair in cornrows with white leather braiding, and he played up the unfamiliarity of his coif. "He was telling people it had been tied up with some white people's skin," Lily recalled. "And it made all these people in suits just blanch. They didn't know what to do."

The sketch's most provocative moments—the ad libs that called out the threat of interracial sex—were edited out, but the larger sketch survived, and with it, a quick portrait of an unlikely intimacy. "I don't believe a thing you're saying," says the Tasteful Lady, to which Lightning Bug responds, "I don't, either." The sketch ends on a promising note, the Tasteful Lady softened by Lightning Bug's roguish charm:

> **LIGHTNING BUG**: I may be a wino, but I am a gentleman, believe that. I'm going to give you my card and if you're down Philadelphia way—a little expression—I want you to look me up. My motto is, "You can always share a jug with Lightning Bug."
> **THE TASTEFUL LADY** [*saving the card in her purse*]: Keep in touch, Mr. Lightning Bug.

The courtship is improbable but believable, since these two socially distant characters share a hidden affinity. Like so many of Richard's and Lily's characters, they are misfits who speak their own truth, and with a beguiling confidence and authority. "I always want them to be strong," Lily said of her characters. "I never like to do anybody who's defeated. . . . The person I love most of all is somebody who conventionally looks out of place, and who thinks she's wonderful. There's nobody more beautiful than that."

She might as well have been speaking of the headstrong characters who populated Richard's stage, from his wino to his chippies to the members of his family he impersonated—characters who, through the force of their personality, acted as if no stigma were attached to them. By trapping the Tasteful Lady and Lightning Bug in an elevator together, Richard and Lily dramatized the secret solidarities that cut across lines of class.

The Lily Tomlin Show was a winner in the Nielsen ratings, a solid eleventh for the week, and when CBS asked her to deliver another show in the fall, she was determined to leverage her success and gain more artistic freedom on her second special, titled simply *Lily.* She brought in new writers like Off-Off-Broadway playwright Rosalyn Drexler and future *Saturday Night Live* producers Lorne Michaels and Herb Sargent. The "Juke and Opal" sketch, she decided, would not be cut this time; the producer who'd deleted it from the first special was not invited back. Plotting her moves strategically, Lily also decided to bring back "War Games," an antiwar sketch that network execs had previously quashed, scandalized by the idea of a mother telling her son, playing soldier in the backyard, "Come on, leg or no leg, supper's on the table." Perhaps Lily could use "War Games" as a bargaining chip if the network tried to block "Juke and Opal" for a second time.

As on the previous special, Richard's improvising spirit put him at loggerheads with CBS. In a new sketch, featuring Lily's Edith Ann and Richard as a young kid, Richard made up the guileless riff "I have titties bigger than your titties . . . boys have titties—first, boys have titties . . . then girls." The network reps panicked and put a stop to the scene, and Richard felt so deflated that he left the soundstage. When Lily met him in his dressing room and urged him to give it another try, he said, "I can't do more." He told a journalist later, "I can't go onstage and it be in my mind that this kid can't say something, 'cause the kid is wrecked, as a kid. I mean, I was ready to cry as a kid, 'cause I was the kid, you dig. That's the way I see kids; I just get fascinated talking to 'em, 'cause it'll be honestly sweet, and whatever they say is innocent. And if they say 'tittie,' you can't tell a kid you can't say 'tittie.' They deal with real shit." The sketch was scrapped; Lily recorded Edith Ann solo instead.

"Juke and Opal" had no off-color language to which the network could object. It was remarkably restrained as it tracked the arm's-length intimacy between Juke, a man struggling to throw off a heroin addiction and get a job, and Opal, who operates her diner with a mix of sensitivity and bottom-dog wit. ("Don't hand me that jive about job training," she tells Juke. "You trained, all right. You highly skilled at not working.") Still, "Juke and Opal" was troubling to the network for other reasons. During its taping, Lily was standing on its set, waiting for another take, when she noticed that everyone else had left. "I go into the hall, and everyone is standing around in a huddle," she recalled. "They had just got the word to 'stop taping this. We don't want this on the air.' "

What had so inflamed the network's executives? A critic praised *Lily*, later, as "probably the most radical departure from television and comedic conventions we will see on the tube this season," and

A radical departure from TV conventions: Lily Tomlin as Opal, Richard Pryor as Juke. (Courtesy of the author)

"Juke and Opal" was Exhibit A for how wayward the special became, how much it purposefully ran off the rails. "Everybody kept saying it wasn't funny, but we wanted to do little poems," said Jane Wagner.

As a "little poem," the sketch doesn't explain, much less overexplain, its two main characters. The nature of Juke and Opal's relationship is subtly enigmatic, starting with the question of Opal's racial identity: Lily deliberately left Opal's race open-ended, disguising her hair behind a scarf and giving her a clipped accent that could be either poor white or poor black. (Some viewers thought Opal mixed-race or black; others assumed she was white.) The two might be former lovers, or prospective lovers. They're reaching, albeit gingerly, toward some new intimacy: Juke plays Al Green's "Let's Stay Together" on Opal's jukebox, and after she turns down his invitation to dance, she hangs back behind the counter, looking at him slyly and dancing with herself. Both of them have a generally wounded look to them, but we can't tell whether they've been wounded by one another or simply the world. "The world" arrives at Opal's diner in the form of two young social workers, a pair of well-meaning types who would never enter her Silver Spoon Café for the food. Here they come armed with a community questionnaire. As soon as they arrive, an invisible thread snaps; the dancing stops; "Let's Stay Together" fades out. We feel the fragility of what Juke and Opal have, and the value of Opal's diner as a haven for irregulars, a warm spot in a cold city.

Opal has a wry working-class knowingness to her. When one of the social workers, defending himself, says about his questionnaire, "Try to understand—we don't make up these questions," she counters, "Try to understand—we do make up these answers." Yet Opal also looks beyond her world. Her greasy spoon is named, with who knows how much irony, "Opal's Silver Spoon Café." The sketch begins and ends with a similarly free-floating juxtaposition: the hash slinger Opal watching, on her TV, a Julia Child–like chef instruct viewers on how to prepare a cold lobster salad and bananas flambé.

As Juke, Richard was at his best as an actor. He modulated the junkie character he'd performed in his stand-up, preserving that character's vulnerability but making him more multifaceted. With the social workers, Juke is acerbic; he steals the questionnaire out of their hands and puts them on the defensive with improvised questions like "Who's Pigmeat Markham's mama?" With Opal, he's undefended, transparently working through his conflicting needs. He wants both her affection and the heroin he craves, and for most of the sketch, he's willing to leverage the former for the latter, angling to borrow ten dollars from her so he can get high.

By the end, though, a gear has shifted in Juke's mind; he has started to see himself through Opal's watchful and loving eyes. He gives her back the ten dollars and makes a modest promise: that he'll try to stay clean. The end of the sketch is filled with similar small but meaningful gestures; nothing is italicized for our benefit. Juke leans in, and the two kiss briefly, their faces obscured by the camera angle. Then, exiting the diner and heading into a swirl of cold wind outside, Juke leaves her musing on better times to come: "I'll think about you. Be glad when it's spring, flower."

All told, "Juke and Opal" was closer to the best stage drama than the usual sketch comedy, and CBS hoped to have none of it. A CBS executive, on seeing the special as a whole, called it a "$360,000 jerk off." "Juke and Opal" in particular was objectionable in so many ways: it was too long, it wasn't funny, and to top it off, it smuggled in a kiss between a black actor and a white actress. Lily negotiated like Talleyrand to preserve the sketch. She offered to can "War Games" if she could keep "Juke and Opal," and the network agreed to this lesser of two evils—under the condition that she sweeten the sketch with a laugh track (so that viewers would think it was, indeed, funny) and move it to the end of the show (where it wouldn't spoil the ratings). Lily took the deal.

Lily premiered, with "Juke and Opal" intact, on November 3, 1973. To CBS's chagrin, it attracted few viewers, ranking fifty-first out of sixty-six shows on prime time that week. Yet those in the know noticed. Six months later, *Lily* picked up Emmy Awards for best comedy-variety special and for the best writing on a comedy-variety special. A year after that, *Lily* writer Lorne Michaels used Lily's specials as a model for his own *Saturday Night Live*, inspired by how she threw together "political stuff and mood pieces and moments of truth."

It was probably no coincidence that Richard and Lily's two sketches together revolved around courtships that were bold but hazy: their own relationship had the same tenor. For Richard, Lily was one of his few unrequited adult crushes. "I love Lily," he told *Rolling Stone* in 1974, then confessed:

> I'd like to ball her in all them different characters she does sometimes. Wouldn't you? I mean, have her around the house and have her do all that—be Ernestine one minute. [*Imitating Ernestine*] "Oh [*snort, snort*], just put it in the proper place. Thank you" [*snort, snort*].

Witnessing Lily's creativity was "sensual" for Richard. "[T]he deeper and funnier it got," he wrote of their collaboration, "the more I wanted to get in her pants." Fortunately, one might say, Lily didn't return those particular affections. Though instantly seduced by Richard as a performer, she was never seduced by him as a man: by 1973 she had been committed to Jane Wagner for several years and would remain so. As a consequence, Richard and Lily had a less troubled connection, uninflected by the possessiveness that Richard felt toward the other women in his life.

The only strains in their relationship, in fact, came when Lily was acting not as an artist onstage but rather as a feminist in conversation, questioning the prerogatives of men. When at one point Richard took her to an after-hours joint, she engaged some working girls with a rap about how they should consider keeping their earnings for themselves. Richard hustled her out, intuiting that she was taking them, and herself, to a dangerous place. And when she trespassed on Richard's own prerogatives, even his darling Lily wasn't granted a free pass. At a restaurant on Sunset Boulevard once, she started talking feminism with Patricia. Richard became so incensed that he turned their table over, letting the dishes clatter to the floor, and stormed out of the restaurant.

For Richard, there was life onstage and life off-, and the onstage life was where he had the license to check his ego and admit his vulnerabilities. Collaborators like Lily Tomlin and Jane Wagner offered him the equivalent of an airtight alibi: with them he could flow into characters and explore his better self, with no worries of getting caught. It was no easy thing to bridge the worlds of on- and offstage. Even Lily, who had a more integrated sense of herself than Richard, acknowledged the difficulty of being at home with her variousness. When an interviewer asked her how she felt when she saw herself on TV, she shot back a riddle of her own: "What does a chameleon see when it looks into a mirror?"

Richard's collaboration with Lily was a shaft of light in an otherwise dim time for his career. In 1972 he had worked on six films; after *Hit!* wrapped in February 1973, he worked on none for nine months, and the only role he could anticipate was a small, low-paid cameo in Sidney Poitier's *Uptown Saturday Night.* The stalling of his film career puzzled him. "I've been trying to be a booty star," he said in October 1973. "I was in about three movies and thought, 'Shit, you get one movie, you get a whole bunch of motherfuckin' movies'. . . . I ain't had a motherfucker call me about nothin'." Richard had done more, too, than simply wait for the phone to ring. Fresh off his work on *Blazing Saddles,* he wrote and tried to peddle *The Black Stranger,* a revisionist Western wherein the odd team of a voodoo woman and a black gunfighter drive out a villain who, suspiciously, acts a whole lot like John Wayne. The *Los Angeles Times* announced that Richard was setting up a production deal; none materialized publicly.

It was out of desperation that Richard came back to stand-up comedy. "I was starving to death," he said, explaining why he'd returned to the stage after years of avoiding it. "Kiss my ass, Jack! I have to get back to work." His manager Ron DeBlasio had a more sanguine view of Richard's situation: he saw Richard as a breakout performer and, given the recognition of his film and TV work, thought he should now play concerts, not club dates. DeBlasio booked Richard for a midnight concert at Washington, DC's Kennedy Center. It was an intense scale-up in capacity, from a DC club like the Cellar Door (220 seats) to the Kennedy Center's stately Concert Hall (2,465 seats). Richard wondered if he was ready.

As preparation for the Kennedy Center show, Richard played a series of woodshedding dates at LA's Comedy Store in October 1973, and you can hear his nerves and rustiness as a performer on the recording of his first show there. He opened with "Wino and Junkie," a routine that had customarily been his closer, and raced through it at a jumped-up clip. Then, for apparently the first time, he welcomed the audience with what became his signature greeting during his heyday: "Hope I'm funny . . . 'cause [this] audience has been known to kick a little ass." Later, perhaps, this line became a mere reflex, but at this point he truly feared having to face the music. His new routines were untested or unelaborated, his old routines polished past the point of feeling fresh to him. Half an hour into the show, he made another unprecedented gesture: he asked the audience for requests. "Whoah, horsey," a line from "Rumpelstiltskin," his oldest and tamest of routines, bounced back at him—reminding him why he never asked for requests. They lashed him to an older version of himself, one he'd long tried to outrun.

Richard barely made it to DC for his Kennedy Center gig, delaying his trip to the LA airport to the last possible minute. In the run-up to the show, he was "a nervous wreck," according to DeBlasio. He couldn't eat; he was irritable; he turned away from conversations or joined them to deliver insults. Backstage at the Kennedy Center, though, he came upon some head-turning news: his midnight concert was a sellout. In DC's black community—and especially among those for whom the witching hour marked just the start of their Saturday night—the name "Richard Pryor" was golden.

Onstage, Richard beheld an almost exclusively black audience packing the lower level, box seats, and two balconies, and he kicked into gear. He rode the crests of laughter, loosely switching between his established routines and his riffs on news of the day, like the energy crisis: "Ain't gonna affect us, 'cause I don't know no nigger buys more than $2 worth of gas anyway." The *Washington Post* wrote that he kept the audience "guffawing in the aisles," and couldn't help observing that "his scatological, outrageously lewd humor struck an interesting note of contrast in the Center's sedate Concert Hall." Never before, it's fair to say, had a comic speculated frankly on a president's sexual prowess (or lack thereof) from its stage.

The tide was turning for Richard. Shortly after the concert, DeBlasio fielded a phone call from Murray Swartz of Queen Booking, possibly the top agency representing black talent and certainly the top black-owned agency. After drifting nearly four years without an agent, Richard signed with Queen, and found himself in the illustrious company of Aretha Franklin, Ray Charles, Sammy Davis Jr., and Gladys Knight and the Pips. Soon he was routinely selling out large venues like New York's Lincoln Center and playing still-bigger arenas like the Oakland Coliseum. But it wasn't simply Queen's muscle that opened doors: Richard's breakthrough as a stand-up was powered by a live show that slayed audiences and by a little album that forever altered the DNA of American comedy.

"*That Nigger's Crazy*" was recorded in February 1974 at a San Francisco nightclub operated by *Soul Train* host Don Cornelius, and in front of an audience that was 90 percent black. Richard's instructions to DeBlasio, who was in charge of producing the record, were minimal but insistent: "Remember black people." After his experience with his first album, he wouldn't allow his material to be cherry-picked for the so-called mainstream. Richard himself came up with the album's title (sometimes forcibly abbreviated in ads as *"That N—— Crazy"*) and with the album's cover, on which his face opens up in a grin that falls halfway between impish and diabolical. Shamelessness was his starting point and his forte.

"That Nigger's Crazy" was an Everlasting Gobstopper of an album, changing flavors the more one savored it. On the first pass, it simply floored contemporary listeners with its audacity. When Richard confessed how he prayed to God after a too-quick ejaculation ("Lord, don't let her know . . . just let it stay heavy if not hard"); when he imitated a cop in naked love with his power ("Put your hands up, take your pants down and spread your cheeks!"); or when, in the character of the swaggering Oilwell, he taunted a cop ("Boy, you hit me with that stick, I'm gonna bite your dick!"), he was uttering the unutterable. As the crazy nigger, he gave voice to repressed anxieties, affronts, wishes—things too painful to remember or too dangerous to dwell upon.

On second and third hearing, *"That Nigger's Crazy"* revealed itself as a set of variations on a theme that Richard announced eleven minutes into the record: "white folks do things a lot different than niggers do." Here he was less the crazy nigger than a sort of comic anthropologist, elaborating on the cultural divide between white and black America. The terms of that divide were familiar—whites were repressed, blacks flamboyant; whites were brittle, blacks unflappable ("nothin' can scare a nigger after 400 years of this shit")—but Richard's examples were fresh and vivid, with no plaster saints or tinhorn villains in sight. He directed much of his attention to black folks who were earthy, homegrown characters. There was his aunt Maxine, who sucked a neck bone with such gusto that, by the time she threw the bone to the family dog, he looked at it puzzled ("What am I supposed to do with that motherfucker?"). There was the wino who, chancing upon Dracula in the ghetto, told him to hightail to an orthodontist. There was the black preacher who, transposed into a black version of *The Exorcist*, informed the Lord that "the devil is just acting the motherfuckin' fool," and asked, "Could you exorcise this motherfucker to Cleveland or some place?" And so on: characters whose bravado came from embracing their idiosyncrasies. Black comedians in the generation after Richard—whether they performed on *Saturday Night Live* or *Def Comedy Jam*, *MADtv* or the *Kings of Comedy* tour—have drawn upon the example that he set here.

Less obviously, perhaps, *"That Nigger's Crazy"* operated like a set of neon-lit folktales, shaking insight and laughter out of the harshest of predicaments. Just as folktales often surprise us with their ghastliness—stepmothers who banish their children, ogres who feed on a diet of bones—so Richard captivated the listener with a vision of the world that, from one angle, was beyond bleak. Thus the final line in his story of a black man getting frisked while out on the town: "What nigger feel like having fun after that? *'Let's just go home, baby.'* You go home and beat your kids and shit—you gonna take that shit out on somebody." He dramatized the desperation and violence of the world, which wasn't simply color-coded by race. In an absurdly grim scene, his junkie vomits in the unemployment bureau, then argues with a black security guard about who should clean up the mess. "[If] you don't clean up that shit," the guard threatens, "I shoot your ass." The junkie replies, "Well, then, who gonna clean up the blood, nigger?" and laughs with self-satisfaction. For the moment he has, like a modern-day Brer Rabbit, bested the guard by outwitting him.

"That Nigger's Crazy" was unquestionably a comedy landmark, but it might have been better still, more searching and provocative, if it had included his routine on dropping acid for the first time. Richard first developed "Acid" around late 1973, and while he later performed it on *Saturday Night Live* and recorded a dazzling version on 1976's *Bicentennial Nigger*, the original version probed deeper. In both versions of "Acid," Richard hits many of the same marks: he takes the drug with bluster ("Baby, I can handle any motherfuckin' thing!"); feels a trippy rush; falls into terror ("I don't remember how to breathe!"); then loses himself in a parallel scene of a mind unspooling, the climax of *2001: A Space Odyssey*. In this last section, Richard's personal voice drops out, and for a long minute his stage routine has the suspended-in-air pacing of the Kubrick film. His audience is made to sit mute with concentration as Richard performs the scene in which Dave the astronaut deactivates Hal the computer:

[*The sound of labored breathing, Dave in a space suit.*]

HAL [*gently and matter-of-fact as ever*]: Dave, don't. I'm losing my mind, Dave.

Hi, my name is Hal 9000. I was embedded in 1992. My teacher taught me a song. Would you like to hear it?

One critic described Richard's performance as "like a ballet, his hands floating slow motion out of control, his head jerking this way and that as if possessed."

In the original version of "Acid," Richard had inserted an extra existential twist to the tale. During his reckoning with the abyss, a powerful voice comes out of a howling wind and assails Richard, urging him to let go of his identity as a "nigger":

VOICE FROM BEYOND [*whispering furiously, with an accusatory tone*]: I've been waiting for about 22 years to meet your ass. You've been bullshittin' me, you know, with all that old jive nigger shit? You know, hidin' behind them shields and shit? Instead of coming *forward* with all this *energy*?

You been layin' back, posin' an' *shit*, bullshittin', motherfucker, well you're DEAD tonight. . . . I'm gonna free you, brother. I'm taking over where I rightfully belong; you givin' up all that phony psychology you didn't learn.

RICHARD [*speaking as if trapped in a slow-motion film*]: Wha-uh-tin-the-fu-kis-sap-ning-to-me-ee?

VOICE FROM BEYOND [*calm now, comforting*]: You becoming a man. You just born. But I'm afraid . . . you won't be a nigger no more. But you won't be ignorant, either. The truth . . . is everlasting.

In this version, Richard was pushed to be reborn—and into a startling discovery about the fictions that ruled his life. In the mid-1960s he had been Mr. Congeniality onstage; then, after his identity crisis in Las Vegas, he had embraced the persona of the "crazy nigger," a persona that allowed him to speak his own truth and violate whatever taboos required violation. Or so he thought. But what if "nigger" itself were just another mask, just another bit of jive? What if being "that crazy nigger" were a mere gimmick, designed to keep the deepest of anxieties at bay?

For a different sort of artist, this moment in "Acid" would have been unthinkable or untenable—the equivalent of those cartoon scenes where a character saws away at the branch he is sitting upon. But for Richard, "Acid" was a fulfillment of his larger program as an artist and a "crazy nigger" both. Once he settled on a truth, he was compelled to unsettle it. Once the foundation seemed solid under his feet, his mind turned to thoughts of earthquakes, quicksand, dynamite.

For a seeker like Richard, there was no easy resolution to the contradiction: race was both the thinnest of fictions and the hardest of truths. During an acid-induced dialogue with a voice from beyond, it might seem a mere illusion. But in the world, it raised your blood pressure, kept you unemployed, and got your ass strip-searched and hauled off to jail.

In early March of 1974, Richard was in Washington, DC, for a set of concerts when he was approached by a friend who'd just been released from the Lorton Correctional Complex in Fairfax County, Virginia. The inmates, his friend said, were Pryor fans and wanted him to perform inside. Would he consider playing there?

A few days later, Richard was in a packed gymnasium at Lorton, surrounded by a thousand inmates; he'd coaxed the promoter behind his DC shows to whip together a concert, and now he was on a bill with a local go-go band, a model, and Inner Voices, an inmate singing group. The inmates in the audience wore Lorton's unofficial uniform—wool caps, fatigue jackets, jeans, and work boots or sneakers—and sat with the utmost attention for this rare reprieve from prison routine.

The men of Inner Voices filed onstage, some in long white robes, one in black, another without a shirt, and sang the just-released ballad by the Stylistics, "You Make Me Feel Brand New." The lead singer reached out, at a tender moment, to one of the two women in the hall, and a wave of applause swelled in the room. On every other day at Lorton, there were no women to serenade.

Richard started weeping and didn't stop. "Look at these guys," he told Ron DeBlasio. "They'll never get out. Look at the life they lead, how terrible it is."

When he took the stage, Richard connected with the men in the crowd, animating a set of characters familiar to them from their life before prison. With his pitch-perfect impersonations, he gave them a taste of the families in which they'd grown up, the players they'd known, the electricity of the streets they'd left behind. It was as if, through the magic of the stage, he had smuggled the world outside Lorton into Lorton.

The full show lasted three hours, or as long as the warden would allow. When it ended, an inmate presented to Richard a painting he'd done. "We wish we had more," he announced, "but we give you our love and this is a token of it."

After the show, the inmates "crowded around Pryor and the other performers," wrote the *Washington Post*, "talking, touching, exchanging addresses." Then they exchanged something more: Richard had been wearing an expensive studded leather shirt, and he traded it for the shirt worn by a young inmate.

Richard left Lorton wearing prison denim. Seven weeks later, he arranged to have Inner Voices transported—with a contingent of armed guards for security—to the Apollo Theater in Harlem, where they served as his opening act for four nights of performances. Richard introduced their act personally at the Apollo, an unusual move for a headliner.

Seven weeks later still, Richard himself was Prisoner No. 2140-875 in the Los Angeles County Jail and wearing prison denim not by choice. He was serving a ten-day sentence for tax evasion, the result of the early years of his career, when he had acted like his grandmother in her brothel and kept his earnings—an alleged $250,000 over four years—off the books. The judge, making an example of Richard around tax season, had mandated prison time.

CHAPTER 18

Number One with a Bullet

Los Angeles, Peoria, 1974–1975

A telling coincidence: in the summer of 1974, as Richard Pryor's *"That Nigger's Crazy"* surged to the No. 1 position on *Billboard*'s R&B charts, Richard Nixon's presidency collapsed under the weight of the Watergate scandal. One Republican senator likened Nixon—protesting his innocence while his associates were linked to a squalid campaign of spying and sabotage—to "a piano player in a whorehouse who claims not to know what's going on upstairs." After August 5, 1974, absolutely no one believed the piano player anymore. The "smoking gun" tape had been made public, and with it, evidence that Nixon had blocked a FBI investigation that could ensnare him. On the night of August 8, Nixon resigned as president. Richard was playing an intimate Philadelphia nightclub called the Bijou, and rather than give his usual show, he brought a TV onstage. Everyone watched, transfixed. Richard supplied color commentary as the politician he'd long lampooned for his diabolical ambition—using red lighting when portraying him onstage—slinked off the stage of history.

The fall of Nixon landed America in a funk, and Richard was the funk's unexpected beneficiary: his peak years as a comedian aligned with the post-Watergate years of Presidents Ford and Carter. "Nixon took justice and broke its jaw," he said, when asked now about the profanity in his act. "Now *that* is profane." A surprising number of Americans agreed with Richard's spin on the morality of the day. His streetwise talk, his cynicism toward those in power, his no-holds-barred wrestling with his own inner truths—all these had a larger purchase after Watergate. An NAACP activist in Peoria captured the prevailing mood: "[Watergate was] a shock and it's leaving our country wide open. If things don't change the attitude is, 'Well, nothing's going to change and I'll free myself *my* way, *any* way I have to.'" Over the next five years, Richard's audience spread outward from its black core to a mainstream that, having just watched its president devolve into a mere conspirator in chief, was looking to free itself any way it had to. *"That Nigger's Crazy"* set the table for a run of albums that won Grammy after Grammy, exploded the possibilities for stand-up comedy, and turned Richard into the most unlikely of avatars.

Or maybe not that unlikely. Who better to lead the way, in an uncertain time, than a performer who called things by their proper names and was quite honest about how he moved through the world? Mudbone, Richard's most famous comic creation, dated from this period, and was a grizzled street corner philosopher who delivered wisdom through the tallest of tales. In a world of trickery—or Tricky Dickery—the self-styled trickster was at least candid about his appetites and open about his love of the extravagant lie, and that was refreshing.

From a business standpoint, the success of *"That Nigger's Crazy"* was a minor miracle. Because of the obscenities that riddled every track, the album carried a "Rated X" label, and radio stations refused to play it. And because of a slew of problems involving Stax, Richard's record company, it barely benefitted from other forms of promotion. The once-mighty Stax was beginning to circle the drain, its financial resources consumed in battles with CBS, with the bank it relied upon for credit, and with the federal government. Just a year earlier, Stax executives had been arranging screenings of *Wattstax* for the United Nations and the U.S. Congress, and offering their company as a model black-owned business. Now they were under investigation by the IRS and the U.S. Attorney's Office, and their company's cash flow had slowed to a trickle. When a Stax rep came to a Pryor show in the summer of 1974, he reversed the usual dynamic by acting the mooch, sticking Richard with the bill for his expenses—including not only his hotel room and dinner but also his prostitute for the night.

On a quite basic level, too, Stax failed to get Richard's album in the hands of record buyers. CBS had arranged to distribute other Stax albums but balked at Richard's. "They flatly refused [the] Richard Pryor project because they didn't understand the dollar impact of it," remembered a Stax executive. "[A]nd once they listened to it they were absolutely certain that they didn't want to be part of it." According to Richard's manager Ron DeBlasio, there was "no promotion, no nothing. They didn't have [the album] in record stores."

Fortunately for Richard, he could generate some buzz for himself by touring. He island-hopped across the archipelago of urban America—Detroit, Philadelphia, Cincinnati, San Jose—and performed, night after night, for largely black crowds. He saw hustlers and their women filling the most expensive seats in the front rows: they were the core of his core audience, and especially good at working the word on "the street" on his behalf. He started feeling something new and electric, something he'd tasted with his *Wattstax* experience—black America coming together around his humor:

> I noticed going around working for black people who're in a depression now, they all laughed at the same things wherever I was working. There's a kind of unity. In different cities, wherever I am, they be laughing at the same [shit], so I know we all know what's happening. I say, "Well, now, Huey [Newton] done went crazy. Whipped his tailor 'cause the pants was too long." And they laughed all over 'cause they knew who I was talking about. They knew about all the niggers who died following after him, and here he is beating up a tailor.

Richard gave pleasure—the pleasure of shared disenchantment—to those who had expected little from Richard Nixon, more from Huey Newton, and been disappointed by both.

The tour in support of *"That Nigger's Crazy"* was a runaway success: sold-out concert halls, crowds caught up in "thunderous roars of laughter and applause," his best-ever reviews in the black press ("the number one comedian in the world"). There was just one snag. On August 4 he was set to perform, on a rare stop south of the Mason-Dixon Line, for a sell-out audience of twelve thousand in Richmond, Virginia, when the venue's manager warned DeBlasio that a municipal ordinance prohibited the use of foul language in a city-owned building. DeBlasio passed on the message to Richard, who was not interested in censoring himself. His act was his act, and he had not trimmed swear words from his live show since 1968, the last time he played Vegas. That night at Richmond's Coliseum, he began with some swipes at Nixon, then was moved by the rowdy spirit of the crowd to his raunchiest and raciest material. He delivered a "blue—no, purple—routine," what the *Richmond Post-Dispatch* called "porn."

For whatever reason, the police held back. Richard had his own explanation: "They was going to arrest me during the show, but with 12,000 niggers there enjoying themselves, they had second thoughts." Richard returned to his hotel room, seemingly having tempted fate and won. At 1:30 in the morning, however, Richmond police turned up at his hotel room and arrested him for "conducting himself in a disorderly manner in public." A black cop, slapping handcuffs on Richard, said, "Listen, brother, this pains me." At booking, another black cop told Richard he loved *"That Nigger's Crazy,"* then sent Richard off to his first stint in a southern jail. Richard spent a long fifteen minutes in lockup while the police processed the five-hundred-dollar bond posted by DeBlasio. At his release, the state scheduled a trial date for August 19.

Then the prosecution did nothing: on August 19 the state attorney's office announced it was dropping the charges against Richard. The decision was a sign that performers like him now held the upper hand; strictures against obscenity had relaxed since his flameout at the Aladdin and the demise of Lenny Bruce. In a world where *Deep Throat* was a date movie, it was hard to convict a performer for swearing in front of consenting adults. Adults-only entertainment—XXX films, peep shows, massage parlors, underground nightclubs for those of every erotic predisposition—had taken hold in major cities across

America, assisted by a 1973 Supreme Court ruling that gave the local community, not the federal government, the right to determine what counted as obscene. The Richmond Coliseum's manager had tried to get the old machinery in motion, but even in the Old Dominion, the principle of free speech carried the day.

With the wind at his back, Richard took the opportunity to repay a long-standing debt. On August 23 he journeyed to his hometown of Peoria, carrying with him the Emmy he'd won in May for cowriting his second special with Lily Tomlin. For the first time, his name was up on the marquee of the Shrine Mosque, one of the city's larger venues. Officially he was there as part of "Richard Pryor Days," a celebration sponsored by Peoria's Ashanti Umoja Center. Yet Richard didn't milk the occasion to grandstand. The afternoon of his show, he presented his Emmy to Juliette Whittaker, his old mentor from the Carver Center, at a ceremony at a preschool that Juliette had established. "It was our award," Richard explained later. His first experience of a writers' room had been in Juliette's upstairs office at Carver.

Juliette accepted the Emmy on behalf of all those black children who'd been involved in Peoria's youth theater. "This is an inspiration for all of us," she said. "Not that everyone can win an Emmy, because we know that's impossible, but this is the impossible dream come true." Then Richard cut the ribbon on another gift he'd provided for Juliette: a redwood playground set, with a steep slide and fireman's pole. (Fearless in many ways, Richard was yet afraid of heights and refused to slide down the slide.) He proved eager to provide for the children who came into Juliette's care. The next year, when Juliette founded a progressive elementary school named the Learning Tree, Richard became its financial angel, providing need-based scholarships for as many as seventy children at a time. Miss Whittaker unlocked the generosity within him; she touched that part of Richard that yearned for the innocence of childhood, an innocence he'd never been allowed.

Richard's performance at the Shrine Mosque capped the hoopla of "Richard Pryor Days" with an anticlimax. The Ashanti Umoja Center, an institution born out of the defiance of Black Power but now promoting, in the spirit of the times, a program of self-help through craft making, presented Richard with a large plaque. Richard promised, jokingly, to wear it in good health. Then he performed a set that, at twenty minutes, was breathtakingly short—a replay of his twenty-minute performance at the Carver Center in 1969. He had just slayed audiences from Oakland to Harlem, but at the Shrine Mosque, he checked himself, as if unable to relax into the artist he'd become. Juliette Whittaker and his family sat in the audience, and after a salty routine about the differences between black sex and white sex, Richard worried aloud, "Boy, my grandmother's gonna beat my ass when I get home." For a performer wedded to the ideal of flowing in the moment, the internal censor was the least welcome of guests—harder to handle, perhaps, than stodgy enemies like the manager of Richmond's Coliseum.

Richard would return to Peoria for family occasions—birthdays, funerals, graduations—but he never gave a concert there again.

It was just Richard's luck to have his first hit album released by a record company at the exact moment that its assets were frozen or otherwise tied up. By the end of September, *"That Nigger's Crazy"* had spent four weeks in the number one R&B slot, and he had some two hundred thousand dollars in unpaid royalties owed him by Stax. His mind-set at the time is suggested by the name of the corporation he founded to pry those monies from Stax's grip: Pay Back Inc. Stax gave Richard possession of his master tapes in an attempt to settle its debt, but Richard still pressed forward with legal action, suing various Stax-related entities for ninety-five thousand dollars in remaining obligations. One day, seething at home, he pointed a gun at the framed gold record of *"That Nigger's Crazy"* hanging on his wall, and from that point forward, the record had two holes: the one given to play it on a turntable, the other supplied by the impact of his bullet.

Still, the breakout success of the record created a set of remarkable opportunities for Richard—among them the chance, in November, to cohost *The Mike Douglas Show* for a week. A few months before, he had appeared on the show as part of a panel that included Martha Mitchell, the free-talking wife of Nixon's attorney general, and the wives of three leading U.S. senators. Mike Douglas worried that the mix of guests was "like nitro and glycerin," but Richard and Martha surprised everyone with their rapport. One of the senators' wives said, "We live, eat, sleep, and breathe politics," and Martha chimed in naughtily, "Together?" That was Richard's cue:

RICHARD [*trying to help*]: She thought you were talking about an orgy.
MARTHA: Thank you, Richard.
RICHARD: Sure . . . You know, we've met before, on the first Amtrak train to Chicago.
MARTHA: I remember that. I christened that train. You were on that train?
RICHARD: Yaz, ma'am. I was the porter.
MARTHA: How nice. Did you carry my bags?
RICHARD: Oh yes'm.
MIKE DOUGLAS: Did she give you a tip?
RICHARD: Uh-huh. Blue Boy in the fifth.

Tickled by such repartee and aware that *"That Nigger's Crazy"* had raised Richard's profile considerably, Mike Douglas asked him to come back as a cohost, and gave him the latitude to choose a number of his guests. He drew from his family in Peoria (his grandmother Marie, his uncle Dickie), his teenage idols (Sammy Davis Jr., Harry Belafonte), younger, hip performers (Ben Vereen, Sly Stone, Freddie Prinze), and some fellow partisans in the battle for free speech (gadfly Gore Vidal and actor George C. Scott, fresh from a tussle with the Motion Picture Association of America Ratings Board over his latest film). And so, in the last week of November 1974, *The Mike Douglas Show* became considerably blacker and more unpredictable than usual. Effectively, Richard had been given the chance to curate his life, his world, on national TV.

Several segments offered access to parts of Richard he rarely displayed in public. Juliette Whittaker came on as the week's surprise first guest and set the tone by reducing him to tears with her mere presence. He choked up when Sammy Davis Jr. praised him as "one of the finest straight actors we have in this business," shone with pride as his grandmother cooked a soul food meal of greens and fried chicken on set, and took obvious pleasure in playing mentor to Freddie Prinze. On the other side of the emotional spectrum, he threw down his drumsticks in frustration when a jokey performance with Sly Stone went awry. And it wasn't just Richard who felt loose. In the middle of the week, he sparred on camera with boxer Joe Frazier, whom he had teased earlier at a club date in Philadelphia. Frazier got his revenge by knocking the wind out of Richard with a dead-serious punch to the gut.

In a week of unanticipated interactions, no exchange was more unusual, or more telling, than a tense skirmish between Richard and Milton Berle. Berle was one of the guests whom Richard *hadn't* suggested. In the 1950s, Berle had been, with his outlandish costumes and his file of more than four million jokes, the king of prime-time TV as host of *Texaco Star Theater.* Now the sixty-seven-year-old comedian was appearing on the show to promote his autobiography, a sobering book in which Uncle Miltie dropped his toothy grin and told of his soul-crushing Jewish mother and his desultory if star-studded sex life. In an age that preferred topicality and candor to vaudevillian japes, he was coming clean—and refurbishing his reputation by revealing the agony-rich inner life he had hidden from view.

From the moment he stepped on *The Mike Douglas Show,* Berle tried to control its tone. He addressed George C. Scott as "Sir Walter Scott" and hailed Richard with "Oh my God, Dick Gregory—haven't seen you in years." He joked that, just as Richard had won an Emmy for writing the Lily Tomlin special, he'd won an Emmy for writing a Pinky Tomlin special years ago. But the one-liners fell flat. (Mike Douglas had to remind the audience that Pinky Tomlin was a 1940s crooner.) "Is this the real audience?" Berle asked Douglas in a stage whisper.

When Berle described getting roughed up by two mobsters who hated his act, Douglas pulled Richard into the conversation, and it careered into unforeseen territory:

> **MIKE DOUGLAS**: Anything like that every happen to you, Richard?
> **RICHARD**: Never happened to me, no.
> **MILTON BERLE**: I saw your act—it should have.
> **RICHARD**: I think Milton Berle is a funny man. I've seen him work—I've been on shows where all us young guys were dying, trying to get laughs, and Milton was there with cards, trying to help us out.
> **MIKE DOUGLAS**: I saw Milton do one of the kindest things . . .
> **RICHARD**: I never saw him do anything kind.
> **MILTON BERLE**: You mean for "your kind."
> **RICHARD**: Oooh.
> **MILTON BERLE**: No, I'm kidding.
> **RICHARD** [*mock-speechifying, raising his finger*]: "Black people of America . . ."
>
> [*Berle silences Richard by putting his hand over Richard's mouth, then looks at his hand disdainfully, as if it were dripping with germs, and shakes it.*]

This scuffle—in which Richard tendered a compliment, then hedged it, and Berle played a number of race cards clumsily—was a prelude to what Mike Douglas called "one of the strangest moments that I've ever experienced." Berle started talking about a central tribulation of his life, a love affair that produced a child whom he had never met, and Richard couldn't abide the seriousness that attended its telling. He failed to stifle a nervous laugh. Berle bristled, "I wish, I wish, Richard, that I could have laughed at that time at your age," then gathered himself and picked up his story. And again Richard punctured the solemnity. When Berle made a point of refusing to name the woman involved, Richard blurted out, "Eleanor Roosevelt."

The audience tittered at the absurd suggestion; the hostilities between the two comics escalated. Berle oozed a sense of his own moral superiority, but somehow he couldn't come out on top:

> **MILTON BERLE**: Richard, let me tell you something, baby. I told you this nine years ago and I'm going to tell you this on the air in front of millions of people. Pick your spots, baby.
>
> **RICHARD** [*imitating Humphrey Bogart*]: All right, sweetheart.
>
> **MILTON BERLE**: Pick your spots . . .
>
> **RICHARD**: I'm sorry, Milton, I'll be honest, I'm crazy.
>
> **MILTON BERLE**: No, you're not crazy. . . . [*Taking Richard by the chin and forcing him to look into his own eyes*] I want to ask you why you laugh.
>
> **RICHARD**: I laugh because it's funny, man. It's funny to me. It ain't nothing to do with you.
>
> **MILTON BERLE**: Because it never happened to you.
>
> **RICHARD** [*turning away from Berle, eyes lifting up to the ceiling*]: No, no, it's just the insanity of all this is funny. Do you understand? I'm funny and I laugh, and so I'm crazy and so I apologize because I don't want to hurt your feelings and because I respect what you do. But I don't want to kiss your ass.

The audience roared at Richard's final obscenity. Berle threw up his hands, pivoted toward Douglas, and shut Richard out of the rest of the conversation. Given that the talk show had lost its usual bearings, there was no more need for the schmoozy civility that was its default setting.

The dustup between the two comedians was the talk of the comedy circuit for weeks after. Older comedians thought Berle had put Richard in his place, while younger comedians thought Richard had held his ground. Inadvertently, as they jousted for position on *Mike Douglas*, the two comedians had revealed the contours of the generation gap in American comedy.

Berle represented a generation of largely Jewish comics who, rooted in vaudeville, catered to mainstream audiences with routines that were wacky and physically witty but not topical or edgy. He kept asking Richard why he'd laughed because the older comedian seemed to know in advance the right answer and was angling for a confession: Richard was ill-mannered, inconsiderate. There could be nothing funny about fathering an illegitimate son, and so the laughter had to be a marker of insensitivity and disrespect—an up-and-coming comedian thinking he had the right to steal Berle's "spots." Deepening the indignity from Berle's point of view, Richard was stealing those spots with obscenities like *ass*, the cheapest of comic shortcuts. A decade earlier, Berle had counseled Lenny Bruce to save his act by editing out the dirty words.

For Richard, his laughter was a genuine enigma. Just as he struggled to explain the laughter at his stand-up shows, where the audience howled when he talked about being beaten by his father, strip-searched in jail, or low-rated sexually by his woman, so he struggled to explain why he laughed on *Mike Douglas*. Pressed by Berle to defend himself, he responded by searching the ceiling: he was laughing at his own "craziness" and at "the insanity of all this," the cosmic machinations that had put him on a talk show with Uncle Milty as he bared his soul on national TV. He certainly wasn't laughing for the reason Berle posited—"because it never happened to you." Berle might always have cordoned off his personal experience in the making of his comedy, but Richard's method was exactly the opposite: post-Aladdin, he had tunneled into his experience, again and again, rescuing laughter from what others might see as mere affliction. Unlike Berle, he wouldn't need to wait until he was sixty-seven to speak his personal truth.

The rest of the week on *Mike Douglas* was a great vindication for Richard. He had long considered himself an outsider to mainstream America: the boy born to brothels, the black artist in white Hollywood. Now he was enjoying pride of place on national TV, able to invite friends and family to join him at the welcome table. In particular he wanted everyone to see his beloved grandmother Marie through the lens of his love—as a savvy woman of the world, tough and self-possessed and admirable. When Marie appeared on *Mike Douglas* on Richard's final day as cohost, she rose to the challenge and then some, acting as if it were the most natural thing to regale the studio audience with tales of Richard's delinquency, or to guide Mike Douglas through the ins and outs of soul food cooking. She wore muted colors, a mink stole that Richard had given her, and a sly, guarded smile that suggested she had gone toe to toe with Life and had never backed down. Sammy Davis Jr., slated to perform after her, said it was "unbelievable" how she commanded the stage: "There ain't no sense in nobody going on. The show belongs to her." Two years later, when talking with an interviewer about how much his family mattered to him, Richard said, "Having my grandmother with me on *The Mike Douglas Show* was the greatest moment in my life."

At the end of his week as cohost, Richard was set to turn thirty-four, and his agent, Murray Swartz, threw together a birthday party for him at his home in Philadelphia, where *Mike Douglas* was taped. Richard's grandmother and uncle Dickie attended, along with fellow *Mike Douglas* guests like Sammy Davis Jr. and pianist-composer Michel Legrand.

Legrand sat in with a jazz trio that Swartz had hired for the party, and it was as if Richard were swept back to the jazz clubs in Peoria where, a decade earlier, he had begun his career as an entertainer and sometimes scatted to Clark Terry's "Mumbles," a comic tune and one of Richard's favorites. At the party, in front of an audience that embraced both his family and his showbiz accomplices, he started scatting in full seriousness and didn't stop. For five minutes, he was part of the ensemble, winging the chord changes and riding them, reaching for something beyond himself. The party carried on until close to daybreak.

Now that he was a bona fide sensation, Richard left behind his modest bungalow on the grounds of Yamashiro and moved, with Patricia, to a larger home above the Sunset Strip with a swimming pool, billiards room, and a gym outfitted with a punching bag. In his bedroom, he placed a large aquarium in which saltwater fish glided serenely back and forth. On his front door he posted a sign that began on a decorous note: "To avoid ill feeling and/or unpleasantness, please be aware that *uninvited guests* are not welcome at any time, whatsoever. To avoid rejection, please do not take the liberty of 'dropping by.' Sincerely and Respectfully, Occupant." Then an addendum: "Yeah, nigger—this means you."

The new home did not arrest the tailspin of Richard and Patricia's relationship, just gave it a new, smarter setting. In the middle of one dinner party with Sammy Davis Jr. and his wife, Altovise, Richard punched Patricia twice, the first time for laughing at apparently the wrong joke, the second for asking why he had hit her. (The Davises sent Patricia a bouquet of two dozen purple roses and a card that read, "You deserve a purple heart for being able to deal with the nigger we love so much.") It was hard, too, for her to avoid the spectacle of Richard's infidelities. After she organized swimming lessons for his children Elizabeth and Rain, she discovered that he was dallying with the swimming instructor in the pool house. Another afternoon, she stumbled upon him in bed with a man, a *Jet* editor. The scene did not provide an occasion for Richard to reflect upon the state of their relationship or the depth of his sexual need. Furious, he accused Patricia of "fuck[ing] up my fun" and beat her for the intrusion.

In these difficult last days of their relationship, Richard's cruelty to Patricia was sharpened by his theatrical imagination. While in a low mood, he would hibernate in their bedroom, alone with his saltwater fish and his guns. Patricia would bring him his meals on a tray, knowing that if she incurred his displeasure, for whatever reason—the wrong food, the wrong time—he might throw the tray at her. One afternoon she heard a couple of gunshots and ran to the bedroom, fearing the worst. The drapes were drawn, the room shrouded in darkness, the floor covered by water. The glass in the aquarium had shattered, leaving the fish to wriggle helplessly on the floor. Richard was lying in bed, his face blood red, his body limp.

Patricia gasped, then did a double take. When she looked more closely, she saw that Richard had merely slathered himself with ketchup. The gunshots were a ruse, a test of her love and loyalty: he wanted to catch her expression at the moment she thought she'd lost him. He was unharmed, though the same couldn't be said of his fish or the hardwood floors, which buckled after absorbing an aquarium's worth of saltwater, and had to be replaced.

If the women in Richard's life saw the worst of his vindictiveness, Patricia perhaps saw the worst of the worst. In their final fight as lovers, he ripped her nightgown from her body and her jewelry from her ear, yelling, "Bitch, I bought this," then threw her, bleeding and naked, out the front door. Desperate for clothes, Patricia climbed the fence of their home and stole into the pool house, where she put on a bathing suit and terrycloth robe, then hoisted herself back over the fence and walked down to Sunset Boulevard, a refugee dressed as if for a pool party. A while later, she called Richard to see if she could pick up her clothes; he surprised her by saying yes. When she arrived at the door, a sickening smell rose up at her. Her floor-length sable coat—the gift Richard had tendered in apology in Sausalito—was burning in the fireplace. Her other clothes had been slashed with scissors.

Richard's dark mood encroached on his relationship with his manager Ron DeBlasio, too. DeBlasio had recently put to bed the messy business with Stax and had negotiated a generous deal (including a fifty-thousand-dollar advance) with Warner Bros. for the rights to *"That Nigger's Crazy."* As late as March 1975, the bond between Richard and his manager had seemed solid: when DeBlasio informed Richard that *"That Nigger's Crazy"* had won the Grammy, the two erupted into giddy laughter and Richard said, significantly, "We did it." But during Richard's depressive episodes, DeBlasio's sanguine attitude to his career rang hollow. When DeBlasio called him up with "three great things" to "jump him out" of his depression, Richard shot back, "Is that all you got?" and hung up the phone. He felt damaged by his tax troubles and remarked, to the press, that he had yet to find his financial footing: "My house is rented and I don't have a whole lot of money in the bank. Let me put it this way. I ain't rich enough to worry about nobody kidnapping my kids hoping for some big ransom."

Their relationship unraveled in a single conversation. Freddie Prinze, then breaking out as the star of TV's *Chico and the Man*, had courted DeBlasio as his own manager, and Richard felt DeBlasio's attentions wandering to the younger actor-comic. DeBlasio came to the conversation with a sense of blamelessness: Richard had personally introduced him to Prinze and had agreed to his taking on Prinze as his client. And Prinze was asking DeBlasio to manage his career because he considered Richard "my best friend in the business" and admired what DeBlasio had done for him.

"Our relationship has changed," Richard told DeBlasio, in a mood for summary judgments. "We're not fucking anymore."

"So that's it?" asked DeBlasio.

"Yeah, motherfucker, that's it," Richard said.

"I'm sorry you feel that way. I just don't understand it. I thought it was okay." DeBlasio paused, then noticed a piece of lint on his pants, which he picked off.

"That's right, that's how I feel," Richard said. He mimicked DeBlasio by picking a piece of lint off his own pants. And with that, he gave the brush-off to the manager who, he felt, had done the same to him. DeBlasio might have helped elevate Richard from someone blackballed by the industry to a Grammy-winning star, but in Richard's mind, he was also guilty of a betrayal, and their intimacy had come to an end.

The firing of DeBlasio created a vacuum that Richard filled by engaging the services of David Franklin, a black businessman-lawyer who proudly wore the nicknames Big Dollar Dave and the Smiling Cobra. Franklin was, in his line of work, as extraordinary a personality as Richard. He was short, husky, light-skinned, baby-faced, and blue-eyed, and spoke with a disarming stutter. Yet he knew how to command a room and close a deal; he talked often of what it meant to have "real power." Unlike Richard, he came from the world of the black middle class—his grandfather had sat on the Presbyterian Board of Missions—and he had brash self-confidence, which he described as a necessity. "A Black man in this country can hardly afford to be modest," he explained in an *Ebony* profile that dubbed him "The Man Who Makes Multimillionaires." "If you don't do it for yourself, nobody is going to do it for you."

By the time Richard met him, Franklin had made his name in politics and entertainment. As a ringleader of Atlanta's "Young Turks," he had masterminded the successful mayoral campaign of his law partner Maynard Jackson and helped break the back of the old racial order there. And in 1973, just a few years after starting to represent talent, he had negotiated a $5.5 million, ten-album deal with Atlantic Records for Richard's friend Roberta Flack—the most lucrative contract ever for a black female performer. In the context of that coup, Richard's fifty-thousand-dollar advance from Warner Bros. didn't seem quite so generous. Flack herself set the wheels in motion for Pryor and Franklin's partnership, telling Richard that if his business matters were handled by Franklin, he wouldn't need to worry about being "ripped off . . . by white people" again. She wanted Richard to "have someone around who'd protect him."

Franklin came to Richard's home and proposed a novel business arrangement. He would himself handle the duties of manager, agent, lawyer, and tax accountant, so Richard could dispense with paying for these services separately. Unlike the usual manager, too, he would be paid a salary rather than a percentage of Richard's earnings; Richard would therefore not face ever-escalating costs as a by-product of his success. And the two of them would operate without a written agreement: Franklin assured Richard that, in Richard's words, "we would always be brothers and everything would be all right . . . If we didn't want to be together then we wouldn't need any paper to keep us together."

For the next six years, Richard and David Franklin forged a high-profile partnership, the power performer paired with the power manager. They were sealed together through mutual admiration, a shared love of capital accumulation, and their common self-understanding as black men working the angles of a white world. Franklin had seen Richard at the San Francisco gig that produced *"That Nigger's Crazy"* and had fallen on the floor, laughing. For his part, Richard thought Franklin "one of the most brilliant men I have ever met," with a "great love for black people." He believed Franklin when he promised not to "take a percentage or advantage of anybody, any black brothers or sisters."

Their word would be their bond. At least, that was the idea. Richard caught an inkling of future troubles when, a few months after starting Franklin with a monthly salary of $2,000, Franklin said that there was more work than he expected and raised his salary to $5,000. A little while later, it became $7,500. Franklin explained that it was no simple task to untangle Richard's finances and restructure them—for instance, by devising a shelter for his earnings in the form of a corporation. (Pay Back Inc. was replaced by "Richard Pryor Enterprises.")

"I wish you would let me be the one to decide to give you a raise or not," Richard said.

"A man has got to know his worth, and that is what I'm worth," Franklin replied.

Fortunately for Richard, that same self-assurance made Franklin a valuable ally in the boardrooms of Hollywood, where he was the rare black man capable of simultaneously driving a hard bargain and calming white people's nerves. He could impress the likes of Sam Weisbord, the head of the William Morris Agency, an entertainment industry fixture who had mentored everyone from Al Jolson and Frank Sinatra to Marilyn Monroe and Elvis Presley; Weisbord publicly called Franklin "one of the most brilliant, able, astute men I've met in my life" and "one of the most honorable men I've ever known." Thom Mount, who later dealt with Franklin as head of Universal Studios, testified that he was "a very tough negotiator," "absolutely one of the best."

For many years—until their relationship had to be litigated in front of California's Labor Commissioner's Office, with $3.1 million of Franklin's earnings in dispute—Richard would agree with these admiring assessments.

In the spring of 1975, while developing some new material at the Comedy Store, Richard experienced a visitation. He felt an old man, familiar from his days in Peoria, standing next to him onstage, beckoning to be noticed. "Over here, Rich. Look at me."

At home afterward, Richard turned over memories of the time he'd spent as a child at a barbecue shack, observing a goateed and toothless old-timer who sat in front of the entrance. The old man whiled away the hours by playing a guitar and a taped-up harmonica, and by singing of the world down south that he'd left, a world of hard luck and tough vengeance:

Killed a guard in Lou-ez-ze-ana
Stabbed him fifteen times
Wouldn't of stabbed him so much
If he had of been a friend of mine

"Say, boy," the old man called out. "Wanna talk to you 'bout them fields." His voice carried the drawl of the Mississippi Delta and was dredged with the wisdom of the blues, the awareness that what goes around comes around—and that a boomerang will pick the darnedest time to knock you upside the head.

This old-timer was the source, the first draft, of the earthy character who came to be known as Mudbone, one of Richard's most famous creations. Mudbone began as a figure from Richard's past, an ancestor who carried with him, like so many black migrants to the urban North, a full cargo of southern folkways and folklore, along with whatever could be stuffed into a battered suitcase. As

Richard embellished his character in live performance, he dropped the harmonica, the guitar, and the stoicism of the bluesman; Mudbone became kinetic, in words if not in body. (Richard sat down while performing the old man.) The drawl remained—one critic quipped that Mudbone's "inebriated diction made it seem like he had created a new set of vowels"—but the character became a fast-talking trickster who appreciated that lies were a form of creativity and could knit people together in pleasure. As Mudbone said of his friend Toodle-ums, "that nigger could tell a lie. That's how we became friends. He'd tell a lie, I'd tell a lie, and we'd complement each other's lies." Whenever Mudbone assumed the stage in Richard's stand-up, the audience knew it was being welcomed into the realm of storytelling, of tall tales that revealed sideways truths. Mudbone was equal parts moralist and fabulist. Richard described his voice, aptly, as "somethin' between a preacher's Sunday mornin' sermonizin' and a grizzled seen-it-all coot sittin' at a bar drinkin' and spinnin' some wild bullshit."

By the time Richard first recorded his Mudbone routines, in May 1975, he had so mastered the nuances of the character that it could seem that Mudbone took on the character of Richard, rather than the other way around. Alone among his characters, Mudbone made Richard speak in his voice as he was introduced. "I was *boan* in Peoria, Illinois. . . . And when I was little, there was an old man, his name was *Mud-boan*": so Richard introduced Mudbone by sucking in his mouth and taking on Mudbone's elongated vowels, his southern inflections and rhythms. It was a slightly disorienting move—Richard talking about being born in Peoria in the voice of a character obviously born in the South—but it had the effect of closing the distance between the two of them and signaling a cultural debt. The self-styled "crazy nigger" of the 1970s had his roots in Mudbone, with his peasant cunning. Or, to put it another way, Mudbone was Richard's vehicle for transmitting the black past, that history of wild invention and wily rebellion that lived on in him.

Richard split his first Mudbone act into two segments, which captured two different facets of black history. The first was an origin tale, the story of why Mudbone had come to Peoria from Tupelo in a tractor, driving "746 miles on one tank of gas." While working for a white man named Cock-Eyed Junior ("His eyes went every which-a-way: he'd say, 'Nigger, pick that up,' and four, five niggers bend down"), our humble narrator had been tasked with picking up Junior's 460-pound fiancée at the depot:

> I walked over to her, introduced myself, said, "Ma'am, my name's Mudbone." And I tipped my hat—bitch slapped me across my head! Said, "Nigger, pick up the bag."
>
> I said, "Goddamn—what kind of shit? I ain't never . . . Goddamn—what kind of shit"—said it to *myself*. 'Cause in them days, that's all a nigger could do—was get mad, see? So I got mad.
>
> And I tried to help her into the buggy. The bitch snatched away from me, old uppity bitch. She stepped on the buggy and the goddamn thing turned over on her.
>
> Well, I couldn't laugh [*laughing*]. I had to bite a hole in my goddamn lip.

This was the segregated South in a nutshell: blacks made to hide their laughter as well as their anger, to act gracious in the face of abuse.

After the fiancée slaps Mudbone a second time, he plots his revenge. He finds a jigsaw, saws away at the bottom boards of an outhouse, and lies in wait so he can observe his triumph:

> Along about 8:30, she come this way to go to the bathroom. I'm in the bushes, looking at her. She wobbled out to the outside, then opened the door, went in. Shut the door. I heard a big splash. That's when I got into the tractor and drove up here. I wasn't mad no more either.

Mudbone takes satisfaction in watching his enemy sink to her true level, even as he knows that his satisfaction had a price. He has to go on the lam, having violated a principle the Jim Crow South holds dear: the sanctity of white womanhood.

Mudbone's second bit, "Little Feets," was a spectacular riff, over ten minutes long, in the form of a conjure tale. It evoked the hidden black world that developed outside the scrutiny of white eyes from slavery times onward: a world of amulets, fetishes, herbs, and potions; a world ruled by the invisible force known, variously, as mojo, voodoo, hoodoo, or conjure. Conjure tales have long been a feature of black folklore and literature, from Charles Chestnutt's *The Conjure Woman* to Ann Petry's *Tituba of Salem Village*; they tend to be meditations on how, through the force of the imagination or the spirit, the powerless can assume some form of power. Richard spiked his conjure tale with an extra dose of ribaldry, irreverence, and surreal imagination. His voodoo woman was, like Mudbone himself, an earthy, outrageous character—utterly human as she did her spirit work.

In Mudbone's telling, his friend Toodle-ums comes to him, laid low by a hex: "My goddamn feets are swole up—look like elephant foot. My arms is weak, blood comin' out of my eye. Plus, I'm in love with a bitch I can't stand." And so Mudbone escorts his friend to the home of Miss Rudolph, the voodoo lady, to reverse the curse. When Miss Rudolph asks for a Thanksgiving turkey as payment for her services, Mudbone agrees quickly, chuckling to himself: Thanksgiving is half a year away, he muses, and he'll be long gone from Miss Rudolph's neighborhood when it arrives. Then a tarantula crawls over Mudbone's body and disappears. When he asks Miss Rudolph where it has gone, she answers, "None of your goddamned business. But if you don't bring that turkey, you will see him again." The trickster has been outtricked.

When it comes to her healing potion, Miss Rudolph herself furnishes the crucial ingredient. She brings out a wash pan, squats over it, and relieves herself with fifteen minutes' worth of "old strong ammonia piss," then instructs Toodle-ums to dunk his feet in the pan.

Toodle-ums obliges, and a chemical reaction unknown in the annals of science commences:

> The water come to bubblin' and boilin', sparks start flyin'. Goddamn bugs runnin' all crazy, bat was flyin' around, monkey started shittin' everywhere—that's when I took my knife out!
>
> And she ran over and stroked this nigger with the monkey's foot. And he was trembling. I tried to get the door open; it was locked. . . .
>
> Then, all of a sudden, it got real quiet. And the piss turned blue. And I said, "Holy Jesus! Holy Jesus!" 'Cause I ain't never seen no blue piss.
>
> Well, the boy eased his feets out the piss, and they was healthy. The nigger had healthy feets. But they was real tiny. The nigger had little baby feets!

Now that the conjure itself has gone awry, Toodle-ums goes berserk. He kills the monkey, hurls the bat out the window, and literally kicks Miss Rudolph in the ass, his tiny feet whipping through the air. He rips the monkey's foot from her neck and swallows it. But in trying to destroy her powers, he makes himself their final victim: "they came and got his ass and took him to the zoo. And you can see him if you go down there. He's the polar bear—with little tiny feets." Mudbone spoke the punch line with a mix of disbelief and pleasure, as if both amazed and amused by the logic of his own tale.

With Mudbone, Richard experienced a new level of freedom onstage and achieved a new sort of resonance. The freedom came from releasing himself into a character unburdened by the present because he lived in and through his past, and unburdened, too, by the demands of "reality." With Mudbone, Richard stepped out of the history he had personally endured and let his imagination take wing in a fantastic kingdom of the past. At the same time, it was through Mudbone that Richard brought the larger scope of black history into his comedy, connecting the country South to the urban North, the Jim Crow past to the inner-city present.

Mudbone was a one-man cultural revival. He pointed backward, teaching black Americans about their "roots" (as did Alex Haley, in his blockbuster book of the following year). Yet he also pointed forward, suggesting through his example that it was still possible to conjure, to tap invisible forces and make them your own—if only the imagination were willing.

PART FIVE

THE FUNNIEST MAN ON THE PLANET

CHAPTER 19

Every Nigger Is a Star

Los Angeles, Macon, New York City, 1975

Between 1973 and 1975, Richard Pryor managed the ambiguously impressive feat of sowing different forms of havoc across the three major TV networks. In 1973, while working on Lily Tomlin's two specials, he maddened CBS executives with his obscenities, his arrival on set in cornrows, and his refusal to play scenes for laughs. In March 1974 he riled ABC when, as emcee of a Redd Foxx roast that was to be televised, he was completely blotto—"so far out," said comic Steve Allen, "as to be close to totally noncommunicative." Then, in February 1975, Richard completed his trifecta of TV mayhem when, as a guest on a Flip Wilson special for NBC, he precipitated a chaotic meltdown on set. The debacle began innocently enough: in a lull between taping, Richard performed an uncensored part of his stage act—as a gift, with no cameras rolling—for the studio audience. Fellow guest star McLean Stevenson did not take kindly to the gift; he fumed "I won't be on the same stage as that man" and walked off the set. A street-fighting mood fell over Richard. When an NBC page refused to let him open a fire door—Richard had some family at the taping and wanted to let them through the door to where their car was parked—Richard swung at him, and pandemonium erupted on the set. Fellow guest star Cher fled to her dressing room and locked herself in. Richard was restrained in a bear hug, but not before causing enough harm, mental and physical, for the NBC page to win thousands of dollars in an ensuing legal settlement.

Remarkably, Richard's track record did not scare off NBC executive Dick Ebersol and producer Lorne Michaels, who in early 1975 were putting together, for the fall, a new Saturday late-night program to replace reruns of Johnny Carson's *Tonight Show.* A mere twenty-seven years old and in line to become the youngest vice president in NBC history, Ebersol wanted to target his new show—what became *Saturday Night Live*—at the under-thirty demographic, and thought Richard would give the show "credibility"; Michaels knew Richard from the Lily Tomlin specials and considered him "the funniest man on the planet." Ebersol and Michaels needed to fight a battle on two fronts if they wanted to land Richard as a guest host for their program. On one side, they would have to budge the NBC higher-ups who were vehemently against Richard hosting the show in its first months on air: even the late-night slot, the execs thought, was too early for such a radioactive performer. On the other side, they would have to soften Richard, who felt, along with his new manager, David Franklin, that network TV was no match for his talents as a comic.

As summer passed into fall, Lorne Michaels broke NBC's resistance by playing hardball: he said, "I can't do a contemporary comedy show without Richard Pryor" and resigned, only to be wooed back when NBC caved. With Richard, Michaels needed a gentler strategy. He flew out to Miami and visited Richard backstage at a jai alai fronton where he was performing. Richard laid out his conditions for committing to the show: Paul Mooney would come on as a writer; Richard's friend Thalmus Rasulala would be hired as an actor; the soul-jazz griot Gil Scott-Heron would be the musical guest; Richard's ex-wife Shelley, who had started to take the stage again, would be allowed to deliver a monologue; and he would be given a great number of tickets—so many that he would be in control of more than half the studio audience. Michaels agreed in the moment, though not without some queasiness. "He'd better be funny," he said on the plane back to New York.

The negotiations stand as a parable for how, after "*That Nigger's Crazy*," Richard leveraged his growing stardom. From one angle, he was being "difficult." But from another, he was exhibiting a greater mindfulness about the worlds he was now navigating and, even, doing his part to desegregate American culture. He knew that his success as a performer had been driven by a core audience of black fans, and so now he was forcibly integrating *Saturday Night*'s audience, under the reasonable assumption that it would skew white. He knew that he'd felt at home on *The Mike Douglas Show* because, as co-host, he had altered the complexion of the ensemble onstage until he was no longer a token presence, and he was committed to do the same with the actors on *Saturday Night*. Last, he knew that a writers' room was the incubator of all sketch ideas, so he wanted Paul Mooney as an ally in it. The audience, the stage, the *SNL* writers' room—all needed more than a little color if they were to swing away from the educated lunacy of *National Lampoon* and toward Richard's sensibility. He would become, on December 13, 1975, the host of the show's seventh, and unforgettable, episode.

Richard had considerably less pull as a movie actor than as a stand-up comic. Yet he was beginning to benefit from the shift, in Hollywood, away from a particular kind of blaxploitation flick, the action movie in which a black hero exacts violent revenge on the white world. In 1974, inner-city theaters were saturated with black-themed knockoffs—of *The Godfather* (*The Black Godfather*), of *Enter the Dragon* (*Black Belt Jones*), of *The Exorcist* (*Abby*), and, especially, of earlier blaxploitation hits like *Coffy* (*Foxy Brown*). The excitement that had greeted *Shaft* or *Superfly* was yielding to a sense of déjà vu. Box office receipts tailed off, and production companies stopped financing movies in the blaxploitation vein: in the words of film historian Ed Guerrero, "Blaxploitation went brain dead and was subsequently euthanized." Richard was arguably the premiere black actor who found his footing in this post-blaxploitation terrain, as filmmakers hunted for the elusive formula of the "crossover" picture, the black-themed movie that nonetheless drew whites to the theater.

His change in fortunes began, modestly, when at the end of 1973, Sidney Poitier asked him if he would play a small part, the role of flimflam artist Sharp Eye Washington, in this new film *Uptown Sat-*

urday Night. Richard might have landed a much meatier role: while punching out the first draft of the script, *Uptown*'s screenwriter imagined Richard as one of its two leads. But Bill Cosby, Poitier's good friend, expressed interest in the part, and as with *Blazing Saddles,* Richard was shouldered aside for the safer casting choice.

With *Uptown Saturday Night,* Poitier was betting early against the blaxploitation vogue and clashing with the executives at his production company, who begged him to abandon the project. Poitier wanted to offer a "healthier exploration of black life," one without the "pimps, prostitutes, and dope pushers who represent only a minuscule portion of the black community." The film's protagonists are not superspades who plug Whitey full of holes; they're two working men, a factory hand and a taxi driver, searching for a lost lottery ticket and bouncing their way through an inner city that is less a scene of lurid corruption than simply the setting for a wild-goose chase. Wide-eyed at first, the two average Joes get properly jostled by a private detective who's actually a con man (Richard's role), a double-dealing congressman who supports both Nixon and Malcolm X, and a pint-sized karate expert. When they trigger gang warfare between a black godfather and his rival, no real blood is spilled; the plot twist is played strictly for laughs.

As a production, *Uptown* had the flavor of a noble cause. Poitier was the motor force behind the film—its star, director, and executive producer—and he thought Hollywood needed integrating. For *Uptown,* he assembled what was billed as "the largest black all-star cast in Hollywood history"—some thirteen hundred black actors, including extras—and hired black technicians to fill almost half the behind-the-camera jobs. The film was a new and rare thing: a decently budgeted, black-directed film that aimed to be, in the words of Cosby, "a picture for the general audience. You can take anybody from your seven-year-old to your 87-year-old to see it." Like several of the film's actors, Richard was offered expenses only, but agreed to the job.

"I almost went into overtime because the man kept me laughing so much I couldn't attend to any of my duties as an actor or director," Poitier said of Richard's performance. For the short while that Richard is in *Uptown*, he steals the film from Poitier and Cosby with his twitching vitality. His con man lights up with naked greed each time he mentions his private detective's fee; he trembles with the anxiety of a hustler on the lam and the excitement of an actor testing how willing his audience is to suspend disbelief. "Look at my eye, my right eye! See how bloodshot it is," he says, selling the wreck that he is. "Know how it got that way? From sleeping with one eye open, baby." Sharp Eye is the blaxploitation hero deflated, a husk of black manhood rather than its strutting embodiment. As Sharp Eye explains in the movie's most self-conscious moment, "The movies always got some super nigger killing some white boy in the Mafia. Ha ha ha! Beating up the crooked police. That's not true, and it don't help me either. And women—they all got women. . . . I might as well be a monk."

Sharp Eye Washington's riff on the reality deficit in blaxploitation captured the spirit of *Uptown Saturday Night* as a whole. The movie had no black-on-white violence, no sultry sex scenes. Its heroes were congenial, lovable, fundamentally decent—and box office gold to the tune of seven million dollars, more than three times the film's budget. Between *Uptown*'s conception and its release in the summer of 1974, the blaxploitation trend had begun to sputter out, and Poitier's film seemed to offer a new formula for success in black film: family-friendly comedy. His gamble paid off, and handsomely. A sequel went into the works.

Richard's next project, the Western spoof *Adíos Amigo*, was an attempt to capitalize on the soft-edged filmmaking niche that *Uptown* had begun to carve out. Fred Williamson, its writer, director, and co-star, had made his name as the hunky, pistol-toting star of such blaxploitation films as *The Legend of Nigger Charley* and *Boss Nigger*, and was stretching himself with this rambling comedy about a frontier settler duped repeatedly by a con man. Richard himself had a long-standing love of the Western and an equally long-standing appreciation for its comic possibilities. Here he was asked to take his con man character from *Uptown* and transport him back a century to the Wild West of the 1870s; and for the first time in his film career, he was a true second lead, not merely a sidekick.

But *Adíos Amigo* was a sloppy film, shot in nine days in the New Mexico desert, then slapped together with a carelessness that led *Variety* to grumble that "there are dozens of scenes that should have been outtakes." It was not a piece of serviceable entertainment like *Uptown*, much less a madcap gem like *Blazing Saddles*. Its poster promised "two sharp dudes taking turns with chicks and tricks," but there was nothing sharp to the picture; the editing was so slipshod that Williamson's character wins a gunfight while being the slowest draw in the West. As director, Williamson seemed to have hoped that, in the absence of a solidly written script, Richard would pick up the slack by ad-libbing, but Richard needed more—a stronger character, or a better comic partner than the granite-like Williamson. Too often, Richard was left to his own devices and simply made funny faces. The low-budget film earned back its costs, but for Richard it was an embarrassment. After its release, he asked *Ebony* to pass along a message to his fans: "Tell them I apologize. Tell them I needed some money. Tell them I promise never to do it again."

Richard's luck in Hollywood improved when, in the spring of 1975, producer Rob Cohen, a protégé of Motown's Berry Gordy, approached him with a script for *The Bingo Long Traveling All-Stars & Motor-Kings*, an ambitious Motown-Universal coproduction. *Bingo Long* was a raffish, socially conscious comedy about a group of 1930s Negro League baseball players who break free of their black bosses ("The slaves done run off," a veteran player exults) and form their own barnstorming team. After this opening premise, the film became, in part, an explicit parable about what it means to be a black crossover performer. On the barnstorming circuit, the players need to attract white crowds to survive, and decide to alter their style of play so that they're not too good or too serious. They bat backward, pitch in a gorilla suit, throw firecrackers instead of baseballs, and parade into town with a "kick the mule" dance. And they have to ask themselves if, in putting on a show, they have sacrificed their dignity in the bargain. "We'll only be pretending," offers Bingo Long, in defense of their clowning before whites. "And since we'll *know* we're pretending, we'll be one up on them." His teammate Leon Carter, played by James Earl Jones, is not so sure, and the tension between the two drives the movie forward.

For Rob Cohen, *Bingo Long* was not just about crossing over; it was also his attempt, as the Harvard-educated white executive in charge of Motown Pictures, to change the economics of crossover, to prove that quality films with largely black casts could break through a box office ceiling that contemporary estimates put at $9 million. He wanted to demonstrate that Motown's magical accomplishments in musical crossover—Marvin Gaye, the Supremes, the Jackson Five—could be duplicated in Hollywood. "We have a real uphill battle to make high budget black films," he told the *Los Angeles Times*, "because there has never been such a thing as a high budget black film. We aren't making 'Superfly' or the story of violent high school kids in Detroit strung out on dope for a budget of $500,000. We are making classy films with glamour and love that whites and blacks can identify with." A "classy" film required top-shelf talent: for *Bingo Long*, Cohen lined up Hal Barwood and Matt Robbins, fresh from winning the best screenplay award at Cannes, to adapt the novel of the same name. With their script in hand, he finagled a $3.5 million financing deal from Universal—an extraordinary budget for a "black" film. He signed Billy Dee Williams and James Earl Jones in the two lead roles, and a young Steven Spielberg, then finishing *Jaws*, as the film's director.

From the start, Richard was fundamental to Cohen's dream of cracking the code of the crossover film. Cohen had been captivated by Richard's performance in *Lady Sings the Blues* and so had instructed Barwood and Robbins to have Richard in mind while filling out the character of Charlie Snow, a Negro League player who hopes to break into the majors by passing himself off as Cuban. In the novel, the character is incidental, a bit of filigree; Barwood and Robbins enlarged him into a jive artist who takes few taboos seriously. Their Charlie tries not only to slip past the major league ban on black ballplayers ("Yo soy el baseballito supremo!") but also to slip into the beds of white women ("Buenas knockers, señorita"). Though a figure of fun, he may also be the most dangerous player on the team: the one for whom the game extends well beyond the baseball diamond, and whose ambitions are not simply noble.

Richard was slow to commit to the part that had been written for him. Officially the difficulties were logistical: schedules needed shuffling, the money needed to grow. For the shoot, Richard was uncomfortable staying with the rest of the cast and crew at the Hilton in Macon, Georgia, and preferred to rent his own home to guard his privacy. But he had another reason to dither, one that couldn't be smoothed over or worked out in a contract. *Bingo Long* would reunite him with Billy Dee Williams, with whom he had had bad blood ever since he discovered that Williams had taken up with his then-girlfriend Patricia Heitman: in Richard's mind, Williams had stolen his woman from him. With Franklin's encouragement, he buried his misgivings and signed on the dotted line. Publicly, he trumpeted how wonderful it was to have "quality actors" and a "quality script": "I don't think anybody ever did a film like this." He lent himself to an experiment in bringing black history to life, and to market.

When Richard arrived on location in Georgia—"James Brown country," he called it—in August 1975, newer misgivings joined his earlier ones. He quickly became suspicious of John Badham, the rookie director who had taken over the film after Steven Spielberg was delayed by unanticipated postproduction work on *Jaws*. Badham, who would direct *Saturday Night Fever* after *Bingo Long*, was by temperament and pedigree Richard's opposite. "It's hard to meet a whiter white man than John," Cohen said. The stepson of an American army general, Badham had grown up in England and Alabama, then studied philosophy and drama at Yale. He was highly

A wary relationship: Richard Pryor eyes Bingo Long *director John Badham. (Courtesy of Bonnie Leeds)*

controlled—the sort of person, according to Cohen, who organized everything in his bedroom in parallel lines or at right angles—and awkwardly reticent. In one of their first conversations, Badham confessed to Richard that he had never seen a black person before he moved to Alabama, and that when, as a child, he caught his first glimpse, he had been stirred by fear. It was not the most graceful way to open up about his past with Richard, who afterward stormed over to Cohen and asked, "What kind of fucking cracker asshole did you hire to do this movie?"

As shooting moved forward in Macon, Richard started to perceive a racial subtext in his interactions with Badham—a subtext to which Badham, who had never worked with a black cast, was oblivious. One night during filming, Badham asked Richard to jump off a balcony and onto a padded platform that was set several feet below. Richard wavered; he had a fear of heights, and here was this director eagerly pushing him to jump over the edge.

Cut to: Cohen, in his production office at the Macon Hilton, receiving Badham's distressed call from a pay phone. "Richard just left the set," Badham reported, "and I think he said he's going back to LA. And we have to shoot with him the rest of the night." Cohen made a beeline for Richard's rental house, in an affluent white area near Mercer University.

"I hate that fucking cracker!" Richard vented to Cohen. "He don't tell no nigger to jump and the nigger jump!" He was ready to quit the film and fly home, he said.

Cohen tried to explain that there had to be a misunderstanding here—a first-time director mishandling his actors—but then spoke honestly about his own stake in the matter. "Do it for me," he pleaded. "Don't ruin my career. This means so much. I've fought so hard to get this movie on—a movie that a year ago Hollywood thought they would never make. We're doing it for a major studio, it's going to get a major release."

Richard relented. "I'm doing this for you," he told Cohen. "So don't forget it."

Convinced that Badham put too low a premium on the well-being of his black actors, Richard remained standoffish. On one occasion, Badham tried to line him up for a shot in which a knife was thrown at Richard's character's foot. Richard said, sensibly, "You don't need me to be my foot"—a point that Badham could not dispute. "He was very concerned about his safety," the director observed later, "and you can't criticize him for that."

Near the end of the shoot, as if to fulfill Richard's prophecies, the director attempted to execute a razzle-dazzle shot of the ballplayers' motorcade as it sped through a country crossroads—and almost killed James Earl Jones. In Badham's plan, the camera car would pass through the crossroads on the path opposite the one taken by the ballplayers' motorcade, pulling the viewer into a tense trajectory and heightening the sense of motion. But the driver of the camera car didn't understand the plan in full—didn't understand that he was supposed to beat the players' motorcade to the intersection. He kept slowing down, and Jones, who led the motorcade, had to swerve off to the side to avoid a head-on collision between his motorcycle and the camera car. The crew rushed to Jones, who was unhurt. Badham apologized profusely, and Jones laughed it off.

Richard had been hundreds of feet behind the near collision and, having stood on the brakes of his character's yellow Franklin convertible, had come to a stop; he was safe. But he had also seen enough; he left the set in a black Cadillac and did not return that day.

The next morning, at 6:30, when Badham strolled out of the Hilton to take his car to the set, a scowling Richard approached him and demanded an apology.

"For what?" Badham said disingenuously.

"You almost got me killed."

"No, it was James Earl."

"Well, you don't care about me, so I'm going home."

Badham mentally calculated how many scenes Richard had left, then said, "Well, I can help you with that. If you do go home, just don't fly out of the Macon airport. Go to Atlanta because it's a lot easier." And, having stood his ground, Badham stepped into the town car and drove off.

Rob Cohen managed to persuade Richard to travel to the set anyway. They were scheduled to film a slapstick scene in which Richard's character rips his pants while sliding into second base, revealing his colorful undershorts. As Charlie Snow, Richard was supposed to shrug off the indignity and laugh with the crowd. As Richard Pryor the actor, he was in no mood for shrugging.

"I'm not doing shit until I get my apology," Richard told Badham. The director wondered if there was menace in Richard's tone—the actor was holding a glass of water, and Badham thought he might throw it in his face—but then he saw, beneath the threat, an undercurrent of sadness. Badham heard himself saying, "I'm really sorry that this is upsetting you a lot." It was more an acknowledgment of

Richard's feelings than a heartfelt admission of regret, but Richard took it as genuine and played his scene.

While Richard's feud with Badham threatened to torpedo the production, his feud with costar Billy Dee Williams threatened much worse. Once, Richard observed Williams speaking to his, Richard's, new girlfriend, who was visiting from out of town, and once was enough: Richard accused Williams of trying to steal her away from him. Given Williams's talents as a charmer, it was easy to understand the source of Richard's panic. Cohen riffed, "If there was a vagina within ten feet of [Billy Dee], he went into a mode, what I call the V-mode—where he starts talking really low and all that. He'd say things like, 'I love your hair. How much time do you spend on it every day?' . . . And you know, he was very successful with women. He was the black man that every white woman who had a black fantasy wanted, because she knew he was good and powerful and charming, a lovely man."

Richard fumed, talking often of bringing his gun with him on the set—to handle the threat of Williams once and for all, to put in the ground the fantasy of suavity he represented. Williams tried to de-escalate the feud. After one altercation, he grabbed Cohen in the film's production offices and insisted, "You got to calm that guy down!" When Cohen asked what had happened, Williams couldn't say; he was so whipped up as to be inarticulate. Cohen decided to put as much physical distance between his two actors as possible, moving Richard to the director's dressing room—unbeknownst to Badham, who alighted upon Richard there and needed to have the situation explained to him by the second assistant director: "We had to move him away from Billy Dee. He was threatening to kill Billy Dee." When the filming of *Bingo Long* wrapped without a violent incident, the crew breathed a collective sigh of relief.

Still, it would be wrong to adduce that Richard was simply seething during *Bingo Long*'s production. He had a warm rapport with the former Negro League and major league ballplayers—people of great gusto and no pretensions—who were cast as his teammates in the film. "We work hard and play hard," said Leon "Daddy Wags" Wagner, formerly of the San Francisco Giants and Cleveland Indians. Unsurprisingly, the "playing hard" portion found a home in Richard's rented house, with the assistance of his grandmother Marie, who joined him in Macon for a spell. One night she prepared a classic soul food feast—fried chicken, oxtail stew, okra, string beans, peach cobbler—for some twenty-five members of the cast and crew. Richard spun a few tracks from his most recent album, but his voice on the stereo had to compete with the wisecracks flying all around him. "We blow Richard's mind," Wagner told a reporter. "He been used to being a funny motherfucker with a quip here and there. But we come on so black, man, that we have to pick Richard up off the ground."

Richard felt at home, too, among the people of "James Brown country." When the crew set up at a four-way intersection in one of Macon's black neighborhoods, its residents started to converge upon the film's three stars. At the first sight of the crowd, Billie Dee Williams and James Earl Jones vanished to their dressing rooms. Richard stood calmly in the center of the intersection as he was enveloped by a crowd that grew from a straggling few to several hundred. He chatted, slipped into a character or two; he enjoyed the back-and-forth with a crowd that cherished him and expressed their love not by gawking but by channeling their warmth. When he was performing for such a crowd, Richard's cynicism and jealousy went into remission, and he rose above his apprehensions about himself and others; he felt magnified into a better and larger version of himself. And as part of the gift of his comedy, he magnified his audience as he reflected them, giving them a sense of the extraordinary in their ordinary lives.

Around this time, Richard distilled that feeling of reciprocity into the form of a motto. He took to wearing a yellow-and-black running suit, inspired by an obscure 1974 Jamaican film and emblazoned with its title: "Every Nigger Is a Star."

While Badham prepared *Bingo Long* for release, Richard rode the tailwind of . . . *Is It Something I Said?*, the follow-up to *"That Nig-*

ger's Crazy," and his first album of new material for Warner Bros. He had recorded the album during a May 1975 run at the Latin Casino, not far from Philadelphia; after so many larger concerts, he'd been amped to play a more intimate club, a dinner theater with terraced tables, in front of a black audience. For him, the recorded show was "one of my best ever," its memory almost sacred: "The comedy gods have many tentacles, you know. And they swoop down and touch you at different times. But when they do it's like salvation. Or deliverance. It's as close to flying as man gets. The magic doesn't happen often, but when you're on and rolling nothing that I've ever touched comes close."

Is It Something was a potent distillation of Richard's latest stand-up act. On it, he recorded for the first time the character of Mudbone, that most garrulous and glorious of his comic creations. He spoke of his cocaine addiction for the first time, too, observing himself with an astonishment that sometimes carried over into bafflement: "I must've snorted up Peru. I could've bought Peru for all the shit I snorted. Could've just given up the money up front and have me a piece of property." He took aim at the legal system, capping his riff on his experience at the courthouse with a stinging one-liner, courtesy of Paul Mooney: "You go down there looking for justice, and that's what you find—just us." And he spoke frankly about sex, the desperation and double-talk of the bedroom. He gave voice to the man who pleads with his girlfriend during a breakup ("Take the TV, but leave the pussy, please"), as well as the woman who hesitates to kiss the mouth that has pleasured her ("It's bad for your teeth"). The negotiations around sex seemed to turn everyone into an absurd version of him- or herself. Witness the father who scolded his daughter for offering up only a kiss to the man who took her out on an expensive date: "Hey, girl, get your ass down here! . . . *Thirty-five dollars is a lot of money, you must be rich. You are?* Wake up your mama, too!"

Released in August 1975, . . . *Is It Something I Said?* rocketed to the No. 1 position on *Billboard*'s R&B chart, sealing the love affair between Richard and his black audience. But its appeal extended further: it broke the Top 15 of *Billboard*'s overall album chart. The record heralded Richard's acceptance by the hip white audience that he hadn't courted for four years, since he left Berkeley behind. In the interim, while he'd been preoccupied with establishing and deepening his connection with black America, that white audience had come to him.

Richard's hosting of *Saturday Night* (later *Saturday Night Live*), in December 1975, was a related experiment in cultural cross-breeding, bringing him in contact with the still-tender, and overwhelmingly white, creative team behind the show. In the run-up to his guest appearance, the mood around the set was tight with worry. Members of Richard's entourage, it was said, were carrying guns; Richard himself was viewed as combustible in the extreme. Michael O'Donoghue, the show's head writer, visited Richard in his hotel room and ran a joke by him, one written for the Weekend Update sketch: "A man should not be judged by the color of his skin, but by the size of his nostrils." Richard bristled and started to object; O'Donoghue cut him off in midsentence. Richard lifted up a cognac bottle and offered, with a burst of laughter that was hard to read, to brain O'Donoghue with it. For the rest of the week, *Saturday Night*'s head writer took a leave from his own show rather than tangle with its host.

Meanwhile, Lorne Michaels was feeling heat from NBC executives, who argued that the show needed a five-second delay so that any expletives could be bleeped. Michaels acceded to the request, unwilling to bet his show's future on Richard's ability to restrain himself. But he did so under conditions of the utmost secrecy. All the clocks in the studio were synchronized to the five-second delay, and the staff who knew of it vowed not to let the secret slip. Michaels feared that his host would walk off if he learned of the delay—an utterly justified concern. In his memoir, Richard said, "If I'd known, I never would've shown up."

The show that Richard delivered did shake up *Saturday Night*, though not in the way NBC execs had feared. (Richard said "ass" twice, but stayed clear of four-letter territory.) With his demands in Miami, Richard had already integrated the show—from the writers' room to the stage to the audience. Now he made the show his own—and race conscious as never before. In a small but symbolic move, he even took control of the photo stills that served as "bumpers" between sketches and commercial breaks, supplying photos of his grandmother, uncle, and children to replace the usual images of New York City street life.

Aptly, the episode began with a staged dispute over the whiteness of *Saturday Night*'s comic formula. Richard and his friend Paul Mooney had noticed that black actor Garrett Morris was often the odd man out, the trouper with no role to play, and they took their frustration public, getting the writers' room to generate a sketch in which Morris stands his ground and Chevy Chase—already emerging as the show's breakout star—plays up his sense of privilege.

"Richard Pryor's here tonight," Morris tells Chase in the sketch, "and I thought I would open the show. I mean, do the fall."

Chase glares and returns, "I *always* open the show. Is it understood?"

In the spirit of comedy, the show settles the argument by splitting the difference. Chase offers to teach Morris how to execute the pratfall and so steals the scene from him, but then, because the fall has ostensibly knocked Chase unconscious, it's Morris who announces the opening of the show. "Live from New York—it's *Saturday Night*!" he says with relish, grinning over Chase's lifeless body.

Most of Richard's *Saturday Night* program toyed with that gap—or was it a chasm?—between how whites and blacks perceived the world and traveled through it. In his opening monologue, Richard put the white half of the studio audience on alert, delivering a version of "Acid" that played off the great distance between Richard's drug-induced panic ("I can't breathe!") and the blithe indifference of his white friend ("Told you it was far out!"). In "Samurai Hotel," John Belushi and Richard were samurai bellhops who duel over which one of them should carry a traveler's suitcase upstairs. After a bit of posturing with their swords, Belushi's samurai yells, "Your mama-san!" at Richard's. The insult is a miscalculation: Richard's samurai is sent into such a rage that he slices the front desk in two—at which point Belushi's samurai concedes the duel. "I can dig where you're coming from," he says, in the only bit of English his character ever spoke. Another running gag featured Richard in an ever-evolving police lineup. In the first bit, he's placed, handcuffed in a bathrobe, alongside a Boy Scout, doctor, and businessman; in the second, alongside a refrigerator, a goose, and a nun; in the last, alongside three policemen, all of whom point an accusing finger in his direction. After every lineup, he appears more battered and bandaged.

The most provocative sketch opened onto a job interview at a desk in a drab office. Richard's Mr. Wilson, in a dress shirt and tie, is apprehensive and obliging, while Chase's interviewer leads him through the beginning of a word association test. "Tree," "dog"; "fast," "slow"; "rain," "snow." Then the interview takes a curious turn, as an ostensibly objective test is revealed to be anything but:

INTERVIEWER: Negro.
MR. WILSON [*meekly*]: Whitey.
INTERVIEWER [*blandly*]: Tar baby.
MR. WILSON [*doing a double take*]: What'd you say?
INTERVIEWER: Tar baby.
MR. WILSON [*testing what's possible*]: Ofay.
INTERVIEWER: Colored.
MR. WILSON [*no longer meek*]: Redneck.

The tension ratchets up; both interviewer and applicant lose their composure, and the mental game of a "word-association test" degenerates into a slashing duel of insults:

INTERVIEWER [*raising his voice*]: Jungle bunny.

MR. WILSON [*leaning in, agitated*]: Honky!
INTERVIEWER [*accusingly*]: Spade.
MR. WILSON [*hollering*]: Honky honky!
INTERVIEWER [*confident, as if playing a trump card*]: Nigger.
MR. WILSON [*grimly serious*]: *Dead* honky.

In a tour de force of physical comedy, Richard then seems to be dismantled by his rage. His nose wrinkles and twitches with a nervous tic that reaches up to his eyebrows; his mouth hangs open, frozen. When Chase's interviewer fumbles, in a conciliatory tone, "I think you're qualified for the job—how about a starting salary of five thousand dollars?" Richard's Mr. Wilson can't arrest the momentum of his anger, even as he looks more aggrieved than incensed. "Yo' mama! Yo' grandmama!" he shouts, his voice catching and his eyes moistening. The sketch ends with a fantastic act of reparations: Chase's interviewer rewarding Mr. Wilson for his trials with an offer to work, at an annual salary of fifteen thousand dollars, as "the highest-paid janitor in America."

"Word Association Test" was the episode's edgiest and most memorable sketch. It suggested that beneath the crust of much American life there was magma boiling; that for many white Americans—and not just pot-bellied sheriffs with thick southern drawls—words like *spade* and *nigger* tripped off their tongues with the same ease as *tree* and *rain*. But it also took this point and drove it home in a way that was witty and unpredictable. Richard's character begins the interview at a disadvantage—the humble applicant trying hard to ingratiate himself and caught off guard by the series of epithets flung at him by his interviewer. He turns the tables not by coming up with more stinging epithets for white people but by refusing to play by the rules dictated to him. "Dead honky" defeats the "nigger" trump card as no single word could do; it transforms the word association test from a language game into a contest of wills, in which righteous courage is bound to prevail. Chase's character crumbles; he is game master no longer.

The sketch—a *Saturday Night Live* classic—has something of a fraught backstory. Both Paul Mooney and Chevy Chase have claimed to have conceptualized the sketch; neither of them has given credit to the other, and the two have gleaned quite different lessons from it. According to Mooney, the sketch was his response to how Lorne Michaels cross-examined him—*How long have you been writing? How long have you been doing comedy?*—when Richard first insisted that Michaels hire Mooney. "Easiest sketch I ever write," Mooney remembered. "All I do is bring out what is going on beneath the surface of that interview with Lorne and the NBC execs in the jai alai greenroom." For Mooney, the sketch was an act of aggression against NBC, one that also allowed Richard to channel the ill will he felt toward his costar: "Chevy Chase was the doll-baby . . . the darling of the discotheque with straight teeth, and Richard wanted to knock them out." Once it was performed, the sketch assumed for Mooney a power that was more than personal, too. It was, he judged, "like an H-bomb that Richard and I toss[ed] into America's consciousness. . . . The N-word as a weapon, turned back against those who use it, ha[d] been born on national TV."

For his part, Chase downplayed any enmity between him and Richard. In his memory, the sketch came about through a meeting of comic minds: "Richard's attitude to it and my attitude toward it were one and the same." And the final product spoke to a dimension in Richard and his art that Mooney didn't mention: his essential generosity. While writing the sketch, Chase recalled "asking Richard for as many slang words for white people as he could come up with. [Richard] hesitated and then realized that there were many more for African Americans than he could think of for 'whities.' This is reflected in the sketch, and it was reflective of the lack of bigotry in the man."

It's a conundrum: Mooney saw Richard as an artist who weaponized comedy to an unprecedented degree, while Chase saw him as an artist who, by nature, did not reach for arms. Could they both have been right—if not about who wrote the sketch, then about the Richard they loved and appreciated? The evidence of the job interview sketch suggests as much. As the slurs pile up, Richard's Mr. Wilson throws off the awkward formality of the interview and comes to speak from a place of genuine, white-hot anger. He seems, as Mooney suggests, energized by his rage. But it's too simple to see the righteously angry Richard as the one and only true Richard. At the opening of the sketch, his character can't believe that the race card is being played, and even his most aggressive gestures are complicated by an internal debate that plays out in the quick ripple of his facial expressions. He's undone by his anger as much as he finds himself through it. Richard's performance might inspire a militant like Mooney, for whom Richard was an apostle of rage, and it might appeal to a writer-actor like Chase, for whom Richard was, at his core, a generous soul. The different fractions of Richard's audience could come together at the crossroads where Richard stood, even if they couldn't agree on where to travel afterward.

Rob Cohen and John Badham caught a hint of the difficulties they faced courting their own crossover audience when they began screening *Bingo Long* at Universal. "What do you expect to do with this nigger epic?" asked Universal's head of distribution, Hy Martin. According to Cohen, Universal president Ned Tanen was beside himself at a private screening. "What the fuck are they saying?" Tanen muttered at the characters on-screen, his ear unattuned to black dialect. "I don't understand a goddamn word!" he said repeatedly, each time pounding the squawk box that was used to communicate to the projectionist—until the squawk box shattered into fragments of plastic and a dangling wire. Tanen stood up, the film still spooling. "Finish this!" he commanded Cohen and Badham, though it was unclear how they might ever satisfy him.

Despite the pushback from Universal execs, the team behind *Bingo Long* had reason to be proud. The final film struck a remarkable balance between sweetness and asperity: it had something of the zip of a screwball comedy—Pauline Kael called it a modern black version of the 1930s football musical *Pigskin Parade*—but its levity was spiked with a hanging sense of raw injustice, of opportunities lost and never recovered. (Badham's next film, *Saturday Night Fever*, was a similarly unstable compound: half Busby Berkeley musical, half Martin Scorsese's *Mean Streets*.) Its tone was set by the 1939 newsreel that opened the film, in which quick reports of the Fascist storm gathering over Europe were juxtaposed with the gee-whiz story of a masochist who swallowed razor blades and stubbed out cigarettes on his tongue for pleasure. The world, it seemed, was breezily perverse.

Onto this historical stage arrived *Bingo Long*'s ballplayers, wayward heroes for a wayward age. Here Badham coaxed unexpected nuances from each of his three principals. Williams was zesty rather than stiffly debonair as team impresario Bingo Long; Jones cut his usual grandiloquence with a joyful sense of mischief; and Richard delivered a performance that was economical and suggestive. "Pryor calculates every line and gesture for small, explosive effect," wrote *Time*. His Charlie Snow was both ingenious and hapless—"a fellow of wit and resource," continued *Time*, whose life is "a slowly losing battle against absurdity." He was also the character who imported a different strain of comedy into the film: it was never Charlie Snow who was shown putting on a high-stepping show for white folks. Instead, he put on a show for himself, "Carlos Nevada" being the alias of the witty lady killer he aspired to be. Whether he was talking about "getting my bat ready" before sliding into bed with a white woman, or cracking wise to a man holding a razor to his chest, he always seemed to be projecting a bravado in which he didn't fully believe. He might pass himself off as Cuban, but he couldn't shed the inner anxieties at his core.

Upon *Bingo Long*'s release in the summer of 1976, critics heaped praise upon it, and on Richard's performance in particular. The *Washington Post* called the film "irresistible," predicting that it "should become one of the most popular movies of the year" and that "Pryor was heading for next year's Academy Award for best supporting actor." *New York*'s tough-minded John Simon commended Badham for the "dizzy old cinematic devices [he kept] up his tricky mitt" and noted the movie's "engagingly bumptious vitality," a "picaresque élan made more unusual by the supersession of the single *picaro* by two sardine-packed cars of pranksters." Similar positive notices could be found from the *New York Times* and the *Wall Street Journal* to the *Chicago Tribune* and *Village Voice*. Universal rolled out a promo campaign that seeded articles on the Negro Leagues in newspapers across the country, and tried to capitalize on the runaway success of *The Bad News Bears*, the summer of 1976's other baseball film, by staging an exhibition game between the casts of the two films and by publicizing a letter, from the actor who played *Bad News* catcher Engelberg, that hailed *Bingo Long* as "the best movie I've ever seen."

All that *Bingo Long* needed, then, was an audience that could appreciate it half as much as Engelberg. In its second week of wide release, boosted by the wave of good press, *Bingo Long* became the third-most popular film in America. But then the audience disappeared: the film had no legs, petering out at a disappointing $2.8 million for Universal. The poor totals couldn't simply be blamed on the failure of the film to cross over to whites, either. Even in its release at the Apollo Theater, the trend was the same: a big opening followed by a trailing off.

What had gone wrong? *Let's Do It Again*, the sequel to *Uptown Saturday Night*, had been released in late 1975 and drawn $11.8 million in rentals, double that of its predecessor. Motown's earlier two vehicles for Diana Ross, *Lady Sings the Blues* and *Mahogany*, had put up impressive box office totals, too: $9.1 million and $6.9 million, respectively. But *Bingo Long*, with its curious mix of the zany and the melancholy, was neither comedy nor melodrama. It was something more interesting, and perhaps harder to digest for audiences on either side of the color line. Or maybe it suffered from being everyone's second-favorite baseball movie of the season. In any case, later bids for the elusive crossover audience would not follow its lead. When Richard became the crossover star par excellence in the next few years, it would be through a fluke that, only in retrospect, would seem like the workings of grand design.

CHAPTER 20

Hustling

Los Angeles, Toronto, Madison, 1976

I'm not a success yet," Richard told a reporter at a train station in Toronto, in May 1976, while filming the scenes in *Silver Streak* that would shoot him into the Hollywood stratosphere. "I've got my foot in the door and a bit of my shoulder and I hope nobody slams it."

It was a peculiar statement, given the dimensions that Richard's life had begun to assume. . . . *Is It Something I Said?* had won for him his second straight Grammy, beating out albums by George Carlin, Lily Tomlin, and Monty Python. Richard felt confident enough to crow to the *Los Angeles Times*, "Some people say there's no 'best' in comedy. They're wrong. I'm the best." With the proceeds of his records and concerts, he opened a sleek office for Richard Pryor Enterprises on the Beverly Hills stretch of Sunset Boulevard, complete with black-and-gold décor and a fishbowl stocked with exotic underwater plants. He bought—with a hefty down payment in cash—a Spanish-style hacienda on a three-and-a-half-acre parcel in the city of Northridge, in the flat northern reaches of the San Fernando Valley. The grounds, formerly owned by an heir of the Wrigley Chewing Gum fortune, encompassed two guest cottages, a tennis court, an Olympic-size swimming pool, a stable for horses, and a large main house equipped with an aviary on the main floor and a screening room in the basement. Visitors approached via a long circular driveway that curved around a front lawn that held an orange grove.

Richard had installed himself in a home fit for a Hollywood star or mogul—with one twist: it had been thirty years since Northridge was a preferred neighborhood of stars or moguls. In the 1930s and '40s, actors such as Barbara Stanwyck, Walter Brennan, and Zeppo Marx had settled in large haciendas like Richard's so that they could own horses and enjoy a semblance of the rural life. Jack Oakie—the Old Hollywood comedian whom Richard didn't want to become—lived just a few miles away from Richard's estate, and had even served as the city's honorary mayor. But Northridge, or "Valleywood," had lost its rustic allure by the mid-1970s, not least because it had been absorbed into the larger suburban explosion of the San Fernando Valley. The actors and producers of Richard's day preferred Malibu, Santa Monica, Beverly Hills, or the elevated neighborhoods that straddled the spine of Mulholland Drive from the Hollywood Hills through Encino. Zealous about his privacy, Richard had, in effect, put at least seven miles between himself and those Hollywood players who might try to court him. An electronic gate rather than a hand-lettered sign now kept the unwelcome away.

For all his achievement, Richard felt his success was just a collapsible illusion. While the main house was being renovated to his specifications, he lived in the guesthouse at the back of his estate, and suffered a recurring dream: men with briefcases coming to his door and asking incredulously, "You mean you *own* this house, Mr. Pryor?" And then there was the matter of his stalled Hollywood career. He had accepted his most recent part, that of thief Grover Muldoon in *Silver Streak*, "because nobody asked me to do anything else." It was a "modern Willie Best," he said of the part, referring to the black bit player who popped up in more than a hundred screen comedies of the 1930s and '40s, always confined to the role of the simple-minded porter, or the simple-minded valet, or the simple-minded deliveryman.

Richard had reason to be dubious about the role as it was handed to him. In screenwriter Colin Higgins's original conception, *Silver Streak* was half romantic comedy and half thriller, the story of an unassuming book editor who takes a train trip for some quiet time and finds himself falling in love and getting entangled in a murder. Higgins was Australian, openly gay, and a graduate of UCLA film school; he had earlier scripted the offbeat *Harold and Maude*, and with *Silver*

Streak he took pleasure in drawing winkingly upon the conventions of classic Hollywood, in particular, Hitchcock's *The Lady Vanishes* and *North by Northwest.* Higgins's script delighted the studios: it was purchased for four hundred thousand dollars, an industry record at the time, and Twentieth Century-Fox budgeted over five million dollars for the film. Gene Wilder, fresh from the successes of *Blazing Saddles* and *Young Frankenstein*, committed to the leading role of book editor George Caldwell. The adept Arthur Hiller (*Love Story*, *The Hospital*, *The Man in the Glass Booth*) agreed to direct.

Unfortunately, Higgins's spirit of winking homage extended to Hollywood's old racial conventions. In his script, Grover Muldoon is a cartoon who wants to be a cartoon—a perfectly self-sacrificing helpmate, devoid of any sense of irony. When the arch villain calls him an "ignorant nigger," Grover shoots back lamely, "Bullshit! I got a high school diploma!" The final proof of the friendship between Grover and Gene Wilder's character is that they can banter in "Amos 'n' Andy" voices and assume the roles of a blackface minstrelsy routine, Tambo and Mister Bones. "Hey, brother, is that a train?" Grover asks, after the Silver Streak has smashed through the wall of the station. Talking now with "black style," George replies, "I don't know, Mister Bones. Looks to me like a kind of bicentennial display." Everyone bursts out laughing.

Nowhere was Higgins's affinity with the racial ways of Old Hollywood more apparent than in what became the film's most famous scene, where Grover blacks up George in a train station men's room, coaxing him to apply shoe polish to his face and then coaching him how to pass as black—all done to help George evade the police on his tail. Here Higgins used the character of Grover to dissolve any qualms that might attach to the use of blackface: it's Grover, the streetwise black man, who gives George permission to become a caricature of blackness. When George shrinks at the disguise, Grover downplays its meaning: "Just think of it as an instant suntan." When George objects that blackface will fool no one, Grover makes himself the butt of a joke: "When I was a kid I thought Al Jolson was a brother." After

Grover instructs George on how to strut his stuff "like you're king of the Shitkicker's Ball," he brightens at how his pupil takes to his lesson. "C'mon, Mister Bojangles. Let's get going," he tells George with an indulgent smile. And when a blacked-up George bops past the cops, Grover smooths his passage by using a phrase that Richard Pryor, as a stand-up comic, made famous: "That is one crazy nigger," Grover tells the cops, who nod in happy agreement.

To his credit, Gene Wilder worried that the scene as scripted would be the film's "Achilles heel." "Before casting started," Wilder recalled, "I told Laddie [producer Alan Ladd Jr.] that I thought there was only one person who could play that scene with me and keep it from being offensive, and that was Richard Pryor." (The producers were already recruiting Richard for the role and worried enough about his reliability that they considered hiring two black actors and shooting every Grover scene twice.) Wilder also advised Higgins, once Richard was cast, to expand the parameters of Richard's part. Higgins obliged, adding Grover to the film's final scene so that its happy ending includes Grover stealing a Dodge Dart and riding off through the wreckage of the train station. Higgins also added more cartoon dialogue: George blesses Grover's getaway just as Grover blesses George's earlier fooling of the cops—with the announcement, "That is one crazy nigger."

Richard, in other words, was being asked to play a role that bowdlerized his main stand-up persona. When he arrived in Canada to shoot the movie, his response to the material was forthright: he would rewrite his part in the moment of acting it, sometimes with grace notes of irony, sometimes with startling revisions. From Gene Wilder's perspective, it was an education in the art of improvisation. On their first day of shooting together, helicopters hovered over them; prop guns were firing in all directions. "I jumped into a ditch next to [Richard]—as I was directed to do—and Richard said his first line, and I answered," Wilder recalled. "Then he said some line that wasn't in the script, and I answered with a line that wasn't in the script. No thinking—just spontaneous reaction. That was the start of our improvisatory relationship on film." Wilder had a bit of practice as an improviser, from a fund-raising tour he had made on behalf of dovish presidential candidate Eugene McCarthy in 1968, but nothing like Richard's expertise from his years as a stand-up. "Richard was my teacher: no thinking—just immediate, instinctive response," Wilder said.

Director Arthur Hiller sensed a special chemistry between his two actors and avoided in-depth rehearsals of their scenes in favor of shorter run-throughs. "I didn't want to lose the spontaneity of their comedic relationships," he said. Their scenes crackle with energy, the nebbishy George always a hair trigger away from a neurotic episode, exasperated but entranced by Grover's heedless cool.

Around six o'clock on May 13, Hiller took his two stars into the men's room of Toronto's train station for a light run-through of the blackface scene, which they were to film the next day. Richard withdrew into himself, so quietly that Hiller didn't notice anything amiss. But Wilder did. On the walk back to the hotel, he probed Richard.

"I'm going to hurt a lot of black people," Richard said.

"How?"

"Doesn't matter. It's too late."

"It's not too late. We can talk to Arthur; I can call Laddie . . . but you have to tell me what it is."

"You're a nice guy, Gene, but I don't want to talk about it. And I don't want to do this film. I want to get out of it."

"I'm in room 1504, Richard. If you change your mind, just call me."

Fifteen minutes later, Richard phoned Wilder. In Wilder's room, he brainstormed a better way to frame the scene. In the original, a white man stumbles into the bathroom and is fooled into thinking that George, in blackface, is actually a black man. In Richard's version, it would be a black man who wanders in and, rather than being fooled, gives the strutting George a bit of further instruction: "You might be in pretty big trouble, fella, but for God's sake, learn to keep time."

The next day, with the cameras rolling, Richard kept reshaping

Playing the American skin game: George Caldwell (Gene Wilder) takes lessons from Grover Muldoon (Richard Pryor) in Silver Streak. *(Courtesy of the author)*

the scene. In the script, the blackface is a goof that Grover Muldoon embraces; in the scene Richard plays, it's a ruse Grover unmasks. When George hesitates to put on the shoe polish, Grover doesn't sell it as an "instant suntan"; he remarks bitingly, "What? Are you afraid it won't come off?" And when George yells, "It'll never work!" Grover doesn't sell the disguise by speaking of his own gullibility as a child. He pivots George to look at his half-blacked-up face in the mirror; George's face relaxes into a sort of guileless curiosity. For a moment, George is a white man entertaining what it would be like to lose his whiteness. "Look at that," Grover says, then snaps George out of his reverie with a cynical lesson about race and Hollywood. "Al Jolson made a million bucks looking like that."

In Richard's reformulation of the scene, blackface was the perfect ruse for George precisely because white people favored a counterfeit of blackness to the truth of it; they preferred not to look too closely at the world around them. In one bit of dialogue that, sadly, was cut from the final scene, George protests, "You dummy, you got oxblood shoe polish!" Grover shoots back that it won't matter: "All the police look for is to see if you got color, any color."

When Richard had finished with it, the scene in the men's room was not just more acerbic than the script had allowed. It was also, in its way, more believably affectionate. Grover offers George the props of cool—his mirrored shades, his purple satin jacket from the Eighty-Second Airborne Division (embroidered with the message "When I Die I'll Go to Heaven Because I've Spent My Time in Hell"), his way of dancing—but he also underscores that props do not make the man. He clues George into how easy it is to perform a caricature, and how ridiculous it is to bear the weight of one. And in revealing something of the complexity of race in America, Grover seems less like a prop himself in the plot—in fact, he seems a better competitor for the love of George than Hilly, the confusingly drawn secretary played by Jill Clayburgh. When, a few scenes later, Grover and George say good-bye on camera for the first time, they moon at each other but say little, as awkward as soldiers who've held one another under fire, embarrassed by how intimate they've become. And when Grover turns up again at the film's end, it seems less like the non sequitur it is than a tying of a knot, a necessary form of emotional closure. The film's more credible love story is between the two men.

It's not too much to say that, with his performance, Richard saved *Silver Streak* from itself. Upon the film's release in December 1976, critics agreed that the film limped along until Richard "goose[d] it into some semblance of life," as Molly Haskell wrote in the *Village Voice*: "Pryor, a comic genius who is turning into one of the great film presences, does what no one else in the film can do: makes it look as if it knew where it was going." Another observed, perceptively, "One suspects Pryor wrote his own material because his scenes are more outrageous, more inventive than the rest of the film." In the consensus view, Richard was the one surprising element of the film: "For about fifteen minutes, Pryor gives the picture some of his craziness. Not much of it, but some—enough to make you realize how lethargic it was without him" (*The New Yorker*); "What furtive sprightliness *Silver Streak* manages to work up is attributable mostly to Pryor, sly-eyed and fast-mouthed, an unbeatable antic spirit" (*Time*).

Even Twentieth Century-Fox seems to have realized that the power of Richard's performance shifted *Silver Streak*'s center of gravity: the final film worked better as a "bromance" than as a standard romantic comedy. A month after its release—as the film defied lukewarm reviews by hauling in tens of millions, on its way to becoming the eighth-highest-grossing film of the year—the film's full-page *New York Times* ad for *Silver Streak* eliminated Jill Clayburgh from view and promoted Richard to top billing instead: "Gene Wilder and Richard Pryor take a train ride from hilarity to mystery and back again." So it was that, with some sleight of hand and considerable finesse, Richard achieved his first starring role in Hollywood. *Silver Streak* represented the culmination of a strategy he had refined with *Lady Sings the Blues* and *Wattstax*: of elaborating a cameo until it was no mere cameo but magnetized everything around it.

Privately, Richard was surprisingly blasé about his first pairing with Wilder. During *Silver Streak*'s production, he shut himself up in his dressing room with a legal pad and pencil, and—as if to compensate for how he felt pigeonholed by Hollywood—wrote a screenplay in which God came down to earth as a black man. (Try turning *that* into a Willie Best role!) The wound inflicted by *Blazing Saddles*, which might have paired him in a buddy comedy with Wilder three years earlier, was still fresh. As they wrapped up filming in LA, Mel Brooks had visited his close friend Gene and hammed it up with his old cowriter Richard. He clinched Richard around the neck and joked that the comic was "wonderful and talented" despite the fact that he wasn't Jewish. Richard smiled in Brooks and Wilder's presence, but once they were gone, he fell on his dressing room bed with a sneer.

He was prepared to be disappointed by whites—prepared to be embraced and then told that he didn't belong and shown the door. After *Silver Streak*, he kept speaking sharply about how he'd known betrayal. "Don't trust too many white folks," he told a black journalist. "[S]tay black in your heart, keep your black friends around you always, 'cause white folks will make you feel that everything is always alright and then they will chop your head off."

Such was the complexity of Richard Pryor: on-screen he could make interracial friendship palpable and believable as never before; off-screen, he warned blacks of the perils of ever trusting whites. *Silver Streak* turned Richard into a bankable Hollywood star. It was the first of four buddy comedies he completed with Gene Wilder; their scene together in the men's room became a classic, a touchstone in the comedy of racial manners, and was perhaps the most prominent vehicle through which Richard tutored a generation of would-be white hipsters to loosen up, go with the flow, and find the rhythm within them. Yet he seemed to want to forget that he'd ever starred in the film. He summed up his experience on it to the *New York Times* with a dismissive quip: "I was looking to hustle, and I got hustled." In his memoir, he mentions *Silver Streak* only glancingly, as a film to which he didn't give his all. Although some imagined that, given his on-screen chemistry with Wilder, the two had to be friends off-screen, in fact they never met outside the context of their working relationship.

When, in 1979, Richard's manager, David Franklin, pressed him to reunite with Wilder for the film that became *Stir Crazy*, the greatest moneymaker of Richard's career, the comic resisted. "It didn't seem like an interesting movie," he said. To which Franklin responded that the studio was offering Richard a million dollars for the part. Richard still was unconvinced.

"Isn't a million dollars enough reason?" Franklin asked.

"Yes, I guess so," said Richard. He felt dragged into the buddy movies that were a crucial piece of his Hollywood legacy. They became his box office calling card, but he longed for another.

As *Silver Streak* wrapped up shooting in June 1976, Richard sensed a new world of possibility opening up for him as an actor. He was wooed in quick succession by a brace of Hollywood dissidents, each of whom had taken his or her own eccentric path from the streets to the producer's suite or director's chair. Having maneuvered their way into the Hollywood system, they were collectively willing to wager millions of dollars that they could slip Richard through its cracks.

First on Richard's dance card was producer Hannah Weinstein, who was putting together a biopic about Wendell Scott, the black stock car racer who broke the NASCAR color bar in 1950s Virginia. The sixty-four-year-old Weinstein shared some of Scott's courage: she was gumption personified—a "woman with no patience for trifles," wrote the *Los Angeles Times*—and a longtime activist. In the 1930s and '40s she had been a speechwriter and campaign organizer for liberal standard-bearers like Fiorello La Guardia and Henry Wallace. In the 1950s, upon migrating to England, she had set up a thriving production company and secretly hired screenwriters who'd been blacklisted in the United States for associating with the Communist Party. She came to Richard as an ambassador of Third World Cinema, the production company she'd launched with black actors Ossie Davis, James Earl Jones, and Diana Sands in 1971, with the mission of opening up the media industries. By 1976, Third World had ushered two hundred people of color into New York's technical unions—quite the achievement, given that the unions had begun with a mere six blacks and two Latinos out of six thousand members. But Third World had less to show for itself as an actual production company. Its output was limited to 1973's *Claudine*, a modest and affecting drama about a welfare mother who falls in love with a sanitation worker.

In her meeting with Richard, Weinstein pitched the film that would become *Greased Lightning*. Melvin Van Peebles, whose *Sweet Sweetback's Baadasssss Song* had so inspired Richard in Berkeley, would be his director. (It was Van Peebles, in fact, who had suggested Richard for the movie.) She started listing the actors whom she saw filling out the picture, and when she dropped the name of Cleavon Little, Richard immediately assumed, perhaps from his experience with *Blazing Saddles*, that Little would play the role of Wendell Scott.

"Who do you want me to play?" he asked.

Weinstein stared at Richard as if he were obtuse. "The lead. You're going to play Wendell Scott."

Richard was stunned. "Well, that fucked me up," he recalled. "I was blown away when a movie that seemed to have substance came along and the producers wanted me to star." He swallowed his misgivings and committed to the film in late June, with production set to begin a mere three weeks away, in Georgia.

While preparing for the role of Wendell Scott, Richard finalized plans to head up a still more audacious project, what became the film *Which Way Is Up?*. Producer Steve Krantz and director Michael Schultz came to him with the idea of translating Lina Wertmüller's *The Seduction of Mimi*, an Italian sex-and-politics satire that had been an art house favorite, into the context of black life in the United States. Schultz, the up-and-coming black director of the moment, was a familiar face to Richard, and made for a compelling pitchman. Richard had thought of Schultz as his director of choice for *The Black Stranger*, his "voodoo western," and had even put up Schultz and his wife, upon their arrival in Los Angeles, in a small Malibu condo he was renting on the side.

Schultz had a calm demeanor, working-class roots, and, most important, a vision for black filmmaking that harmonized with Richard's own. Having cut his teeth as a director on plays, by the likes of Sam Shepard and Derek Walcott, that experimented with odd tonalities, Schultz wanted to depart from the models offered either by blaxploitation films (too lurid) or Sidney Poitier's ghetto comedies (too tame). "My theory is that you can make just as exciting films by dealing with reality, not fantasy," he told the *Hollywood Reporter* in 1975. *Cooley High*, an alternately joyful and sober treatment of black high school life in Chicago, was his breakthrough film. His next, *Car Wash*, likewise marbled together feelings of joy and entrapment. On the one hand, it was a funky pick-me-up, synchronizing a single day at a Los Angeles car wash to a pumping Norman Whitfield soundtrack. On the other—with its pageant of car wash workers moving in and out of the foreground, seeking, with some desperation, their piece of action—it was an inner-city version of Robert Altman's *Nashville*. In its closing scene the militant Abdullah says, with tears on his face, "I know I'm not crazy, but every day I have to come here and watch this clown show. Sometimes I just can't take it."

For *Car Wash*, Schultz had recruited Richard for a day player cameo, one that both lightened the film's mood and gave texture to its politics. As Daddy Rich, an evangelist who arrives in a gleaming limousine bearing the license plate TITHE, Richard turns the car wash workers into an instant congregation by preaching the gospel of Mammon with utter conviction. He is the clown prince of its clown show—and, consequently, is resisted by Abdullah, who calls him out as a pimp in preacher's clothing.

After *Car Wash*, Richard was game for another collaboration with Schultz, and he signed on for the Wertmüller adaptation. To seal their friendship, he presented Schultz with a provocative gift: a rifle with Schultz's name engraved on it, accompanied by a note that read, "I hope you can shoot this better than you can shoot movies." Universal picked up the film; production was set for October, just two months after *Greased Lightning* wrapped. Richard swung the job of adapting Wertmüller's scenario to his Berkeley comrade Cecil Brown, even though Brown had little track record as a screenwriter. As he had done with *Saturday Night*, Richard was using his influence to open up the industry, to help those who had helped him.

Richard's successes with Weinstein and Schultz were preludes to the most consequential business meeting of his summer, with Universal's Thom Mount. By the time he took the meeting, around the beginning of July, Richard was relaxed enough to lounge on a long white sofa while Mount and Richard's manager, David Franklin, hashed out the terms of his future in Hollywood. Mount was all of twenty-eight years old, and a veteran of the sixties. As a college student in North Carolina, he had devoted himself to the Southern Students Organizing Committee, a New Left group whose emblem showed black and white hands clasped together against the background of a Confederate flag. He had been an artist in SoHo, a writer for the Liberation News Service, and an editor for the Indochina Peace Campaign, an antiwar group that saw the Vietnam conflict as "the focal point of a worldwide struggle against imperialism." Now Mount was empowered to represent Universal, a Hollywood studio with a particular reputation for stuffiness; his job was, in part, to unstuff its shirt. Since coming to Universal, he had sponsored two films with largely black casts, *Bingo Long* and *Car Wash*, and a number of movies with absolutely no aspirations to social significance. When he met Richard, he had in his pipeline the Burt Reynolds vehicle *Smokey and the Bandit*, of which he later said, "It is pure junk food, but I *like* Big Macs and Coca-Cola. They mean something to me."

Mount, then, was some combination of activist, populist, and—an essential requirement for his job—opportunist. Richard was an opportunity he felt compelled to seize. Under the unprecedented terms of the deal he struck with Richard, Pryor was guaranteed an eye-popping three million dollars over the next four years. In return, the actor-comedian was obligated to give Universal "first right of refusal" for his creative ideas on six movies. He had the choice of starring in these movies or not; if he did star, he would earn a share of the movie's profits. Should he need help fleshing out his story ideas into a script, Universal would pay a handsome salary to both Richard and the screenwriter collaborating with him. And if Richard chose to act in films for other studios while fulfilling the terms of his Universal contract, that was fine.

The contract was a watershed in Richard's career: an incredible act of faith in his abilities as a writer and performer, not to mention his power as a crossover draw. "We believe it is possible to make money on class A pictures that not only star black people, but are made by black people," Mount told a reporter, explaining the deal as a breakthrough in industry thinking. To which Richard rejoined, "Well, I guess that means if these movies don't make money a whole lot of niggers gonna be in trouble."

A hazy sense of experimentation was in the air in Hollywood. Soon after Mount negotiated the multipicture deal, *New West* magazine profiled him as one of Hollywood's "baby moguls," its "new power elite." Mount was, the article reported, a fresh sort of studio executive, the kind who might wear blue jeans with his tux and sport an old SDS button at the opening of a film festival. Still, it was unclear what sort of changes, outside the wardrobe choices of its executive class, the baby moguls would bring to Hollywood. According to some, the baby moguls would ventilate Hollywood with the spirit of the sixties. "That whole period taught me not to be frightened," said Lisa Weinstein, a young vice president at Twentieth Century–Fox (and Hannah Weinstein's daughter). "It was great training. After a bayonet's stared you up your nose, what's to be scared of taking risks?" Other observers were more skeptical. "I often wondered where all the student radicals would go when they grew up," said one. "Now I know. They came to a place where they never have to grow up."

For Richard, the question of Hollywood's openness to risk took a more personal form: how much, as he started carrying films, would he be made to adapt to Hollywood? And how much would Hollywood be made to adapt to him?

With so much at stake in his career, Richard tried to turn over a new leaf. "I'm through actively messing with my body," he said. He embraced a regimen of "holistic living," hoping to become more fit and trim. Health foods and vitamins were in; cocaine was out. When his Berkeley buddy Claude Brown visited him in his dressing room at a concert, he proudly opened his refrigerator to display what seemed like thirty-some quarts of orange juice.

While he flushed his system clean with OJ, Richard faced a tight deadline. Given his start date on *Greased Lightning* and the terms of his contract with Warner Bros., he had less than two weeks to conceive and produce a new album for the label. *Bicentennial Nigger*, the album that he rushed into existence, is his most uneven, padded with undeveloped riffs on his teenage gang in Peoria and lengthy shout-outs to black celebrities in his audience. "It's not my best work," he complained to a reporter upon its release. "I'm never going to sign a multirecord contract like that again." But it is also his most hard-edged and conceptual album, with several tracks skewering from different angles the patriotic hoopla of America's bicentennial. The album's cover brilliantly captured the slant of Richard's alternative history. It depicted Richard in ten incarnations—as policeman, convict, hustler, boxer, reverend, slave, and so on—with all the incarnations bound together in leg irons fastened by Uncle Sam himself. Richard might contain a multitude in himself, the image suggested, but no matter how much he multiplied himself onstage, Uncle Sam always held the power to yank his chain.

The title track was a stick of dynamite with a slow fuse. "You all know how black humor started," Richard said. "It started in the slave ships. A cat was on his way over here, rowing. And a dude said, 'What are you laughing at?' '*Yesterday I was a king.*'" He connected the dots between that slave ship and the state of black America in 1976:

> They're having a bicentennial. Two hundred years! Gonna have a bicentennial nigger. They will—they'll have some nigger two hundred years old in blackface, with stars and stripes on his forehead.

In the wheezy voice of his bicentennial minstrel, Richard said, "I used to live to be one hundred and fifty. Now I dies of the high blood pressure by the time I'm fifty-two, yuk yuk yuk. And that thrills me to death." He recounted the horrors visited upon black Americans—the Middle Passage, the separation of families under slavery—as if they were all a hilarious joke, with yuk-yuks punctuating every sentence. "The Battle Hymn of the Republic" (an unusual in-studio touch) surged in the background, the dissonant soundtrack to black suffering. "Y'all probably done forgot about it," he said, still in that minstrel chuckle, before speaking normally, truthfully, as if for the first time: "But I ain't never gonna forget."

Silence. The end—of the track and the album. It's hard to think of any other "comedy" record that closes with such a head-snapping reckoning.

While Richard saw the last two hundred years of American history as a blackface horror show, he also wondered if the prospects for the next two hundred were equally bleak. "Hey, Jack, saw *Logan's Run* the other day," Richard riffed in one of the *Bicentennial Nigger* shows.

"Twenty-third century, but there weren't no niggers in it. Guess they're not planning for us to be around." Then a kicker: "That's why *we* got to make movies." Summoning himself to that task, he planned, after *Bicentennial Nigger,* to stick to a three-year moratorium on stand-up so that he could make his mark on Hollywood. "I don't really want to go around the country playing clubs, seeing cities. I did that already. I have this new house. I want to stay put and do films," he told a reporter.

A few weeks later, he was flying to Madison, Georgia, to step into his first role as leading man. Perhaps Third World Cinema could break the old American pattern.

The production of *Greased Lightning* was soon full of drama, but in a change of pace, Richard was not its main instigator. Nervous about carrying a film—and especially worried about how he could absorb a part with so many lines—he aimed to stay on the straight and narrow. He brought his grandmother Marie out to Madison to "take care of things" and, implicitly, keep him in line. He settled with her in a farmhouse on the city's rural outskirts and in his downtime lived a rusticated life, wiling away the hours fishing, or setting off firecrackers, or hunting. He savored where his career had taken him. "When I was a kid," he told an interviewer while making the film, "I always said I would be in the movies one day, and damned if I didn't make it. Sometimes I just sit home and look out the window and say, 'Daaaammmmmm!' " On the set, he was often in the same reflective mood: when waiting for his scenes, he would pull over a chair and sit under a tree.

Given Richard's relative mellowness, *Greased Lightning*'s disturbances at first came from other sources. When the film's largely black cast and crew arrived in Madison, local whites rebelled. They "were creating all kinds of havoc," recalled Michael Schultz, who visited Richard in the early days of shooting to confab about *Which Way Is Up?*. According to Schultz, it took the intervention of the town's white sheriff to calm the waters. " 'Be cool,' " Schultz remembered him saying, " 'these niggers are gonna be out of here in a couple of weeks. Y'all just be cool, it's a lot of money.' "

Director Melvin Van Peebles was the loser in the next skirmish that beset the film. He had wanted to thread an element of fantasy into the biopic, but several weeks into the shoot, Warner Bros. and Hannah Weinstein looked at the rushes and felt the film was rattling off course, with a tone too broadly satirical and stylized. Though radical in her politics, Weinstein was not drawn to formal experimentation. She was happy for *Greased Lightning* to deal forthrightly with the hardships of black life, or to underscore how poor blacks and poor whites could make common cause, but didn't cotton to Van Peebles's ironic vision, and she removed him from the film.

The production came to a standstill; Richard was now a leading man without a director. He phoned Michael Schultz, who had since returned to LA, and asked him to save the movie. Schultz hesitated—he was deep into the preproduction work on *Which Way Is Up?*—then reconsidered. "Here's my star," he thought. "I don't want him to be in a movie that's going to blow. I don't want him to look bad. I guess I'll have to go do it." Schultz told the press that, in his conception, *Greased Lightning* would now follow in the lines of Burt Reynolds's *White Lightning*, but with more of a comic touch—music, no doubt, to the ears of Weinstein and Warner Bros. Schultz arrived in Madison, took stock, and decided there was little he could salvage from Van Peebles's footage; he went on to reshoot 80 percent of it.

Fortunately, Schultz had a star who was generally living outside his "crazy nigger" mystique—and who, when he strayed, had a co-star who kept him in line. Pam Grier, cast as Wendell's wife, Mary, arrived on the set one morning in August, eager to work with Richard for the first time. Then she waited. The sweltering Georgia heat melted her makeup; her dress became wet with sweat. At two o'clock, Richard strolled in and, instead of moving straight into a rehearsal of their scene together, took out a fork and teasingly poked at her eye. Grier snapped: she smacked the fork out of his hand and gave him a tongue-lashing.

"This is an opportunity for you to be a leading man and show what you can do, and you're going to mess with this," she said. "Do you know your lines?"

"No, not . . ." Richard fumbled.

"If not, I'll come back when you're ready," Grier said, and peeled off for her dressing room. As she reflected later, she could not have chosen a better way to impress, or seduce, Richard: "I walked off and respected myself, and that's when he fell in love with me." During the shoot, they were affectionate, curious to get to know one another outside their respective mystiques. "Pam Grier, you're just a farmer. A hick," Richard told her, surprised to glimpse the person behind the persona; she was far from the badass vigilante character he knew from screen roles like Foxy Brown and Coffy. In their screen time together, too, they flirted with finding their less sensational selves.

Aware of all he had to learn, Richard was everywhere looking to add more nuance to his part. He studied the moves of his costar Beau Bridges, who played Hutch, a poor white race car driver who begins as Scott's competitor and ends as his boon companion. "He was beautiful," Richard said of Bridges. "I'd watch him in a close-up and want to kill him, he was so good. He taught me a lot about acting in front of the camera." Richard received another sort of acting tutorial from the race car drivers he met on set—among them Wendell Scott, who served as the film's technical adviser. Richard befriended the man whom he was playing on-screen, and absorbed Scott's geniality. Scott's attitude "was different from how I would do it as a black man today," Richard offered, "because I would have taken a shotgun with me. And he don't have none of that feeling."

All this—Richard's affection for Grier and Bridges, his sense of Scott and the racing world he inhabited—filtered into his performance, which was understated and surprisingly modulated. His Wendell Scott is a dreamer who comes fully alive only when he's hurtling down a road or a track, a sweet soul who lives for an adrenaline rush but not for revenge. Off the track and in the company of family and friends, he's kind and straight-ahead. With his white pal Hutch, for instance, he has a casual, unforced intimacy—nothing like the electric agitation between *Silver Streak*'s Grover Muldoon and George Caldwell. Wendell and Hutch have a bottom-dog connection: they love the sound of humming engines while sensing, at the same time, that their lives are as busted up as the stock cars they're endlessly rebuilding.

Behind the wheel, Richard's Wendell is more animated, bringing a dash of style and good-natured rebelliousness to the task at hand. At his first racing scene, he is a dandy among the grease monkeys, with a newsboy's cap and a long white scarf draped around his neck. When the good ol' boy owner of the racetrack instructs him, as if talking to a small child, about the basics of racing ("One time around is a lap"), Scott calls him "captain" and "sir" with a gamesome spirit: he's involved in a delicate bit of acting, mocking the owner to himself but not so overtly that he trips off any suspicions. White men in positions of authority are pitiable giants to him, so powerful and yet so dumb. He wants to get on with the race. And when white race car drivers push him off the track and nearly kill him, he still wants to get on with it—to coax his smoking and sputtering mess of a car back on the track and across the finish line. Richard's Wendell flickers with a shrewd intelligence, but at his core, he's driven by a simple, uncomplicated love for his sport.

When *Greased Lightning*'s production wrapped in September, Richard had reason to be proud of how he'd handled his first starring role. There was nothing Willie Best–like to his part; and he had defied the rumors of his unreliability and held himself together. Still, a curious irony trailed his debut as a leading man. He had ascended with a role that was as remote from the jagged power of his stand-up comedy as any in his career. His Wendell Scott is free of raunch, free of neuroses, free of cutting edges—as soft and lovable as Richard's "bicentennial nigger" was sharp and disturbing. And that was how Hannah Weinstein liked it: when, in the coming months, Michael Schultz tried to make the film more dynamic in its editing, he suffered a similar fate to that of Melvin Van Peebles. Weinstein fired

Schultz's editor and took over the film, reshaping it according to what Schultz called "the soap opera style of moviemaking," with "a lot of emphasis on the family and on the boring parts of the picture." All this might have made the character of Wendell Scott closer to the real-life Wendell Scott, who by all reports was a good-natured family man, but it did not draw him closer to the real-life Richard, or to the wellsprings of his comedy.

While directing *Greased Lightning* in Georgia, Schultz looked ahead to *Which Way Is Up?*, already in preproduction, and announced to the trade press, with some bite, that "I want to make certain that Richard Pryor . . . has an opportunity to give full play to his comedic talents, and those talents can be very political, and very raunchy. I plan to see his humor is not castrated." For several years, Schultz had conceived of his sex farce as Richard's Hollywood breakthrough: "the whole idea of this picture is to give Richard's talent a vehicle to express itself." By late summer, though, Schultz had a problem on his hands. Richard's friend Cecil Brown had delivered a screenplay that was too prolix—a novelist's idea of a screenplay—and, worst of all from Schultz's perspective, simply not funny. The director brought in Carl Gottlieb, a comedy writer who had just taken an unwieldy script about a shark and, by tightening it and giving its dialogue an improvisational flavor, had helped turn it into *Jaws*. Perhaps if he worked closely with Richard, Gottlieb could cast a similar spell on *Which Way*.

So, in the fall of 1976, Richard set off with Gottlieb for a ten-day vacation at a villa in Barbados. The assignment: to project the characters in Richard's head onto the page, with their profane spirits fully intact.

CHAPTER 21

A Man of Parts

Barbados, Los Angeles, industrial Michigan, 1976–1977

The Richard who arrived in Barbados could feel that the pieces of his life were finally coming together—that he'd passed through the whirlwind and been deposited by a gentle hand on a sun-drenched shore.

At his side was Pam Grier, who, after the shooting of *Greased Lightning*, had transitioned from costar to inamorata, and brought a loving sense of structure to his life. With her support, Richard had committed to a new morning regimen. No more sleeping in until two in the afternoon; now he breakfasted on eggs, bacon, freshly made oatmeal, and freshly squeezed juice, then dashed off to the tennis court for a workout with his trainer. Self-improvement was the order of the day—and not just for his body. Having confessed to Pam that, with his eighth-grade education, it was hard for him to read fluently, he enlisted her to coach and support him. He dreamed big while staying true to his sensibility. "I heard that *War and Peace* is the hardest motherfuckin' novel to read," he told her. "I'm gonna read it. If I can't read it, it's so damned big, at least I can kill someone with it. Use it as a weapon." The circle of his ambition was expanding. He signed on to star in a number of literary adaptations—*Cyrano de Bergerac*, *Arsenic and Old Lace*, even George Orwell's *Animal Farm*.

In Barbados, Richard was the picture of physical and mental discipline. He woke up, dressed himself in tennis whites all the way down to his knee socks and sneakers, and played some games at a nearby court; he took a light lunch (salad, melon) on the terrace of the villa they'd rented; he brainstormed with Carl Gottlieb about *Which Way*

More than costars: Richard Pryor and Pam Grier, circa 1977. (Courtesy of Getty Images)

Is Up? in the afternoon; he went out for a nice dinner with Pam, Carl, and Carl's wife. Then he retired for the evening and began the cycle anew the next morning. He was relaxed and in fine fettle. Once, he broke into a high singsong voice, "As mayor of the Munchkin City"—and entertained Carl with a flawless rendition of the entire Munchkin sequence from *The Wizard of Oz*.

In their afternoons together, Richard and Carl had a creative project into which they could sink their teeth. Wertmüller's *The Seduction of Mimi* was a ripe Italian parable about the idiocy of machismo: its title character was a bumbler in politics and love, confused enough to become, in turn, a Communist and a tool of the Mafia, and foolish enough to think that he can enter the bedrooms of three different women without paying a price for his conniving. But *Mimi* was also inimitably Italian in its plotting and style, and very far from the Hollywood mode of filmmaking, even the "New Hollywood" mode of filmmaking. The main character's buffoonery was rooted in the tradition of the *commedia dell'arte*, with its hopelessly dumb schemers. And Wertmüller, who apprenticed under Fellini, loved to populate her casts with oversize characters who spilled into the realm of the grotesque: at one point in *Mimi*, she aimed a fish-eye lens at the naked and flabby posterior of an overweight actress, so as to fill the screen with it. From Gottlieb's point of view, *Mimi* had "enormous story gaps, covered by music and montage. I mean *real* flaws."

Adapting *Mimi*, then, was no simple affair. It meant translating *commedia dell'arte* into the funky idiom of black American comedy, and Italian art house cinema into Hollywood entertainment. Michael Schultz had already established, with Cecil Brown's help, some of the coordinates of the translation. Mimi's job as a laborer in the quarries of Sicily would become Leroy Jones's job as a fruit picker in the fields of Central California; the Communist struggle would become the migrant farmworkers' struggle; and the Mafia-run world of Italy would become the corporate-run world of America. Now Richard and Carl worked to fill in the other blanks: they needed to Pryor-ize the film's characters—to rewrite Mimi as a black Everyman, to turn Mimi's father into a version of Mudbone, and to turn Mimi's rival into a version of Richard's loquacious reverend.

Carl ran a tape recorder while he and Richard let their imaginations unspool. Carl had a background in improv—he had been involved for half a decade with the political comedy troupe the Committee—and the two played through the script as if it were an extended improv game. "It was a very healthy collaboration because [Richard] was very intent on making the movie work," Gottlieb remembered. Unlike many actors, Richard submerged his ego and was unconcerned with the number of lines allotted to his character.

Their creative idyll was interrupted by a medical emergency. Pam's temperature spiked; her lips became swollen, part of a severe allergic reaction to some shellfish she'd eaten. Richard, who often had much in common with the triple-timing Mimi, stayed by her side. He applied cold compresses to her forehead and reassured her, "It's going to be alright, baby" (and it was: an American doctor arrived the next day to give her an injection, which stabilized her). Nervously but fully, Richard inhabited the role of caretaker—another new leaf turning over. Upon Pam's recovery, the two couples returned to LA, Carl having everything he needed—hours of taped improvisations—for the rewrite.

When Carl Gottlieb delivered his revised script for *Which Way Is Up?*, the cynicism of Wertmüller's original had melted away, and Richard was working on the most explicitly political movie of his career. The farmworkers' union now gave the movie its moral thrust; it was the larger solution to a world where blacks and Latinos worked for poverty wages in the fields while company bosses snaked around in limos, surrounded themselves with goons, and ordered hits on union leaders. The union's adversary in the film is Agrico Industries, a hydra-headed conglomerate whose motto is "We Grow on You" and whose top executive has the all-white suit and decadent manners of a southern plantation owner.

Schultz, meanwhile, was trying to make his film *engagé* in other ways. Averse to having his farmworkers played by "Hollywood extras with their sunglasses," he invited El Teatro Campesino, a radical theater group affiliated with the United Farm Workers, to play Latino characters and rewrite any farmworker dialogue that sounded false. Universal resisted the idea; Schultz won the argument by warning the studio, "I don't want to do a phony representation of [the farmworkers' movement] and neither do you. Because if you do, then theaters are going to get burned." Meanwhile, he assembled a crew that breathed in the spirit of *la causa*. It was high on youthful energy and low on studio veterans—the technicians who, as Gottlieb summed them up, were "the old farts in the baseball caps, named Red and Curly and Mack and Shorty." The crew's average age was thirty-two; many were black, Chicano, or female, the sort of people who wouldn't have been hired on a production ten years earlier. Presiding over the camera operators was cinematographer John Alonzo (*Harold and Maude*, *Chinatown*), himself the child of Mexican migrant workers.

As *Which Way Is Up?* approached its first day of filming in late 1976, Schultz took another creative risk: he asked Richard to play all three characters inspired by his stand-up—father, son, and holy roller—in the sort of virtuosic turn associated with British actors Alec Guinness (*Kind Hearts and Coronets*) and Peter Sellers (*Dr. Strangelove*). If Richard accepted the challenge, it would mean not just that he'd be working harder—filming scenes multiple times, with stand-ins—but also that he'd be carrying a heavier emotional load.

In the scenes between the diffident Leroy and his cocksure father Rufus, he would be replaying a dynamic from his own past, the Peoria of the early 1960s, when as a young man he shared a roof with his father Buck. Rufus might have been originally conceived as a takeoff on Mudbone, but he ended up an amalgam of Mudbone and Buck, with the mannerisms of the former and the harsh swagger of the latter. In the final film, he's a nonstop editorialist whose favorite subject is his son's shortcomings. "Pop, I'm in the paper!" Leroy enthuses as if starstruck with himself, the day after he falls into the arms of a Cesar Chavez–like activist. "You done tore your ass now, boy!" Rufus responds, deflating his son like a toy balloon. When Leroy mutters to Annie Mae, "I hope my kids ain't gonna be like him," Rufus slips in the dagger: "Nigger, you got to get some pussy before you can have some kids!" Leroy flinches; Rufus chuckles. "Shit, I'm knockin' the bottom out of mine." As a father, he's accustomed to getting the last word and the last laugh.

Richard accepted all the challenges of *Which Way Is Up?*—of carrying the movie in triplicate; of revisiting the sore spots of his past and transforming them into comedy. In December 1976, just before filming began, he made another professional gamble: he committed to produce for NBC a special and twelve half hours of other unspecified programming, despite his reservations about TV work. Given how NBC was, for the first time in its history, ranked last among the major networks, he believed that he could defeat the network censors in any skirmishes. "I'm just going to say, 'Here's the shit, take it or leave it.' NBC will go for anything right now because they're in trouble," he predicted.

His future seemed so bright that even the prospect of his own crack-up caused him no anxiety. "I'm going to be big. What I'm happy about is I don't owe nobody, and I got enough money to go crazy with. If I have a nervous breakdown, I can be in a private hospital."

The set of *Which Way Is Up?* was kept closed, the usual forbidding sign ("No Admittance—Cast and Crew Only") embellished with a red skull and crossbones. *Time*, *Newsweek*, and the *Washington Post* pestered Universal to interview the film's players, to no avail. The growers put in calls to the studio, anxious how the film would represent their interests, and also were put off. Schultz played his cards close to his vest; he was just making "a harmless little comedy," he said. He didn't want to rile anyone until he'd pulled off the film's tight shooting schedule: "minor miracles in 33 days," he called it.

In his element: on the set of Which Way Is Up? *with director Michael Schultz and costar Lonette McKee. (Courtesy of Marcia Reed)*

For Richard, *Which Way Is Up?* was both grueling and delightful as an acting experience. He looked at the young, multiracial crew, so similar to his usual stand-up crowd, and every moment he was on camera—a great proportion of the shoot—he took upon himself the near-impossible task of keeping them in stitches. As Carl Gottlieb observed, "In the master [take], when we finished a scene and the director yelled, 'Cut!,' everybody who was holding in their laughter would let it out. The whole set would laugh—the grips, the cameramen, everybody." Then it was time to reshoot the scene, with close-ups and cutaway shots, for coverage. "He'd do the scene," Gottlieb continued, "and the laugh that he was used to getting wasn't there. No fault of Richard, but everybody had heard the joke ten times. They were professionals. So in an effort to win the crew back, Richard would start ad-libbing. And he would always win them back." A reporter for *Mother Jones* saw the crew "us[ing] sweaters to stifle their laughter at [Richard's] elaborations and taradiddles"; given Richard's refusal to repeat himself, she thought, the "script supervisor's pencil must be down to a nubbin." Schultz later said, "My hardest job on [*Which Way Is Up?*] was keeping the crew from laughing and spoiling the sound, or keeping the actors from cracking up." Richard, he judged, was an actor who "can do the same scene ten different ways—all of them right."

When Richard was done with it, *Which Way Is Up?* was more anarchic and unpredictable than *The Seduction of Mimi.* It still had the bones of a political film, as its creators had intended, but in its guts it was a sex comedy, about the spectacles unleashed by human appetites. Richard's Leroy Jones is a man at the mercy of his impulses, a chameleon whose foolishness takes on the color of each world he passes through. With his wife, Annie Mae, at the beginning of the film, he's a fool for sex. When she lies in bed with her back to him, he wheedles her to uncross her ankles and serenades her with "Just a little lovin', early in the mornin'"; rebuffed, he tortures himself by eavesdropping on the lovemaking between his father and stepmother in the next room. With his lover Vanetta, the liberated woman who supports the farm workers and subsists on a diet of carrot juice and organic food, Leroy is a fool for romance. He tries to jog alongside her until he plotzes headfirst into the ground; he dresses in flowing caftans that match hers; he promises his undying fidelity to her. And with "Sister Sarah," the wife of the preacher who has given Annie Mae a child, he's a fool for revenge—the fool of fools. He breaks his promise to Vanetta by courting Sister Sarah extravagantly, and the full weight of his confused life crashes down upon him. In trying to have it all, he loses everything.

With *Which Way Is Up?*, Richard finally had license to be as sharp, vulgar, and as outré on-screen as he wished. He was free, as *Newsweek* later put it, to "gobble[] up his triple parts like a happy hog let loose in the garden." There's no Hollywood film that better testifies to his gifts as a comedian. In hilarious moments of physical comedy, he showed how he'd begun, in the 1950s, by studying the examples of Sid Caesar and Jerry Lewis. As Leroy, he scrunches up his face to make himself unrecognizable to a goon; as the Reverend Lennox Thomas, he sways with gleeful self-love while performing a guitar solo next to his pulpit; as Rufus, he tumbles like a bowling pin in the back of a pickup truck, his eyes wide with surprise yet flashing with anger. At the same time, the film revealed Richard as a disciple of Redd Foxx and other older black comedians of the Chitlin Circuit. In the roles of Rufus and the Reverend especially, he exhibits their ability to play with a cartoon of a character, to give an exaggerated performance but keep the language razor-edged and nimble.

And then there was all that was original to Richard's stand-up and that charged his performance as Leroy, the working-class everyman who can detect everyone's bullshit but his own. Sometimes Leroy acts dumb because that's how the powerful want him to act; sometimes he acts dumb because his appetites have led him astray; but even in his foolishness there is a winsome desire to figure out who he truly is, to solve the mystery of his potential. As one reviewer put it, Leroy might have been "a total heel, a coward, and an opportunist," but he was also "a personification . . . of our own venal (and human) instincts." We laugh not at the mayhem that Leroy causes—and that the film does not minimize—but at the all-too-human confusions within his character. Leroy wants to be both sensitive and macho, a man of the people and his own boss; he pulls on every string and watches his life unravel from all sides. Somehow Richard managed, as a performer, to stand within that confusion enough to make it sympathetic and stand apart from it enough to make it laughable.

When *Which Way Is Up?* wrapped in early March, Richard could not have been more happy with the film or the people who had helped him make it. He took out a two-page ad in the trade papers, thanking by name the 117 members of the production, from studio executive Thom Mount to the film's electricians, prop men, and makeup artists. He asked its still photographer for an eight-by-ten copy of every photograph she'd taken over the course of the production—all twenty-five hundred of them—so as to affix every aspect of the experience in his memory. "I'm going to save them for the rest of my life," he said. "This film is the most special thing I've ever done."

Whoever tuned into NBC at nine o'clock on May 5, 1977, saw this: Richard pacing through the studio in a tuxedo, musing fitfully over how he might program his own TV special. Within the space of an hour, he was beset by all manner of black folks. He was thumped by a churchwoman until he promised to give a guest slot to her televangelist pastor; waylaid by a fan who informed him that his special would flop without her favorite music group; challenged by two kids to stay away from clowns and offer something "socially relevant"; and, lastly, browbeaten by a posse of militants who demanded that he deliver a message of "black unity and dignity and pride" through a humorless script of their own devising. On *The Richard Pryor Special?*, Richard played himself as the befuddled artist, helpless before the demands of all the people he had to answer to. He was a quizzical fellow in the country of the confident.

In point of fact, while working on his first prime-time special, Richard had been fully in command. In the writers' room, he had fielded ideas—from his right-hand man, Paul Mooney; from head writer, Rocco Urbisci—then played with them until they were his own. "Every time a writer would come up with something," director

John Moffitt remembered, "Richard would turn it around and make it better. So ultimately everything filtered through Richard." He was determined to follow his own nose, to deliver a TV special that tossed variety show formulas out the window. As with his work on Lily Tomlin's specials, he wanted his audience to think, not just slap their knees. When Mooney suggested adding Maya Angelou to a sketch centered on Richard's wino, Richard embraced the idea—and kept embracing it even as Angelou composed a hard-hitting monologue, from the perspective of the wino's wife, about the humiliations her husband had endured and then inflicted on her through his abuse. For its first seven minutes, Richard's Willie is a wino in the tradition of stage drunkards; for its last four minutes, under the spell of Angelou's monologue, he is an alcoholic who tears his wife's heart to shreds. There is no effort to smooth out the difference or reconcile the viewer's conflicting emotions. "The comedy turns into a touching essay, with reverberations within reverberations," noted the *New York Times*.

Angelou's monologue wasn't typical for the special, but then again, nothing was: the tone of the program was unpredictable in the extreme. The special could be dreamy, as when a group of beautiful black women danced languorously in a soft-focus adaptation of Langston Hughes's poem "Harlem Sweeties." It could be high-concept absurd, as when an announcer presented "And the Pips"—the Pips without Gladys Knight—and the tuxedoed backup singers performed by themselves with impeccable nonchalance, the camera bouncing between them and an unattended microphone. It could be folksy-absurd through Mudbone, here materializing as a gray-haired NBC shoeshine who related coming out to California with a traveling circus of black midgets. Or it could be confusingly offbeat, as when Richard played Ugandan dictator Idi Amin, offering a rebuttal to news reports of his derangement before shooting the announcer and ordering the execution, by machine gun, of a roomful of NBC executives.

The machine-gunning of NBC execs was just one way that Richard's program took aim at television itself. The question mark in the special's title was well-earned; Richard was willing to question everything. For the special's cold opening, John Belushi played the captain of a slave ship, lustily cracking his whip while his shackled slaves row his boat forward. The captain selects one of his captives for some unnamed task, but the slave prefers to leap into the ocean and be eaten by sharks. "He got off easy," the captain says, and seizes another slave, played by Richard. Now he names the terrible fate for which the slave has been chosen: "You're going to NBC, you're going to do your own special!" Richard's face convulses in horror: "No!" Richard enjoyed toying with the notion that being a crossover star was a fate worse than death.

In his televangelist sketch, Richard took aim at the crossover urge from a different angle. As the Right Reverend James L. White, Richard arrived wearing an afro the size of Rhode Island, a white cape that belonged in the wardrobe of James Brown, and a white jumpsuit sparkling with gold sequins. Lit up with self-satisfaction, he danced down to a phone bank and delivered a fund-raising sermon on the wonder of money—when it boogalooed into his bank account and his alone. Reverend White was a glittering and glorious fraud, mocking those who told him to unload his hotels, boats, and flashy clothes: "That's easy for you to say because you have none of those things." And the surest sign of his fraudulence was the endpoint of his sermon, in which he went after the "crossover bucks," "the Billy Graham dollar." He petitioned to whites not on behalf of the "crippled children" or the "black orphans of Watts," appeals that were fund-raising duds. Instead, he asked whites to support the "BTAM," the Back to Africa Movement—and the phones rang off the hook. For all his soulful mannerisms, Reverend White was happy to exploit the idea of a black-free America if it could line his pockets. His last name was no coincidence.

From one angle, Richard took absolutely nothing seriously on his special. He spoofed militants and fellow travelers, preachers and soul sisters, Idi Amin and slave drivers, himself and the network that had written him a fat check. From another angle, Richard was absolutely serious about his commitments—as serious as a firing squad. There was nothing ironic about the Maya Angelou monologue or the Langston Hughes adaptation, which together honored the grit and beauty of black women; nothing ironic about the sketch in which a multiethnic ensemble of kids sang the Stevie Wonder refrain "this world was made for all men." It was a strange and unusual balance, this blend of irreverence and political seriousness, and Richard was willing to fight to achieve it. When John Belushi, the special's lone guest star, felt himself upstaged by the actor Falstaff Wilde and threatened to leave the special, Richard told him simply, "John, I'm not changing anything. I hope you do the show." Head writer Rocco Urbisci observed that once Richard thought a sketch was right, he was completely committed to it. "It's not about your ego, it's about the piece," Richard would say. "If you are contributing to the piece, then screw your ego. Just do the job."

Which Way Is Up? and *The Richard Pryor Special?* spoke to a unique moment in Richard's career. On-screen he was dramatizing the traps of success, the lures of "selling out" for the highest dollar or strongest ego boost. Meanwhile, off-screen he was trying to be as professional as a banker, and coming close enough to celebrate some of the biggest paydays of his life. He had found a way if not to bite the hands that fed him, then at least to nibble on them with pleasure. It all seemed to be working out beautifully. NBC was so happy with *The Richard Pryor Special?* that it asked him to deliver a series of hour-long programs, at the rate of three hundred thousand dollars each, and offered him the extraordinary sweetener of two million dollars to remain exclusively with the network for the next five years. Richard's manager, David Franklin, having driven a hard bargain, compared Richard with the kings of TV comedy: "We wanted Richard to have an exclusive personal services contract with the network similar to what Bob Hope, Jack Benny, and Milton Berle have had. Richard is the first Black performer to have such a deal." Richard celebrated the deal by presenting Franklin with the gift of a $52,000 Rolls-Royce Silver Shadow, complete with red leather interior.

It was a time to be generous and repay old debts. For Mother's Day weekend, Richard traveled back home to Peoria and gave his grandmother Marie the keys to a three-bedroom ranch house he'd bought for her in the suburb of Bartonville. He dressed in a suit and watched his fifteen-year-old son, Richard Jr., in a school play; he posed for *Jet* with Juliette Whittaker, his drama teacher from the Carver Center, both of them holding the Emmy he'd given her three years earlier. Marie exulted in how Richard had followed the advice she'd given him years before: "Now, baby, look. You're going up and you can come down a lot faster than you come up, so don't forget where you come from. Peoria is your home, these are your friends around here." "Richard Pryor Proves You Can Always Go Home Again," *Jet* sang in its headline.

The one jangly note to Richard's trip was supplied by the woman on his arm—who was not Pam Grier. As recently as March, Richard had told a reporter, "I adore [Pam Grier], she has meant so much to me. . . . I am thinking seriously about marriage"; the two would continue to figure as a couple in magazines through September. But their relationship had frayed. A clue to their difficulties was supplied by a response Richard gave, around the time of their trip to Barbados, to the question "What about women's rights?" "As far as I'm concerned," Richard told the interviewer, "somebody's got to be in charge. I'm the man and I'm in charge. That's the way I am and every woman that is mine will do what I say, my way." His competitiveness with Pam could take extreme forms. After Pam beat him in tennis, he refused to talk to her for a day; when she gave him pointers, he barked back, "I'm supposed to take instructions and have you beat my ass too? No way."

From Richard's point of view, Pam was too career-minded, too self-absorbed. "I was put off by how much I thought Pam believed that stardom belonged to her," Richard reflected later, with some regret. "In my head there was only one Numero Uno, and it wasn't her." From Pam's perspective, Richard was still an unknown quantity, a former addict who might yet relapse. When Richard pressed her to move in with him, she told him, "I don't feel safe living here yet because I don't know who you are." As Pam took her distance from Richard, the structure she'd brought to his life began to dissolve. There were fewer healthy breakfasts, fewer morning tennis matches, and fewer drug-free afternoons.

In Peoria, Richard was instead accompanied by Deboragh McGuire, a young black model whom he'd dated a year earlier; he introduced her to family and friends as his fiancée. Unlike Pam Grier, a proudly independent spirit, McGuire was accustomed to leaning on her man. When he met her, Richard recalled, she had been supported for years by a wealthy, older white man. Now, in Peoria, she was with a black version of the same.

Juliette Whittaker observed the two of them together and asked Richard, "Why her?"

"She's young," Richard said. "She loves me and she's young."

"All right, if that's your criteria," said Whittaker.

Whittaker tried to make conversation with McGuire but found her standoffish, always slipping away from a one-on-one chat. "She was afraid of me," Whittaker concluded later. "She was afraid that if I didn't like her, I would influence him. Why she thought I wouldn't like her is something only she could answer, because I approached her with the greatest neutrality."

The film *Blue Collar*, which preoccupied Richard from mid-May through mid-July 1977, was a profoundly double-edged experience. Artistically, it was a triumph, the culmination of Richard's quest to discover his capacities as a serious actor. Personally, it was a catastrophe, breaking his spirit and throwing him back into the hole of his cocaine addiction. Perhaps the most perplexing aspect of *Blue Collar*, for Richard, was that the genius behind it and the person who crushed his spirit were one and the same: screenwriter Paul Schrader, who was making his directorial debut with the film.

Schrader was a uniquely seductive and unnerving presence within the art colony of New Hollywood. He had grown up in a hardcore midwestern fundamentalist household where whippings were common and worldly entertainments forbidden; it was only as a junior in high school that he sneaked into his first movie. In his twenties, after leaving behind the priesthood for film school, Schrader became an unusual mix of stern Calvinist and voluptuary aesthete. Fascinated with the spectacle of fire and brimstone, of punishers and punishment, he wrote some of the most memorably lurid scenes in 1970s cinema—a hand pushed down a sink's garbage disposal and cut into pieces (*Rolling Thunder*); a cabbie on a murderous, blood-soaked rampage through a grimy New York City brothel (*Taxi Driver*). As an artist he was drawn, like Richard, to the darker corners of experience, but unlike Richard, he came to them with a heavy load of guilt and without the inclination to laugh at the inky abyss. His life and art were tightly coiled. On the butcher-block table where he wrote *Taxi Driver,* Schrader kept two props: a Smith & Wesson .38 (loaded when guests were not present) and a crown of thorns pounded out of brass, with thorns sharp enough to prick the skin and draw blood. A depressive and a control freak, he had gone through a period when he talked of blowing his brains out with the Smith & Wesson through a towel wrapped around his head. He liked big gestures but hated big messes.

When, in the summer of 1976, Schrader pitched Richard a starring role alongside Harvey Keitel and Yaphet Kotto in a heist drama about three auto workers who rob their union local, Richard leapt at the chance. He idolized Robert De Niro and was eager to work with the screenwriter who had conjured *Taxi Driver*'s Travis Bickle. Schrader and his brother Leonard went to work tailoring for Richard the part of Zeke Brown, a workingman twitchy with desires for a better life. They put Richard's comedy albums on heavy rotation and modeled Zeke's talk and rhythms after Richard's own. When they were done, Schrader felt it was inconceivable for anyone else to play the part. He and his brother had taken Richard's stage persona, the trickster undone by his appetites, and moved that persona to the gritty and clanging floor of a factory in Detroit, where it took on a new weight.

At its core, the film is a study in disintegration—the disintegration of friendship, the disintegration of idealism under the fire hose–like pressure of larger forces. The three workers at its center start with a complex and fragile bond. Richard's Zeke is the live wire and schemer, a man who emits a pure surge of riotous energy. Feeling his debts, he pads his tax form with a few extra kids and hopes the IRS will never darken his door; frustrated with a locker door that has injured his pinky, he breaks up a listless union meeting with a fuming, hilarious monologue on his tribulations. Jerry (Harvey Keitel) is the laugher and the worrier. He loves Zeke's jokes but would never crack a joke himself; he's not that loose or cynical yet, and is holding down a second job to make ends meet. Smokey (Yaphet Kotto) is the smartest and strongest of the three, and also the most watchful. While Zeke blows his top at the union meeting, Smokey leans back and absorbs the show; he's tight-lipped while others guffaw. It's never clear how much these three like one another, but it's clear that they *need* one another: who else can understand their gripes, the losing hands they've all been dealt? They're motivated to rob their union by a common sense of desperation, which, unfortunately, turns out to be a weak solvent. *Blue Collar* played as working-class tragedy: the heist goes bad, friendships go sour, a man is killed, solidarity proves an illusion. Upon its release, the *Village Voice* called it "the single most overtly political movie made for a major studio in a decade."

As Schrader moved the film into production, he found it most useful to have Richard on board. When other studios refused to touch such a hard-hitting project, it was Richard's risk-taking booster at Universal, Thom Mount, who agreed to cofinance and distribute it. And when Detroit's automakers froze out Schrader from filming on location in their auto plants, it was Richard who, indirectly, saved the day. The wife of the owner of the Checker Motor Company had loved *Silver Streak* and convinced her husband to open his plant in Kalamazoo for what promised, in their minds, to be a fun production.

The production was not fun. The contrast with Richard's last two films—where he had happily collaborated with the easygoing (and

A director leaning on his actors: Harvey Keitel, Paul Schrader, Yaphet Kotto, and Richard Pryor on the set of Blue Collar. *(Courtesy of Universal Pictures)*

black) Michael Schultz—could not have been more extreme. He told Schrader repeatedly, during the production, that it was "the most difficult, unpleasant and distasteful thing he had done in his life."

Schrader himself called the experience of making *Blue Collar* "unrelentingly unpleasant" and likened it to trench warfare. The set was oppressively hot, the feeling there explosive. Scuffles between the three leads were a daily occurrence. "Right after you said 'Cut,' a fight would start," remembered Schrader. After a few weeks, the three lead actors refused to speak with one another, and Schrader had to engage in "shuttle diplomacy, much like the Middle East, going from hotel room to hotel room, trailer to trailer, relaying each other's feelings toward each other because they won't speak directly." The liberal intake of cocaine on set did little to lower its temperature. Twice Richard smashed a chair over the heads of an actor during the shoot—once over the head of Kotto, who was a little drunk and just fell down; another time, over the head of George Memmoli, who filed a one-million-dollar lawsuit against Richard for a fractured skull. Around the time his three main actors stopped speaking with one another, Schrader started crying uncontrollably on set. He was checked by Richard, who said, "You pussy—are you gonna be a man or what?"

What had gone wrong? In some sense, the hostilities on set were part of Schrader's grand strategy for his film:

> As a first-time director, I knew I wasn't going to teach anybody how to act and I knew I wasn't going to get a big star actor. So I went to three actors, each of whom was pushing for his career and each of whom was not independently bankable but who as a group were somehow bankable. Then I took all three of these bantam roosters, dropped them into the same pit and made sure that nobody got out first. After a couple of weeks, you can imagine what it got like down in that pit, because they each wanted to put their stamp on the film. In fact, it was a clash of egos which got transferred, as it always does, onto race.

For Schrader, the actors' cockfight was an experiment in controlled sadism, conducted for art's sake. There was no small irony here: *Blue Collar* was a parable, he declared, about how "big organizations . . . get away with poorer working conditions, because everyone is sort of going at each other, everyone's trying to outmaneuver his fellow worker." As a director, he had adopted a similar strategy of provocation—setting actor against actor—without being in control of the consequences.

For Richard, the tension with his fellow actors was a shock to his system. In his previous films, he had been the king of the scene stealers, often playing to a straight man or a group of actors who gave his lines extra bounce. In *Blue Collar,* partly because Schrader encouraged the rivalry, his costars viewed every scene as a zero-sum game, with every point to Richard debited straight from their personal accounts.

Keitel and Kotto were, according to Schrader, "very trained, and very professional, and also very greedy. If they both ate and gorged themselves, and there was one piece of rice left on the table, they'd fight each other for it. So Richard had to come on the set every day absolutely prepared with improvs he'd worked out the night before, so he could fight. Because if he ever relaxed, Harvey or Yaphet would slip into the vacuum, and take the scene from him. And they would have no qualms about leaving him on the floor; they'd love that, as he would love to do it to them."

Apart from the matter of their competing egos, Richard and Harvey Keitel came to blows over their nearly opposite approaches to the craft of acting. Richard hated repeating himself and hated overthinking a role; he liked to surprise his director, his fellow actors, and even himself with a new twist on a scene. He exploded with energy and kept it up for four or five takes, then started waning. Keitel was more deliberate, and much slower to warm up. As a consequence, for his scenes with Richard, he needed to run through his scenes eight or nine times with a stand-in. Once Keitel was ready, the red-hot Richard would be brought in for his first take—and his ad libs would make a mess of Keitel's thoughtful preparation. At one point, after a particularly inspired ad lib on Richard's part, Keitel looked into the camera, went out of character, and deliberately spoiled the take. A split second later, Richard jumped on Keitel; fists flew; Richard's bodyguard and Schrader dove into the scrum to pull the actors off each other. It was just another muggy, hot-tempered day on the set of *Blue Collar.*

On top of Richard's struggles with his costars and director was his struggle with the very character he was playing, the once-rebellious but ultimately accommodating Zeke Brown. He thought that his character flipped too easily from trickster to sellout—that Zeke risked being seen as a mere weasel rather than as a black man in a bind. He worried that if black audiences were to reject Zeke, they would be rejecting him, too. Schrader wasn't sympathetic; he thought Richard worried too much about being likable, that he confused being an actor with being a public figure.

Ultimately, though, Richard reshaped the last act of the film in thoughtful and consequential ways. "If you're going to imply that I've done something," he suggested pointedly, "then the audience should see me do it so they aren't left to imagine it for themselves." A light went off in Schrader's head, and he instantly wrote an extra scene in which Zeke confronts the union boss, then is pushed back into a corner. (Richard played it beautifully; he captured the poetry of a defeated soul without saying a word, just in the way he shut his eyes, then folded his hands over his face.) And Richard did much to deepen his next scene, a slow-burning tour de force in which Zeke explains his choice to Keitel's character, Jerry. The scene was a mere three pages in the screenplay. It became five minutes long after the two actors elaborated it with their improvs. "If I gotta kiss ass," Zeke explains to Jerry, "I'm gonna pick the ass I'm gonna kiss, and it ain't gonna be the motherfuckin' police because they ain't gonna do nothing but shit in my face." The words spill out quickly, but there's a hush to his tone that suggests a new quality to his character: circumspection.

Schrader, one might say, was both a horrible director and a marvelous director—horrible in how he made his actors suffer, marvelous in how he used and framed what his actors gave him. He had the good judgment to let his actors treat his script, when it served them, as if it were merely guideline writing. With Richard, Schrader allowed him to "set sail from the script, just take a good jump," even though Richard's spontaneity meant that Schrader had less "coverage" and less latitude in the editing room: "better to cut for the performance," he concluded, "than have a smoothly cut film of blandness." These improvisations meant that *Blue Collar* had a different texture from Schrader's earlier films, a crackle to it. *New York*'s Molly Haskell observed that the film had "30 very funny lines," which was "30 more than in any previous Schrader screenplay."

All told, Schrader created a dark-tinted working-class world in which the contradictions of Richard's stage persona—his vulnerability and his aggression, his likability and his rascality, his seriousness and his refusal to take anything seriously—made perfect sense. In so many of his earlier movies, Richard played a cameo figure because there was no way to register the range of his stage act within the central premises of the film; he was an outlier. In *Blue Collar*, Richard had a setting that was close in spirit to the working-class Peoria in which he had grown up, the low-ceilinged world whose ethic he summed up as "work, pension, die." As an actor, he could tap into—and flash across—his many moods.

Take the shape-shifting scene in which destiny arrives at Zeke's household in the form of a nebbishy IRS agent. Zeke begins by playing the affable host: "Always glad to help the government," he says gamely. Then the agent sticks him with a $2,460 bill in penalties and late payments, and the fizz goes out of the conversation. Zeke looks queasy; he asks searchingly, "Man, where am I gonna get that kind of money? You're talking about my *life*." His wife brings in three of their neighbor's kids, thus upping their total to the six he's claimed as deductions, and he brightens for the performance: "start checking off them names," he instructs the agent. When the agent refuses to play along, Zeke's back to his vulnerable self: "I'm left with about thirty bucks after all the fucking bills are paid. Give me a break, will you, mister?" When the agent rebuffs him again ("I work for Uncle Sam"), the energy trapped within Zeke explodes: "Fuck Uncle Sam! They give the fuckin' politicians a break! Agnew and them don't pay shit! The workingman's gotta pay every goddamn thing!" He pushes the agent out the door, but before the agent has left the premises, Zeke seems exhausted by the explosion and flooded by worry. His voice breaks on his last line: "If I had the navy and the marines behind me, I'd be a motherfucker too!" With another actor playing Zeke, this scene might have merely reinforced the ugly stereotype of the black man as tax cheat. But Richard's Zeke was many things at once: a schemer, an open book, a powder keg, a wreck. It was fascinating to watch the play of his emotions.

Perhaps the greatest surprise in Richard's performance in *Blue Collar* was that, in tune with Schrader's own temperament, Richard exposed the depressive within himself. It was a strong facet of his self that, for all his candor onstage, he'd kept hidden from his audiences. In the film's most claustrophobic scene, the three friends sit on a couch after a night of bingeing on cocaine, booze, and women. For three long minutes, the camera remains fixed on them in their stillness. None of them looks the others in the eye; they're close enough to be touching but pointedly alone. When Richard's Zeke speaks, it's to confess, under his breath, his sense of inadequacy: "Sometimes I get so depressed. I start thinking about the shit I promised Carolyn and shit I ain't never going to be able to do, and I know a man's supposed to take care of his family. I never was good with money, man. I'm just always broke. I can't fuckin' get the knack of that shit. God knows I tried." Church bells toll in the distance; Keitel's Jerry puffs on a final cigar; Kotto's Smokey broods with heavy-lidded eyes. Zeke has named the desperation that is their common baseline. On that couch, they'll start plotting to rob their union and, by reaching for a

On the couch: Smokey (Yaphet Kotto), Jerry (Harvey Keitel), and Zeke (Richard Pryor) in Blue Collar*'s morning-after scene. (Courtesy of the author)*

dream of release, throw their old lives away.

The "couch scene" was the last scene filmed for *Blue Collar.* By that point, in mid-July, the movie's leads disliked one another so much they couldn't stand to make eye contact, and they disliked Schrader so much that they couldn't bear to film standard cutaway shots. The scene was shot, by necessity, in one seemingly endless take: Schrader's actors wouldn't give him anything else. After Schrader said, "Cut," Richard made for his car and drove off. The movie was over. In the can was an indelible film that took one of Richard's great themes onstage, self-sabotage, and projected it onto a broader canvas, until it seemed like self-sabotage was the worrisome fate of the American working class.

"It changed my life," Richard said of his work on *Blue Collar.* "I had a whole struggle going on—getting that deep, revealing that pain." According to Schrader, Richard later accused the director of putting him back on cocaine, a charge that Schrader dismissed as "a stretch." Still, it was true that working on *Blue Collar* was a shattering experience for him, one that left him uncertain as to who he was or what he would become. Reflecting on his career and the way forward, he told one interviewer that no line of work was safe. His own bruised feelings were part of a bigger picture: "the world around us is crumbling to make way for new life."

CHAPTER 22

Giving Up Absolutely Nothing

Los Angeles, 1977

In early July, after another exhausting day on the set of *Blue Collar*, Richard returned home for a meeting with the creative team behind his TV series. *The Richard Pryor Show* was set to premiere in two months, and the meeting was framed as your average brainstorming session; a reporter for *Newsweek* sat in. After batting around ideas for the first of ten shows, Richard cut everyone off. "I don't feel this in my heart. It just stops *here*," he said, pointing to his head. "Two years ago there was great shit on TV. Now people walk around being outraged, numb from the shock." He confessed to having an epiphany while watching comic Flip Wilson in a small role on *The Six Million Dollar Man* as a special guest star. Flip had recently been a giant, with his own TV show. Now he was chewed up and used up, a nonentity. "I don't want that to happen to me," Richard said.

He started thinking aloud. "You know something? I don't want to be on TV. I'm in a trap. I can't do this—there ain't no art." He broke into tears. "I bit off more than I can chew. I was turning into a greedy person. They give you so much money you can't refuse." The creative dynamic in the room, he felt, was all wrong: "I need a straight, square person like Bob Ellison"—the esteemed script doctor, an alum of *The Mary Tyler Moore Show*, who had punched up Richard's special and then been removed from the team for the series. "I hated Bob Ellison's motherfucking guts, but he made me work. Y'all love me, sit around nodding and smiling."

When a writer begged him to think about what the show might accomplish, Richard said, unforgettably, "You want to see me with my brains blown out? I'm gonna have to be ruthless here because of what it does to my life. I'm not stable enough. I don't want to drink and I don't want to snort and I can't do it no other way." He was pulling out of the show. That decision made, Richard announced it was time to relax. His housekeeper fetched a sock, filled with cocaine, that he kept hanging in his closet. Richard emptied it on the table and encouraged everyone to help themselves.

Over the next several days, Richard discovered that it wasn't so easy to walk away from NBC. His manager, David Franklin, had already invested a great deal of the network's first payment in a parcel of Atlanta real estate. NBC, reeling from an especially poor season, didn't cotton to having a hole in its new programming schedule. The show's writers, with their own hopes for the series, hired a plane to buzz over Richard's house with a banner that read "Surrender Richard." After several weeks of negotiations with the network, Richard agreed to continue with the show; NBC agreed to whittle his commitment down from ten episodes to four, with the possibility of more if Richard wanted. Somewhere in the shuffle of summer, too, NBC seems to have decided to hedge its bets with Richard's show: the network shifted it from 9:00 p.m. on Thursday to the more daunting time slot of 8:00 p.m. on Tuesday, where *The Richard Pryor Show* would now compete against ABC's two nostalgia-fueled hits, *Happy Days* and *Laverne and Shirley*. It was an unlikely matchup that one columnist called "electronic hari kiri" for NBC: Richard facing the Fonz in America's family hour. The series moved forward, with the first episode to be taped in late August.

Meanwhile, Richard's personal life was as vexed as his professional life. Around the time of *The Richard Pryor Special?* he had been balancing three different women: Pam Grier, Deboragh McGuire, and aspiring actress Lucy Saroyan. Once, all three of them had converged at his home to meet his grandmother Marie, who was visiting, and had sat chatting with her in his den while Richard hid in his bedroom like a little boy. Afterward, Richard asked Marie which one he should marry. The queen maker of the Pryor family tossed out the premise of the question. "I wouldn't give a nickel for any of those bitches," she said.

By August, Richard's love life had become still more crowded and confused. Pam remained in the picture, albeit at the edges of the frame; Deboragh had become his "fiancée," then had fallen away, but was alive in his mind; Lucy was working to remodel his home and was still enmeshed in his affairs; a new woman, Lucy's friend and assistant Jennifer Lee, had caught his eye; and then there were many more women who were partners for a night. When Jennifer Lee began working on Richard's home remodel, she noticed that, on most mornings, a different woman would straggle out of his bedroom and out of his house, never to be seen again. For his part, producer-writer Rocco Urbisci remembered that, every day on the set of *The Richard Pryor Show*, a new woman would materialize at his office, announcing that Richard had promised her a job as a production assistant. Urbisci eventually created "Satin Doll," a production number that required comely ladies as dancers in its jazz nightclub, in order to put this company of women to work as extras on the TV show.

Somehow Richard kept up appearances on the publicity tour that he undertook in August to promote the release of *Greased Lightning*, the first film he'd carried. To the outside world, he was not a ticking bomb but a "new black superstar," "one of Hollywood's hottest properties." If *Silver Streak* had sparked mainstream America's curiosity with Richard, *Greased Lightning* eased him into its good graces. Ultimately, producer Hannah Weinstein had created, over the objections of director Michael Schultz, a quite old-fashioned piece of Americana, a heartwarming Capraesque fable about a little guy from a small town who bucks the system with the help of friends and family. *Time*'s Richard Schickel wrote, in a representative review, that "it is impossible to believe that any real life could so unerringly follow the classic lines of so many biopix past. The cheerfully determined young man struggling to support his family while trying to fulfill his ambitions, the opposition from the Establishment in his field, the early heartbreaks, the ultimate triumph—all this is the familiar stuff of a hundred celluloid dreams."

Yet it was also true that Richard put a wry spin on those old formulas. He gave *Greased Lightning* a bottom note of black pride and inflected the movie with just enough of his loose-limbed energy to make it an invigorating ride. "There is not a more likable movie currently on view than *Greased Lightning,*" concluded Schickel in the same review that noted its slavish embrace of biopic conventions. Filmgoers agreed: the movie went on to gross almost triple its four-million-dollar budget. Warner Bros. took notice, too: the studio signed Richard to a contract for a minimum of four films at a million dollars per film, an impressive pendant to his lucrative contract with Universal.

In interviews of the time, Richard managed to radiate an alternately humble and embattled confidence. He was an artist following his own path, whatever the consequences. Sure, "NBC would love to make me a household word. . . . But I'm not interested in being a household word. I'm interested in my art." And yes, Warner Bros. had signed him to a multipicture deal, but "[i]f I disappoint them, it'll become a *one*-picture deal." With so much at stake, then, was he taking a risk by splitting himself between comedy and more serious acting jobs? "Hell, the atom split. Why shouldn't I?" he asked.

At this peak moment of his career, he still carried within him the sense of being an underdog—still felt as if he was flirting with oblivion. "Hey, you know what I feel like?" he told the *New York Times.* "You ever drop a dime and can't find it? That's me, the dime you can't find. Rolling down the road, and landing in the hobo's pocket." He lit up mischievously at the comparison. It tickled him to think of himself as a hobo's treasure, something lost and barely found.

Never edit yourself in these meetings," Richard instructed his writers, in the conference room at NBC's Burbank studios. "Please don't do that." His writers followed Richard's gonzo lead: the four episodes of *The Richard Pryor Show* constitute one of the oddest cultural experiments ever to be sponsored by a major network. NBC's Dick Ebersol, the young executive who had worn down Richard's resistance to TV through an extended charm offensive, later turned on the very show he'd labored so hard to bring into existence. By the time Richard delivered the fourth episode, Ebersol told the show's director, lividly, "I'll never work with him again."

And yet: Ebersol couldn't have asked for a stiffer blast of fresh air in NBC's prime-time lineup. The *New York Times* judged it a "cause for wonder" that "so much social complexity could be presented as comedy to a mass audience." The *Washington Post* praised *The Richard Pryor Show* as "the most perilously inventive comedy hour to hit prime time in years." At its best, Richard's series was weirdly riveting and brilliant. At its worst, it was unpredictable to the point of seeming purposeless. And sometimes its best and its worst were one and the same. TV critics couldn't agree on which sketches worked, perhaps because few of them "worked" in the standard ways. A sketch that one critic hailed as a "devastating, bittersweet episode—beautifully played, beautifully designed" could register, with another critic, as mere "icky wistfulness." Richard was following his muse and sowing bewilderment in his wake.

In this experiment, Richard was supported by a multiracial ensemble recruited by Paul Mooney from the pool of stand-ups at the Comedy Store, Richard's preferred club for trying out new material. Some in the ensemble—Robin Williams, Sandra Bernhard, Tim Reid (*WKRP in Cincinnati*), Martha Warfield (*Night Court*)—later achieved some measure of fame in film or on TV; at the time, all of them were scuffling comedians. "He loved them," said director John Moffitt of the feeling between Richard and the rest of the cast. "He tried to give those comics as much presence as possible. And they loved him." For Richard, the dynamic harkened back to his apprentice days at New York's Improv, where he larked onstage until the early hours of the morning, riffing and rolling. Tim Reid remembered a feeling of pure discovery on set: "We came in with no structure, no rules. Most of the stuff was improv. We would have a theme, and we would all come out, and we would just go. And they would run the tape. Sometimes the tape would run for thirty minutes and then Moffitt had to figure out how to get a sketch out of it." The mood on set was devil-may-care—and yet the actors knew that the devil did, in fact, care. Reid continued: "We all knew that we were too far. We were beyond the point of the network being able to accept and absorb what we were doing. You know, they sent spies on the set. They had guys dressed in street clothes to come to our rehearsals to try and find out what the hell we were doing. And we would always pick them out. We would laugh and make fun of them."

It's not hard to imagine what worried the cautious-minded at NBC. In "Star Wars Bar," the first sketch of the first show, Richard dropped Mudbone into the *Star Wars* cantina, where he was a bartender ministering to a pack of intergalactic irregulars. (Director George Lucas loved Richard's comedy so much that he loaned the show the actual masks from the film.) The sketch brought the raw atmosphere of the Famous Door, the Pryor family's bar in 1940s Peoria, to a galaxy far, far, away. Brushing up against a troglodyte in a monk's hood, Richard's bartender declares, "You look just like a nigger from Detroit I know." The troglodyte grunts and motions to his companion, an imp with a bald and horned head. "Oh, I see," returns Richard. "Well, why don't you go upstairs and get a room? . . . If that's your type, well alright." Later, a huge, tentacled creature starts devouring Richard, who calls desperately for his bouncer, Fuzz, to remove him from its grip. Rescued, he suggests to Fuzz, "Take him in the back room. And while you're back there, get a little octopussy." Suffice it to say that, over on ABC, the Fonz was not making double entendres about interspecies sex.

In the show, Richard was drawn to explore the full spectrum of off-color humor: the silly, the risqué, the politically pungent, the macabre. In a spoof of spaghetti Westerns, a smart-alecky villain asks Richard's gunslinger, "How's your ass?" To which Richard replies, after a pregnant pause, "You mean my donkey? It wasn't nice of you boys to shoot my donkey." In "The 40th President of the United States," Richard played the first black president at a press conference, trying to project an air of competence. The sketch begins as a satire of political doubletalk (the neutron bomb is a "neo-pacifist weapon"), but evolves into an exercise in ever-more-improbable racial fantasies: under President Pryor, the jazz of Miles Davis will be piped into space; there will be more black NFL quarterbacks; Huey Newton will be head of the FBI. White reporters wriggle in their seats. A southern newsman uses his question to launch the ultimate insult—"Now, after your tenure, if your mother goes back to being a maid, right, will your momma do my house?"—and the presidential press conference degenerates into a miniature race riot, with black and white reporters at one another's throats.

And then there was Bo Jaws, a faith healer preying on the poor, sick, and maimed in a bayou tent revival. "Let Bo Jaws handle it!" shrieked Richard, in a Rastafarian fright wig and with a crazed gleam in his eye, in the strangest sketch of the show's premiere. "Handling it," for Bo Jaws, means pitching a cripple out of a wheelchair and telling her to crawl; molesting a pair of Siamese twins (they complained they never had any fun); and putting a brown paper bag over the head of an ugly woman. Like the Reverend James L. White from Richard's TV special, Bo Jaws is a fraud, but he has been so consumed by his own fraudulence that there's no longer any daylight between him and his act. The sketch closes with Bo Jaws exorcising the devil within himself by slicing his body three times with a knife, wrapping the "devil's serpent" around his neck, and kissing a live snake. (Urbisci swapped out the fake one used in rehearsal, unbeknownst to Richard.) Bo Jaws's congregation moans and writhes in ecstatic worship as the sketch fades out; there's no end in sight to their pain. "As a vitriolic lampoon of pseudo-religious fervor this is not particularly funny," wrote the *Washington Post* appreciatively, "but it is unquestionably alarming." The sketch made a singular impression: comedian Dave Chappelle, who had his own struggles with television as a medium, later told Urbisci that it was his favorite.

As Richard was pushing his show to the edge of what network TV might handle, he was also pushing his own body to the brink—drinking and snorting just as he had predicted. He had a habit of filling

"Let Bo Jaws handle it!": the twisted imagination of The Richard Pryor Show. *(Courtesy of the author)*

up a water glass with vodka (no ice) and draining it over the course of the meeting in the writers' room. Cocaine, though it could be found everywhere on set, was especially plentiful in his dressing room. Sometimes he finished the day passed out on the floor. While filming "Star Wars Bar," he delayed getting into his makeup, then was so blotto with the cameras rolling that he spoiled much of a first run-through of the scene. John Moffitt pleaded with Richard for one more take; Richard felt he couldn't do it, then reluctantly agreed. A few days later, when Moffitt showed Richard a meticulously edited version of the sketch, Richard was shocked. "I don't remember doing it," he told Moffitt. He had ad-libbed, with fitful brilliance, then blacked out.

And yet it would be wrong to conclude that Richard was less than fully invested in his show. When informed that the first episode had run eighty-five thousand dollars over budget—in part because, with "Satin Doll," he confected a glossy twenty-minute mini-movie complete with song-and-dance numbers in period style—Richard turned to his manager and deadpanned: "write a check." The check was written.

Though Dick Ebersol tried to protect the first episode of *The Richard Pryor Show* from network interference, there was a limit to Ebersol's power, and Richard breached it with the visual joke set to open the program. As with his special, Richard wanted to launch his show by making fun of TV itself. At first he and his writers came up with the idea of NBC executives pressing Dr. Frankenstein to operate on Richard and a white man. The doctor would hook up their brains and, after a mysterious medical procedure, the white man would rise and talk jive; Richard would rise and say, in a voice closer to Andy Williams's than his own, "I'm so glad to be on TV." Richard ditched the Frankenstein idea in favor of a more pointed treatment of what exactly network TV threatened to do to him:

> **RICHARD** [*in close up*]: Good evening, ladies and gentleman, and welcome to *The Richard Pryor Show*. . . . People say, "Well, how can you have a show? You've got to compromise, you've got to give up everything!"
>
> Is that a joke or what? Well, look at me. I'm standing here naked.
>
> [*Camera pulls back to take in the top half of Richard's body; he's wearing no clothes.*]
>
> I've given up absolutely nothing.
>
> [*Camera pulls back to take in Richard's entire body; instead of having genitalia, he's as smooth and sexless as a doll.*]
>
> So enjoy the show!
>
> [*Richard breaks into a wide grin; theme music starts up; Richard starts wincing; his grin now looks tortured.*]

NBC's West Coast office had originally approved the segment in a slightly less explicit form—without the lines about "standing here naked" and "not giving up anything"—but it refused to air the final version. The show's producers appealed the decision by sending the video to the New York office of NBC chief censor Herminio Traviesas, who was categorical in his judgment: the sketch was unacceptable in any form; it had to be cut. A vice president of broadcast standards explained the logic of the decision: "We don't do genital jokes. . . . [W]e just think television is not quite ready for that. It's a matter of either compromising our principles or his production company realizing its responsibility to present programming that is suitable for television."

Richard was in no mood for compromise, either. Four years earlier, he had seen Lily Tomlin locked in a similar skirmish, fighting for the integrity of her own show, but while Tomlin battled her network as if in a chess game, Richard's preferred strategy was to threaten to go nuclear. On the Monday before his first show was set to air, he held a press conference at NBC studios in which he screened the censored segment and said he was prepared to walk away from the series unless NBC reconsidered its decision: "if we can't find a reasonable means of dealing with it, then Tuesday night's (taping of the second episode) probably will be the last. Everybody will say I'm crazy if I quit, that I'm the crazy nigger who ran off from NBC, but this is stifling my creativity and I can't work under these conditions." When a journalist asked whether NBC shouldn't have some control over what it aired, Richard broke up the audience with his reply: "They do, and that's why they're Number 3." Over the next two days, NBC didn't budge, and neither did Richard: he refused to create an alternative opening segment.

Still, the offending segment did air—on the local CBS affiliate in LA, which covered the dustup in its early-evening and late-night newscasts. The press coverage favored Richard. "Maybe if NBC hired Farrah Fawcett-Majors they'd ask her to cut her hair," wrote *Washington Post* critic Tom Shales. "Maybe they'd give Nureyev a desk job. Maybe if they reunited The Beatles it would be on condition that they promise not to sing. It makes as much sense as giving Richard Pryor a prime-time hour of comedy and then expecting him to be safe, sane, and squeaky-clean."

As always for Richard, censorship was felt as both a political and a personal affront. He told *Jet*, "I'd like to get the names of these people who say they're protecting the public by trying to prevent my form of communication. That's a political decision, not a moral one." "It's an insult to me," he told Shales. "[W]e don't intend to do any further work for NBC if we can't get it on the air the way we do it. They're treating us like children." A more judicious soul might have looked at the first episode of *The Richard Pryor Show* and marveled at how much—references to "octopussy" and a threesome with Siamese twins!—had slipped past the censor's blank gaze. But Richard had an all-or-nothing approach to his art; he would not back down, even though the battles took their toll. "All of us could use some bandages," said a NBC executive. "If each program causes this much consternation, I don't see how any of us can continue."

The following week was, relatively speaking, a cooling-off period for Richard and NBC. The second episode of *The Richard Pryor Show* did not generate another battle between him and the network; it was outré but not risqué. It also gave the network a sense of how little it could use one episode of *The Richard Pryor Show* to predict the next. "Every piece that Richard did was different," director John Moffitt observed. "You will find that in every variety show there's a safe corner, we go to this little element week after week . . . and that never happened with Richard. And I don't think it would have happened if we did the ten shows or more." Averse to the usual variety show formulas, Richard had no interest in recruiting "special guest stars" or in generating the sort of easy chatter that other shows used as filler or segues. His show was structured instead like a collage, with the viewer left to make his or her own connections between the parts and the whole. NBC's executives might have questioned the entertainment value of such a collage-like approach, but its censors put up no roadblocks.

The one sketch that did rile the network was also the most memorable segment of the second show: a satire of rock fandom so disturbing that it was cousin to the midnight movie emanations of Richard's Berkeley period. In "Black Death," Richard plays the leader of a glam-metal band, modeled after KISS, whose musicians make their stage entrance by popping out of coffins. His bandmates are ghoulish monks in cowls, robes, and white pancake makeup. Richard sports a thick reddish mane of hair, teased out with spikes, and his body is encased in a skintight purple and metallic costume that is at once ludicrous and heavily armored. After strutting his stuff onstage, Richard's singer proceeds to exterminate his audience; the sketch is about overkill, in every sense of the word. "I've got some reds, they're bad for you," he sings in a voice that is halfway between Dylan and Hendrix, then throws bags of poison pills at his audience. Bodies fall limp to the ground. Richard's singer sprays toxic gas at the audience, and more bodies fall. Then he machine-guns the crowd until there is no one left standing. All the while, Black Death kicks out the jams, and every audience member bops until he or she drops. Surveying the final pile of corpses, Richard's singer mutters the stock countercultural response to the world's strangeness: "Far out." But there was nothing stock to the sketch. It took the logic of heavy metal's fascination with the dark side and stretched it to the grimmest of conclusions.

In its original form, the sketch was harsher still. Richard and his writers had wanted to start it with a public hanging—with the promoter asking for a volunteer from the audience to be hanged, and with the audience watching as a young man was sacrificed for the show. The noose went up, the banner for Black Death came down, and the music began. NBC objected, understandably. "We crossed the line on that one," Rocco Urbisci reflected. "You can't hang somebody on TV."

Richard did not threaten to quit over this edit. The sketch was still pungent and brutal—a dream of murdering your audience for loving you too much, too blindly, too voraciously. It was not strictly autobiographical (Richard was a fan of jazz and soul music, not heavy metal), but it spoke to the aggression that was never far from the

Ludicrous and armored: Pryor as the lead singer of Black Death. (Courtesy of the author)

surface of his stand-up after the late 1960s. Whenever his audience seemed to be enjoying itself too easily, Richard felt something must be wrong. Often, whether motivated by cruelty or anger or simply a desire for his version of a dynamic equilibrium, he searched for his audience's weak spot and, finding it, lashed out.

On the night of September 18, when Richard took the stage of the Hollywood Bowl as a headliner of the "Star-Spangled Night for Rights," the event had, according to one journalist, "all the makings of a 'cabaret' version of Woodstock." Less than fifteen minutes later, when Richard ended his ten-minute performance by asking the audience to "kiss my happy, rich black ass," the benefit concert was closer to "a 'cabaret' version of Altamont." The good vibes had dispersed; a night of unity had turned into a hot, steaming mess. Many in the crowd booed or shouted curses: "Richard Pryor, you just committed professional suicide!" "Kiss your ass, hell! I'd like to put a hot poker up it!" Others cheered a provocateur who, before he had dismissed the crowd as self-serving "faggots," had spoken bravely about the joy of gay sex and exposed the fault lines of the gay rights movement. And still others sat pole-axed, trying to grasp how, in coming to the Hollywood Bowl, they had taken a detour into the Twilight Zone. "In more than 14 years of covering the great, near-great and terrible of show business, I have never seen anything like it," wrote John Wasserman in the *San Francisco Chronicle.* "To call what happened bizarre would not, for me, do it justice. It was like watching a person come unglued in front of you and then, as in a cartoon, disappear piece by piece."

Richard's meltdown at the Hollywood Bowl was, in its own way, a vintage Pryor performance: artful and impulsive, merciless and hapless, and above all, devilishly attuned to the hidden dynamics of the moment. The driving force behind the benefit concert had been the Save Our Human Rights Foundation, a San Francisco group composed largely of gay professionals, formed in response to the antigay crusade spearheaded by Anita Bryant and other Christian conservatives in Florida. The foundation hoped to do for gay rights what the American Cancer Society had done for cancer: "to educate people, but in a nice glossy way." Dignity was of utmost concern. When the show's producer discovered that one of his performers, a comedy act, would satirize Anita Bryant directly, the act was removed from the bill; the appeal for "human rights" meant always aiming for the moral high ground.

Until Richard strolled onstage, the foundation's "Star-Spangled Night" had occupied that rarefied perch without anyone questioning the thinness of the air in the upper altitudes. The seventeen thousand people assembled at the Bowl, mostly gay men, sang the national anthem "with the volume and fervor usually associated with conventions of the veterans of foreign wars." Actor Christopher Lee launched the evening's entertainment by reciting, to the swell of an orchestra, a solemn monologue titled "The Ascent of Man" ("What is life? . . . it is to be free . . . every life shall be a song"). Performers before Richard avoided specific mention of gay life, much less gay

Unglued: Pryor asking his Hollywood Bowl audience to kiss his "happy, rich black ass." (Courtesy of AP Photo/Lennox McLendon)

sex; in the words of another observer, it was "an evening of unspoken assumptions." Richard's friend Lily Tomlin came the closest to striking a direct chord when she reminisced about the 1950s as a time "when sex was dirty . . . and, of course, no one was gay, only shy."

Over the course of the evening, Richard grew increasingly allergic to the atmosphere of moral superiority. He despised euphemisms, and yet here he was headlining a gay rights benefit that couldn't put the word *gay* in its title. He felt the victim of a bait and switch; like at least one other black artist on the program, he'd originally been asked to perform for a human rights rally, pure and simple. Other resentments gathered on top of the first one. He scanned the sea of faces in the audience and spotted only a handful of black people, which alarmed him. And he noticed that the Lockers, a young black dance group on the bill, kept suffering from poor treatment. When the dancers asked stagehands for help with the lights, the stagehands paid no notice; when the dancers performed their high-spirited moves onstage—one jumped over six chairs in a single bound—the audience sat in their seats. An hour later, just before Richard was set to perform, the formerly indifferent stagehands leapt to fix the lights for two white ballet dancers; and the formerly blasé audience applauded them, with their delicate pas de deux from *Le Corsaire*, as if they were "some bad motherfuckers." Backstage Richard saw the fire marshal dress down a Locker for setting off a small explosive onstage as a special effect, and he saw the show's promoters refuse to come to the dancer's defense. To Richard, all this was racism in action. He simmered, and awaited his turn onstage.

When he walked in front of the audience, finally, Richard didn't speak for a little while; he prowled back and forth like a pent-up animal. Then he pounced with a one-liner that had tongues wagging across West Hollywood the next day. "I came here for human rights," he said, "and I found out what it was really about was about not getting caught with a dick in your mouth." The crowd erupted in laughter. "You don't want the police to kick your ass if you're sucking the dick, and that's fair," Richard continued. "You've got the right to suck anything you want!" With three sentences, Richard had outflanked all the other performers on the bill—some of whom, like Lily Tomlin, had open ties to the gay community—by stripping away the airy talk of "human rights." He had brought into the open the basic demand of the gay struggle: sexual freedom in the face of police harassment.

Then he went even further. "I sucked one dick," he said. "Back in 1952. Sucked Wilbur Harp's dick. It was beautiful, but I couldn't deal with it. Had to leave it alone." The crowd roared. Richard minced no words and spared few details: "It was beautiful because Wilbur has the best booty in the world. Now I'm saying booty to be nice. I'm talking about ass-hole. Wilbur had some good ass-hole. And Wilbur would give it up so good and put his thighs against your waist. That would make you come quick." With that confession, Richard became perhaps the first major Hollywood celebrity to talk graphically about his own positive experience of gay sex—and certainly the first to do so in front of tens of thousands of people. (He himself had talked, on '*Craps*,' of "fucking the faggot," but it was a sheepish confession, not a proud one.) Having spoken of the joy of gay sex, Richard then spoke of the romance it kindled in him: "I was the only motherfucker that took Wilbur roses. Everybody else was bullshitting. I took Wilbur [the roses] and said, 'Here, dear.'" Again the crowd hooted in delighted disbelief.

Now that he had worked the audience into the palm of his hand, Richard became indecisive. He appeared diffuse, addled by some combination of drugs, alcohol, and the complexity of his feelings. Speaking softly into the microphone, as if musing to himself, he asked, "How can faggots be racists?" He recounted what he'd observed with the Lockers—the disinterest of the crowd, the intimidation of the fire marshal, the disrespect of the show's promoters—and then his tone shifted. His anger grabbed hold of him, and he aimed pure scorn at the audience: "I hope the police catch you motherfuckers and shoot your ass accidentally, because you motherfuckers ain't helpin' niggers at all." Howls rose up from the crowd. He won back some of their sympathy by reminding them that, while everyone else had "skirted the issue," he was ready to say, "I have sucked a dick." Then he threw that sympathy away with a rant that pitted women's rights against welfare rights ("Motherfuck women's rights. The bitches don't need no rights. What they need to do is pay the people on welfare."). The crowd booed in response, and Richard goaded them back: "Yeah, get mad. 'Cause you're going to be madder than that when [Police Chief] Ed Davis catches you motherfuckers coming out of here in the lot."

It was hard to tell where Richard's allegiances lay. Was he on the side of the police or the side of sexual freedom? Or simply on the side of Richard? "I wanted to test you to your motherfuckin' soul," he continued, as if the anger he'd unleashed was a thought experiment on his part, a trial he'd designed to winkle out the truth in their hearts. The gay people in the audience, he determined, were the same gay people who, a decade earlier, had looked the other way at the black community's desperation: "When the niggers were burning down Watts, you motherfuckers were doing what you wanted on Hollywood Boulevard, didn't give a shit about it." With that, he hoisted his backside into the air, asked the crowd to kiss it, then walked off to a chorus of boos, a smattering of applause, and thousands of sullen faces. The show's choreographer came onstage and cried in anguish, "I hope you realize that was unplanned and everybody involved is very, very embarrassed about it." He was promptly booed, too. A producer came on to apologize, and he was shouted down as well. Richard had left a mess that no apology could clean up.

It took two weeks for the firestorm sparked by Richard's performance to blow through the LA and Bay Area press. (The *Los Angeles Times* devoted over a full page to the original event, then ran seventeen letters in two installments in response to it.) The bad feeling lingered. Among the commentators, most numerous were the moralists who judged Richard an obscene homophobe who should never have been permitted onstage at the Bowl. "His 'street' language was abusive, filthy, and racist," wrote one audience member, typically, in the *Los Angeles Times*. "It takes a certain talent, genius (if you will) to insult 17,000 people—black, white, male, female, straight, gay, rich and poor—at one time." Others thought Richard wrong in his sweeping comments about gay racism. "[M]ost of us in the gay rights movement (which does not include all gay men and women) were previously involved in other civil rights movements such as those for black and women's liberation," an activist explained. "Now we are fighting for our own rights and we need support, especially from those we have supported in the past."

Yet Richard did have his defenders among the gay community's outliers, those further from its power centers, who praised him for forcing the community to examine its own blind spots. A member of

Bay Area Gay Liberation, a group to the left of the Save Our Human Rights Foundation, wrote that "Much too often we see the gay rights movement trying only to get a bigger piece of the pie for ourselves—only too willing to do so at the expense of Third World peoples and of women"; the campaign against Anita Bryant had failed, he observed, for precisely this reason. A *Los Angeles Times* reader wrote, on a more personal note: "Being a black homosexual and living here practically all my life, I can say that the California homosexual is the most extreme of bigots. He hates blacks, fats, women, and himself most of all. Pryor's actions were crude, but sadly true. If one refuses to believe, let any person who is fat, black, ugly or female try going to a gay club alone." (In fact, as LA's gay activists noted to their displeasure on other occasions, the city's biggest gay disco admitted few nonwhites or women, and its gay baths tended to have a "pull up your shirt" rule that excluded any man who wasn't well toned.) Lily Tomlin was closest to this third camp: she felt that gay men tended to look down upon lesbians, and she appreciated how Richard had asked everyone to consider their prejudices. "When you hire Richard Pryor, you get Richard Pryor," she'd told the show's producer before the event. When her prophecy was fulfilled, she was bemused rather than horrified.

Lost in the swirl of postmortems was the taboo Richard had broken and the fact of his early life that he had revealed. Part of the silence is understandable: a family newspaper, for instance, was not about to quote a line like "Wilbur had some good ass-hole." But other distortions were more complicated. The outrageousness of Richard's remarks seems to have inspired either mishearing or disbelief. Several journalists reported that Richard had said that he experimented with a gay man and "didn't like it"—a twisting of his actual remark that it was "beautiful" but that he "couldn't handle it." *Jet*'s correspondent called Wilbur Harp a "presumably fictitious Midwestern homosexual," as if a male sex partner for Richard Pryor had to be a figment of the comic's crazed imagination.

Yet Richard was not confecting his story out of thin air. According to his friend Cecil Grubbs, Wilbur Harp was a gay teenager in Peoria in the 1950s, at a time when there was little in the way of a gay community there. In the late 1950s, he and Richard whiled away the hours at the Blue Shadow bar in Peoria. In the mid-1960s, according to Harp's brother Hillis, Richard and Wilbur crashed for weeks at the same apartment in Chicago, the would-be comedian bunking with the would-be cosmetologist. Even after Richard moved to his Northridge estate in 1976, the two were still close enough for Richard to invite Wilbur out to Los Angeles for a weeklong vacation. Whether or not Richard and Wilbur truly had sex is probably unknowable—Harp is dead, so he cannot speak for himself—and is perhaps less important than the fact that Richard *wished*, on that night, for it to be true. He was seeking to convey something about himself and the world in which he was raised, a world distant from the affluent gay audience at the Bowl. "In my neighborhood whatever you were was cool," he said in a related 1975 interview. "You could be a thief, murderer, or closet queen. There was a faggot . . . that turned more tricks than the prostitutes but nobody ridiculed him. Dudes avoided him during the day but could be seen creepin' around his house late at night. It didn't matter. We were all part of a community."

Sometimes, as at the Hollywood Bowl, Richard slammed into the fact that he wasn't in Peoria anymore and that he had lost that community; that no matter how large his estate in the San Fernando Valley, he would continue to feel out of place; that no matter how high he rose in Hollywood's pecking order, his sensibility would never match up with that of its right-thinking, liberal precincts. The debacle at the Bowl left him reeling, besieged. Several days later, he continued to justify himself to the *Sentinel*, LA's black newspaper, by emphasizing how poorly the Lockers had been treated: "My feeling is that they cannot pay me enough to keep quiet when something is wrong. And this was wrong." (The Lockers, for their part, kept out of the fracas.) As the controversy raged on, Richard did not calm the waters by issuing an apology of his own.

Instead, Richard continued to act out the polarities of his Hollywood Bowl performance in his own life. In the week following the gay rights benefit, he made two impulsive and startling commitments. The first was to Deboragh McGuire, whom he proposed to and married within the space of a few days. The second was to an experimental piece of gay theater, which he included in his prime-time TV show in total defiance of NBC.

CHAPTER 23

Can I Speak to God Right Away?

Los Angeles, New York City, Peoria, 1977–1978

When a star in a galaxy takes on too much mass, it begins to collapse into itself. Its core becomes weaker until it can no longer support the weight of its outer layers, which fly into the core and crush it. Sometimes, though, in one of nature's mysteries, the star's life does not end there: the collapse touches off a fresh nuclear reaction, a process of runaway fusion that flings the outer layers back out into the universe. A supernova is born, a galaxy illuminated.

This seems a fair description of Richard Pryor's life starting in mid-September 1977. He was consumed in the flurried motions of his own collapse: he married one woman while falling in love with another; he finished off his TV show with two episodes that careened between slapstick, satirical diatribe, experimental theater, and the most tender of pantomimes; he wasted himself on drugs to the point of hospitalization and near death. And then, through a chain reaction that remained mysterious even to him, he produced a brilliant account of his life in the form of a low-budget, seventy-eight-minute film that dispensed with all the frills of Hollywood moviemaking in favor of giving the audience a single man alone on a stage with just his microphone, his talent, and his demons for company. *Richard Pryor: Live in Concert* defeated *Superman* at the box office and gave birth to more comics, good and bad, than any other film in history. It even gave birth to a new Richard.

Richard's wedding, on September 22, 1977, was both a product of his inner chaos and an attempt to manage it. For over two years, he and the twenty-five-year-old Deboragh McGuire had been on-again, off-again lovers. In August, during one of their frequent "off" periods, Richard had dreamed of prying her from the grip of her other lovers, of possessing her once and for all. Yet he was curiously passive, relying on the mechanisms of his celebrity to reconnect with her. In a late-summer interview with *Jet*, he used the magazine to put out a feeler in her direction. "There is a very special lady out there who I'm still really in love with. It's tough trying to get over her," he said, hoping that Deboragh might read the interview and discern that he was talking about her.

In the meantime, Richard was drawn to the sharp, tough-minded Jennifer Lee, who was supervising his home renovation. He felt that she'd "seen things," that she'd tapped into experiences beyond him. In fact, Jennifer had grown up in an affluent pocket of upstate New York, the daughter of a lawyer father who defended civil rights workers and a mother who traced her lineage back to white abolitionist John Brown. Jennifer came by her tough-mindedness honestly. During her childhood, her mother had suffered violent mood swings, and self-medicated with Miltown and cocktails. In the early 1970s, the family had fragmented, her mother institutionalized after a psychotic break, her father traveling to Europe to find himself. Jennifer had been floating since dropping out of Manhattan's Finch College—a little modeling here, some acting there, and, according to her memoir, a full dose of the freedom and heartache that arrived with the sexual revolution. In her film work, she carried herself with a hard-won, slightly aloof intelligence.

Richard approached Jennifer gingerly. For their first date, he invited her to a political fund-raiser for UN ambassador Andrew Young at the Beverly Wilshire hotel, a subdued and high-class affair; the two held hands under the table. On the limo ride home with David Franklin and his black date, the evening turned sour when Franklin's companion questioned whether Jennifer could ever truly understand a black man like Richard. At the door to Jennifer's bungalow, Richard tried to make things right. He brought her closer, kissing her, and opened up: "I'm sorry for what she said in the car. I don't know what you've heard or read about me. But I don't see colors. I don't believe in prejudice. We're all people, you know? That's hard enough."

At summer's end, Richard's thoughts on the state of his love life were captured in a question-and-answer session with the audience of his TV show. Asked if he had plans to marry in the near future, he felt free to be indecently casual: "If the pussy good," he quipped. When a black woman asked him to divulge one of his "wildest dreams," he replied—perhaps with his budding romance with Jennifer in mind—"One of my wildest dreams is to be able to fuck a white woman and y'all don't fuck with me." Deboragh did not appear to be on his radar.

Then, around the time of the Hollywood Bowl benefit, the issue of *Jet* carrying Richard's appeal to a "very special lady" arrived on newsstands—"like a drumbeat going out," in Richard's words. Deboragh heard the drumbeat and phoned him. "I told her," Richard said later, "we couldn't go on any longer the way we had been and that we had to get married." Deboragh hesitated at Richard's proposal; she felt she needed to think it over. Richard hung up, got hammered on cocaine and vodka, worked himself into a lather, then drove to her home and banged on her door. When he got no answer, he screamed for her through it. The door opened a crack; Deboragh refused to let him in. Several days later, she yielded. "Okay, you win," she told him over the phone. "I'll marry you."

The wedding was scheduled in a few days' time, as if both of them were uncertain they could hold together their engagement for much longer. Richard worried about disturbing the fragile equilibrium that had led her to agree to marry him. Slated to start filming the title role on Motown's *The Wiz* just after his scheduled wedding, he told *Wiz* producer Rob Cohen that he had to back out of the upcoming shoot in New York; he needed to give his bride her honeymoon. Cohen, who had befriended Richard on *Bingo Long*, begged him to reconsider: "We can't shoot without you. If you don't show up, that's a week down on the movie. We're so over budget. We're all going to die." Richard refused to budge. Cohen promised to get back to him with some sort of workaround.

While Richard played the devoted husband-to-be in his conversation with his producer, his commitment to Deboragh wavered in the company of Jennifer Lee. The night before his wedding, he stood in his bedroom with Jennifer, the two of them admiring an antique child's desk she had placed there. The desk made him feel like a happy kid, he told her. Their eyes locked in silence. "I'm feeling something dangerous I shouldn't be feeling," he confessed, then pulled her into their first kiss since his engagement to Deboragh.

She asked, with genuine perplexity, "You're getting married, right?"

"Supposed to be," Richard said.

"So how come you're kissing me like this?"

"I guess I want it all."

Soon the two were kissing in the bathroom, with Jennifer pressed against the black marble. The bell at the gate rang, the intercom crackled, "It's me, Deboragh"—and the electric circuit of their connection was broken. Jennifer ran out of the bathroom and through the living room to the kitchen, where she collided with a tetchy Deboragh, who was absorbed in her own woes. "I've got the worst hangover," she complained. "Never again."

A sudden affair: Richard Pryor and Deboragh McGuire at their post-wedding reception. (Courtesy of AP Photo)

The next morning, bride and groom were joined in holy matrimony, and in total intoxication. Richard showed up drunk; Deboragh arrived an hour late and, according to Richard, "had to be revived after taking too many Quaaludes." One of Richard's daughters wore black to convey her thoughts on the union. The ceremony took place at his home, with little effort made to disguise the fact that it was a construction site. Richard and Deboragh recited their vows surrounded by unfaced cabinets, torn-up floors, and stacks of lumber. "Thank God you were drunk when I got there," Richard remembered Deboragh saying afterward, "because if you'd seen what I looked like . . ."

For their wedding reception, Richard and Deboragh traveled to NBC studios in Burbank, where Richard was responsible for wrapping up the third episode of his TV show. Earlier, producer Rocco Urbisci had made preparations for a party with confetti and a cake; he'd assumed Pam Grier was the bride, so the cake carried the frosted message "Congratulations Richard and Pam." Apparently Grier, too, had thought she was in contention to be the bride: Urbisci recalled fielding, on the morning of the wedding, a phone call from an incensed Grier, in which she explained that she was going to visit a certain "motherfucker" and "shoot his ass." Urbisci notified security; Grier was kept at bay. But he forgot about the infelicitous inscription on the cake. When the bride and groom arrived at the studio and the cake was brought out, Urbisci had to grab some roses from a prop table and hurriedly scatter them over the cake to cover the name "Pam."

On the occasion of his third formal marriage, Richard told the cast members of his show, "This is the first time I've been married—in my heart." Deboragh, a first-time bride, owned up to her bewilderment at the speed of things. "I'm still in shock," she said, her eyes glassy. "It's unbelievable . . . I got him."

After finishing the taping of his show, Richard went with his bride to the airport, where they were treated to the workaround that *Wiz* producer Rob Cohen had orchestrated, with Richard's permission. A private jet stood waiting for them, its cabin transformed into an airborne honeymoon suite. Seats were cleared out to make room for a large bed; candles, white balloons, and white chocolate set the mood; curtains were closed. The newlyweds took off on a red-eye for Oz, via LaGuardia Airport.

The next day in New York City, Cohen telephoned Richard about picking him up for rehearsal, and got no answer. He ran over to Richard's hotel room and pounded on the door, and received the same nonresponse. At last, a bleary-eyed Richard arrived at the door and joined Cohen for the drive over to the rehearsal space at the Hotel St. George, in Brooklyn Heights. In the limo, Richard brooded; his wedding night hadn't lifted him out of his dark mood. He vented to Cohen about how NBC had promised him freedom and yet censored him to bits.

Cohen tried to convince Richard that *The Wiz* would be different, that there was fabulous energy on the set, a wildness of ambition. The producer had plenty of material to work with: the day Richard arrived in town, the *New York Times* reported that *The Wiz* was laying down twenty-six miles of yellow-brick vinyl across the city's boroughs and remaking the World Trade Center's plaza into the Emerald City's main square, with a dance sequence that required four hundred dancers, twelve hundred costumes, and thirty-eight thousand colored-lightbulbs. Richard shrugged at Cohen's patter.

Then Cohen had an idea. When they reached the St. George, he didn't hand Richard over to *Wiz* director Sidney Lumet. Instead he promised to show Richard how much everyone appreciated his presence, and led him through the corridors of the hotel. Richard followed, exhausted to the point of docility, incognito in a baseball cap and T-shirt.

Cohen arrived at the hotel's ballroom and opened its doors, revealing an astonishing scene: four hundred dancers sashaying and pirouetting to the burbling funk of Quincy Jones in a rehearsal of the Emerald City sequence. Four hundred lithe, black bodies, clothed in unitards and tights that advertised just how beautiful they were. It was a pageant of black grace.

"Welcome," Cohen said to his star.

Some of the dancers in the front row noticed the man in the baseball cap next to Cohen, and stopped dancing. Another five stopped; another twenty, fifty, one hundred stopped—until the entire would-be population of Emerald City stopped to stare at their Wiz. A ripple of applause swelled into the cascade of a standing ovation.

Richard nodded and smiled at the dancers. When the applause died down, he switched into character to address the crowd. "We are gathered here today," he declaimed in the voice of his silver-tongued reverend. Before he could finish his sentence, the dancers fell down on the floor in laughter. They knew the character, the routine, the wicked wit to come, and they tingled with anticipation. Richard stretched out into an impromptu monologue, preaching to a congregation that delighted in his every turn of phrase. The dynamic was the opposite of that at the Hollywood Bowl a week before. The worries he had carried within him—a TV show on the rocks, a marriage that seemed to be spinning off course from its very first moments—melted away as he met an audience that loved him as one of their own and, in loving him that way, put him back in the flow of character, the flow of life.

After a few days on *The Wiz*'s set, Richard returned to the purgatory of his own making in Los Angeles: he needed to complete the fourth, and final, episode of *The Richard Pryor Show.* Though he was submitting to an obligation that, by all reports, he would have preferred to be released from, he was never someone who "worked to rule." In fact, the last two episodes of his program showcase his imagination at its most chaotic—as experimental as he ever allowed himself to be in his stand-up. And in some ways, they are even more revealing of the full compass of his imagination. Whereas onstage he was often anchored by the details of his actual life, in his TV show Richard used the freedom of sketch comedy, the freedom of implausibility, to project himself into a series of fantasies.

The second-to-last episode, taped just after the Hollywood Bowl fiasco, was the series' most exploratory moment, and arguably its finest. Five of the episode's segments were driven by pantomime, as if Richard were curious to see what he could express without opening his mouth. In "Mr. Fixit," the spirit is Chaplinesque—the bowler hat on Richard's head, the cranked-up action, and the rickety piano soundtrack all point back to the era of silent comedy. Richard plays a mechanic who, as he goes about repairing Paul Mooney's car, dismantles it instead with his every touch—until, at the end, he pats Mooney casually on the shoulder and Mooney's arm falls off. In "Separate Tables," a vivid parable of civilization and its discontents, Richard and his team paid homage to the famously sensual eating scene in the 1963 comedy *Tom Jones*. Richard sits facing Marsha Warfield at an upscale restaurant, both of them dining alone. After some coy eye contact, they communicate with each other through their food: Richard slowly slurping a spaghetti noodle, Warfield savoring a bite of her corn on the cob. As their passion builds, Richard becomes more frustrated and discombobulated—not just delighting in his food à la *Tom Jones*, but rubbing his salad over his face, or squeezing his grapes in his fist until they squirt at him. The two diners dive at each other and start writhing on the restaurant's floor, at which point the maître d' takes a hose and nonchalantly sprays them with the equivalent of a cold shower. The diners return to their tables, their respective dates arrive, and they carry on as if nothing happened—as if they were obedient creatures of decorum. Their sopping clothes tell a different story.

More poetic was a sketch that Rocco Urbisci and John Moffitt considered a disappointment, though it might be better to consider it a sketch *about* disappointment. "Once Upon a Time" lasted eight slow-moving minutes and aimed to return viewers to a time in their lives when they could be stirred by the simplest of amusements. The setting: a washed-out junkyard, a depressive's version of the habitat of Bill Cosby's Fat Albert. A calliope toots mechanically in the distance. A handful of kids watch as a gray-haired Richard, wearing a battered top hat and tails, plays the roles of ringmaster, lion tamer, tightrope walker, and clown in a traveling circus that is pure make-believe. With a toy whip and toy pistol, Richard evokes a lion tamer bringing an imaginary beast to heel on an upturned garbage pail; with the simple prop of a chair, he becomes a high-wire artist balancing himself with one leg raised in the air. The children clap enthusiastically, but the piece is forlorn in mood, mourning the loss of childhood even as it celebrates the pleasures of it. The spell of Richard's imaginary circus is broken by the shout of a mother offstage, telling the kids to stop playing in "that dirty junkyard." The kids flee, leaving Richard alone. Though the sketch ends on a somewhat optimistic note—with a lone black boy, presumably a younger version of Richard, coming back to the junkyard, finding Richard's top hat on the ground, and putting it on—it's mostly a sobering meditation on the power of play, a power that can seem life-giving one moment and trivial the next. At the age of thirty-seven, Richard had created a portrait of the artist as an old man, so out of phase with the world of responsible adulthood that he seemed unreal, or unbelievable.

The searching qualities of "Once Upon a Time" found an echo in "New Talent," the strangest of all sketches ever aired on *The Richard Pryor Show.* The curious segment had a curious backstory to match: Rocco Urbisci had received an audition tape from actress Kres Mersky and had been riveted by an experimental monologue of hers, part of a one-woman show she'd performed in LA. In the piece, Mersky's character sits in a bathrobe and talks intensely to an unseen person, or perhaps just to herself, about how she's "fallen in love again"—this time with a woman in her rooming house. With some graphic detail, she recounts a tryst with her lover in a clearing in a park. Then she toys with her audience by revising her story repeatedly, each time promising to divulge what "actually" happened. Actually the woman took her by force; no, actually she took the woman by force; no, actually she never went to the park at all but instead just stayed at home, reading a book on "violence and seduction." Urbisci played the monologue for Richard, who loved it and brightened at the subversive idea of smuggling it into their series. In a testament to his freethinking spirit, Richard did not bat an eyelash at turning four minutes of his show over to a little-known actress performing a monologue that nowadays would be labeled performance art, and queer performance art at that.

Once Richard and Urbisci had agreed to feature Mersky's piece, the practical question then became: how to segue into it? They settled on an ingenious solution: Richard would camp it up as Little Richard, in a high pompadour and glittering cape, singing "Good Golly Miss Molly"; his performance would quickly dissolve into static and snow; and Mersky's monologue, presented in black and white, would fade in. When her monologue was over, the static and snow would return, and Little Richard would finish his song. For unsuspecting viewers at home, it might seem that their TV set had begun to fail or that NBC's signal had been jammed by a local public-access station. Yet, at the same time, the figure of Little Richard was more than just a comic non sequitur. With his pancake makeup, tweezed eyebrows, and leering lusciousness, the early rock-'n'-roller was a rollicking example of the sexual confusions that, in a more minor key, drove Mersky's monologue. One good gender bender deserved another; "Miss Molly" wasn't the only one who loved to ball. And so, just a few days after Richard's crack-up at a gay rights benefit, his director shot Mersky delivering her monologue about gay desire and Richard whooping and blowing air kisses as the glammy rock-'n'-roller.

NBC tried to kill the segment as it was being produced, but Richard was adamant, threatening, as ever, to pull out of his show. Kres Mersky looked on, astonished that her little piece was causing such a ruckus. Apparently NBC didn't think Richard was bluffing; the sketch went through. The strength of Richard's commitment to it begs the obvious question of why, in the context of the fallout from his Hollywood Bowl appearance, he was willing to endanger his show for a provocative piece of gay theater. If it was a statement, what sort of statement was it? Perhaps we might simply say that Mersky's sketch was the sort of "gay culture" Richard could get behind. It suggested that when a woman fell in love with another woman, the result was just as complicated, just as riddled with the problems of power and submission, as when a man fell in love with a woman, or a woman with a man. The sketch did not glide over gay sex with euphemisms or vague talk, but came back again and again to that clearing in the park, where the two women met for something between good sex and rape. (In the final version that aired, these graphic moments were blacked out, emphatically, with the silent message "Censored"—a decision that forced the viewer's imagination to fill in the blanks.) Like Richard's own "Wino and Junkie," Mersky's monologue was explicit but elusive, and a far cry from the sort of self-congratulatory bombast—"The Star-Spangled Banner," "The Ascent of Man"—that set the tone for the Hollywood Bowl benefit. It beguiled the viewer into a space of troubling uncertainty.

By the time Richard started taping the final episode of his show on October 11, both he and the network were looking forward to the end of their relationship. *The Richard Pryor Show* had shed viewers until it was in the basement of the Nielsen ratings; Richard was as volatile as a tropical weather system, flashing between indifference and defiance, resignation and anger. His last show had both more filler and more minutes of caustic performance that had to be left on the cutting-room floor. As part of his kiss-off to NBC, he expanded one of his Mudbone monologues into a sixty-five minute, expletive-soaked "sustained sleight of comic imagination," in the words of the *New York Times*. Exactly twenty-two words of it were suitable for broadcast.

Richard's mixed feelings were in full evidence at the comic roast held on his behalf and aired, in severely edited form, on the last episode. At the event Marsha Warfield teased Richard about his compulsive womanizing: "Richard Pryor is a real humanitarian. He's raised a lot of money for young students. In fact, he's paid half the girls at the local high school to keep their mouths shut." Robin Williams offered, under the cover of a jibe, some wisdom about the nature of Richard's talent: "This man's a genius. Who else can take all the forms of comedy—slapstick, satire, mime, and stand-up—and turn it into something that would offend everyone? . . . All he wants is a loose director, a tight script, and a warm place to rehearse." And Paul Mooney took the occasion to deliver a heartfelt tribute: "Richard Pryor is a lot like a child. . . . He's innocent in a lot of ways, and in a lot of ways he's not so innocent, and he's a beautiful human being and I love him dearly. I'm really glad we did this, and I really mean that." He hugged Richard, who rose to a standing ovation from the cast.

Richard took the podium and cut the mood with an improvised, and never-aired, series of insults that started light and became increasingly savage. "Thank you, I'm thrilled. It's not often that amateur people get a chance to be on television," he began. A few minutes later he was mocking Tim Reid's manhood ("We wanted to give him a job because he had the shortest thing of any black man in America, and we didn't want white people to know"); cutting down Marsha Warfield as "a big black gorilla" whom the show had adopted from the zoo ("We fixed her hair, and she's been acting the fool ever since"); skewering a tubby cast member without mercy ("He has a wedding band on him, but Mrs. Hippo isn't here tonight"); and eviscerating his friend David Banks as the ultimate pimp ("I first met him in church—he tried to get an angel to sit on my face"). It was an exercise in over-the-top cruelty, virtuosic in its spontaneity but hitting uncomfortably close to the bone. Then Richard reversed himself and turned sentimental: "I have a special place in my heart for everyone here. I really love them because they are brilliant people and they have made the show possible." Just as he had thanked the whole crew of *Which Way Is Up?* when it wrapped, so he singled out his show's set and lighting designers along with the writers and actors. The show had wrecked him—afflicted him with a set of responsibilities he couldn't manage—but it had also put him at the center of a singular troupe of young artists, who had thrilled at the risks he took for his art and had buoyed him up.

The last two sketches of the final episode stand as a fitting emblem of all that Richard accomplished on his show and all that he suffered for it. In the haunting "Gun Shop," he played a man who, as he walks through the shop and peruses the merchandise, hears each gun talking to him. A rifle drawls, "I don't like you, boy. Come on down to my part of the country—I'll show you law and order." A pearl-handled pistol murmurs, "Mrs. Mercer said I used to make her feel sexy. We finally got a mugger. The last thing he saw was the fire that came out of my eyes." Richard continues to drift and be assailed by voices. A Saturday-night special, afflicted with status anxiety, jabbers, "You don't think I have class—I got class! I killed more people than anybody in this room"; a Luger pistol brags of itself as "a weapon of ethnic purity." Each gun, it seems, is trapped in its own pathology, hungering to visit its particular brand of destruction on the world. The sketch ends with Richard leaving the store, rattled and empty-handed; a gun revolves on a carousel until it's pointed straight at the viewer.

Haunted by voices: Richard Pryor in "Gun Shop." (Courtesy of the author)

With "Gun Shop," Richard was taking aim at himself. The actor spooked at the gun shop was, after all, the same person who had pistol-whipped an early manager, shot up his first gold record over frustrations with his record label, and acquired an arsenal that encompassed a Walther .380 automatic, a Colt .357 Magnum, an antique flintlock, and a shotgun. It takes nothing away from the power of the sketch to note that, at a New Year's Eve party just ten weeks after "Gun Shop" aired, Richard seized a gun and, in a fury, unloaded it into a Mercedes that had previously contained his wife and friends. Demons are not so easily cast out that they can be ventilated and exorcised in a six-minute sketch. But what is remarkable is that Richard was able to see those demons with such piercing clarity and get others to share his vision of himself. In his art, he achieved the sort of ironic distance that was impossible to maintain in the churning slipstream of his life.

"A Rebuttal," the final sketch of *The Richard Pryor Show*, was a fitting send-off—an encapsulation of Richard's experience on the TV show as a whole. A white-whiskered Richard came on the news in the person of Santa Claus to offer an "editorial," which in his case was a rant about the difficulties of pleasing the multitudes. A flask of whiskey sat conveniently at Santa's elbow; toy cars and airplanes were scattered everywhere in front of him. He talked, with faux cheeriness, of being overworked to a breaking point:

> Advertisers and businessmen are beginning to celebrate the holiday season a little earlier every year—'long about July 12, I would say—and it's a pain for Santa. Not that I mind it, because I love each and every one of you dearly, but it puts a lot of pressure on lovable Santa.
>
> [*Takes a swig from the flask.*]
>
> You know, boys and girls, I have to work a little harder every year. Not that I mind, 'cause I love each and every one of you. Ho ho ho! But I work my f—
>
> [*CENSORED flashes on the screen with a long beep.*]
>
> Huh? Did you ever think about how hard I have to work? Or do you give a [*CENSORED*] I work my Rudolph off?

Confessing that he had gone "dingy," Santa groused about having, every day, to answer four million letters (many composed by children with extremely poor handwriting!); explained that Rudolph's nose was red because, like Santa, he was a sniffer; talked leeringly of the "ho" in "ho ho ho"; and then blacked out at the news desk. The whiskey—or was it the burden of having to try to please everyone in the world on an impossible schedule?—had felled him. He couldn't hold the stage.

In early November, *Which Way Is Up?*—the movie Richard had called "the most special thing I've ever done"—opened to the most stinging mainstream reviews of his career. Producer Steven Krantz had fretted, before its release, that the film might antagonize critics with its ripe dialogue, ribald plot, and clear put-down of big business. What he hadn't anticipated was that among a certain set of critics—white, older—it would be labeled racist and intolerable. The *Los Angeles Times*' Charles Champlin, who had earlier applauded Richard in *Wattstax* and *Greased Lightning*, wrote, "If 'Which Way Is Up' isn't racially offensive, what in God's name is? It takes the oldest stereotype of all—of blacks as oversexed or sexually obsessive children, and I would expect the NAACP to be in the streets with placards." *Variety*'s Arthur Murphy blew a gasket: "Pryor's career seems now at a crossroads, where his increasingly annoying brand of reverse racism must vanish. . . . [T]his film brings into focus the fact that a lot of his material exploits in a shallow fashion the very character stereotypes that, literally, millions of people have, not without difficulty in many cases, managed to overcome." About the character of Richard's reverend, Murphy huffed: "a Ku Klux Klan propaganda film couldn't do it better."

And yet—the NAACP did not protest; the Ku Klux Klan did not claim *Which Way* as its own; and though Universal partly dumped the movie in second-string theaters in black neighborhoods, *Which Way* succeeded beyond the wildest expectations of its creative team. Five months after its opening, Krantz could tout it as the most commercially successful black film in history, with twenty-three million dollars in domestic and foreign rentals. And in some circles—left-leaning or black—it was seen as the exact opposite of racist. The *Village Voice* hailed the film as director Michael Schultz's "first major" black film, one which invited the black audience to identify with its spirit of "chastened survival" rather than the "defeatism" of Wertmüller's *Seduction of Mimi.* The black-themed magazine *Cause* celebrated *Which Way* for moving beyond the "false and empty macho images" of blaxploitation; it was an "upbeat, positive film of Black identification." As with his TV show and performance at the Hollywood Bowl, Richard had cleaved audiences apart, delighting some in the act of antagonizing others.

Critics like Champlin and Murphy saw only the outer mask of the movie. They asked if the film offered, in the characters Richard played, role models for black life, and they just as quickly determined that it didn't: Leroy Jones was a weak-willed opportunist; his father, Rufus, a self-satisfied satyr; the Reverend Lenox Thomas a hypocrite of the highest order. These critics missed that, far from the Hollywood mainstream, there had long been a comic tradition in which black performers played with the most shameful of stereotypes—the dissolute preacher, the cheating gambler, the hot-tempered "coon"—and in a complex move, both entertained the stereotypes and shuffled them off. Richard located himself in this tradition of self-conscious caricature: after *Which Way*'s release, he expressed interest in making a biopic about the vaudevillian Bert Williams, who was the tradition's most gifted turn-of-the-century exponent, a black man turning blackface to account.

For Richard, the demand to be a "role model" was a trap that would have him forever playing safe parts like *Greased Lightning*'s Wendell Scott. He was an artist, not a spokesman, and as an artist, he was drawn to the poetry of failure. His major theme was self-sabotage, and it was difficult for him to play a self-saboteur without coming in the vicinity of stereotypes about black foolishness. In a perceptive review of *Which Way*, the *New York Times*' Vincent

Canby noted the difficulty and delicacy of Richard's balancing act. Canby judged Richard "one of the few actors . . . who manages to be funny—sometimes outrageously so—while giving every impression of being furious with his audience and removed from his material. This distance from his characters, however, allows him to play black stereotypes in a way that sends up the stereotypes while getting every last laugh from them." This balancing act had its dangers: Bert Williams described himself as "whittling on dynamite." Richard was a fellow whittler. His caricatures, if not handled with the proper finesse, always threatened to blow up in his face.

A great number of contemporary black-themed comedies might claim *Which Way Is Up?* as their Hollywood ancestor. The *Barbershop* movies, *Friday* and its sequels, the spoofs produced by the Wayans brothers, the Madea films of Tyler Perry—all these have rooted themselves in the sort of gutbucket humor that takes everyday buffoonery and magnifies its dimensions to the point of cartoonishness. They've also courted critical disapproval and controversy as a result—been derided, like *Which Way Is Up?*, as low-brow, or been faulted for refusing to offer positive images of the black community.

Yet the comparison also reveals the uniqueness of *Which Way Is Up?*. Unlike these other movies, *Which Way* was both a sex comedy and a film grounded in the spirit of *la causa*. The farmworkers' struggle was the backdrop against which Richard's Leroy Jones proved himself a fool, so trapped within his macho psychodrama that he couldn't see how he'd become a pawn in the larger power play between a corporation and its workers. In its final scene, Leroy had to watch his soul mate, Vanetta, drive off with his friend Chuy, a pro-union firebrand who has none of Leroy's wishy-washiness. Leroy's only heroic gesture is his very last: he tells his corporate patron to "shoot me in the ass 'cause that's the only part of me you're ever gonna see" and walks down the open road, jaunty for once, no longer pulled by someone else's string. Leroy may not have the faintest idea where he is going, but at least he feels himself moving forward. The credits roll over his image as it recedes into the horizon.

With his TV series in the can, Richard had hopes of pulling himself away from the bad habits that had gotten him through its production. He anticipated that when he and Deboragh traveled to Maui for a true honeymoon, his soul might find some rest. Instead, the bad habits clung to him. On the first night, he found himself reeling—drunk and covered with his own vomit in the shower while his new wife complained about the shabbiness of their accommodations. There were bugs, apparently, and their bungalow had no room service. "Are we going to eat cornflakes for a week?" she demanded. That night set the tone for the week that followed. Richard's mind wandered from his honeymoon and his bride: he kept telephoning LA to speak with Jennifer Lee, who came to feel that Richard's marriage was, oddly, "bringing us even closer together."

Back in New York City for another shoot on *The Wiz*, Richard journeyed farther down the road of excess. "I caroused with sleazy, doped-up nogoodniks all night," he recalled. "I was as lit as the white suit I wore playing the Wiz himself. I answered my wake-up calls by saying, 'Oh, shit, I made it again.'"

On November 9, with Deboragh at his side, Richard flew to Peoria for a belated celebration of his grandmother Marie's seventy-eighth birthday. The next afternoon, he went fishing with Deboragh, Marie, and Uncle Dickie. The day was beautiful, the weather bracing and fresh, but Richard was unable to relax into the peaceful rhythm of casting lines. Back in his hometown, he itched to satisfy the cravings that his early years had planted in him. He and Dickie skipped out on the fishing trip to have some private time with two women who, according to Deboragh, were the "two most unattractive white women ever—dogs." In his memoir, Richard himself called his partner an "ugly whore." It was as if he were a prisoner of his drift, spiraling down into the black hole of his addictions and testing his new wife to see how much she would mutely bear witness to his vanishing act. Deboragh refused to look on passively; she packed her bags for LA.

In the middle of sex with the prostitute, Richard felt his heart race and hammer. He gasped for air and had trouble finding it; he felt sick.

He was reprising the family theme—death by sex—that his father had established a decade earlier. Still, he paid little attention at first to the discomfort; a racing heart was nothing new to him. Then the pain arrived—a starburst of pain in his chest—and he dropped the pretense that this was his body's business as usual. Somehow he brought himself to his grandmother and cried, "Mama! Mama! Help me, Mama!"

When everyone in his family rallied to rush him to the hospital, Richard saw a dark subtext. "They were probably closer to death than I was," he observed. "They saw their money supply gasping for air, moaning, and writhing in pain. They probably wondered if this wasn't some sick joke. Me coming home to die in front of them. They weren't going to have none of that shit. Not about to lose my fame and money." Richard was thirty-six years old, the most sensational rising star in black Hollywood, and at risk of frittering himself to death.

On November 10, the day after Richard was admitted to the emergency room of Methodist Medical Center, a radio station in Los Angeles reported that he had died. The news was false: Richard was at that moment recovering, in the hospital's coronary care unit, after a restless night. Five hundred phone calls poured into the hospital from various friends and well-wishers, among them Aretha Franklin, Olivia Newton-John, and Sammy Davis Jr. According to the *Peoria Journal Star*, every caller seemed to believe that they had a special relationship with Richard—that he would return their calls if only the hospital took the care to pass along their number. But Richard was in no mood to plug back into the world. After being discharged from the hospital, he told a reporter, "I was on a treadmill, and you often just get on it and don't look back for a while." He was ready to dial back on his commitments. Talking to himself as much as the reporter, he said, "Success is no good if you don't have your health."

Thirteen months later, Richard took the stage of Long Beach's Terrace Theater and performed his experience of his heart attack. In the interim, he had publicly destroyed his marriage to Deboragh—had shot it full of holes on New Year's Eve, just a little while after

A new act in the making: Jennifer Lee and Richard Pryor in 1978. (Courtesy of Jennifer Pryor)

telling an *Ebony* reporter, "We're going to be very happy together a long time, because it's the first time I've admitted I don't know anything." Without skipping a beat, he had taken up with Jennifer Lee, who matched him in her appetite for the drama of life: the two were swept up in the blizzard of Richard's cocaine use, and for years ran themselves ragged with the intense form their love took. (Lee's memoir, *Tarnished Angel*, is at once a love story and a wiredrawn account of the insanities unleashed by cocaine—how, under its influence, petty jealousies get magnified into crazed vendettas.)

Then, starting in the summer of 1978, Richard righted himself by returning to stand-up. He had been mandated, by the judge in the car-shooting case, to submit to psychological counseling, and in tandem with those private therapy sessions, and with Jennifer at his side, he used the stage of the Comedy Store to retell the story of his life. After a month of woodshedding—a fever of lucidity—he had come up with a new act: over an hour of fresh material, which he then performed in concerts across America.

Richard's account of his heart attack sat at the core of a show that, as *Rolling Stone*'s David Felton noted, was something of a departure from his earlier concerts. Previously, Richard had let his imagination wander into woollier characters like Mudbone, his preacher, or his wino—a fact that gave those shows a wild, centripetal energy. In this show, which became the film *Richard Pryor: Live in Concert*, Richard flowed centrally into the character of himself. The concert was a set of riffs on the trials of his life: the trials of becoming Richard Pryor. Its sketches ranged from the primal memories of his childhood—being beaten by his grandmother and father—all the way to the more recent tribulations of his heart attack and his New Years' Eve shooting of the Mercedes. Yet the show was clear-eyed and free of self-pity. Out of his suffering, Richard had extracted the story of a man who, having been pained into self-knowledge, did not rue the foolishness of his past selves or begrudge those who had walloped him into wisdom.

In the stage version of Richard's heart attack, his wife and family in Peoria were pared away to make room for a different story of crime and punishment. The heart attack opened onto a fable about cosmic payback. The setting: a backyard, not a bedroom. A heavy voice ambushes Richard from out of the blue, like a sadistic mugger: "Don't *breathe*." Richard's right fist strikes the left side of his body with an uppercut.

"Hunh?" Richard says. His eyes search for his invisible assailant.

The heart is a disciplinarian tougher than Marie or even Buck: "You heard me, motherfucker, I said don't *breathe*." It lands another heavy blow to his chest.

Richard is unmanned by his pain. His voice tightens into a quick, high-pitched rasp: "Okay, I won't breathe, I won't breathe."

"Then shut the fuck *up*!"

"Okay, okay, don't kill me, don't kill me."

"Get on one knee and *prove* it!"

"I'm on one knee, I'm on one knee, don't kill me."

"You're thinking about dying now, aren't ya?"

"Yeah, I'm thinking about dying, I'm thinking about dying."

"You didn't think about it when you was eating all that *pork*!" A crushing punch—the punch of comeuppance—belts Richard to the floor. (In other performances, the heart adds Richard's drinking and drugging to its list of offenses.) Richard grimaces in agony, flat on his back. The routine slows. Richard's mouth opens and closes in a silent howl. His body cramps up in the form of a writhing question mark.

Richard sits up, shifts into his normal voice, and says, laughing, "You be thinking about shit like that when you think you're gonna die. You put an emergency call into God, too, right?"

The desperate voice again: "Can I speak to God right away, please?"

The call makes it to heaven but gets stuck at the celestial switchboard. An angel with the soul of a bureaucrat sniffs in a very white voice, "I'll have to put you on hold."

"Was you trying to talk to God behind my back?" the heart asks, suspiciously.

"Nooo . . . ," Richard says.

"You're a lyin' mother*fucker*!" the heart says, and slams Richard on the ground one last time.

Richard sits up, no longer in the moment of agony, and speaks of his reprieve from pain: "I woke up in an ambulance, right? And there wasn't nothing but white people staring at me. I say, 'Ain't this a bitch? I done died and wound up in the wrong motherfuckin' heaven. Now I got to listen to Lawrence Welk the rest of my days.' "

The sketch delivered a happy ending with a tart twist. Richard was no longer in the clutches of death, but he was still in the clutches of race. Saved, he was still left seeking. Perhaps it was the trickster's fate to slip from one snare only to be faced with another.

For seven years, Richard had tried to crack the code of the Hollywood film, to bend the industry around the shape of his talent. From *Lady Sings the Blues* to *Blue Collar*, he had aimed to infuse his films with the same spirit of creative improvisation that fired his stage act, and when he had met the right collaborators, he produced some remarkable successes. But *Richard Pryor: Live in Concert* suggested a cruder yet more elegant solution: set up a few cameras, point them at the stage, and create a new genre in Hollywood entirely. Rather than crack an old code, write a fresh one. Critics experienced *Live in Concert* as the shock of the new. The *Village Voice*'s Andrew Sarris called it "one of the most exhilarating experiences of my moviegoing life." Jonathan Rosenbaum compared the film favorably to *The Deer Hunter* (on a trajectory to win the Best Picture Oscar): "Working entirely without props, gimmicks, or excuses, [Pryor] creates a world so intensely realized and richly detailed that it puts most recent million-dollar blockbusters to shame." *The New Yorker*'s Pauline Kael was moved, by Richard's performance, to name him "the only great poet satirist among our comics." When the film went on to gross thirty-two million dollars off a tiny budget (it had been put together in a month, with little in the way of postproduction), it seemed a sort of box office miracle, too, one that might change the calculus of Hollywood. *Rolling Stone*'s David Felton named it a "low-budget, short-order masterpiece, a powerful argument for spontaneity in mass entertainment."

For Richard, *Live in Concert* was a miracle for a reason completely separate from its critical raves or box office returns. His beloved grandmother Marie had died from a stroke three weeks before filming, leaving him with a prophetic warning: "Son, you just don't know. It's ugly out there. You've got to protect yourself from it now. You're on your own now, Richard. Be careful." He had managed to ride the momentum of his concert tour into the making of the film, and it had launched him definitively as an artist. But from now on, he had to stare at the haunting question: Who was he without the woman who had grounded him—loved him, beat him, braced him, and, by her own account, shielded him from the true ugliness of the world?

EPILOGUE

When, early in the morning of December 9, 1978, his grandmother Marie drew her last breath, Richard Pryor was not ready to let her go. He'd been holding her hand in her hospital room at Peoria's Methodist Medical Center, and four people "couldn't pry him loose without a struggle," his aunt Maxine recalled. "They couldn't get him out of that room and when they did, he broke and come right back in there. . . . And when the wagon table came to take mamma to the morgue, they had to pull Richard out." In the hospital lounge afterward, Richard was gutted with grief. "Everything I've had and everything I've got is gone," he cried to Maxine. Then, calling out to the woman he'd lost: "Mama, I did everything I could for you. Everything! I prayed and I prayed, and I prayed, Mama. I prayed so hard. I didn't even know I could pray."

The coming days brought the rituals of mourning—a night funeral at Peoria's Morning Star Baptist Church, presided over by the reverend who had helped inspire Richard's grandiloquent stage minister; a second funeral the next day, at Decatur's Church of the Living God, the ministry that had sanctified Marie's first marriage to Roy Pryor sixty-five years earlier. On December 14, Marie Carter Pryor Bryant was interred under cloudy winter skies at Decatur's Greenwood Cemetery, her body returning to the city where she had acquired her depth as a woman.

With Marie no longer there to exert her influence, the post-funeral gatherings took on a looser air. Richard played host by filling a bowl with cocaine and setting it on a table next to a full complement of reefer; guests were invited to snort or toke to their hearts' content. The party was on, with Richard leading by example.

The post-funeral festivities opened onto eighteen months in which Richard did not dwell in his grief so much as lose himself in it, aided by his cocaine and, starting in November 1979, the freebasing pipe that, by heightening the rush of the drug, drew him into a fevered form of oblivion. Often in his life, a phase of personal confusion had yielded a moment of artistic discovery. In 1968 he had spun, like a whirligig, from his crack-up at the Aladdin into a period of onstage experimentation that produced the multi-character sketches of his first album and the breakthrough ghetto playlet "Hank's Place." In 1975 he had emerged, out of the debris of his wrecked relationships with Patricia Heitman and Ron DeBlasio, with the triumphant invention of Mudbone and his inspired work on *Bingo Long* and *Saturday Night Live*. The success of *Live in Concert*, following upon the emotional chaos of the previous year, continued the pattern. But the depression that followed the death of Marie was different. It led Richard, in an instant, to sear away a crucial part of his artistic self: the love of experiment that had pushed him through his changes as a performer.

In the early evening of June 9, 1980, Richard had been, by his own account, awake for somewhere in the vicinity of five days straight, much of that time spent locked in his bedroom with the essentials for freebasing—cocaine, pipe, and Bic lighter—and a bottle of hard liquor. A paranoid dementia overtook him: "Voices swirled in my head so that I wasn't able to tell which came from me and which were hallucinations. My conversations became animated, like those crazy people on the street. I heard people who had worked for me talking outside the bedroom window. They were loud, rude, laughing, angry. They made fun of my helplessness. I yelled at them, louder and louder, and still they refused to answer."

Into this inner pandemonium came the flash of an idea. What

transpired next was not, as many continue to think, a drug-related accident. It was more akin to a terrible act of improvisation—one that, horribly, killed the urge to improvise. According to Richard's bodyguard Rashon Khan, Richard was sitting in the living room watching a program that showed scenes from the Vietnam War, including footage of a Buddhist monk setting himself on fire. "You have to have a lot of courage to light that shit," Khan said to Richard. "You have to have more courage not to flinch when you light it!" Richard replied. In his memoir, Richard recalled that the precipitating event was a dialogue he was trying to have with God—the one voice he couldn't find in the swirl of voices. He repeatedly asked, "What do you want me to do?" Receiving no answer, he boasted, "I'll show you" and laughed with a demented sense of giddiness.

Richard poured the liquor over his head so that it soaked his hair, his neck, and a shirt that, fatefully, was a polyester weave. He flicked a cigarette lighter once, twice—no spark. The third try was a success: his shirt blazed into flames that reached up to his head. In an instant, Richard no longer wished to toy with death; he felt himself burning up and wanted desperately to stay alive. When Khan and Richard's aunt Dee threw a sheet on him to smother the flames, he resisted, because he thought they were trying to smother him, not the flames. Then he shocked them by bolting, in a delirium of pain, out of the house, down the estate's long curving driveway, through its ten-foot-high iron gates, and into the street.

A gathering mass of drivers on Parthenia Street were baffled by the pedestrian they beheld. A man who bore an uncanny resemblance to Richard Pryor was walking briskly on the sidewalk. Most of his polyester shirt had melted onto his skin; the rest of it had been reduced to a few singed tatters. To the cops on routine traffic detail who came across him, he appeared to be wearing some strange makeup. When one of them, Officer Richard Zielinski, approached him on foot, he caught the stench of scorched flesh and burnt polyester. Zielinski asked Richard, gently, to stop. An ambulance's siren pealed in the distance.

Whether because he was never one to welcome policemen into his life or because his rational faculties had deserted him, Richard refused Officer Zielinski's entreaty. "If I stop, I'll die," he said, then broke into a jog. According to the *Los Angeles Times*, he continued jogging for a full half mile, Zielinski and the police car following alongside him as he raved and pleaded, loud enough for neighbors to hear him, "Lord, give me another chance. There's a lot of good left in me. Haven't I brought any happiness to anyone in this world?" He had to be physically subdued to be lifted into the ambulance that arrived on the scene, and was in deep shock by the time it had carried him to the burn unit of Sherman Oaks Community Hospital.

This book is about the shaping of a talent until it rose to the level of its full genius, and for that reason the thrust of its story ends with the film *Live in Concert* and the harrowing depression that followed it. Of course, the era of Richard Pryor's greatest commercial success still lay ahead of him. *Stir Crazy*, his first full-fledged pairing with Gene Wilder, became the third-highest-grossing film of 1981; the family feature *Bustin' Loose* made him the only star to have two films in that year's top twenty. *Richard Pryor Live on the Sunset Strip*, his follow-up to *Live in Concert*, earned five times its budget in its first three weeks and bested the returns of the earlier concert film. "Whatever happened to the black film?" the *Los Angeles Times* asked rhetorically in 1981. "It seems to reside these days in the person of Richard Pryor."

At the height of Richard's stardom, it could seem that the future of Hollywood itself was bound up with the riddle of his appeal. *Time* commented in 1982 that "In a troubled period for movies, when attendance is slipping and not even the presence of Burt Reynolds or Clint Eastwood can guarantee box office gold, Richard Pryor is the one actor whose name spells HIT." The great director Billy Wilder quipped that studio executives had a surefire formula for making a box office smash: they "approach it very scientifically—computer projections, marketing research, audience profiles—and they always come up with the same answer: Get Richard Pryor."

Yet the arrival of Richard as a Hollywood star coincided with a new artistic cautiousness on his part. Arguably there are more jaw-dropping surprises—more moments of off-kilter ingenuity—in the last episode of *The Richard Pryor Show* than in all his 1980s comedies combined. His work in the 1970s could be raw to the point of being sloppy or outré to the point of being almost indigestible, but even its sloppiest, most indigestible moments seemed to derive from Richard's integrity as an artist, his unwillingness to settle for easy jokes and prefab emotions. By contrast, his oeuvre in the 1980s seemed too concerned with hitting the expected marks. For those who knew his earlier work, the delights these later films offered were familiar pleasures rather than uneasy or deeper ones. And as the decade wore on, even these familiar pleasures started wearing out their welcome.

It was the odd film critic who, after 1982, didn't muse on the disheartening disconnect between the power of Pryor as an artist and the feebleness of his latest film. After *The Toy* (in which Richard plays an unemployed reporter who becomes a rich boy's plaything), Michael Sragow asked, "What's wrong with Richard Pryor?" and answered that he was "becoming the Toy of the studios," his raw energy processed into unthreatening corn. After *Brewster's Millions* (for which Richard instructed its screenwriters to write his character without any racial cues), Vincent Canby wrote that the experience of watching Richard in the film was "like watching the extremely busy shadow of someone who has disappeared. The contours of the shadow are familiar but the substance is elsewhere." By the time of the semiautobiographical *Jo Jo Dancer, Your Life Is Calling* in 1986, the tone of critical disapproval had slipped into a harsher register. The *Boston Phoenix* called Richard "a victim of the very screen personality he forged in more than a dozen wearyingly mediocre comedies," and offered that Richard had "come close to turning himself into a media-age minstrel show: a cross between the early Woody Allen and Buckwheat." Pauline Kael, a great booster of Richard since *Lady Sings the Blues*, lamented, "If I'd never seen Richard Pryor before, I couldn't have guessed—based on what Jo Jo does here—that he has an excitable greatness in him."

What had happened to that greatness? A simple and not untrue answer would be that the fire burned a good deal of excitability out of him. Richard was temperamentally different, more reticent and withdrawn, after the trauma—a situation that, on a personal level, he interpreted as a change for the better. When asked, on a movie set in 1981, where he was born, he replied, "The Sherman Oaks Burn Center." Director John Badham, with whom Richard had feuded on the set of *Bingo Long*, described the new Pryor as "gentle" and "mellow"—adjectives that would have been absurd to apply to the comedian at any earlier point in his life. In 1983, Richard observed, "People call me up and say, 'You're not like you used to be.' I say to them, 'That's right, but do you know what I was really like then? Do you know what kind of insanity I was into, with the drugs and liquor? I'm not going to start doing that again. I'm going to be nice to myself. I don't have the same desire to succeed any more. I don't have that push, push, push I used to have. I think I had it until I burned up." Three years later, he reflected on the general mellowing effect: "Sure, my moods go up and down, but at least I know where I'm at . . . I'm not waking up saying, 'Oh, no, did I kill someone last night?' " Whatever the personal benefits, the artistic benefits were more minimal. The new Richard was less brave and open—less willing to improvise, or wander into strange terrain, or risk the red-hot act of creative aggression that makes an audience howl in shock and astonishment.

Yet it wasn't only Richard who became more risk-averse after 1980. Hollywood itself struggled through a transition that, according to one of its foremost historians, was as wrenching as the coming of sound in the 1920s. Between the release of the first *Star Wars* movie in 1976 and the third *Indiana Jones* movie in 1989, Hollywood evolved from an industry that produced movies to an industry that generated entertainment-related "product." Theater distribution became just one revenue stream among many. Home video sales and cable licensing fees, tie-ins with everything from videos games and amusement park rides to fast food, toys, and pajamas—these new sources of profit changed the industry calculus, pushing studios to invest in films that could be exploited in as many ways as possible. Often this meant blockbusters on the model of the movies of George Lucas and Steven Spielberg. Sci-fi and fantasy films boomed in the 1980s, dominating the box office. Those films that weren't fantasy-driven blockbusters tended to fit snugly into other genres, like comedy (*Ghostbusters*, *Porky's*), horror (often of the slasher variety), or action-adventure (*Rambo*, *Top Gun*).

While it's difficult to generalize about a decade of filmmaking that produced *E.T.* and *Blade Runner*, *Red Dawn* and *Platoon*, *Friday the Thirteenth* and *The Shining*, one trend bears noting: the decline of a certain sort of "1970s movie" that sat uneasily within its supposed genre. There were fewer films that danced on the line between entrancing spectacle and affecting drama, like *The Mack* and *Saturday Night Fever*; fewer films that infused moments of jittery laughter into otherwise bleak stories of working-class life, like *Blue Collar* and *Mean Streets*; and fewer films that mixed low comedy and high politics, like *Blazing Saddles*, *Car Wash*, and *Little Big Man*.

As these examples suggest, Richard thrived in precisely the sorts of films that became increasingly rare in the 1980s. For another index of the changes afoot in Hollywood, one might compare him to Eddie Murphy, his successor as the big marquee name among black actors after 1983. Murphy was clearly a comic in the Pryor mold: a talented physical comedian radiating a certain streetwise sass and cool, his mouth his weapon of choice. But Murphy, in 1980s roles like Axel Foley, had little of Richard's bottom notes—his fragility, tenderness, or openness to emotional confusion. Or one might compare the two showbiz biopics, *Lady Sings the Blues* and *Jo Jo Dancer*, that framed Richard's career in Hollywood. Both films, notably, were parables about the perils of being a black entertainer. In the first, the young Richard injected levity and some moral complexity into a movie that otherwise risked becoming a formula melodrama. In the second, the older Richard stripped out the complexity from his own life story. The character of his grandmother was made over as a simple, warmhearted soul full of the milk of human kindness—a far cry from the prickly, forceful woman whom Richard had known. Meanwhile, Richard largely erased from view his own capacity for violence and self-sabotage, portraying himself as the sad-faced victim of drugs and women. *Jo Jo Dancer* desperately needed the irreverent spirit of the young Richard Pryor to save it from itself. After 1980, that actor was unavailable.

One would like to assign a happy ending to Richard's acting career. Perhaps if he had stayed healthy into his sixth decade, his fearlessness might have come back, like a sleeping virus awakened, with the arrival of the post-Reagan era in entertainment. His TV series, though short-lived, was yet the godfather of cable comedy shows like *In Living Color, Chappelle's Show,* and *Key and Peele,* and it's easy to imagine a middle-aged Pryor as a wildly avuncular guest on them, goosing along the young'uns and stepping into a new version of himself. Perhaps, too, a healthy older Pryor might have fulfilled his dream of being a character actor—on the cast of *Homicide* or *The Wire,* say, or in the films of black-oriented directors like Spike Lee, John Singleton, or Lee Daniels. Between 1967 and 1986, Pryor's work in Hollywood was largely split between cameos and starring roles, and it would have been nice for him to find his stride, at the end of his career, as an ensemble player.

Yet Richard never had the chance to age gracefully in public view. In August 1986, after experiencing some trouble with his motor control and eyesight, he went to the Mayo Clinic in Minneapolis for tests. The diagnosis that came back: multiple sclerosis, or MS, a degenerative disease of the nervous system. One of his first responses was to wonder if the MS was karmic payback. "[A]t the outset of life God gives you a certain number of angels," he speculated. "They hover above you, protecting your ass from danger. But if you cross a certain line too many times, they get the hell away. Say, 'Hey, motherfucker, you've abused us too many times. From here on, you're on your own." Part of the medical community might agree, in a way, with Pryor's conjecture. Recent studies have suggested that, while MS has a strong genetic basis, individuals who engage in risk-associated behavior such as alcohol use, drug use, and smoking are more susceptible to the disease. In Utah, non-Mormons are roughly four times more likely to get it than Mormons—and Richard was no Mormon in the years preceding his diagnosis.

MS is a cruel disorder for anyone: it slowly strips the sufferer of the ability to walk, to talk, or to control his bowels. But there was an extra layer of cruelty to Pryor's coming down with it. From an early age, Richard had, like any number of humbly born athletes, actors, and dancers, made a future for himself by discovering and exploiting the resources of his body. His native expressiveness—the emotions he made instantly legible on his face, the energy he concentrated in his gestures—had always been at the foundation of his act. Now he felt his physical grace slipping away: he told one interviewer that the hardest part of having MS was not being able to jump around as he used to. By spring 1991, he was emaciated—a mere 115 pounds—and, though barely able to walk ten yards without help, living alone in a rented mansion at the summit of Bel Air. He spent his days holed up in his bedroom, clutching a .357 Magnum and worrying that, if he tried to move around, he might crack his head on his Spanish marble floor. He was close to broke from all his medical bills. It was, he later reflected, "the lowest point of my life."

With the help of old friends and lovers, Pryor shook off his solitude and rallied in 1993 for what became his farewell tour as a comedian. Sitting in an easy chair at center stage, he floated through a set of riffs on his life with MS. For the great part of Pryor's career, he had seemed preternaturally youthful, the vulnerability of a child never far from the surface of his performances. Now he was prematurely aged: ancient at fifty-two, his legs giving out from under him, vulnerable because his frailty put him uncomfortably close to death's door. "I don't want to be alone when I die," he said onstage at one point, and the audience knew that this was no idle conjecture. Then, Pryor-style, he cut the solemnity with a sacrilegious confession: "I want some motherfuckers fighting over my money." The old, discomfort-inducing honesty was still there, charged now with a nearly unbearable pathos. One critic observed that when Pryor's audience gave him a standing ovation at the end of his short set, it was "as emotionally drained as the comedian himself."

After that tour, itself abbreviated because he became too fatigued, Pryor kept an exceedingly low profile. When asked if he still saw himself as an entertainer, he spoke of that part of himself as if it were a ghost: "It's not gone, but it's *fa-a-ar* away. Like it's through this veil and I can't see it. I know where it is, but I can't reach it." "I'm going through a humbling experience these days," he told another interviewer. "There was a time in my life when I thought I had everything—millions of dollars, mansions, cars, nice clothes, beautiful women, and every other materialistic thing you can imagine. Now I struggle for peace."

In 1994, he asked Jennifer Lee to return to him, and she did, taking on the roles of caretaker and, in the words of one journalist, "general aide-de-camp." It was a time for looking backward and taking stock. Richard published his memoir in 1995, and then, in 2000, Jennifer helped pull together the boxed set . . . *And It's Deep Too!*, a retrospective of his recording career as a stand-up. The following year, the two were married in secret—without the knowledge, even, of Richard's children, several of whom had never warmed to the idea of Jennifer as a stepmother. As the MS took its remorseless course, Richard often withdrew into himself, the burden of company more weight than he wished to bear. He might take in a movie once a week, but rarely went out otherwise. He saw his children just once a month as his condition deteriorated—a limitation that frustrated them. His daughter, Rain, concluded that her father had become Jennifer's "prisoner," locked up in his own home. For her part, Jennifer maintained that she was just trying to protect Richard from undue stress.

On December 10, 2005, nine days after his sixty-fifth birthday, Richard suffered a heart attack in the early morning. He was pronounced dead later that day at a nearby hospital. Newspapers and magazines mourned his passing in terms befitting the death of an icon. (Former senator and presidential candidate Eugene McCarthy died the same day, and Pryor's death trumped his on front pages across America.) "The comic voice of a generation," judged the *Washington Post*. In the *New York Times*, Mel Watkins underlined how Pryor had transformed black and white America both: "He unleashed a galaxy of street characters who traditionally had been embarrassments to most middle-class blacks and mere stereotypes to most whites. And he presented them so truthfully and hilariously that he was able to transcend racial boundaries and capture a huge audience of admirers in virtually every ethnic, economic, and cultural group in America."

For all the glory of Pryor's achievement as an artist, his funeral was a small, private affair at Hollywood's Forest Lawn Cemetery. Mourners lit candles to help guide Richard's passage to the spirit realm; Diana Ross broke spontaneously into a rendition of "Amazing Grace." Richard's casket was covered with sunflowers—flowers that he'd loved ever since, as a child, he discovered a patch of them in a vacant lot near his grandmother's brothels. "I don't know how they got started or who watered them, but every summer they headed up toward the sky as if they were trying to escape the ghetto," he'd written in his memoir. "After realizing they couldn't get out, they bloomed. Big. Like giant sunbursts." Those hardy sunflowers spoke to the beautiful side of Richard, the side that brought startling radiance to places where few expected to find it.

Of course there was another side to Richard, one darker and messier, and that lived on after his death, too. He had declared, on his 1993 concert tour, that he hoped to have "some motherfuckers fighting over my money," and he got his wish. Upon discovering that Richard had named Jennifer as his executor and principal heir, his eldest daughter, Elizabeth, charged Jennifer, in civil lawsuits, with forging Richard's name on their marriage license, committing elder abuse as his caretaker, and exploiting his frailty to gain control of his assets. Jennifer fought the allegations in court and prevailed. Unsurprisingly, the legal battle left a rift between Jennifer and several of Richard's children: four years later, only Richard Jr. agreed to participate in *Omit the Logic*, the documentary Jennifer produced about their father. Richard Pryor had never led an uncomplicated life, and he did not die an uncomplicated death.

There are two periods in comedy in America: before Richard Pryor and after Richard Pryor." So declared actor-comedian Paul Rodriguez, and few practicing comics, whether born in 1929 or 1969, would beg to differ. Among the generation before Pryor, Mel Brooks has classed Pryor as "the funniest comedian of all time," ahead of Charlie Chaplin, Buster Keaton, and Harpo Marx; Bob Newhart has named him "the single most seminal comedic influence in the past 50 years." Among the generation after Pryor, he has been called "the Picasso of our profession" (Jerry Seinfeld) and "the Rosa Parks of comedy" (Chris Rock). Comedians from Eddie Murphy and Damon Wayans to George Lopez and Margaret Cho have recalled the impact Pryor made on their young selves and offered a version of Bernie Mac's economical tribute: "Without Richard, there would be no me."

But if Pryor was, in Wayans's words, the artist who "started it all," what exactly did he start? It's easier to nod to the scale of Pryor's achievement than to capture its precise contours. His artistic legacy is extremely various—and as packed with complexities as the personality he presented onstage. Pryor could be foul-mouthed and delicate, cruel and tender, straight-ahead and experimental. He could be the most hilarious and the most troubling of comedians. He could be soul brother number one and a trickster who slipped the bonds of race. How to encompass all these Pryors?

We might start by refusing to pigeonhole him in the most obvious way. Conducting interviews for this book, I commonly heard the complaint that Pryor was misunderstood as an artist—that too often people mistook the headline-generating part of Pryor's style, his use of obscenity, for the whole. "All they remember is the profanity," said the poet-critic Amiri Baraka, "and they can't get to the profundity." Actor Tim Reid went so far as to suggest that "Richard has probably spawned more bad comics than any comic in history": "they listened to his words but they didn't understand his creativity." For his part, Pryor himself grew frustrated when hip critics kept grouping him with Lenny Bruce, the other pioneer of obscenity in stand-up; he said he suffered from "the Lenny Bruce syndrome." And considering Pryor's approach to the stage, one can understand why the comparison rankled. Lenny Bruce was a satirist who made points; Pryor was a searcher who explored, in the words of Mudbone, how oftentimes "there is no point to be made."

Perhaps it's best, for clarity's sake, to isolate three different aspects of Pryor's achievement: his legacy as a stand-up comic, as a social critic, and as a crossover artist.

As a stand-up, Pryor was a revolutionary in the spirit of the high 1960s, suggesting that nothing was off-limits. Not only did he refuse to respect the boundaries of "good taste," but more powerfully, he turned his own powers of scrutiny on himself and declared that nothing was off-limits there, either. His anxiety and his fury, his self-loathing and his cravings for intimacy, sex, and power—in other words, the parts of him that might have shamed or endangered him—were the lifeblood of his stage act. There was a swirling, centrifugal energy to Pryor's stand-up; audiences were pulled deep into his inner drama. At the same time, Pryor had a finely honed capacity to fling himself outward and into character. His stage instantly became a carnival of working-class black life, or a free-fire zone where the battle of the sexes played out. Often, even a personal soliloquy evolved into a multicharacter playlet, his angels and demons manifesting as characters with their own voices and body language.

To create these well-populated worlds, Pryor didn't merely unzip his brain and let the characters out. Rather, he used his craft. In the tributes from his fellow comedians, one hears the admiration of those who understand the effort that goes into the look of effortlessness. In Pryor's case, his craft was mastered over three decades, through lessons with a succession of teachers and collaborators. Over his first twenty years, he absorbed, from his grandmother, a gift for storytelling; from his father, an eye for the cruel yet telling detail; and from the examples of Jerry Lewis and Sid Caesar, an antic expressiveness that made caricature come alive. Over the next ten years, he discovered, with his comic friends in Greenwich Village, how to lose himself in improv; with Redd Foxx, how to make dirty jokes his own; and with Paul Mooney and his Berkeley writer friends, how to sharpen the political edge of his satire. Later, as he collaborated with the likes of Mel Brooks and Lily Tomlin, he remained open to what each could give him, whether as catalyst or sounding board. He perfected the art of dramatizing his own imperfections, and the world's.

As a social critic, Pryor is best summed up by the epithet his friend Paul Mooney coined for him: Dark Twain. Just as Mark Twain looked at the aftermath of the Civil War and meditated, with wit and troubling insight, on how people remained unfree after the watershed of emancipation, so Pryor skeptically sized up America in the moment after the freedom movements of the 1960s had washed over it. Having grown up in brothels, he never lost the raw, brothel-oriented point of view. The ugliness of the world was not something to be flinched at or avoided. He detested euphemisms because they dulled the hard smack of the truth; he wanted to bring his audience to its senses. And so he became, for many in the 1970s, a guide to how much and how little the world had changed after Black Power and Flower Power. Blacks might have a new set of rights on paper, but they were still brutalized by police, criminalized by the media, shunted off to prisons, or caught in the gears of the welfare bureaucracy. Lovers might talk more frankly about sex and pleasure, but they still talked past one another or stung one another with insults. And as for drugs, well, they might open the doors of perception, but they might also drop you into the abyss, or worse.

With material like "Bicentennial Nigger" and "Black Death," Pryor could be severe as he followed the logic of American violence to its brutal end. (Another connection with Twain: the finale of *A Connecticut Yankee in King Arthur's Court* has the self-satisfied hero electrocuting twenty-five thousand knights until they have fused into "homogeneous protoplasm, with alloys of iron and buttons.") Yet Pryor wasn't the sort to deliver a message in italics or hand down a judgment from a mountaintop. He was allergic to self-righteousness and shuddered to find it in himself. Rather than hold himself up as a model of integrity, he presented himself as someone in danger of cracking up, reduced to a lesser version of himself, with just his mother wit to save him. Here he showed a way of handling the pressure of stereotype that later performers, of all backgrounds, found liberating. "The comedian who really moved me was Richard Pryor," recalled Roseanne Barr. "I knew that he was inside the stereotype and fighting against it, that he was going to blow it up from the inside. I got that immediately. I thought, By God, I'm going to do the same thing being a woman."

Pryor's work as a crossover artist is probably the most misunderstood and underappreciated aspect of his career. His Berkeley friend Ishmael Reed captured the common view when he wrote, upon Pryor's death, that Pryor was a "comic genius who let Hollywood use him." (Reed wished, for Pryor's legacy as an artist, that the comic had resisted the charms of the film industry and stayed in Berkeley.) Reed's view has taken hold for reasons that are easy to understand. Pryor was generally more unbuttoned on the concert stage than the sound stage, and he himself disavowed many of his films upon their release, offering that he'd been "hustled" or that he'd done a project just for the money. As he grew older he didn't seem to shed these misgivings: in his memoir, he spent shockingly little time on the films that consumed much of his energy in the 1970s and after. And as few critics would dispute, Pryor's movies after 1983 were often weak tea. It can be tempting, then, to draw a line between the "genius" Pryor and the "sellout" Pryor, with the "genius" Pryor conveniently color-coded as the "blacker" Pryor. His stand-up albums and concert films, powered by the creativity of a black man alone onstage, would fall in the "genius" category; his non-concert films would stand as evidence of how an obtuse Hollywood failed to adapt to the arrival of a formula-shattering black talent.

There are two problems with this view. First, while one can lament all that Pryor didn't accomplish on-screen, the more remarkable story is how Pryor became one of the most unlikely stars in Hollywood history, jimmying a window open, sneaking into the dream factory, and taking over one of its projection rooms. *Lady Sings the Blues*, *Wattstax*, and *Silver Streak*—each of these breakthrough films for Pryor had been conceived with him in a minimal role at best, then were jolted into a new shape by his improvisations. In his Hollywood career, Pryor was aided and abetted by a wide range of collaborators, mostly Jewish or black, who believed in his wayward talent and sometimes staked their credibility upon it. The list of these collaborators is long, and might start with the names John Badham, Mel Brooks, Michael Campus, Rob Cohen, Berry Gordy, James B. Harris, Arthur Hiller, Max Julien, Thom Mount, Sidney Poitier, Paul Schrader, Michael Schultz, Mel Stuart, and Hannah Weinstein. And while it would be wrong to underplay the tension Pryor felt toward many of them, especially white directors like Badham, Campus, and Schrader, it would be churlish to deny that they were crucial intercessors. By trusting in Pryor's talent, they gave him a new platform, one often conceived with the brazen character of his stand-up in mind. *Bingo Long*, *Which Way Is Up?*, and *Blue Collar* were all scripted with Pryor's stand-up crackling in the background, and the finished films have a good deal of its bounce and bite.

The second problem with the dismissal of Pryor's crossover work is that it can lead us to misconstrue the nature of his creativity. In some sense, all his creative projects—not just his films for Hollywood—were the result of his hunger to "cross over." He grew up in the tough-minded world of Peoria's red-light district, and though he held tight to his native knowledge as the grandson of Marie Pryor, madam and matriarch, he yearned for an alternative to the dominion of Marie—a world where he might discover his freedom. His first major crossover performance was at Blaine-Sumner elementary school, before a group of white classmates; his second, at the Carver Center, before a "respectable" black audience of parents and children; his third, at Harold's Club, before a mixed audience looking to escape respectability. He never stopped from there. "Pryor's career in total," sums up critic Greg Tate, "was a masterpiece of how to keep it moving."

The stage attracted Pryor because it was a place to experiment with his identity, to make himself as large and as various as his imagination allowed. He pushed beyond the boundaries of his blackness even as he dramatized the extraordinary richness of black life—a balancing act that made him an "off-color" comedian in a different, more profound sense. He was an unusual combination: a trickster in love with the power of disguise and a seeker driven to push beyond surfaces and get to the bottom of things, where he hoped to find something like love, or a state of sheer connection.

When asked by Barbara Walters, not long after he burned himself alive, if he saw the world in terms of black people and white people, Pryor answered by reframing the question.

"I see people," he said searchingly, "as the nucleus of a great idea that hasn't come to be yet."

ACKNOWLEDGMENTS

Writing this book has been an intensely collaborative effort, and it gives me great pleasure to acknowledge those who helped give it shape.

Richard Pryor's own family was extraordinarily generous, adding much insight to my sense of Pryor and his formative years. I would like to thank his great-uncle Allen Pryor, his daughter Elizabeth Pryor, his daughter Rain Pryor, and his son Richard Pryor Jr. for their gracious response to my inquiries. In particular, I would like to thank his sister Barbara McGee for the trove of family photographs she shared; his sister Sharon Wilson Pryor for her brave choice to revisit painful memories with me; and his wife Jennifer Pryor, whose assistance allowed me to procure Pryor's school and U.S. Army records.

One of the joys of writing this book is that it gave me a reason to meet a small galaxy of fascinating people and ask questions—often extremely impertinent ones—about their past. The book would be inconceivable without the generosity of those who agreed to reflect on their past involvements with Richard Pryor and the circles he inhabited. I wish to thank Bob Altman, Irving Arthur, Michael Ashburne, John Badham, Bill Banks, the late Amiri Baraka, Pete Barbutti, Pat Benson, Andrew Bergman, the late Harvey Bernhard, Jimmy Binkley, Michael Blum, Ben Caldwell, Caryl Camacho, Joe

Camacho, Ralph Camilli, Don Campbell, Michael Campus, Matt Clark, Rob Cohen, Loren Cornish, John Davidson, Ron DeBlasio, Jim Demetropolis, Henry Diltz, Paul Dorpat, Rick Edelstein, the late Alan Farley, Susan Fink, Jane Fishbeck, Silver Saundors Friedman, Sandy Gallin, Carl Gottlieb, Dick Green, Hillis Griswold, Michael Grussemeyer, Cecil Grubbs, Paul Hampton, James Harris, Patricia Heitman, Bert Heyman, Thomas Henseler, Arthur Hiller, Maria Höhn, Henry Jaglom, Margaret Kelch, Craig Kellem, the late Zalman King, Harvey Levine, Robert Marchese, Lonette McKee, Kres Mersky, John Moffitt, Joe Mosley, Sam Mosley, Sonya Nesbit, Harold Parker Jr., Ishmael Reed, Tim Reid, the late Manny Roth, Michael Schultz, Kirk Silsbee, Willis Smith, Penelope Spheeris, Dave Sprattling, Norman Steinberg, the late Mel Stuart, Murray Swartz, Judy Tannen, Renee Taylor, Ros Taylor, Joan Thornell, Fred Tieken, Cathryn Timmes, John Timmes, Lily Tomlin, Rocco Urbisci, Melvin Van Peebles, Jeff Wald, Hollie West, and Bruce Scott Zaxarides.

The research for this book took me through a maze of archives large and small, public and private, where I found no shortage of material that begged to be deciphered. For helping me to locate, interpret, and/or reprint such material here, I owe a special debt to the following individuals and institutions: Pam Adams, Linda Aylward and Elaine Sokolowski of the Peoria Public Library, the Bahai Center of Peoria, the Bradley University Special Collections Library, Don Cannon, the City of Peoria's Records Office, the Decatur Circuit Court's Office, Brian DeShazor of Pacifica Archives, Deborah Dougherty, Dan Einstein of UCLA's Film and Television Archive, Zephyr Frank, John Glover of Fort Leonard Wood, Martha Hammer of the Peoria Police Department, Edie Harris, David Houston of the *Los Angeles Daily Journal*, Rick Hunter and Amy Schwegel of the Billy Rose Theatre Division of the New York Public Library, Tal Kahana, Norm Kelly, Harry Langdon, Tammy Lomelino of the Peoria County Circuit Clerk's Office, the Los Angeles County District Attorney's Office, the Margaret Herrick Library of the Academy of Motion Pictures Arts and Sciences, Mary Ann Mason, Rachel McPherson, the Paley Center for Media, Richard Peek of the University of Rochester, the *Peoria Journal Star*, the Peoria Public Schools Office, Dylan Penningroth, Jim Ralph, Marcia Reed, Loni Shibuyama of ONE National Gay and Lesbian Archives, and USC's Cinematic Arts Library and its David L. Wolper Center for the Study of Documentary. I would like to give an extra tip of the cap to Rhino's Reggie Collins, who has often lent me his expert knowledge of Richard Pryor's recordings, released and unreleased.

I owe another sort of debt to the following writers, some of whom counseled me on the art and mechanics of biography, others of whom generously opened up their Rolodexes and shared their contacts: Robin D. G. Kelley, Harvey Kubernik, Gerald Nachman, Ann Powers, Arnold Rampersad, Carlo Rotella, R. J. Smith, Steve Stanley, James Sullivan, Mike Weatherford, Oliver Wang, Eric Weisbard, Richard White, Jon Wright, and Richard Zoglin. A related thanks go out to those whose writings on Pryor were an especially generative source of insights and leads: Hilton Als, Cecil Brown, David Felton, James Haskins, James McPherson, Paul Mooney, Fran Ross, Jeff Rovin, Mel Watkins, and the father-son team of John A. Williams and Dennis Williams.

A project of this magnitude would have been impossible to incubate and develop without assorted forms of material support. I am grateful to the Andrew W. Mellon Foundation for crucial seed funding; the Stanford Humanities Center for providing the most clean, well-lighted place imaginable; and Stanford's Spatial History Project for helping sponsor the development of the book's companion website and for loaning the services of Erik Steiner, cartographer extraordinaire. At UC-Berkeley, I've benefitted from the support of the Office of the Dean of the Arts and Humanities, the Doreen B. Townsend Center for the Humanities, and the Department of English. Special thanks go to UC-Berkeley's Janet Broughton, Anthony Cascardi, Samuel Otter, Katherine O'Brien O'Keeffe, and Sue Schweik for all their kind offices.

I have been blessed to work, over the past five years, with a remarkable group of research assistants—William Bottini, Camille

Brown, Alex Catchings, Ismail Muhammad, Jonathan Shelley, and Alex Tarr—who often served as my closest advisers and helped me refine my ideas enormously. Bottini deserves special thanks as he continued to contribute to the project, with intelligence and good humor, long after leaving UC-Berkeley and its employ.

I wish to thank my tremendous team at HarperCollins: editor David Hirshey, for his galvanizing faith in the project; editor Barry Harbaugh, for his scrupulous sculpting of my prose; editorial assistant Sydney Pierce, for her graceful help with the mechanics of publication; and copy editor Jenna Dolan, for her meticulous labors. My agent Chris Calhoun gave this project a great boost three years ago and has been a continuous source of sage counsel ever since.

For forms of moral support too various and mind-boggling to enumerate, I would like to thank the following friends and family: Kathy Donegan, Joseph Entin, Dan Fishman, Ethan Goldstine, Melissa Hillier, Dave Landreth, Waldo Martin, Louis Matza, Marjorie Perloff, Gautam Premnath, Corey Robin, my brother Lawrence Saul and his family, my parents, Beth and Ronald Saul, Penny Sinder, Dan Smith, and Bryan Wiley. Ken Parille read each chapter as it rolled off the printer and was both rigorous and generous in his feedback. A special sort of writerly thanks go to the Beanery, a happy local oasis at which I consumed roughly 100 gallons of fine coffee while writing this book, day-in and day-out, on its premises.

My wife, Elana, has lived the writing of this book on an intimate level; her contributions to it, and to me, are incalculable. I could not have written this book without her. And last, I would like to thank my seven-year-old son, Maxie, who, having listened to much Richard Pryor while in the womb, proceeded then to grow in mass along with my manuscript. Unfailingly he gave me a fresh perspective on it. I dedicate this book to him lovingly.

NOTES

ix **"A trickster does not live":** Lewis Hyde, *Trickster Makes This World: Mischief, Myth, and Art* (New York: Farrar, Straus and Giroux, 1998), p. 6.

ix **"The world around us":** Nancy Anderson, " 'Lightning' Is Not a Black Film," *Mt. Vernon Register-News*, Aug. 17, 1977, p. 7A.

Author's Note

xii **Pryor himself had declared that he'd reinvented himself:** Richard Pryor, with Todd Gold, *Pryor Convictions and Other Life Sentences* (New York: Pantheon, 1995), pp. 115–18 (hereafter *Pryor Convictions*); **His previous biographers couldn't even agree:** John A. Williams and Dennis A. Williams, *If I Stop, I'll Die: The Comedy and Tragedy of Richard Pryor* (New York: Thunder's Mouth Press, 1991), p. 63; Fred Robbins and David Ragan, *Richard Pryor: This Cat's Got 9 Lives!* (New York: Delilah Books, 1982), pp. 48–49; Jeff Rovin, *Richard Pryor: Black and Blue: The Unauthorized Biography* (New York: Bantam, 1983), pp. 77–78; Jim Haskins, *Richard Pryor: A Man and His Madness* (New York: Beaufort Books, 1984), pp. 57–61.

xii **His struggle was that of an artist searching for his true medium:** For more on Pryor's time in Berkeley, see chapter 14.

xiii **He hated the standard format of Q&A:** David Felton, "This Can't Be Happening to Me," *Rolling Stone*, Oct. 10, 1974, p. 44; Frederick D. Murphy, "Richard Pryor: Teetering on Jest, Living by His Wits," *Encore American & Worldwide News*, Nov. 24, 1975, p. 27; **J. Edgar Hoover:** John H. Corcoran Jr., "The Peoria Stroker Has Arrived," *National Observer*, May 24, 1975; **when film critic Elvis Mitchell:** Tirdad Derakhshani, "Godfather of Soul Guilty of Domestic Abuse," *Philadelphia Inquirer*, June 15, 2004.

xiv **"It's hard to get information from these people":** "John A. Williams interview with Steve Logue, Nov. 29, 1983," Box 171, John A. Williams Papers, Special Collections Library, University of Rochester, Rochester, NY.

xiv **John A. Williams was the one early biographer:** Williams and Williams, *If I Stop, I'll Die*, pp. 20–23; see also the interviews collected in Box 171, John A. Williams Papers. In the last year, as I was putting the finishing touches on this book, two other Pryor biographies were published: David Henry and Joe Henry,

Furious Cool: Richard Pryor and the World that Made Him (Chapel Hill, NC: Algonquin Books, 2013), and Cecil Brown, *Pryor Lives! How Richard Pryor Became Richard Pryor* (CreateSpace, independent publishing platform, 2013). Unfortunately, these appeared too late for me to incorporate their insights.

xvi **A recent documentary film on Pryor:** *Richard Pryor: Omit the Logic*, directed by Marina Zenovich (Fresh One Productions and Tarnished Angel, 2013).

Prologue

1 **the most celebrated stand-up comedy performance of all time:** *Richard Pryor: Live in Concert*, directed by Jeff Margolis (Special Events Entertainment, 1979) (hereafter *Richard Pryor Live in Concert*). For more on *Live in Concert*, see chapter 23.

2 **At this point the routine:** For a related take on the complex morality of this sketch, see Jonathan Rosenbaum, "The True *Auteur*," *Take One*, May 1979, p. 14.

3 **"25 or 30 different people":** Louie Robinson, "Richard Pryor Talks," *Ebony*, Jan. 1978, p. 122.

Chapter 1: Dangerous Elements

7 **On the morning of October 19, 1929:** "Boy Slapped, Woman Routs Proprietor of Confectionary," *Decatur Herald*, Oct. 20, 1929, p. 3.

8 **The city's black citizens were expected to stay "in their place":** Sundiata Keita Cha-Jua, "A Warlike Demonstration: Legalism, Violent Self-Help, and Electoral Politics in Decatur, Illinois, 1894–1898," *Journal of Urban History* 26, no. 3 (July 2000).

8 **a straight razor she reportedly stashed in her bra:** Author's interview with David Sprattling, July 16, 2010; author's interview with Rob Cohen, Aug. 18, 2010.

8 **Richard's "Mama" was born Rithie Marie Carter:** *The Mike Douglas Show*, aired Nov. 29, 1974, DVD in author's possession; **only three survived:** 1900 U.S. Federal Census (Population Schedule), Decatur City, Decatur Township, Macon County, IL, ED 46, Sheet23b, Family 480, Dwelling 495, S. Colfax, Richard Carter household. Marie's mother had better luck with her next four children: three of them survived. See 1910 U.S. Federal Census (Population Schedule), Decatur City, Decatur Township, Macon County, IL, ED 104, Sheet 8A, Family 191, Dwelling 191, S. Colfax, Richard Carter household.

8 **Marie's grandfather Abner Piper had been a Union volunteer:** *Consolidated Lists of Civil War Registrations, 1863–1865,* NM-65, entry 172, 620 volumes, Records of the Provost Marshal General's Bureau (Civil War), Record Group 110, National Archives, Washington, DC; "Historical Register of National Homes for Disabled Volunteer Soldiers, 1866–1938," Records of the Department of Veterans Affairs, Record Group 15, National Archives, Washington, DC; **lived at home with Marie:** "The Death Record," *Decatur Herald*, Jan. 5, 1906, p. 6.

9 **early settlers felt:** Otto John Tinzmann, *Selected Aspects of Early Social History of DeKalb County* (Chicago: Loyola University of Chicago, 1986), p. 106; **it prospered by attracting cereal mills:** Mabel E. Richmond, *Centennial History of Decatur and Macon County* (Decatur, IL: Decatur Review, 1930), pp. 368–69; "F. P. Howard Returns to Business," *The Soda Fountain* 20 (June 1921): 78; Dan Guillory, *Decatur* (Chicago: Arcadia, 2004); **black Decaturites were shunted to a shabby part of town:** Cha-Jua, "A Warlike Demonstration," p. 599.

9 **The lynching of Samuel Bush in 1893:** "A Dastard's Deed," *Decatur Weekly Republican*, June 28, 1894, p. 1; Cha-Jua, "'A Warlike Demonstration," pp. 599–

604. Even as late as 1929, the lynching of Bush was described in the official *Centennial History of Decatur and Macon County* as "one of the exciting events" of the 1890s (Richmond, *Centennial History of Decatur and Macon County*, p. 357). Cha-Jua, "'A Warlike Demonstration," pp. 609–13.

10 **a ten-chapter history of the city's black population:** Aug. 27–Sept. 3, 1929; see also Richmond, *Centennial History of Decatur and Macon County*.

10 **worked as a bouncer in the city's brothels . . . yelling obscenities in public:** "Are Sorry They Spoke," *Daily Review* (Decatur), Apr. 27, 1895, p. 1; **beating his wife:** "Presto Chango," *Decatur Bulletin-Sentinel*, Feb. 1, 1896, p. 1; **whipping his wife:** "Pleaded Guilty," *Decatur Evening Republican*, June 26, 1899, p. 2; **assaulting someone with brass knuckles:** *Decatur Daily Review*, Oct. 3, 1906, p. 10; **pointing a firearm at his brother:** "At Peddecord's," *Decatur Bulletin-Sentinel*, Feb. 1, 1896, p. 1; **A tall, wiry amputee:** "Bothered the Dago," *Herald-Dispatch*, (Decatur), Aug. 22, 1896, p.6; "A Strange Burglary," *Bulletin-Sentinel* (Decatur), July 13, 1895, p. 4; **bootlegged liquor:** "Carter Arrested for Selling," *Decatur Review*, Oct. 26, 1908, p. 8; **gaming room:** "Mayor M'Donald Stops Craps Game," *Decatur Review*, Dec. 24, 1907, p. 3; "Negroes and Whites Captured in Raid," *Decatur Review*, July 7, 1912, p. 19; **when Congress passed the Opium Exclusion Act:** On the 1909 Opium Exclusion Act, see David Courtwright, *Dark Paradise: A History of Opiate Addiction in America* (Cambridge, MA: Harvard University Press, 2001 [1982]).

11 **"opium joint":** "Opium Seized in Opium Joint," *Decatur Sunday Review*, Oct. 26, 1908, p. 8. The fact that police discovered opium ashes, or *yenshee*, rather than fresh smoking opium suggests that Carter's clientele ran to the down-and-out, not the sporting classes.

11 **"disturbing element":** "'Tip' Carter Says He Will Vote 'Dry,'" *Decatur Review*, Mar. 31, 1910, p. 4; **arrested simply for taking a room:** "Two Arrested," *Decatur Evening Republican*, May 29, 1899, p. 3; **a robbery:** "Even Took His Teeth," *Decatur Review*, Nov. 23, 1903, p. 8; "Two Arrested," *Daily Review* (Decatur), Nov. 24, 1903, p. 8; "Carter Arrested for Selling," *Decatur Review*, Jan. 27, 1904, p. 5.

11 **a stunning 150 times:** "Events of 1903 in Decatur in Short Sentences," *Decatur Herald*, Jan. 5, 1904, p. 2; **a "cakewalk" party:** "Tip's Cake Walk," *Decatur Herald*, July 2, 1902, p. 5. Tip Carter was even the local Republican Party's nominee for pound master, the city official responsible for the management of loose livestock ("Republican Ticket," *Daily Review* [Decatur], Mar. 18, 1903, p.2).

11 **"It is a noticeable fact":** "Capture a Crap Game," *Herald-Dispatch* (Decatur), Jan. 13, 1897, p. 4.

12 **evening of August 15, 1914:** "Married," *Decatur Review*, Aug. 17, 1914, p. 12; **Church of the Living God:** "Barbecue," *Decatur Review*, July 10, 1914, p. 14; **"using bad language":** "Is Fined $6.30," *Decatur Review*, June 22, 1916, p. 11; **altercation with a police officer:** "Chauffeur Talked Back to Policeman," *Daily Review* (Decatur), Apr. 1, 1910, p. 1.

12 **born in June of the following year:** "LeRoy Pryor Jr.," *Peoria Journal Star*, Oct. 2, 1968; **"grand ball":** "Claimed Wife Attended Ball," *Decatur Herald*, Dec. 6, 1915, p. 12; **another assault charge:** *Decatur Herald*, Apr. 3, 1917, p. 10.

13 **carrying a revolver:** *Decatur Review*, May 27, 1917, p. 5.

13 **struck him on the head with a common hammer:** "Wife's Hammer," *Decatur Review*, Mar. 10, 1904, p. 7; **"on a ripsnorter":** "Dick Carter in Trouble," *Decatur Herald*, Dec. 8, 1905, p. 5. Julia Carter may have been something of a hell-raiser herself: at one point her husband had *her* arrested for disturbing the peace (*Decatur Review*, March 10, 1904, p. 10).

13 **A madam herself:** "Donahue Pleads Not Guilty," *Decatur Review*, Feb. 10, 1914,

p. 10; **pressed assault charges:** "Colored Woman Stabs Her 'Hubby,'" *Decatur Review,* Mar. 23, 1916, p. 4; **"the only time" . . . Jim shot an elderly man:** "Last Escapade for Jim Carter," *Decatur Review,* Feb. 13, 1919, p. 4; **"Why wait until they kill?":** "Why Wait Until They Kill?," *Decatur Review,* Feb. 14, 1919, p. 6; **filed for divorce:** *Decatur Review,* Oct. 19, 1919, p. 11. More on Jim Carter's assault and criminal record can be found at *People v. James Carter,* Case No. 9046, Circuit Court, Macon County, IL (1919).

14 **year-old baby:** "LeRoy Pryor Jr.," *Peoria Journal Star,* Oct. 2, 1968 (Pryor's father was born June 7, 1915); **"gathering of the colored brethren":** "Got Affectionate with Baby," *Daily Review* (Decatur), Nov. 19, 1916, p. 1.

14 **Marie and Roy had three more children together:** Birthdates of Marie's children are from 1920 U.S. Federal Census (Population Schedule), Decatur Township, Macon County, IL, ED 143, Sheet 1b, Family 16, Household 18, 448 E. Orchard St., Roy Pryor household; 1930 U.S. Federal Census (Population Schedule), Precinct 31, Decatur City, Decatur Township, Macon County, IL, ED 58-33, Sheet 16b, Family 32B, Household 342, 1604 East Sangamon St., Thomas Bryan household; **But then Julia died, on May 4, 1921:** *Daily Review* (Decatur), May 4, 1921, p. 14; **a sting on their home:** "Seven Colored Men Arrested," *Decatur Review,* Jan. 5, 1919, p. 8.

14 **Marie filed for divorce:** "Asks Divorce," *Decatur Review,* Apr. 20, 1922, p. 16; **cook at a restaurant:** "Indictment for Nick Economos," *Decatur Review,* Oct. 18, 1925, p. 25; "Dismiss Economos Case," *Decatur Herald,* Nov. 20, 1925, p. 3.

15 **grand larceny:** "One Prisoner of Fourteen Pleads Guilty," *Decatur Herald,* June 6, 1928, p. 3; "Pryor and Storey Given Probation," *Decatur Daily Review,* July 7, 1928, p. 10; **she went back to her maiden name:** "Three Are Arrested in Raid Sunday Night," *Decatur Herald,* Oct. 14, 1929, p. 5.

15 **He had married his first wife:** "Divorcees Are Given Warning," *Decatur Herald,* June 7, 1927, p. 2; **three months on the Vandalia prison farm:** "Police Notes," *Decatur Daily Review,* Feb. 16, 1927, p. 13; **milked cows and grew corn:** Charles L. Clark and Earle Edward Eubank, *Lockstep and Corridor: Thirty-Five Years of Prison Life* (Cincinnati, OH: University of Cincinnati Press, 1927), p. 130.

15 **fighting with another black woman:** "Police Notes," *Decatur Review,* Aug. 21, 1919, p. 8; **Jazz Bone Minstrel Company:** *The Mike Douglas Show,* aired Nov. 29, 1974.

16 **crushed between two train cars:** "Richard Carter Dies of Injuries," *Daily Review* (Decatur), Sept. 20, 1925, p. 11; **family legend:** *Pryor Convictions,* p. 18. Richard Carter is misidentified as Pryor's grandfather "LeRoy Pryor" in the family legend, though the circumstances of the death fit exactly with his great-grandfather's accident on the job.

16 **a swing city:** "Saloons Win with Record Vote Cast," *Decatur Daily Review,* Apr. 6, 1910, p. 1; "Jail Terms End Reign of Booze," *Chicago Daily Tribune,* Jan. 24, 1915, p. 3; **"canned heat" . . . the Sterno trash mounds . . . loaf of bread:** "New Generation of Criminals, New Kind of Crime Has Developed during Last Decade, Chief Wills Has Found," *Decatur Herald,* May 27, 1928, p. 25. On Prohibition more generally, see Daniel Okrent, *Last Call: The Rise and Fall of Prohibition* (New York: Scribner, 2010).

16 **It didn't take much . . . "buffet flat":** Okrent, *Last Call,* p. 208; **a raid on her home:** "Three Are Arrested in Raid Sunday Night," p. 5.

17 **she pleaded not guilty:** "Boy Slapped, Woman Routs Proprietor of Confectionary"; **struck back with a countercharge of assault:** "Tit for Tat," *Decatur Herald,* Nov. 4, 1929, p. 16; "Three Arrested on Assault Charges," *Decatur Herald,* Nov. 5, 1929, p. 5.

17 **Marie eventually lost in court:** "Woman Fined $50 on Assault Charge," *De-*

catur Herald, Nov. 13, 1929, p. 3.

18 **factory payrolls plunging:** Richard J. Jensen, *Illinois: A History* (New York: W.W. Norton, 1978), pp. 124–25; **Class war broke out:** Andrew Hemingway, *Artists on the Left: American Artists and the Communist Movement, 1926–1956* (New Haven, CT: Yale University Press, 2002), p. 160; **blacks who held on to work:** author's interview with Allen Pryor, Nov. 10, 2010.

18 **"Diamond Lil," a stout black madam:** "Peoriana" binder, Peoriana collection, Peoria Public Library, pp. 2342–43; Norman V. Kelly, "Miss Diamond Lil'," *News & Views* (Peoria), Feb. 2011, p. A18; **"largest and liveliest black and tan resort":** " 'Diamond Lil' Found in Cell; Keeps Silence," *Chicago Daily Tribune*, Dec. 27, 1931, p. 9; "She Refuses to Tell of Drainage Board Whoopee," *Chicago Daily Tribune*, Dec. 28, 1931, p. 26.

18 **located at 200 Eaton Street:** Legend of photograph of Eaton Street, c. 1920, in personal collection; **130 Eaton:** Polk's Peoria City Directory (1936), p. 716; **"sinkhole of midwestern vice":** "Peoria Vice Hit by Government," *The Christian Century*, March 18, 1942, p. 362.

19 **the Bumboat:** John Bartlow Martin, "The Town That Reformed," *The Saturday Evening Post*, Oct. 1, 1955, p. 27.

Chapter 2: The Backside of Life

20 **"Sweet as far-off bugle note":** Edna Dean Proctor, *Poems* (Cambridge, MA: H. O. Houghton and Company, 1890), p. 64; **On the vaudeville circuit . . . "I spent four years there one night":** George H. Scheetz, "Peoria," in Edward Callary, ed., *Place Names in the Midwestern United States* (Lewiston, NY: Edwin Mellon Press), pp. 43–70; **"it rained all week":** John M. Sumansky, "Peoria: The Growth and Development of a River Town," in Daniel Milo Johnson and Rebecca Monroe Veach, eds., *The Middle-Size Cities of Illinois: Their People, Politics, and Quality of Life* (Springfield, IL: Sangamon State University, 1980), p. 137.

21 **"the rube and the boob":** Elise Morrow, "Peoria," *The Saturday Evening Post*, Feb. 12, 1949, p. 20; **America's most unchecked sin city:** On sin cities, see Mara Keire, *For Business and Pleasure: Red-light Districts and the Regulation of Vice in the United States, 1890–1933* (Baltimore, MD: Johns Hopkins University Press, 2010; **"talk[ed] about corruption":** Martin, "The Town That Reformed," p. 27; **divorced at a rate:** Clarence Wesley Schroeder, *Divorce in a City of 100,000 Population* (Chicago: University of Chicago, 1939), pp. 7–9.

21 **"city of good spirits":** Morrow, "Peoria," pp. 20–21; **whiskey tax:** "Peoria Is Busier Than Ever, but It's Much Drier," *Chicago Daily Tribune*, Sept. 8, 1926, p. 4; **half the federal government's internal revenue:** Jerry Klein, "Made in Peoria: The Birth of Industry," *Peoria Magazine*, Jan. 2011.

21 **city of violent contrasts:** Morrow, "Peoria," pp. 20–21, 119.

22 **outhouses:** *1950 United States Census of Housing, Peoria, Illinois Block Statistics,* 1950 Housing Report, Vol. 5, Part 142 (U.S. Government Printing Office, 1952).

22 **"Don't bother my racket":** "This Was Peoria," *Peoria Journal Star*, Apr. 15, 1956, p. A8.

22 **it had the votes: Ed Woodruff . . . . "Peoria likes to live":** "Illinois: By the River," *Time*, Feb. 26, 1945, p. 17; **"bums cluttered its steps":** Betty Friedan, "Now They're Proud of Peoria," *Reader's Digest*, Aug. 1955, p. 93.

22 **"wide open as the gateway to hell" . . . the sex trade:** "Old Peoria? As Wide Open as the Gateway to Hell," *Peoria Journal*, Apr. 14, 1956, p. 1.

23 **"When I had left Chicago":** Anonymous with John Bartlow Martin, *My Life in Crime: The Autobiography of a Professional Criminal* (New York: Harper and Brothers, 1952), p. 219.

23 **Madams . . . register their girls:** "Old Peoria: Fixed Cops, Gang Murders, Wholesale Kidnappings," *Peoria Journal*, Apr. 15, 1956; **by a doctor for venereal disease:** "This Was Peoria," p. A8; **twenty dollars a month . . . "Special Miscellaneous":** Wayne Slater, "Oldest Profession Amateurish Now," *Peoria Journal Star*, Nov. 2, 1980, p. D1; **newsstands and neighborhood drugstores:** "This Was Peoria," p. A8; **even near local schools:** "Old Peoria? As Wide Open," p. 1.

23 **its black residents:** Romeo B. Garrett, *The Negro in Peoria* (Peoria, IL: self-published, 1973), pp. 80, 93–95. **Like many northern cities before World War II:** On segregation in the North, see Thomas Sugrue, *Sweet Land of Liberty: The Forgotten Struggle for Civil Rights in the North* (New York: Random House, 2008).

24 **a city of grudging compromises:** Garrett, *The Negro in Peoria*, pp. 47–48, 93–94; **There might be black policemen:** Author's interview with John Timmes, May 15, 2011; **could not arrest white people:** Author's interview with Loren Cornish, May 19, 2011.

24 **"queen of Peoria's half world":** "Underworld—Women," Peoriana collection, Peoria Public Library, pp. 2335–42.

25 **butcher . . . chauffeur . . . entertainer:** *Polk's Peoria Directory* (St. Louis: Polk, 1938), pp. 79, 392; **elevator operator:** *Polk's Peoria Directory* (St. Louis: Polk, 1941), p. 127; **"the backside of life":** Maureen Orth, "The Perils of Richard Pryor," *Newsweek*, Oct. 3, 1977, p. 62. Unlike Marie's other children, her son William does not appear to have become involved in the businesses she ran.

25 **over two hundred pounds:** Author's interview with Cecil Grubbs, July 9, 2010; **Golden Gloves boxing tournament:** "LeRoy Pryor Jr.," *Peoria Journal Star*, Oct. 2, 1968; **recruiting the girls and the johns:** Author's interview with Allen Pryor, Nov. 10, 2010; **six feet tall . . . six foot two:** Author's interview with Cecil Grubbs, July 9, 2010

25 **"Don't mess with my money" . . . whites were not to be harassed:** Ibid.; **her straight razor . . . "a lot of men":** Author's interview with David Sprattling, July 16, 2010; author's interview with Rob Cohen, Aug. 18, 2010; **customary 50 percent:** Anonymous, *My Life in Crime*, p. 222; **upgraded to a pistol:** Author's interview with Sharon Wilson Pryor, Dec. 15, 2010.

26 **"I'll put my twelves":** Author's interview with Barbara McGee, Dec. 14, 2010.

26 **"I was raised to hate cops":** James McPherson, "The New Comic Style of Richard Pryor," *New York Times Magazine*, Apr. 27, 1975, p. 34; **"all the political people":** Felton, "This Can't Be Happening to Me," p. 44; **"As fast as they would come in":** Author's interview with Cecil Grubbs, July 9, 2010.

26 **One of Richard's neighbors recalled:** Author's interviews with Rosalyn Taylor, Nov. 30, 2010, and Dec. 2, 2010.

26 **background of Richard Pryor's mother:** 1930 U.S. Federal Census (Population Schedule), Pilot Township, Vermilion County, IL, Robert Thomas household; **A more attainable sort of glamour:** Edie Harris, e-mail communication with author, Nov. 11, 2010.

27 **the Thomas family relocated to Peoria:** *Polk's Peoria Directory* (St. Louis, Mo.: Polk, 1940), p. 572; *Polk's Peoria Directory* (St. Louis, Mo.: Polk, 1941), pp. 651, 821; **Gertrude was light-skinned:** Description of Gertrude taken from photograph in author's possession; **Peoria madams preferred:** Anonymous, *My Life in Crime*, p. 224; **the professional name of Hildegarde:** Rovin, *Richard Pryor*, p. 12.

27 **And what did Gertrude see:** Description of Buck taken from photographs in author's possession.

28 **"If I Didn't Care":** Phil Doubet, *My Pryor Year: A 333 Soul Anthology* (Lincoln, NE: iUniverse, 2006), p. 552; **wooed another woman who would carry his**

child: Author's interview with Barbara McGee, Dec. 14, 2010.

28 **Marie took Gertrude's side:** Rovin, *Richard Pryor*, p. 13.

28 **Richard Franklin Lennox Thomas Pryor:** "Births," *Peoria Daily Record*, Dec. 4, 1940.

28 **"I wish" . . . "made it her job":** *Pryor Convictions*, pp. 15, 20. In interviews, Pryor often referred to both Gertrude and his stepmother Ann as his "mother." This has bred some confusion among previous biographers. Gertrude was largely out of his life after his parents' divorce, when he was five; Ann was a presence in his life for almost twenty years, from the late 1940s until her death in 1967. Biographers have tended to conflate the two in a single portrait of a mother who worked for his grandmother as a prostitute, but Gertrude's life as a prostitute seems to have been considerably briefer than Ann's, and Ann appears to have worked largely for Richard's father in the 1950s and '60s.

Previous biographers (and even Pryor himself) have also made the understandable mistake of identifying Gertrude as a bookkeeper: there was another "Gertrude Thomas," who is found in Peoria directories well before Pryor's mother arrived in town and who is listed as a bookkeeper and accountant, but I've found no evidence that points to Pryor's mother working in that profession as well.

28 **"At least Gertrude":** *Pryor Convictions*, p. 20.

29 **"I chose you, so be cool":** *The Tonight Show Starring Johnny Carson*, aired July 21, 1978 (NBC); **four more, by four different women:** Author's interview with Sharon Wilson Pryor, May 13, 2011.

29 **Caterpillar jumped into high gear:** Klein, "Made in Peoria"; **the opening of nearby Camp Ellis:** Camp Ellis brochure in author's possession; **so many soldiers:** Mary Watters, *Illinois in the Second World War, Vol. 1: Operation Home Front* (Springfield, IL: State of Illinois, 1951), p. 163.

29 **Regional military officials noticed:** William McLinden, "Report U.S. Plans to Close City to Men on Leave Unless Prostitution Is Checked," *Peoria Journal-Transcript*, Jan. 28, 1942; "Carson Orders Resorts Closed," *Peoria Journal-Transcript*, Mar. 5, 1942; "Peoria Vice Hit by Government," p. 362; **"Why Peoria's Vice District Must Go!":** Peoria Junior Chamber of Commerce poster, Junior Chamber of Commerce materials, Peoria Public Library; **a form of wartime sabotage:** "Vice Termed Sabotage," *Peoria Star*, Dec. 7, 1943, p. 3. On military efforts to curb venereal disease during World War II, see Allan Brandt, *No Magic Bullet: A Social History of Venereal Disease in the United States* (New York: Oxford University Press, 1985), pp. 161–70; **the foxlike Mayor Woodruff:** "Council-Mayor Fight Widens as New Edict on Vice Is Ignored," *Peoria Journal-Transcript*, Dec. 17, 1941; "Council Votes Cleanup Power," *Peoria Journal-Transcript*, Dec. 1, 1943, p. 5; **a two-hundred-dollar instead of a five-dollar fine:** "Police Ordered to Enforce Ban," *Peoria Journal-Transcript*, Nov. 30, 1943, p. 13.

30 **They jacked up their prices:** Anonymous, *My Life in Crime*, p. 223; **his grandmother had her own strategy for skimming:** Murphy, "Richard Pryor," p. 28.

30 **A good number of Camp Ellis men were black:** Author's interview with Allen Pryor.

30 **Buck married Gertrude:** "Marriage Licenses," *Peoria Daily Record*, Dec. 28, 1943, p. 4; **practical concerns:** John Modell, *Into One's Own: From Youth to Adulthood in the United States* (Berkeley: University of California Press, 1989), pp. 185–86; **fifty-dollar . . . ten-thousand-dollar life insurance policy:** Steven Mintz and Susan Kellogg, *Domestic Revolutions: A Social History of American Family Life* (New York: Free Press, 1988), pp. 154, 168.

31 **the Peoria newspapers announced:** see, for instance, *Peoria Star*, Dec. 24, 1943.

31 **as early as 1931:** "Arrest Four Negroes in Wabash Sand House," *Decatur Herald*, Mar. 17, 1931; **One intriguing detail:** "Final Payment Roll, Voucher No. 1904, Fort Devens, Mass., 19-035, July 25, 1944," National Personnel Records Center, St. Louis, MO. LeRoy Pryor's full army record was lost in a fire, so we will likely never know the full circumstances under which he left the service.

32 **On the afternoon of February 12, 1945:** "Ellis Sergeant Slugged, Robbed," *Peoria Journal-Transcript*, Feb. 13, 1945, p. 13; **Buck was indicted by a grand jury:** State of Illinois, Peoria County v. Fred Pinkerton and LeRoy Pryor, Peoria County Circuit Clerk, Peoria, IL (Feb. 12, 1945).

32 **worked together at the Famous Door:** Richard Pryor school records, Peoria school district (in author's possession) (hereafter "Pryor school records"); **Typically, in the heat of argument:** Author's interview with Allen Pryor; **Gertrude's divorce papers:** "Bill of Complaint," *Gertrude Pryor v. Leroy Pryor*, Gen. No. 30372, Peoria County Clerk's Office archives, n.p. (Jan. 1946). **"Gertrude drank a lot":** *Pryor Convictions*, pp. 20, 23.

33 **"Okay, motherfucker . . . confused my ass just by being so nice to me":** *Pryor Convictions*, pp. 26–27.

33 **"He felt that deep kind of love . . . would've killed her":** Ibid., p. 19.

33 **She fled North Washington Street with her son:** "Answer and Counterclaim for Divorce," *Gertrude Pryor v. Leroy Pryor*, n.d., n.p.

33 **sharing space with livestock:** *Pryor Convictions*, p. 33.

34 **"always conducted herself" . . . "extreme and repeated cruelty":** "Bill of Complaint," *Gertrude Pryor v. Leroy Pryor*, n.p.

34 **In his counterclaim:** "Answer and Counterclaim for Divorce," *Gertrude Pryor v. Leroy Pryor*, n.p.

34 **Her one formal response:** "Affidavit of Non-Military Service," *Gertrude Pryor v. Leroy Pryor*, Jan. 17, 1946, n.p.

34 **a future Illinois Supreme Court judge:** "Judge Culbertson dies at age 90," *Peoria Journal Star*, July 27, 1980.

35 **"I'd like to be with my grandma, please":** *Pryor Convictions*, pp. 32–33.

35 **this recollection:** Ibid., p. 32; **"at the present time":** "Decree for Divorce," *Gertrude Pryor v. Leroy Pryor*, Mar. 26, 1946.

35 **In his ruling:** Ibid.; **a presumption, in custody battles:** Mary Ann Mason, *From Father's Property to Children's Rights: The History of Child Custody in the United States* (New York: Columbia University Press, 1994); Mary Ann Mason and Ann Quirk, "Are Mothers Losing Custody? Read My Lips: Trends in Judicial Decision-Making in Custody Disputes—1920, 1960, 1990 and 1995," *Family Law Quarterly* 31, no. 2 (Summer 1997): 215–36; **"custody, control and education":** "Decree for Divorce," *Gertrude Pryor v. Leroy Pryor*, Mar. 26, 1946.

36 **"He had a child":** *The Barbara Walters Special*, aired May 29, 1979 (ABC); **adultery among war brides . . . a divorce rate without precedent in American history:** Mintz and Kellogg, *Domestic Revolutions*, pp. 171–73; **It was tempting to believe:** Culbertson's decision can additionally be explained by the law's relative nonchalance in the face of spousal abuse. Spousal abuse was not deemed a factor in custody battles until the 1960s (author's e-mail communication with Mary Ann Mason, Nov. 10, 2010).

36 **"I got my bizarre sense of humor":** *The Tonight Show Starring Johnny Carson*, aired July 21, 1978 (NBC).

Chapter 3: The Law of the Lash

37 **From an early age:** Rovin, *Richard Pryor*, p. 21; **John Wayne . . . Boris Karloff:** *Pryor Convictions*, p. 44; Rovin, *Richard Pryor*, p. 23; **Funky London:** Dick

Kleiner, "Richard Pryor Back on Top," *Merced Sun-Star*, Jan. 6, 1977, p. 10; **"I used to live in the movie houses":** Robbins and Ragan, *Richard Pryor*, p. 30; **"No movie opened":** Kleiner, "Richard Pryor Back on Top," p. 10.

37 **"I wanted to be just like him":** Robbins and Ragan, *Richard Pryor*, p. 30; **unlikely leading man:** *Law of the Lash* (1947), *King of the Bullwhip* (1950).

38 **LaRue was strictly B-grade:** On LaRue and the B Westerns, see Roderick McGillis, *He Was Some Kind of a Man: Masculinities in the B Western* (Waterloo, Ontario: Wilfred Laurier University Press, 2009), pp. 88–91; **woo a lady:** *Wild West* (1946).

38 **In his home life, violence:** Jennifer Lee, "Trouble Man," *Spin*, May 1988, p. 46.

38 **she was good at getting screams to stop:** Ibid., p. 46; **"hell" . . . "Richard Franklin Lennox Thomas Pryor":** *The Barbara Walters Special*, aired May 29, 1979 (ABC).

39 **late 1970s diary entry:** Richard Pryor, *. . . And It's Deep Too!: The Complete Warner Bros. Recordings*, Rhino R2 76655 (2000) (hereafter *. . . And It's Deep Too!*). I have standardized the spelling and punctuation from Pryor's diary entry; as a result of his intermittent schooling, Pryor never mastered basic rules of spelling and grammar.

39 **"It's so much easier":** Rovin, *Richard Pryor*, p. 32; **"You had to be an adult":** Sander Vanocur, "Richard Pryor: It's a Long Way from Peoria—and It's Your Serve," *Washington Post*, Mar. 20, 1977, p. F3.

39 **"strange, dark, big feel":** *Pryor Convictions*, p. 22; **Formerly a dance hall:** Rovin, *Richard Pryor*, p. 11; **"peck on the windows":** *The Barbara Walters Special*, aired May 29, 1979 (ABC).

39 **shared one of these bedrooms with "Pops":** Richard Pryor, "Unwed Mutha," *Details*, Feb. 1996, p. 86. According to Pryor, Marie stopped sleeping with Pops after she caught him in bed with one of her girls. Part of his punishment was to be paired in bed with "the kickingest kid ever"; **peeking through keyholes:** Vanocur, "Richard Pryor," p. F3.

40 **"watching things when I didn't exactly know what they were":** *The Barbara Walters Special*, aired May 29, 1979 (ABC); **"I saw my mother":** Janet Maslin, "'Didn't Cut Nobody's Throat,' Says a Proud Pryor," *New York Times*, Aug. 18, 1977, p. 76.

40 **"messed me up sexually":** *The Barbara Walters Special*, aired May 29, 1979 (ABC).

41 **elegant suits:** Author's interview with Dave Sprattling; **a one-dollar mistake:** "Waitress Says Parker 'Sapped Her," *Peoria Journal-Star*, July 21, 1957; **China Bee had her own sense of style:** Author's interviews with Harold Parker Jr., Dec. 14, 2010, and May 26, 2011; **Peoria's finer department stores . . . "anything you needed, sexually":** Author's interview with John and Kathryn Timmes, May 15, 2011.

41 **three-hundred-pound bouncer:** Author's interview with Dave Sprattling; **"Bulldog" Shorty:** "Bris Collins Surrenders to Serve Term," *Chicago Defender*, Sept. 11, 1954, p. 5; **boxing manager:** "In St. Louis," *Chicago Defender*, June 3, 1939, p. 9; **procurer:** "'Lack of Prosecution' Kills Case on Collins," *Peoria Journal Star*, Oct. 14, 1959; **counterfeiter:** "Collins Gets Year, Day on Money Count," *Peoria Journal*, July 2, 1954, p. A3; **hundred-thousand-dollar numbers racket:** "Bris Collins Surrenders to Serve Term," p. 5; **Kefauver investigations:** Ibid.; **military and federal penitentiaries:** People of the State of Illinois v. Arthur Anderson, Supreme Court of Illinois (May 27, 1971); **According to musicians:** Author's interview with Cecil Grubbs, July 9, 2010.

42 **police raided:** "Bris Collins' Tap Raided, Closed; Baseball Pool Czar Fined $1000," *Peoria Star*, May 23, 1953.

42 **"As a comedian":** *Pryor Convictions*, p. 24.

43 **"Come on, man":** Ibid., pp. 24–25.

43 **an eclectic mix of businesses:** *Polk's Peoria Directory* (St. Louis, MO: Polk, 1943), p. 538; **a larger location, at 319-21 North Adams:** *Polk's Peoria Directory* (St. Louis, MO: Polk, 1946), p. 170; **all the accoutrements of a smart business:** Pryor family photographs in author's possession; **small jazz-blues combos:** Author's interview with Jane Fishback, Feb. 1, 2011.

43 **Famous Door's clientele, which departed sharply:** Family photograph in author's possession; **Especially after 1:00 a.m.:** Author's interview with John Timmes, May 15, 2011.

44 **One of the smoothest operators:** Author's interview with Harold Parker Jr., Dec. 14, 2010.

44 **a world where blacks and whites might pair up as lovers:** On antimiscegenation laws and the long history of interracial intimacy, see Rachel F. Moran, *Interracial Intimacy: The Regulation of Race and Romance* (Chicago: University of Chicago Press, 2001); Randall F. Kennedy, *Interracial Intimacies: Sex, Marriage, Identity, and Adoption* (New York: Pantheon, 2003); Kevin Mumford, *Interzones: Black/White Sex Districts in Chicago and New York in the Early Twentieth Century* (New York: Columbia University Press, 1997).

45 **Morning Star Baptist Church:** *Pryor Convictions*, p. 26; author's interview with Cecil Grubbs, Oct. 15, 2010; **a soul kitchen feast:** Author's interview with Cecil Grubbs, July 9, 2010; **Richard always dressed nicely:** Author's interview with Margaret Kelch, Jan. 21, 2011; **pair of new shoes:** Author's interview with Ron DeBlasio, Jan. 8, 2011.

45 **"Son, one thing a white man":** Joyce Maynard, "Richard Pryor, King of the Scene-Stealers," *New York Times*, Jan. 9, 1977, p. 18.

46 **ma'am or sir:** Kleiner, "Richard Pryor Back on Top," p. 10; **had to perform his chores:** *The Mike Douglas Show*, aired Nov. 29, 1974; **"If you couldn't put the worm":** *The Tonight Show with Johnny Carson*, aired Sept. 19, 1973 (NBC).

46 **she would try to beat the disobedience out of him:** Vanocur, "Richard Pryor," p. F5; **"Anything you want to know about fear":** Scott Cohen, "Richard Pryor," *High Times*, Dec. 1977, p. 61.

46 **Richard walked on eggshells:** *Richard Pryor Live in Concert*; **"The guy says you have no soul":** Interview with Richard Pryor, on *Only in America, with Greg Jackson*, aired Dec. 12, 1985 (CBS) (in author's possession; hereafter "*Only in America* interview"); **"scared to death" . . . "afraid to make a sound":** Author's interviews with Matt Clark, Dec. 6, 2010, and Dec. 28, 2010.

47 **rustle and straighten out his newspaper:** *Kraft Summer Music Hall*, aired June 13, 1966; *Tonight Show with Johnny Carson*, aired Jan. 12, 1979 (NBC).

47 **"If you don't go to sleep":** *Kraft Summer Music Hall*, aired June 13, 1966.

47 **When other kids . . . His father would brag:** Richard Pryor, "Peoria," *Evolution/Revolution: The Early Years (1966–1974)*, Rhino R2 78490 (2005) (hereafter *Evolution/Revolution*); **A Peoria police officer:** Rovin, *Richard Pryor*, p. 17.

47 **"I was weird":** *The Mike Douglas Show*, aired Nov. 11, 1974.

48 **he had been playing by himself:** *Pryor Convictions*, pp. 28–31.

48 **Red Skelton:** Ibid., p. 44; **lifelong fascination with cartoons . . . twenty-five cartoons in a row:** McPherson, "The New Comic Style of Richard Pryor," p. 41.

49 **would delight himself by drawing:** Author's interview with Michael Grussemeyer, May 27, 2011; **imitating the Road Runner:** Lurlena Pieters, "'Hurt Pride' Leads to Comic Career," *Cleveland Call and Post*, Apr. 20, 1974, p. 3A.

49 **a compelling backstory:** *Oregon Trail Scouts* (Republic Pictures, 1947); **rescuing Red Ryder:** *Cheyenne Wildcat* (Republic Pictures, 1944), *Vigilantes of Dodge*

City (Republic Pictures, 1944), *California Gold Rush* (Republic Pictures, 1946).

49 **pointed lesson:** *Pryor Convictions*, p. 44; **"one of my first big traumatic experiences":** Maynard, "Richard Pryor: King of the Scene-Stealers," p. 11.

50 **first performance as a comic:** *Pryor Convictions*, pp. 14–15; **"That was my first comedy routine":** "Slippin' in Poo Poo," *Evolution/Revolution*.

50 **Richard was one of a minority of blacks:** Author's interview with Michael Grussemeyer, May 27, 2011; **the minstrelsy behind popular radio programs like *Amos 'n' Andy*:** Melvin Patrick Ely, *The Adventures of Amos 'n' Andy: A Social History of an American Phenomenon* (New York: Free Press, 1991), pp. 11–13. The year that Richard arrived at kindergarten, Peoria's high school tried to stage a blackface minstrel show complete with "pickaninnies," and revised its script only under pressure from the local chapter of the Congress of Racial Equality. See Jim Ralph, "Patterns of Protest: The Civil Rights Struggle in Peoria, Illinois, 1945–1970," African American history folder, Peoria Public Library, p. 11; Hazel Fritchell, letter to George Houser, June 3, 1946, Congress of Racial Equality Papers (microfilm), Reel 14, Series III, No. 67.

51 **"Apparently unstable emotionally":** Pryor school records.

51 **During the middle of his second try:** Ibid.; **"The farm" . . . "Yes, sir":** *Pryor Convictions*, p. 33; David Handelman, "What Happened to Richard Pryor?," *Lakeland Ledger*, Jan. 29, 1992, p. 5C.

51 **back in Peoria schools:** Pryor school records; **third grade:** Author's interview with Michael Grussemeyer.

52 **sole brothel with white prostitutes:** *The Barbara Walters Special*, aired May 29, 1979 (ABC); "Joe Eagle Indicted on Lie Charges," *Peoria Journal*, July 2, 1954, p. 1.

52 **"three oddball brothers":** Author's interview with Michael Grussemeyer.

52 **relatively decent grades . . . two Cs, four Ds, and one F:** Pryor school records.

52 **Richard's poor grades in "conduct":** Rovin, *Richard Pryor*, p. 24; author's interview with Michael Grussemeyer.

53 **Irving School's basketball team:** Interview with Michael Grussemeyer; **the toast of the black community:** Rob Thomas, *They Cleared the Lane: The NBA's Black Pioneers* (Lincoln: University of Nebraska Press, 2002); John Christgau, *Tricksters in the Madhouse: Lakers vs. Globetrotters, 1948* (Lincoln: University of Nebraska Press, 2004).

53 **Richard found trouble in a whole new way:** *Pryor Convictions*, pp. 43–44. Another account of the same incident is given in Maynard, "Richard Pryor, King of the Scene-Stealers," p. 11.

54 **saw his father unleash his anger in his defense:** *Pryor Convictions*, pp. 43–44.

54 **"You could almost set your watch by it":** Author's interview with Michael Grussemeyer; **"S[tudent] can't return":** Pryor school records.

54 **the realm of private fantasy:** Rovin, *Richard Pryor*, pp. 22–23.

55 **"I'd write a lot":** Pieters, "'Hurt Pride' Leads to Comic Career," p. 3A.

55 **Born in New Orleans:** "Mrs. Viola Pryor," *Peoria Journal Star*, Jan. 3, 1968; **a prostitute at China Bee's,** *Pryor Convictions*, p. 34; **a freckled Creole . . . elegant dresses cinched with belts:** Family photographs in author's possession; author's interview with Margaret Kelch, May 15, 2011.

55 **pleaded with the principal:** Author's interview with Michael Grussemeyer; **calling her "Mom":** *Pryor Convictions*, p. 34.

56 **"Why'd they kick me out of school?":** Ibid., pp. 40–41.

56 **Peoria's longtime mayor was defeated:** "Triebel and Madden Win Mayor Races," *Peoria Journal-Transcript*, Feb. 14, 1945, p. 1.

57 **by 15 percent:** "Bluff Outvotes 'Valley' Wards," *Peoria Journal-Transcript*, Feb. 14.

1945, p. 17; **cleared out the city's slot machines:** Frank Sturdy, "Gamblers Tell Why They Quit Peoria Rackets," *Chicago Daily Tribune*, Oct. 20, 1948, p. 21; **sharpshooter hiding in some nearby underbrush:** "Dry Era Gangster Killed in Ambush," *New York Times*, July 27, 1948, p. 46; "2d Shelton Brother, Leader of Gang, Slain in Ambush," *Chicago Daily Tribune*, July 27, 1947, p. 1; **a recording of an emissary:** "Shelton's 'Voice from Grave' Charges $25,000 Bribe Plot," *Chicago Daily Tribune*, Aug. 8, 1948, p. 1; **a sweeping investigation:** "State Names 2 to War on Crime, Vice," *Chicago Daily Tribune*, Sept. 13, 1948, p. 1; **bombed a year after:** "Bomb Blasts Peoria Home of Prosecutor," *Chicago Daily Tribune*, Dec. 17, 1949, p. 1.

57 **ex-GIs returning to Peoria:** Friedan, "Now They're Proud of Peoria," pp. 94–95; **breaking the hammerlock:** "John C. Parkhurst Memoir, Volume I," Illinois General Assembly Oral History Program, Norris L. Brookens Library, University of Illinois at Springfield, pp. 43–46; Herbert Gamberg, "The Escape from Power: Politics in the American Community" (Monticello, IL: Council of Planning Librarians, 1969), pp. 6–9; Martin, "The Town That Reformed," p. 26; **thirty-five raids:** "Eleven 'All-American' Cities of 1953," *The American City*, Feb. 1954, p. 113.

58 **Since the early 1940s:** "Business and Civic Leaders Join in Call for Solution of Midtown Bridge Problem," *Peoria Journal-Transcript*, Sept. 1, 1940; **In 1951:** "Fayette-Jackson Is Area for New Span," *Peoria Star*, July 26, 1951; **Fourteen buildings:** "State to Clear 14 Buildings Here," *Peoria Star*, July 9, 1953; **1950 U.S. Census:** *1950 Housing Census Report: Block Statistics, Peoria, Illinois*, Volume V, Part 142 (Washington, DC: U.S. Government Printing Office, 1952), p. 6.

58 **In late 1951:** Pryor school records; **Famous Door had closed . . . beauty shop:** *Polk's Peoria Directory* (St. Louis, MO: Polk, 1948), p. 106; *Polk's Peoria Directory* (St. Louis, MO: Polk, 1950), p. 14; **cheaper rents and less ramshackle housing:** *1950 Housing Census Report: Block Statistics, Peoria, Illinois*, pp. 6. 14; **pool hall:** *Polk's Peoria Directory* (St. Louis, MO: Polk, 1952), p. 115.

58 **Blaine-Sumner elementary:** Pryor school records.

Chapter 4: Glow, Glow Worm, Glow

59 **Mrs. Yingst struck a deal with him:** Eric Sandstrom, "Deal with Teacher Gave Pryor First Audience," *Peoria Journal Star*, Dec. 26, 1982; *Pryor Convictions*, p. 47; **rarely late for school again:** Pryor school records.

60 **especially inspired by Jerry Lewis:** *The Merv Griffin Show*, aired Aug. 1, 1966. When Pryor met Lewis in person on *The Merv Griffin Show* in 1966, he earnestly recounted how he "fell in love" with him while watching the 1952 film *Sailor Beware* and called him "the god of comedy."

61 **a prime-time show:** "Classmate Recalls Pryor's School Days," *Peoria Journal Star*, May 10, 1985; author's interviews with Margaret Kelch, Jan. 21, 2011, and May 15, 2011.

62 **"When I heard their laughter":** *Pryor Convictions*, p. 47.

63 **Cs in reading:** Pryor school records.

63 **and the bottom fell out again:** "Classmate Recalls Pryor's School Days"; interview with Margaret Kelch, Jan. 21, 2011; "Dempsey" was not the surname of Pryor's seventh grade teacher; I have changed her name, as I was unable to contact her to confirm her treatment of Pryor.

63 **target of a federal narcotics sting:** "Eight Arrested Here in Narcotics Raid," *Peoria Journal*, Apr. 8, 1953, p. A1, A4; "8 Jailed Here in Narcotic Raid," *Peoria Star*, Apr. 9, 1953, p. B6; **twenty-nine heroin capsules:** On the 1950s heroin trade and law enforcement, see Eric Schneider, *Smack: Heroin and the American*

City (Philadelphia: University of Pennsylvania Press, 2008). Dickie's alleged fellow "ringleader" was Jimmy Bell, a jazz musician who had fronted a group that played regularly at the Famous Door ("Bell Sought, Six Held in Dope Case," *Peoria Journal*, Apr. 9, 1953, p. B1; and "Bell Captured in St. Louis on Dope Charges," *Peoria Journal*, Apr. 10, 1953, p. B1).

64 **box of counterfeit money:** *Pryor Convictions*, p. 52; **confrère Bris Collins:** "Collins Gets Year, Day on Money Count," p. A3; **federal penitentiary:** *Pryor Convictions*, p. 52.

64 **"What happened?" she asked:** "Classmate Recalls Pryor's School Days"; author's interviews with Margaret Kelch, Jan. 21, 2011, and May 15, 2011.

64 **she followed the precedent:** Author's interview with Margaret Kelch, Jan. 21, 2011.

46 **"He wanted to be included" . . . she might have fallen for him:** Ibid.

65 **One day, Marie received a phone call:** *The Mike Douglas Show*, aired Nov. 29, 1974; Pryor school records.

65 **He was placed in Roosevelt Junior High:** Pryor school records.

66 **"closely split":** E-mail communication with Willis Smith, May 15, 2011.

66 **spring of 1955:** Sidney Baldwin, "In My Opinion: Children's Theater of Carver Center," March 15, 1955, p. 10; **a squat, unassuming brick building:** "Push Plan for Negro Center," *Peoria Journal Transcript*, Nov. 30, 1943, pp. 1, 16; "**Mecca of the black community":** Author's interview with Kathryn Timmes, July 21, 2011; **three-quarters of black Peorians . . . "teenage hangout":** "Push Plan for Negro Center," pp. 1, 16; "Tenth Anniversary Report of Carver Community Center," Carver Center folder, Peoria Public Library; Eunice Wilson, "Red Feather Agency Builds Useful Life," *Peoria Journal*, Oct. 15, 1952; "Carver Center Given 'Once Over' by Student," *Peoria Journal Star*, Oct. 20, 1957, p. 5; "Billy Smiles," Carver Center pamphlet, Juliette Whittaker folder, Bahai Center, Peoria, IL.

67 **behest of a friend:** Author's interview with Matt Clark, Dec. 6, 2010; **Colored Women's Aid Society:** "George Washington Carver Community Center Association" pamphlet (n.d.), Carver Center folder, Peoria Public Library; **Carver's teachers:** Author's interview with Kathryn Timmes, May 15, 2011; **black women's club movement:** Wanda A. Hendricks, *Gender, Race, and Politics in the Midwest: Black Club Women in Illinois* (Bloomington: Indiana University Press, 1996); Nikki Brown, *Private Politics and Public Voices: Black Women's Activism from World War I to the New Deal* (Bloomington: Indiana University Press, 2006); Elizabeth Lindsay Davis, *Lifting as They Climb: The National Association of Colored Women* (Washington, DC: National Association of Colored Women, 1933).

67 **Juliette Whittaker:** Steve Strahler, "Juliette Whittaker: 'If You Shoot for the Moon, You're Bound to Hit a Star,'" *Peoria Journal-Star*, Mar. 8, 1981, p. B1; "F. S. Whittaker, Lawyer, Father of Peorian, Dies," *Peoria Journal Star*, Apr. 7, 1965; Channy Lyons, "Whittaker's Expressive Arts," *Peoria Times-Observer*, Nov. 27, 2002, p. B1.

68 **"made you forget about things":** *Pryor Convictions*, p. 48; **dashikis:** Author's interview with Cecil Grubbs, May 13, 2011; **bongo drums:** "She Lends Many Talents to Corn Stock," *Peoria Journal Star*, June 11, 1957; **Tchaikovsky . . . Miles Davis:** Author's interview with Cecil Grubbs, May 13, 2011; author's interview with Matt Clark, May 25, 2011; **"When we're putting a play together":** *The Mike Douglas Show*, aired Nov. 11, 1974.

69 **her father, a Harvard Law alum:** Amilcar Shabazz, "Carter Wesley," in Ty Cashion and Jesus F. de la Teja, eds., *The Human Tradition in Texas* (Wilmington, DE: Scholarly Resources, 2001), p. 167.

68 **someone who walks onstage:** *Pryor Convictions*, pp. 48–49; **never a good reader:** Author's interview with Carl Gottlieb, Aug. 25, 2010.

69 **Starting with this, his very first role onstage:** *The Mike Douglas Show*, aired Nov. 11, 1974.

69 **"Yeah, it's true" . . . "That's the way":** Strahler, "Juliette Whittaker." Whittaker assumed that Pryor had read and memorized the dialogue from the script, but this seems unlikely: even as a leading man in Hollywood, he struggled with written scripts.

69 **a woman who did everything:** Author's interview with Matt Clark, Dec. 6, 2010.

70 **Her *Rumpelstiltskin*:** Baldwin, "Children's Theater of Carver Center."

70 **"His elevator doesn't go":** Author's interview with Matt Clark, May 25, 2011; author's interview with Kathryn Timmes, May 15, 2011; **"slap him away":** Scott Hilyard, "'A Quiet Storm': Woman Who Mentored Richard Pryor Remembered at Service," *Peoria Journal Star,* May 8, 2007, p. B5; **"I never even heard him mentioned":** Rovin, *Richard Pryor,* p. 32.

70 **"We've got a new one!":** Author's interview with Kathryn Timmes, May 15, 2011.

71 **sat in her office's big chair:** Author's interview with Kathryn Timmes, July 28, 2011; **field trips:** Author's interview with Kathryn Timmes, May 15, 2011; Strahler, "Juliette Whittaker," p. B1; **"When I would come into that pool hall":** *The Mike Douglas Show,* Nov. 11, 1974.

71 **Juliette tried to slip in some moral instruction:** Strahler, "Juliette Whittaker," p. B1; *The Mike Douglas Show,* aired Nov. 11, 1974.

72 **Richard took in Juliette's method:** Author's interviews with Kathryn Timmes, May 15, 2011, and July 21, 2011.

73 **Richard's apprenticeship as a stage actor:** Rovin, *Richard Pryor,* p. 33.

73 **chalked up to the gender norms:** Strahler, "Juliette Whittaker," p. B1.

73 **role of emcee:** John A. Williams interview with Juliette Whittaker, Oct. 31, 1983, Box 171, John A. Williams Papers, University of Rochester, Rochester, NY; **Local gangs:** Author's interview with David Sprattling, July 16, 2010.

74 **in a class of his own:** Author's interview with Cecil Grubbs, July 9, 2010; **"The kids would come":** John A. Williams interview with Juliette Whittaker, Oct. 31, 1983.

74 **He did "impressions":** Author's interview with David Sprattling; **Rummage Sale Ranger:** *Pryor Convictions,* p. 50.

74 **"Miss Whittaker was just a magic lady":** *The Mike Douglas Show,* aired Nov. 11, 1974.

Chapter 5: The Boot

75 **one of 9 blacks:** *The Crest of 1956: Centennial Year* (Peoria, IL: Peoria High School, 1956); **even its custodians:** Ibid.; **its controlled environment:** Author's interview with Loren Cornish, May 19, 2011; **"Richard had something":** Rovin, *Richard Pryor,* p. 31; **best marks:** Pryor school records.

75 **Mr. Fink:** *Pryor Convictions,* p. 50; **A former air force colonel:** Author's interview with Susan Fink, May 25, 2011; **experimented with model airplanes:** *The Crest of 1957: Yearbook of Peoria High School* (Peoria, IL: Peoria High School, 1957); *The Crest of 1958: Yearbook of Peoria High School* (Peoria, IL: Peoria High School, 1958), p. 17; **"didn't put up with foolishness":** Author's interview with Loren Cornish; **clown . . . in the classroom's back row:** *Pryor Convictions,* p. 50.

76 **mid-March . . . 129 days:** Pryor school records; **Frank Sinatra . . . Roseanne Barr:** John Lahr, *Show and Tell: New Yorker Profiles* (Berkeley: University of California Press, 2000), pp. 53, 113–14. Pryor gives another account of his expulsion in Pieters, "'Hurt Pride' Leads to Comic Career," p. 3A.

76 **None of the eight other blacks:** *The Crest of 1958: Yearbook of Peoria High*

School; **a paltry crop:** Garrett, "The Negro in Peoria"; "Ministers Lament Small Number of Negro High School Graduates," *Peoria Journal Star*, Jan. 4, 1962; **a dropout rate:** Bill Conver, "Teenagers Need to See Value of School Work," Apr. 10, 1957; Bill Conver, "School Dropouts among Negroes Highest Here," *Peoria Journal Star*, Nov. 2, 1964.

76 **"It's okay":** *Pryor Convictions*, p. 51; **mid-'50s survey:** *Industrial Resource Survey of Metropolitan Peoria, Vol. 1* (Peoria, IL: Association of Commerce, 195[]), pp. 539–42.

77 **"I can do the sweeping":** *Pryor Convictions*, p. 51.

77 **designed by the same architect:** "National Register of Historic Places Inventory—Nomination Form: Pere Marquette Hotel," June 24, 1982 (document in author's possession); **"made the shine cloth":** *Pryor Convictions*, p. 51; **always dreamed:** Author's interview with Joe Mosley, Dec. 10, 2010. In the mid-1950s, the Pere Marquette started suffering from the squareness of the time, quite literally so: its domed lobby was outfitted with a drop ceiling, in an aesthetically cruel renovation that foisted midcentury modern style on a Greek Revival building.

77 **"the jingle-jangle of possibilities":** *Pryor, Convictions*, p. 53; **his grandmother told him to clean a skillet:** *The Mike Douglas Show*, aired Nov. 29, 1974.

78 **"So I'm sitting on the front porch":** Ibid.

79 **Around the summer of 1956:** Jerry Tallmer, "Richard Pryor: When It Rains," *New York Post*, Dec. 18, 1976, p. 23; **"an attractive little package":** *Pryor Convictions*, pp. 54–55; **"What's wrong with the boy, Buckie?":** *The Barbara Walters Special*, aired May 29, 1979 (ABC).

79 **a family meeting:** Ibid.; **who himself had fathered four children:** Author's interview with Sharon Wilson Pryor, May 13, 2011; **April 1957:** Tallmer, "Richard Pryor: When It Rains."

79 **For a while:** "Enlisted Qualification Record," Apr. 14, 1959, Richard Pryor U.S. Army records (in author's posession) (hereafter "Pryor army records"); **"I never knew":** Sidney Fields, "Kook from Peoria," (New York) *Daily News*, Mar. 5, 1966, p. 19; **"It was nasty work":** *Pryor Convictions*, p. 53.

79 **the kid with the frail body and the smart mouth:** Author's interview with Matt Clark, Dec. 27, 2010.

80 **ride on your scooter:** Author's interview with Loren Cornish **"the perfect friendship":** Matt Clark, "Richard Pryor Practiced His Life's Work on Peoria Streets," *Peoria Journal-Star*, Dec. 18, 2005, p. A5. One of Clark's brothers was Mark Clark, who was killed in an infamous raid by the FBI and Chicago police on the apartment of Black Panther Party leader Fred Hampton; Matt Clark himself also later joined the Black Panthers (author's interview, Dec. 27, 2010).

80 **he made his barber:** Pam Adams and Sarah Okeson, "Tears of Laughter," *Peoria Journal Star*, Dec. 11, 2005; **stationed himself . . . State Park:** Clark, "Richard Pryor Practiced His Life Work on Peoria's Streets"; **Silver Satin:** Author's interview with Matt Clark, Dec. 27, 2010; **movies that the city projected:** Author's interview with Loren Cornish; **clear sight lines:** Author's interview with Matt Clark, Dec. 27, 2010. Some remember the curfew as starting at 10:00 p.m.; Pryor and others pegged the time as 11:00 p.m.

80 **The curfew:** Author's interview with John Timmes, Aug. 4, 2011.

81 **lived in fear:** Author's interview with Loren Cornish; author's interview with David Sprattling, July 16, 2010; *Kraft Summer Music Hall*, aired July 3, 1968.

81 **"until three minutes before eleven":** *Kraft Summer Music Hall*, aired July 3, 1968.

82 **April 13, 1959:** "Report of Medical Examination," Apr. 13, 1959, Pryor army records; **a third of its restaurants:** Garrett, *The Negro in Peoria*, p. 95; **turned**

away from the Pantry: Author's interview with Rosalyn Taylor, Nov. 30, 2010; **spent half his take-home pay . . . "Work, pension, die":** *Pryor Convictions*, pp. 53–54.

82 **"Yes, I was in Deutschland":** "The Army," *Evolution/Revolution*; **"Man, when I was in Germany":** "White Chicks," *Outrageous*, Laff Records A206, 1979 (hereafter *Outrageous*); **Clark had lied about his age:** Author's interview with Matt Clark, Dec. 27, 2010.

82 **subversive organizations:** "Armed Forces Security Questionnaire," Apr. 13, 1959, Pryor army records. The list of "subversive organizations" included the Committee for the Negro in the Arts, a cultural group that sponsored black theater in New York and had given key boosts to Sidney Poitier and Pryor's idol Harry Belafonte; **flat feet . . . 126 pounds:** "Report of Medical Examination," Apr. 13, 1959, Pryor army records; **specialized in training:** Jerold E. Brown, ed., *Historical Dictionary of the U.S. Army* (Westport, CT: Greenwood, 2001), p. 190; **"one of the most racist bases":** Curtis Morrow, *What's a Commie Ever Done to Black People?: A Korean War Memoir* (Jefferson, NC: McFarland and Co., 1997), p. 90. For material related to Pryor's time at Fort Leonard Wood, see *Operation Entertainment*, aired Dec. 20, 1968 (WABC-TV); and *Operation Entertainment*, aired Nov. 8, 1968 (WABC-TV).

83 **"I learned to kill":** "Army Life," *Richard Pryor*, Dove Records RS 6325 (1969) (hereafter "*Richard Pryor* [album]".

83 **"When I was in World War II":** *Operation Entertainment*, aired Dec. 20, 1968 (WABC-TV).

83 **another physical:** "Report of Medical History," Aug. 11, 1959, Pryor army records; **"Once again I was covered":** *Pryor Convictions*, p. 55.

83 **embarked from an army terminal:** "Service Record," Apr. 14, 1959–Aug. 20, 1960, Pryor army records; **thirty thousand black GIs:** Maria Höhn and Martin Klimke, *A Breath of Freedom: The Civil Rights Struggle, African American GIs, and Germany* (New York: Palgrave Macmillan, 2010), p. 83.

84 **"For black GIs":** Colin Powell, *My American Journey* (New York: Random House, 1995), p. 53.

84 **former Nazi stronghold:** Maria Höhn, *GIs and Fräuleins: The German-American Encounter in 1950s West Germany* (Chapel Hill: University of North Carolina Press, 2002), pp. 19–24; **"It's about time you got here, boy":** "The Army," *Evolution/Revolution*. In *Pryor Convictions*, Pryor gives a similar but more telegraphic account: the sergeant simply tells him that he looks forward to Pryor's arrival, since "I've been working with a nigger for the last three years" (p. 56).

84 **Mississippi-ish double standard . . . felt intensely isolated:** Author's interview with Maria Höhn, Aug. 9, 2011; Höhn, *GIs and Fräuleins*, p. 96.

85 **black entertainer Timmie Rogers:** Arthur Olsen, "Army Will Court-Martial Major for Attack on Club Entertainer," *New York Times*, Aug. 16, 1958; **"What's the matter, man?":** "Officer Struck Rogers for Calling Him 'Man,'" *Baltimore Afro-American*, Oct. 4, 1958, p. 17.

85 **threatened German bar owners:** Höhn, *GIs and Fräuleins*, pp. 96–97; **"miscegenation" punishable by death:** Maria Höhn, "Love Across the Color Line: The Limits of German and American Democracy, 1945–1968," in Larry Greene and Anke Ortlepp, eds., *Germans and African Americans: Two Centuries of Exchange* (Jackson: University Press of Mississippi, 2011), p. 112; **a proud neo-Nazi in its legislature:** "Neo-Nazis' Gains Laid to Radicals," *New York Times*, May 3, 1959, p. 8; **"Little Harlem":** Höhn, *GIs and Fräuleins*, p. 192; **black GI bars were often raided . . . "Bimbo City":** Ibid., pp. 195–98. A German girlfriend of a black GI could beat the prostitution charge only if she could prove that she and the black GI were in a committed

relationship, and since white commanding officers rarely granted wedding permits to black soldiers in interracial relationships, she rarely had that proof at hand.

85 **Private Pryor stumbled:** *Pryor Convictions*, pp. 56–57.

86 **new black recruit wandering . . . military police . . . New Year's Eve in 1955:** Höhn, *GIs and Fräuleins*, pp. 98, 100, 262.

86 **Richard went to the dispensary:** "Chronological Record of Medical Care," Oct. 7, 1959, Pryor army records.

86 **Siberia of Germany:** Author's interview with Maria Höhn, Aug. 9, 2011; **horse-drawn wagons:** Höhn, *GIs and Fräuleins*, p. 33.

87 **numbing routine:** Norbert Flatow, *What Next Big Guy* (West Conshohocken, CT: Infinity, 2004), p. 105; **one and a half packs a day:** "Chronological Record of Medical Care," June 9, 1960, Pryor army records; **twenty-six pounds:** "Report of Medical Examination," Aug. 1, 1960, Pryor army records.

87 **military career unraveled:** "Unit Punishment Record," Jan. 1960, Pryor Army records; "Enlisted Personnel Data," July 12, 1960, Pryor army records; **there to push the red buttons:** Author's interview with Maria Höhn, Aug. 9, 2011.

87 **"Gringo monkey" . . . "*Chingada madre*":** "Donald D. Edington, Statement," Jan. 29, 1960, Pryor army records; "William Wagoner, Statement," Jan. 29, 1960, Pryor army records; "John E. Walter, Statement," Jan. 29, 1960, Pryor army records. The soldiers who testified against Pryor remembered the Spanish insult as "*chingawa madre*," a sign either that Pryor got his slang wrong or that it was so unfamiliar they didn't hear it quite right.

87 **posing as a Puerto Rican recruit:** "White Chicks," *Outrageous*.

87 **"Are you tired of living":** "William Wagoner, Statement," Pryor army records.

88 **"lacks the ability":** "John E. Walter, Statement," Pryor army records; "Recommendation for Reduction," Jan. 29, 1960, Pryor army records.

88 **picked up some basic German:** *Pryor Convictions*, p. 59; **their motives were decidedly mixed:** Höhn, *GIs and Fräuleins*, pp. 105–8, 206–8; author's interview with Maria Höhn, Aug. 9, 2011.

88 **"Boy, don't you ever kiss" . . . "a revelation":** *Pryor Convictions*, p. 57.

88 **July 9, 1960:** Ibid., p. 57.

89 **a lush melodrama of the time:** *Imitation of Life*, directed by Douglas Sirk (Universal, 1959). With its powerful combination of sentimentality and irony, *Imitation of Life* has become a touchstone in the study of film melodrama. See, for starters, Lucy Fischer, ed., *Imitation of Life* (New Brunswick, NJ: Rutgers University Press, 1991).

89 **According to Richard's memoir:** *Pryor Convictions*, pp. 57–58.

89 **Private Pryor had, for no reason, stabbed:** "Bert K. Crisp, Statement," July 12, 1960, Pryor Army records; "Kenneth D. Teague, Statement," July 12, 1960, Pryor army records.

90 **Like other soldiers:** Author's interview with Maria Höhn, Aug. 9, 2011; **Black soldiers . . . NAACP charged:** Höhn and Klimke, *A Breath of Freedom*, pp. 156–62.

90 **"has a history of violence":** "Recommendation for AR 635-209 Elimination Action," July 19, 1960, Pryor army records; **Race often went unmentioned:** Author's interview with Maria Höhn, Aug. 9, 2011.

90 **Confined to a cell:** *Pryor Convictions*, p. 58; **plenty of time:** "Service Record," Apr. 14, 1959–Aug. 20, 1960, Pryor army records; **a host of ailments:** "Report of Medical History," July 28, 1960, Pryor army records.

91 **On two previous occasions:** "Report of Medical History," Apr. 13, 1959, Pryor army records; "Report of Medical History," Aug. 11, 1959, Pryor army records; **"actor":** "Report of Medical History," July 28, 1960, Pryor army records.

Chapter 6: The Measure of a Man

92 **Fort Dix . . . twenty-five days of back pay:** Pryor army records; **took his half-sister Barbara to a movie:** Author's interview with Barbara McGee, Dec. 14, 2010; **broke out a few snatches of German:** *Pryor Convictions*, p. 59.

92 **Richard was back under Buck's roof:** Author's interview with Barbara McGee, Dec. 14, 2010.

93 **"I came up to him":** Author's interviews with Sharon Wilson Pryor, Dec. 15, 2010; and May 13, 2011.

93 **aficionado . . . Rialto Theater:** Ibid.; **"We had to sit there":** Doubet, *My Pryor Year*, p. 551.

94 **a hangover-cure chili:** Author's interview with Cecil Grubbs, Nov. 17, 2010; **his friend Wilbur Harp:** Author's interview with Hillis Grismore, Nov. 17, 2010.

94 **the Villa . . . "Big Irma" . . . Sylvester "Weasel" Williams:** Author's interview with Rosalyn Taylor, Dec. 2, 2010; **"Kiss my ass, nigger!" . . . "You funny in that hat" . . . "Now what you gonna do" . . . "a beautiful place":** "Hank's Place," *Evolution/Revolution*.

94 **sweet white wine:** Author's interview with Sharon Wilson Pryor, Dec. 15, 2010; **"Preacher" Brown:** Author's interview with Rosalyn Taylor; Pam Adams, "Peoria's Storyteller," *Peoria Journal Star*, June 10, 1993, p. A4; author's interview with David Sprattling; **Wade's Inn:** Author's interview with Joe Mosley, Dec. 10, 2010.

95 **"Man, I know Jesus":** *Richard Pryor: Live and Smokin'*, directed by Richard Blum, MPI Home Video, 1985 (filmed Apr. 29, 1971) (hereafter *Live and Smokin'*).

95 **"What do you do?":** *Pryor Convictions*, pp. 59–60; **bartender:** Author's interview with David Sprattling..

96 **"Boy Wonder of Peoria" . . . "hottest thing this side of Khrushchev" . . . Chicago-bred chorus girl:** Ole Nosey, "Everybody Goes When the Wagon Comes," *Chicago Defender*, Sept. 26, 1959, p. 18; **"give ward residents":** "Fourth Ward," *Peoria Journal Star*, Feb. 11, 1961. Parker lost the aldermanic election.

97 **Regal Theater . . . Chorus girls:** Author's interview with Cecil Grubbs, Sept. 6, 2011; **Musicians suited up:** Author's interview with David Sprattling; **elegance itself:** Photograph of Harold's Club in author's possession; **about one-third white and two-thirds black:** Author's interview with Fred Tieken, Sept. 8, 2011; **scent of cologne . . . Cab Calloway . . . framed portrait:** Ibid.

98 **bribed the musicians' union . . . "Sometimes when he didn't pay":** Author's interview with David Sprattling; **"meanest cats":** Pieters, "'Hurt Pride' Leads to Comic Career," p. 3A; **Parker's own mother:** Author's interview with Fred Tieken.

99 **"anything goes" attitude:** Author's interview with Fred Tieken.

99 **Santa Claus:** Author's interview with David Sprattling; **jackleg preacher . . . car salesman:** Author's interview with Jimmy Binkley, July 1, 2010.

99 **wino character:** Author's interview with Cecil Grubbs, July 9, 2010.

100 **Bob Hope:** Lahr, *Show and Tell*, p. 202; **Caesar . . . Winters:** Gerald Nachman, *Seriously Funny: The Rebel Comedians of the 1950s and 1960s* (New York: Pantheon, 2003), pp. 105–7, 240–53.

100 **not even the house musicians:** Author's interview with David Sprattling.

100 **In the spring of 1961:** Author's interview with Richard Pryor Jr., Oct. 4, 2011; author's interview with Cecil Grubbs, Sept. 6, 2011.

101 **"for better, for worse, and forever":** Pryor, "Unwed Mutha," p. 86. Like Pryor, Patricia Price grew up in an environment that made 1950s sitcoms seem

like broadcasts from another planet. According to Richard and Patricia's son Richard Jr., Patricia's father, Gladstone "Fox" Watts, often drank himself into a rage and then brutalized her mother, Jessie; as an older man, he served time in a penitentiary for having gunned down someone who slandered his manhood (author's interview with Richard Pryor Jr.).

101 **"Son, you don't have to" . . . "If Buck hadn't said that":** Pryor, "Unwed Mutha," p. 86; **ill equipped his son was . . . Fewer than ten people . . . the ceremony had already ended . . . dressed more formally than the bride:** Author's interview with Barbara McGee, May 13, 2011.

101 **June 11, 1961:** "Complaint for Divorce," Richard F. Pryor v. Patricia B. Pryor, No. 66D 746, Peoria County Circuit Clerk's Office archives, (Mar. 4, 1966), p. 1 (hereafter "Complaint for Divorce").

102 **moving into Marie's:** Author's interview with Barbara McGee, May 13, 2011; **paper from clothes hangers . . . the hospital was closed:** Author's interview with Richard Pryor Jr.

102 **"I'm sick of potatoes" . . . "The next time he hits you":** Ibid.

102 **He broke into song:** Ibid.

103 **Around September 1:** "Complaint for Divorce," p. 1; **Fourth Street:** Author's interview with Barbara McGee, May 13, 2011; **"It's part of show business":** *Pryor Convictions*, p. 61; Author's interview with Rosalyn Taylor, Dec. 2, 2010. In his autobiography, Pryor misspells Stenson's last name and misidentifies him as a singer.

103 **On April 1, 1962:** "Fatally Shot," *Chicago Defender*, Apr. 3, 1962; author's interview with David Sprattling; author's interview with Cecil Grubbs, Oct. 3, 2011; "Churchman, Father of 5, Dies Grabbing Tap Interloper's Gun," *Peoria Journal Star*, Apr. 2, 1962; "Grand Jury Recommended on Shotgunning," *Peoria Journal Star*, Apr. 5, 1962.

104 **"looked like a little ape":** *Pryor Convictions*, p. 62.

104 **stopped by the home:** Author's interview with Barbara McGee, Sept. 8, 2011.

104 **Harold Parker lost his liquor license:** "Cop in Closet Sees Bribe Try as Club Owner Faces Charge," *Peoria Journal* Star, June 26, 1961; "Harold's Club Liquor License Revoked," *Peoria Journal Star*, July 21, 1961; *Day v. Illinois Liquor Commission*, Illinois Appellate Court, Second District, Second Division (Jan. 24, 1963), accessed at http://il.findacase.com/research/wfrmDocViewer.aspx/xq/fac.19630124_0000026.IL.htm/qx. **Caterpillar Corporation would build:** Steve Tarter, "Caterpillar Still Studying Options for New Peoria Headquarters," *Peoria Journal Star*, Jan. 13, 2014.

105 **died a few years later:** Author's interview with Harold Parker Jr., Oct. 6, 2011.

105 **operated a tavern . . . since 1939:** *Polk's Peoria Directory* (St. Louis, MO: Polk, 1939), p. 645; **Richard's grandfather Pops took over:** *Polk's Peoria Directory* (St. Louis, MO: Polk, 1954), p. 91; **seventy-two dollars a week:** Vanocur, "Richard Pryor," p. F5; Bill Knight, "Musicians Remember Pryor's Friendship," *Peoria Journal Star*, May 11, 1985; "Carbristo Collins, Former Restaurant Owner, Dies at 72," *Peoria Journal Star*, Dec. 3, 1980; **he had recently opened:** Al Monroe, "So They Say," *Chicago Defender*, Mar. 26, 1962, p. 16.

105 **supporting the Carver Center:** Author's interview with Kathryn Timmes, May 15, 2011; **refusing to carry any liquor:** John L. Clark, "John L. Clark Discovers Negroes Now Talking; Ike Gets 'Suggestions,'" *Pittsburgh Courier*, Oct. 11, 1952, p. 19; **white strippers who straggled in:** Author's interview with Jimmy Binkley, July 1, 2010; **a handful of whites:** Author's interview with Fred Tieken, Sept. 8, 2011; author's interview with David Sprattling, July 16, 2010; **house band . . . "Bris Collins would say":** Author's interview with Jimmy Binkley, July 1, 2010.

105 **For Richard**, Collins Corner was: Ibid.

106 **a baby being born:** *Jo Jo Dancer, Your Life Is Calling*, directed by Richard Pryor (Columbia Pictures, 1986) (hereafter *Jo Jo Dancer*); author's interview with Tim Reid, Oct. 4, 2010; author's interview with Jimmy Binkley, July 1, 2010. For a different inflection on a similar idea, listen to "Being Born," *Richard Pryor: Are You Serious???*, Laff Records A196 (released 1976, recorded late 1960s) (hereafter *Are You Serious???*).

107 **asked him to beat her:** *Pryor Convictions*, pp. 63–64; **"She hit me":** Vanocur, "Richard Pryor," p. F5.

107 **"What the fuck are you doing?":** *Pryor Convictions*, p. 64.

107 **Richard scrambled to gather a few things:** Author's interview with Barbara McGee, May 13, 2011.

107 **His head swimming:** *Pryor Convictions*, p. 64; **Juliette Whittaker, Grossinger's:** Author's interview with David Sprattling, July 16, 2010; Haskins, *Richard Pryor*, p. 31; author's interview with Jimmy Binkley, July 1, 2010; author's interview with Richard Pryor Jr., Oct. 4, 2011.

108 **"One day you'll pay to see me":** Author's interview with Cecil Grubbs, July 9, 2010; **they expected him to return, humbled:** Author's interview with Loren Cornish, May 19, 2011; **a *South Pacific*–style burlesque show:** "Richard Pryor interviewed with Congress of Wonders, 08/25/71, Berkeley, Calif.," transcript in author's possession (hereafter "Congress of Wonders interview").

108 **"probably the best thing we ever did for him":** Jean Budd, "Young TV Comic Richard Pryor Visiting Family Here," *Peoria Journal Star*, Oct. 28, 1966, p. A5.

108 **For Richard, Peoria would always be:** Phil Luciano, "Comedic Genius," *Peoria Journal Star*, Dec. 12, 2005.

Chapter 7: In Search of Openness

111 **"good Negro folks":** Mel Watkins, *On the Real Side: A History of African American Comedy* (New York: Simon and Schuster, 1994), pp. 488–89; **the Chitlin Circuit:** See Preston Lauterbach, *The Chitlin' Circuit and the Road to Rock 'n' Roll* (New York: W.W. Norton, 2010); **"We was so poor":** Haskins, *Richard Pryor*, p. 33.

111 **"Every day was different":** *Pryor Convictions*, pp. 64–66; **"Hey, y'all can boo me now":** Watkins, *On the Real Side*, pp. 488–89.

112 **"You've got to talk":** *Pryor Convictions*, pp. 64–66.

112 **taken his clothes with them:** Fields, "Kook from Peoria," p. 19; **owners of the Casablanca Club:** The incident at the Casablanca was replayed for laughs in Pryor's film *Live on the Sunset Strip* and in his autobiographical film, *Jo Jo Dancer, Your Life Is Calling*, and Pryor seems to have embroidered the tale for these performances. Much of the humor in his retelling came from the incongruity of seeing him dropped into a scene from *The Godfather*—"Look at the pair of *gaguzzis* on that kid . . . What a pack of *zingis* . . . Hey, Paolo, fix up some *frono*"—but the Casablanca's owners were Lebanese, not Sicilian, Watkins, *On the Real Side*, pp. 488–89; **"Hey, do it again, Rich":** *Richard Pryor Live on the Sunset Strip*, directed by Joe Layton (1982) (hereafter *Live on the Sunset Strip*); *Jo Jo Dancer*. Though it was not unusual for performers to be underpaid by club owners on the Chitlin Circuit, I have found no evidence that the owners of the Casablanca were involved in any wrongdoing.

112 **December 1962:** George E. Pitts, "Negro Stars Must Give Negro Promoters Break," *Pittsburgh Courier*, Dec. 8, 1962, p. 16; **Civic Arena:** Sharon Eberson, "Arena Timeline," *Pittsburgh Post-Gazette*, May 30, 2010; **"Officer, about that young fellow":** *On Broadway Tonight*, aired Aug. 31, 1964 (CBS) (viewed at UCLA Film and Television Archive; hereafter *On Broadway Tonight*).

112 **Davis let him bum a cigarette:** *Pryor Convictions*, pp. 67–68; **"a hard grind at best":** *On Broadway Tonight.*

112 **in Pittsburgh, he started dating a singer:** *Pryor Convictions*, pp. 66–67; "Black Panther Racial Matter," Richard Pryor FBI file, Feb. 5, 1969, p. 3. In his memoir, Pryor claimed that he gambled his way out of jail by playing "313" (the number of his childhood address on North Washington Street), using his winnings to secure his release. This account of events does not jibe with how the legal system tends to work. Convicted defendants are generally asked, by the terms of their sentence, to serve jail time *or* pay a fine—not to serve jail time *until* they can pay a fine.

113 **"hillbilly bar" . . . gay wrestlers:** Vanocur, "Richard Pryor," p. F5.

113 **flipped open *Newsweek*:** *Pryor Convictions*, p. 68.

114 **"Riiight,"** *Newsweek*, June 17, 1963, p. 89.

114 **"sick" humor:** On the sick comics, see Nachman, *Seriously Funny*; and Stephen Kercher, *Revel with a Cause: Liberal Satire in Postwar America* (Chicago: University of Chicago Press, 2006).

114 **"Goddamn it":** *Pryor Convictions*, p. 68; **"composed mainly of Bohemian youths":** Paul Gardner, "Comic Turns Quips into Tuition," *New York Times*, Jun. 25, 1962, p. 23.

115 **train ticket . . . ten dollars:** *Pryor Convictions*, p. 69.

115 **"It was a lot to take in":** Ibid.

116 **"In two blocks, I saw more black people":** *Only in America* interview.

116 **At the Apollo:** *Pryor Convictions*, pp. 69–70.

116 **"It was a time":** Orth, "The Perils of Richard Pryor," p. 61.

117 **the incubator of the new comics:** "Greenwich Village Becoming Top N.Y. Showcase for New Acts," *Variety*, Oct. 9, 1963.

117 **"Coney Island, carnival atmosphere":** Edith Evans Asbury, "Greenwich Village Argues New Way of Life," *New York Times*, Aug. 4, 1963, pp. 1, 62; **"One good mistress":** Bitter End menu in author's possession (proverbs originally written by surrealists Paul Eluard and Benjamin Péret); **open until midnight:** Beth Bryant, *The New Inside Guide to Greenwich Village* (New York: Oak Publications, 1965), pp. 10–14; **the local avant-garde:** Sally Banes, *Greenwich Village 1963: Avant-Garde Performance and the Effervescent Body* (Durham, NC: Duke University Press, 1993); John Strausbaugh, *The Village: A History of Greenwich Village* (New York: Ecco, 2013).

117 **tried every drug:** Author's interview with Bruce Scott Zaxariades, Feb. 14, 2012.

118 **"with jacket sleeves":** Joan Rivers with Richard Meryman, *Enter Talking* (New York: Dell, 1987), p. 332; **a small, dark apartment:** Author's interview with Bruce Scott Zaxariades, Feb. 14, 2012; **"I didn't make the Village scene":** David Felton, "Jive Times: Richard Pryor, Lily Tomlin and the Theater of the Routine," *Rolling Stone*, Oct. 10, 1974, p. 46.

118 **"The man was amazing":** *Pryor Convictions*, p. 72.

118 **"Richard Cosby":** Ibid., pp. 72–73; **studying Cos's records:** Harvey Pack, "History of Negro Humor on Special," *Winona Daily News*, Apr. 2, 1967, p. 14; **"screaming takeoffs":** Henry Benjamin, "Del Shields' Jazz Show Is Mighty Fine," *Philadelphia Tribune*, May 9, 1964, p. 17.

118 **"I grabbed the crook":** *On Broadway Tonight*, aired Aug. 31, 1961 (CBS).

119 **"I'm going for the bucks":** *Pryor Convictions*, pp. 72–73.

119 **first media coverage of Richard's career:** Robert Salmaggi, "After Sunset," *New York Herald Tribune*, Mar. 19, 1964; **"You can't be Cos":** Author's interview with Manny Roth, July 17, 2010.

119 **an air of unqualified success:** Nachman, *Seriously Funny*, p. 563.

120 **Jaglom:** Author's interview with Henry Jaglom, Jan. 8, 2011; **"upright hippo of a man":** Mike Thomas, *The Second City Unscripted: Revolution and Revelation at the World-Famous Comedy Theater* (New York: Villard Books, 2009), p. 33; **Altman:** Gene Palatsky, "Stage and Finance," *Newark Evening News*, Sept. 9, 1963, p. 16; **Friedberg:** Author's interview with Pat Benson, Oct. 27, 2011; author's interview with Henry Jaglom, Oct. 25, 2010; **Heyman:** Author's interview with Burt Heyman, Oct. 21, 2011.

120 **spring of 1963:** Keith Scott, *The Moose That Roared: The Story of Jay Ward, Bill Scott, a Flying Squirrel and a Talking Moose* (New York: St. Martin's Press, 2000), p. 212; **"everyone you haven't seen":** *Village Voice*, Oct. 17, 1963, p. 10; **"happy espresso oasis":** Salmaggi, "After Sunset"; **"the dregs":** Author's interview with Henry Jaglom, Oct. 25, 2010.

121 **"Come on up":** Jeffrey Sweet, *Something Wonderful Right Away: An Oral History of the Second City and Compass Players* (New York: Avon, 1978), p. 354; **for nothing other than the joy of performance:** Richard Zoglin, *Comedy at the Edge: How Stand-Up in the 1970s Changed America* (New York: Bloomsbury USA, 2008), p. 47. Pryor once accused Improv owner Budd Friedman of taking advantage of him because he was black, to which Friedman replied that he paid Pryor what he paid all the comedians: nothing.

121 **"to almost fool spontaneity":** Viola Spolin, *Theater Games for the Classroom: A Teacher's Handbook* (Evanston, IL: Northwestern University Press, 1986), p. 5.

121 **"He would just investigate":** Author's interview with Henry Jaglom, Oct. 25, 2010; **a fortune-telling vending machine:** On the Vend-a-Buddy sketch and improv theater more generally, see Lee Gallup Feldman, "A Critical Analysis of Improvisational Theatre in the United States from 1955–1968," PhD dissertation University of Denver, 1969, pp. 144–47; and Janet Coleman, *The Compass: The Improvisational Theatre That Revolutionized American Comedy* (New York: Alfred Knopf, 1990).

121 **soldiers:** Sweet, *Something Wonderful Right Away*, p. 355; **Mafioso and his mark:** Author's interview with Bob Altman, Oct. 21, 2010; **samurai warriors:** Sweet, *Something Wonderful Right Away*, p. 355.

122 **make-believe aquarium:** Author's interview with Pat Benson, Oct. 27, 2011; **sat eating an entire meal:** Ibid.

123 **edgier performance scenes:** Stephen Bottoms, *Playing Underground: A Critical History of the 1960s Off-Off-Broadway Movement* (Ann Arbor: University of Michigan Press, 2004); **"flesh jubilation":** Banes, *Greenwich Village 1963*, p. 197.

123 **button-down shirt, sports coat:** Photograph in author's possession; **"there goes another myth":** Author's interview with Silver Saundors Friedman, Oct. 20, 2010.

123 **"I think I'll go downtown":** Ibid.

123 **Jaglom came from a spectacularly wealthy family:** Author's interview with Henry Jaglom, Oct. 25, 2010, and Jan. 8, 2011.

124 **an intellectual and an idealist:** "Letters," *New York Times*, Aug. 18, 1963, p. 176; **Congress of Racial Equality:** "CORE Wants Negroes Used in Soap Commercials on TV," *Wall Street Journal*, Aug. 20, 1963, p. 10; and Jason Chambers, *Madison Avenue and the Color Line: African Americans in the Advertising Industry* (Philadelphia: University of Pennsylvania Press, 2008), pp. 133–41.

124 **Richard started spilling condiments:** Author's interview with Henry Jaglom, Oct. 25, 2010.

125 **At Jaglom's home:** Ibid., and interview with Jaglom, Jan. 8, 2011; **November 1964:** "Cosby to Appear in TV Spy Series," *New York Times*, Nov. 16, 1964, p. 63.

125 **CORE leaders . . . set up training workshops:** Marilynn S. Johnson, *Street*

Justice: A History of Police Violence in New York City (Boston: Beacon Press, 2003), p. 230.

126 **Jaglom thought he might "get killed":** Author's interview with Jaglom, Oct. 25, 2010.

126 **improv became more than an art form:** Author's interview with Pat Benson, Oct. 27, 2011; and author's interview with Burt Heyman, Oct. 21, 2011.

Chapter 8: Mr. Congeniality

128 **"scared little black kid":** Author's interviews with Manny Roth, May 23, 2010, and July 17, 2010; **one of the Village's many Jewish entrepreneurs:** Paul Colby with Martin Fitzpatrick, *The Bitter End: Hanging Out at America's Nightclub* (New York: Cooper Square Press, 2002), pp. 24–33; Greenwich Village was no interracial idyll in the late 1950s: if an interracial couple walked into the Cock-n-Bull, Roth advised them, "I'm sorry but I can't let you sit in the window, because there's going to be a brick coming in the window if you sit there." On the history of the tension between blacks and Italian Americans in New York City, see Robert A. Orsi, "The Religious Boundaries of an In-Between People: Street *Feste* and the Problem of the Dark-Skinned Other in Italian Harlem, 1920–1990," in Robert A. Orsi, ed., *Gods of the City: Religion and the American Urban Landscape* (Bloomington: Indiana University Press, 1999), pp. 257–88; **Indiana . . . Ku Klux Klan:** On the Ku Klux Klan and segregation in Indiana, see Emma Lou Thornbrough, "Segregation in Indiana during the Klan Era of the 1920's," *Mississippi Valley Historical Review* 47, no. 4 (Mar. 1961): 594–618; Leonard Joseph Moore, *Citizen Klansmen: The Ku Klux Klan in Indiana, 1921–1928* (Chapel Hill: University of North Carolina Press, 1991).

128 **"a subterranean cavern . . . facial acrobatics":** Bob Dylan, *Chronicles, Volume 1* (New York: Simon and Schuster, 2004), pp. 9, 11; Robert Shelton, *No Direction Home: The Life and Music of Bob Dylan* (New York: William Morrow, 1986), p. 93.

129 **fifteen dollars a set:** Author's interview with Manny Roth, May 23, 2010; **"I was the craziest of the crazies":** Author's interview with Manny Roth, July 17, 2010; **His friends . . . had groomed Bill Cosby:** Author's interview with Manny Roth, May 23, 2010.

129 **"What Pryor needed most was a father figure":** Author's interview with Manny Roth, July 17, 2010.

130 **the Living Room:** Harold H. Hart, *Hart's Guide to New York City* (New York: Hart Publishing Company, n.d.), p. 899; **"everything for the big time":** *Richard Pryor: Comic on the Edge* (*A&E Biography*, 1996). **"half-assed show":** Author's interview with Manny Roth, July 17, 2010; **"walked out with our tails between our legs":** Author's interview with Manny Roth, May 23, 2010; **"avant garde viewpoint":** *Variety*, March 24, 1964.

130 **attacked someone in the audience with a fork:** Author's interview with Manny Roth, July 17, 2010; **threaten to skip his gigs . . . cab fare:** Phil Berger, *The Last Laugh* (New York: William Morrow, 1975), p. 141; **a second chance to impress:** *On Broadway Tonight.* It's hard to prove, beyond a shadow of doubt, that Pryor's comedy routines were never broadcast on U.S. Army radio, as these radio broadcasts were not archived, but this is a claim that Pryor never repeated, to my knowledge.

135 **they had tuned their TV:** Budd, "Young TV Comic Richard Pryor," p. A5.

135 **Bitter End:** *Variety*, Oct. 21, 1964; **Café au Go-Go:** *Billboard*, Sept. 19, 1964; *Variety*, May 5, 1965.

136 **"self-imposed curb" . . . "a racial balancing":** *New York Times*, Feb. 4,

1964, p. 32; Clarence Taylor, *Knocking at Our Own Door: Milton Galamison and the Struggle to Integrate New York City Schools* (New York: Columbia University Press, 1997); **middle ground . . . seemed to be disappearing:** On the fraying black-white civil rights coalition in New York City in 1963–64, see Tamar Jacoby, *Someone Else's House: America's Unfinished Struggle for Integration* (New York: Free Press, 1998), pp. 15–32; Daniel Perlstein, *Justice, Justice: School Politics and the Eclipse of Liberalism* (New York: Peter Lang, 2004), pp. 101–5; **the shooting of a black ninth-grader:** Fred C. Shapiro and James W. Sullivan, *Race Riots, New York, 1964* (New York: Crowell, 1964).

136 **"[The artist] is a man":** LeRoi Jones, *Home: Social Essays* (Hopewell, NJ: Ecco Press, 1998 [1966]), p. 183.

136 **a prominent voice of black radical disenchantment:** Lorraine Hansberry, "The Black Revolution and the White Backlash," *National Guardian*, July 4, 1964, pp. 5–7; Amiri Baraka, *The Autobiography of LeRoi Jones* (Chicago, IL: Lawrence Hill Books, 1997), p. 278.

136 **introduced Richard to Jones:** E-mail communication with Henry Jaglom, Aug. 31, 2011; author's interview with Henry Jaglom, Oct. 25, 2010.

138 **"Reality is best dealt with":** Author's interview with Amiri Baraka (LeRoi Jones), Jan. 25, 2011; Sylviane Gold, "Richard Pryor Finds a Lot Not to Laugh About," *New York Post*, Aug. 6, 1977, p. 32.

138 **Malcolm X was assassinated:** Manning Marable, *Malcolm X: A Life of Reinvention* (New York: Viking, 2011), p. 436; **"[b]ack in the homeland":** Baraka, *Autobiography of LeRoi Jones*, p. 295.

138 **the freedom to date white women:** According to Pryor's friend and neighbor in his New York days, Pryor "never went with chocolate" when it came to romance (author's interview with Bruce Scott Zaxariades, Feb. 14, 2012).

138 **Maxine Silverman:** Author's interview with Elizabeth Pryor, Sept. 30, 2011.

139 **the cutest white girl" . . . "grooved right along":** *Pryor Convictions*, pp. 77–78.

140 **classy doorman building:** Author's interview with Bruce Scott Zaxariades, Feb. 14, 2012.

140 **high drama:** Author's interview with Elizabeth Pryor, Sept. 30, 2011; **"white lady":** *Pryor Convictions*, pp. 75–81; author's interview with Sandy Gallin, Nov. 11 2010.

140 **Maxine got the last jab:** *Pryor Convictions*, pp. 80–81; author's interview with Bruce Scott Zaxariades, Feb. 14, 2012.

141 **they considered themselves . . . husband and wife:** Author's interview with Elizabeth Pryor, Sept. 30, 2011. There is some dispute as to whether Maxine Silverman and Richard Pryor were "really" married. In later interviews, Pryor did not count her among his wives. But according to their daughter, Elizabeth, the two referred to each other as husband and wife when they were together—a judgment confirmed by an *Ebony* profile from September 1967, in which Pryor claimed to be married ("Beyond Laughter," *Ebony*, Sept. 1967, p. 90).

141 **calling card as a comic:** "George Carlin Interview," Archive of American Television, accessed at http://www.emmytvlegends.org/interviews/people/george-carlin.

142 **"My name is Rumpelstiltskin":** *Kraft Summer Music Hall*, Aug. 8, 1966 (audio in author's possession).

143 **Richard *looked* young:** Photograph of Pryor on *The Ed Sullivan Show* in author's possession. Tellingly, when Pryor remembered his first encounter with Lenny Bruce, he recalled being blown away not by Bruce's obscene language—the connection many critics use to link the two—but by his affectionate impersonation of a kid who couldn't help but reveal his deepest desires. In the Bruce sketch, the

kid, a glue-sniffer, goes to a toy store and can't bring himself to order airplane glue outright, so he buys a clutch of random things (a nickel's worth of pencils, some Jujubes) before asking for two thousand tubes of airplane glue. *Pryor Convictions*, pp. 71–72; Lenny Bruce, "Airplane Glue," *Lenny Bruce—American* (Fantasy Records, 1961).

143 **more than twenty appearances:** Fields, "Kook from Peoria," p. 19; **General Artists Corporation:** Author's interview with Craig Kellem, Nov. 5, 2010.

144 **"lean, literate, quick-witted":** Fields, "Kook from Peoria" p. 19; **"most elastic face in show business":** "TV Previews," *Milwaukee Journal*, Nov. 7, 1966; **"stormed by teen-agers":** "New York Beat," *Jet*, Sept. 23, 1965, p. 64.

144 **the police were cracking down:** "Prostitution Down from Year Ago, Survey Unit Says," *Peoria Journal Star*, Dec. 2, 1965; "Open City's Merry-Go-Round Never Stopped," *Peoria Journal Star*, Jan. 26, 1986; **where Peoria's brothels had migrated:** Bill Mitchell, "'70s Reform Took Its Toll, but These Days a New Fear Emerges from the Shadows," *Peoria Journal Star*, Oct. 3, 1993, p. A1.

144 **Sheriff Ray Trunk:** "Guilty Verdict in Trial of Alleged 'Madam,'" *Peoria Journal Star*, Oct. 6, 1965; "Appellate Court Upholds Vice Count Conviction, Sentence," *Peoria Journal Star*, Sept. 24, 1966; "Upholds Ruling in Vice Case," *Peoria Journal Star*, Oct. 3, 1967.

144 **another impromptu raid:** "Prostitution Counts Name 5 Defendants," *Peoria Journal Star*, Sept. 19, 1965; "5 of 10 Vice Raid Counts Dismissed," *Peoria Journal Star*, Nov. 10, 1965.

145 **not so fortunate:** "Guilty Verdict in Trial of Alleged 'Madam'"; **attending night school:** "Convicted Madam Out as Student," *Peoria Journal Star*, Oct. 8, 1965; *People of the State of Illinois v. Viola Ann Pry* [*sic*] (alias Jane Doe), Case No. 65A 1463, Peoria County Circuit Court (Oct. 6, 1965), handwritten note in case file.

145 **Ramrod-straight Peoria:** "Convicted Madam Out as Student"; "Convicted Madam Draws 1 Year Term," *Peoria Journal Star*, Oct. 27, 1965.

145 **headlining the Blue Angel:** "Refreshing Comic Graces Blue Angel," *Chicago Daily Defender*, Nov. 1, 1965, p. 20; **"Sure enough":** Budd, "Young TV Comic Richard Pryor," p. A5.

146 **twenty thousand in cash:** *Pryor Convictions*, p. 103. Buck and Ann's new home at 1319 Millman was purchased between Richard's 1965 date at the Blue Angel and his October 1966 visit to Peoria.

Chapter 9: An Irregular Regular

147 **in a West Hollywood high-rise:** Author's interviews with Henry Jaglom, Oct. 25, 2010, and Jan. 8, 2011; **little known outside certain bohemian circles:** Jay Stevens, *Storming Heaven: LSD and the American Dream* (New York: Grove Press, 1998).

147 **a set of gigs down the hill at the Troubadour:** Advertisement, *Los Angeles Times*, Oct. 17, 2012, p. Q23; **a hotbed of the new comedy:** Barney Hoskyns, *Waiting for the Sun: Strange Days, Weird Scenes, and the Sound of Los Angeles* (New York: St. Martin's Press, 1996); Barney Hoskyns, *Hotel California: Singer-Songwriters and Cocaine Cowboys in the LA Canyons, 1967–1976* (New York: HarperCollins, 2007). Pryor's time in LA seemed to loosen him up a bit: at the Troub, he started cracking jokes about smoking weed—speculating, for instance, on what would happen if a pilot started "flying high in the friendly skies" (author's interview with Harvey Levine, Jan. 22, 2012).

147 **Later that night:** Author's interviews with Jaglom, Oct. 25, 2010, and Jan. 8, 2011.

148 **How differently these two friends traveled:** Eight years after he dropped

acid with Jaglom, Pryor began to perform a stand-up routine about the first time he took acid, one in which the person who gives Pryor the drug is merely a generic white hippie—a revision to his life story that reflects both the dissolution of his friendship with Jaglom and Pryor's engagement with a certain strain of black radicalism in the interim. For more on Pryor's routine, see chapter 17.

148 **writing new material constantly:** Author's interview with Bruce Scott Zaxariades, Feb. 14, 2012; **Dolly Parton, Lily Tomlin, and Michael Jackson:** Claudia Eller, "Managing in Turbulent Times," *Los Angeles Times*, Jan. 16, 1994, p. 8; **"What are you going to do with him?":** Author's interview with Sandy Gallin, Nov. 11, 2010;.

149 **"I cannot call a waitress":** *The Merv Griffin Show: The Greatest Comedians*, 2006, DVD.

149 **His "Cary Grant" thing:** *Kraft Summer Music Hall*, aired July 25, 1966; *The Merv Griffin Show: The Greatest Comedians.*

149 **Jerry Lewis movies in marathon sessions:** Author's interview with Bruce Scott Zaxariades, Feb. 14, 2012; **"the first man on the sun":** Author's interview with Renee Taylor, Dec. 15, 2011; *Kraft Summer Music Hall*, aired Aug. 8, 1966; "Man on the Sun," *Holy Smoke,* Laff Records A212, 1976; **"shark-fighting championship":** *Kraft Summer Music Hall*, aired June 6, 1966; **"Japanese robot who's a karate expert":** *Kraft Summer Music Hall*, aired Aug. 8, 1966.

150 **"Novocaine Martinovich":** *Kraft Summer Music Hall*, aired June 6, 1966.

150 **"unraveled":** Dorothy Ferenbaugh, "Merv Griffin: Man of 1,000 Faces," *New York Times*, July 18, 1965, p. X15; **"I just want to thank you":** Merv Griffin with David Bender, *Merv: Making the Good Life Last* (New York: Simon and Schuster, 2003), pp. 58–59.

151 **he invited British philosopher Bertrand Russell:** Bernard M. Timberg with Robert J. Erler, *Television Talk: A History of the TV Talk Show* (Austin: University of Texas Press, 2002), pp. 76–77; **a direct pipeline:** Author's interview with Bruce Scott Zaxariades, Feb. 14, 2012; author's interview with Burt Heyman, Oct. 21, 2011.

151 **"impression of my sweater talking to my ass":** "Sick," *Outrageous*; **"five hundred guys would be in there":** Pryor, "Nudie Movies," *Insane*, Laff Records A209, 1976 (hereafter *Insane*).

151 **"Did you hear the one about":** "Did Ya Hear the One About," *Insane.*

152 **"You ever take a long ride":** Author's interview with Bob Altman, Oct. 21, 2010.

152 **"I would like to make you laugh":** "Intro," *Are You Serious???*; **"I would like to make you":** "The Operation," *Outrageous.*

152 **"This is a game" . . . "Why don't you go to Vegas?":** "Improv, Part I," *Evolution/Revolution.*

153 **so thrilled:** *Pryor Convictions*, pp. 73–74.

153 **"making faces and all kinds of funny sounds":** Jerry Butler with Earl Smith, *Only the Strong Survive: Memoirs of a Soul Survivor* (Bloomington: Indiana University Press, 2000), pp. 196, 198. The management at the Apollo waited almost a full decade to bring Richard back to its stage (Marie Moore, "Richard Pryor: The Funniest of Them All," *New York Amsterdam News*, May 4, 1974, p. D8).

154 **March 1966:** E-mail communication with Nathan Thomas, Merv Griffin Entertainment, July 13, 2010; **"Hey, Zorro!":** "*Only in America* interview"; Pryor, "Interview" (1983); . . . *And It's Deep Too!.*

154 **mother and father both were Baptist ministers:** James Sullivan, *Seven Dirty Words: The Life and Crimes of George Carlin* (New York: Da Capo Press, 2010),

pp. 75–76; **"showcase of rising young stars" . . . "spontaneous and multi-talented":** NBC publicity material in author's possession.

154 **where he could more easily audition:** Author's interview with Sandy Gallin, Nov. 11, 2010.

155 **He journeyed out to LA:** Author's interview with Elizabeth Pryor, Sept. 30, 2011; **officially filed in Peoria County Court:** "Complaint for Divorce." In the complaint, Richard accused Patricia of having "committed adultery with divers other unknown male persons" and argued that she was "not a fit person to have the care, custody, control . . . of the education" of Richard Jr.—perhaps an opening gambit in the negotiations over alimony, as it seems unlikely that Richard wished to have custody of Richard Jr.

155 **dumping a suitcase of clothes:** Author's interview with Elizabeth Pryor, Sept. 30, 2011.

155 **Ferrari Drive:** Ibid.; Richard Pryor FBI file, memo dated June 29, 1970; "Consumer Credit Clearance," Richard Pryor FBI file, memo dated June 8, 1970; **a black population of 1 percent:** *Report 3: Social Indicators for Planning and Evaluation, 1980 Census of Population, Beverly Hills City, California* (Beverly Hills, CA: National Technical Information Service, 1982), p. 1; **Baldwin Hills:** Josh Sides, *L.A. City Limits: African American Los Angeles from the Great Depression to the Present* (Berkeley: University of California Press, 2003), pp. 161–62, 190.

155 **"like oil to water":** "Bottoms Up," *Time*, Apr. 3, 1964; **befriended Hanson and his wife, Sally:** Author's interview with Zalman King, Aug. 18, 2010; William Murray, "Jack Hanson, the Man behind the Daisy," *Los Angeles Times*, Apr. 16, 1967, p. A22.

156 **"The Daisy, on any given night":** Dan Jenkins, "Life with the Jax Pack," *Sports Illustrated*, July 10, 1967.

157 **"sensational catch":** Nancy Adler, "Sunday Batters Score in the Affluence League," *New York Times*, July 4, 1966, p. 11; Jenkins, "Life with the Jax Pack"; author's interview with James B. Harris, July 30, 2010.

157 **joked with Sandy Gallin:** Author's interview with Sandy Gallin, Nov. 11, 2010; **skipped rehearsals . . . "really in his own world":** Author's interview with John Davidson, May 9, 2011.

158 **cross-eyed:** *Kraft Summer Music Hall*, aired June 6, 1966; **medley of "river songs":** *Kraft Summer Music Hall*, aired Aug. 8, 1966; **children's circle games:** *Kraft Summer Music Hall*, aired July 25, 1966.

159 **"Rumpelstiltskin," the pantomimes:** *Kraft Summer Music Hall*, aired Aug. 8, 1966; **pickup artist:** *Kraft Summer Music Hall*, aired July 25, 1966.

159 **"Nobody Knows You When You're Down and Out":** *Kraft Summer Music Hall*, aired Aug. 1, 1966.

159 **the singer Bobby Darin:** Pryor had long been captivated by Darin as a performer: he did an imitation of Darin in his early act. See "Pryor," *Cause Magazine*, n.d., p. 57 (Richard Pryor file, Margaret Herrick Library, AMPAS). On Darin, see Michael Starr, *Bobby Darin: A Life* (Lanham, MD: Rowman and Littlefield, 2004); David Evanier, *Roman Candle: The Life of Bobby Darin* (Albany, NY: SUNY Press, 2010 [2004]); David Hadju, *Heroes and Villains: Essays on Music, Movies, Comics, and Culture* (Cambridge, MA: DaCapo Press, 2009), pp. 45–49.

160 **$2,400 a week:** *Pryor Convictions*, pp. 83–84.

161 **"the constellation Talent" . . . "wing-dang-doodle" . . . head-turning celebrity summit:** Invitation and photographs in author's possession; **his wife, Sandra Dee, had filed for divorce:** "Sandra Dee Files Suit to Divorce Bobby Darin," *Los Angeles Times*, Aug. 13, 1966, p. B8; **uncomfortable with all the attention:** *Pryor Convictions*, pp. 83–84.

161 **"the god of comedy":** *The Merv Griffin Show*, aired Aug. 1, 1966.

161 **"Young man, you're a comic?":** *Pryor Convictions*, pp. 84–85.

162 **"as big a thrill":** Ibid., p. 83; **Caesars Palace:** Margaret Malamud and Donald T. McGuire Jr., "Living Like Romans in Las Vegas: The Roman World at Caesars Palace," in Sandra R. Joshel, Margaret Malamud, and Donald T. McGuire Jr., eds., *Imperial Projections: Ancient Rome in Modern Popular Culture* (Baltimore, MD: Johns Hopkins University Press, 2001), pp. 249–55.

162 **basking in an air:** *Pryor Convictions*, p. 83; on the Flamingo and Vegas in this era, see Mike Weatherford, *Cult Vegas: The Weirdest! The Wildest! The Swingin'est Town on Earth!* (Las Vegas, NV: Huntington Press, 2001); Jeff Burbank, *Las Vegas Babylon* (London: Robson Books, 2006); Hal Rothman and Mike Davis, eds., *The Grit beneath the Glitter: Tales from the Real Las Vegas* (Berkeley: University of California Press, 2002); **demolished the all-time attendance record:** Joy Hamann, "Wheeling around Las Vegas," *The Hollywood Reporter*, Aug. 29, 1966, p. 4.

162 **"wonderfully kookie style":** "Nitery Reviews," *Variety*, Aug. 22, 1966, p. 6; **"It's uncanny":** *Pryor Convictions*, p. 83.

163 **Back in LA:** "Dick Pryor's 'Busy' Bow," *Daily Variety*, Sept. 15, 1966; "Comic Pryor Signs for Movie Role," *Chicago Daily Defender*, Oct. 5, 1966.

163 **"tiptoe[ing]":** *Pryor Convictions*, p. 85; **Acting in a film didn't come as naturally:** Budd, "Young TV Comic Richard Pryor," p. A5; **"I did every actor":** Rovin, *Richard Pryor*, p. 66.

163 **"tasteless Runyonesque rehash":** "To Bury Caesar," *Time*, June 9, 1967; **"Producer-director William Castle":** Clifford Terry, "'Busy Body' Film Is Gangster Spoof," *Chicago Tribune*, Sept. 4, 1967, p. E11.

163 **fall 1966 premiere:** "Night of the Eccentrics," *The Wild, Wild West*, aired Sept. 16, 1966.

164 **"For real-life stuff":** "Telepix Reviews," *Daily Variety*, Sept. 19, 1966, p. 12.

164 **for the first time since he'd left:** *Pryor Convictions*, pp. 85–86; **conquering hero . . . cops who had treated him:** Pack, "History of Negro Humor on Special," p. 14; **"the thrill of our son":** Budd, "Young TV Comic Richard Pryor," p. A5; **he played cards:** *Pryor Convictions*, pp. 85–86.

164 **the Pere Marquette hotel:** Author's interview with Joe Mosley, Dec. 10, 2010.

164 **"It's a sham":** Budd, "Young TV Comic Richard Pryor," p. A5.

164 **"I can walk two blocks":** Ibid.

Chapter 10: The Person in Question

166 **"If America don't come around":** H. Rap Brown speech at Cambridge, Maryland, July 24, 1967, archived at http://msa.maryland.gov/megafile/msa/speccol/sc2200/sc2221/000012/000008/media/00080003.mp3; Peter B. Levy, *Civil War on Race Street: The Civil Rights Movement in Cambridge, Maryland* (Gainesville: University of Florida Press, 2003). Ironically, the flames in Cambridge ended up consuming a great number of black-owned businesses.

166 **"These rebellions are but a dress rehearsal":** Levy, *Civil War on Race Street*, p. 83. On the 1967 wave of riots, see Kerner Commission, *Report of the National Advisory Commission on Civil Disorders* (Washington, DC: U.S. Government Printing Office, 1968). **"On certain corners":** David Llorens, "Miracle in Milwaukee," *Ebony*, Nov. 1967, p. 29.

167 **no countercultural hole-in-the-wall:** James P. Craft, *Vegas at Odds: Labor Conflict in a Leisure Economy, 1960–1985* (Baltimore, MD: Johns Hopkins University Press, 2012), p. 23; **prime sirloin:** Menu from New Year's Eve show at the Sands, in author's possession; **a woman whose son was posted in Vietnam, Bobby Darin was on hand:** Starr, *Bobby Darin: A Life*, p. 162; **bearish,**

Mob-connected: Alanna Nash, *The Colonel* (New York: Simon and Schuster, 2003), p. 193.

167 **"swinging from chandeliers" . . . "the top place in the United States":** Author's interview with Sandy Gallin, May 4, 2012; **left Vegas with his reputation intact:** Forrest Duke, "Comic Richard Pryor Axed at Aladdin," *Las Vegas Review-Journal*, Oct. 3, 1967, p. 11.

167 **A month later:** "Name Change for Negro Humor Spec," *Chicago Daily Defender*, Feb. 22, 1967, p. 10.

168 **Belafonte:** Jeff Sharlet, "Voice and Hammer," *Virginia Quarterly Review* (Fall 2013); **William Attaway:** Richard Yardborough, "William Attaway," in Steven Tracy, ed., *Writers of the Black Chicago Renaissance* (Champaign: University of Illinois Press, 2011), pp. 39–52; **"A whole people" . . . "Negro humor has often been loud and bitter":** Allan Morrison, "Negro Humor: An Answer to Anguish," *Ebony*, May 1967, pp. 110 and 99; Paul Gardner, "Dark Laughter in Snow White Land," *New York Times*, Apr. 2, 1967, p. 117.

168 **Foxx and Mabley . . . making their prime-time TV debuts:** Henry Louis Gates Jr. and Evelyn Brooks Higginbotham, eds., *African American Lives* (New York: Oxford University Press, 2004), p. 552; Michael Seth Starr, *Black and Blue: The Redd Foxx Story* (Milwaukee: Applause, 2011), p. 81; **"They wanted Bill Cosby":** Pack, "History of Negro Humor on Special," p. 7.

168 **comedy . . . developed along two tracks:** *A Time for Laughter: A Look at Negro Humor in America (ABC Stage 67)*, Apr. 6, 1967 (hereafter *A Time for Laughter*). The program's take on blackface minstrelsy is most eloquently supported in Robert Toll's *Blacking Up: The Minstrel Show in Nineteenth-Century America* (New York: Oxford University Press, 1974). Some of the complexities of blackface minstrelsy, glossed over in *A Time for Laughter*, are explored in Annemarie Bean, James V. Hatch, and Brooks McNamara, eds., *Inside the Minstrel Mask: Readings in Nineteenth-Century Blackface Minstrelsy* (Hanover, NH: Wesleyan University Press, 1996); Eric Lott, *Love and Theft: Blackface Minstrelsy and the American Working Class* (New York: Oxford University Press, 1993).

169 **where he fit into this two-track model:** *A Time for Laughter.*

170 **Here he was a young funeral director:** Ibid.; **"would be equally at home":** "Negro Humor's Written in Black, White," *Chicago Defender*, March 28, 1967, p. 10.

170 **"Working in a show like the Belafonte special":** Pack, "History of Negro Humor on Special," p. 14.

170 **"shocked by the lie" . . . "I never thought":** "Beyond Laughter," pp. 88–92.

171 **"vignettes of a boyhood":** Aaron Sternfield, "Mitchell Mixes His Tunes in Winning Combo," *Billboard*, June 24, 1967, p. 24.

171 **"could barely commit to being me":** *Pryor Convictions*, p. 86; **hit a final breaking point:** Author's interview with Elizabeth Pryor, Sept. 30, 2011.

172 **April 24, 1967:** Ibid.; **"big orange balloon":** *Pryor Convictions*, p. 87; **For four or five days:** Pryor's FBI file notes that he was arrested or received by the San Diego Police Department on April 29, 1967—five days after the date of the full moon (Pryor, FBI file, "Black Panther Matter," p. 2).

172 **sixteen thousand pounds of marijuana:** Robert Berrellez, "Tijuana Marijuana Mecca," *Daytona Beach Morning Journal*, July 7, 1968, p. 21; **"I was black":** *Pryor Convictions*, p. 87; **in jail for six days:** Pryor, FBI file, "Black Panther Matter," p. 2; **reminded, by a deputy:** *Pryor Convictions*, p. 87.

172 **"the most luxurious apartment[s]":** *Los Angeles Times*, Oct. 26, 1958; *Los Angeles Times*, Oct. 7, 1956.

173 **shot himself in the head:** *Los Angeles Times*, May 7, 1968, p. 2; **hijack a**

Chicago-bound plane: "Agents Nab Skyjacker at O'Hare," *Chicago Tribune*, Apr. 18, 1972, p. 1; "Jury Brings Quick Indictment of O'Hare Skyjacking Suspect," *Chicago Tribune*, Apr. 19, 1972, p. A14.

173 **Dirty Dick . . . "fairly well fucked up":** *Pryor Convictions*, p. 91; **the full amount he:** Pryor made $1,500 for every six nights of work at the Village Gate in May 1967 (images of checks in author's possession); **Around 11:30 on the night of July 26:** "Reporter's Transcript, Preliminary Hearing," *The People of the State of California v. Richard Frank Pryor,* Case A 051 511 (Sept. 12, 1967) (hereafter *California v. Pryor*), pp. 1–17.

173 **Richard muttered a single word:** Ibid., pp. 17–39.

175 **Trosper had been terminated:** Ibid., p. 28; **"Come on, nigger":** *Pryor Convictions*, p. 91.

175 **Tholkes ended up:** *California v. Pryor*; **suspicion of assault:** "Actor Held on Charge of Assault," *Los Angeles Times*, July 28, 1967, p. 22; "Actor Arrest Ordered in Assault Case," *Hollywood Citizen-News*, Dec. 12, 1967.

175 **"the pith of Pryor legend":** Mark Jacobson, "Richard Pryor Is the Blackest Comic of Them All," *New West*, Aug. 30, 1976, p. 58; Duke, "Comic Richard Pryor Axed at Aladdin," p. 11; "Aladdin, Vegas, Cancels Dick Pryor for 'Obscene' Gab," *Daily Variety*, Oct. 3, 1967, p. 1; "Aladdin Snuffs Its Pryor Lamp," *Arizona Republic*, Oct. 4, 1967, p. 28; William Sarmento, "CBS Cuts Back Its TV Output," *Lowell Sun*, Oct. 27, 1967, p. 27; Richard Pryor, "Blackjack," *'Craps' (After Hours)*, Laff Records, 1971 (hereafter *'Craps'*).

176 **eighteen-hole golf course . . . forty thousand lightbulbs:** Eugene P. Moehring, *Resort City in the Sunbelt: Las Vegas, 1930–2000* (Reno: University of Nevada Press, 2000), pp. 115–16; **Redd Foxx was a Bagdad Room mainstay:** Hamann, "Wheeling around Las Vegas," p. 9; John L. Scott, "Redd Foxx in Room," *Los Angeles Times*, Apr. 2, 1968, p. D14.

176 **Godfrey Cambridge:** Murray Hertz, "Comic Loses Pounds—Career Soars," *Las Vegas Review-Journal*, Sept. 14, 1967, p. 15; **Rusty Warren:** John L. Scott, "'The Odd Couple' on Reno Stage," *Los Angeles Times*, July 1, 1967; Jacob Smith, *Spoken Word: Postwar American Phonograph Cultures* (Berkeley: University of California Press, 2011), pp. 88–95; **two adults-only albums:** Foxx, *Redd Foxx—Live in Las Vegas*, Loma 5906, 1967; *Rusty Rides Again*, Jubilee JGM 2064, 1967.

176 **"blonde beguiler":** "Hypnotist Is Favorite of the Stars," *Las Vegas Review-Journal*, Sept. 22, 1967, p. 20.

176 **first seven minutes:** Forrest Duke, "Comic Richard Pryor Axed at Aladdin," p. 11; **"I was doing material":** Dennis Hunt, "Black Comedy and the Pryor Commitment," *Los Angeles Times*, Apr. 11 1974, p. 92; **"The life I was leading":** Felton, "This Can't Be Happening to Me," p. 46.

177 **According to his memoir:** *Pryor Convictions*, pp. 94–95.

177 **"You can't get through there!":** Felton, "This Can't Be Happening to Me," p. 41.

177 **Jim Murray:** Author's interview with Sandy Gallin, March 4, 2012.

178 **"What about us":** Felton, "This Can't Be Happening to Me," p. 41.

178 **"Everybody was worried about themselves" . . . "the minors":** Ibid.; **He needed to look after himself:** Kleiner, "Richard Pryor Back on Top," p. 10.

178 **"I was blackballed":** Hunt, "Black Comedy and the Pryor Commitment," p. 92.

178 **returned in August 1968 to play Caesars Palace:** *Variety*, Aug. 12, 1968, p.8; **hefty advance:** Author's interview with Robert Marchese, Mar. 1, 2011; for other details, see chapter 11.

179 **"just the right pairing":** Joy Hamann, "Las Vegas," *Hollywood Reporter*, Sept. 21, 1967, p. 6.

180 **"abusive to his audience" . . . "at least four times":** Duke, "Comic Richard Pryor Axed at Aladdin," p. 11.

180 **"blister the ears":** Joy Hamann, "Las Vegas," *Hollywood Reporter,* Oct. 11, 1967, p. 13. Unfortunately, when asked if it had the recording of Pryor's expletive-soaked monologue in its possession, the Las Vegas branch of the American Guild of Variety Artists told the author that it did not.

180 **"mother-frockers" and "cork-soakers":** Foxx, *Live in Las Vegas;* **Lenny Bruce:** Edward de Grazia, *Girls Lean Back Everywhere: The Law of Obscenity and the Assault on Genius* (New York: Random House, 1992), pp. 444, 455–56, 460, 462–63, 477.

181 **"feed on the corpse" . . . "an overdose of police":** Ronald K. L. Collins and David M. Skover, *The Trials of Lenny Bruce: The Fall and Rise of an American Icon* (Napierville, IL: Sourcebooks, Inc., 2002), pp. 339–40.

181 **"Mickey Mouse material":** Hunt, "Black Comedy and the Pryor Commitment," p. 92.

182 **"Be clean":** "Beyond Laughter," p. 90.

182 **In only one interview:** Author's interview with Cynthia Dagnal Myron, May 17, 2012; Cynthia Dagnal Myron, "A Memory of Richard," http://rogerebert.suntimes.com/apps/pbcs.dll/article?AID=/20051211/PEOPLE/512110307.

183 **Richard felt the hand of God:** Myron, "A Memory of Richard."

183 **"flittamajitter":** *Pryor Convictions,* p. 78; **he didn't show up:** "'That Girl' Their Girl from the Start," *Waterloo Sunday Courier,* Nov. 19, 1967, p. 3. Pryor dated his "flittamajitter" to an earlier moment, but Sandy Gallin suggested that Pryor's memory was faulty, and the *Waterloo Sunday Courier* article dates his no-show to November 1967; **a clause was simply stitched into his next contract:** Author's interview with Sandy Gallin, Mar. 4, 2012.

183 **legal fees and a regular child support payment:** John A. Williams papers, University of Rochester; **bench warrant:** "Actor Arrest Ordered in Assault Case."

184 **police raided his father's brothel:** "Vice Raid Nets Man, 56, Woman," *Peoria Journal Star,* Nov. 15, 1967; **trial by jury:** "Jury Demand," *City of Peoria v. LeRoy Pryor,* Case No. 67Q 2769 (Dec. 13, 1967); **Illinois Supreme Court:** "Upholds Ruling in Vice Case."

184 **Ann received last rites:** Author's interview with Thomas Henseler, Feb. 12, 2012.

184 **"Dad, I ain't going":** *Pryor Convictions,* pp. 97–98.

Chapter 11: The King Is Dead

187 **a stunning go-go look:** Rain Pryor with Cathy Crimmins, *Jokes My Father Never Taught Me: Life, Love, and Loss with Richard Pryor* (New York: HarperCollins, 2006), pp. 23–25.

187 **"So what're you writing":** Ibid., pp. 24–26.

188 **"a classic psychedelic pad":** Author's interview with Robert Marchese, Mar. 1, 2011; **"rock-and-roll salon":** Michael Walker, *Laurel Canyon: The Inside Story of Rock-and-Roll's Legendary Neighborhood* (New York: Faber and Faber, 2006), p. 25.

189 **"made me feel free":** *Pryor Convictions,* p. 97.

189 **fourteen below:** *The Tonight Show with Johnny Carson,* aired July 21, 1978 (NBC); **Two hundred friends:** Author's interview with Thomas Henseler, Feb. 23, 2012; **fur-lined coat . . . cornrows:** Author's interview with Sharon Wilson Pryor, June 6, 2012.

189 **gray gloves:** Author's interview with Thomas Henseler, Feb. 23, 2012; **"the dirt" . . . "brutally honest":** *The Tonight Show with Johnny Carson,* aired July 21, 1978 (NBC).

191 **introducing her with great pleasure:** Author's interviews with Sharon Wilson Pryor, Dec. 15, 2010, May 13, 2011, and June 6, 2012.

191 **On January 13:** "Richard Pryor Sued for Divorce," *Los Angeles Sentinel*, June 25, 1970, p. A1; **Shelley was the white romantic:** Pryor, *Jokes My Father Never Taught Me*, p. 29.

192 **a delicate, circling dance:** Van Gosse, *Rethinking the New Left: An Interpretative History* (New York: Palgrave Macmillan, 2005); Simon Hall, "On the Tail of the Panther: Black Power and the 1967 Convention of the National Conference for New Politics," *Journal of American Studies* (Apr. 2003): 59–78; **"short-circuited the ghetto's mental hate syndrome":** David McBride, "Death City Radicals: The Counterculture in Los Angeles," in John Campbell McMillan and Paul Buhle, eds., *The New Left Revisited* (Philadelphia: Temple University Press, 2003), pp. 121–22; Dave McBride, "Counterculture," in William Deverell and Greg Hise, eds., *A Companion to Los Angeles* (Malden, MA: Blackwell, 2010), pp. 327–45; **a stone thrown at a white photographer:** "Ghetto Love-In," *Open City*, Aug. 4–11, 1967, p. 9; "Diggery Is Niggery," *Open City*, Oct. 21–27, 1967, p. 16.

192 **"politically irrelevant":** McBride, "Death City Radicals."

193 **audiences that, for him, were half white and half black:** Author's interview with Marchese, Mar. 1, 2011.

193 **When news of Martin Luther King Jr.'s assassination:** Author's interview with Jeff Wald, May 9, 2011; **the beginning of a riot:** Janet Abu-Lughod, *Race, Space, and Riots in Chicago, New York, and Los Angeles* (New York: Oxford University Press, 2007), pp. 79–127.

193 **canceled a scheduled appearance:** Author's interview with Jeff Wald, May 9, 2011; **audience of ten thousand:** "Hollywood Stars Aid King Fund," *El Paso Herald-Post*, Apr. 22, 1968, p. 10; **"we are here today":** "Showfolk in Free King Fund Benefit," *Washington Afro-American*, Apr. 23, 1968, p. 5; "Martin Luther King Friendship Rally," *Los Angeles Sentinel*, Apr. 25, 1968, p. A3.

194 **"All these people here":** Leonard Feather, "King Concert Memorial Stirs Bowl," *Los Angeles Times*, Apr. 28, 1968, p. D34; Nat Freedland, "Wailing," *Los Angeles Free Press*, Apr. 26, 1968, p. 25. It would not be the last benefit, or even the last Hollywood Bowl benefit, whose mood of unity was disrupted when Pryor instinctively recoiled at what he perceived as the sanctimony of the occasion.

194 **a fifty-thousand-dollar, two-album contract:** Author's interview with Robert Marchese, Mar. 1, 2011; Freedland, "Wailing."

195 **"Bam-da-boom":** "I Feel," *Evolution/Revolution*.

196 **the term *nigger baby*:** "Nigger Babies," *Evolution/Revolution*.

196 **The most elaborate:** "Prison Play," *Richard Pryor* (album).

197 **Marchese had grown up:** Author's interview with Robert Marchese, Mar. 1, 2011.

197 **calmer, if equally iconoclastic:** "T.V. Panel Show," *Richard Pryor* (album).

200 **Marchese didn't have an easy time:** Author's interview with Robert Marchese, Mar. 1, 2011; **"uncomfortable or perhaps even hostile":** *Daily Variety*, Apr. 18, 1968, p. 6.

200 **So Marchese and Roberts struggled:** Author's interview with Robert Marchese, Mar. 1, 2011.

200 **Frankenstein's monster on LSD:** "Frankenstein," *Richard Pryor* (album).

201 **"be careful":** *Under the Covers: A Magical Journey*, directed by Bill Day and Terry Schwartz (Triptych Pictures, 2002); **At a first photo shoot:** Author's interview with Henry Diltz, Aug. 4, 2009. Diltz and Burden became one of the most celebrated album design teams, whose credits include the Doors' *Morrison Hotel*, Crosby, Stills, and Nash's debut album, and the Eagles' *Desperado*.

202 **"real authentic stuff":** Author's interview with Henry Diltz, Aug. 4, 2009; *Under the Covers.*

203 **On the night of September 27:** Unless otherwise specified, all details in this section are from author's interviews with Sharon Wilson Pryor, Dec. 15, 2010, May 13, 2011, and June 6, 2012.

205 **11:25 p.m.:** "LeRoy Pryor Jr.," *Peoria Journal-Star,* Oct. 2, 1968.

206 **"I know you got more money than this":** Author's interview with Sharon Wilson Pryor, June 6, 2012; author's interview with Barbara McGee, Dec. 14, 2010.

206 **Upon hearing the news:** *Pryor Convictions,* p. 102–3.

206 **"Your father fucked everything":** Ibid., p. 103.

206 **it fell to Richard . . . to make the funeral preparations:** Ibid., pp. 103–4.

207 **Section 8:** *Tonight Show,* aired July 21, 1978; **a compromise was found:** Author's interview with Thomas Henseler, Feb. 23, 2012.

207 **Six days:** "LeRoy Pryor Jr.," *Peoria Journal Star,* Oct. 2, 1968; **center court . . . a hundred people:** Author's interview with Thomas Henseler, Feb. 23, 2012; **no small number of whom were prostitutes:** Author's interview with Barbara McGee, Dec.14, 2010; **practicing layups:** *Tonight Show,* aired July 21, 1978.

207 **expected his father to wink:** Ibid.; **stashed a little money:** *Pryor Convictions,* p. 105; **a single five-hundred-dollar bill:** Author's interview with Thomas Henseler, Feb. 23, 2012.

208 **"the conversation flowed":** *Pryor Convictions,* pp.104–5.

Chapter 12: Black Sun Rising

209 **one of his favorite routines:** Ibid., pp. 106, 113; "Super Nigger," *Richard Pryor* (album).

209 **war movie:** *Evolution/Revolution.*

210 **a trickster in the tradition of Brer Rabbit:** Hyde, *Trickster Makes This World*; Lawrence Levine, *Black Culture and Black Consciousness: Afro-American Folk Thought from Slavery to Freedom* (New York: Oxford University Press, 1977), pp. 102–32.

210 **Below the surface, Richard's routine:** Pryor, *Jokes My Father Never Taught Me,* pp. 30–31.

211 **"Wallace is president":** Jim Merriam, "Disenchantment of Being Black," *Lethbridge Herald,* Nov. 15, 1968, p. 4.

211 **Sky River Rock Festival:** E-mail communication with Paul Dorpat, June 23, 2010; Walt Crowley, *Rites of Passage: A Memoir of the Sixties in Seattle* (Seattle: University of Washington Press, 1995); Paul de Barros, "1968's Sky River Rock Festival Revisited Friday," *Seattle Times,* Aug. 11, 2011.

212 ***Tonight Show*****:** "Program Files, 1939–1985," NBC microfiche, UCLA Film and Television Archive, Los Angeles, CA; **headlined a benefit:** Advertisement, *Los Angeles Free Press,* Dec. 5, 1968, p. 5; **Diggers:** Michael William Doyle, "Staging the Revolution: Guerrilla Theater as a Countercultural Practice," in Peter Braunstein and Michael William Doyle, eds., *Imagine Nation: The American Counterculture of the 1960s and 70s* (New York: Routledge, 2001), pp. 71–97; "Trip without a Ticket," *The Digger Papers,* Aug. 1968, p. 3; "Hippie Happy Hour Makes Glide Glow," *Berkeley Barb,* Mar. 3, 1967, pp. 1–2; "The Post-Competitive, Comparative Game of a Free City," *The Digger Papers,* Aug. 1968, p. 15. Given the Diggers' emphasis on free goods, it's perhaps unsurprising that the LA benefit was poorly attended (author's interview with Caryle Camacho, Oct. 25, 2010; author's interview with Joe Camacho, Oct. 25, 2010).

212 **demanded to see the commanding officer:** Author's interview with Sandy

Gallin, Nov. 11, 2010; **his zany "Kill Class" routine:** *Operation: Entertainment*, WABC-TV, Dec. 20, 1968 (in author's possession).

213 **wished people could play his first album's *cover*:** Author's interview with Ron DeBlasio, Dec. 28, 2010; **didn't even crack the Top 100:** Liner notes, *Evolution/Revolution*, p. 18; **co-owner of the album's imprint:** "W-7 to Distribute the Dome Label," *Billboard*, Nov. 23, 1968, p. 3. *Billboard*'s misconstruing *Dove* Records as *Dome* Records in its announcement of the imprint's arrival was inauspicious, and prophetically so. *Richard Pryor* (Dove RS 6325) appears to have been the only record released on the imprint. The album did not chart until November 1973, four years after its original release, when it climbed to forty-one on the R&B chart.

213 **why . . . had he gotten so little money up front?:** Author's interview with Robert Marchese, Mar. 1, 2011.

213 **pistol-whipped his manager:** Author's interview with Sandy Gallin, Nov. 11, 2010; **For a while afterward:** Ibid.

214 **"Let's all get in bed":** Paul Mooney, *Black Is the New White* (New York: Simon and Schuster, 2009), pp. 10–13; *Pryor Convictions*, p. 90. Pryor remembered his invitation as "Let's take off all our clothes and have an orgy!"

214 **Mooney was raised:** Mooney, *Black Is the New White*, pp. 39, 51.

215 **"I get Mooney's share":** Ibid., pp. 18–19.

215 **"a black Playboy Mansion":** Carla Rivera, "A Distinction of Note for a Musical Landmark," *Los Angeles Times*, June 18, 2000, p. 1; Steve Kawashima, "Historic Night Life Echoes at Maverick's Flat," *Los Angeles Times*, Feb. 25, 2000; "A Place of Daring Vision," *Los Angeles Sentinel*, May 20, 1971, pp. 21, 126; **beauty pageants:** *Los Angeles Times*, Aug. 30, 1970, p. L37; **casting calls:** Mary Murphy, "Movie Call Sheet," *Los Angeles Times*, Oct. 26, 1972, p. E28; **redevelopment of the ghetto:** "Plans Offered for 2,000 Watts Jobs," *Los Angeles Times*, Aug. 20, 1967, p. E8; **"Psychedelic Shack":** Ericka Blount Danois, *Love, Peace and Soul: Behind the Scenes of America's Favorite Dance Show Soul Train* (Milwaukee, WI: Backbeat Books, 2013).

216 **small black Derringer:** Starr, *Black and Blue*, pp. 85–92; **"ran the club like a gangster":** *Pryor Convictions*, pp. 98–99; **"an aisle":** Starr, *Black and Blue*, p. 87; **a comic with his wits:** Ibid.; **"I loved getting on that stage":** Joe X. Price, *Redd Foxx, B.S. (Before Sanford)* (Chicago: Contemporary Books, 1979), p. 85; **"coke Olympics":** *Pryor Convictions*, pp. 98–99

216 **his two favorite words:** Mooney, *Black Is the New White*, p. 25; **"Say, nigger" . . . "Niggers nowadays":** "After Hours" and "Wino Panthers," *'Craps.'*

217 **"had an act":** Russ Wilson, "Pryor Serves Up a Fun Assortment," *Oakland Tribune*, Mar. 31, 1969, p. 14; Starr, *Black and Blue*, p. 90.

217 **In a dope-fueled brainstorming session:** *Pryor Convictions*, pp. 106–7.

218 **Black Sun:** C. Verne Bloch, "Richard Pryor Returns to Peoria Stage," *Peoria Journal Star*, Mar. 9, 1969, p. B1.

218 **Roth remembered him wandering:** Author's interview with Manny Roth, July 27, 2010. In the September 1967 *Ebony* profile of Pryor, he is shown training a camera that appears to be a sixteen-millimeter Bolex upon the brown coils left by a neighbor's dog; **new types of low-budget movies:** Marshall Fine, *Accidental Genius: How John Cassavetes Invented American Independent Film* (New York: Hyperion, 2005); David K. Frasier, *Russ Meyer: The Life and Films* (Jefferson, NC: McFarland and Co., 1990); Yannis Tzioumakis, *American Independent Cinema: An Introduction* (New Brunswick, NJ: Rutgers University Press, 2006); Chris Nashawaty, *Crab Monsters, Teenage Cavemen, and Candy Stripe Nurses: Roger Corman, King of the B Movie* (New York: Harry N. Abrams, 2013).

218 **his involvement with the AIP film:** "Night Club Comic Joins Stellar Stars in

AIP's 'Wild in the Streets,'" exhibitor manual for *Wild in the Streets*, Pacific Film Archive (Berkeley, CA), p. 4.

219 **"cheap commodity":** Pauline Kael, "Trash, Art, and the Movies," in *For Keeps* (New York: Dutton, 1994), p. 203. Ironically, the same film that inspired Pryor to rhapsodize about the technical perfection of American moviemaking was held up by Kael as an instance of trash cinema (whose vitality she appreciated).

220 **"What's that stuff?":** Mooney, *Black Is the New White*, p. 89.

220 **"an angel is financing it":** Bloch, "Richard Pryor Returns to Peoria Stage," p. B1.

220 **"House of Pain":** *Pryor Convictions*, pp. 111–12; **Lady Cocaine:** Pryor, *Jokes My Father Never Taught Me*, pp. 30–38; **spent long nights:** *Pryor Convictions*, pp. 111–12.

221 **she could invest her parents' wedding present:** Pryor, *Jokes My Father Never Taught Me*, pp. 31–32.

221 **Danny Kaye . . . Borscht Belt . . . *The Watermelon Fantasy*:** Martin Gottfried, *Nobody's Fool: The Lives of Danny Kaye* (New York: Simon and Schuster, 1994), pp. 17, 25.

221 **"a documentary . . . of black people":** *Under the Covers.*

222 **"White American, listen":** Mark Weiner, *Black Trials: Citizenship from the Beginning of Slavery to the End of Caste* (New York: Alfred A. Knopf, 2004), pp. 303–15.

223 **Richard began contributing concretely:** "Black Panther Racial Matter," Richard Pryor FBI file, Feb. 5, 1969. We have the FBI to thank for documenting his donation: as part of their surveillance of the Black Panther Party, they noted it in the file they opened on Richard. According to Pryor's FBI file, the Panthers were somewhat disappointed by the scale of his support: they had anticipated that he would join the party and write them a ten-thousand-dollar check. **special trip to Peoria:** "Peoria Negro Comic Slated at Carver Center," *Peoria Journal Star*, Feb. 25, 1969; **headlined a Congress of Racial Equality fund-raiser:** "CORE's 'Encore,'" *New York Amsterdam News*, May 17, 1969, p. 24; advertisement, *New York Amsterdam News*, May 24, 1969, p. 20; Alex Poinsett, "Ralph Innes: Nation Builder," *Ebony*, Oct. 1969, pp. 170–76.

223 **a spiral notebook:** Mooney, *Black Is the New White*, p. 92; **"The film opened":** *Pryor Convictions*, p. 107.

224 **winos, and drug addicts:** Hollie West, "Comic Pryor," *Washington Post*, July 28, 1969, p. B5; author's interview with Penelope Spheeris, Apr. 6, 2011.

Chapter 13: Irreconcilable Differences

225 **"I'm looking for film students":** Author's interview with Penelope Spheeris, Apr. 6, 2011.

225 **Shooting began in February 1969:** Mooney, *Black Is the New White*, p. 92; author's interview with Patricia Heitman, Sept. 17, 2011; author's interview with Penelope Spheeris, Apr. 6, 2011.

226 **one actor on the film recalled:** Daryl Littelton, *Black Comedians on Black Comedy: How African-Americans Taught Us to Laugh* (New York: Applause Books, 2006), p. 135.

226 **"I can make whatever I want":** Bloch, "Richard Pryor Returns to Peoria Stage," p. B1.

226 **The trip to Peoria:** Ibid., pp. B1, B2.

227 **Gertrude had reentered the Pryor family circle:** Author's interview with Sharon Wilson Pryor, Dec. 15, 2010.

227 **"You've got it on her too long":** Jennifer Pryor, "Trouble Man," *Spin*, May 1988, p. 49.

227 **"Hiya, mom":** Bloch, "Richard Pryor Returns to Peoria Stage," p. B1; **Two photographs hint:** Photograph in author's possession (courtesy of Barbara McGee).

228 **His old Carver mentor:** Bloch, "Richard Pryor Returns to Peoria Stage," p. B1; **Nation of Islam:** "Black Muslim Group Opens South Side Temple," *Peoria Journal Star,* Feb. 5, 1968; **"Afro-American Service Patrol":** "The Black Guards," *Peoria Journal Star,* Dec. 11, 1968; **Black high school students:** Tom Edwards, "School Board Agrees to Race Meeting After Singing Sit-In Demonstration," *Peoria Journal Star,* July 19, 1966; "200 Manual Students Walk Out of School for Protest March," *Peoria Journal Star,* Nov. 9, 1967, p. D1; "Schools Free of Demonstrators," *Peoria Journal Star,* Nov. 15, 1967, p. C1; **Bradley University:** Bernadine Martin, "BU Establishes Black Culture House, Sets Afro Degree Plan," *Peoria Journal Star,* Mar. 7, 1969, p. B1; **the Struts:** Bloch, "Richard Pryor Returns to Peoria Stage," p. B2.

229 **ABC had signed Spelling to create:** Aaron Spelling with Jefferson Graham, *A Prime-Time Life* (New York: Macmillan, 1996), pp. 79–81.

230 **"Season of Social Relevance":** Aniko Bodroghkozy, *Groove Tube: Sixties Television and the Youth Rebellion* (Durham, NC: Duke University Press, 2001), pp. 199–235; Todd Gitlin, *Inside Prime Time* (Berkeley: University of California Press, 2000 [1983]), pp. 203–20; Christine Acham, *Revolution Televised: Prime Time and the Struggle for Black Power* (Minneapolis: University of Minnesota Press, 2004); Donald Bogle, *Prime Time Blues: African Americans on Network Television* (New York: Farrar, Straus and Giroux, 2001); "The Connection," *The Mod Squad,* aired Sept. 14, 1972 (ABC); "Soul Club," *The Partridge Family,* aired Jan. 29, 1971 (ABC); *The Young Lawyers,* aired Oct. 28, 1969 (ABC); *Carter's Army,* aired Jan. 27, 1970 (ABC).

230 ***Carter's Army* was an exception:** Pamela Haynes, "'Carter's Army,' ABC Mini-Movie, Is Saga about Black GI's at War," *Philadelphia Tribune,* Jan. 31, 1970, p. 22.

232 **Negro Ensemble Company:** Ellen Foreman, "The Negro Ensemble Company: A Transcendent Vision," in Errol Hill, ed., *The Theatre of Black Americans: A Collection of Critical Essays* (New York: Applause, 1987), pp. 270–82; **"We got to calling ourselves":** "No Time for Comedy for Comic Richard Pryor in Guest Star Role on 'Movie of the Week," ABC press release, Jan. 16, 1970, Richard Pryor clippings file, Billy Rose Theatre Collection, New York Public Library.

232 **"I play a coward":** Ibid.

232 **after the weather:** Author's interview with Penelope Spheeris, Apr. 6, 2011; **For the first time:** *Pryor Convictions,* p. 108.

233 **five days later:** Pryor, *Jokes My Father Never Taught Me,* pp. 35–38.

233 **For twelve hours a day:** Author's interviews with Penelope Spheeris, Apr. 6, 2011, Apr. 11, 2011.

233 **"the White Lady":** Mooney, *Black Is the New White,* p. 88

234 **ran naked to his car . . . grabbed an extra coat:** Author's interview with Penelope Spheeris, Apr. 6, 2011; Pryor, *Jokes My Father Never Taught Me,* pp. 40–41.

234 **Penelope spliced back together:** Author's interview with Penelope Spheeris, Apr. 6, 2011; *Pryor Convictions,* p. 107.

235 **off-center, X-rated exercise:** Melvin Van Peebles, *Sweet Sweetback's Baadasssss Song: A Guerrilla Filmmaking Manifesto* (New York: Thunder's Mouth, 2004 [1971]), pp. 91–92.

235 **"I liked it":** "Talking to the Secret Primps: An Interview with Richard Pryor," *Good Times,* July 23, 1971, p. 12.

235 **citing "irreconcilable differences":** "Richard Pryor Sued for Divorce," p. A1; "Ex-Peoria Comic Ordered to Pay Back Alimony," *Peoria Journal Star,*

Nov. 13, 1969; **his companion Maxine:** "*If I Stop I'll Die* Research," Box 171, John A. Williams Papers, University of Rochester.

235 **let his phone be disconnected:** "Subscriber by credit," Richard Pryor FBI file, Sept. 1, 1970.

236 **cutting off his relationship:** Earl Calloway, "Brown and Pace Replace Pryor at Mister Kelly's," *Chicago Defender*, Dec. 30, 1969, p. 11; **premier supper club:** Author's interview with Tim Reid, Oct. 4, 2010; **"keep it clean":** *Good Times* interview with Richard Pryor and the Congress of Wonders, July 15, 1971, Berkeley, CA (transcript in author's posession) (hereafter "*Good Times* interview"); **Lennie's on the Turnpike:** Author's interview with Ralph Camilli, June 7, 2011; **"Just listening":** Hollie I. West, "Pryor's Comedy," *Washington Post*, Oct. 7, 1970, p. B9.

236 **who had earlier enthused about Richard's comedy:** *The Rosey Grier Show*, aired Sept. 21, 1968; **"could use some self-discipline":** James Brown, "Richard Pryor on Troubadour Stage," Feb. 21, 1969, p. J15; **Redd Foxx groused:** *Los Angeles Sentinel*, May 5, 1970, p. B3A; **"pandering":** Todd Everett, "LA Concert Capsules," *Los Angeles Free Press*, Jan. 15, 1971, pp. 31, 44.

237 **"in the world":** *Good Times* interview.

237 **Laff Records . . . "When we signed":** Littleton, *Black Comedians on Black Comedy*, pp. 87–88, 137; "A Short Laff History," *Billboard*, Jan. 7, 1978, p. 43.

237 **The four-album contract:** Contract between Richard Pryor and ALA Enterprises, Inc., Dec. 7, 1970 (in author's possession).

238 **"Masturbating" . . . "Jackin' Off":** *'Craps.'* Laff labeled *'Craps'* as recorded at the Redd Foxx Club, but the provenance of the album as a whole may be more complicated. On December 7, 1970, Richard entered into his contract with Laff; sometime in December, the Redd Foxx Club burned to the ground (Starr, *Black and Blue*, p. 106). In "Blow Our Image," Richard talks as if he were performing at the Redd Foxx Club, but given the other references to Mongo Santamaría and Richard's ongoing marriage, it seems quite possible that the recording dates to a mid-April 1970 double bill with Santamaría. On the second side of the album, meanwhile, Richard's references to the Osmond Brothers suggest a recording date of January 1971—by which time the Redd Foxx Club was defunct. Richard did perform on January 22–23, 1971, at the York Club, a cocktail lounge with a vibe similar to that of "Redd's Place" (Billy Rowe, "Billy Rowe's Notebook," *New York Amsterdam News*, Apr. 25, 1970, p. 18; advertisement, *Los Angeles Sentinel*, Jan. 14, 1971, p. B2A).

238 **a young black man in the pincers of the law:** "I Spy Cops" and "Lineup," '*Craps*.' Over the past seven years, Pryor had spent time in jail in Pittsburgh, at the San Diego border, and in Los Angeles as a result of the assault at the Sunset Towers West—all of which he may have drawn upon in these routines.

239 **"We used to think" . . . "Blacks are the same":** Michael Sherman, "Pryor Appearing at Club," *Los Angeles Times*, Jan. 1, 1971, p. H12.

240 **Being married is hard:** "F**k from Memory," *'Craps.'*

240 **Richard's vision of sex:** "Gettin' Some," "Gettin' High," and "Big Tits," *'Craps'*.

241 **"I was the only dude in the neighborhood":** "F**king the Faggot," *'Craps'*.

241 **living in the Sunset Tower:** Contract between Richard Pryor and ALA Enterprises, Inc., Dec. 7, 1970.

241 **John Wayne . . . best-kept prostitutes:** Laurie Ochoa, "Tawdry Tales of the Sunset Tower," *Los Angeles Times*, June 19, 1988, p. L98. According to Mötley Crüe bassist Nikki Sixx, Pryor carried on a highly charged relationship with Sixx's mother, who also lived in the Tower at the time ("Dear Superstar: Nikki Sixx," *Blender*, Sept. 2007).

242 **episode of *The Partridge Family*:** "Soul Club," *The Partridge Family*, aired Jan. 29, 1971.

243 **Around forty-two seconds after 6:00 a.m.:** "Death Toll 33 in Massive Earthquake," *Los Angeles Times*, Feb. 10, 1971, p. B1; **"the valley of the damned," "knew God or something":** *The Tonight Show with Johnny Carson*, aired Jan. 12, 1971 (NBC).

243 **The Sylmar Earthquake:** Special San Fernando Earthquake edition, *California Geology* 24 (April/May 1971): 4–5.

243 **"It was as if":** *Pryor Convictions*, pp. 113–14.

244 **shaggy-browed:** Alan Farley, "Divided We Stand: A Sketch of the History of the Disunity of Broadcasters in the Face of Threats to the First Amendment," *KPFA Folio* 22, no. 4 (Apr. 1971): 5; **math degree . . . chairman:** Author's interview with Alan Farley, Feb. 13, 2007; **production assistant:** *KPFA Folio* 22, no. 2 (Feb. 1971): 1; **Gaslight:** *New York*, Feb. 22, 1971, p. 15; **Basin Street West:** Alan Farley, "Media Monitor," *KPFA Folio* (Mar. 1971): 8, 46. In his memoir, Pryor remembers driving up to Berkeley with Paul Mooney. While it is probably true that Mooney and Pryor did drive up to Berkeley together at some point, Farley's recollection fits better with the timeline set by the earthquake, Pryor's performances at Basin Street West, and the beginnings of Farley's recordings of Pryor (pp. 113–14).

Chapter 14: I'm a Serious Mother

245 **"learn to live":** "Talking to the Secret Primps," p. 12; **"an apple a day":** Author's interview with Alan Farley, Feb. 13, 2007; **"to cast off everything":** *Pryor Convictions*, p. 115.

245 **Starting in the fall of 1967:** W. J. Rorabaugh, *Berkeley at War: The 1960s* (New York: Oxford University Press, 1989), pp. 145–66.

246 **"crackling with information":** Author's interview with Ishmael Reed, Feb. 20, 2007.

246 **By 1971, the left in Berkeley:** Rorabaugh, *Berkeley at War*, pp. 155–66; **three hundred demonstrators:** em, "People Return FBI Call," *Berkeley Barb*, Feb. 12–18, 1971, p. 5; "Turnabout's Fair Play," *Good Times*, Feb. 12, 1971, pp. 14–15.

246 **more than three thousand:** "Stone Cold Revolutionaries," *Good Times*, Feb. 12, 1971, p. 2; **"Smash the State!":** "Women Lead Action," *Berkeley Barb*, Feb. 12–18, 1971, p. 5; **clobbered a policeman:** Wittol, "They Bleed Too . . . ," *Berkeley Barb*, Feb. 12–18, 1971, p. 3.

247 **"a schizophrenic with multiple personalities":** C.D., "Chaos Over Laos," *Berkeley Barb*, Feb. 12–18, 1971, p. 3; **A young woman composed a poem:** em, "Stone Cold Revolutionaries."

248 **a survey of electoral preferences:** The Sellerses (Nancy Sellers and Charles Sellers), "Black Berkeley: Shifting Left?," *Berkeley Monitor*, Dec. 3, 1971, p. 8; **a separate police department for black Berkeley:** David Mundstock, "Berkeley in the 70s: A History of Progressive Electoral Politics," http://www.berkeleyinthe70s.homestead.com.

248 **played out this chemistry:** Author's interview with Alan Farley, Feb. 13, 2007; **a fledgling social critic:** Farley, "Divided We Stand," pp. 4–5, 47; Farley, "Media Monitor," *KPFA Folio* (Feb. 1971): 7, 43; **Richard was free speech incarnate:** Farley, "Media Monitor," *KPFA Folio* (Mar. 1971): 8, 46.

249 **The *Examiner*'s Phil Elwood:** Joel Selvin, "Phil Elwood, 1926–2006: Beloved Bay Area Jazz and Blues Critic," *San Francisco Chronicle*, Jan. 11, 2006; Alan Farley, "Vignettes Amidst the Pimps," *San Francisco Examiner*, May 16, 1971, p. 5.

249 **"unfunny and not original":** Cecil Brown, "Remembering Richard Pryor: A True Friend and Comic Genius," *AOL Black Voices*, Dec. 12, 2005; **"a major figure":** Philip Elwood, "Comic Pryor Is Young, Black and Outrageous," *San Francisco Examiner*, Feb. 20, 1971, p. 8.

249 **"endless creativity":** Alan Farley, "Media Monitor," *KPFA Folio*, Mar. 1971, p. 46.

249 **"master of a hundred voices":** Grover Sales, "Stage & Screen," *San Francisco*, Jan. 1971, p. 40; Grover Sales, "Stage & Screen," *San Francisco*, Apr. 1971, p. 56; **"nervous, light-brown ferret":** Grover Sales, "Stage & Screen," *San Francisco*, July 1971, p. 42.

250 **approached by a producer:** Author's interview with Alan Farley; ***The Great American Dream Machine*:** John J. O'Connor, "Who's Inside the 'Dream Machine,'" *New York Times*, Apr. 11, 1971, p. D21; *Pioneers of THIRTEEN—The '70s: Bold and Fearless* (THIRTEEN/WNET, 2013); **Writing on spec for the show:** Richard Pryor with Alan Farley, "Uncle Sam Wants You Dead, Nigger," *The Realist* 90 (May–June 1971): 39–41.

250 **Richard's screenplay tracked the life of Johnny:** Ibid., pp. 39–41.

251 **Richard's most straightforward political statement:** "Uncle Sam Wants You Dead, Nigger," recorded June 16, 1971, Museum of Performance and Design, Performing Arts Library, San Francisco, CA.

251 ***The Great American Dream Machine* rejected the script:** Farley, "Uncle Sam Wants You Dead, Nigger," p. 39; **At Alan Farley's suggestion:** Author's interview with Alan Farley. The producers of *The Great American Dream Machine* did not lack political courage: the same year they rejected Richard's script, they battled against the FBI to air an investigation of its undercover agents, one that alleged that "some of the violence blamed on the New Left movement was actually the work of police and F.B.I. undercover agents" (O'Connor, "TV: Report on F.B.I. Raises Questions," p. 63).

252 **underground magazine that had just published:** "Disneyland Memorial Orgy," *The Realist*, April/May 1967, pp. 12–13.

252 **Richard was approached by Improv regular:** Author's interview with Michael Blum, Feb. 20, 2007.

252 **In Blum's film:** *Live and Smokin'*; **describes how the white johns:** "Whorehouse, Part I," *Evolution/Revolution*.

253 **"Remember the old days" . . . "this ain't shit!":** Author's interview with Ralph Camilli, June 7, 2011.

253 **"I hate to see folks leave":** *Live and Smokin'*.

253 **caught in another jam:** Author's interview with Alan Farley; Charles Burress, "Mary Moore—Founder of Berkeley Nightclub Mandrake's," *San Francisco Chronicle*, Dec. 28, 2001; Ed Ward, liner notes to *Joy of Cooking* (Capitol/Evangeline Records, 2003 [1971]).

254 **Pied Piper:** E-mail communication with Ed Ward, Feb. 27, 2007.

254 **Moore called to the stage . . . "Louie, Louie":** Cecil Brown, "Running Buddy," in Benj Demott, ed., *First of the Year: 2008* (New Brunswick, NJ: Transaction, 2008), p. 204.

254 **"A slim shadow" . . . "under the spell" . . . "I was one of the only":** Ibid., pp. 204–7.

254 **After the show, Brown followed Richard:** Ibid., pp. 206–7.

255 **"a nightmare":** Christopher Lehmann, "If You're Black, Get Back, and Jive to Survive," *New York Times*, Jan. 14, 1970, p. 45; **protagonist, George Washington:** Cecil Brown, *The Life and Loves of Mr. Jiveass Nigger* (New York: Ecco Press, 1991 [1969]), pp. 206, 212; **"flimflamboyantly erotic":** Lehmann, "If You're Black, Get Back," p. 45; **fielding raves:** Richard Rhodes, "Does Everybody Lie? Yes, Says George Washington," *New York Times*, Feb. 1, 1970, p. BR3; Ardie Ivie, "The Uncle Remus Reality Updated," Mar. 8, 1970, p. N47; ***The Tonight Show*:** *Chicago Tribune*, Mar. 6, 1970, p. B19; **screen rights:** A. H. Weiler, "A-Jive in Denmark," *New York Times*, Feb. 22, 1970, p. D15; **hosted the sort of parties:** Author's interview with Ishmael Reed.

255 **"He had never been around":** Author's interview with Joan Thornell, Feb. 28, 2007; **"uncompromisingly black":** *Pryor Convictions*, p. 117.

256 **"was not on the curriculums":** Author's interview with Ishmael Reed; **"Hey, motherfucker":** "John Williams interview with Claude Brown," recorded July 29, 1983, Box 171, John A. Williams Papers, University of Rochester.

256 **"Perhaps the most soulful word":** Claude Brown, "The Language of Soul," *Esquire* vol. 69, Apr. 1968, p. 88; Ishmael Reed, ed., "Introduction,"*19 Necromancers from Now: An Anthology of Original American Writing for the 1970s* (Garden City, NY: Doubleday, 1970), p. xv.

256 **"I don't think I have a style yet":** "Talking to the Secret Primps," p. 14; **"I'm a serious mother":** "John Williams interview with Claude Brown."

257 **"Dracula, Frankenstein, the Wolfman":** "Prelude," *Evolution/Revolution.*

257 **$110-a-month rental . . . "the soundtrack for my life":** *Pryor Convictions*, pp. 115–16; **a dingy clapboard rooming house:** Author's interview with Patricia Heitman, Sept. 17, 2011.

257 **"like drinking out of two cups":** "Congress of Wonders interview"; **"I'm using the money":** "Talking to the Secret Primps," p. 13; **"freest time of my life":** *Pryor Convictions*, p. 114.

257 **"very high on cocaine and whiskey":** "'The Assassin' and Other Musings, 6/13/1971," transcript in author's possession.

258 **"Back up on myself":** "Stream of Consciousness," *A Snapshot of Richard Pryor*, produced by Alan Farley, KALW, Feb. 13, 2003 (recording in author's possession).

258 **wild fable of black payback:** *Sweet Sweetback's Baadasssss Song*, directed by Melvin Van Peebles (Cinemation, 1971).

259 **crisp takedown:** Lerone Bennett Jr., "The Emancipation Orgasm: Sweetback in Wonderland," *Ebony*, Sept. 1971, p. 118; J. Hoberman, *The Dream Life: Movies, Media, and the Mythology of the Sixties* (New York: The New Press, 2005), pp. 299–304.

259 **"That was as exciting to me":** "Talking to the Secret Primps," p. 12.

259 **a day in the life of a black guerrilla:** "'The Assassin' and Other Musings, 6/13/1971."

260 **The screenplay begins:** Felton, "This Can't Be Happening to Me," p. 44.

261 **screenplay's final scene:** Ibid., p. 69.

261 **he kept his cocaine close:** "John Williams Interview with Claude Brown"; **"like a deranged wizard":** *Pryor Convictions*, p. 116; **on Telegraph Avenue:** Author's interview with Joan Thornell.

262 **"You know how Dracula":** "Talking to the Secret Primps," p. 12. In another interview, when a white comedian compared his "straight, middle-class college scene" to Richard's "ghetto scene," Richard took offense, snapping "my scene isn't no fucking ghetto scene" ("Congress of Wonders interview").

262 **Then the routine would hang:** *Live and Smokin'.*

264 **"I repeated a single word":** *Pryor Convictions*, p. 116.

265 **On the morning of September 9, 1971:** Tom Wicker, *A Time to Die* (New York, Quadrangle, 1975), pp. 9–18, 286–92, 315–16; **one shower . . . one roll of toilet paper:** *Transcript of New York State Special Commission on Attica*, Hearings of Apr. 12, 1972, pp. 83, 87; **"orgy of brutality":** David W. Chen, "Judge Approves $8 Million Deal for Victims of Attica Torture," *New York Times*, Feb. 16, 2000, p. B6.

265 **packed his few possessions":** Author's interview with Patricia Heitman, Sept. 11, 2011.

266 **where he went to meet his drug connection:** Author's interview with Patricia Heitman, Mar. 7, 2013; **"talked to a black man":** Author's interview with

Patricia Heitman, Sept. 11, 2011; **"What the fuck are you doing?":** *Pryor Convictions*, p. 119;.

266 **biweekly show on KPFA:** *KPFA Folio*, Nov. 1971, p. 8.

266 **"Murder the dogs":** "Richard Pryor Program," recorded Sept. 15, 1971, Museum of Performance and Design, Performing Arts Library, San Francisco, CA; "Richard Pryor Program," recorded Sept. 29, 1971, Museum of Performance and Design, Performing Arts Library, San Francisco, CA.

267 **"get even with white folks":** "Richard Pryor Program," recorded Sept. 15, 1971.

267 **In his second and last KPFA program:** "Richard Pryor on Attica"; R.W. Apple, "Attica—A Judgment on America," *New Statesman*, Oct. 1, 1971, p. 424. **Oswald's hand-wringing sense:** Oswald's anguished liberalism has continued to live on in American pop culture: the prison on HBO's *Oz* was named after Oswald, and much of the show revolved around the question of whether it was possible to rehabilitate prisoners in the hyperviolent environment of the maximum-security prison.

268 **"People's Park":** Rorabaugh, *Berkeley at War*, pp. 155–66; **in April 1971:** Mundstock, "Berkeley in the 70s".

269 **"Let's see that little shuffle":** "Richard Pryor Program," recorded Sept. 29, 1971.

269 **renovate his stage act:** Hollie I. West, "Richard Pryor at Cellar Door," *Washington Post*, July 28, 1971, p. B8.

269 **tour some college campuses:** "Talking with the Secret Primps," p. 13; **a small independent film:** Hunt, "Black Comedy and the Pryor Commitment," p. S1; **give up her stewardess job:** Author's interview with Patricia Heitman, Sept. 17, 2011.

270 **no bank account:** Author's interview with Patricia Heitman, Mar. 7, 2013; **"I talked about being a star":** *Pryor Convictions*, p. 131.

Chapter 15: The More I Talk, the Less I Die

273 **felt his whole body tense up:** Author's interview with Sandy Gallin, Nov. 11, 2010; **a well-connected friend called:** Author's interview with Ron DeBlasio, Dec. 28, 2010; **"I don't know what they're laughing at":** Author's interview with Norman Steinberg, July 6, 2010.

273 **"The movie industry was more on its ass" . . . "These were aging gentlemen":** Peter Biskind, *Easy Riders, Raging Bulls: How the Sex-Drugs-and-Rock 'n' Roll Generation Saved Hollywood* (New York: Simon and Schuster, 1998), pp. 20, 125. On the crisis of the studios and the New Hollywood of the 1970s, see also David A. Cook, *Lost Illusions: American Cinema in the Shadow of Watergate and Vietnam*, 1970–1979 (Berkeley: University of California Press, 2002); Mark Harris, *Pictures at a Revolution: Five Movies and the Birth of the New Hollywood* (New York: Penguin, 2008); Thomas Elsaesser et al., eds., *The Last Great American Picture Show: New Hollywood Cinema in the 1970s* (Amsterdam: Amsterdam University Press, 2004); Lester Friedman, ed., *American Cinema of the 1970s: Themes and Variations* (New Brunswick, NJ: Rutgers University Press, 2007); Timothy Corrigan, *A Cinema without Walls: Movies and Culture after Vietnam* (New Brunswick, NJ: Rutgers University Press, 1991).

274 **"Because of the catastrophic crisis" . . . "ground was in flames":** Biskind, *Easy Riders, Raging Bulls*, pp. 14, 22.

275 **"bananaland":** Felton, "This Can't Be Happening to Me," p. 71. With the exception of Paul Schrader, Pryor was brought into Hollywood by directors who stood outside the most well-known circles of "New Hollywood": he was not approached by the likes of Francis Ford Coppola, Martin Scorsese, Robert Altman,

Hal Ashby, William Friedkin, or Steven Spielberg. (In fact, Spielberg backed out of a commitment to work on a film that would have starred Pryor in a supporting role.) Understanding Pryor's rise as part of the story of New Hollywood, then, shifts our sense of that larger story.

275 **"Believe it or not":** Author's interviews with Patricia Heitman, Sept. 11, 2011, and Mar. 7, 2013.

276 **exactly . . . one line:** Author's interview with Jay Weston, Mar. 14, 2013; **modeling his character after Jimmy Binkley:** *Pryor Convictions*, p. 130.

277 **"in such a funny, drawling way":** Author's interview with Jay Weston, Mar. 14, 2013; **"mumbly-magical":** Andrew Sarris, "Films in Focus," *Village Voice*, Nov. 23, 1972.

277 **became Billie's best friend:** Berry Gordy, *To Be Loved: The Music, the Magic, the Memories of Motown: An Autobiography* (New York: Warner, 1994), pp. 313–14;

277 **Signed originally for five hundred dollars . . . multiples of that amount:** Author's interview with Patricia Heitman, Sept. 11, 2011; **"We became real close":** "Behind the Blues: *Lady Sings the Blues*," *Lady Sings the Blues*, directed by Sidney J. Furie (Paramount, 1972), DVD (hereafter *Lady Sings the Blues*).

277 **alone among the film's actors:** Author's interview with Jay Weston.

278 **a choice much disputed . . . "I was as strong":** Nat Hentoff, "The Real Lady Day," *New York Times Magazine*, Dec. 24, 1972, p. 18; **The movie's villains are many:** Hollie I. West, "No Way to Treat Billie Holiday," *Washington Post*, Nov. 2, 1972, pp. C1, C10.

279 **the hidden strengths of director Sidney Furie:** Herbert G. Luft, "Interviewing Sidney Furie," *Foreign Cinema*, May 31, 1968, p. 4; **belonged to a different film:** Pauline Kael, "*Lady Sings the Blues*: Pop Versus Jazz," *New Yorker*, Nov. 4, 1972.

279 **Berry Gordy broke the impasse:** Author's interview with Jay Weston.

280 **the former gardener's cottage . . . Richard was attracted to the serenity:** Author's interview with Patricia Heitman, Sept. 11, 2011.

280 **Patricia tried to rouse him:** Author's interview with Patricia Heitman, Sept. 11, 2011.

281 **Steinberg called:** Author's interview with Norman Steinberg; **"I decided":** Kenneth Tynan, *Profiles*, ed. Kathleen Tynan and Ernie Eban (New York: HarperCollins, 1990), p. 393.

281 **"If you have three Jews":** Author's interview with Andrew Bergman, July 12, 2010; **"I said, 'I can't say the N-word'":** *Mel Brooks and Dick Cavett Together Again* (HBO Films, 2011).

281 **"lock a bunch of weirdos up together":** Brad Darrach, "Playboy Interview with Mel Brooks," *Playboy*, Feb. 1975, p. 64; **needed train fare:** Mel Brooks commentary track, *Blazing Saddles*, directed by Mel Brooks (Warner Bros., 1974), DVD (hereafter *Blazing Saddles*).

282 **666 Fifth Avenue, sixth-floor:** Mel Brooks commentary track, *Blazing Saddles*; **Richard arrived late:** Author's interview with Steinberg; **executive conference room . . . "Did you see that?":** Author's interview with Bergman.

282 **four men who gathered:** Dentist Alan Uger was a fifth writer who received a screen credit on *Blazing Saddles*. He spent only a little while in the writers' room (ibid.); **had just failed to land an academic job:** Ibid.; **"for two weirdos in the balcony":** Darrach, "Playboy Interview with Mel Brooks," p. 64.

283 **"My God, I'm not a writer":** Tynan, *Profiles*, p. 385; **"like a one-armed paper hanger":** Author's interview with Bergman.

283 **"very brave and very far-out and very catalytic":** Tynan, *Profiles*, p. 393; **In Bergman's original treatment:** Author's interview with Bergman; **"one crazy nigger":** "*Blazing Saddles* script, July 26, 1972," Margaret Herrick Li-

brary, Academy of Motion Picture Arts and Sciences (Beverly Hills, CA) (hereafter "*Blazing Saddles* script"), pp. 31, 41, 76, 78, 90.

284 **"My family was poor":** "*Blazing Saddles* script," pp. 24–27.

285 **he'd learned it in prison:** Author's interview with Steinberg; **first collected . . . two years later:** Bruce Jackson, *Get Your Ass in the Water and Swim Like Me: Narrative Poetry from Black Oral Tradition* (Cambridge: Harvard University Press, 1974).

286 **"We would never have done [that bit]":** Author's interview with Bergman.

286 **"concentrated on Mongo":** "Back in the Saddle," *Blazing Saddles*; **preference for dancing with men:** "*Blazing Saddles* script," pp. 58–60.

287 **"You really believed":** Author's interview with Bergman.

287 **"What happened?":** Author's interview with Steinberg.

287 **"Where ya' headin'?":** "*Blazing Saddles* script," p. 118.

288 **"That was about as much *sitzfleisch*":** Author's interview with Bergman; **Brooks had enthused**: Felton, "This Can't Be Happening to Me," p. 71; **"Richard Pryor" was placed second:** "*Blazing Saddles* script," title page. In the final film, the order of credits on the screenplay ran as follows: Mel Brooks, Norman Steinberg, Andrew Bergman, Richard Pryor, Alan Uger.

288 **former pimp Robert Poole:** Ron Pennington, "'Mack's' Boxoffice Strength Activates Planning for Sequel," *Hollywood Reporter*, Apr. 27, 1973, p. 3; **on toilet paper:** "Michael Campus," in David Walker, Andrew J. Rausch, and Chris Watson, eds., *Reflections on Blaxploitation: Actors and Directors Speak* (Lanham, MD: Scarecrow Press, 2009), p. 17; **$120,000:** Comments by "ARDATH" on Robert Poole script, *Black and Beautiful* (1969), cover page (script held at USC Cinematic Arts Library, Los Angeles, CA) (hereafter "*Black and Beautiful* script").

288 **the script itself:** "*Black and Beautiful* script," pp. 1, 111.

289 **"To say I was cold":** Joseph McBride, "Campus, Director with Hit 'Carson,' Wants Pix 'That Make My Blood Boil,'" *Daily Variety*, Aug. 20, 1974; **sang the Internationale:** "Michael Campus handwritten notes (1972)," Michael Campus Papers, Special Collections, Bancroft Library, University of California at Berkeley, p. 4; **cried with his parents . . . father blacklisted:** Author's interview with Michael Campus, July 27, 2010; **in the back of a police car:** "Interview with Michael Campus, Tape no. 1 of 4, April 6, 2002," "Interviews—*Making of the Mack*" folder, Michael Campus Papers, Special Collections, Bancroft Library, University of California at Berkeley; **under one condition:** Author's interview with Michael Campus, Aug. 28, 2009.

289 **considered several actors:** "Original Casting" folder, Michael Campus Papers, Special Collections, Bancroft Library, University of California at Berkeley; **killed in a robbery:** Author's interview with Campus, Aug. 28, 2009; **brash and longstanding self-confidence:** "For Max Julien, from Wish to Fact," *Los Angeles Herald Examiner*, Aug. 24, 1968.

290 **a close friend of Huey Newton:** Commentary soundtrack, *The Mack*; **"There could be":** "Expatriate Black Actor Max Julien Says Film Industry behind the Times," *Variety*, July 15, 1971, p. 3; **"I can't play Goldie as a fop":** Author's interview with Michael Campus, Aug. 28, 2009.

290 **Julien insisted:** Commentary soundtrack, *The Mack*; **Richard in turn demanded:** "Making of the Mack" screenplay, Michael Campus Papers, Special Collections, Bancroft Library, University of California at Berkeley; **all-night rewrite sessions:** Author's interview with Michael Campus, Aug. 28, 2009; **yet to go to Oakland:** "Michael Campus handwritten notes (1972)," pp. 2, 9–10.

290 **"three musketeers":** Author's interview with Michael Campus, Aug. 28, 2009.

290 **"Richie says nothing" . . . avoided the eyes of Campus . . . "White Boy":** "Michael Campus handwritten notes (1972)," pp. 4, 10, 15.

291 **Gradually . . . the film took shape:** "*Black and Beautiful* script."
291 **pitch-perfect sense of street talk:** Author's interview with Michael Campus, Aug. 28, 2009.
292 **they had never formally discussed:** "Michael Campus handwritten notes (1972)," p. 7.
292 **"You're gonna pay me" . . . "I'm the director," . . . "Get me my money":** "Michael Campus handwritten notes (1972)," p. 1.
292 **"Richie is the human submarine":** Ibid., pp. 13–17.
292 **"one of the coldest movies":** *Vibe*, Apr. 2005, p. 123; **bodyguards carried firearms:** Commentary on *The Mack*; **bottles started raining down:** *Mackin' Ain't Easy*, directed by Laura Nix (2002).
293 **"base of operations" . . . "liberating the territory of Oakland":** Joshua Bloom and Waldo Martin, *Black against Empire: The History and Politics of the Black Panther Party* (Berkeley: University of California Press, 2013), p. 380; **secured the Ward Brothers' protection:** Ron Pennington, "Producer of 'Mack' Gains Confidence of Oakland Gang Lords to Shoot Film," *Hollywood Reporter*, Sept. 14, 1972; **"You're in Panther territory":** Author's interview with Harvey Bernhard.
293 **the next day at noon:** Ibid.
294 **set up pickets . . . "The Black Community Will Not Be Exploited Anymore" . . . "silver coated form of oppression":** "Blaxploitation," *The Black Panther*, Oct. 7, 1972, pp. 2, 9, 11.
294 **"What are you doing?":** Author's interview with Michael Campus, July 27, 2010.
294 **needed to prop him up:** Author's interview with Michael Campus, Aug. 28, 2009.
295 **at 3:00 a.m., he knocked:** Commentary track, *The Mack*.
295 **"I was going to throw the coffee table on top":** Author's interview with Bernhard.
295 **The manager of the Marriott . . . would have to be written out:** Author's interview with Michael Campus, Aug. 28, 2009.
296 **which Richard in fact was doing:** Robert Poole, "*The Mack* shooting script," Michael Campus Papers, Special Collections, Bancroft Library, University of California at Berkeley, pp. 44–45; **"we're gonna get the motherfucker":** *The Mack*.
297 **"I know ladies who've been abused":** Commentary track, *The Mack*.
297 **fourth-highest-grossing film:** "50 Top Grossing Films," *Variety*, Apr. 25, 1973, p. 10.
297 **"Bitch," he said:** Unless otherwise noted, all details of this episode come from the author's interview with Patricia Heitman, Sept. 11, 2011.
298 **a writing friend of Richard's:** Author's interview with Rick Edelstein, Mar. 15, 2013.

Chapter 16: Black Goes First

300 **"Shoulders stooped":** [Paramount Pictures], "Richard Pryor Emerges as a Dramatic Actor," *Hit!* publicity materials (1973), n.p., Cinematic Arts Library, University of Southern Calfornia, Los Angeles, CA.
300 **"a half-empty room":** Author's interview with Mel Stuart, July 16, 2009.
301 **"on one condition":** Ibid.; **held an open call:** Wattstax publicity brochure, p. 1, Box 131, Folder 10, David L. Wolper Collection, David L. Wolper Center for the Study of the Documentary, University of Southern California, Los Angeles, CA (hereafter DLWC); "Wattstax '72' Film Shot by 90% Black Crews; 250G Budget for Docu," *Variety*, Sept. 27, 1972; Larry Clark commentary on *Wattstax*, directed by Mel Stuart (Columbia, 1973), DVD (hereafter *Wattstax*).

301 **ninety-two thousand people:** William Earl Berry, "How Watts Festival Renews Black Unity," *Jet*, Sept. 14, 1972, p. 54; **one hundred thousand feet of film:** "'Wattstax '72' Film Shot by 90% Black Crews"; **not unlike later film reviewers:** Dennis Hunt, "Pryor Highlight of 'Wattstax' Collage," *Los Angeles Times*, Feb. 21, 1973, p. G10; John Hartl, "'Wattstax' Owes a Lot to Pryor," *Seattle Daily Times*, June 8, 1973; **"It's a newsreel":** Author's interview with Stuart.

302 **"There are directors I could name":** Bridget Byrne, "Celebration Turned into Social Commentary," *Los Angeles Herald-Examiner*, Mar. 4, 1973, p. D1.

302 **"Gentlemen, we need Shakespeare":** Author's interview with Stuart.

302 **felt he'd found his chorus figure:** Ibid. The site of Pryor's performance—identified at the Summit Club in *Wattstax*'s records—has been mistakenly linked to the Summit Club of Hollywood. However, this Summit Club was closed by 1972; the Summit Club of Pryor's performance was located at the intersection of La Brea and Stocker in the upscale black enclave of Baldwin Hills.

303 **I think that niggers:** For whatever reason, Pryor did not repeat this parable about the origins of *nigger* in any of his recorded performances onstage (Reggie Collins, e-mail to the author, July 11, 2013).

304 **"side-splittingly funny":** Arthur Knight, "Facing Reality," *The Saturday Review*, Apr. 1973, p. 72.

305 **"Here and Now Black Man":** Sandra Haggerty, "1972 for Blacks: Gains and Losses," *Los Angeles Times*, Dec. 31, 1972, p. B1. On the state of the Black Power movement in 1972, see Peniel Joseph, *Waiting 'Til the Midnight Hour: A Narrative History of Black Power in America* (New York: Henry Holt, 2006).

305 **Not long after Richard tried to choke:** Author's interview with Patricia Heitman, Sept. 11, 2011.

305 **ran a boutique label . . . made a list:** Author's interviews with Ron DeBlasio, Dec. 28, 2010, and Jan. 8, 2011.

306 **"Richie, you were a sensation":** Author's interview with DeBlasio, Dec. 28, 2010.

306 **Richard popped by:** Ibid.; **glowing reviews:** Charles Champlin, "Two Ladies Who Sing the Blues," *Los Angeles Times*, Oct. 25, 1972, p. E1; Gene Siskel, "A Nice 'Lady,' but She's No Billie," Oct. 27, 1972, p. B1; Andrew Sarris, "Films in Focus"; Kael, "*Lady Sings the Blues*: Pop Versus Jazz."

306 **the Pied Piper:** Gertrude Gipson, "Gertrude Gipson's Candid Comments," *Los Angeles Sentinel*, Nov. 23, 1972, p. B3A.

307 **near the end of 1972:** "Cleavon Little Plays 'Black Bart' Title Role," *Daily Variety*, Dec. 19, 1972; **an amiable, classically trained actor:** Glenn Collins, "Cleavon Little, Award-Winning Actor, Dies at 53," *New York Times*, Oct. 23, 1992; **"acting out so many things,"** Felton, "This Can't Be Happening to Me," p. 71; **asked [Warner Bros.] on bended knee:** Jacoba Atlas, "Mel Brooks Interview," *Film Comment* (Mar.–Apr. 1975); **even flew out to New York:** Mel Brooks commentary track, *Blazing Saddles*; **"Very simply . . . they're afraid":** Felton, "This Can't Be Happening to Me," p. 71.

307 **"Warner Bros. wouldn't touch him":** Author's interview with Andrew Bergman, July 12, 2010.

307 **"a thorn in my heart" . . . "They used me and that's not fair":** Martin Weston, "Richard Pryor: Every Nigger Is a Star," *Ebony*, Sept. 1976, p. 56; Mooney, *Black Is the New White*, pp. 154–55; **claiming credit later for the film's most famous scene:** *Pryor Convictions*, p. 132.

307 **"Nobody takes credit":** Author's interview with Norman Steinberg, July 6, 2010.

308 **"Good morning, ma'am":** *Blazing Saddles*; **"Richie had a dark side":** Author's interview with Bergman.

308 **"Cleavon is not a threatening figure":** Author's interview with Bergman. Earlier in 1972, Pryor had actually shared screen time with Little on "The Connection," the season-premiere episode of *The Mod Squad*. Richard played a jazz trumpeter with a lucrative sideline in heroin smuggling; Cleavon, his squirrelly right-hand man. In their scenes together, the difference between them as actors is striking. Richard is streetwise and rugged, spitting words with earned authority; Cleavon is stagy and broad, an actor putting curlicues on his tough-guy role. ("The Connection," *The Mod Squad*, aired Sept. 14, 1972.)

308 **disappointed with the scripts:** *Pryor Convictions*, p. 133; **"I don't want to become Jack Oakie":** Gregg Kilday, "Richard Pryor—Rapman without an Exit Line," *Los Angeles Times*, Mar. 15, 1973, p. H29.

309 **"Lincoln-doctor's-dog of a movie":** Charles Champlin, "Billie Dee and the Soiled Six," *Los Angeles Times*, Oct. 3, 1973, p. D1; **allowed to improvise:** "Hit!," *Hollywood Reporter*, Sept. 19, 1973, pp. 3, 8.

309 ***Hit!*'s production in late 1972:** "Richard Pryor in Paramount's 'Hit!,'" *Hollywood Reporter*, Nov. 29, 1972; **Richard served as best man . . . "Me and Billie":** Author's interview with Patricia Heitman, Sept. 11, 2011.

309 **jealous of Billie:** Author's interview with Rob Cohen, Aug. 18, 2010; **"I didn't know anyone more aware":** *Pryor Convictions*, p. 108; **turned often to Richard for advice:** Author's interview with Patricia Heitman, Sept. 11, 2011; **called Richard a "genius":** James J. Murray, "Williams Says 'Hit' Film Puts Drugs Down," *New York Amsterdam News*, Sept. 29, 1973, p. C6.

309 **poker:** Ponchitta Pierce, "A Look into the Private Life of Billie Dee Williams," *Ebony*, Apr. 1974, p. 64; **drawn into an affair:** Author's interview with Patricia Heitman, Sept. 11, 2011.

310 **Then, one day, . . . burning up:** Ibid.

310 **"The secret of the film's success":** Judith Crist, "Seasonal Slurp," *New York*, Sept. 23, 1973, p. 89; **a typical pan . . . "made the bizarre choice":** "Hit!," p. 3; Vincent Canby, "Furie's 'Hit!' Is a Caper Film without Style," *New York Times*, Sept. 19, 1973, p. 38.

310 **"Pryor's humor pierces through":** Jay Cocks, "Bad Dope," *Time*, Oct. 29, 1973.

311 **"His work may relieve the tension":** "Hit!," p. 9; **spent three hours . . . "fashion free-for-all":** Beth Ann Krier, "'Wattstax' Outdoes Premiere-Goers," *Los Angeles Times*, pp. F1, F8; **range of politicians:** Leah Davis, "Wattstax Premiere," *SOUL*, Mar. 12, 1973; "'Wattstax' to Open at Music Center's Ahmanson Theater," *Hollywood Reporter*, Jan. 19, 1973; Marvene Jones, "The V.I.P.'s," *Hollywood Reporter*, Feb. 6, 1973; Norma Lee Browning, "Is This an Offer Brando Can't Refuse?," *Chicago Tribune*, Feb. 12, 1973; Marilyn Beck, "Cream of Filmland Society, Watts Residents to Preview *Wattstax*," *San Jose News*, Dec. 5, 1972—all in Box 131, Folder 1, DLWC.

312 **"I'm not equipped":** Kilday, "Richard Pryor—Rapman without an Exit Line," p. H29.

312 **grand marshal:** "Eighth Watts Festival to Open Aug. 15," *Los Angeles Times*, July 29, 1973; **Richard was chosen to headline it:** *Los Angeles Sentinel*, Feb. 15, 1973, p. B4A.

313 **"wickedly funny":** Arthur Cooper, "Watts Happening," *Newsweek*, Feb. 26, 1973; **"breathtakingly irreverent and ironic":** Charles Champlin, "Vibrations from a Black Woodstock," *Los Angeles Times*, Feb. 27, 1973, p. H1; **"the most talented black comedian":** Ronald E. Butler, "Viewpoint," *Tulsa World*, June 23, 1973.

314 **Even those less captivated:** Vincent Canby, "'Wattstax,' Record of Watts Festival Concert," *New York Times*, Feb. 16, 1973, p. 17; **"Without Pryor's wise**

rudder": Peter Herbst, "'Wattstax' Tells Life-Style," *Boston Herald-American*, Mar. 23, 1973; **"Perhaps Pryor should have directed":** Hartl, "'Wattstax' Owes a Lot to Pryor."

314 **in London:** James Bacon, "Ayres Turmoil Recalled by Amnesty Controversy," *Los Angeles Herald Examiner*, Feb. 15, 1973; **United Nations:** "Wattstax," *Richmond African-American*, May 12, 1973; **Washington, DC:** "Previewing 'Wattstax' for Washington Brass," *Daily Variety*, Jan. 19, 1973; **"You Can't Judge a Movie by Its Color":** Unidentified clipping, Box 131, Folder 9, DLWC.

314 **So Richard journeyed:** Marilyn Beck, "Hollywood Closeup," *Milwaukee Journal*, May 2, 1973.

314 **roulette wheels spun:** Rex Reed, "Drop a Bomb over Cannes and There Goes Show Biz," *Chicago Tribune*, May 27, 1973, p. E9; **Wolper asked Richard:** Author's interview with Ron DeBlasio, Dec. 28, 2010.

314 **took in the Cannes parade:** Ibid.; **Ladies of the night . . . see-through swimsuits:** Norma Lee Browning, "Standing on the Corner Watching the Girls," *Chicago Tribune*, May 21, 1973, p. B26; **garrulous and open . . . sad-faced girl:** Dorothy Manners, "Tourists Star-Hunting at Festival," *Los Angeles Herald-Examiner*, May 18, 1973; "'WATTSTAX' ou Cent Milles Noirs en Couleur . . . ," unidentified clipping, Box 131, Folder 9, DLWC.

314 **talked with African filmmakers:** Author's interview with DeBlasio; **exulted at seeing writer James Baldwin:** Brown, "Remembering Richard Pryor"; **"one of the uproarious delights":** Charles Champlin, "Merv's Glimpses of the Cannes Festival," *Los Angeles Times*, July 31, 1973, p. C12.

315 **at Richard's urging . . . "No, black goes first":** Author's interview with Mel Stuart; Commentary track, *Wattstax*.

316 **he'd made films for both Lyndon Johnson and Richard Nixon:** David L. Wolper, *Producer: A Memoir* (New York: Scribner, 2003), pp. 75–80, 183; **large enough for forty but holding eight:** Author's interview with DeBlasio; **"Princess Grace can't see you today":** Author's interview with Mel Stuart.

316 **La Chaumière . . . "What's wrong?":** Wolper, *Producer*, p. 183.

317 **No one knew how to translate:** Author's interview with Patricia Heitman, Sept. 11, 2011.

Chapter 17: Be Glad When It's Spring, Flower

318 **James B. Harris:** Author's interview with James B. Harris, July 30, 2010; **Mel Stuart:** Author's interview with Mel Stuart, Oct. 4, 2010; **he would remove some cocaine:** Author's interview with Ron DeBlasio, Dec. 28, 2010; **"I had to jump through hoops with him":** Author's interview with Lily Tomlin, Nov. 4, 2010.

318 **took Lily to a black part of Los Angeles:** Ibid.; **"meant, if you were a girl":** Jeff Sorensen, *Lily Tomlin: Woman of a Thousand Faces* (New York: St. Martin's Press, 1989), p. 14.

318 **only if she could pay her own way . . . "Nude Live Girls":** Author's interview with Lily Tomlin, Nov. 4, 2010.

319 **Pussycat Theater:** David Handelman, "The Last Time We Saw Richard," *Premiere*, Jan. 1992, p. 87.

319 **"We had conversations":** *Pryor Convictions*, p. 136; **"We are soul mates":** "Lily . . . Ernestine . . . Tess . . . Lupe . . . Edith Ann . . . ," *Time*, Mar. 28, 1977.

320 **"The networks feel":** Sorensen, *Lily Tomlin*, p. 65; **"the 11 o'clock news":** Cecil Smith, "Barbra, Lily in Tandem Specials," *Los Angeles Times*, Nov. 2, 1973, p. F25.

320 **"something he'd be proud of":** Author's interview with Lily Tomlin, Nov. 4,

2010; **A white Tennessean by birth:** Sorensen, *Lily Tomlin*, p. 60; **an unusually bracing TV movie:** Jane Wagner, *J.T.* (New York: Random House, 1969); **"the most profound meditation":** Hilton Als, "A Pryor Love," *The New Yorker*, Sept. 13, 1999, p. 70; **the script came back:** Author's interview with Lily Tomlin, Nov. 4, 2010.

321 **"You ever kiss a black man?" . . . "You better get off":** David Felton, "Lily and All the Funny Women," *Rolling Stone*, Oct. 24, 1974, p. 84; **"He was telling people":** Handelman, "The Last Time We Saw Richard," p. 87.

321 **The sketch's most provocative moments:** Felton, "Lily and All the Funny Women," p. 84; *Lily*, directed by Joseph Hardy, aired Mar. 16, 1973 (CBS).

321 **"I always want them to be strong":** Sorensen, *Lily Tomlin*, p. 54.

322 **a winner in the Nielsen ratings:** "The Bunkers and CBS Top Nielsen Poll," *Los Angeles Times*, Mar. 28, 1973, p. 31; **she was determined:** Author's interview with Lily Tomlin, Nov. 4, 2010; **"Come on, leg or no leg":** Sorensen, *Lily Tomlin*, p. 65.

322 **"I have titties":** David Felton, "This Can't Be Happening to Me," p. 72.

323 **"Juke and Opal":** Felton, "Lily and All the Funny Women," p. 84; **"Don't hand me that jive":** *Lily*, directed by Bill Davis, aired Nov. 2, 1973 (CBS).

323 **"probably the most radical departure":** Felton, "Lily and All the Funny Women," p. 50; **"Everybody kept saying":** Als, "A Pryor Love," p. 81.

324 **Lily deliberately left Opal's race:** Author's interview with Lily Tomlin, Nov. 4, 2010; **mixed-race:** TV Scout, "Barbra and Lily Present Specials on Channel 7," *Lowell Sun*, Nov. 2, 1973, p. 33; **black:** Felton, "Jive Times," p. 38.

325 **improvised questions:** The questions that Juke the character improvises were, in fact, improvised by Richard Pryor the actor (author's interview with Lily Tomlin, Nov. 4, 2010).

325 **"$360,000 jerk off":** Felton, "Lily and All the Funny Women," p. 50; **the network agreed to this lesser of two evils:** Author's interview with Lily Tomlin, Nov. 4, 2010.

325 **ranking fifty-first:** Ernie Kreiling, "A Closer Look at Television," *Van Nuys News*, Nov. 15, 1973, p. 20; **"political stuff and mood pieces":** Sorensen, *Lily Tomlin*, p. 74.

326 **"I love Lily":** Felton, "Lily and the All the Funny Women," p. 49.

326 **"sensual":** *Pryor Convictions*, p. 136.

326 **The only strains in their relationship:** Author's interview with Lily Tomlin, Nov. 4, 2010; **At a restaurant on Sunset Boulevard:** Author's interview with Patricia Heitman, Sept. 11, 2011.

327 **Even Lily . . . acknowledged the difficulty:** "Lily . . . Ernestine . . ."

327 **six films:** *Lady Sings the Blues*, *Blazing Saddles*, *The Mack*, *Some Call It Loving*, *Wattstax*, and *Hit!*; **low-paid cameo:** *The Mike Douglas Show*, aired Nov. 26, 1974; **"I've been trying to be a booty star":** *Richard Pryor Live at the Comedy Store*, recorded Oct. 29, 1973, Shout! Factory, 2013 (hereafter *Live at the Comedy Store*).

327 **Western wherein the odd couple:** Author's interview with Michael Schultz, Sept. 4, 2010; **The *Los Angeles Times* announced:** Mary Murphy, "Movie Call Sheet," Feb. 28, 1973, p. G15.

327 **"Kiss my ass, Jack!":** *Live at the Comedy Store*; **he saw Richard as a breakout performer:** Author's interview with Ron DeBlasio, Dec. 28, 2010; **a midnight concert:** Tom Zito, "Street Talk," *Washington Post*, Dec. 17, 1973, p. B4; **Cellar Door (220 seats):** Author's interview with Ralph Camilli, June 6, 2011; **wondered if he was ready:** *The Tonight Show with Johnny Carson*, aired Jan. 17, 1974 (NBC).

328 **you can hear his nerves:** *Live at the Comedy Store*.

328 **barely made it . . . a "nervous wreck":** Author's interview with Ron DeBlasio, Dec. 28, 2010.

329 **"Ain't gonna affect us" . . . "guffawing in the aisles":** Zito, "Street Talk," p. B4.

329 **DeBlasio fielded a phone call:** Author's interview with Ron DeBlasio, Dec. 28, 2010; **Queen Booking:** "First Lady of Talent Booking," *Ebony*, June 1974, pp. 73–80; author's interview with Murray Swartz, Mar. 14, 2011; **Lincoln Center:** "Richard Pryor Naughty but Funny," *New York Amsterdam News*, Oct. 19, 1974, p. B16; **the Oakland Coliseum:** Kathie Staska and George Mangrum, "California Jam a Smooth Show," *The Daily Review* (Hayward, CA), Apr. 12, 1974, p. 40.

329 **90 percent black:** Felton, "This Can't Be Happening to Me," p. 43; **"Remember black people" . . . Richard himself came up with the album's title . . . abbreviated in ads:** Author's interview with Ron DeBlasio, Dec. 28, 2010.

330 **"Lord, don't let her know" . . . "Put your hands up" . . . "Boy, you hit me":** "Black & White Life Styles," "Niggers vs. Police," "The Back Down," *"That Nigger's Crazy,"* recorded Feb. 1974, Partee PBS-2404 (hereafter *That Nigger's Crazy*).

330 **"nothin' can scare a nigger" . . . :** "Flying Saucers," "Black and White Life Styles," "Wino Dealing with Dracula," "Exorcist," on *That Nigger's Crazy.*

330 **"What am I supposed to do" . . . hightail to an orthodontist . . . "the devil is just acting":** Ibid.

331 **"What nigger feel" . . . "[If] you don't clean up that shit":** "Niggers vs. Police," "Wino and Junkie."

331 **"Baby, I can handle any motherfuckin' thing":** "Acid," *Live at the Comedy Store;* **"I don't remember how to breathe":** "Acid," *Bicentennial Nigger.*

332 **"like a ballet":** Felton, "This Can't Be Happening to Me," p. 43.

332 **In the original version:** "Acid," *Live at the Comedy Store.*

333 **approached by a friend:** "Richard Pryor: A Sensitive and Serious Man . . . at Times," *New Pittsburgh Courier*, May 4, 1974, p. 18.

333 **A few days later . . . Lorton's unofficial uniform:** Joel Dreyfuss, "Of Men and Longing," *Washington Post*, Mar. 6, 1974; **coaxed the promoter:** "Richard Pryor: A Sensitive and Serious Man," p. 18.

334 **some in long white robes:** Dreyfuss, "Of Men and Longing," p. B9.

334 **"Look at these guys":** Author's interview with Ron DeBlasio, Jan. 8, 2011.

334 **he had smuggled . . . "We wish we had more":** Dreyfuss, "Of Men and Longing," p. B9; **as long as the warden would allow:** Author's interview with Ron DeBlasio, July 31, 2013.

334 **"crowded around Pryor":** Dreyfuss, "Of Men and Longing," p. B9.

334 **Richard left Lorton:** "Richard Pryor: A Sensitive and Serious Man," p. 18; Moore, "Richard Pryor the Funniest of Them All," p. D8.

334 **Prisoner No. 2140-875:** "Jail Comedy: Inmates Flip as Flip Does a Panty Flip," *Los Angeles Times*, June 14, 1974, p. A7; **$250,000 over four years:** "Comic Pleads Guilty to U.S. Tax Charges," *Los Angeles Times*, Apr. 16, 1974; **making an example of Richard:** Author's interview with Ron DeBlasio, July 31, 2013.

Chapter 18: Number One with a Bullet

336 **surged to the No. 1 position:** See, for instance, "Soul LPs," *Billboard*, July 13, 1974, p. 56; "Soul LPs," *Billboard*, Aug. 3, 1974, p. 29; "Soul LPs," *Billboard*, Sept. 7, 1974, p. 29; **"a piano player in a whorehouse":** David Greenberg, *Nixon's Shadow: The History of an Image* (New York: W.W. Norton, 2003), p. 200; Richard G. Zimmerman, *Plain Dealing: Ohio Politics and Journalism Viewed from the Press Gallery* (Kent, OH: Kent State University Press, 2006), p. 70; **no one believed the piano player:** Stanley Kutler, *The Wars of Watergate* (New York: Alfred

A. Knopf, 1990), pp. 527–44; **playing an intimate Philadelphia nightclub:** John Fisher, "This Week in Music," *Bucks County Courier Times*, Aug. 4, 1974, p. C12; **he brought a TV onstage:** Author's interview with Ron DeBlasio, Jan. 8, 2011; **lampooned for his diabolical ambition:** "Nixon," *Live at the Comedy Store*; author's interview with Joan Thornell, Feb. 28, 2007.

336 **"Nixon took justice and broke its jaw":** Murphy, "Richard Pryor," p. 27.

337 **"[Watergate was] a shock":** Haynes Johnson, "The View from Peoria: It's Not Playing Well," *Washington Post*, June 30, 1974, p. C4.

337 **"Rated X" label:** "'That Nigger's Crazy'," *Philadelphia Tribune*, June 25, 1974, p. 11; **radio stations refused to play it:** "Richard Pryor . . . Latest Record a $1 Million Hit," *Peoria Journal Star*, Nov. 2, 1974; **beginning to circle the drain:** Rob Bowman, *Soulsville, U.S.A.: The Story of Stax Records* (New York: Schirmer, 1997), pp. 320–33; **a Stax rep came to a Pryor show:** Author's interview with Ron DeBlasio, Dec. 28, 2010.

338 **"They flatly refused":** Bowman, *Soulsville, U.S.A.*, p. 323; **"no promotion, no nothing":** Author's interview with Ron DeBlasio, Dec. 28, 2010.

338 **hustlers and their women fill up:** Author's interview with Ron DeBlasio, Dec. 28, 2010; **He started feeling something new and electric:** "Interview between James McPherson and Richard Pryor," c. 1975 (in author's possession); **"I noticed going around working":** McPherson, "The New Comic Style of Richard Pryor," p. 32.

338 **"thunderous roars" . . . "the number one comedian in the world":** "Richard Pryor Naughty but Funny," p. B16; "Pryor on Extensive Tour," *New Pittsburgh Courier*, June 15, 1974, p. 19.

339 **sell-out audience of twelve thousand . . . "blue—no, purple":** C. A. Bustard, "Music," *Richmond Post-Dispatch*, Aug. 5, 1974, p. A5; **a municipal ordinance prohibited:** "Richard Pryor Charged for Disorderly Conduct," *Jet*, Aug. 22, 1974, p. 61; **was not interested in censoring himself:** Author's interview with Ron DeBlasio, Jan. 8, 2011.

339 **"They was going to arrest me":** Tallmer, "Richard Pryor: When It Rains," p. 23; **1:30 in the morning:** "Richard Pryor Charged for Disorderly Conduct," p. 61; **"Listen, brother":** Author's interview with Ron DeBlasio, Jan. 8, 2011; **another black cop told Richard:** "Interview," recorded fall 1974, on *Richard Pryor—No Pryor Restraint: Life in Concert*, Shout Factory, 2013 (hereafter *No Pryor Restraint*); **fifteen minutes . . . five-hundred-dollar bond . . . trial date:** "Comic Arrested after Concert," *Richmond Post-Dispatch*, Aug. 5, 1974, p. A5.

339 **dropping the charges against Richard:** "Comedian's Case Not Prosecuted," *Richmond Post-Dispatch*, Aug. 20, 1974, p. B4; **Adults-only entertainment:** Peter Braunstein, "'Adults Only': The Construction of an Erotic City in New York during the 1970s," in Beth Bailey and David Farber, eds., *America in the 70s* (Lawrence: Univ. of Kansas Press, 2004), pp. 129–46.

340 **on the marquee of the Shrine Mosque:** "Interview with Juliette Whittaker," recorded May 16, 1983, Box 171, John A. Williams Papers, Special Collections Library, University of Rochester, Rochester, NY; **"Richard Pryor Days":** Theo Jean Kenyon, "Ashanti Umoja Center: From Act of Defiance to Sense of Identity," *Peoria Journal Star*, Aug. 23, 1974; **"It was our award":** *The Mike Douglas Show*, aired Nov. 25, 1974.

340 **"This is an inspiration for all of us" . . . playground set:** Ibid.; "Interview with Juliette Whittaker"; **the Learning Tree . . . seventy children:** Strahler, "Juliette Whittaker," pp. B1, B4.

341 **born out of the defiance of Black Power:** Kenyon, "Ashanti Umoja Center"; **presented Richard with a plaque, "Boy, my grandmother's gonna beat my ass":** "Skit on Race, Sex a Hit at Mosque," *Peoria Journal Star*, Dec. 25, 1974.

341 **some two hundred thousand dollars in unpaid royalties . . . Stax gave possession:** Bowman, p. 323; **Pay Back Inc.,:** "Stax Sued by Comedian Pryor," *Billboard*, Nov. 9, 1974, p. 14; **gold record:** "Richard Pryor Naughty but Funny," p. B16; **two holes:** Author's interview with Rob Cohen, Aug. 18, 2010.

342 **"We live, eat, sleep":** Mike Douglas, *I'll Be Right Back: Memories of TV's Greatest Talk Show* (New York: Simon and Schuster, 2000), pp. 109–10.

342 ***The Mike Douglas Show* became:** *The Mike Douglas Show*, aired Nov. 25–26, 28–29, 1974 (in author's possession).

343 **Joe Frazier, whom he had teased:** Author's interview with Murray Swartz, Mar. 30, 2011.

343 **more than four million jokes . . . sixty-seven-year-old comedian:** Tom Shales, "Replay on Mr. Television," *Washington Post*, Nov. 11, 1974, p. B1; **a sobering book:** Milton Berle with Haskel Frankel, *Milton Berle: An Autobiography* (New York: Delacorte Press, 1974).

343 **"Is this the real audience?":** *The Mike Douglas Show*, aired Nov. 25, 1974.

344 **"one of the strangest moments":** *The Mike Douglas Show*, Nov. 26, 1974.

344 **"I wish . . . I could have laughed":** *The Mike Douglas Show*, Nov. 25, 1974; **"Eleanor Roosevelt":** Douglas, *I'll Be Right Back*, p. 111.

345 **the talk of the comedy circuit:** Ibid., pp. 111–12.

346 **Berle had counseled Lenny Bruce:** Shales, "Replay on Mr. Television," p. B11.

347 **"There ain't no sense in nobody going on":** *The Mike Douglas Show*, aired Nov. 29, 1974; **"Having my grandmother with me":** Lisa Collins, "Time Out for Richard Pryor," *Black Stars Magazine*, June 1976, p. 44.

347 **threw together a birthday party:** Author's interview with Murray Swartz, Mar. 30, 2011.

347 **sometimes scatted to Clark Terry's "Mumbles":** Author's interview with Jimmy Binkley, July 1, 2010; **one of Richard's favorite tunes:** *The Tonight Show*, aired July 22, 1968 (NBC).

347 **a larger home above the Sunset Strip:** Author's interview with Patricia Heitman, Sept. 11, 2011; **a swimming pool, billiards room:** Robert A. DeLeon, "Richard Pryor Looks to '75," *Jet*, Jan. 9, 1975, pp. 60–61; **a large aquarium:** Author's interview with Patricia Heitman, Sept. 11, 2011; **"To avoid ill feeling":** McPherson, "The New Comic Style of Richard Pryor," p. 20; **"Yeah, nigger—this means you":** Collins, "Time Out for Richard Pryor," p. 41.

348 **tailspin of Richard and Patricia's relationship:** Author's interview with Patricia Heitman, Sept. 11, 2011

348 **cruelty to Patricia was sharpened:** Ibid.

349 **the worst of his vindictiveness:** Ibid.

349 **fifty-thousand-dollar advance . . . "We did it" . . . "three great things":** Author's interviews with Ron DeBlasio, Dec. 28, 2010, and Jan. 8, 2011; **damaged by his tax troubles:** Ron Kisner, "The Money Problems of the Stars," *Ebony*, May 1977, p. 148; **"My house is rented":** DeLeon, "Richard Pryor Looks to '75," p. 61.

350 **Their relationship unraveled in a single conversation:** Author's interview with Ron DeBlasio, Jan. 8, 2011; **"my best friend in the business":** *The Mike Douglas Show*, aired Nov. 28, 1974.

350 **"That's right, that's how I feel":** Author's interview with Ron DeBlasio, Jan. 8, 2011.

350 **proudly wore the nicknames Big Dollar Dave and the Smiling Cobra:** Author's interview with Michael Ashburne, May 7, 2011; Orde Coombs, "The Voice of the New Vulnerability," *New York*, Feb. 15, 1982, p. 47; **baby-faced**

. . . **"A Black man in this country":** Ronald Harris, "The Man Who Makes Multimillionaires," *Ebony*, June 1979, p. 61; **"real power" . . . his grandfather had sat:** Peter Ross Range, "Making It in Atlanta: Capital of Black-Is-Bountiful," *New York Times Magazine*, Apr. 7, 1974, p. 70.

351 **masterminded the successful mayoral campaign:** Ibid., pp. 70–72; **a $5.5 million, ten-album deal:** Harris, "The Man Who Makes Multimillionaires," pp. 56.

351 **"ripped off . . . by white people":** "Reporter's Transcript of Proceedings, Vol. III," *Richard Pryor v. David McCoy Franklin*, Case No. TAC 17 MP 114 (Mar. 3, 1982), p. 271 (hereafter *Pryor v. Franklin*); **"have someone around who'd protect him":** Harris, "The Man Who Makes Multimillionaires," p. 60.

351 **a novel business arrangement . . . operate without a written agreement:** "Reporter's Transcript of Proceedings, Vol. I," *Pryor v. Franklin*, Mar. 1, 1982, p. 32.

352 **Franklin had seen Richard:** Author's interview with Michael Ashburne, May 7, 2011; **"one of the most brilliant men" . . . "take a percentage":** "Reporter's Transcript of Proceedings, Vol. IV," *Pryor v. Franklin*, pp. 563–65.

352 **a monthly salary of $2,000 . . . "I wish you would let me be the one":** "Reporter's Transcript of Proceedings, Vol. I," *Pryor v. Franklin*, pp. 28–30.

352 **had mentored everyone from Al Jolson:** "Sam Weisbord Dead; William Morris Aide," *New York Times*, May 9, 1986; **"one of the most brilliant," "a very tough negotiator":** Harris, "The Man Who Makes Multimillionaires," p. 56.

353 **litigated in front of California's Labor Commissioner's Office:** "Determination," *Pryor v. Franklin* (Aug. 12, 1982), p. 36; "Ex-Talent Agent Told to Pay Richard Pryor $3.1 Million," *Los Angeles Times*, Aug. 20, 1983, p. A13.

353 **"Over here, Rich":** *Pryor Convictions*, p. 143.

353 **"Killed a guard in Lou-ez-ze-ana," "Say, boy":** McPherson, "The New Comic Style of Richard Pryor," p. 20.

354 **"inebriated diction made it seem":** William Jelani Cobb, "Richard Pryor's Mudbone," *NPR News & Notes*, aired Jan. 2, 2008; **"something between a preacher's Sunday mornin' sermonizin'":** *Pryor Convictions*, p. 3.

354 **Mudbone made Richard speak in his voice:** "Mudbone," . . . *Is It Something I Said?*, Warner Bros., MS 2227, 1975 (hereafter *Is It Something*).

356 **a spectacular riff:** "Little Feets," *Is It Something*; **have long been a feature:** Charles Chestnutt, *The Conjure Stories*, ed. Robert B. Stepto and Jennifer Rae Greeson (New York: W.W. Norton, 2011); Eric Sundquist, *To Wake the Nations: Race in the Making of American Literature* (Cambridge: Harvard University Press, 1998); Glenda Carpio, *Laughing Fit to Kill: Black Humor in the Fictions of Slavery* (New York: Oxford University Press, 2008).

356 **"My goddamn feets":** "Little Feets," *Is It Something.*

Chapter 19: Every Nigger Is a Star

361 **he riled ABC . . . "so far out . . . as to be close":** Steve Allen, *Funny People* (New York: Stein and Day, 1981), pp. 232–33; Aaron Gold, "Tower Ticker," Mar. 20, 1974, p. B2; **"I won't be on the same stage":** Author's interview with Carl Gottlieb, Aug. 25, 2010; **fled to her dressing room:** Gertrude Gipson, "Gertrude Gipson's Candid Comments," *Los Angeles Sentinel*, Feb. 27, 1975, p. B5.

362 **putting together . . . a new Saturday late-night program:** Tom Shales and James Andrew Miller, *Live from New York: An Uncensored History of Saturday Night Live* (Boston: Little, Brown, 2002), pp. 19, 64; Doug Hill and Jeff Weingrad, *Saturday Night: A Backstage History of Saturday Night Live* (New York: William

Morrow, 1986); **"the funniest man on the planet":** Jeff Sorensen, *Lily Tomlin*, p. 66; author's interview with Craig Kellem, Nov. 5, 2010.

362 **"I can't do a contemporary comedy show" . . . laid out his conditions . . . "He'd better be funny":** Shales and Miller, *Live from New York*, pp. 63–64; Hill and Weingrad, *Saturday Night*, pp. 76, 116; Mooney, *Black Is the New White*, pp. 160–61.

363 **the shift, in Hollywood:** Ed Guererro, *Framing Blackness: The African American Image in Film* (Philadelphia: Temple University Press, 1993), pp. 69–101; **"Blaxploitation went brain dead":** Ed Guerrero, "The So-Called Fall of Blaxploitation," *Velvet Light Trap* (Fall 2009): 90.

364 **Richard might have landed:** *The Lowdown on Uptown: A Retrospective* (2003), on *Uptown Saturday Night* DVD.

364 **clashing with the executives:** Aram Goudsouzian, *Sidney Poitier: Man, Actor, Icon* (Chapel Hill: University of North Carolina Press, 2004), p. 345; **"healthier exploration of black life":** Carol Kramer, "For a Black Pioneer, the Burden Turns Gold," *Chicago Tribune*, June 30, 1974, p. E16; **"pimps, prostitutes, and dope pushers":** Goudsouzian, *Sidney Poitier*, p. 345.

364 **"the largest black all-star cast":** "Uptown Saturday Night," *Ebony*, July 1974, pp. 52–53; **almost half the behind-the-camera jobs:** T. Prescott Simms, "The Living Arts," *Chicago Tribune*, Aug. 11, 1974, p. O19; **"a picture for the general audience":** "Uptown Saturday Night," *Ebony*, July 1974, pp. 52–53; **Richard was offered expenses only:** *The Mike Douglas Show*, Nov. 26, 1974.

364 **"I almost went into overtime":** *Uptown Saturday Night* promotional short, Nov. 6, 1973.

365 **"Look at my eye":** *Uptown Saturday Night*, directed by Sidney Poitier (Warner Bros., 1974).

365 **box office gold:** Mark A. Reid, *Redefining Black Film* (Berkeley: University of California Press, 1993), pp. 28–30; Goudsouzian, *Sidney Poitier: Man, Actor, Icon*, p. 345; **blaxploitation trend had begun to sputter:** Guerrero, *Framing Blackness*, pp. 103–10.

366 **shot in nine days:** Weston, "Richard Pryor: 'Every Nigger Is a Star,'" p. 57; **"there are dozens of scenes":** *Filmfacts* 19, no. 1 (1976): 35; **"two sharp dudes":** Gerald Martinez, Diana Martinez, and Andres Chavez, *What It Is . . . , What It Was: The Black Film Explosion of the '70s in Words and Pictures* (New York: Hyperion, 1998), p. 90; **earned back its cost:** Weston, "Richard Pryor," p. 57; **"Tell them I apologize":** Weston, "Richard Pryor," p. 57.

366 **a protégé of Motown's Berry Gordy:** Gregg Kilday, "Motown Simplifies the Complex," *Los Angeles Times*, Aug. 3, 1974, p. A7; **a raffish, socially conscious comedy . . . "The slaves done run off":** *The Bingo Long Traveling All-Stars & Motor-Kings*, directed by John Badham (Motown Productions-Universal Pictures, 1976).

367 **"We have a real uphill battle":** Mary Murphy, "Motown Firms Film Commitment," *Los Angeles Times*, Sept. 3, 1975, p. G14; **top-shelf talent:** Bruce Cook, "The Saga of Bingo Long and the Traveling All-Stars," *American Film*, June 1976, pp. 10–12; **a $3.5 million financing deal:** Author's interview with Rob Cohen, Aug. 18, 2010; **an extraordinary budget for a "black" film:** Hollie I. West, "The Bingo Long All-Stars Wind Up for a Grand Slam," *Washington Post*, Aug. 24, 1975, p. H2.

367 **From the start, Richard was fundamental:** Author's interview with Rob Cohen; "Richard Pryor in 'Bingo Long' to Roll June 30," *Hollywood Reporter*, June 17, 1975; **in the novel:** William Brashler, *The Bingo Long Traveling All-Stars and Motor Kings* (Urbana: University of Illinois Press, 1993 [1973]).

368 **slip into the beds of white women:** Hal Barwood and Matthew Robbins,

The Bingo Long Traveling All-Stars & Motor Kings screenplay, n.d., Writers Guild Library, Los Angeles, CA.

368 **preferred to rent his own home:** West, "The Bingo Long All-Stars Wind Up for a Grand Slam," p. H2. **"quality actors" . . . "quality script" . . . "I don't think":** Mary Murphy, "'Julia' Role Next for Jane Fonda," *Los Angeles Times*, June 14, 1975, p. A8;

368 **"James Brown country":** Murphy, "'Julia' Role Next for Jane Fonda," p. A8; **the rookie film director who had taken over:** Joan E. Vadeboncoeur, "Debut Brings Film Success," *Syracuse Herald-Journal*, July 22, 1976, p. 35; **"It's harder to meet a whiter white man" . . . who organized everything in his bedroom . . . :** Author's interview with Cohen.

370 **One night during filming:** Author's interview with Badham; **"Richard's just left the set":** Author's interview with Cohen.

370 **in an affluent white area near Mercer University:** West, p. H2.

370 **"You don't need me to be my foot" . . . "He was very concerned":** Author's interview with Badham.

370 **almost killed James Earl Jones:** John Badham and Craig Modderno, *I'll Be in My Trailer: The Creative Wars Between Directors and Actors* (Studio City, CA: Michael Weise Productions, 2006), pp. 10–11; author's interview with Badham; director's commentary, *The Bingo Long Traveling All-Stars and Motor Kings*.

371 **"For what?":** Author's interview with Badham; Badham and Modderno, *I'll Be in My Trailer*, pp. 10–12.

372 **Once, Richard observed Williams:** Author's interview with Badham; **"If there was a vagina":** Author's interview with Cohen.

372 **talking often of bringing his gun . . . "You got to calm the guy down!":** Author's interview with Cohen; **"We had to move him away":** Author's interview with Badham; **a collective sigh of relief:** Marilyn Beck, "Beck's Show Business Beat," *Cedar Rapids Gazette*, Sept. 3, 1975, p. 5C.

373 **"We work hard":** West, "The Bingo Long All-Stars," p. H2.

373 **Richard felt at home:** Author's interview with Badham; **expressed their love:** Maslin, "'Didn't Cut Nobody's Throat,'" p. 76. Notably it was Pryor, not his costars, who organized a batting and throwing contest for some ninety kids in the neighborhood of the *Bingo Long* shoot—a contest complete with real prizes, such as a trip to the World Series (Dave Distel, "Ashford Behind Plate in Front of Camera," *Los Angeles Times*, Jan. 30, 1976, p. A6).

373 **running suit:** Weston, "Richard Pryor: 'Every Nigger Is a Star,'" p. 55.

374 **amped to play a more intimate club:** Author's interview with Murray Swartz, Mar. 30, 2011.

374 **"one of my best ever":** *Pryor Convictions*, pp. 143–44.

374 **No. 1 . . . Top 15:** *. . . And It's Deep Too*, booklet.

375 **Richard's hosting of *Saturday Night*:** Hill and Weingrad, *Saturday Night*, p. 116.

375 **Lorne Michaels was feeling the heat:** Ibid., pp. 116–17; **"If I'd known":** *Pryor Convictions*, p. 145.

375 **The show that Richard delivered:** *Saturday Night*, aired Dec. 13, 1975 (NBC); **Richard said "ass" twice:** Hill and Weingrad, *Saturday Night*, p. 118.

376 **photos of his grandmother, uncle, and children:** *Saturday Night*, aired Dec. 13, 1975 (NBC).

376 **Richard and . . . Paul Mooney had noticed:** Mooney, *Black Is the New White*, p. 161.

376 **In "Samurai Hotel":** *Saturday Night*, aired Dec. 13, 1975 (NBC). Richard, who had his own collection of samurai swords, had loved Belushi's imitation of

Japanese actor Toshiro Mifune, and the writers had created "Samurai Hotel" as a vehicle for it.

378 **"Dead honky" defeats the "nigger" trump card:** Randall Kennedy, *Nigger: The Strange Career of a Troublesome Word* (New York: Pantheon, 2002), pp. 24–25.

379 **the sketch was his response . . . "Easiest sketch I ever write":** Mooney, *Black Is the New White*, pp. 159–65; **"the doll-baby":** Steve Echeverria Jr., "Paul Mooney on Pryor, Chappelle and the State of Black America," *Tampa Herald-Tribune*, May 26, 2006. **"like an H-bomb":** Mooney, *Black Is the New White*, pp. 159–65;

379 **"Richard's attitude to it":** "He Was Chevy Chase, and You Weren't," *Hollywood Outbreak*, Mar. 15, 2013; **"asking Richard for as many slang words":** *. . . And It's Deep, Too!*.

380 **"What do you expect to do," "What the fuck":** Author's interview with Cohen.

381 **modern black version:** Pauline Kael, *5001 Nights at the Movies* (New York: Picador, 1991), p. 75

381 **Badham coaxed unexpected nuances:** Jay Cocks, "Infield Hit," *Time*, Aug. 2, 1976.

382 **"irresistible":** Gary Arnold, "A High-Flying 'Bingo Long,'" *Washington Post*, July 16, 1976, p. B1.

382 **"dizzy old cinematic devices":** John Simon, "Batting Average," *New York*, July 26, 1976, p. 55; **positive notices:** Vincent Canby, "Film on Black Baseball Is a 'Bingo,'" *New York Times*, July 17, 1976, p. 10; Joy Gould Boyum, "Playing Ball in Jim Crow's Day," *Wall Street Journal*, July 19, 1976, p. 7; Gene Siskel, "'Bingo' Scores in an Off-the-Wall Fashion," *Chicago Tribune*, July 16, 1976, p. B3; Andrew Sarris, "'Bingo Long' Deserves Wider and Whiter Distribution," *Village Voice*, Aug. 2, 1976, p. 93; **seeded articles on the Negro Leagues:** See, e.g., West, "The Bingo Long All-Stars," pp. H1–H2; "Baseball Barnstormers Remembered," *Colorado Springs Gazette Telegraph*, July 17, 1976, p. 3D; **exposition game:** Karen Jackovich, "It's a 'Jovial Battle' When Bears Tangle with Bingo's Boys," *Valley News*, June 20, 1976, pp. 4–5; **"the best movie I've ever seen":** *Bingo Long* advertisement, *Los Angeles Times*, July 23, 1976. The film's handling of race did provoke a few critics to pan the film. See Stephen Farber, "Minstrels on the Mound," *New West*, Aug. 2, 1976, p. 103; Robert Taylor, "'Bingo Long'—A Mixture of Slapstick and Violence," *Oakland Tribune*, July 21, 1976, p. 22.

382 **third-most popular film:** "50 Top-Grossing Films," *Variety*, Aug. 4, 1976, p. 12; "50 Top-Grossing Films," *Variety*, Sept. 22, 1976, p. 9; **Even in its release at the Apollo:** "Bway at Slow Crawl but 'Bingo Long,' in 41, Big 300G," *Variety*, July 28, 1976, p. 8.

383 **$11.8 million in rentals:** Cook, *Lost Illusions*, p. 500; **impressive box office totals:** Frank Segers, "Will 'The Wiz' Ease on Down the Road to Box-Office Ahs?," *Variety*, Oct. 10, 1978, p. 2.

Chapter 20: Hustling

384 **"I'm not a success yet":** Debbi Snook, "Richard Pryor Thinks Things Are Coming His Way," *Albany Times-Union*, May 23, 1976, p. G2.

384 **a sleek office:** Jacobson, "Richard Pryor Is the Blackest Comic of Them All," p. 58; "Black Press Mailer," Richard Pryor folder, Jack Hirshberg Papers, Margaret Herrick Library, Academy of Motion Picture Arts and Sciences, Los Angeles, CA, p. 3; **a hefty down payment in cash:** Author's interview with Patricia Heitman, Sept. 11, 2011; **a Spanish-style hacienda:** Jennifer Lee Pryor, *Tarnished Angel* (New York: Thunder's Mouth, 1991), pp. 97–98; *Pryor Convictions*, p. 151; Weston, "Richard Pryor: 'Every Nigger Is a Star,'" pp. 57–58; Gertrude

Gipson, "The Serious Side of Richard Pryor," *Los Angeles Sentinel*, Mar. 17, 1977, p. B; "A New Black Superstar," *Time*, Aug. 22, 1977; Robinson, "Richard Pryor Talks," p. 116.

384 **it had been thirty years since Northridge:** Kevin Roderick, *The San Fernando Valley: America's Suburb* (Los Angeles: Los Angeles Times Books, 2001); Kevin Roderick, "Hometown Memories," *Los Angeles Times*, Jan. 24, 1994; Dana Bartholomew, "Oakie House Saved from Destruction," *Los Angeles Times*, Jan. 30, 2010; Laura Barraclough, *Making the San Fernando Valley: Rural Landscapes, Urban Development, and White Privilege* (Athens: University of Georgia Press, 2011).

385 **lived in the guesthouse:** Gibson, "The Serious Side of Richard Pryor," p. B; **a recurring dream:** Jacobson, "Richard Pryor Is the Blackest Comic," p. 58; **"because nobody asked me":** Joyce Maynard, "King of the Scene-Stealers," p. 11; **"modern Willie Best":** Guy Flatley, "Peoria's Booty Star Plays a One-Man Film Festival," *New York Times*, Aug. 6, 1976, p. C4.

385 **screenwriter Colin Higgins's original conception:** "Colin Higgins," *Cinema Papers*, Dec. 1982, p. 535.

386 **four hundred thousand dollars:** Charles Higham, "What Makes Alan Ladd Jr. Hollywood's Hottest Producer," *New York Times*, July 17, 1977, p. D9. For a list of the films that inspired Higgins, see the early notes wherein he calls both *The Lady Vanishes* and *North by Northwest* "The Big One!" in "Super Chief," Box 115, Folder 3, Colin Higgins Papers, Department of Special Collections, Charles E. Young Library, UCLA, n.p. (hereafter "Colin Higgins Papers").

386 **"Bullshit! I got a high school diploma":** "REVISED—'THE SILVER STREAK'—4/2/76," Box 40, Folder 4, Colin Higgins Papers, p. 86; **"Hey, brother":** "Silver Streak script, master," Box 114, Folder 4, Colin Higgins Papers, p. 141.

387 **"Achilles' heel" . . . "I told Laddie":** Gene Wilder, *Kiss Me Like a Stranger* (New York: St. Martin's Press, 2005), p. 163; **they considered hiring two black actors:** Patrick Goldstein, "Higgins: Writer-Director on a Hot Streak," *Los Angeles Times*, Jan. 24, 1981, p. B15; **Wilder also advised Higgins:** "Interoffice Correspondence, Twentieth Century Fox," Box 116, Folder 4, Colin Higgins Papers, n.p.; **"That is one crazy nigger":** "REVISED—'THE SILVER STREAK'—4/2/76," p. 116.

387 **On their first day of shooting together:** Wilder, *Kiss Me Like a Stranger*, pp. 164–65. Two of Pryor's most telling ad libs, which get at how he made his role more multidimensional: First, when the villain calls Grover an "ignorant nigger," he doesn't reply by revealing his own ignorance but instead pushes back, with savvy, against the other side of the insult: "You don't know me well enough to call me no nigger! I'll slap the taste out your mouth!" Second, when George confesses how quickly he's fallen for Hilly, Grover doesn't say excitedly, "That's the way it is with love. Fast! I always feel like I swallowed the Fourth of July." Instead, he ruminates, more poetically, "I always lose my memory when I fall in love" ("REVISED—'THE SILVER STREAK'—4/2/76," pp. 70, 85–86).

388 **"I didn't want to lose the spontaneity":** E-mail communication from Arthur Hiller, May 25, 2011.

388 **May 13:** "'The Silver Streak' Shooting Schedule," Box 116, Folder 4, Colin Higgins Papers, pp. 14–15.

388 **"I'm going to hurt a lot of black people":** Wilder, *Kiss Me Like a Stranger*, pp. 165–66.

388 **Fifteen minutes later:** Ibid., p. 166; **"you might be in pretty big trouble":** *Silver Streak*, directed by Arthur Hiller (Twentieth Century-Fox, 1976).

389 **"What? Are you afraid":** *Silver Streak*.

389 **"All the police look for":** Alex Thein, "Color No Problem for Black Comic," *Milwaukee Sentinel*, Aug. 17, 1976, p. 16.

390 **"goose[d] it into some semblance of life":** Molly Haskell, "The Orient Express It Isn't," *Village Voice*, Dec. 20, 1976; **"One suspects":** Howard Kissel, "Arts and Pleasures," *Women's Wear Daily*, Dec. 7, 1976, p. 16; **"For about fifteen minutes":** Pauline Kael, "Processing Sludge," *The New Yorker*, Jan. 17, 1977, p. 98; **"What furtive sprightliness":** Jay Cocks, "Milk Train," *Time*, Dec. 13, 1976.

391 **"Gene Wilder and Richard Pryor take a train ride":** *New York Times*, Jan. 25, 1976, p. D10.

391 **he shut himself up in his dressing room:** "Black Press Mailer," p. 2. Pryor's screenplay about a black God never came to fruition; *Oh, God!*, with George Burns as the deity, was released late in 1977 and became that year's seventh-highest-grossing film. **Mel Brooks had visited his buddy Gene:** Jacobson, "Richard Pryor Is the Blackest Comic," p. 62.

391 **"Don't trust too many white folks":** Gipson "The Serious Side of Richard Pryor," p. B.

392 **"I was looking to hustle":** Maslin, "'Didn't Cut Nobody's Throat,'" p. 76; **he mentioned *Silver Streak* only glancingly:** *Pryor Convictions*, pp. 146, 149; **they never met outside the context of their working relationship:** Wilder, *Kiss Me Like a Stranger*, pp. 182–83.

392 **"It didn't seem like an interesting movie":** "Reporter's Transcript of Proceedings, Vol. IV," *Pryor v. Franklin*, Case No. TAC 17 MP 114 (Mar. 3, 1982), pp. 56–57.

392 **Hollywood dissidents:** Barbara Zheutlin and David Talbot, *Creative Differences: Profiles of Hollywood Dissidents* (Boston: South End Press, 1978).

393 **"woman with no patience for trifles":** Linda Gross, "She Battles for Minorities," *Los Angeles Times*, July 18, 1977, p. F14; **longtime activist . . . Third World Cinema:** Dale Pollock, "Woman Studio Chief Is Remembered," *Los Angeles Times*, Apr. 14, 1984, p. C7; Michael Seiler, "Hannah Weinstein Dies at 73," *Los Angeles Times*, Mar. 11, 1984, p. A14; Steve Neale, "Swashbuckling, Sapphire and Salt: Un-American Contributions to TV Costume Adventure Series in the 1950s," in Frank Kurtnik et al., eds., *"Un-American" Hollywood: Politics and Film in the Blacklist Era* (Piscataway, NJ: Rutgers University Press, 2007), pp. 199–204; **Third World Cinema:** "Ossie Davis Gets Unions to Allow Trainees on Set," *Daily Variety*, Feb. 23, 1971, pp. 1, 13; A. H. Weiler, "The Whole 'World' in Their Hands," *New York Times*, Jan. 2, 1972, p. D9; Gregg Kilday, "Women as Film Producers: A Success Story," *Los Angeles Times*, May 29, 1974, pp. E1, E11; Barbara Campbell, "Third World Pins Movie Hopes on 'Claudine,'" *New York Times*, June 5, 1975, p. 49; Gross, "She Battles for Minorities," p. F14; "Four-Yr.-Struggle Behind Filming of Black Comedy-Drama 'Claudine,'" *Daily Variety*, Apr. 15, 1974.

393 **It was Van Peebles:** Haskins, *Richard Pryor*, p. 110.

393 **"Who do you want me to play?":** *Pryor Convictions*, p. 149.

394 **committed to the film:** "Pix, People, Pickups," *Daily Variety*, June 25, 1976, p. 1.

394 **While preparing for the role:** "Universal Acquires Wertmuller Comedy," *Hollywood Reporter*, June 30, 1976; **an Italian sex-and-politics satire:** Peter Biskind, "Lina Wertmuller: The Politics of Private Life," *Film Quarterly* (Winter 1974/1975): 10–16; **into the context of black life:** Sheila Benson, "Richard Pryor, Who Is Co-Starring with Richard Pryor and Richard Pryor in Michael Schultz's Next Film," *Mother Jones*, June 1977, p. 52; **director of choice:** Author's interview with Michael Schultz, Sept. 4, 2010. Steve Krantz was himself something of an iconoclast—a former joke writer for Milton Berle who became

an impresario of countercultural and black filmmaking, producing *Fritz the Cat*, the first X-rated animated feature, and Schultz's directorial debut, *Cooley High*. In the spirit of Richard's comedy, *Fritz the Cat* used actual winos, junkies, and Black Panthers to voice the lines of street people and militants ("Obituaries: Steve Krantz, 83," *Los Angeles Times*, Jan. 15, 2007, p. B11; Earl Gottschalk Jr., "What If They Showed Cartoons and No Kids Could Come?," *Los Angeles Times*, Dec. 12, 1971, pp. 42–43; Earl Gottschalk Jr., "Move Over, Mickey—Sex, Drugs, and Violence Come to Cartoonery," *Wall Street Journal*, Sept. 13, 1971, pp. 1, 29).

394 **"My theory is":** Zheutlin and Talbot, *Creative Differences*, pp. 191, 197–203; *Cooley High*, directed by Michael Schultz (American Independent Pictures, 1974); *Car Wash*, directed by Michael Schultz (Universal, 1976); **an inner-city version of Robert Altman's *Nashville*:** Author's interview with Michael Schultz.

395 **he signed on for the Wertmüller adaptation:** "Universal Acquires Wertmuller Comedy"; **"I hope you can shoot this better":** Author's interview with Michael Schultz.

395 **around the beginning of July:** "U Signs Richard Pryor as Actor and Scripter," *Daily Variety*, July 7, 1976; **relaxed enough to lounge on a long white sofa:** Weston, "Richard Pryor: 'Every Nigger Is a Star,'" p. 57; **a college student in North Carolina:** Zheutlin and Talbot, *Creative Differences*, p. 147; **an artist in SoHo:** Maureen Orth, "Hollywood's New Power Elite: The Baby Moguls," *New West*, June 19, 1978, p 20; **"the focal point":** Charles DeBenedetti, *An American Ordeal: The Antiwar Movement of the Vietnam Era* (Syracuse, NY: Syracuse University Press, 1990), p. 338; **a particular reputation for stuffiness:** Charles Schreger, "Killer Shark Gets Lampooned," *Los Angeles Times*, Apr. 4, 1979, p. G12.

396 **"It is pure junk food":** Zheutlin and Talbot, *Creative Differences*, pp. 150–51;

396 **unprecedented terms:** Jacobson, "Richard Pryor Is the Blackest Comic of Them All," p. 58; **an eye-popping three million dollars . . . "We believe it is possible" . . . "Well, I guess":** Weston, "Richard Pryor: 'Every Nigger Is a Star,'" p. 57; Will Tusher, "Richard Pryor's Contractual Way of Life: Pay or Play or Vice Versa," *Daily Variety*, Aug. 21, 1979, p. 6.

396 **one of Hollywood's "baby moguls":** Orth, "Hollywood's New Power Elite," pp. 20, 23–24.

397 **"I'm through actively messing with my body":** Jacobson, "Richard Pryor Is the Blackest Comic of Them All," p. 58; **"holistic living":** "John Williams interview with Claude Brown."

397 **less than two weeks . . . "It's not my best work":** Gene Siskel, "Cary Grant's First Acid Trip—and Other Untold Star Tales," *Chicago Tribune*, Jan. 5, 1977, p. A1; *Bicentennial Nigger*, Warner Bros. BSK 3114 (1976).

398 **title track:** "Bicentennial Nigger," *Bicentennial Nigger.*

399 **"Twenty-third century":** Jacobson, "Richard Pryor Is the Blackest Comic of Them All," p. 64; **a three-year moratorium:** Snook, "Richard Pryor Thinks Things Are Coming His Way," p. G2; **"I don't really want to go":** Jacobson, "Richard Pryor Is the Blackest Comic of Them All," p. 64.

399 **A few weeks later:** "Bridges, Julien to Costar in Third World Cinema Pic," *Hollywood Reporter*, July 1, 1976.

399 **worried about how he could absorb a part:** "Pam Grier interviewed by John Wildman" (video), Walter Reade Theater, New York City, Mar. 16, 2013; **"take care of things":** *Pryor Convictions*, p. 150; **setting off firecrackers:** Author's interview with Schultz; **"When I was a kid":** Flatley, "Peoria's Booty Star Plays a One-Man Film Festival," p. C4; **he would pull over a chair:** *Richard Pryor: A Man and His Madness*, p. 111.

399 **"were creating all kinds of havoc":** Author's interview with Schultz.

400 **wanted to thread an element of fantasy:** "Pam Grier interviewed by John Wildman"; **felt the film was rattling off course:** Sue Reilly, "Schultz Directing Wendell Scott Pic," *Hollywood Reporter*, Aug. 19, 1976, pp. 1, 13; Gregg Kilday, "Substitutions," *Los Angeles Times*, Aug. 16, 1976; **Weinstein was not drawn to formal experimentation:** Zheutlin and Talbot, *Creative Differences*, pp. 203–4.

400 **"Here's my star":** Author's interview with Michael Schultz; **reshoot 80 percent of it:** Zheutlin and Talbot, *Creative Differences*, pp. 203–4; In *Pryor Convictions*, Pryor recalls that Van Peebles was fired because he wanted there to be more blacks on the crew. In interviews with the author, Schultz and Van Peebles remembered differently, and the press reports of the time all point to "creative differences." It seems unlikely, too, that Weinstein and Van Peebles would butt heads on this score, as she had been a leading advocate of minority-led casts and crews (*Pryor Convictions*, p. 150; author's interview with Melvin Van Peebles, Sept. 30, 2010).

401 **"This is an opportunity":** "Pam Grier interviewed by John Wildman."

401 **"Pam Grier, you're just a farmer":** Pam Grier, *Foxy: My Life in Three Acts* (New York: Grand Central Publishing, 2010), p. 160.

401 **"He was beautiful":** Maynard, "Richard Pryor, King of the Scene-Stealers," p. 11; **"was different from how I would do it":** Jean-Claude Bouis, "Richard Pryor Returns from a Busy 'Vacation,'" *Toledo Blade*, Sept. 18, 1977, p. G1; Jerry Wayne Williamson, *Hillbillyland: What the Mountains Did to the Movies and What the Movies Did to the Mountains* (Chapel Hill: University of North Carolina Press, 1995), pp. 142–43; Gold, "Richard Pryor Finds a Lot Not to Laugh About," p. 12.

401 **filtered into his performance:** *Greased Lightning*, directed by Michael Schultz (Universal, 1977).

402 **wrapped in September:** Reilly, "Schultz Directing Wendell Scott Pic," pp. 1, 13.

403 **"the soap opera style of moviemaking":** Zheutlin and Talbot, *Creative Differences*, pp. 203–4.

403 **"I want to make certain":** Sue Reilly, "Director Won't Castrate Pryor's Humor," *Hollywood Reporter*, July 30, 1976; **"the whole idea":** Benson, "Richard Pryor, Who Is Co-Starring," p. 57; **too prolix:** Author's interview with Carl Gottlieb, Aug. 25, 2010; **simply not funny:** Author's interview with Michael Schultz. For his part, Cecil Brown has written an account of his experience on *Which Way Is Up?*, arguing that the failure to realize his vision for the film speaks to Hollywood's inability to represent the black experience in its complexity. See Brown, "Blues for Blacks in Hollywood," *Mother Jones*, Jan. 1981, pp. 20–28, 59.

403 **ten-day vacation:** Author's interview with Carl Gottlieb, Aug. 25, 2010.

Chapter 21: A Man of Parts

404 **Self-improvement was the order of the day . . . "I heard that *War and Peace*":** Grier, *Foxy*, p. 162; Gipson, "The Serious Side of Richard Pryor," p. B; ***Cyrano de Bergerac*:** "Richard Pryor Seeks $250,000 for Breach of 'Cyrano' Movie Contract," *Jet*, Oct. 27, 1977, p. 56; ***Arsenic and Old Lace . . . Animal Farm*:** Maynard, "Richard Pryor, King of the Scene-Stealers," p. 11.

405 **broke into a high singsong voice:** Author's interview with Carl Gottlieb, Aug. 25, 2010.

405 **a ripe Italian parable:** Biskind, "Lina Wertmuller," pp. 10–13; Grace Russo Bullaro, *Man in Disorder: The Cinema of Lina Wertmüller in the 1970s* (Leicester, UK: Troubadour, 2007), pp. xv–xvi, 1–27; **"enormous story gaps":** Benson, "Richard Pryor, Who Is Co-Starring," p. 56.

406 **Michael Schultz had already established:** Zheutlin and Talbot, *Creative Differences*, p. 205.

406 **Carl ran a tape recorder . . . "It was a very healthy collaboration":** Author's interview with Carl Gottlieb. The name "Leroy Jones" invokes the real-life Leroi Jones, who renamed himself Amiri Baraka after devoting himself to the black struggle; it is the name of a character who has not come to full consciousness.

406 **Their creative idyll was interrupted:** *Pryor Convictions*, p. 150; author's interview with Carl Gottlieb.

407 **revised script:** "*Which Way Is Up?* Revised Final Draft Screenplay by Carl Gottlieb," dated Jan. 10, 1977 (in author's possession) (hereafter "*Which Way Is Up?* final draft screenplay"); Zheutlin and Talbot, *Creative Differences*, p. 207.

407 **"Hollywood extras with their sunglasses":** Benson, "Richard Pryor, Who Is Co-Starring," p. 56; **"I don't want to do a phony representation":** Zheutlin and Talbot, *Creative Differences*, pp. 205–6; Louis Torres, "Farm Workers in Sharp Focus," *Los Angeles Times*, Oct. 28, 1977; **"the old farts":** Benson, "Richard Pryor, Who Is Co-Starring," p. 56; **the child of Mexican migrant workers:** *The Man Who Shot* Chinatown*: The Life and Work of John A. Alonzo*, directed by Axel Schill (Montagnola Productions, 2007).

408 **Schultz took another creative risk:** Author's interview with Carl Gottlieb; author's interview with Michael Schultz; **"Pop, I'm in the paper!":** *Which Way Is Up*? It's worth noting that, while filming *Which Way Is Up?*, Pryor's ad libs consistently made Rufus more cutting and cruel (see "*Which Way Is Up?* final draft screenplay," pp. 5, 15, 18).

408 **for the first time in its history:** Hill and Weingrad, *Saturday Night*, p. 13; **"I'm just going to say":** "What's Cooking?," *People*, Dec. 27, 1976, p. 110.

409 **"a harmless little comedy":** Benson, "Richard Pryor, Who Is Co-Starring," p. 52.

410 **"In the master [take]":** Author's interview with Carl Gottlieb; **"us[ing] sweaters to stifle their laughter":** Benson, "Richard Pryor, Who Is Co-Starring," pp. 57–58; **"My hardest job":** Author's interview with Michael Schultz; **"can do the same scene":** "A New Black Superstar."

411 **When Richard was done with it:** *Which Way Is Up?*, directed by Michael Schultz (Universal, 1977) (hereafter *Which Way Is Up?*).

411 **"gobble[] up his triple parts":** David Ansen, "Pryorities," *Newsweek*, Nov. 14, 1977.

412 **"a total heel":** Lynn Minton, "Which Way Is Up?," *McCall's*, Jan. 1978, p. 53.

412 **wrapped in early March . . . "I'm going to save them":** Lee Grant, "Richard Pryor Thanks His Crew," *Los Angeles Times*, Mar. 5, 1977, p. B6; **two-page ad:** *Daily Variety*, Mar. 1, 1977, pp. 10–11.

412 **his own TV special:** *The Richard Pryor Special?*, directed by John Moffitt, aired May 5, 1977 (NBC, 1977). All other references are to this program.

412 **fully in command . . . "Every time a writer":** Author's interview with Rocco Urbisci, Aug. 30, 2010; author's interview with John Moffitt, Aug. 20, 2010.

413 **Mooney suggested adding Maya Angelou:** Mooney, *Black Is the New White*, p. 177; **"The comedy turns into a touching essay":** John O'Connor, "TV: Pryor and Chase Take Their Pot Shots," *New York Times*, May 5, 1977, p. C27.

415 **"John, I'm not changing anything" . . . "It's not about your ego":** Author's interview with Urbisci.

415 **series of hour-long programs:** "Lindbergh Talks with Sevareid," *Los Angeles Times*, May 19, 1977, p. G20; **two million dollars to remain exclusively:** "Pryor Surprises Manager with $52,000 Rolls," *Jet*, May 26, 1977, p. 57; **red leather interior:** Author's interview with Michael Ashburne, May 7, 2011.

416 **for Mother's Day:** "Pryor Proves You Can Always Go Home Again," *Jet*, June 2, 1977, pp. 22–23.

416 **"I adore [Pam Grier]":** Gipson, "The Serious Side of Richard Pryor," p. B; **continue to figure . . . in magazines:** Bob Lucas, "Pam and Richard: Movie Love Turns into Real Thing," *Jet*, June 2, 1977, pp. 58–61; "People Are Talking About . . . ," *Jet*, Sept. 29, 1977, p. 28; **"What about women's rights?":** Ace Burgess, "Richard Pryor: An Explosive, Angry Interview," *Gallery*, Jan. 1977, p. 124; **After Pam beat him in tennis:** Orth, "The Perils of Richard Pryor," p. 61; **"I was put off":** *Pryor Convictions*, p. 151.

416 **"I don't feel safe living here yet":** Grier, *Foxy*, pp. 163–67.

417 **accompanied by Deboragh McGuire:** Haskins, *Richard Pryor*, pp. 130–31; **supported for years by a wealthy, older white man:** *Pryor Convictions*, p. 139.

417 **"She was afraid of me":** Haskins, *Richard Pryor*, p. 131.

417 **grown up in a hardcare midwestern fundamentalist household:** Biskind, *Easy Riders, Raging Bulls*, pp. 286–93; Karen Koshner, "Writer Pursues Different Direction," *Syracuse Herald-Journal*, Sept. 6, 1977, p. 24.

418 **the most . . . lurid scenes in 1970s cinema:** Charles Higham, "When I Do It, It's Not Gore, Says Writer Paul Schrader," *New York Times*, Feb. 5, 1978, p. D15. On Schrader, see Paul Schrader, *Schrader on Schrader*, ed. Kevin Jackson (London: Faber and Faber, 2004); George Kouvaros, *Paul Schrader* (Champaign: University of Illinois Press, 2008).

418 **in the summer of 1976:** Gary Crowdus and Dan Georgakas, "Blue Collar: An Interview with Paul Schrader," *Cineaste* (Winter 1977/1978): 36; **He idolized Robert De Niro:** Author's interview with Patricia Heitman, Sept. 11, 2011; **put Richard's comedy albums on heavy rotation:** "*Blue Collar* Production Notes," Jan. 6, 1978, pp. 2–3, *Blue Collar* file, Pacific Film Archive, Berkeley, CA; **Schrader felt it was inconceivable:** "Entretien avec Paul Schrader," *Positif* (Dec. 1978), p. 22.

419 **"the single most overtly political":** Terry Curtis Fox, "Blue Collar Fever," *Village Voice*, Feb. 27, 1978, p. 31. While no critic has doubted how "political" *Blue Collar* is, there has been a rich debate over the meaning of its politics. See, for starters, Peter Biskind, "Blue Collar Blues," *Seven Days*, Apr. 7, 1978, pp. 31–32; Pauline Kael, "The Cotton Mather of the Movies," *The New Yorker*, Feb. 27, 1978, pp. 84–86; Andrew Sarris, "Off the Assembly Line: One Lemon, One Authentic Model," *Village Voice*, Feb. 27, 1978, pp. 32–33; Richard Schickel, "Union Dues," *Time*, Feb. 13, 1978, p. 66; Molly Haskell, "Toward a More Imperfect Union," *New York*, Feb. 20, 1978, pp. 78–79; James Monaco, "*Blue Collar*," *Take One* (Mar. 1978): 9–10; and more recently, Jefferson Cowie, *Stayin' Alive: The 1970s and the Last Days of the Working Class* (New York: New Press, 2012); Derek Nystrom, *Hard Hats, Rednecks, and Macho Men: Class in 1970s American Cinema* (New York: Oxford University Press, 2009).

419 **other studios refused to touch such a hard-hitting project:** Zheutlin and Talbot, *Creative Differences*, pp. 160–61; **loved *Silver Streak*:** Crowdus and Georgakas, "Blue Collar: An Interview with Paul Schrader," p. 36; Gregg Kilday, "The Ring around the 'Collar,'" *Los Angeles Times*, June 22, 1977, pp. D1, D12.

419 **The contrast with his last two films:** Haskins, *Richard Pryor*, pp. 135–36.

420 **"the most difficult, unpleasant and distasteful thing":** Kilday, "The Ring around the 'Collar,'" p. D12.

420 **"unrelentingly unpleasant":** "Paul Schrader," *Film Comment* (July–Aug. 1978): 46; **trench warfare:** "Paul Schrader interviewed by Maitland McDonagh," commentary track, *Blue Collar*, directed by Paul Schrader (Universal, 1978), DVD; **"Right after you said 'Cut'":** Biskind, *Easy Riders, Raging Bulls*, p. 349; **"shut-**

tle diplomacy" . . . over the head of Kotto: "Paul Schrader interviewed by Maitland McDonagh."

421 **over the head of George Memmoli:** Robbins and Ragan, *Richard Pryor*, p. 104; **"You pussy":** Biskind, *Easy Riders, Raging Bulls*, p. 349.

421 **"As a first-time director":** Crowdus and Georgakas, "Blue Collar: An Interview with Paul Schrader," p. 37.

421 **"big organizations":** Ibid., p. 34.

422 **"very trained and very professional"**: "Paul Schrader," *Film Comment* (July–Aug. 1978): 47.

422 **nearly opposite approaches to the craft of acting:** "Paul Schrader interviewed by Maitland McDonagh."

422 **He worried that if black audiences:** Robbins and Ragan, *Richard Pryor*, pp. 115–16.

423 **"If you're going to imply":** Kilday, "The Ring around the 'Collar,'" p. D12; **The scene was a mere three pages:** "Paul Schrader interviewed by Maitland McDonagh."

423 **"set sail from the script":** "Paul Schrader," *Film Comment*, p. 47; **"30 very funny lines":** Haskell, "Toward a More Imperfect Union," p. 78.

424 **"work, pension, die":** *Pryor Convictions*, pp. 53–54.

425 **the last scene filmed for *Blue Collar*:** "Paul Schrader interviewed by Maitland McDonagh."

426 **"It changed my life":** Orth, "The Perils of Richard Pryor," p. 63; **"a stretch":** "Paul Schrader interviewed by Maitland McDonagh"; **"the world around us is crumbling":** Anderson, "'Lightning' Is Not a Black Film," p. 7A.

Chapter 22: Giving Up Absolutely Nothing

427 **"I don't feel this":** Orth, "The Perils of Richard Pryor," p. 61; **having an epiphany:** Author's interview with John Moffitt, Aug. 20, 2010; Fran Ross, "Richard Pryor, Richard Pryor," *Essence*, April 1979, pp. 92–95.

427 **"You know something?":** Orth, "The Perils of Richard Pryor," p. 61; **"I need a straight, square person":** Ross, "Richard Pryor, Richard Pryor," p. 92; **punched up Richard's special . . . housekeeper fetched a sock:** Author's interview with John Moffitt; "Interview with John Moffitt, Nov. 20, 2003," Archive of American Television, www.emmytvlegends.org.

428 **had already invested a great deal:** Author's interview with John Moffitt; **reeling from an especially poor season:** Jack E. Anderson, "NBC Makes an Event of Replacing Its Regular Prime-Time Programs," *Chicago Tribune*, July 5, 1977, p. A8; **"Surrender Richard":** Orth, "The Perils of Richard Pryor," p. 61; **from ten episodes to four:** James Brown, "NBC 'Stifling My Creativity,'" *Los Angeles Times*, Sept. 14, 1977, p. G12; **from 9:00 p.m. on Thursday:** Cecil Smith, "NBC Schedule for Fall TV," *Los Angeles Times*, May 5, 1977, p. H26; **"electronic hari kiri":** James Bacon, "Elvis' Girlfriend Threatened," *Los Angeles Herald-Examiner*, n.d. (Sept. 2[], 1977), Richard Pryor file, ONE National Gay and Lesbian Archives, University of Southern California, Los Angeles, CA.

429 **"I wouldn't give a nickel":** *Pryor Convictions*, p. 152.

429 **Pam remained in the picture:** Author's interview with Matt Clark, Dec. 27, 2010; **When Jennifer Lee began working for Richard:** Lee, *Tarnished Angel*, p. 100; **a new woman would materialize at his office:** Author's interview with Rocco Urbisci, Aug. 30, 2010.

429 **Richard kept up appearances:** Maslin, "'Didn't Cut Nobody's Throat,'" p. 76; Anderson, "'Lightning' Is Not a Black Film," p. 7A; Gold, "Richard Pryor Finds a Lot Not to Laugh About," p. 12; Bouis, "Richard Pryor Returns from

a Busy 'Vacation,'" p. G1; **"new black superstar":** "A New Black Superstar"; **over the objections of director Michael Schultz:** Zheutlin and Talbot, *Creative Differences*, pp. 203–4; **"it is impossible to believe" . . . "There is not a more likable movie":** Richard Schickel, "Vroomy Movie," *Time*, Aug. 15, 1977.

430 **went on to gross almost triple its four-million-dollar budget:** Louie Robinson, "Michael Schultz: A Rising Star Behind the Camera," *Ebony*, Sept. 1978, p. 95; **a contract for a minimum of four films at a million dollars:** "Four Pics For Pryor," *Variety*, Aug. 3, 1977, p. 4; "Richard Pryor: Sensational New TV Show," *Jet*, Sept. 29, 1977, pp. 58–59. For more *Greased Lightning* reviews, see John Simon, "Don't Shoot the Actor, He's Doing the Best He Can," *New York*, Aug. 29, 1977, pp. 58–59; Steven Schaefer, "Stock Schlock," *SoHo Weekly*, Aug. 18, 1977; Pat Aufderheide, "Greased Lightning," *Cineaste* (Fall 1977): 48; David Ansen, "Out of My Way," *Newsweek*, Aug. 15, 1977; and (for the picture's biggest rave) Penelope Gilliatt, "The Current Cinema," *The New Yorker*, Aug. 22, 1977, p. 66.

430 **"NBC would love to make me":** "Richard Pryor: Sensational New TV Show," pp. 58–59; **"[i]f I disappoint them":** Maslin, "'Didn't Cut Nobody's Throat,'" p. 76; **"Hell, the atom split":** Gold, "Richard Pryor Finds a Lot Not to Laugh About," p. 12.

430 **"Hey, you know what I feel like?":** Maslin, "'Didn't Cut Nobody's Throat,'" p. 76.

430 **"Never edit yourself":** Author's interview with Rocco Urbisci; **Dick Ebersol:** Tom Shales, "A Pryor Restraint," *Washington Post*, Sept. 14, 1977, p. B1.

431 **"I'll never work with him again":** Author's interview with John Moffitt.

431 **"cause for wonder":** Joseph Lelyveld, "Off Color," *New York Times Magazine*, Nov. 6, 1977, p. 44; **"the most perilously inventive comedy hour":** Tom Shales, "Pryor's Angry Humor, the Savagery of 'Soap,'" *Washington Post*, Sept. 13, 1977, p. B9; **TV critics couldn't agree:** Jay Sharbutt, "Pryor Show Revolts against Family Hour," *Daily Sitka Sentinel*, Sept. 14, 1977, p. 2; "The Richard Pryor Show," *Variety*, Sept. 14, 1977, p. 8; "The Richard Pryor Show," *Hollywood Reporter*, Sept. 15, 1977, p. 6; Gary Deeb, "NBC and Pryor Make Peace for Now, but Their War Promises to Rage On," *Chicago Tribune*, Sept. 16, 1977, p. A10; **"devastating, bittersweet episode":** Brown, "NBC 'Stifling My Creativity,'" p. G18; **"icky wistfulness":** James Wolcott, "The New Season (3): Uprooted," *Village Voice*, Sept. 26, 1977, p. 42.

431 **recruited by Paul Mooney:** Mooney, *Black is the New White*, p. 176; **"He loved them":** Author's interview with Moffitt; **"We came in with no structure":** Author's interview with Tim Reid, Oct. 4, 2010.

432 **the first sketch of the first show:** Episode one, *The Richard Pryor Show*, aired Sept. 13, 1977 (NBC).

433 **Urbsici swapped out the fake one:** Author's interview with Rocco Urbisci; **"As a vitriolic lampoon":** Shales, "Pryor's Angry Humor," p. B9.

433 **a habit of filling up a water glass with vodka:** "Interview with John Moffitt, Nov. 20, 2003."

434 **everywhere on set:** Author's interview with Bob Altman, Oct. 21, 2010; **delayed getting into his makeup:** Author's interview with Rocco Urbisci; **"I don't remember doing it":** "Interview with John Moffitt, Nov. 20, 2003."

435 **"write a check":** "Richard Pryor: Sensational New TV Show," p. 60.

436 **without the lines:** Shales, "A Pryor Restraint," pp. B1, B9; **"We don't do genital jokes":** Brown, "NBC 'Stifling My Creativity,'" p. G12.

436 **"stifling my creativity":** Ibid., p. G12; **"They do":** Jay Sharbutt, "Pryor Angry at NBC Censorship," *Oakland Tribune*, Sept. 14, 1977, p. 22.

436 **"Maybe if NBC hired":** Shales, "A Pryor Restraint," p. B1.

437 **"I'd like to get the names":** "Richard Pryor: Sensational New TV Show," pp. 58–59; **"It's an insult":** Shales, "A Pryor Restraint," p. B9; **"All of us could use some bandages":** Deeb, "NBC and Pryor Make Peace for Now," p. A10.

437 **"Every piece that Richard did was different":** Author's interview with John Moffitt.

438 **"We crossed the line on that one":** Author's interview with Rocco Urbisci. Pryor's scenario—of a charismatic leader leading his followers to a grisly murder-suicide—was echoed, horribly, in November 1978 in Jonestown, Guyana, when Jim Jones drove, or forced, his followers into a ritual death. Airing when it did, "Black Death" was prophecy. If it had aired fifteen months later, it would have been in the worst possible taste—and unimaginative.

439 **"all the makings of a 'cabaret' version of Woodstock":** Robert Kemnitz, "Rights Wronged at Benefit," *Los Angeles Herald-Examiner*, Sept. 22, 1977.

439 **"Kiss your ass, hell!":** Randi Rhode, "Pryor: Clever (?) to Obnoxious," *Los Angeles Free Press*, Sept. 23, 1977, p. 7; **sat pole-axed . . . "To call what happened":** John L. Wasserman, "Pryor's Gay Shocker," *San Francisco Chronicle*, Sept. 20, 1977, p. 1.

440 **"to educate people":** Nancy Friedman, "They Had a Gay Time at the Bowl," *San Francisco Examiner*, Sept. 20, 1977.

440 **"with the volume and fervor":** Friedman, "They Had a Gay Time at the Bowl"; **"Ascent of Man":** Ron Pennington, "Pryor Tirade Mars Hollywood Bowl Benefit for Gays," *Hollywood Reporter*, Sept. 20, 1977, p. 23; **"What is life?":** Lee Grant, "'A Night for Rights' at the Bowl," *Los Angeles Times*, Sept. 20, 1977, p. F11; **"an evening of unspoken assumptions":** Ronald E. Kisner, "Pryor Adds Fireworks to Star-Spangled 'Gay Night,'" *Jet*, Oct. 6, 1977, p. 54; **"when sex was dirty":** Grant, "'A Night for Rights' at the Bowl," p. F11.

441 **the victim of a bait and switch . . . he noticed that the Lockers:** James H. Cleaver, "Richard Pryor Lashes Out at 'Gay' Rally," *Los Angeles Sentinel*, n.d. (Sept. 2[?], 1977), pp. A1, A10, Richard Pryor file, ONE National Gay and Lesbian Archives; author's interview with Don Campbell, Mar. 23, 2011; **"some bad motherfuckers":** "Performance at the Star-Spangled Night for Human Rights, Hollywood Bowl," Tape No. A00503, International Gay Information Center collection, New York Public Library. All subsequent quotes are from this archival audiotape. Pryor's performance was often misquoted or bowdlerized in press coverage.

442 **prowled back and forth:** Kisner, "Pryor Adds Fireworks to Star-Spangled 'Gay Night,'" p. 54; **a one-liner that had tongues wagging:** James Bacon, "Gays Go into Closet to Laugh at Richard Pryor's Putdown," *Los Angeles Herald-Examiner*, Sept. 21, 1977, p. B3.

443 **first major Hollywood celebrity:** On the reticence that characterized Hollywood in the 1970s, see David Ehrenstein, *Open Secret: Gay Hollywood, 1928–1998* (New York: HarperCollins, 1998).

444 **A producer came on to apologize:** Wasserman, "Pryor's Gay Shocker," p. 5.

444 **a full page:** "Pryor's Performance: The Rights and Wrongs," *Los Angeles Times*, Oct. 2, 1977, p. 47; **an obscene homophobe:** Michael Kearns, "Michael Kearns" column, *Los Angeles Free Press*, Sept. 23, 1977; Polly Warfield, "Actor's Verbal Violence Assaults Bowl Audience," *Los Angeles Free Press*, Sept. 23, 1977, p. 5; **"His 'street' language was abusive":** "Pryor Furore at 'Rights Night,'" *Los Angeles Times*, Sept. 25, 1977, p. 2; **"[M]ost of us in the gay rights movement":** "Letters to the Editor," *San Francisco Chronicle*, Sept. 26, 1977.

445 **"Much too often":** Ibid.; **"Being a black homosexual":** "Pryor's Perfor-

mance: The Rights and Wrongs," p. 47; **the city's biggest gay disco:** Lillian Faderman and Stuart Timmons, *Gay L.A.: A History of Sexual Outlaws, Power Politics, and Lipstick Lesbians* (New York: Basic Books, 2006), pp. 234–38; **Tomlin was closest to this third camp:** Author's interview with Lily Tomlin, Nov. 4, 2010; **"When you hire Richard Pryor":** Orth, "The Perils of Richard Pryor," p. 60.

445 **"didn't like it":** Liz Smith, "Rolling in Daddy's Tracks," (New York) *Daily News*, Sept. 20, 1977, p. 6; Todd Everett, "'Star-Spangled Night' Gets a Taste of Pryor's Verbal Rights," *Daily Variety*, Sept. 20, 1977, pp. 1, 4.

445 **"presumably fictitious Midwestern homosexual":** Kisner, "Pryor Adds Fireworks to Star-Spangled 'Gay Night,'" pp. 54–55.

446 **Wilbur Harp was a gay teenager:** Author's interview with Cecil Grubbs, Nov. 11, 2010; author's interview with Hillis Grismore, Nov. 17, 2010; **"In my neighborhood whatever you were was cool":** Murphy, "Richard Pryor," p. 27.

446 **left him reeling:** Lee, *Tarnished Angel*, p. 108; **"My feeling is that they cannot pay me":** Cleaver, "Richard Pryor Lashes Out at 'Gay' Rally," p. A10.

446 **The Lockers . . . kept out of the fracas:** Author's interview with Don Campbell.

Chapter 23: Can I Speak to God Right Away?

448 **When a star in a galaxy:** Laurence Marshall, *The Supernova Story* (Princeton, NJ: Princeton University Press, 1988).

448 **defeated *Superman*:** David Felton, "Richard Pryor's Life in Concert," *Rolling Stone*, May 3, 1979, pp. 54–55; Linda Ruth Williams and Michael Hammond, eds., *Contemporary American Cinema* (New York: McGraw Hill, 2006), pp. 186–87.

449 **possessing her:** *Pryor Convictions*, pp. 155–57; **"There is a very special lady out there":** "Richard Pryor's Sensational New TV Show," *Jet*, Sept. 29, 1977, p. 61.

449 **"seen things":** *Pryor Convictions*, p. 157; **Jennifer had grown up:** Lee, *Tarnished Angel*, pp. 3–93; **slightly aloof intelligence:** *The Man in the Glass Booth*, directed by Arthur Hiller (1975).

449 **their first date:** *Pryor Convictions*, p. 154; Lee, *Tarnished Angel*, pp. 108–9.

450 **At summer's end:** "Audience Q&A," *Richard Pryor TV Show* DVD.

450 **"I told her":** *Pryor Convictions*, pp. 155–56.

450 **"We can't shoot without you":** Author's interview with Rob Cohen, Aug. 18, 2010.

451 **"You're getting married, right?":** *Pryor Convictions*, pp. 156–57.

452 **"had to be revived":** *Pryor Convictions*, p. 157; **wore black:** Author's interview with Patricia Heitman, Sept. 11, 2011; **a construction site:** Lee, *Tarnished Angel*, p. 109; **"Thank God you were drunk":** *Pryor Convictions*, p. 157.

452 **their wedding reception:** *Jet*, Oct. 13, 1977, p. 33; "Pryor Stuns Friends with Wedding," pp. 56–57; **he'd assumed Pam Grier was the bride . . . "shoot his ass":** Author's interview with Rocco Urbisci, Aug. 30, 2010.

452 **"This is the first time":** Roger Piantadosi, "Personalities," *Washington Post*, Sept. 24, 1977, p. C3; **"I'm still in shock":** "Pryor Stun Friends with Wedding," p. 57.

453 **airborne honeymoon suite:** Author's interview with Cohen.

453 **The next day in New York City:** Robbins and Ragan, *Richard Pryor*, pp. 124–25; Author's interview with Cohen.

453 **Cohen tried to convince Richard:** Author's interview with Cohen; **plenty of material to work with:** Dee Wedemeyer, "The Emerald City Comes to New York," *New York Times*, Sept. 23, 1977, p. 29.

453 **Then Cohen had an idea:** Author's interview with Cohen; *Richard Pryor: This Cat's Got 9 Lives!*, p. 125; William Brashler, "Berserk Angel," *Playboy*, Dec. 1979, p. 296.

454 **The second-to-last episode:** Episode three, *The Richard Pryor Show*, Sept. 27, 1977.

455 **famously sensual eating scene in . . . *Tom Jones*:** Author's interview with Reid.

455 **a sketch that Rocco Urbisci and John Moffitt considered a disappointment:** Author's interview with Urbisci; author's interview with Moffitt.

456 **a curious backstory to match:** Author's interview with Kres Mersky, Sept. 30, 2010; author's interview with Urbisci. Mersky's monologue was adapted from Marcia Blumenthal, "Tearing," in the feminist short story anthology *Bitches and Sad Ladies*, ed. Pat Rotter (New York: Harper's Magazine Press, 1975), pp. 394–402. Interestingly, Blumenthal's original story involved a relationship between a woman and a man; it was Mersky's idea to keep alive the question of sexual violation but transfer it onto a relationship between a woman and a woman.

457 **They settled on an ingenious solution:** Author's interview with Urbisci; **a rollicking example of the sexual confusions:** Mary Beth Hamilton, "Sexual Politics and African American Music: or, Placing Little Richard in History," *History Workshop* (Autumn 1998): 161–76. There's no reason to think that Richard knew specifically that Little Richard had performed as a drag queen, or that "Tutti Frutti" was originally written as a paean to "good booty," or that "Miss Molly" was slang for a gay man, but there's also no reason to think, given his friendship with Wilbur Harp and his time sharing the bill with female impersonators at Harold's Club in Peoria, that he was unperceptive on these and related matters.

457 **NBC tried to kill the segment:** Author's interview with Kres Mersky.

458 ***The Richard Pryor Show* had shed viewers:** "Soap, Betty White Debut amid Top 10," *Los Angeles Times*, Sept. 21, 1977, p. I18; Gary Deeb, "Rickles Earning Top Loser Stripes with 'Sharkey,'" *Chicago Tribune*, Oct. 27, 1977, p. A13; **"sleight of comic imagination":** Lelyveld, "Off Color," p. 44.

458 **the comic roast:** "Richard Pryor Roast," *The Richard Pryor Show*, Oct. 20, 1977.

459 **Richard took the podium:** "Richard Pryor Roast."

459 **hears each gun talking:** "Gun Shop," *The Richard Pryor Show*, Oct. 20, 1977.

460 **pistol-whipped an early manager:** see chapter 12; **shot up his first gold record:** see chapter 18; **an arsenal that encompassed:** Felton, "This Can't Be Happening to Me," pp. 40–41.

461 **at a New Years' Eve party:** "Gun Charge Dropped, Pryor Faces 'Assault by Auto' Rap," *Jet*, Mar. 9, 1978, p. 55; *California v. Pryor.*

461 **the final sketch:** "Rebuttal," *The Richard Pryor Show*, Oct. 20, 1977.

462 **the most stinging mainstream reviews:** Richard Cuskelly, "Richard Pryor Misfires, Again," *Los Angeles Herald-Examiner*, Nov. 7, 1977; Charles Champlin, "Wall-to-Wall Stereotypes." *Los Angeles Times*, Nov. 4, 1977, p. G27; **Producer Steven Krantz had fretted:** Marilyn Beck, "Pryor Power," *Los Angeles Herald-Examiner*, Nov. 7, 1977; **"Pryor's career seems":** Arthur Murphy, "Which Way Is Up?," *Variety*, Nov. 2, 1977, p. 17.

462 **though Universal partly dumped the movie:** Mark A. Reid, *Redefining Black Film* (Berkeley: University of California Press, 1993), pp. 39–40; **the most commercially successful black film in history:** "Calls 'Which Way Is Up?' Top Black Grosser; Pryor Not Hurt," *Variety*, Apr. 26, 1978, pp. 7, 40; ***Village Voice* hailed the film:** "Which Way Is Up?," *Village Voice*, Nov. 14, 1977; **"false and empty macho images":** "The Black Male Image Wins in 'Which Way Is Up,'" *Cause*, n.d., pp. 22–24, in "Which Way Is Up" production file, Margaret Herrick Library, AMPAS.

463 **there had long been a comic tradition:** W.T. Lhamon Jr., "Whittling on Dynamite: The Difference Bert Williams Makes," in *Listen Again: A Momentary History of Pop Music*, ed. Eric Weisbard (Durham, NC: Duke University Press, 2007); W. T. Lhamon Jr., *Raising Cain: Blackface Performance from Jim Crow to Hip Hop* (Cambridge: Harvard University Press, 1998); Watkins, *On the Real Side*; Camille Forbes, *Introducing Bert Williams: Burnt Cork, Broadway, and the Story of America's First Black Star* (New York: Basic Civitas Books, 2008); **expressed interest in making a biopic about the black vaudevillian:** Brown, " Remembering Richard Pryor." Richard also committed to a biopic of jazz saxophonist Charlie Parker, which suggests another, competing tradition that attracted him: the black avant-garde. Kenneth L. Geist, "The Charlie Parker Story," *Films in Review*, May 1989, pp. 279–84.

464 **"one of the few actors":** Vincent Canby, "Comic Film 'Which Way Is Up?' Loses Way," *New York Times*, Nov. 5, 1977, p. 13.

464 **courted critical disapproval and generated controversy:** Erica Renee Edwards, *Charisma and the Fictions of Black Leadership* (Minneapolis: University of Minnesota Press, 2012), pp. 147–66; David J. Leonard, *Screens Fade to Black: Contemporary African American Cinema* (Westport, CT: Praeger, 2006), pp. 141–60; Catherine John, "Black Film Comedy as Vital Edge," in *A Companion to Film Comedy*, ed. Andrew Horton and Joanna Rapf (Malden, MA: Wiley-Blackwell, 2012), pp. 343–64.

464 **"shoot me in the ass":** *Which Way Is Up?*, directed by Michael Schultz (Universal, 1977).

465 **when he and Deboragh traveled to Maui:** *Pryor Convictions*, p. 159; **he kept telephoning . . . Jennifer Lee:** Lee, *Tarnished Angel*, p. 110.

465 **"I caroused with sleazy, doped-up nogoodniks":** *Pryor Convictions*, p. 159. Photographs suggest that the carousing began at Studio 54, the legendary discotheque, then at the height of its glamour. (Photograph of Richard Pryor and Deboragh McGuire, in author's possession.)

465 **Richard flew to Peoria:** "Pryor Suffers Reported Heart Attack," *Peoria Journal Star*, Nov. 10, 1977; **he went fishing with Deboragh:** Pryor *Convictions*, p. 159.

466 **"Mama! Mama!":** *Pryor Convictions*, pp. 159–60.

466 **"They were probably closer to death":** *Pryor Convictions*, pp. 160–61.

466 **a radio station in Los Angeles reported that he had died:** Felton, "Richard Pryor's Life in Concert," p. 50; **Five hundred phone calls:** "Pryor in Stable, Good Condition," *Peoria Journal Star*, Nov. 11, 1977; **every caller seemed to believe:** "Pryor Released, Returns to Beverly Hills Home," *Peoria Journal Star*, Nov. 13, 1977; **"I was on a treadmill":** Haskins, *Richard Pryor*, pp. 153–54; "Pryor Denies He Was Hospitalized for Heart Attack," *Peoria Journal Star*, Nov. 21, 1977.

466 **had publicly destroyed his marriage:** "Gun Charge Dropped, Pryor Faces 'Assault by Auto' Rap," p. 55; **"We're going to be very happy together":** Robinson, "Richard Pryor Talks," p. 122.

467 **Without skipping a beat:** Lee, *Tarnished Angel*, pp. 114–27; **he used the stage of the Comedy Store . . . after a month of woodshedding:** *Pryor Convictions*, pp. 167–69.

467 **Richard's account of his heart attack:** *Richard Pryor Live in Concert*, directed by Jeff Margolis (Special Event Entertainment, 1979); Lee, *Tarnished Angel*, pp. 156–60; **something of a departure from his earlier concerts:** Felton, "Richard Pryor's Life in Concert," p. 50.

468 **In the stage version:** *Richard Pryor Live in Concert*; Felton, "Richard Pryor's Life in Concert," p. 52.

469 **in other performances:** Richard Pryor, "Heart Attacks," *Wanted: Live in Concert* (Warner Bros., 1978).

470 **"one of the most exhilarating experiences":** *Richard Pryor Live in Concert* pamphlet, *Richard Pryor Live in Concert* clipping file, Pacific Film Archive, Berkeley, CA; **"Working entirely without props":** Rosenbaum, "The True *Auteur,*" p. 14; **"the only great poet satirist among our comics":** Pauline Kael, *For Keeps: 30 Years at the Movies* (New York: Penguin, 1994), p. 933; **thirty-two million dollars:** *Contemporary American Cinema,* pp. 186–87; **put together in a month . . . "low-budget, short-order masterpiece":** Felton, "Richard Pryor's Life in Concert," p. 54.

470 **had died from a stroke three weeks before filming:** "Richard Pryor Joins Grieving Family for Grandmother's Funeral," *Jet,* Jan. 4, 1979, pp. 14–16; "Pryor's Grandma Expires," *Los Angeles Sentinel,* Dec. 14, 1978, p. A16; **"Son, you just don't know":** "Richard Pryor Talks about Richard Pryor (the Old, the New), Rejection That Led to Loneliness and Drugs, God, Prayer, 'Nigger,' and How He Was Burned," *Ebony,* Oct. 1980, p. 36; **floated weightless:** *Pryor Convictions,* pp. 171–72

Epilogue

471 **"couldn't pry him loose without a struggle":** "Richard Pryor Joins Grieving Family," pp. 14–15.

471 **a night funeral:** Ibid., pp. 14–16; "Rites Set for Grandmother of Comedian Richard Pryor," *Peoria Journal Star,* Dec. 12, 1978; **the reverend who had helped inspire Richard's grandiloquent stage minister:** Author's interview with Cecil Grubbs, Nov. 16, 2010; "Peoria, Ill. Church Split into Two Warring Groups," *Jet,* July 22, 1991, p. 18; **a second funeral:** "Richard Pryor Joins Grieving Family," pp. 14–16; **cloudy winter skies:** www.wunderground.com.

472 **Richard played host:** Author's interview with Rosalyn Taylor, Dec. 2, 2010.

472 **Richard did not dwell in his grief so much as lose himself in it:** *Pryor Convictions,* pp. 170–72, 177–91; **starting in November 1979:** Lee, *Tarnished Angel,* pp. 208–32.

472 **awake for somewhere in the vicinity of four days straight:** "Richard Pryor Talks about Richard Pryor," p. 42; **"Voices swirled in my head":** *Pryor Convictions,* p. 187.

473 **"You have to have a lot of courage":** Handleman, "The Last Time We Saw Richard," p. 84.

473 **Richard poured the liquor:** *Pryor Convictions,* pp. 188–90.

473 **A gathering mass of drivers:** Jerry Belcher, "Chemical Set off Fire That Burned Pryor, Police Say," *Los Angeles Times,* June 11, 1980, pp. B3, B20.

474 **"Lord, give me another chance":** Haskins, *Richard Pryor,* pp. 187–89; *Pryor Convictions,* pp. 190–91; **deep shock:** "Comedian Richard Pryor Found Afire, Critically Hurt," *Los Angeles Times,* June 10, 1980, p. B3. Though it's hard to imagine how Pryor physically jogged half a mile after setting himself aflame, the Associated Press likewise reported that he was found "more than a mile from home" ("Richard Pryor in Critical Condition After Explosion of Drug Mixture," *New York Times,* June 11, 1980, p. A20).

474 **the third-highest-grossing film of 1981 . . . "In a troubled period for movies":** Richard Corliss, "Pryor's Back—Twice as Funny," *Time,* Mar. 29, 1982, p. 62; ***Live on the Sunset Strip:*** Lee Grant, "Looking Down from the Top," *San Francisco Chronicle,* Apr. 11, 1982, p. 17; **bested the returns:** Linda Ruth Williams and Michael Hammond, eds., *Contemporary American Cinema* (New York: McGraw-Hill, 2006), p. 187; **"Whatever happened to the black film":** Dale Pollock, "Pryor in High Demand as Black Film Declines," *Los Angeles Times,* May 8, 1981, p. G1

474 **"approach it very scientifically":** Stephen Farber, "Success Holds No Laughter for Richard Pryor," *New York Times*, June 12, 1983, p. H1.

475 **"What's wrong with Richard Pryor?":** Michael Sragow, "What's Wrong with Richard Pryor?," *Rolling Stone*, Feb. 17, 1983, pp. 37, 41; **After *Brewster's Millions*:** Vincent Canby, "Richard Pryor in Search of His Comic Genius," *New York Times*, June 2, 1985, p. H19; Owen Glieberman, "Poor Richard's Almanac," May 6, 1986, pp. C1, C12; "The Current Cinema," Pauline Kael, *The New Yorker*, May 5, 1986, p. 114. See also David Ehrenstein, "Beginning of the End of Richard Pryor," *Los Angeles Reader*, Apr. 9, 1982, pp. 17, 19; Jonathan Rosenbaum, "The Man in the Great Flammable Suit," *Film Comment* (July/Aug. 1982): 17–20; David Edelstein, "Torched Song," *Village Voice*, May 6, 1986; **for which Richard instructed its screenwriters:** Interview with Herschel Weingrod, "Natsukashi" podcast, posted Mar. 20, 2009, at http://natsukashi.wordpress.com.

476 **"The Sherman Oaks Burn Center":** Fred Robbins and David Ragan, "Man on Fire," *US Weekly*, May 11, 1982, p. 30; **"gentle . . . mellow":** Corliss, "Pryor's Back—Twice as Funny," p. 63; **"People call me up and say":** Farber, "Success Holds No Laughter for Richard Pryor," p. H1; **"Sure, my moods go up and down":** David T. Friendly, "Richard Pryor—Your Life Is Calling," *Los Angeles Times*, Apr. 27, 1986, p. Z4.

476 **it wasn't only Richard who became more risk-averse:** Biskind, *Easy Riders, Raging Bulls*, pp. 408–39; Peter Biskind, "Blockbuster: The Last Crusade," in Mark Crispin Miller, ed. *Seeing through Movies* (New York: Pantheon, 1990), pp. 112–49; **as wrenching as the coming of sound:** Stephen Prince, *A New Pot of Gold: Hollywood under the Electronic Rainbow, 1980–1989* (Berkeley: University of California Press, 2000), pp. xi–xvii, 287–340; Geoff King, *Spectacular Narratives: Hollywood in the Age of the Blockbuster* (New York: St. Martin's, 2000); Tom Shone, *Blockbuster: How Hollywood Learned to Stop Worrying and Love the Summer* (New York: Free Press, 2004). For a correction to the overemphasis on how the blockbuster changed Hollywood style, see David Bordwell, *The Way Hollywood Tells It: Story and Style in Modern Movies* (Berkeley: University of California Press, 2006).

477 **Eddie Murphy, his successor as the big marquee name:** Guerrero, *Framing Blackness*, pp. 114–33; **the older Richard strips out the complexity:** Jennifer Lee, "Richard Pryor, Now Your Ex-Wife Is Calling," *People*, June 16, 1986.

478 **his dream of being a character actor:** Jack Hirshberg interview notes (1976), Richard Pryor folder, Jack Hirshberg Papers, AMPAS, p. 2.

478 **The diagnosis:** *Pryor Convictions*, pp. 220–24; C. H. Hawkes, "Are Multiple Sclerosis Patients Risk-Takers?," *Quarterly Journal of Medicine (QJM)* 98 (Oct. 2005): 895–911; Christopher H. Hawkes and David Boniface, "Risk Associated Behavior in Premorbid Multiple Sclerosis: A Case-Control Study," *Multiple Sclerosis and Related Disorders* (Jan. 2014): 40–47; Lawrence Steinman, "Multiple Sclerosis: A Coordinated Immunological Attack against Myelin in the Nervous System," *Cell* 85 (May 3, 1996): 299–302.

479 **the hardest part of having MS:** Greg Tate, "Richard Pryor, 1940–2005," *Village Voice*, Dec. 14–20, 2005, p. 38; **a mere 115 pounds:** Handelman, "The Last Time We Saw Richard," pp. 79–80; David Kleinberg, "Alive and Fighting," *San Francisco Chronicle*, Oct. 25, 1992, p. 20; Craig Wolff, "Still Laughing through the Pain, A Comedian Returns," *New York Times*, Feb. 18, 1993, pp. B1; **a rented mansion:** Als, "A Pryor Love," Sept. 13, 1999, p. 81; **close to broke:** "Richard Pryor's Biggest Fight," *Ebony*, Sept. 1993, pp. 100, 105; **"the lowest point of my life":** Handelman, "The Last Time We Saw Richard," pp. 79–80; Kleinberg, "Alive and Fighting," p. 20; Wolff, "Still Laughing through the Pain, p. B5.

479 **Sitting in an easy chair:** *Pryor Convictions*, pp. 241–42; **"I don't want to be**

alone" . . . "as emotionally drained": Kleinberg, "Alive and Fighting," pp. 20–21.

480 **"It's not gone":** Greg Tate, "Richard Pryor," in *The Vibe Q: Raw and Uncut* (New York: Kensington Books, 2007), p. 74; **"I'm going through a humbling experience":** "Richard Pryor's Biggest Fight," p. 106.

480 **he asked Jennifer Lee to return to him:** Als, "A Pryor Love," pp. 80–81; **"general aide-de-camp":** "Pryor Engagement," *The New Yorker,* July 10, 1995, p. 26; **the two were married in secret:** *Elizabeth Pryor v. Jennifer Pryor,* No. B207398, Court of Appeal, Second District, Division 4, CA (Sept. 29, 2009); *Elizabeth Pryor v. Jennifer Pryor,* No. B207402, Court of Appeal, Second District, Division 4, CA (Sept. 29, 2009); **He saw his children just once a month . . . "prisoner":** Pryor, *Jokes My Father Never Taught Me*, pp. 191–202.

481 **"The comic voice of a generation":** Matt Schudel, "With Humor and Anger on Race Issues, Comic Inspired a Generation," *Washington Post*, Dec. 11, 2005, p. A1; **"He unleashed a galaxy":** Mel Watkins, "Richard Pryor, Who Turned Humor of the Streets into Social Satire, Dies at 65," *New York Times*, Dec. 12, 2005, p. A24.

481 **a small, private affair:** "Family and Close Friends Celebrate Pryor's Life at Private Ceremony," *Jet*, Jan. 9, 2006, pp. 59–60; e-mail to author from Ron De-Blasio, Mar. 21, 2014; Pryor, *Jokes My Father Never Taught Me*, p. 204; **"I don't know how they got started":** *Pryor Convictions*, p. 23.

481 **in civil lawsuits:** *Elizabeth Pryor v. Jennifer Pryor,* No. B207398; *Elizabeth Pryor v. Jennifer Pryor,* No. B207402.

482 **only Richard Jr. agreed to participate:** Joel Keller, "An Uneasy Collaboration: The Creative Pull of Making a Richard Pryor Documentary," *Co.Create*, May 30, 2013 (http://www.fastcocreate.com/1683057/an-uneasy-collaboration-the-creative-push-and-pull-of-making-a-richard-pryor-documentary).

482 **"There are two periods in comedy":** . . . *And It's Deep Too!*; **"the single most seminal comedic influence":** Jim Cheng, "Comedians Praise Pryor's Groundbreaking Humor," *USA Today*, Dec. 11, 2005; **"the Picasso of our profession":** Allison Samuels, "Richard Pryor, 1940–2005," *Newsweek*, Dec. 18, 2005; **"the Rosa Parks of comedy":** Jesse McKinley, "Admiration for a Comedian Who Knew No Limits," *New York Times*, Dec. 13, 2005, p. E1; **Eddie Murphy . . . Margaret Cho:** . . . *And It's Deep Too!*; **"Without Richard, there would be no me":** McKinley, "Admiration for a Comedian Who Knew No Limits," p. E1.

482 **"started it all":** Handelman, "The Last Time We Saw Richard," p. 81.

482 **"All they remember is the profanity":** Author's interview with Amiri Baraka, Jan. 25, 2011; **"Richard has probably spawned more bad comics":** Author's interview with Tim Reid, Oct. 4, 2010; **"the Lenny Bruce syndrome":** Alan Farley, "Vignettes amidst the Pimps," *San Francisco Examiner*, Datebook section, May 16, 1971, p. 5; **"there is no point to be made":** *Live on the Sunset Strip.*

484 **Mark Twain looked at the aftermath of the Civil War:** Stephen Railton, *Mark Twain: A Short Introduction* (Malden, MA: Blackwell, 2003); Shelley Fisher Fishkin, ed., *A Historical Guide to Mark Twain* (New York: Oxford University Press, 2002); Mark Twain, *The Adventures of Huckleberry Finn,* ed. Gerald Graff and James Phelan (New York: St. Martin's Press, 2004); Susan Gillman and Forrest G. Robinson, eds., *Mark Twain's* Pudd'nhead Wilson*: Race, Conflict, and Culture* (Durham, NC: Duke University Press, 1990). Fittingly, Pryor was the first recipient of the Mark Twain Prize for American Humor in 1998.

485 **"homogeneous protoplasm":** Mark Twain, *A Connecticut Yankee in King Arthur's Court* (Berkeley: University of California Press, 1979), p. 478; **"The co-**

median who really moved me": John Lahr, "Dealing with Roseanne," *The New Yorker*, July 17, 1995, p. 45.

485 **"comic genius who let Hollywood":** Ishmael Reed, "Richard Pryor—Comic Genius Who Let Hollywood Use Him," *San Francisco Chronicle*, Dec. 19, 2005.

486 **scripted with Pryor's stand-up:** See chapters 15 through 22.

486 **"Pryor's career in total":** Tate, "Richard Pryor, 1940–2005," p 50.

487 **"I see people":** *The Barbara Walters Special*, aired Aug. 5, 1980 (ABC).

INDEX

RP = Richard Pryor
Page numbers of illustrations are in *italics*.

ABOUT THE AUTHOR

Scott Saul is an associate professor of English at the University of California–Berkeley. His writing has appeared in *Harper's*, the *New York Times*, and the *Nation*, among other publications. He is the author of *Freedom Is, Freedom Ain't: Jazz and the Making of the Sixties*. He lives in Berkeley, California.

For more on Richard Pryor's life, please visit www.becomingrichardpryor.com.